ARISTOTLE'S *PROBLEMATA*
IN DIFFERENT TIMES AND TONGUES

MEDIAEVALIA LOVANIENSIA

Editorial Board

Geert H.M. Claassens - Jean Goossens
Carlos Steel - Werner Verbeke

SERIES I / STUDIA XXXIX

KATHOLIEKE UNIVERSITEIT LEUVEN
INSTITUUT VOOR MIDDELEEUWSE STUDIES
LEUVEN (BELGIUM)

ARISTOTLE'S *PROBLEMATA*
IN DIFFERENT TIMES AND TONGUES

Edited by

Pieter DE LEEMANS
and
Michèle GOYENS

LEUVEN UNIVERSITY PRESS
2006

Published with the support of the K.U.Leuven Commissie voor Publicaties
and Universitaire Stichting van België

ISBN 90 5867 524 6
ISBN 978 90 5867 524 8
D/2006/1869/7
NUR: 684-694

In Memory of Jozef Brams (1937-2003)

CONTENTS

Pieter DE LEEMANS and Michèle GOYENS
Introduction   IX

Joan CADDEN
Preliminary Observations on the Place of the Problemata in Medieval Learning   1

Robert W. SHARPLES
Pseudo-Alexander or Pseudo-Aristotle, Medical Puzzles and Physical Problems   21

Lou S. FILIUS
The Genre Problemata in Arabic: Its Motions and Changes   33

Graziella FEDERICI VESCOVINI
L'Expositio Succinta Problematum Aristotelis de Pierre d'Abano   55

Maaike VAN DER LUGT
Aristotle's Problems in the West: A Contribution to the Study of the Medieval Latin Tradition   71

Iolanda VENTURA
Aristoteles fuit causa efficiens huius libri: On the Reception of Pseudo-Aristotle's Problemata in Late Medieval Encyclopaedic Culture   113

Françoise GUICHARD-TESSON
Évrart de Conty, poète, traducteur et commentateur   145

Caroline BOUCHER
Des problèmes pour exercer l'entendement des lecteurs: Évrart de Conty, Nicole Oresme et la recherche de la nouveauté   175

Joëlle DUCOS
Lectures et vulgarisation du savoir aristotélicien: les gloses d'Évrart de Conty (sections XXV-XXVI)   199

Geneviève DUMAS
Évrart de Conty et Pierre d'Abano: commentateurs d'Aristote   227

Annelies BLOEM
À la recherche de la subjectivité dans les Problèmes d'Évrart de Conty: un commentateur juché sur les épaules d'Aristote?   247

John MONFASANI
    George of Trebizond's Critique of Theodore Gaza's
    Translation of the Aristotelian Problemata   275

Selected Bibliography   295

Index codicum manu scriptorum   319

Index auctorum   322

Pieter DE LEEMANS and Michèle GOYENS

INTRODUCTION

Knowledge is relevant if, and only if, you can share it with others. Evolution in knowledge is tributary to communication: exchange of knowledge leads to fresh findings.

In the Middle Ages, things were not different. The inheritance of ancient knowledge deeply influenced medieval thought; scientific knowledge, for instance, was based on the legacy of ancient philosophers and scientists like Aristotle, Galen, Hippocrates. Their writings and theories reached medieval man primarily through translations: translations from Greek into Arabic, from Arabic into Latin, from Greek into Latin, from Latin into the vernacular, ... These translations were then submitted to critical analyses; they became the subject of commentaries, and were incorporated into medieval thinking, which was inspired by but certainly did not blindly accept the ancient original. Translators had to interpret their source-text. Commentators had to interpret the translations. These interpretative acts carried the danger of misinterpretations, but they also offered the possibility to discuss the source-text and to develop a personal approach. Moreover, in a time in which no standard editions existed, translators and commentators necessarily relied on manuscripts, with all their particularities. It is this complex web of relations between source-texts, translations, commentaries, and manuscripts that has to be grasped in order to evaluate how thinking, and more specifically, scientific thinking evolved during the Middle Ages.

The present volume is dedicated to a treatise of which the transmission perfectly illustrates this process: Aristotle's *Problemata*, a multi-faceted text asking various questions about scientific or everyday topics. As it was recently underlined by Jeanine Bertier[1], this text is one of the most neglected Aristotelian treatises, because of its heterogeneous character and its so-called 'inauthenticity'. Indeed, the genesis of the *Problemata* is a complex history. The text as we have it today is a combi-

---

1. BERTIER J., 'Problemata Physica', in: *Dictionnaire des philosophes antiques. Supplément.* Publié sous la direction de Richard GOULET, en collaboration avec Jean-Marie FLAMAND et Maroun AOUAD, Paris: CNRS éditions, 2003, p. 575-593.

nation of materials from different sources and different periods, in which genuine Aristotelian texts have been mixed with later texts, e.g. by Theophrast.

During the Middle Ages, the treatise was translated several times, into Arabic, Latin, and the vernacular. David of Dinant made a first Latin translation in the second half of the 12th century, which might have been only partial and of which only fragments have been preserved[2]. More important was the Latin translation by Bartholomew of Messina, active at the court of King Manfred of Sicily (1258-1266), which circulated at the University of Paris and of which many copies are still extant[3].

Although this translation was certainly read, used, and quoted in the decades after its completion, the first integral commentary was published not earlier than 1310 by the Italian scholar and physician Peter of Abano. In the introduction to this commentary, Peter stresses the originality of his work: he states that he is the first to have undertaken this task, and seeks an explanation for the absence of previous commentaries in the fact that the work deals with nearly every aspect of Aristotle's philosophy. An analysis of the commentary itself shows that Peter based his interpretation on Bartholomew's translation, of which he might have had several manuscripts at his disposal, or at least one annotated manuscript. Peter's commentary soon became a standard work, and it deeply influenced later translators and commentators.

The influence of Peter is strikingly illustrated by the translation of the *Problemata* into Middle French. If knowledge of this and other Latin texts was at first intended for a scholarly elite, the development of vernacular traditions started to make them available to a larger public. In this light, Charles V, also known as the 'Wise', gathered at his court several translators; he ordered them to translate into the French vernacular a series of scientific treatises. The most famous of these translators was Nicole Oresme who translated several Aristotelian works. Charles' personal physician, Evrart de Conty, who was also 'maître régent' at the

2. For a discussion on this translation, see VUILLEMIN-DIEM G., 'Zum Aristoteles Latinus in den Fragmenten der *Quaternuli* des David von Dinant', *Archives d'Histoire Doctrinale et Littéraire du Moyen Age* 71 (2004), p. 27-135.

3. About Bartholomew of Messina, see BRAMS, J., *La riscoperta di Aristotele in Occidente* (Eredità Medievale 03/22), Milano: Jaca Books, 2003, Ch. 7, p. 89-96. For a description of his translation technique, see GOYENS M. – DE LEEMANS P., 'Traduire du grec au latin et du latin au français: un défi à la fidélité', in: P. ANDERSEN (ed.), *Pratiques de traduction au Moyen Age*, Actes du colloque de l'Université de Copenhague (25 et 26 octobre 2002), Copenhagen: Museum Tusculanum Press, University of Copenhagen, 2004, p. 204-224 (here p. 206-213).

University of Paris, worked around the 1380's on the translation of the
Problemata. He used simultaneously Bartholomew's Latin translation
and Peter of Abano's Latin commentary to write his own commented
translation. For each problem, he divided his translation into two parts:
texte and *glose*. The *texte* consists of Aristotle's problem and response
and corresponds to both Bartholomew's translation and Peter of Abano's
rephrasing of it[4]. The *glose* is the commentary to the problem, largely
inspired by Peter of Abano's comment but also developing Evrart's personal ideas, drawn from his reading and experience as a physician.

In the Renaissance, the *Problemata* remained to be read and studied,
yet not as often as most other Aristotelian treatises. Of special interest
are the 15th-century translations made by two leading humanist scholars,
Theodore of Gaza and George of Trebizond. Of these, Gaza's translation
became the standard version, whereas George's translation faded into
obscurity. Commentaries were written by four Italian medical doctors
who also showed some interest in philology: Domenico Montesauri,
Giovanni Manelfi, Giulio Guastavini, and Lodovico Settala. Peter's
commentary kept playing a role, as it is clear from several printings and
from comments by the humanist scholars on their medieval predecessor.

The present volume results from the interdisciplinary workshop that
took place at the Institute of Philosophy of the University of Leuven
(K.U.Leuven) on 30-31 October 2003. The initiative to organize this
meeting was taken within the framework of a linguistically orientated
research project about the Latin translation of the *Problemata* by
Bartholomew and the Middle French translation of it by Evrart de
Conty, in which the *Aristoteles Latinus* (Union Académique Interna-
tionale) and the Department of Linguistics (French historical linguistics)
collaborate[5]. By organizing the workshop, we wanted to gather other
researchers who are studying the *Problemata* in order to exchange information and to stimulate collaboration. The invitation was accepted by
several scholars from Europe, Canada, and the United States. Most of
the papers presented at the workshop are to be found in this book. They
examine the transmission of the *Problemata* in different time periods

---

4. Cf. DE LEEMANS P. – GOYENS M., '*Et samble qu'il woeille dire...*: Evrart de Conty
comme traducteur de Pierre d'Abano', in: O. BERTRAND (ed.), *Théorie et Pratique de la
traduction au Moyen Age* (The Medieval Translator), Turnhout: Brepols Publishers,
forthcoming.

5. Research project G.0110.03 'From source- to goal-language in the Middle Ages:
expressing motion and change in the Medieval translations of Aristotle's *Problemata*',
promoter M. Goyens; co-promoters W. Van Hoecke, J. Brams (†), and P. De Leemans.

and in different languages, covering most aspects of the transmission process described above, from Antiquity to the Renaissance.

The volume opens with a paper by Joan Cadden, who discusses the position of the *Problemata* in medieval learning. She first asks where intellectuals located the text in relation to other texts and domains of learning, and argues that, although the *Problemata* do not figure in late medieval works that articulate the *divisio* of philosophy, medieval authors found satisfactory ways to fit the text into a larger scheme of medieval learning, but not all in the same way. The second question concerns the social locations of the *Problemata*; in which intellectual environments did the *Problemata* circulate, and what did readers hope to find when they copied, bought, read, or glossed it? Cadden analyses the use of the text at the University, by physicians, and at the courts. She concludes that the wide variety of subjects dealt with in the text, its association with authority, and its power to delight resulted in various ways of using the text.

Returning to Antiquity, Robert W. Sharples focuses on the history of the genre of *Problemata* in general, and more concretely on one particular area of their transmission: the transmission of the text edited by U.C. Bussemaker as pseudo-Aristotle, *Problemata Inedita*, but by H. Usener as Books 3-4 of the *Problemata* by Alexander of Aphrodisias, of which Sharples and Sophia Kapetanaki are preparing an edition and translation. In the manuscripts that are extant, the texts are attributed to Aristotle, to Alexander, or to Alexander and Aristotle. These various attributions can be explained by the association of materials from a different source in one collection. The collection seems to consist of two parts, one of which is probably more recent; yet, the authorship of Alexander can be excluded.

The *Problemata Inedita* also play a role in the paper by Lou S. Filius, who examines the genre of *Problemata* in Arabic. In Arabic, different collections of *Problemata* circulated. The *Problemata Physica* might have been translated by Ḥunain ibn Isḥāq, as one Hebrew manuscript tells us. This translation substantially differs from the Greek text; the translation is incomplete – it corresponds with only the first fifteen books of the Greek text –, the individual *problemata* have been reordered, and the translator often searched to elucidate the meaning of the text. Moreover, there is a collection of 91 *problemata inedita* in Arabic, translated from Greek by an unknown translator. Like the Arabic *Problemata Physica*, this is not a literal translation but rather an adaptation. Filius closes his paper with some remarks on the *Problemata* of pseudo-Alexander of Aphrodisias in Syriac, and on the reception of the *Problemata* in Arabic literature.

The reception of the *Problemata* in the Medieval West cannot be fully understood without considering the role played by Peter of Abano, yet his commentary on this text still raises many questions. In her paper, Graziella Federici Vescovini offers a *status quaestionis*. She first asks the question whether Peter of Abano himself made a translation of the *Problemata*; in this respect, she examines some of the expressions used by Peter, such as 'traduxi' or 'translinguavi'. Secondly, she considers the intellectual and philosophical profile of Peter's commentary. The appendix offers the text of the introduction of Peter's commentary as it is found in the 1475 edition.

Peter was not the only commentator in the medieval Latin West who paid attention to the *Problemata*. Maaike van der Lugt presents four other texts: a Latin adaptation from Italy, a commentary attributed to Walter Burley, and two anonymous commentaries that circulated in Central and Eastern Europe. All these writings confirm the status of Peter's *Expositio* as a standard work for the interpretation of the text. In the Italian adaptation, for example, Bartholomew's translation is combined with Peter's commentary in order to produce a clearer and more understandable text of the *Problemata*. Van der Lugt also offers some comments on the text division of the *Problemata* found in Burley's and in the two anonymous commentaries. Three appendices illustrate the relations between the different texts.

Iolanda Ventura focuses on another aspect of the transmission of the *Problemata*, viz., its influence on the collections of *Quaestiones naturales*. This genre of encyclopaedia was extremely popular, since it presented different subject matters in a very clear and systematic way. Yet, within this genre, many variations are found; popular collections, manuals for preachers, but also collections for a cultural and intellectual elite. Ventura offers a survey of the evolution of this genre in Latin from the fourteenth until the sixteenth century.

By the end of the 14th century, the vernacular translation by the physician Evrart de Conty appeared. The next five contributions show that this text is not merely a commented translation, but also a personal commentary and even an entirely original creation on several occasions, combined with a didactic concern to make the text accessible to a larger public.

Françoise Guichard-Tesson was the first to analyse the French translation, since she already wanted to undertake the edition of the text a decade ago. She was one of the first specialists of Evrart de Conty, having published an edition of one of his other writings. In her contribution, she discusses the author's work, since he was not only the first French translator of the *Problemata*, but also seems to have been the author of an allegoric poem, the *Eschés amoureux,* and of an extended commentary on that poem, the *Eschez amoureux moralisés*, which was published by the contributor. More specifically, she analyses, for the three works, the conception and the objectives of the commentary elaborated by Evrart, as well as the audience to which they were addressed, and explores the common elements in his 'œuvre'. She shows that Evrart's *Problemes* is the connection between the three texts. If his translation had to be made in narrow confines, it enabled him to develop a technique and made him write a work for a broader audience, in which he could synthesize his moral and scholarly preoccupations.

The originality Evrart put into his translation is the object of Caroline Boucher's contribution. She analyses the image Evrart, as well as his contemporary Nicole Oresme, gives of himself as a translator, always concerned about the novelty of his developments. In his *Problemes*, and in Nicole Oresme's *Livre du ciel et du monde*, another translation of an Aristotelian text, both translators claim the originality of their comments and try to initiate a dialogue with the reader. Boucher shows that both translations can be considered as key works in the vernacularization process of Latin scientific texts.

An equal concern about originality is found in the article of Joëlle Ducos, who studied Evrart's commentary in Parts XXV and XXVI, concerned with meteorological questions, more specifically air and water. Since those matters concern both Aristotelian meteorology and Hippocratic medicine, where air and water are causes of diseases or good health, Evrart, as a physician, was highly interested in them. Ducos shows that Evrart's commentary is a kind of readers' guide, joining learned findings and developments on the one hand, and more anecdotal passages on the other, which leads to different writings, destined to different readers. As such, the process of vulgarization or vernacularization is seen as a mixture of different types of writing, where readers of various cultures or backgrounds can meet their needs or interests. It provides Evrart with a true quality of physician, popularizer, and writer.

The relationship between Evrart and Peter of Abano, the Latin commentator, is in the centre of Geneviève Dumas' paper. More specifically, Evrart's sources are analysed, with respect to those cited by Peter. Indeed, Evrart de Conty frequently refers to authorities, of which he gives a marginal reference, in Latin. Analysing some 225 references which appear in the first section of Evrart's *Problemes*, dedicated to medical problems, Dumas compares Evrart's way of referring to sources with Peter of Abano's, in his Latin commentary of the *Problemata*. Both scholars emerge from the same educational milieu, the medical studies at the University of Paris, but seem to write for a different audience. Peter has more references to sources, and seems to write for a learned audience; in this first part, Evrart offers rather a kind of introductory course in medicine for future students, where his didactic qualities and concern about scientific vulgarization are more than obvious.

Evrart's subjectivity is studied in Annelies Bloem's article. The way Evrart adopts Aristotle's ideas or discusses them shows indeed how the translator balances between his respect for the great philosopher and his own critical ideas concerning several topics. The author focuses on the first section, devoted to medical questions: given the fact that Evrart was a physician, this domain is the most likely to have triggered his critical remarks. The analysis shows that, most of the time, Evrart follows rather faithfully Peter of Abano's example with respect to criticizing Aristotle. Evrart's personal touch appears then more through his didactic approach of the medical matter, organizing and popularizing knowledge in such a way that he practically guides the reader through Aristotle's *matere obscure*. In this respect, he does not hesitate to shorten Peter's commentary if he believes that it is necessary in order to understand the text better.

The volume closes with a paper devoted to the reception of the *Problemata* in the Renaissance. John Monfasani examines the critique George of Trebizond formulated on the translation of the *Problemata* by his rival Theodore Gaza. The former even wrote a *Protectio Problematum Aristotelis* (Rome, 1456), a polemic work, meant to discredit Gaza. An analysis of the *Protectio* reveals two different personalities: Gaza was an alien to the medieval tradition, who wanted to recreate Aristotle in a completely new Latin vocabulary, whereas George of Trebizond greatly admired medieval scholasticism.

This volume would not have been possible without the stimulating contributions of the authors during and after the workshop, nor without the financial support of the University Foundation (Belgium). We express our gratitude to the Fund of Scientific Research – Flanders, for its financial support of our research project and of the workshop. We also gratefully acknowledge the other sponsors of the workshop for their kind grants: the Faculty of Arts of our University, the Department of

Linguistics, the Institute of Philosophy, the De Wulf-Mansion Centre, and the *Aristoteles Latinus*. Last but not least, we thank the collaborators of our research projects, as well as Daniël De Smet, for their help in the preparation of this volume. Special thanks to Prof. Werner Verbeke, the indefatigable secretary of the Institute of Medieval Studies.

Katholieke Universiteit Leuven

Joan CADDEN

PRELIMINARY OBSERVATIONS ON THE PLACE OF THE *PROBLEMATA* IN MEDIEVAL LEARNING

Où se trouvèrent les Problemata *dans la taxonomie des connaissances aux 14ᵉ et 15ᵉ siècles? Quelles fonctions servirent-ils dans les milieux sociaux variés? Afin de répondre à ces questions, l'article examine non seulement les textes qui ont été produits autour de l'ouvrage aristotélicien, mais aussi les manuscrits dans lesquels ces écrits ont survécu. Auteurs, autant anonymes que connus (Pietro d'Abano, Évrart de Conty, Walter Burley), commanditaires, possesseurs et lecteurs témoignent des significations et usages de ce livre qui n'était guère conforme à la catégorisation habituelle des sciences ou des genres. Pour certains, les* Problemata *servirent d'encyclopédie de phénomènes hétéroclites; pour d'autres ils constituèrent un site de recherches de philosophie naturelle. Ces derniers ont dû faire face à la forme de l'œuvre composée de questions sans solution définitive. Les lecteurs associés aux facultés des arts y recherchèrent les causes naturelles; les médecins se tournèrent vers les théories et faits médicaux; le public aristocratique s'amusa des curiosités qui y étaient inscrites et s'imagina les biens qui pourraient résulter de telles connaissances naturelles.*

Introduction*

Manuscripts of the Aristotelian *Problemata* circulated widely and commanded considerable attention from the late thirteenth through the fifteenth century. There are more than a hundred twenty extant copies or fragments of the standard Latin translation and the commentaries, abbreviations, and other texts dependent on it. This study offers a preliminary account of the nature of medieval interest in these texts. Its suggestions are tentative for a number of reasons. First, it is based on consultation of only about three quarters of the manuscripts. Second, information about provenance is often fragmentary, conjectural, or both. Finally, it results from a study that has centered on a single *problema*, pt. IV, probl. 26, so that the observations are often dependent on limited examination of the texts and manuscripts. It is nevertheless possible to draw some conclusions concerning the meaning and value the *Problemata* had for those who copied, read, and owned it.

One way to address the subject is to ask: Where was the work situated on the medieval map of knowledge? Where did intellectuals locate it in

* This material is based upon work supported by the U.S. National Science Foundation under Grant No. 0115556.

relation to other texts and domains of learning? This is the approach of the first part of the paper, which explores the position of the *Problemata* in medieval taxonomies of knowledge. Readers took various stances toward the aspects of the work that might have made it difficult to place – its scattered subject matter, its inconclusive responses to particular questions, and its imperfect claim to Aristotelian authenticity. But the subject can also be investigated at the social level: Who were its readers and what did they hope to find in the *Problemata*? This approach will be the subject of the second part of the paper, which explores the social locations of the manuscripts. Here too answers varied. At universities scholars used it as the basis for non-teleological natural philosophy; among physicians it was a source for theory and practice; and at court it brought together a sense of wonder and an interest in utility.

Much of the evidence available resides in the manuscripts of the Latin translation made by Bartholomeus de Messina in the 1260s and in texts and manuscripts of the main commentaries upon it, produced in the course of the fourteenth century. The physician and natural philosopher Pietro d'Abano, whose career is associated with the universities of Padua and Paris, completed the first of these in 1310. Within a few decades Walter Burley, who taught philosophy at Paris and Oxford and wrote extensively on Aristotelian texts, prepared a summary of the text that relied at least in part on Pietro's commentary. Finally, in the 1380s, Evrart de Conty, who had studied Pietro (and perhaps other expositors), produced a version of the *Problemata*'s text in French and supplied extensive glosses on its contents. Evrart, who had ties to the University of Paris, served as a physician to Charles V for whom he originally undertook his project. In addition to these prominent works of which we have multiple manuscripts, other more modest, less well circulated, and anonymous texts relating to the *Problemata*, as well as occasional information about owners or readers, provide evidence about how the work was conceived of and used.

1. The Problemata *in Taxonomies of Knowledge*

The *Problemata* does not figure in late medieval works or diagrams that articulate the *divisio* of philosophy – its parts and the relations among them. It had many features that placed it at or beyond the margins of the well-defined and systematic disciplines that qualified as *scientie*. First, as a member of the species *compilatio*, its subject matter ranges from sneezing to justice and from olive oil to melancholy. Second, as a member of the textual genre of natural questions, its treatment of those subjects was particular, rather than general. Furthermore its answers took the form of suggestions rather than the arguments characteristic of so much late medieval learned literature. Finally, its status as an authoritative text, already called into question by its inchoate subject and its indecisive approach, could have been undermined by certain doubts concerning Aristotle's authorship. Such difficulties may partially explain why fewer copies of the work have come down to us than of a number of other books on natural philosophy. Its late appearance in Latin relative to the main Aristotelian corpus may also help to account for its marginality, though other late-comers, such as the *De motu animalium*, circulated far more widely. Similarly, its extraordinary length made it expensive to copy and daunting to read, though the comparably bulky *De animalibus* enjoyed more success. For those who did take an interest in it, however, its character as a compilation, the unresolved contents of its chapters, and its shaky relationship with Aristotle, though serious questions, did not tarnish its value as a source of knowledge.

1.1. 'Compilatio'

We know that medieval readers took seriously the designation of the *Problemata* as a compilation. Pietro d'Abano identified the work's subject matter simply as 'what is knowable' (*scibile*), and commented on its 'variety' and 'particularity' (*diversitas* and *singularitas*)[1]. Evrart de Conty was more specific about the composition of the work, calling it 'une assemblee' of questions that Aristotle selected from various disciplines[2]. The same notion is conveyed in some pictorial representations. At the opening of Bartholomeus's text, found in a Bruges manuscript, the illuminator has altered or even reversed the commonplace scene of a master imparting knowledge to a group of students (figure 1)[3]. The young, beardless, untonsured men whom the master (Aristotle) addresses are offering him scrolls, presumably containing knowledge from their respective domains of expertise. In an intellectual environment increasingly conscious of the taxonomy of knowledge, this work did not conform to such familiar distinctions as those between the liberal and mechanical arts, between mathematical and physical sciences, or even

1. PIETRO D'ABANO, *Expositio Problematum Aristotelis*, Paris, Bibliothèque Nationale, ms. lat. 6540, fol. 1ra and 1rb.
2. ÉVRART de Conty, *Les Problemes d'Aristote*, The Hague, Koninklijke Bibliotheek, ms. 133A3, vol. 1, fol. 1rb.
3. Bruges, Openbare Bibliotheek, ms. 476, fol. 92ra.

Figure 1
Aristotle as a master, receiving scrolls. Opening initial of
Aristotle's *Problemata*, Latin translation by Bartholomeus
of Messina. Bruges, Openbare Bibliotheek, ms. 476,
fol. 92ra. Reproduced by permission of the library.

among logical, physical, and ethical knowledge. Although almost all of the
more than eight hundred questions inquire about natural phenomena, the
work also contains problems on such topics as justice and moderation.

Medieval authors and readers answered the question of the work's
proper place in different ways. In a deluxe copy of Evrart's version, the
artist celebrated the miscellaneous diversity of the subject matter, apparently undisturbed by its lack of a well-defined relation to any schema of
knowledge. Arrayed before the seated Aristotle are male figures bearing

implements or attributes of subjects dealt with in the text: a physician (medicine), a monk (moral philosophy), a musician (the liberal arts), two knights (justice), and a clerical astronomer (mathematics). In addition, the artist, perhaps speculating that Aristotle would not have omitted so important a science, has included a naked figure who appears to be a hermetic hermaphrodite representing magic or alchemy (neither of which figures in the text), as well as two other enigmatic individuals[4]. Thus, in a courtly context, the *Problemata* could play the role of an encyclopedia, even though it lacked the structure of such works.

Although more learned audiences were also conscious of the great range of the work, they were readier to acknowledge its overwhelmingly scientific content than were the artists who produced illustrations for aristocratic patrons. In his preface, Pietro (and those who copied his work) struggled with his own sweeping claim that the problems pertained to every branch of knowledge (*circa unamquamque artem et scientiam*). In most manuscripts, the prologue says that philosophy is *almost* completely covered in the work, explaining that 'almost' refers to the absence of grammar and metaphysics. Three manuscripts, however, omit the qualification, thus implicitly defending the universal scope of the text[5]. One of the scribes who included the subject-limiting sentence seems to have had the dominance of natural philosophy in mind. Where Pietro alluded to the work's many 'revelations and remarkable things' (*declarationes et notabilia*), this copyist read 'revelations and remarkable natural things' (*declarationes et naturalia notabilia*)[6]. Although Pietro himself reiterated the comprehesive nature of the compilation, as a natural philosopher, he saw in the text the familiar form of a book of natural questions[7].

---

4. Jena, Thüringer Universitäts- und Landesbibliothek, ms. El.f.81, fol. 1r. See DEXEL W., *Untersuchungen über die französischen illuminierten Handschriften der jenaer Universitätsbibliothek vom Ende des 14. bis zur Mitte des 15. Jahrhunderts* (Zur Kunstgeschichte des Auslandes 115), Strasbourg: J. H. Ed. Heitz, 1917, p. 19-23.

5. PIETRO D'ABANO, *Expositio Problematum...*: 'Sed in eo pene sermo philosophie totius simpliciter reperitur... Dixi autem *pene* quoniam rationem non invenio explicitam in ipso de his que sunt gramatice et philosophie supreme parumper'. Paris, BN, lat. 6540, fol. 1rb. Similarly Paris, Bibliothèque Nationale, lat. 6541A; Cesena, Biblioteca Malatestiana, mss. D.XXIV.2. and S.VI.2.; Vatican, Biblioteca Apostolica, ms. lat. 2175; Venice, Biblioteca Marciana, ms. 2465. The mss. Paris, Bibliothèque Nationale, ms. lat. 6541, Nürnberg, Stadtbibliothek, ms. Cent. III.38, and Vatican, Biblioteca Apostolica, ms. lat. 2174 omit *pene* in the first sentence, as well as the entire second sentence.

6. PIETRO D'ABANO, *Expositio Problematum...*, Paris, BN, lat. 6540, fol. 1ra.

7. PIETRO D'ABANO, *Expositio Problematum...*, Paris, BN, lat. 6540, fol. 1ra-b: 'Forma autem huius est duplex, videlicet tractatus consistens in distinctione partium libri naturalium et pertinentium [Vatican lat. 2175: particularium] ut videbitur subsequenter. Et forma tractandi...'.

Jean de Jandun, to whom Pietro sent a copy of his commentary, had earlier given some thought to the work's fundamental character. While not denying the presence of other subjects, he included the *Problemata* among Aristotle's natural works, and described it as mainly composed of 'many natural accidents'[8]. Evrart too specified that the book contains 'questions one can ask about things seen in nature'[9]. Walter Burley asserted more precisely that the work belongs to the domain of the natural philosopher (*physicus*), even though, like Pietro, he identified the main divisions of the work as medical, natural, mathematical, and moral. By associating it with a recognized discipline Burley rendered respectable what he feared would be perceived as the trivial, base, and even scandalous content of the compilation[10]. Thus, for him, the justification of the work – in social as well as theoretical terms – depended on its subject being *physica*, the study of the natural world. Indeed it was Burley who made the only explicit statement I have found about the text's specific location on the map of learning, saying, 'The order is such that this book follows the book *On Animals and Plants*'[11]. That is, it occupies a place towards the bottom of, but nevertheless within, the hierarchy of Aristotelian natural philosophical texts as reflected in tracts on the sciences and in manuscript anthologies. In fact, it is often found in the company of all or part of the *De animalibus*[12]. Readers thus confronted the particular character of the compilation in various ways: some by celebrating its prodigious array of curiosities, others by confining it within familiar disciplinary categories.

1.2. 'Problema'

There remained the problem that, even if natural philosophy as a whole was taken to be its primary domain, the subject of the work was

8. JOHANNES DE JANDUNO, *Quaestiones super 8 libros Physicorum Aristotelis*, Venice: Iuntas, 1551; reprinted Frankfurt: Minerva, 1967, Preface, pt. 2, fol. [x]rb.

9. EVRART DE CONTY, *Les problemes...*, The Hague, KB, 133A3, vol. 1, fol. 1ra: 'les questions qui se peuent faire des choses c'on voit en nature'.

10. PIETRO D'ABANO, *Expositio Problematum...*: 'In hoc libro invenitur fere totius philosophye' (Paris, BN lat. 6540, 1rb). [Walter BURLEY], *Problemata Aristotilis*, Oxford, St. John's 113, fol. 1ra. Elsewhere in this text, manuscripts place the *Problemata* among *medicinalibus vel philosophicis* (Oxford, St. John's 113, fol. 12va) or *medicinalibus vel physicis* (Oxford, Bodleian Library, ms. Digby 153, fol. 110r). See CADDEN J., '«Nothing Natural Is Shameful»: Vestiges of a Debate about Sex and Science in a Group of Late-Medieval Manuscripts', *Speculum* 76 (2001), p. 82-4.

11. [BURLEY], *Problemata Aristotilis*, Oxford, St. John's 113, fol. 1rb: 'Ordo talis est quod iste liber librum *De animalibus et vegetabilibus* subsequitur'.

12. Material from the *Problemata* and the *De animalibus* are associated in at least seventeen manuscripts, for example: Paris, BN, mss. lat. 14,725 and 14,728; Bruges, OB 476; Vatican, Biblioteca Apostolica, ms. Borghese 37.

not really the natural world itself. Rather it was a state of mind: uncertainty about the causes of recognized natural phenomena. As Burley, following Pietro, explains: 'The material cause or subject of the *Book of Problems* is something commonly knowable subjected to doubt'[13]. For this reason, the work could not even fully claim membership in the general category of *scientia* in its strict sense. That is, it is not rationally systematized; it does not present arguments; and the explanations it offers cannot aspire to any degree of certainty. By their very nature, the answers to its questions cannot be definitively determined. In the simplest terms, 'A *problema* is a question that is difficult to solve'[14]. Pietro d'Abano explained that a *problema* could 'devour and ensnare', and an anonymous expositor emphasized the unresolved nature of questions that 'battle in the mind'[15].

Once again, medieval authors and readers took various approaches. Intellectuals who operated within the formats of scholastic philosophy, such as the quodlibetal question, were never far from the older traditions of problem literature described by Brian Lawn[16]. Authors and readers of some of the more abbreviated treatments of the Aristotelian work may well have regarded these problems as appropriate exercises for students[17]. Pietro d'Abano approached the *Problemata* very differently – as an occasion for advanced exploration of natural phenomena. Indeed, he asserts that the work cannot be fully understood by readers not familiar with all parts of philosophy. As is apparent in his earlier work, the *Conciliator*, he had a special intellectual appetite for confronting difficult questions and contradictory explanations. But in his exposition of the *Problemata* he was far less likely to settle a question. Rather, where the

13. [BURLEY], *Problemata Aristotilis*, Oxford, St. John's 113, fol. 1ra: 'Causa materialis sive subiectum libri *Problematum* Aristotelis secundum Petrum Badulanensem [sic] est scibile commune sub dubitatione prolatum'. Cf. Oxford, BL Digby 153, fol. 102r: 'est stabile quoddam sub dubitatione prolatum'. Cf. PIETRO D'ABANO, *Expositio Problematum...*, Paris, BN lat. 6540, fol. 1ra: 'Materia sive subiectum huius libri vel scientie est scibile pene commune sub dubitatione prolatum'.

14. [BURLEY], *Problemata Aristotilis*, Oxford, St. John's 113, fol. 1ra: 'Problema est questio difficilis ad solvendum'. Cf. PIETRO D'ABANO, *Expositio Problematum...*, Paris BN lat. 6540, fol. 1rb: 'Est enim questio difficilis aliquid continens quod disputatione solvendum [est]'.

15. PIETRO D'ABANO, *Expositio Problematum...*, Paris, BN lat. 6540, fol. 1rb: 'voret et decipiat'; and Erfurt, Universitätsbibliothek Erfurt/Gotha, ms. Ampl. F. 263, fol. 35vb: 'problema est speculacio contendens ad mentem'.

16. LAWN B., *The Salernitan Questions: An Introduction to the History of Medieval and Renaissance Problem Literature*, Oxford: Oxford University Press at the Clarendon Press, 1963.

17. For example, Vatican, Biblioteca Apostolica, ms. lat. 901, fols. 122v-135v.

text gives alternative or even contradictory responses, Pietro often appears content to develop the logic of each. In that regard, his commentary mirrors the uncertainty conveyed by the very nature of the text itself.

Others were not as comfortable as Pietro with the lack of resolution provided by the Aristotelian work. One anonymous author tried to fit the work into the mold of a scholastic disputation, conveying confidence that every *questio* could produce a *determinatio*. In a gloss on pt. IV, probl. 21, where an answer strikes him as non-Aristotelian, he says, 'As he often does, Aristotle answers first according to the opinion of others'[18]. He thus implies that the last alternative stated is normally the correct one. In the same spirit, Evrart uses simple terms to convey the idea that, for each question, Aristotle 'respont et met la solution'[19]. Evrart himself is also more inclined to reach a determination than Pietro. He is reflecting his own convictions – not Aristotle's or Pietro's – when he asserts that the homosexual desires described in pt. IV, probl. 26 can be defeated by the individual will[20]. Thus, faced with a work that failed or even refused to provide definitive knowledge, medieval readers were able to assimilate the *Problemata* to various available models – some that accommodated uncertainty, others that resolved it.

1.3. 'Aristotelis'

Aristotle's authorship of the *Problemata* unquestionably lent status to the work and thus affected its place among learned texts; conversely, expulsion from the Aristotelian corpus would have meant even greater marginalization. Medieval scholars were aware of doubts about the attribution, but seem to have been untroubled by them. Most manuscripts of the Bartholomeus translation and the texts dependent on it mention Aristotle in a medieval heading or table. Perhaps because he is conscious of being the first to integrate the text into the discourse of scholastic philosophy, Pietro d'Abano draws attention to the issue of authorship, calling those who deny it 'mendacious' and invoking references to the *Problemata* in authentic Aristotelian works as evidence[21]. The person

18. Krakow, Biblioteka Jagiellońska, ms. 2095, fol. 227r: 'Ut frequenter respondit Aristotiles primo secundum opinionem aliorum'. Pietro uses the term *disputatio* in his preface, but does not allude to the formal practices of the scholastic *questio*. See above, note 14.

19. EVRART DE CONTY, *Les Problemes*..., The Hague, KB 133A3, vol. 1, fol. 1va.

20. EVRART DE CONTY, *Les Problemes*..., The Hague, KB 133A3, vol. 1, fol. 137va.

21. PIETRO D'ABANO, *Expositio Problematum*..., Paris, BN lat. 6540, 1rb: 'Neque est quod hic liber non fuerit Aristotilis sicut estimant quidam mendaciter abnegantes cum de ipso in secundo *Metheororum* ac in plerisque locis *Parvorum naturalium* et *Libris animalium* faciat multotiens mentionem ac in his quidem derelicta in hoc opere compleantur'.

who made the copy and glosses of the Bartholomeus text in a late four-teenth-century manuscript uses (perhaps borrows) the same evidence, concluding, 'This book, the assertion of certain people to the contrary not withstanding, was compiled by Aristotle'[22]. (One version of the Burley text may also be alluding to the doubts about authorship with its virtuoso elaboration on Aristotle's name, although it is possible that the author is just showing off[23]). Evrart, writing after the text's position was well established, did not even discuss the controversy, and his view of the nature of the compilation would explain the intrusion of non-Aristo-telian ideas into the text.

Medieval authors thus found satisfactory ways to fit the *Problemata* into the larger scheme of medieval learning, but they did not all do so in the same way. Some treated it as an encyclopedia of natural phenomena, others gave it a specific location within the Aristotelian corpus; some were content with the open-ended form that answered questions with other questions, others chose to understand Aristotle's responses as deci-sive; some evaded the question of authenticity, others answered it. This flexibility allowed the work to find a home in a variety of intellectual environments.

2. *The Social Locations of the* Problemata

Understanding where medieval authors placed the *Problemata* on the conceptual map of knowledge helps us to see what readers were after when they copied, bought, read, or glossed it. But this approach gives only a partial picture, which can be supplemented by looking at medi-eval practices relating to the work. This section treats some ways in which the *Problemata* functioned in relation to universities, medical cir-cles, and courts. Omitted here is the presence of manuscripts in religious houses. The prior of St. Victor of Paris, for example, purchased a copy of the work in the second quarter of the fifteenth century as part of an aggressive acquisition policy for the monastery's library in conjunction with its academic mission[24]. In such cases, the books were probably viewed in ways similar to those in the hands of university students and masters. Many more copies found their way into monastic libraries as

22. Vatican, Biblioteca Apostolica, lat. 2112, fol. 1r: 'Iste liber non obstante dicto aliquorum in oppositum compilatus fuit ab Aristotele'.

23. [BURLEY], *Problemata Aristotilis*, Oxford, St. John's 113, fol. 1ra-b.

24. Paris, BN, lat. 14,728. See OUY G., *Les manuscrits de l'abbaye de Saint-Victor: Catalogue établi sur la base du répertoire de Claude de Grandrue (1514)* (Bibliotheca Victorina 10), Turnhout: Brepols Publishers, 1999, vol. 1, p. 27 and vol. 2, p. 64, H5.

gifts and bequests or through the agency of university-educated clerics, such as a canon of Prague who had studied arts and medicine[25]. Whether they were used and how they were understood is more difficult to determine.

2.1. Universities

The production of *Problemata*-related texts was clearly associated with the environment of the arts faculties, where the compilation was treated as a work of natural philosophy. This is the case not only for Paris, where an official version of the Bartholomeus translation is known to have circulated[26], but also for Padua, Oxford, Erfurt, Prague, and Krakow. From there they spread to Flanders, Bavaria, Lombardy, and other parts of Europe. Like other texts on the fringes of the Aristotelian corpus, the *Problemata* did not merit a place in the regular curriculum, but it was at least occasionally the subject of public academic discussion. The controversial philosopher Jean de Jandun may or may not have carried out his intention to offer Paris students a series of lectures based on Pietro's exposition. His wish to do so indicates that such a program was not only conceivable but worth Jean's efforts – however slight – to review and modify Pietro's text[27]. In 1334, not long after Jean had fled France, sixty Paris students are said to have attended the lectures of Jan van Berblengheen, a master of arts and medical student who was later a chaplain at Mechelen (Malines) in the diocese of Cambrai[28]. Further evidence that the text was put to public academic use survives in the form of a set of *reportata* contained in a manuscript from later in the fourteenth century[29].

25. Wycbold owned Erfurt, Universitätsbibliothek Erfurt/Gotha, ms. Collectio Amplonia Fol. 15. Other likely examples are Bruges, OB 476 and Oxford, Bodleian Library, ms. Digby 206.

26. DE LEEMANS P. – GOYENS M., 'La transmission des savoirs en passant par trois langues: le cas des *Problemata* d'Aristote', in: P. NOBEL (ed.), *La transmission des savoirs au Moyen Âge et à la Renaissance*. Vol. 1. *Du XIIe au XVIe siècle*, Besançon: Presses Universitaires Franche-Comté, 2005, p. 231-57.

27. KUKSEWICZ Z., 'Les *Problemata* de Pietro d'Abano et leur "rédaction" par Jean de Jandun', *Medioevo* 11 (1985), p. 113-37.

28. I am grateful to A. Derolez for information about him. See also WICKERSHEIMER E., *Dictionnaire biographique des médecins en France au moyen âge* (Centre de Recherches d'Histoire et de Philologie de la IVe Section de l'École pratique des Hautes Études 5; Hautes Études Médiévales 34/1), Geneva: Droz, 1979 (reprint of 1936 edition), p. 360-61.

29. Erfurt, UB CA F. 263, fols. 16ra-29va (for *reportata* see fol. 19vb). Perhaps associated with Aachen. SCHUM W., *Beschreibendes Verzeichniss der Amplonianischen Handschriften-Sammlung zu Erfurt*, Berlin: Weidmann, 1887, p. 170-72. See also

What were the interests and motives of the university segment of the *Problemata*'s audience? In one sense, they cannot be distinguished from the more general academic appetite for natural philosophy. Yet this is a work very different from Aristotle's *De celo* or *De anima*, which are both systematic and dogmatic. Indeed, its quirky, miscellaneous character was no doubt part of its appeal for young students, as it is for modern readers. The absence of structured argument allowed the various questions to occupy a space outside the ordered coherence of nature that was conveyed by the central works of the Aristotelian canon. Perhaps more important, the *Problemata* and its Latin commentaries place their emphasis almost entirely upon material and efficient causes. Other Aristotelian works, particularly the *Historia animalium* and parts of the *Parva naturalia*, offered comparable intellectual opportunities. But the *Problemata*, because of its fragmented form and its array of concrete natural particulars, was especially free from the imperatives of teleology.

This is not to say that Latin commentators denied the importance of final cause or the existence of divine providence, but simply that the text attracted intellectuals for whom the investigation of proximate efficient and material factors was the primary concern. The mechanical workings of nature occupy a place of honor in a Prague commentary, for example[30]. Pietro d'Abano, whose penchant for naturalistic explanations is visible in all his works, often slighted teleological reasoning in favor of more immediate and concrete forces. Thus, in his introduction to Part IV, *De coitu*, he puts *generatio filiorum* and *sanitas* – the two higher purposes of sexual intercourse – in second and third place, saying: 'Coitus is the mutual action of male and female in which the excess material from the third stage of digestion is expelled. It is engaged in for the sake of pleasure, as is usually done; and sometimes for the sake of producing children; and also occasionally for the sake of health'[31]. His commentaries on the questions of Part IV reflect an even greater lack of concern for procreation. We cannot know how many of the *Problemata*'s readers were sympathetic with Pietro's outlook. Certainly Evrart was not. He consistently used the term *œuvre de generation* for the Latin *coitus*.

Markowski M., *Repertorium commentariorum medii aevi in Aristotelem latinorum quae in Bibliotheca Amploniana Erffordiae asservantur*, Wrocław: Zakład Narodowy im. Ossolińskich – Wydawnictwo Polskiej Akademii Nauk, 1987, p. 174.

30. Prague, Národní Knihovna, ms. I.C.25.

31. Pietro d'Abano, *Expositio Problematum...*, IV.1, Paris, BN lat. 6540, fol. 53ra: 'Notandum est quod coytus est mutua actio maris et femelle qua tertie digestionis expellitur superfluum, quod delectationis causa exercetur ut plurimum fit et aliquando causa generationis filiorum interdum etiam causa sanitatis'.

Nevertheless, at universities, the text was clearly the site of some aggressive naturalism that was encouraged by its location at the edge of the Aristotelian corpus.

2.2. Medicine

Some textual practices thus positioned the *Problemata* firmly within the domain of the university, but others placed it in the territory of medicine. Not only were Evrart and Pietro physicians themselves, but medical men are among the few identifiable individual owners and users for the Bartholomeus translation and Pietro's exposition[32]. To be sure, the university and medical worlds were not entirely distinct. The physicians who possessed copies of *Problemata*-related texts were likely to have been ones who, like Amplonius de Berka, took an interest in the areas where medical theory overlapped with natural philosophy[33]. But several types of evidence suggest that the work was understood to be a specifically medical resource. The *Problemata* and, especially, its derivatives were often copied or bound together with medical works[34]. For example, by the fifteenth century, an anonymous summary derivative of Pietro's commentary was bound with recipes, *consilia*, and other medical material[35].

More decisive than the juxtaposition with medical texts are the structures of the text and the patterns of annotation. Those who created versions of the *Problemata* or made copies of them were concerned with the organization of the subjects treated, disagreeing about whether the two sections of the modern standard Part I were one *particula* or two, and whether the distinction was between theory and practice, disease and cure, or airs and medicines[36]. That some medieval users regarded the *Problemata* as a source of specifically medical wisdom is further suggested by the existence of what seems to be a free-standing commentary on Part I in a medical collection that eventually belonged to

32. For example, Petrus Roselli (Paris, Bibliothèque Nationale, ms. lat. 15,454) and Vincentus de Pistorio (Nürnberg, Stadtbibliothek, ms. Cent. III.38). On the former, see D'ALVERNY M.-T., 'Avicenna Latinus II', *Archives d'Histoire Doctrinale et Littéraire du Moyen Âge* (1963), p. 224-6.

33. The Collectio Amploniana contains seven manuscripts that include the Bartholomeus *Problemata* and derivative texts: Erfurt, Universitätsbibliothek Erfurt/Gotha, mss. CA F. 15, F. 16, F. 26, F. 236, F. 263, Q. 16, Q. 237.

34. For example, Erfurt, UB CA F. 236 and 263; Oxford, BL Digby 153 and 206; Paris, Bibliothèque Nationale, mss. lat. 14,725 and 15,081; Vatican, Biblioteca Apostolica, mss. lat. 2481 and Chigi E.VIII.254.

35. Munich, Bayerische Staatsbibliothek, ms. Codices Latini Monacenses 12021.

36. For example, theory and practice, Erfurt, UB CA F. 236; disease and cure, Erfurt, UB CA F. 263, 35vb-39vb; airs and medicines, Munich, BSB, ms. CLM 12021.

Amplonius de Berka[37]. When readers intervened in the manuscripts, their attention was preponderantly focused on Part I. Exclamations of 'nota', *manicula*, and other signs of active interest are sometimes dense, though substantive glosses are rare. Readers of Pietro's exposition especially give evidence of such interest, even when we discount for the fact that people are more likely to have read the beginning of a text than its middle or end. Some noted general principles of health and disease, others specific conditions or treatments. The problema on *pestilencia*, for example, attracted some attention[38]; and, at another point, one reader of the *Problemata* remarked 'It is like this in Jacob of Verme's sister'[39]. In his treatise on conception, the fifteenth-century French physician Bernard Chaussade cited the *Problemata* (IV.5) as his authority for a recommendation against having sexual intercourse barefoot[40].

Thus, in a sense, the existence and practices of medical readers turned this unconventional Aristotelian work into a medical text. Such an adaptation did not sever its ties with university-based natural philosophy, but did place it in a new social, as well as conceptual, environment. To be sure, physicians studied and enjoyed natural philosophy, but they also practiced medicine. Furthermore, in the fifteenth century, physicians in Northern Italy and elsewhere were prominent among the urban intellectuals who integrated the *Problemata* into the emerging world of humanism. Amplonius de Berka and Giovanni Marco da Rimini each owned several copies of *Problemata*-related books[41]. And, at his home in Venice, another physician, Jacobo Suriano, copied into a single manuscript both the old translation of Bartholomeus and the new ones of George of Trebizond and Theodore Gaza[42].

2.3. Courts

Aspects of humanism are also present in some of the courts of Europe, the third and final medieval social environment in which works derived from the Bartholomeus translation of the *Problemata* took root.

37. Erfurt, UB CA F. 236, 24r-35v.
38. For example, a reader has called attention to I.7 with a marginal label, 'pestilentia'; Vatican, Biblioteca Apostolica, ms. lat. 10,452, fol. 1ra.
39. Vatican, lat. 2112, fol. 4r: 'Ita est in sorore domini Iacobi de Verme'.
40. Paris, Bibliothèque Nationale, ms. lat. 7064, fol. 41v. I am grateful to Amy Lindgren for calling my attention to this citation.
41. On Amplonius, see above, note 33. Giovanni Marco da Rimini: Cesena, Biblioteca Malatestiana, mss. D.XXII.2 and D.XXIV.2. See MANFRON A., *La biblioteca di un medico del quattrocento: I codici di Giovanni di Marco da Rimini nella Biblioteca Malatestiana* (Archivi di Bibliofilia), Turin: Umberto Allemandi for the Instituzione Biblioteca Malatestiana, Cesena, 1998, p. 176-7 and 193.
42. London, British Library, ms. add. 21978.

The manuscripts of Evrart's version are the most notable and beautiful of these, finding a place in libraries of the French royal family and also in those of the counts of Nassau and the dukes of Cleves[43]. But his was not the only work to be so honored. Handsome copies of Pietro's commentary belonged to the dukes of Milan and to a leading patrician of Bruges[44]. To some extent their presence at court can be attributed to the influence of university-trained counselors, and at times they may have served no more noble purpose than as objects of material adornment. Furthermore, their readers at court may have had some of the same motives as the arts students and medical men who read them elsewhere. Yet the physical features of these manuscripts, as well as clues in Evrart's text, suggest that the work took on distinct meanings in the courtly context.

The first was the pleasurable enjoyment of natural curiosities. Some texts that circulated in more modest environments also mentioned the marvelous character of the phenomena treated. For example, Walter Burley, whose work is found in simple quarto volumes, declares (citing Aristotle) that in even the vilest objects of nature there is something 'divinum et mirabile'[45]. But it is Evrart, writing in French for a broader and less specialized audience, who insists repeatedly, in his general prologue and in the introductions to many of the book's parts, that the work is filled with things to wonder at. The marvels are far more often the objects and events of everyday experience than singular or exotic phenomena, but these too are capable of exciting curiosity and producing delight in an elite audience.

The pleasure associated with hearing the *Problemata* expounded would have been consistent with general edification, not only in the domain of natural philosophy but also in the area of proper conduct. Given how few of the questions in the work actually relate to subjects like justice and virtue, it is remarkable what prominence they receive in the frontispieces for Evrart's work. An illumination in a Paris manuscript, for example, illustrates the nature of the work as a compilation. In addi-

43. Charles d'Orléans possessed a copy (see DELISLE L., *Inventaire général et méthodique des manuscrits français de la Bibliothèque Nationale*, Paris: H. Champion, 1876-78, vol. 1, p. lxxi and vol. 2, p. 163). The Hague, KB 133.A.3 was owned by the house of Nassau; Jena, ULB El.f.81 by the house of Cleves.

44. On Paris, Bibliothèque Nationale, mss. lat. 6540, 6541, and 6543 see PELLE-GRIN E., *La Bibliothèque des Visconti et des Sforza, ducs de Milan, au XVe siècle* (Publications de l'Institut de Recherche et d'Histoire des Textes 5), Paris: Service de Publications du C.N.R.S., 1955, *passim*; on Ghent, Bibliotheek van de Rijksuniversiteit, ms. 72, see DEROLEZ A., *The Library of Raphael de Marcatellis, Abbot of St. Bavon's, Ghent, 1437-1508*, Ghent: E. Story-Scientia, 1979, # 10, p. 78-80 and 83-85.

45. [BURLEY], *Problemata Aristotilis*, Oxford, St. John's, 113, fol. 1rb.

tion to the practitioners of medicine, music, and astronomy, it includes one figure, with a sword, representing justice and another, with a balance, representing either temperance or justice again[46]. The opening image in the manuscript that belonged to the counts of Nassau may reflect Evrart's vague declaration that the book 'fait moult a la perfection humaine' (figure 2)[47]. Standing on Aristotle's right is a physician, representing Part I; on his left stands a scholar (perhaps an astrologer, since he points to the heavens), with one book on natural philosophy and one on moral philosophy. However meager the work's treatment of ethics and decorum, the households of the higher nobility enjoyed the suggestion that the *Problemata* bore some relation to virtue.

This was not, however, the only value conveyed by Evrart's work or by the illustrations that accompanied his and Pietro's texts. Evrart occasionally stresses the practical utility of the material (an aspect of the work not lost on its Latin audience[48]). Thus, for example, before the discussion of a method for making celery root grow large, he announces, 'In this chapter, Aristotle shows us clearly how good tools and good preparation of plants improve and perfect them'[49]. Or, 'In this chapter Aristotle teaches us how, by skill and ingenuity, one can produce big fat pumpkins and cucumbers, and also teaches us the cause'[50]. It is not likely that anyone in the entourage of Charles VI, to whom the work is dedicated, intended to put this knowledge into practice. Nevertheless, the aristocracy of fifteenth-century France and Flanders regarded it as appropriate to contemplate the prudent management of their lands. Military devastation, economic decline, and political instability strengthened the links among peace, prosperity and social order in the imagination of the ruling class. In court circles, the *Problemata* came to be colored with such concerns, at a time when those concerns themselves were coming

46. Paris, Bibliothèque Nationale, ms. fr. 211, fol. 1r.

47. The Hague, KB 133.A.3, vol. 1, fol. 1r (illumination) and 1va (quotation). Cf. KORTEWEG A. S., *Boeken van Oranje-Nassau: De bibliotheek van de graven van Nassau en prinsen van Oranje in de vijftiende eeuw*. The Hague: Museum van het Boek/Museum Meermanno-Westreenianum and Koninklijke Bibliotheek, 1998, p. 31 and figure 28. I am grateful to Dr. Korteweg for advice about this manuscript.

48. The colophon of the *Problemata* in Vatican, BA, lat. 2112, fol. 34vb reads: 'Explicit iste liber utilis ad multa'. I am grateful to Dr. Pieter De Leemans for calling my attention to this *explicit*.

49. EVRART DE CONTY, *Les Problemes...*, XX.8, The Hague, KB 133A3, vol. 2, fol. 65ra-b: 'Aristote en cest probleme nous moustre clerement comment les bons instrumens et la bonne preparation des plantes les amende et parfait'.

50. EVRART DE CONTY, *Les Problemes...*, XX.9, The Hague, KB 133A3, vol. 2, fol. 65vb-66ra: 'Aristote nous aprent en cest probleme comment on poeut par art et par engin humain les couhourdes et les comcombres faire grosses et grandes et nous aprent aussy la cause et la raison de ceste chose'.

Figure 2

Aristotle with a physician and a philosopher. Frontispice to Evrart de Conty's *Les Problemes d'Aristote*. The Hague, Koninklijke Bibliotheek, ms. 133A3, vol. 1, fol. 1r. Reproduced by permission of the library.

to be associated with natural and technical knowledge. These emerging ties may explain the presence of a ship with full sails on the opening page of the Jena manuscript, suggesting a connection between navigation and the lengthy *particula* on winds[51]. Less ambiguous is the scene before which Aristotle and his colleagues pose in the Hague manuscript (figure 2), which was made in the late fifteenth century and was not long thereafter in the possession of the Count of Nassau. An orderly and fruitful landscape is marked by neat orchards and powerful towns. Above the heavens govern; below, in the distance, the unruly winds are tamed and put to work by a windmill[52].

Nor is it only the vernacular manuscripts that convey the association between the phenomena investigated by Aristotle and the results of good stewardship and good government about which the courtly audience dreamed. Similar themes are conveyed by the images in the manuscript of Pietro's commentary commissioned by Raphael de Marcatellis (1434-1508) – bastard son of Philip the Good of Burgundy, and sometime student of the arts and theology at Paris. He held the titles of Abbot of Saint Bavon and Bishop of Rhosus, but lived as a prosperous burgher of Bruges, taking advantage of his connections to an Italian merchant family, and collecting a library that included magnificent manuscripts of some humanist texts. In his copy of Pietro's exposition, illustrations convey a serene prosperity: a group of problems on fruit-bearing plants is introduced with a depiction of six baskets, each filled with a different kind of fruit; a group on seed-bearing plants with a sack of grain, a sack of flour, and a sack of bread loaves; and a group of horticultural questions with a well-ordered, walled garden overlooking a harbor in which ships are moored[53].

In the first illumination of this work, many of the principal themes discussed here converge (figure 3)[54]. The *Problemata* thrived and multiplied in medieval Europe, in part because it played so many different roles. It was a compilation presided over by the Philosopher himself, enthroned on the cathedra at the center of the scene. The book that Aristotle

51. Jena, ULB El.f.81, fol. 1r. Cf. DEXEL, *Untersuchungen über die französischen …*, p. 19-23 and plate 4.

52. The Hague, KB 133A3, vol. 1, fol. 1r. A similar landscape appears at vol. 2, fol. 1r. I am grateful to Prof. Gregory Clark for his judgement that the manuscript was produced in Hainaut between about 1480 and 1490.

53. Ghent, UB, ms. 72, pt. XXII (fruit), fol. 268v; pt. XXI (grain), fol. 261r; pt. XX (garden), fol. 249v. See DEROLEZ, *The Library of Raphael…*, p. 1-2, no. 10 (p. 78-85), and figures 16, 17, and 20.

54. Ghent, UB 72, fol. 1r. See DEROLEZ, *The Library of Raphael…*, p. 80, figure 17.

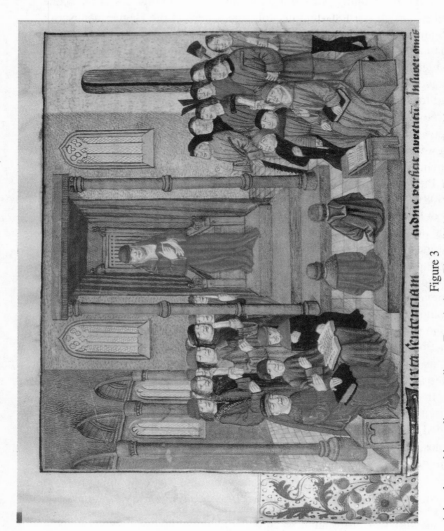

Figure 3

Aristotle teaching a diverse audience. Frontispice to Pietro d'Abano's *Expositio Problematum Aristotelis.* Ghent, Bibliotheek van de Rijksuniversiteit, ms. 72, fol. 1r. Reproduced by permission of the library.

is expounding served as a source of intellectual exercise for the young, who are seated in the foreground facing the master. Seated on either side, completing an inner circle of academic listeners, are mature scholars who possess their own copies. For this group, then, the work is the basis of serious scholarly investigation. But Aristotle's audience is also a source of his knowledge, for many of its members, standing to Aristotle's left and right behind the rows of scholars, offer him scrolls. That is, he draws upon the wisdom of experts from a wide array of occupations, represented on one side by artisans and laborers carrying implements of their trades – a mallet, a saw, a spade, and so forth. Whether in relation to the agriculture of the countryside or in the context of urban artisanal production, the *Problemata* thus evoked the skill and the docility of an ideal labor force. Also in attendance is a group of dignitaries standing to Aristotle's right. These are the men – all with long robes, and some with fur collars and chains of office – who presided over economic life and civil society. From them too, the Aristotelian text drew wisdom, represented by scrolls, and to them, as well as to the scholars and artisans, it offered usable knowledge. (Physicians, though not explicitly depicted here, are present in manuscripts of Evrart's version[55].) At the same time, they lend their prestige to the contents of the elaborately illuminated volume.

Conclusion

The *Problemata* was not all things to all men, but its curious structure, its peripheral subject matter, its association with authority, and its power to delight and edify allowed it to fit – intellectually and socially – into an exceptionally wide range of medieval environments. Academic, medical, and aristocratic audiences owned and used the text in a variety of ways, taking advantage of its encyclopedic contents, its challenges to natural philosophy, its distillation of medical wisdom, its body of practical lore, and its focus on the marvellous in everyday experiences. Marginal to the established canon of medieval academic learning, the *Problemata* nevertheless enjoyed considerable status in the medieval culture of knowledge.

University of California at Davis

---

55. The Hague, KB 133A3, vol. 1, fol. 1r; Paris, BN, ms. fr. 211, fol. 1ra; Jena, ULB El.f.81, fol. 1r.

Robert W. SHARPLES

PSEUDO-ALEXANDER OR PSEUDO-ARISTOTLE, MEDICAL PUZZLES AND PHYSICAL PROBLEMS

Cette contribution concerne, dans le contexte d'une édition à paraître de Sophia Kapetanaki et de moi-même, des textes édités par Bussemaker comme étant des Problèmes inédits *du pseudo-Aristote, mais par Usener comme le 3ᵉ et le 4ᵉ livre des* Problèmes *du pseudo-Alexandre d'Aphrodise. La dernière partie du 2ᵉ livre chez Bussemaker, et la plus grande partie du 3ᵉ, sont beaucoup plus similaires aux problèmes pseudo-aristotéliciens édités par Bekker que le sont le 1ᵉʳ livre et la première partie du 2ᵉ; mais il paraît, surtout par des parallèles avec les* Problèmes *de Bamberg et avec les versions arabes étudiées par Lou Filius (dans ce volume), que jadis, aussi la source de la première partie du 2ᵉ livre était déjà attribuée à Aristote. L'association des deux parties de l'actuel 2ᵉ livre, et puis du 2ᵉ au 1ᵉʳ, attribué déjà lui-même à Alexandre, peut expliquer la variation des attributions dans les manuscrits que nous possédons maintenant. Le 1ᵉʳ livre et la première partie du 2ᵉ sont, semble-t-il, plus tardifs que le reste; mais il n'est pas possible qu'ils soient des œuvres d'Alexandre lui-même.*

This contribution is a report on work in progress by Sophia Kapetanaki (Athens) and myself, to produce an edition and translation of the texts here discussed[1]. Material summarised here will be discussed in full, with supporting evidence, in the introduction to the edition[2]. The present

---

1. A similar summary was presented both at a conference on ancient medicine at Reading in August 2003 and at the conference in Leuven in October 2003. This is a heavily revised version of that summary. Although the present paper is chiefly concerned with the problems edited by Bussemaker and Usener, for reasons that will become apparent it will be necessary to consider the problems edited by Ideler as well. A new edition of these is currently being prepared by Carl-Gustaf Lindqvist of Gothenburg. I am grateful for discussion and advice on various points to Dr Lindqvist and also to Bruce Barker-Benfield, Dr A.T. Bouwman, Charles Burnett, John Dudley, Philip van der Eijk, Lou Filius, Antonio Garzya, Alan Griffiths, Inna Kupreeva, John Monfasani, Marlein van Raalte, Harold Tarrant, Stephen White and Jürgen Wiesner. The *Thesaurus Linguae Graecae* database has given incalculable help in searches for parallels and for points of word-usage. The present paper could not have been written without the contribution Sophia Kapetanaki has made to our joint research; in particular, she has undertaken by far the greatest part of the work involved in collating MSS and constructing a critical apparatus, on which all reconstruction of the transmission of the material must necessarily depend.

2. To be published in the series *Peripatoi* by Walter de Gruyter (Berlin). I am grateful to the publisher for permission to include here material from this forthcoming volume. Research on an earlier project to catalogue the MSS of the *scripta minora* attributed to

paper is offered as a contribution to the history of the genre of *Problems* and as a clarification of one particular area of their transmission.

In 1841 Ideler published two books of *Medical Puzzles and Physical Problems* attributed to Alexander of Aphrodisias, the commentator on Aristotle who flourished around 200 A.D[3]. In 1859 Usener published two more books which he argued were books 3 and 4 of the same collection[4]. But in 1857 Bussemaker had appended to his edition of the pseudo-Aristotle *Problems*, as contained in Bekker's edition[5], three extra books of *Problemata inedita* – i.e. *hitherto* inedita – the first two of which are the same as the two subsequently edited by Usener[6]. Here, and in the forthcoming edition, we use Bussemaker's numbering for the books, in accordance with the majority of scholars[7] and in order to recognise the 'Aristotelian' character of some of the texts. However, we use Usener's numbers for the individual problems within the books; Bussemaker did not give separate sequential numbers to some problems that are preserved in only one of the MSS he himself used, presumably regarding them as late additions in this MS, but they appear in other MSS too, as Usener discovered, and in any case a single continuous sequence of numbers is desirable. We distinguish the two books edited by Ideler by using the lower-case numerals i and ii. Since we cannot go on calling problems first edited in 1857 *problemata inedita*, however exciting that may make them sound, here and in the edition we use the title *Supplementary Problems*.

The extent to which any of these problems is 'medical' needs to be heavily qualified. The topics selected are indeed predominantly concerned with the functioning of animal bodies; but we are definitely not dealing with any sort of therapeutic manual, and what motivates the discussion is intellectual curiosity. For example, the two problems concerned with nausea are (2.105) why some people feel nausea and hunger

Alexander was generously supported by grants from the British Academy and the A.G. Leventis Foundation, and that on the *Problemata* has been supported by a grant from the Leverhulme Trust. We are also grateful to the many libraries that have provided prints or microfilms of the various MSS.

3. IDELER J.L. (ed.), *Physici et medici graeci minores,* Berlin: Reimer, 1841-2, vol. 1, p. 3-80.

4. USENER H. (ed.), *Alexandri Aphrodisiensis quae feruntur Problematorum libri 3 et 4,* Berlin: Typis Academiae Regiae, 1859.

5. BEKKER I. (ed.), *Aristotelis Opera,* Berlin: Reimer, 1831, vol. 2, p. 859-967.

6. BUSSEMAKER U.C. (ed.), *Aristoteles, Opera Omnia,* vol. IV.1, Paris: Didot, 1857, p. 291-332.

7. FLASHAR H. (tr.), *Aristoteles: Problemata Physika* (Aristoteles Werke in Deutscher Übersetzung 19), Berlin: Akademie-Verlag 1962 ([4]1991), p. 362 n.1.

at the same time, and (2.106) why the vomit of those who are sea-sick on ships is bilious while other vomit is phlegmatic. I have not been able to find any parallels for discussion of these issues in the medical literature, which discusses nausea and vomiting rather in the practical contexts of disease and of antidotes to poisoning.

Although Bussemaker included his three books in an edition of Aristotle, he none the less distinguished in his introduction between those items which he regarded as 'Aristotelian' and those which he regarded as 'Alexandrian'. It has indeed been generally recognised that Bussemaker's three books contain material of two different types. A new preface separates the greater part of book 2, introduced as a discussion of 'common symptoms', from the first 38 problems, and the problems in the greater part of book 2, and the first 45 problems of book 3[8], are similar in structure and approach to the pseudo-Aristotle *Problems* included in Bekker's edition. Like these, they are divided into sequences on specific topics. Some of these sequences include a high proportion of problems also found in the Bekker collection while others do not; in the case of some of the latter, there is reason to ask whether they may not be linked with lost works of Theophrastus in the way in which some of the Bekker *Problems* are linked with his surviving works[9]. 2.104 is a single statement of an explanation which, as Marenghi 1991, 134 notes, appears *twice* in the Bekker *Problems*, at 12.5 in connection with good odours and at 13.12 in connection with bad ones. It seems more likely that it has been duplicated there, as part of an editorial process, than that our text has combined two Bekker *Problems*.

In the majority of the MSS book 1 begins with a preface which Dietz edited from a Vienna MS (med. gr. 49) where it occurs rather as a preface to Hippocrates' *Aphorisms*. The view that this was in fact its original context has been challenged by Flashar[10]. The book itself contains

8. The latter are indeed preserved in only one MS (Paris, BN, ancien gr. 2047A), separate from the material there attributed to Alexander and with no explicit attribution of their own. 3.46-49 Bussemaker, together with two further problems added in an appendix by Usener, are a collection of odds and ends that occur in the non-standard sequence only (see below), four of the six being extracts from or paraphrase of Olympiodorus' commentary on the *Meteorologica*. For 3.50-52 Bussemaker see below at n. 25. 3.53-54 Bussemaker, taken by him from Valla's translation and printed in Latin, presumably on the basis that he supposed that the Greek did not survive, are in fact – as he belatedly realised: BUSSEMAKER, *Aristoteles...*, vol. IV.1, p. xviii n. 1 – simply the second and third parts of i.88 Ideler, which Valla had divided into three sections.

9. See SHARPLES R.W., 'Evidence for Theophrastus On Hair, On Secretion, On Wine and Olive-Oil?', *Bulletin of the Institute of Classical Studies* 47 (2004), p. 141-151.

10. DIETZ F.R. (ed.), *Commentarii in Hippocratis aphorismos* (Scholia in Hippocratem et Galenum 2), Königsberg: Bornträger, 1834, p. 244.16-245.29; FLASHAR H., 'Bei-

22 miscellaneous problems, some medical and some concerned with food, wine and the like. Book 2 Usener starts with 38 miscellaneous physiological problems. Both in book 1 and in the first 38 problems of book 2 there are relatively few parallels either with the [Aristotle] *Problems* in Bekker's edition or with the [Alexander] *Problems* in books i-ii Ideler; most of the *Problems* in 2.1-38 are much shorter than those in the latter part of the book, and in 1 and 2.1-38 the answer to the problem begins simply 'Because' (ὅτι) whereas in 2.39-192 it begins with 'Is it because' (ἢ ὅτι), as in the Bekker *Problems*. Parallels with ancient medical literature also seem different in character in the two groups of texts. In the discussion of purging and excretion in 2.105-126 there are parallels in the Hippocratic writings to a number of the alleged facts that provide the problems, though not to the solutions. This section regularly uses for 'excessively purged' the term ὑπέρινος, which was used by Hippocrates, Aristotle (*GA* 3.1 750a29) and Theophrastus (*HP* 9.14.2) but is not part of standard later vocabulary; it is one of the Hippocratic terms that Galen explains[11], and also occurs in the lexicographical tradition. In the case of 1 and 2.1-38, on the other hand, while there are a few parallels from the classical and Hellenistic periods[12], the majority are to be found in the writings of Galen[13] or even later[14]. Flashar sees Christian influence in the reference to God as making Hippocrates 'nature incarnate' (τὴν φύσιν σαρκώσας) in the prologue to book 1[15]. Even Usener recognised that 2.39ff. were different from 1 and 2.1-38 and in some sense 'Aristotelian', but in order to uphold the attribution to Alexander he argued that these 'Aristotelian' problems had been *fraudulently* incorporated into a four-book collection attributed as a whole to Alexander.

It has long been known that some of the individual problems are referred to at an early date, and attributed to Aristotle, in an Oxyrhynchus

---

träge zur spätantiken Hippokratesdeutung', *Hermes* 90 (1962), p. 402-418, especially 412. Cf. also USENER, *Alexandri Aphrodisiensis...*, p. xi-xii; I. SLUITER, 'Two Problems in Ancient Medical Commentaries', *CQ* 44 (1994), p. 270-275, who notes parallels with Galen's commentary on the *Aphorisms*.

11. Galen, *Ling. Hippocr. explic.*, vol. 19, p.148.15-149.1 Kühn.

12. 2.20 ~ Plato, *Timaeus* (question and solution); 2.19 ~ Erasistratus (question only); 2.14 (question ~ Hippocrates, answer ~ Galen).

13. 1.1, 1.4, 1.6, 1.8, 1.18, 2.14, 2.19 (question and solution); 1.12 (question; solution ~ Stephanus, 7[th]cent. AD).

14. 1.9 has an etymology for 'spleen' from 'attract' which occurs in the lexicographer Orion (5[th]cent. AD) and the medical writers Meletius (7[th]cent. AD or later) and Leo (9[th]cent.). The terms 'spleen' and 'attract' are also used in close proximity, without any explicit allusion to the etymology, by Galen, *Meth. med.* 11.16 (vol. 10 p. 796.16-17 Kühn).

15. FLASHAR, 'Beiträge...', p. 413. This is however questioned by SLUITER, above n. 10.

papyrus[16], in Plutarch[17] and in Athenaeus[18]; there is also an apparent cross-reference from the Bekker *Problems* themselves[19]. Flashar rightly observes that such citations prove nothing about the antiquity of the entire books in which they are now found; they do however suggest that the problems referred to formed part of *some* collection attributed to Aristotle (since they can hardly have circulated in isolation), even if we cannot rule it out that material from this was subsequently incorporated into an 'Alexander' collection. A *terminus ante quem* for the existence of some of the texts is also provided by parallels with book 7 of Macrobius' *Saturnalia*; Linke noted 24 such parallels in books i and ii Ideler, arguing that only four of these are close enough to suppose that Macrobius might have been dependent on 'Alexander', and that we should therefore rather think of a common source[20]. There are also parallels between Macrobius and books 2 and 3 Bussemaker, but these are fewer in number[21].

16. Oxyrhynchus papyrus 2744, from the 2nd century A.D., quotes a fuller version of problem 2.156; ROSELLI A., 'Ps.-Aristotele Problemata Inedita 2.153 in POxy 2744', *Zeitschrift für Papyrologie und Epigraphik* 33 (1979), p. 9-12. LUPPE W., 'Der Kommentar Pap. Oxy. 2744', *Archiv für Papyrusforschung* 20 (1970), p. 29-42 (cf. LUPPE W., 'Nochmals ps.-Aristoteles *Problemata inedita* 2.153 in POxy 2744', *Zeitschrift für Papyrologie und Epigraphik* 36 (1979), p. 55-56) argued that the text in the papyrus which contains this quotation is a commentary written by Didymus Chalcenterus in the first century B.C.

17. Plutarch, *Quaest. Nat.* 12 may (because it does not link Aristotle himself with the specific point made about divers, and goes on to attack those who make this particular connection) refer to 3.47 Bussemaker, rather than to Bekker *Problem* 32.11 as argued by FLASHAR, *Aristoteles: Problemata...*, p. 360 n. 1. Plutarch, *De prim. frig.* 13 950b seems to be a reference to 3.29; cf. FLASHAR, *Aristoteles: Problemata...* BUSSEMAKER, *Aristoteles: Opera...*, p. xviii argued that Plutarch, *Quaest. Nat.* 21 917d is a reference to 2.145, but FLASHAR, *Aristoteles: Problemata...*, p. 360 that it refers to Aristotle, *HA* 6.28 578a32-b5. 3.9 may be an abridged remnant of the fuller discussion reported by Plutarch, *Quaest. conviv.* 7.3. 701e-702b = Aristotle fr. 224 Rose[3]. On the other hand, FLASHAR suggests (*Aristoteles: Problemata...*, p. 367) that Plutarch, *De fac. in orb. lun.* 19 932bc (= Aristotle fr. 210 Rose[3]) refers to ii.46; and if this is correct we have an example of an 'Alexander' problem which was earlier attributed to Aristotle.

18. The citation of Aristotle at Athenaeus 14.72 656ab is, as BUSSEMAKER, *Aristoteles: Opera...*, p. xix and FLASHAR, *Aristoteles: Problemata...*, p. 367 note, closer to 3.43 than to Aristotle, *Meteor.* 4.3 380b21.

19. Bekker *Problem* 27.4 seems to refer to 3.14; BUSSEMAKER, *Aristoteles: Opera...*, p. xix, FLASHAR, *Aristoteles: Problemata...*, p. 694.

20. LINKE H., *Quaestiones de Macrobii Saturnaliorum fontibus*, Bratislava: G. Koebner, 1880, p. 52-54.

21. LINKE, *Quaestiones...*, p. 54 n. 2. 2.4, on eunuchs, is parallel to Macrobius 7.7.8, and Macrobius 7.12.9-10, on wine and honey, is closer to 3.22 Bussemaker than to ii.70 Ideler. However Macrobius 7.10.13, also on eunuchs, is closer to i.8 and i.97 than to 2.5; Macrobius 7.10.5, on baldness at the front of the head, is closer to i.2 than to 2.80; and Macrobius 7.6.9 contradicts 2.12, the former arguing that wine causes trembling because it is cold, the latter that it does so because it is hot.

Three extant collections, (a) problems 2.1-38 Bussemaker, (b) the eighth century Latin problems known as the *Problemata Bambergensia* or *Problemata vetustissima* and edited by Rose[22] and Stoll[23], and (c) the Arabic problems soon to be edited by Lou Filius, are each a subset of a collection which also included some of the problems of Cassius the Iatrosophist. There are also parallels between texts from book 2 and the medieval Latin *Prose Salernitan Questions*, all but one coming from 2.1-38 and involving texts also included in the *Problemata Bambergensia*. Although the problems correspond, the answers in the *Prose Salernitan Questions* are different to a greater or lesser extent. In at least one case our Greek text is compressed to a point where it is only comprehensible with the aid of the Latin: 2.19 explains the cravings of pregnant women for strange food (*pica*) as follows: 'Because the conception is unnatural, and the effect is in the region of the womb. The inward part is sinewy. Craving is an affection of the stomach, like appetite and loss of appetite.' This is so compressed that the argument, and particularly the relevance of 'the inward part is sinewy', is difficult to understand. However, several other discussions give the cause of the craving as the retention of blood when menstruation ceases with pregnancy; and *Prose Salernitan Question* B295 (Lawn 1979) explains the fact that the effect is felt *in the stomach* by arguing that the womb and the stomach are close to each other, cold, and *sinewy* (*nervosi*). *Problemata Bambergensia* 23, though not specifically mentioning the retained blood, says slightly more than *Problem* 2.19, observing that because the womb is sinewy, 'therefore the stomach is affected in sympathy through the sinews that extend to it'. It looks very much as if *Problem* 2.19 is a compressed version of a fuller original text better preserved in the *Problemata Bambergensia,* and as if the *Salernitan Question* has preserved even more of the original or (more probably) has coupled the explanation given there with the point about retained blood from another source. What is significant for the question of attribution, however, is that both (ii) the *Problemata Bambergensia* and (iii) the Arabic version of the *Supplementary Problems* are attributed to Aristotle, not Alexander; which suggests that the putative collection from which they and 2.1-38 derive was attributed to Aristotle as well.

---

22. ROSE V., *Aristoteles Pseudepigraphus*, Leipzig: Teubner, 1863, p. 666-676.
23. STOLL U., *Das "Lorscher Arzneibuch": ein medizinisches Kompendium des 8. Jahrhunderts (Codex Bambergensis medicinalis 1)* (Sudhoffs Archiv, Beihefte 28), Stuttgart: F. Steiner, 1992, p. 68-75.

The Greek MSS of the *Supplementary Problems*[24] fall into two groups. Those in the first group, the 'standard sequence', contain the texts, or excerpts therefrom, in the order in which they appear in the modern editions, allowing for minor variations. Five MSS attribute books 1 and 2 to Aristotle while attributing Ideler's two books to Alexander; two more contain parts of books 1 and 2 only, and attribute them to Aristotle. Two MSS attribute book 1 to Alexander and treat books 1 and 2 as a single book; two treat both book 1 and book 2 as a continuation of Ideler's second book attributed to Alexander. Three MSS apparently attribute all or part of books 1 and 2 to Alexander, but may do so in their present state only as the result of omissions or losses. One late MS attributes book 1 to *both* authors and book 2 to Aristotle; one attributes Bussemaker's book 1 to Alexander and leaves book 2 unattributed; three contain excerpts from all four books, all attributed to Alexander. Three MSS attribute to Alexander five books altogether, of which 'books 1 and 2' are Ideler's i and ii, with omissions; 'book 3' is a selection from the first part of Bussemaker's book 1 in the standard sequence followed by a selection from [Galen], *Def. med.* in question-and-answer form and then by 3.50-52 Bussemaker, which occur only here attributed to Alexander and turn out actually to be extracts from Psellus[25]. 'Books 4 and 5' in these three MSS are material from *earlier* in [Galen] *Def. med.* with a selection from Palladius' *Synopsis on Fevers* intervening in book 4[26].

There are good reasons, on the basis of readings and omissions, to suggest that at least some of the MSS which attribute books 1 and 2 to Aristotle are not dependent on any other extant MSS, and that those that do so belong to two distinct branches of the tradition, so that it cannot at

24. The Bussemaker/Usener *Problems* and the Ideler *Problems* have often, not surprisingly, been confused in catalogues with the *Quaestiones* and *Ethical Problems* attributed to Alexander; see SHARPLES R.W., 'Alexander and pseudo-Alexanders of Aphrodisias: *Scripta minima. Questions* and *Problems*, makeweights and prospects', in: W. KULLMANN – J. ALTHOFF – M. ASPER (eds.), *Gattungen wissenschaftlicher Literatur in der Antike* (ScriptOralia 95), Tübingen: Gunter Narr, 1998, p. 383-408, at p. 389-90 and n. 37. Only four of the MSS containing all or part of books 1-2 Bussemaker do not contain books 1-2 Ideler; but there are 7 MSS which contain all of books 1-2 Ideler, and 16 which contain part of these, without books 1-2 Bussemaker. The leaves (18-25) containing part of book 2 in MS Leiden, Voss. misc. 16 (see H. Wegehaupt, 'Zur Überlieferung der pseudo-Aristotelischen προβλήματα ἀνέκδοτα', *Philologus* 75 [1918], p. 469-473) are in fact the first eight of those missing from Oxford, New College MS 233; see the introduction to our forthcoming edition (above, n. 2). The Leiden MS is therefore not included as a separate item in the enumeration that follows.

25. WESTERINK L.G. (ed.), *Michael Psellus: De omnifaria doctrina*, Nijmegen: Centrale Drukkerij, 1948, p. 6.

26. On this, and a related collection in two other MSS, cf. SHARPLES, 'Alexander and pseudo-Alexanders...', p. 391-393.

any rate be *demonstrated* that the attribution of these books to Aristotle
is secondary and that to Alexander primary. That the attribution to Alexander, as well as that to Aristotle, is early as far as the Greek tradition is
concerned is however suggested by the fact that MS Oxford, Baroccianus 131 contains, at 441v-446, a paraphrase of much of the Ideler/
Usener material, attributed to Psellus[27]. The sequence in this paraphrase
is based on the standard tradition, but dislocated in a way that seems to
bear no close relation to that in any other known MS. Nevertheless, the
fact that Psellus (who lived from 1018 to 1097) drew on all four books
suggests that all four had already been united into a single corpus by his
time, the 11th century AD; and *if* he regarded that corpus as attributed to
a single author, that author would seem to have been Alexander.

There are also twelve MSS which contain material from some or all
of the four books in non-standard sequences, which can be traced back
to two MSS, one extant (Paris, BN, suppl. gr. 690), the other hypotheti-
cally reconstructed. The first group is not really relevant to the present
discussion, for it includes nothing from books 1 and 2 Bussemaker, and
only two problems which were included by Bussemaker in his third
book, as 3.46 and 3.47, occurring in this group of MSS only. The second
group however includes material from Bussemaker 1 and 2, as well as
Ideler i and ii; and the important point for the present argument is that in
it *all* this material is attributed to Alexander. It is clear on grounds of
arrangement and content that the standard sequence is not the result of
rearrangement of and addition to the non-standard ones; and if the non-
standard sequences are the result of selection from and rearrangement of
the standard one, it seems more reasonable to suppose that the compiler
of the second sequence attributed to Alexander material all of which he
found already attributed to him, rather than that he found some of it attributed to Alexander, some to Aristotle, and disregarded that fact.

While 2.39ff. are more Aristotelian in character than 1 and 2.1-38,
2.1-38 as well as 2.39ff. were attributed to Aristotle at some point before

27. Edited by DUFFY J.M. (ed.), *Michaelis Pselli philosophica minora I*, Stuttgart and
Leipzig: Teubner, 1992, p. xxxvii-xxxviii, and WILSON N.G., 'A Byzantine Miscellany:
MS Barocci 131 revisited', *Jahrbuch der Österreichischen Byzantinistik* 27 (1978), p. 157-
179, at p. 171. This material is to be distinguished from two other sections containing
material from the pseudo-Aristotle / pseudo-Alexander *Problems* in the same MS (!): that
in the second 'non-standard sequence' (see below) at 62v-64v, and i.85-99 Ideler in dialogue form at 404v-405 (cf. PONTIKOS I.N., *Anonymi miscellanea philosophica, a miscellany in the tradition of Michael Psellos (Codex Baroccianus graecus 131)* (Corpus
philosophorum medii aevi, Philosophi Byzantini 6), Athens: Academy of Athens, 1992,
p. 2-6).

28. Later, because of the similarity of the prefaces to ii Ideler and 1 Bussemaker – if
indeed the latter was already attached to this collection; see above, n. 10.

the eighth century. Perhaps 2.1-38 and 2.39ff. were subsequently joined together, and attributed as a whole to Aristotle; if they were then united with book 1, already attributed to Alexander, this would explain how these books came later still[28] to be connected with the two books edited by Ideler both in the Greek MSS transmission at the stage where it becomes directly accessible to us and in the excerpts made by Psellus and by the compiler of the non-standard sequence. If a heading for books 1 and 2 Bussemaker referred both to Alexander and to Aristotle, this could explain both the variations in attribution in the MSS we have and the double attribution in one of our MSS. But this is highly speculative, and other explanations are possible.

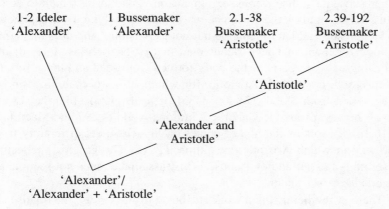

1-2 Ideler	1 Bussemaker	2.1-38	2.39-192
'Alexander'	'Alexander'	Bussemaker 'Aristotle'	Bussemaker 'Aristotle'

'Aristotle'

'Alexander and Aristotle'

'Alexander'/ 'Alexander' + 'Aristotle'

There is no reason to suppose that the 'Aristotelian' problems in 2.39ff. have any more connection with Aristotle himself than do the better-known problems edited by Bekker (above, n. 5); some of them may well derive from the early Peripatetic school, and Aristotelian authorship of individual items cannot perhaps be excluded, but we have no way of telling. But what of the possible connection of any of this material (including, now, books i and ii Ideler) with Alexander of Aphrodisias himself? Against this are (1) references to providence and the influence of the heavens, in the preface to 1 Bussemaker[29] and in 1.16, along with gross materialism, like that in the argument in i.26 Ideler that small people are wiser because their souls are concentrated into a smaller space.

29. Not actually included in Bussemaker's edition, even though it is present in all but one of the MSS which contain the whole of book 1, and the exception is probably only due to damage. Bussemaker was no doubt influenced by the view of DIETZ, Commentarii..., that the prologue was not originally written for this book; see above, n. 10.

Alexander might allow some influence from the heavens[30], but what is said about providence and about the soul does seem inconsistent with his views. (2) Rose 1863, 219 detected Neoplatonist tendencies in books i and ii Ideler, and even though not all his examples are equally telling, they seem sufficient to rule out both the connection with Alexander of the problems to which this applies, and also, in combination with (1), a unified origin for all the material. (3) The allegorical explanation of myth in 1.17 Bussemaker and i.87 Ideler does not seem consistent with Alexander's authorship. (4) In 1 and 2.1-38 there are divergences from Aristotelian doctrine on specific points, which are strikingly in contrast with Alexander's own tendency to defend Aristotelian orthodoxy even when subsequent discoveries, e.g. in anatomy, had made it hard to do so. Thus 1.1 recognises the existence of 'female testes', i.e. ovaries, known to Hellenistic and later medicine but not to Aristotle, and uses the terminology for them of Galen rather than that of Herophilus. 1.18, distinguishing between parts of the body formed from seed and those formed from blood, contradicts Aristotle, for whom *all* parts including sinews are formed from blood (*GA* 2.6 743a18); a distinction like that in our text is however found in Galen[31]. 2.5 (along with i.8, i.97 and Macrobius 7.10.13)[32], explains the higher voices of eunuchs quite differently from the way in which Aristotle does himself[33]. (5) The general intellectual level of 1-2 Ideler and of 1 and 2.1-38 Bussemaker does not seem characteristic of Alexander.

There is another medical work attributed to Alexander, the treatise *On Fevers*. The most recent editor, Tassinari[34], came to the conclusion that this treatise was probably written by someone who lived at approxi-

30. Cf. GENEQUAND C., 'Quelques aspects de l'idée de la nature, d'Aristote à al-Ghazali', *Revue de Théologie et de Philosophie* 116 (1984), p. 105-129, at p. 114; GENEQUAND C., *Alexander of Aphrodisias On the Cosmos*, Leiden: Brill, 2001, p. 18; SHARPLES R.W., 'Schriften und Problemkomplexe zur Ethik', in: P. MORAUX†, ed. posth. J. WIESNER, *Der Aristotelismus bei den Griechen,* vol. 3. *Alexander von Aphrodisias* (Peripatoi 7/1), Berlin: De Gruyter, 2001, p. 513-616, at p. 526-9; FAZZO S., 'Alessandro di Afrodisia e Tolomeo: Aristotelismo e astrologia fra il II e il III secolo d.C.', *Rivista di storia di filologia* 4 (1988), p. 627-649; FAZZO S. – ZONTA M., *Alessandro d'Afrodisia, Sulla Provvidenza*, Milan: Rizzoli, 1998, p. 41, 63-68.

31. GALEN, *Ars medica* 26 (BOUDON V. (ed.), *Galien: Exhortation à l'étude de la médecine, Art médical*, Paris: Les Belles Lettres, 2000, p. 358.8-10); similarly Oribasius, *Coll. med. libri incerti* 15.17 (RAEDER I. (ed.), *Oribasii Collectionum medicarum reliquiae*, vol. 4 (Corpus Medicorum Graecorum 6.2.2), Leipzig and Berlin: Teubner, 1933, p.105.14-17).

32. Cf. LINKE, *Quaestiones...*, p. 54 n.2.

33. ARISTOTLE, *GA* 5.7 787b20-788a15.

34. TASSINARI P., *Ps.-Alessandro di Afrodisia. Trattato sulla Febbre*, Alessandria: dell'Orso, 1994, p. iii-vi.

mately the same time as Alexander of Aphrodisias, who had a particular interest in philosophical analysis, rather than in medical treatment, and who held distinctively Peripatetic views concerning natural philosophy and the status of forms. Tassinari did not himself go as far as accepting the conclusion to which these facts might seem to point, namely that the author *was* Alexander, and perhaps we should not do so either; but if Tassinari was right to accept the suggestion that the treatise *On Fevers* is in fact by an unknown namesake and contemporary of Alexander of Aphrodisias, we may have a candidate for the authorship of parts of our material as well[35]. It may however be that we are simply dealing with just one more example of the tendency for texts to be ascribed to famous individuals.

University College London

---

[35] The author *could* be Alexander's father; a recently discovered inscription informs us that he was also named Alexander, and was described as a philosopher. See A. CHANIOTIS, 'Epigraphic evidence for the philosopher Alexander of Aphrodisias', *BICS* 47 (2004), p. 79-81, and R.W. Sharples, 'Implications of the new Alexander of Aphrodisias inscription', forthcoming in *BICS* 48 (2005).

Lou S. FILIUS

THE GENRE *PROBLEMATA* IN ARABIC:
ITS MOTIONS AND CHANGES

Dans cette contribution, j'esquisse tout d'abord le développement du genre
Problemata *en grec, mais transmis en arabe. Ce développement permet de conclure que dans l'histoire grecque, les textes du genre* Problemata *ont été sujets à
des changements par leur forme souvent concise de question et réponse. Les
textes qui ont été conservés en arabe présentent des suppléments explicatifs,
mais également des modifications, à cause de changements de points de vue
pendant le deuxième siècle. Sur le plan terminologique, ces suppléments et modifications ressemblent beaucoup aux textes des* Problemata Inedita, *comme C.
Bussemaker les a édités. Je conclus que l'auteur connaissait à fond la langue
grecque et les sciences de son époque. Voilà pourquoi ces textes me semblent
d'origine grecque. Plus tard le genre a eu son propre développement dans la
littérature arabe.*

Introduction

The genre *Problemata* is one of the most transformed types of literature. From earlier times we have known the genre as e.g. *Aporemata
Homerica*[1], later on as e.g. *Problemata Physica*. We also know about a
book Ἰατρικῶν Ἀπορημάτων καὶ φυσικῶν προβλημάτων from the
third or fourth century A.D., ascribed to Alexander of Aphrodisias[2]. In
the Semitic world, too, the genre of *Problemata* existed in all its different
forms and with all different changes, as the article 'masā'il w-adjwiba'
by H. Daiber has shown[3]. In this paper, I will discuss the *Problemata*

---

1. Cf. PRANTL C., 'Ueber die Probleme des Aristoteles', *Abhandlungen der philoso-
phisch-philologischen Klasse der königlichen Bayerischen Akademie der Wissenschaften*
6 (1852), p. 353; FLASHAR H. (tr.), *Problemata Physica* (Aristoteles Werke in deutscher
Übersetzung 19), Berlin: Akademie-Verlag, 1962 (reprint: Darmstadt, Wissenschaftliche
Buchgesellschaft, 1975-1991), p. 297-303.
2. Alexander Aphrodisiensis, Ἰατρικῶν Ἀπορημάτων καὶ φυσικῶν προβλημάτων,
in: IDELER I.L. (ed.), *Physici et Medici Graeci Minores,* vol. I, Berlin, 1841 (reprint: Amsterdam, A.M. Hakkert, 1963), p. 3-80.
3. See DAIBER H., *The Encyclopaedia of Islam* (EI2), Leiden-Boston: Brill, 1979ff,
vol. VI, p. 636a-637b. Cf. also, e.g., OESTERLEY W.O.E. – BOX G.H., *A short survey of
the literature of Rabbinical and Mediaeval Judaism*, New York: Macmillan, 1920 (reprint: New York: Lenox Hill, 1973), p. 211-212, about the Jewish *Responsa*-literature.

translated in Arabic, which were derived from the Greek *Problemata Physica* and those related to it, and the Arabic and Syriac forms derived from it:

1. The *Problemata Physica* from the *Corpus Aristotelicum*[4];
2. The Arabic version of the *Problemata Physica*, supposed to be translated by Ḥunain ibn Isḥāq;
3. The Greek-Latin *Problemata Inedita*, known in the edition of Bussemaker and Usener, the *Problemata* of Cassius Iatrosophista, and the *Problemata Bambergensia* in the Arabic version;
4. Briefly about the *Problemata* ascribed to Alexander of Aphrodisias in the edition of Ideler and in the Syriac version;
5. Briefly about the reception of the Greek *Problemata* genre in the Middle Eastern world.

1. Problemata Physica Graeca (PG)

The *Problemata Physica* was edited by Immanuel Bekker in the *Corpus Aristotelicum*, but it was clear, probably also for the editor, that largely it did not originate from Aristotle, but rather from his successors, e.g. Theophrastus[5]. Probably it has been a kind of encyclopaedia or a textbook, used for instruction and probably intended to give subjects for discussion. That latter point can be observed not only in the questions, nearly all of which begin with διὰ τί and are often followed by a suggested answer, but also in the answers themselves, mostly formulated in the form of a question with a theoretical discussion of these sometimes somewhat strange problems and with different solutions.

In medicine, too, this type of literature was used during the time of Hippocrates to instruct pupils by means of discussion about different medical subjects, as Flashar related in his commentary[6]. It means that in Greek literature for these very reasons the genre of *Problemata* went through many changes in form and contents during a long time, in particular in medicine.

---

4. *The Aristoteles Semitico-Latinus* project (ASL-project) of the University of Leiden in which I participate, intends to edit the various translations of texts of Aristotle in the Semitic languages of the Middle East and its translations in Latin.

5. Cf. FLASHAR, *Problemata Physica...*, p. 333-341 and 356-358. Cf. also FORTEN-BAUGH W.F. – SHARPLES R.W. – SOLLENBERGER M.G., *Theophrastus of Eresus. On sweat, on dizziness and on fatigue* (Philosophia Antiqua. A series of studies on ancient philosophy 93), Leiden-Boston: Brill, 2003, p. 12-15, 178-179, 256 and 259-262.

6. Cf. FLASHAR, *Problemata Physica...*, p. 299.

2. *Problemata Physica Arabica (PPA)*

Renan[7] was the first to write about an Arabic translation of the *Problemata Physica*, translated in Hebrew by Moses ibn Tibbon at Montpellier in 1264[8]. The Arabic translation may have been by Ḥunain ibn Isḥāq, as one Hebrew ms. tells us[9], but the original Arabic text was unknown. M. Steinschneider, too, mentioned this Hebrew translation in his famous book 'Die hebräischen Übersetzungen des Mittelalters und die Juden als Dolmetscher'[10], now with three Hebrew manuscripts[11]. Ibn an-Nadīm, the famous bookseller at Baġdād about A.D. 1000 wrote in his catalogue al-Fihrist that he had a book which was a tafsīr mā bāl of Aristotle, written by Yaḥyā an-Naḥwī or Ioannes Grammaticus[12], containing 10 maqālāt (books)[13], but Steinschneider already concluded that, owing to Ibn Abī Uṣaibiʿa, there were probably 17 books. By the way, a tafsīr in this case is to be interpreted as a commentary on Greek scientific and philosophical works, especially applied to the works of Aristotle[14].

7. RENAN M.E., *Les rabbins français du commencement du quatorzième siècle*, Paris: Imprimerie Nationale, 1877 (reprint Westmead: Gregg International Publishers Limited, 1969), p. 744-745, on the basis of a remark by Casiri in his catalogue.

8. Cf. ms. Oxford, Bodleian Library 2380, Opp. Add. Qu. 141; FILIUS L.S., *The Problemata Physica attributed to Aristotle. The Arabic version of Ḥunain ibn Isḥāq and the Hebrew version of Moses ibn Tibbon* (Aristoteles Semitico-Latinus 11), Leiden-Boston-Köln: Brill, 1999, p. lx-lxii.

9. Cf. FILIUS, *Problemata Physica...*, p. lvi and lx-lxii.

10. STEINSCHNEIDER M., *Die hebräischen Übersetzungen des Mittelalters und die Juden als Dolmetscher*, Berlin: H. Itzkowski, 1893 (reprint Graz: Akademische Druck-und Verlaganstalt, 1960), p. 229-232. Later STEINSCHNEIDER M., *Die arabischen Übersetzungen aus dem Griechischem*, Graz: Akademische Druck- und Verlaganstalt, 1960, p. 112.

11. FILIUS, *Problemata Physica...*, p. lx-lxiv.

12. Although in most cases Ioannes Philoponus and Ioannes Grammaticus or Yaḥyā an-Naḥwī have been considered as the same person by the Arabic writers, it seems that the philosophical commentaries were written by Ioannes Philoponus and the author of medical books has been another Ioannes or Ioannes Grammaticus, but much confusion has been caused by the Arabic writers, cf. ULLMANN M., *Medizin im Islam* (Handbuch der Orientalistik I 6 erster Abschnitt), Leiden-Köln: Brill, 1970, p. 89.

13. Ibn an-Nadīm, *Kitāb al-Fihrist*, edited by R. TAĠADDUD, Tehran, 1391/1971, p. 315, s.v. Yaḥyā an-Naḥwī, l. 5-6 and Ibn abī Uṣaibiʿa, *Kitāb ʿUyūn al-anbāʾ fī ṭabaqāt*, edited by A. MÜLLER, Cairo-Leipzig, al-Maṭbaʿa al-Wahbīya, 1299-1301/1882-1884, vol I, p. 199, where Ḥunain is mentioned as a translator of the *Problemata*. Cf. FILIUS, *Problemata Physica...*, p. xiv-xv and notes 4 and 5.

14. About the tafsīr, PETERS F.E., *Aristotle and the Arabs* (Studies in Near Eastern Civilization 1), New York-London: New York University Press, 1968, p. 92-93 and EI2 X 83b.

The first mention of the existence of the Arabic original was made by R. Kruk in a publication in 1976[15] about a manuscript at Tehran[16], which later appeared to be book X or maqāla XI. Later, I photographed a manuscript with all the maqālāt 1-17 in the Manisa Library in Turkey, having been given a hint by H. Daiber. A summary of this text by Ibn aṭ-Ṭayyib in a manuscript at an Istanbul Library[17] is known, but it contains only the maqālāt 1-15, unfortunately without mentioning any author or translator. In the manuscript, the last two maqālāt, which are short and perhaps incomplete, are missing. This manuscript contained two summaries, firstly that of the *Problemata* ascribed to Alexander of Aphrodisias and secondly that of the *Problemata Physica* in 15 maqālāt. In the Manisa manuscript the first five *problemata* and the first part of *problema* 6 (Greek I 8) are missing, but these *problemata* are transmitted in the Hebrew translation and in the summary of Ibn aṭ-Ṭayyib. The *problemata* ascribed to Alexander of Aphrodisias are transmitted in a Syriac translation, and therefore we could assume that a Syriac link to the Arabic translation of the *Problemata Physica* also existed, but that is not obvious in spite of the summary of Ibn aṭ-Ṭayyib even in the same manuscript. There are no Syriacisms, and even if there were any, such as e.g. *udhn* 'ear' for 'gill' in the *Historia Animalium*[18] or special syntactical and stylistic features[19] to have any assumption about the language of translation, we can have doubts about an intermediate translation, because the translators mostly were Christians and therefore they used mostly Syriac as their mother tongue.

This Arabic translation is substantially different from our Greek version:

15. KRUK R., 'Pseudo-Aristotle: An Arabic version of Problemata Physica X', *Isis* 67 (1976), p. 251-256.

16. FILIUS, *Problemata Physica...*, p. lviii-lix: Tehran University Library 2234 (copy: Leiden University Library Or. 14, 623).

17. Nuruosmaniye 3610 (new numbering 3095). Cf. also DAIBER H., 'A survey of Theophrastean texts and ideas in Arabic: some new material', in: W.W. FORTENBAUGH – P.M. HUBY – A.A. LONG (eds.), *Theophrastus of Eresus, on his life and work* (Rutgers University studies in Classical Humanities 2), New Brunswick-Oxford: Transactions Publishers, 1985, p. 108-109.

18. *HA* 489b3, frequently between 504b28 and 505a19; also 506a19, 506a7, 506a9 and 506a12, cf. DEN HEIJER J., 'Syriacisms in the Arabic version of Aristotle's Historia Animalium', *ARAM* 3 (1991), p.104-106.

19. Cf. e.g. DEN HEIJER, 'Syriacisms...', p. 106-109; cf. also Aristotle, *Generation of animals. The Arabic translation commonly ascribed to Yahyâ ibn al-Bitrîq*, edited by J. BRUGMAN and H.J. DROSSAART-LULOFS (Publication of the 'De Goeje Fund' 23), Leiden: Brill, 1971, p. 10-17 and ENDRESS G., *Die arabischen Übersetzungen von Aristoteles' Schrift De Caelo*, diss. Frankfurt am Main, 1966, p. 32ff.

a) In Arabic, there are 17 maqālāt (but the last two maqālāt are probably incomplete), corresponding with the first 15 books of our Greek text, but the Arabic text is hardly shorter than the Greek text with 38 books. Therefore, to show the differences between the Greek text and the Arabic one, some short texts have been chosen as an illustration.

- The first book in Greek has become two maqālāt in Arabic according to the division also in some Greek manuscripts[20]. In Arabic, the first maqāla is called 'Introduction to (medical) science' and has 28 questions. Maqāla 2: 'About medical treatments and technical facilities'. In the Greek manuscripts, the title of book I is ὅσα ἰατρικά ('all sorts of medical treatments') and it was written above *problema* 30: ὅσα βοηθηματικὰ πρὸς ἴασιν (all sorts of medicines) at the place corresponding with that in the Arabic text. Anyway, this title was written in the most important manuscripts, the Laurentianus LXXXVII,4 and the Parisinus gr. 2036[21]. But perhaps it is a tradition not to split up this book of the Greek text into two different books.
- The same is applicable to book PG 15[22]. In Greek, this book is titled ὅσα μαθηματικῆς μετέχει θεωρίας, (about the theory of mathematics), whereas above problema 5 in the Greek manuscripts, it is written: ὅσα περὶ οὐράνια, (about the phenomena in heaven). But in the Parisinus gr. 2036 exactly the same division exists, precisely the manuscript about which Klek said in the edition which Ruelle prepared[23]: 'omnium codicum praestantissimus et vetustissimus est Parisinus 2036', and P. Louis[24] is still more approving of this ms. It clarifies that there was a good reason for the Arabic translator to keep the text of book 15 split up into maqāla 16 and 17 with the titles 'About mathematics' and 'About the heaven' according to his Greek mss.

b) The individual problemata are not always incorporated in the same order. But those changes in the order may be explained to some extent. For example, the description of the constitution of the seasons is followed by the change of types of water (PPA I 10). Then comes the change of food which is, as it seems, less fundamental than the change of water (PPA I 11), then the effect of food and drink on the body (PPA I 12 and PG I 15b), and finally it is mentioned that exceptional changes bring about diseases (PPA I 13 and PG I 15a). However, though in this case it seems that the order depends on the nature of the change of water

---

20. FLASHAR, *Problemata Physica...*, p. 385.
21. LOUIS P., *Aristote, Problèmes*. Texte établi et traduit par P. LOUIS (Collection des Universités de France), Paris: Les Belles Lettres, 1991-1994, p. xl-xlviii.
22. FLASHAR, *Problemata Physica...*, p. 566.
23. Aristoteles, *Aristotelis quae feruntur Problemata Physica*. Edidit C.A. RUELLE, recognovit H. KNOELLINGER, praefatione ornavit I. KLEK, Leipzig: Teubner, 1922, p. iv.
24. LOUIS, *Problèmes*, p. xl-xliii.

and food and drink, in general it is not always clear why the order is different[25].

c) The occurrence of doubles, two similar *problemata* in the same book or in different books of the *Problemata Physica*, is a strange point in the composition. About this Flashar said: 'Unter den fast 900 einzelnen Problemen finden sich über 200 Wiederholungen, wobei der Charakter der Wiederholung im einzelnen verschieden sein kann. Neben völliger Identität von Fragen und Antworten gibt es auch eine Gleichheit nur der Fragen bei verschiedener Beantwortung.... Bei dieser Lage der Dinge ist es verständlich, daß die Doubletten für die Erklärung der Entstehung des Werkes eine gewichtige Rolle spielen'[26]. Also in the Arabic version some doubles occur and these are also distributed among different books.

To show something of the Arabic version, I copied PG I 18 and XIV 6 and the double in the Arabic version PPA I 16 and XV 6 in translation. The text in italics in the translations of the Arabic texts below is the addition, which is absent in the Greek texts. The Greek text has been translated precisely in Arabic, but the author of the tafsīr, assumed to be Yaḥyā an-Naḥwī according to Ibn an-Nadīm, took the Greek text and when the text was not clear enough, it seems that he made some additions, sometimes very extensive:

> PG I 18 = PG XIV 6:
> Why is it that in marshy districts wounds in the head heal quickly, but those in the legs slowly? Is it because moisture is heavy because its nature is earthy, and what is heavy tends to sink? Hence the upper parts are soon cleared out (I 18) – ἔκκριτα / concocted (XIV 6) – εὔπεπτα – because the moisture sinks downwards, but the lower parts are full of waste product, which readily putrefies (I 18) / easily decomposes[27] (XIV 6).

> PPA I 16:
> Why does somebody among people who drink marsh water recover if one of them has pustules on his head, but only rarely if he has them on his leg? Because the moistures that are formed in their bodies are heavy, because they are akin to the nature of the earth. What is heavy is always characterised by the fact that it sinks. Hence the uppermost parts of the body are free

25. Some *problemata* are split up in two *problemata*, e.g. PG I 27 in PPA I 26 and 27, PG I 55 even in 5 *problemata*, PPA II 28-32. On the other hand e.g. PG I 25 and I 28 have become PPA I 24. Other *problemata* are absent in the Arabic text, e.g. PG I 57, II 32, III 27 and 28.

26. FLASHAR, *Problemata Physica...*, p. 323. Cf. also PRANTL, 'Ueber die Probleme...', p. 345ff.

27. For the translations of the Greek texts I used the translation of W.S. Hett in: Aristotle, *Problems,* with an English translation by W.S. HETT (Loeb Classical Library 216), Cambridge Mass.: Harvard University Press – London: W. Heinemann LTD, 1926 (reprint 1970).

from corruption and from moistures which *are bad in quality. They recover quickly from the pustules which emerge therefrom, because the healing of pustules only takes place through the drainage and absorption of the moistures and the drainage of their moist substance. The effect of all medicines with which pustules are treated is merely to absorb and dry up.* But because the moistures flow to the lower parts of the body *and these moistures then become solid substance and earthy by nature, the body changes the disease. Its substance* is confined in the lower parts of the body, *so that the disease is prolonged and is not cured quickly* on account of the many moistures which have flowed to them and easily corrupt.

PPA XV 6:
Why is it that when pustules grow on the heads of the inhabitants of countries in which there are marshes, they quickly recover from them, and if the pustules appear on their feet, why do they not quickly recover from them? Because the water of the marshes is very thick and earthy. *Hence the composition of what they drink is thick.* Something thick is heavy. It is characteristic of that which is heavy that it always sinks. Therefore, there is little moisture in the head and in all the upper parts of the body, so that they recover quickly when pustules appear on them, *because this moistness dries up out of the vapours which rise up. When dryness prevails in their constitution, it also causes putrid, sticky substance to go away. But because moistness is predominant in the constitution of the feet and* the lower parts of the body and the residues always sink down, bad substances are collected there in abundance. *Therefore their healing is difficult. Hence they do not heal, because pustules do not heal when moistness is predominant in parts.*

The text of the question is the same in Greek and in Arabic, but in Arabic there is some emphasis on the inhabitants because the maqāla XV concerns the people who live in different countries, whereas in the first version in I 16 it could be everyone who drinks marshy water, because he happens to be in that country. Book I / maqāla I deals with different diseases due to changes in country or season. It seems obvious that the author of the tafsīr read the Greek book very well and thus wrote his text.

The answer also contains a good translation of the Greek text:

In Arabic, there is first an explanatory translation of ἔκκριτος (found in PG I 18): 'Hence the uppermost parts of the body are free from corruption and from moistures', and then 'which are bad in quality'. Seligsohn[28] has given the same explanation in his commentary without knowing the Arabic version. The same in PPA XV 6: 'this moistness dries up... so that the dryness also causes the putrid, sticky substance to go away'.

28. SELIGSOHN H., *Die Übersetzung der ps.-aristotelischen Problemata durch Bartholomaeus von Messina*. Text und tekstkritische Untersuchungen zum ersten Buch, Berlin, 1934, p. 82-83: He chooses for ἔκκριτος as the best version, 'denn der Kopf ist eben dadurch, daß die Feuchtigkeit nach unten zieht, leer geworden (gereinigt)'.

The next part is an explanation of curing the disease, namely by dry-ing. But in maqāla XV 6 we find an interesting peculiarity, namely 'be-cause this moistness dries up out of the vapours which rise up'. The va-pours rise up to the brain, as Galen[29] said 'like a roof of a warm house' to stay in the brain which is always moist, as we also find in PPA I 14 and III 10, so that dryness prevails in their constitution beneath the brain. The vapours are the finest moistures that rise up to the brain. Per-haps we can explain that the vapours rising up in Arabic is an explana-tion of εὔπεπτος in PG XIV 6. But because the bad moistness is con-fined to the lower parts of the body, the pustules there do not heal.

It is obvious that in the answer the author of the Arabic text tried to elucidate the Greek text, which was often very short in the 'Aristotelian' version, and possibly also to update the text by quoting Galen.

In general, it seems that the author of the tafsīr did not try to smooth out what we call 'the compositional weakness', but he tried to make the doubles in the text meaningful. Every double gives some other informa-tion depending on the context. The doubles never have the same text, because the author commented on the Greek text.

As an example of updating of the original 'Aristotelian' version, the following one is interesting, because it is possible to find back the origin of the updating (PG III 10 = PG III 30 and PPA IV 11 = PPA IV 32). In both doubles the question is the same, but the answers are different in Greek and in Arabic, but there are also differences between the Greek and the Arabic texts.

PG III 10

Why is it that, to men who are drunk, the one often seems to be many? Is it, as we have said above, because, the sight is moving, the same vision can never remain at rest on the same spot at any time? But that which is seen in a different way at the same moment seems to be later in time; for that which is visible is seen by the touching (ἁφῇ) of the sight, and it is impos-sible for sight to touch several things at the same time. But as the interven-ing time, while the sight touched and passed on from the object seen, is

29. GALENUS, Opera. Edidit C.G. KÜHN, vol. I-XX, Leipzig, prostat in officina libra-ria Car. Cnoblochii, 1821-1833 (Reprint: Hildesheim-Zürich-New York: G. Olms, 1964-1965), vol. III, p. 658 De usu partium IX, (On the usefulness of the parts of the body. De usu partium. Translated from the Greek with an Introduction and a Commentary by M. T. MAY, Ithaca-New York: Cornell U.P., 1967, p. 425-426), cf. also FILIUS L.S., 'The theory of vision in the Problemata Physica. A comparison between the Greek and the Arabic versions', in: G. ENDRESS – R. KRUK (eds.), The ancient tradition in Christian and Islamic Hellenism. Studies on the transmission of Greek philosophy and sciences, dedicated to H.J. Drossaart Lulofs on his ninetieth birthday, Leiden: Research School CNWS. School of Asian, African, and Amerindian Studies, 1997, p. 81-82 and SIEGEL R., Galen. On sense perception, His doctrines, observations and experiments on vision, hear-ing, smell, taste, touch and pain, and their historical sources, Basel-New York: S. Kar-ger, 1970, p. 46ff and 90ff.

imperceptible, the time in which it has been touched and passed on from its object appears to be a single moment; so that, when more than one glance is in contact with the same thing at the same time, the objects seen appear to be more than one, because it is not possible for them to be touched in the same way.

PPA IV 11

Why do drunken people see the single thing as many things? Because perception is even and complete only if it catches, in one glance and evenly, the optic ray of the things which are seen. But if this optic ray moves in a confused manner on account of the drunkenness which occurs, and the vapours arising from the wine grow too thick, that ray changes into various parts and the perception is also different for this reason. If the eye then sees the object which is perceived, it sees (the object) as many different objects. That is because the time that passes between one glance and the other, namely the arrival of the first ray and of the second ray, is very little and imperceptible (...)

PPA IV 32, answer

Because the cone of the sight is moved from inside by the wine, like the movement of the finger when it comes to the eye from outside and makes it go up or down. For just as the finger makes the eye go up or down and the sight is consequently confused, so that it sees the object as two objects – for the pupil, which is located high up, first sees what is opposite to it on the same level, and subsequently it sees what is below it, and for this reason it sees one object as two objects –, so (it is) likewise (with) the phenomena which we have mentioned, which occur as a result of the vapours of the wine, when the eye is consequently compressed from inside (...)

PG III 30, answer

Is it because the sources of sight within are disturbed by the wine, as also is the whole head, and when the sources are disturbed the vision does not focus on the same whole, but as it were upon each part of the object seen in turn; hence it appears double? The same effect is produced if one presses the eye from below; for this disturbs the origin of sight, so that one eye no longer focuses at the same point as the other eye (...)

The theory of vision in the *Problemata Physica* in Arabic shows the most interesting change of the Greek version in the *Corpus Aristotelicum*. In Greek, a theory of touching existed which was called by Flashar[30] 'Fühlfadentheorie', in which the ἀφή – a technical term for the 'touch', the contact with the object – is the cause of seeing, a theory from Empedocles opposite to Aristotle's theory of seeing. For him light is a movement from the objects which are seen through a transparent medium[31].

In fact the Arabic text does not speak about touching, but about sending and catching/receiving optic rays. In PPA IV 11 it is: لان النظر انما لا

---

30. FLASHAR, *Problemata Physica...*, p. 443: W.S. Hett translated this ἀφῆ with 'by contact with the sight'.

31. FORTENBAUGH – SHARPLES – SOLLENBERGER, *Theophrastus of Eresus*, p. 217-218.

.مستويا كاملا اذا استقبل الشعاع الباصر بالاشياء المنظور اليها 'The perception is even and perfect when it receives or meets the optic rays which grasp the percepted things'[32].

In PG III 30 we read: 'Is it because the sources of sight (αἱ ἀρχαὶ τῶν ὄψεων) within are disturbed by the wine, as also the whole head.' Therefore, the vapours of the wine in the head disturb the whole head and thus also the eyesight.

But for the author of the Arabic text the term αἱ ἀρχαὶ τῶν ὄψεων was not quite clear and therefore he has explained 'the sources of sight' as the 'cone of sight' in PPA IV 32: لان صنوبرة الناظر يحركها الخمر من داخل كمثل حركة الاصبع اذا لقيت العين من خارج ونخستها الى فوق او الى اسفل

('Because the cone of the sight is moved from inside by the wine, like the movement of the finger when it comes to the eye from outside and makes it go up and down.'). In PPA XVII 2: لان النور النظرى فى شكله يشبه قونوس اى السروى وكذلك يكون خروجه وانبساطه وقاعدة قونوس السروى مستديرة وقد كان يجب ان كان الشعاع مستويا وسقوطه على خطوط مستقيمة ان ترى مستوية

('Because the light of perception in its form resembles a κῶνος, i.e. cone. The light of perception also emanates and spreads in this way. The base of the κῶνος, the cone, is round. Perhaps it would be necessary for the rays to be straight and for them to fall down in straight lines, if one saw them straight.').

Apparently the eye is the top of the cone of sight, which emits optic rays through its perceiving light to the object that is seen. The rays of al-nūru 'l-naẓarīyu or light of perception (PPA XVII 2 and XV 14) must be straight and fall down in straight lines, if one saw them straight. But there are many things that may confuse the sight, for example things in dark places, and because of the darkness these things are not visible.

Therefore, first there is the optic pneuma (in PPA IV 10 and PPA XI 10: ar-rūḥu 'l-baṣīru PPA XI 10 also: ar-rūḥu 'l-bāṣiru and in PPA XV 14: ar-rūḥu 'l-baṣarī). Normally 'the vapours in the brain move evenly' (PPA IV 10), but that is impossible now because of the drunkenness, 'for the vapours are struck and stopped and assume a circular movement, as water and smoke assume a circular shape at that place where their progress is stopped. That is why, when these vapours are brought to-

---

32. Alexander of Aphrodisias attributes this theory to mathematicians like Hero of Alexandria and Ptolemaeus, cf. Alexander Aphrodisiensis, *On Aristotle, on sense perception*, Translated by A. TOWEY, London: Duckworth, 2000, p. 37 (28, 1-7), p. 167, n. 130 and 139. For a similar theory of seeing in Galen, see FILIUS, 'The theory of vision...', p. 77-83.

gether in the ventricles, the movement of the optic pneuma changes into a revolving movement. When the optic pneuma resolves, it makes the perceived forms like the disposition of the optic pneuma that perceives them, a circular disposition'. But the thick vapours of the wine disturb the regular movement of the optic rays, which means that different rays are sent out by the eye and these rays cannot be combined because of the confusion of the sight, due to the wine.

This short exposé makes it possible to order some issues of the theory of vision given by the author of the tafsīr to explain the short Greek texts:

- The eye is the top of a cone of visual rays sent from the brain with optic pneuma, which is the finest part of the psychic pneuma (ar-rūhu 'n-nafsānīyu). In the brain the visual rays are separated from the psychic pneuma, emitted by visual light to the object that is seen. Subsequently, the rays come back and are received by the eyes, return to the brain where an impression is made in the perceiving sense (PPA IV 8).

- In the pseudo-Alexander of Aphrodisias' *Aporèmata* (ed. Ideler[33]) we have found many similar terms. The pneuma psychikon in the brain is obvious in the terms τὸ ψυχικὸν ἐν ἐγκεφάλῳ πνεῦμα in Id. I 131, where people who are turning around fall down, because this pneuma is disturbed so that it can not receive its percipient power and other faculties (πρὸς ὑποδοχὴν ψυχικῆς δυνάμεως, αἰσθητικῆς καὶ κινητικῆς, Id. p. 45, l. 1-2: I 131) and so apart from other things they see darkness, because its optikon pneuma is disturbed (τῷ τεθολῶσθαι τὸ ὀπτικὸν αὐτῆς πνεῦμα, Id. p. 45, l. 6-7: I 131), as cats can see in the night, because of the optikon pneuma which is τὸ ὀπτικὸν πνεῦμα λεπτότατον καὶ διαυγέστατον ('the optic pneuma is the finest and the most translucent') in Id. I 68, where we find the same term as in Id. I 114: τὸ ὀπτικὸν πνεῦμα διαυγέστατον ὂν καὶ φωτοειδές ('the optic pneuma is the most translucent and most similar to light'). For owing to this light of the pneuma we can see in the night, when we open our eyes (Id. I 69), but when we come from dark into light we cannot see inmediately, because the optikon pneuma is disturbed (Id. II 37). We even find the term αἱ ὀπτικαὶ ἀκτῖνες in Id. II 53, but there the optic rays are mentioned because of their bewitching effect.

Thus we may conclude that this text seems to be a re-edition of the *Problemata Physica* from the *Corpus Aristotelicum* (CA). The text must have been commented in the time after Galenus and during or after the time in which the Aporèmata attributed to pseudo-Alexander of Aphrodisias were written, after 200-250 A.D., but perhaps later because of the possibility of Stoic influence as found in the theory of vision. It is

33. See note 2.

difficult to speak about Stoic influence later than Galenus, because Galenus, too, was strongly influenced by the Stoics[34]. Therefore it is difficult to mention a date of origin that is more exact than 'after Galen', while the *ante quem* is the invasion of the Arabs into Egypt.

Some Greek words and in particular names of countries, not mentioned in the Greek text of the CA, are mentioned in the Arabic text, which confirms the conclusion that this text was originally a revision of the CA-text.

Yet, it is impossible to mention Ioannes Grammaticus as author of this text with certainty, as the Fihrist did. We know only very little about his medical activities and knowledge, as far as I am aware, and perhaps another person, e.g. Ioannes Alexandrinus or another Ioannes, is a greater probability. It was not uncommon to attribute a book to another author. Apart from that, Baumstark has remarked: 'Die gesamte Überlieferung bezüglich der aristotelischen Probleme ist ja unklar genug.'[35].

3. *Problemata Inedita in Arabic (PIA)*

The *Problemata Inedita*[36] is another type of *problemata*, published under that name in the Aristoteles-edition of Didot by Bussemaker[37]. Usener[38] made them book 3 and 4 of the *Problemata*, attributed to Alexander of Aphrodisias.

In Arabic there are 91 *problemata* at this moment. In the survey below, I have included part of the Arabic questions in translation, and I have combined them with the *Problemata Inedita* in Bussemaker-Usener (BU), the *Problemata* of Cassius[39] and the *Problemata Bambergensia*[40], and in some places the *Quaestiones Salernitanae* from Lawn's edition[41]. The different lines in the survey, column 2, show the various mss-groups.

---

34. Cf. Flashar H., 'Beiträge zur spätantiken Hippokratesdeutung', *Hermes* 90 (1962), p. 413ff.

35. Baumstark A., *Aristoteles bei den Syrern vom 5. bis 8. Jahrhundert*, Leipzig: Teubner, 1900 (Reprint: Aalen: Scientia Verlag, 1975), p. 85.

36. I am much indebted to R.W. Sharples for his stimulating comments.

37. Aristoteles, 'Problemata Inedita', in: Dübner F. – Bussemaker C. – Heitz A., *Aristoteles, Opera omnia graece et latine* 4, Paris: Didot, 1857, p. 291-332.

38. Alexander Aphrodisiensis, 'Problemata Inedita. Alexandri Aphrodisiensis quae feruntur liber III et IV', edidit H. Usener, *Jahresbericht über das Königl. Joachimsthalsche Gymnasium*, Berlin 1859.

39. Ideler I.L., *Physici et Medici Graeci minores* I, 1841 (Reprint: Amsterdam: Adolf M. Hakkert-Publisher, 1963), p. 144-167.

40. Rose V., *Aristoteles Pseudepigraphus*, Leipzig: Teubner, 1863 (Reprint: Hildesheim-New York: G. Olms, 1971), p. 666-676.

41. Lawn B., *The Prose Salernitan Questions*, London: Oxford U.P., 1979.

The transmission comprises about 15 manuscripts, one of which is written in Arabic but in Hebrew script largely with the diacritical points. For the time being, I call this manuscript PIAH[42].

The most important and the most complete ms. is that from Leiden (*N* in the survey), which is attributed to ar-Rāzī (Rhazes). This attribution can not be correct, because ar-Rāzī himself in his al-Ḥāwī (Latin: *Continens*) quotes some of these *problemata* as being from Aristotle[43]. The manuscript is from the 14th century[44], titled as 'as'ilatun w'-adjwibatun'[45]. The other important manuscript is that from Tehran[46] from the 19th century (*H* in the survey). Both these texts are nearly in the same order, have almost the same list of *problemata* and are very similar in content. Therefore these mss. are most important for the text constitution.

The other groups are less important, some were known earlier, as e.g. the Baghdād-manuscript, mentioned by H. Daiber in his note in *Gnomon*[47]. Others are known from Daiber's travelling through India, described in *Manuscripts of the Middle East*[48]. In the survey, this group is mentioned α; then there are two mss. forming another group, namely a manuscript from the British Museum (*M*)[49] and one from Lucknow (*L*)[50].

Together they must have had one source from Greek texts and as such, it must be a Greek text translated in Arabic, but the translator is unknown.

Nearly all these texts contain texts belonging to those from Usener IV 1-38 or Bussemaker II B 1-38, and the *Problemata* of Cassius the Iatrosophist[51] and the *Problemata Bambergensia*. Therefore, we can state that these texts must have been part of one *Corpus*. This must be true even more so, because all texts mentioning an author mention Aristotle and besides they are all in the same order, in the Greek and in the

42. STEINSCHNEIDER M., 'Bibliografia Orientale. Manoscritti arabici in caratteri ebraici', *Bollettino italiano degli studi orientali*, N.S. 4 (1878), p. 65-69.
43. E.g. PIA 13 in *al-Ḥāwī* XV 160, 16 and PIA 39 in *al-Ḥāwī* XIV, 14, 6. The edition of *al-Ḥāwī*: Abū Muḥammad ibn Zakariyā ar-Rāzī, *al-Ḥāwī fī 't-ṭibb*, published by DĀ'IRATU 'L-MA'ĀRIFI 'L-ÓSMANIA, vol. 1-23, Ḥaidarabad, 1374-1390/1955-1971.
44. VOORHOEVE P., *Handlist of Arabic Manuscripts*, Leiden-The Hague-Boston-London: Leiden U.P., 1980, p. 25: 958 (11).
45. Thanks to Drs. Monique Janson, who drew my attention to this ms.
46. WITKAM J.J., *Catalogue of Arabic manuscripts,* Leiden: Brill- Leiden U. P., 1986, fasc. 4, p. 357-358: fotocopy: Leiden University Library Or 14.255.
47. DAIBER H., 'Note to F.E. Peters, Aristoteles Arabus', *Gnomon* 42 (1970), p. 538-547, here p. 545.
48. DAIBER H., 'New Manuscripts Findings from Indian Libraries', in: *Manuscripts of the Middle East* 1 (1986), p. 26-48.
49. See MEREDITH-OWENS G., 'A tenth-century Arabic Miscellany', *The British Museum Quarterly* 20 (1955-1956), p. 33-34.
50. See DAIBER, 'New Manuscripts Findings...', p. 38, n. 143.
51. See note 41.

Arabic mss., as you can see in survey below. You will find some
problemata only in Arabic, others only in the collection of Bussemaker-
Usener, and again others only in the *Problemata* of Cassius or in the
Problemata Bambergensia, but the order remains almost the same.
Therefore, we can state that the *Corpus* of these *problemata* must have
been much larger than it seems on the face of it.

These *problemata* are especially interesting, because they are always
short in the source-text, but later on some have become longer and in
such a way that they show the same process of adaptation we have seen
in the *Problemata Physica*.

Another collection of *Problemata* is the collection which I have given
the temporary abbreviation PIAH. It is a ms. from Munich, written in
Arabic with Hebrew characters, containing 18 *problemata*, also attributed to Aristotle[52]. In general these texts are very short and the text is
very similar to the other texts of the *Problemata Inedita*, with only a few
changes. Firstly, it starts with an opening sentence causing it to look like
a series of questions to the philosopher Aristotle whose wisdom is useful.
Secondly, each question begins with: "It is said" and then: "Why…?"
in its shortest form: only 'lima', not 'mā bālu' or 'lima ṣāra'. The answer is always: 'He said', followed by the answer to the question. It
seems to me that these texts are summaries of the Arabic version we
have; and therefore not very important for the constitution of the text.

Survey of a part of the *Problemata Inedita* in the Arabic tradition

Content of problemata	Arabic mss.	Greek texts	similarity
1. Why is someone who suffers from diarrhoea, very thirsty?	α -/ M -; L -/H 1; N 1 PIAH 1	BU 1/Bamb 1	
2. Why do sad people weep?	α 2/ M 6; L 6/ H 2; N 2 PIAH 2	BU 2/ Bamb 2	Id. I 31 SQ 56 (p. 309)
3. What is the difference between a ḫādim-eunuch and a ḫaṣī-eunuch? (eunuch and castrated?)	α 3/ M -; L -/ H 3; N 3	BU 3/ Bamb 3	
4. Why is it that he who has no testicles, does not grow a beard?	α -/ M 20; L 20; φ 51/ H 4; N 4 PIAH 3	BU 4/ Bamb 4	SQ 43 (p. 222) cf. Gal. K. I 339-345; (hairiness, Galen. K. I 344-5)

52. STEINSCHNEIDER, 'Bibliografia Orientale…', p. 66-69; STEINSCHNEIDER M., *Die
hebraeischen Handschriften der königlichen Hof- und Staatsbibliothek in Muenchen*,
München 1875, ad 275 not mentioned, but in STEINSCHNEIDER M., 'Schriften der Araber
in hebräischen Handschriften, ein Beitrag zur arabischen Bibliographie', *Zeitschrift der
Deutschen Morgenländischen Gesellschaft* 47 (1893), p. 342.

Content of problemata	Arabic mss.	Greek texts	similarity
5. Why is the voice of the ḫādim-eunuchs lighter/ higher-pitched than that of the ḫaṣī-eunuchs?	α -/ M 21; L 21; 52/ H 5; N 5 PIAH 4	BU 5/ Bamb 5	Id. I 8; I 97 SQ 40 (p. 221)
6. Why does the thirst of someone who is thirsty, stop when he takes a bath, whereas the bath makes him thirsty who has no thirst?	α 4/ M 22; L 22/ H 6; N 6/ PIAH 5	BU -/ Bamb 6; Cass. 5	Id. I 41 SQ 122 (p. 251)
7. Why do we belch after taking food, moist or dry?	α 5/ M 23; L 23/ H 7; N 7/ PIAH 6	BU 6/ Bamb 7	
8. Why are some people able to have sexual intercourse more frequently than others?	α -/ M -; L – / H 8; N 8	BU 7/ Bamb 9	
9. Why is it that he who comes from a bright place to a dark one, is not able to see immediately and then it is not long before he can see (again)?	α -/ M 7; L 7; φ 45/ H 9; N 9/ PIAH 7	BU 8/ Bamb 10	Id. II 37 SQ P 102 (p. 244)
10. Why is that when a swelling occurs to the toe, it hurts from stumbling, but the swelling of the vena femoris gives no feeling of pain in the toe?	α -/ M -; L – / H 10; N 10	BU -/ Bamb -	
11. Why is it that the woman who is suffering a disease of the uterus, passes out?	α 6 (K -)/ M -; L – / H -; N 11/ PIAH 8	BU 9/ Bamb 8	
12. Why is it that from all living creatures only women menstruate?	α 7 (K -)/ M 8; L 8 / H 11; N 12	BU 10/ Bamb 11	
13. Why is it that eye disease mostly precedes pestilence?	α 8 (K -)/ M -; L – / H 12; N 13	BU 11	Rāzī, al-Ḥāwī XV 160, 16
14. Why do old men better resist fasting?	α -/ M -; L – / H 13; N 14/ PIAH 9	BU -/ Bamb 12; Cass. 46	SQ B 186 (p. 101)
15. Why do young people not resist fasting?	α -/ M -; L – / H 14a; N 15/		or together with 14, because the "Why" is missing?
16.Why do both testicles among the other parts shrink and dry out at death?	α 9 (K -)/ M -; L – / H 14; N 16	BU -/ Bamb 14; Cass. 47	
17. Why does the semen flow out from a man who is dying?	α 10 (K -)/ M -; L – / H 15; N 17	-	
18. Why is the drunk fond of bad wine?	α -/ M -; L – / H 16; N 18	Cass. 48	
19. Why are the dropsicals always thirsty, although their bellies are full of water?	α 11 (K -)/ M 9; L 9 / H 17; N 19 PIAH 10	BU -/ Bamb 15; Cass. 4	Id. I 81

Content of problemata	Arabic mss.	Greek texts	similarity
20. Why do things upon which the stomach acts, contribute to the digestion?	α -/ M -; L – / H -; N 20 PIAH 11	-	
21. Why does someone who is trembling, become steady (in his movements) when he has drunk wine?	α -/ M 10; L 10; φ 46/ H 18; N 21	BU 12/ Bamb 17	
22. Why do non-rational animals walk and creep when they have been born, whereas man does not?	α 1/ M 4; L 4/ H 19: N 22/ PIAH 12	BU 13/ Bamb 18	

Problema 1 reads as follows:

> Why is someone who suffers from diarrhoea, very thirsty? Because when the moistures in these people flow down, the region of the stomach becomes dry and thirst is the result of dryness.

In the Hebrew-Arabic version PIAH 1 is: 'Why are the bodies of people dry in weariness?'. Sometimes, the Hebrew script causes some minor problems. Here it seems that the question is about weariness: 'kulfa' in Arabic, but in Hebrew you can also read 'khilfa', i.e. 'diarrhoea', but all Arabic mss. have the version 'khilfa'. Furthermore, the Greek text has Διὰ τί οἱ τὴν κάτω κοιλίαν ῥευματιζόμενοι ... 'those with a flux' so that it is obviously the right version. Id. II 75 could pose a little problem: The text is about a tired body that is dry. But it is a text about sleep, because tiredness makes the body dry, but dryness causes sleeplessness, which is totally different from our text.

In *Problema* 5, we see the same kind of change that we found in the *Problemata Physica*. The BU-text gives only the reason why the voice of the one is high and the voice of the other is low, but the cause of it, lack of warmth causing the passages of the voice to become wider or by cutting off the testicles to remain narrow, is ignored in the Greek text, but is mentioned in the Arabic one. But the real cause, warmth, is also found in Id. I 97, beside the moistness in Id. I 8, which is necessary to widen the passages, but not in these Greek texts and neither in the Arabic ones. Galen[53] extensively discussed the moistness and the warmth of the testicles in his *Ars Parva*, K. I 339-341, where it is said that the testicles are the warmest parts of the body. Therefore eunuchs are not hairy, as Galen later explains about the hairy bodies.

53. See note 31.

Problema 6 is to be found in Cassius' *Problemata* 5, but somewhat more elaborately than in Arabic. A remarkable expression is διὰ τὸ μετέχειν ζωτικῆς δυνάμεως ('because of the participation to the vital power'). The cause of thirst is mentioned also in Arabic, but the ζωτικὴ δύναμις is absent in Arabic, and also in the *Quaestiones Salernitanae* 122 (Lawn, p. 251). Cassius reads ζωτικὴ δύναμις μετέχει αὐτό (τὸ ὑγρόν ('the moistness') of the bath and thus gives an explanation why τὸ ὑγρόν penetrates into the pores of the body.

Problema 8 is very short in Greek. The reason why they have a more frequent sexual intercourse is, because they are warmer, but in Arabic it is also because these bodies have more moisture according to Galen, *Ars Parva*, K. I 339, l. 13-14.

Problema 9 is also very short in Greek: going from darkness into light we do not see the surrounding things immediately, because they are hidden because of the darkness. In Arabic it is another reason, and here I want to show you the adaptation of the text: it is because first the darkness penetrates into the optic pneuma in spite of its fineness, but the optic pneuma becomes more powerful and that is the reason why we are able to observe the surrounding things later on. This explanation through optic pneuma (τὸ ὀπτικὸν πνεῦμα) is to be found in pseudo-Alexander of Aphrodisias and later on. In the PPA the optic pneuma is the finest type of τὸ πνεῦμα ψυχικόν. It appears to be necessary to add this pneuma to the explanation of the phenomena[54], also according to the explanation in pseudo-Alexander of Aphrodisias. This explanation of the optic pneuma is to be found in all mss., except in the ms. with Hebrew script, but this manuscript is clearly less important.

I did not find *Problema* 10 in BU, Bamb or Cass. I still do not know any parallel.

I am not sure about 14 and 15, whether they are one or two *problemata*, because in the different versions the formula 'lima ṣāra' 'why' is missing.

Interesting is *Problema* 13, because here, too, we have an explanation that is missing in Greek. The Greek text reads:

> Why do eye diseases in most cases begin in times of plague? Because plague is an affliction of the pneuma. So when a change occurs affecting it, the pneuma is carried upwards and disturbs the eyesight; for there it is wider and flows more easily.

The Arabic text has a clear explanation in the real sense of pneuma in the answer:

54. See FILIUS, 'The theory of vision...', p. 80-82.

Because the pestilence only results from corruption of the air. When the air is corrupted, first the pneuma in the body, especially in the eyes among the other parts, is corrupted. In (the eyes) there is the most, the finest and the clearest pneuma. Owing to this the corruption of the air reaches them quickly and thus eye disease occurs.

'Because the pneuma in the eye is the most, finest and clearest pneuma' is the same as we saw in the *Problemata Physica*, in pseudo-Alexander of Aphrodisias and in Galen. The text is obviously corrected according to the knowledge and the views of the time of the author.

Problema 10 (PIAH) seems to be new, but from the answer its is obvious that it deals with dropsy:

Why is the man in whom is yellow water always thirsty? Because the moisture we drink does not go to the place to which it ought to go, but goes to the outside skin. Therefore he becomes thirsty as if he had not drunk.

That 'yellow water' is somewhat strange, but the expression 'Who has yellow water in his belly'[55] is an Arabic term for 'who is dropsical' which is not found in the other Arabic mss. The PIAH must have another tradition than the other Arabic ms., as stated before.

Problema 22 is interesting, because of the differences. The Greek text (IV 13) is in translation:

Why do irrational animals walk around as soon as they are born, but men do not? Because in the case of irrational animals the heat is equal in every part, but in the case of children it is more around the head. So when the heat is equally spread everywhere, they stand up.

The Arabic text (PIA 22) reads:

Why do irrational animals walk and creep as soon as they are born, whereas man does not? Because the heat and the moisture in all parts of the irrational animals are equally spread, but the moisture in the brain of children greatly submerses the warmth. For the brain gets colder to endure thinking and gets moister to facilitate its reception of the imagination which is impressed in it. In childhood there is an excess in moisture in the brain owing to the age and thus moisture is more pressing on the heat. Therefore it (the heat) cannot get out until the child begins to move and to cause to move the other parts, for the beginning of moving originates from the brain. So when the child is getting older and the amount of moisture decreases consequently and the warmth becomes powerful, the brain starts moving and likewise the other parts of the body. At that moment he rises up.

According to the Arabic text of the Leiden manuscript, there is too much moisture in the head and this moisture must be cold. We may un-

55. LANE E.W., *An Arabic-English Lexicon*, 8 Parts and Supplement, London-Edinburgh: Williams and Norgate, 1863-1893 (Reprint: Beirouth, Librairie du Liban, 1980), IV 1097b, cf. also ULLMANN, *Die Medizin...*, p. 243, n. 6.

derstand that the cold moistness of the brain is overwhelming and causes a concentration of heat in the head, because the cold moisture encloses the heat, as an effect of antiperistasis[56], well-known in the Peripatetic School. As a result the heat cannot find its way out to the rest of the body, but when the child is getting older the amount of moisture decreases and the child starts moving. Therefore we may understand the summary in PIAH 12 'The heat in their head is less and also the movement' as 'a part of the brain is colder and and due to the inequality of the heat's distribution over the body the child does not move'.

Besides, it may be an explanation of the faculty of the human brain being different from that of the animals: the concentration of heat makes part of the brain colder and moister to facilitate thinking and imagination[57], two human qualities. You may compare it with the necessity of sleep, because during sleep the brain becomes moister and thus the imagination becomes stronger, Galen K. XVII 169 and 177[58].

In any case, here, too, we may find some adaptation to later thoughts, especially thoughts showing some similarity with pseudo-Alexandrian and Galenic theories. I am uncertain about the relation between this Greek text and the Arabic one, but perhaps we have to explain that in PIA 22 the idea of antiperistasis is correct and that the version of the Leiden-ms. is a later explanation added to the original lack of clarity in the Greek text according to ideas from the Aristotelians, as we find in the time of Alexander of Aphrodisias and later on. Perhaps the Greek text has compressed the cause of human thinking and imagination.

In general it is to say that also the PIA may be a later elaboration of earlier *problemata* as in Buss-Us, and after these had been provided with their explanations, they were translated into Arabic.

56. I am very grateful to R.W. Sharples for his suggestion of antiperistasis here.
57. For the idea of antiperistasis, cf. FLASHAR, *Problemata...*, p. 331; FORTENBAUGH – SHARPLES – SOLLENBERGER, *Theophrastus of Eresus*, p. 104-105 ad 'Theophrastus on Sweat' 23.159-160 and notes. Cf. also Aristoteles, *Meteorologica*, 348b2sqq. and Aristotle, *Meteorologica*, edited with an English translation by H.P. LEE (Loeb Classical Library 397), Cambridge Mass.: Harvard U.P. – London: W. Heinemann LTD, 1952 (Reprint: 1978), p. 82-83, note b; also LETTINCK P., *Aristotle's Meteorology and its reception in the Arab world* (Aristoteles Semitico-Latinus 10), Leiden-Boston-Köln: Brill, 1999, p. 99, note 2. Cf. also PG 867b32 and 962a2.
58. SIEGEL R., *Galen, On psychology, psychopathology, and function and diseases of the nervous system*' (Galen's system of Physiology and medicine 3), Basel–München–Paris–London–New York–Sydney: S. Karger, 1973, p. 144ff. The answer in the *Quaestiones Salernitanae*, ed. LAWN, B228 (p. 115-116) that the menstrual blood can be cleared for the embryo in time, is interesting for the source from which it was deduced.

4. The Problemata of pseudo-Alexander of Aphrodisias in Syriac

The translation of the collection of *problemata* attributed to Alexander of Aphrodisias[59] will not take a long time, because this is a translation in Syriac of the Greek text of Ideler. It is a rather literal translation, although there are some changes in the text, but not so fundamental and not so many as e.g. in the Arabic text of the *Problemata Physica*. Only an Arabic summary by Ibn aṭ-Ṭayyib exists[60]. Ibn aṭ-Ṭayyib knew Syriac. Therefore, he was able to use the Syriac text for his summary. For the text edition of the Syriac it will be important to compare the Syriac text with this summary, because we may be able to establish whether an Arabic translation existed, too.

5. Reception of the Problemata in Arabic literature

The genre *Problemata Physica* has its own history[61]. It would be interesting to examine the reasons why they did change the texts and due to what circumstances, but it seems better to focus on some short comments on two other *Problemata*-texts, which demonstrate the motion and the change of *Problemata* texts. First, I am looking at a text from the *Problemata Inedita* in the Arabic version, no. 45:

> Why do some people become gray-haired quickly? Because in the parts of their heads coldness comes quickly and easily.

In a long story we find an answer to the question: 'Why is it that of all other living beings only men get grey hair?'

> The cause is that there is a difference of moistures in men because of the difference of food and victuals. Thus different moistures and residues result. Nature is pushing him so that he becomes grey through the softness and the warmth of nature, as in the beginning. Thus he has reverted to whom he was, because in the beginning he was a drop of water and grows up through the warmth and then finally he returns to his beginning to come to nothing as in the beginning – namely that drop of water –, because that drop came into the uterus and from that drop man resulted, and becomes perfect but the drop comes to nothing so that there is no drop and becomes

---

59. See note 35. Cf. also DAIBER, 'Note...', p. 545-546. Also CLERMONT J.T., *A checklist of Syriac manuscripts in the United States and Canada* (Orientalia Christiana Periodica 32), Roma: Pontificale Institutum orientalium studiorum, 1966, p. 224-251 and 478-522.

60. Nuruosmaniye 3610 (new numbering 3095), fol. 1v-21v.

61. Cf. BERTIER J. – FILIUS L.S., *Problemata Physica*, in: GOULET (ed.), *Dictionnaire des Philosophes Antiques, Supplément,* Paris: CNRS éditions, 2003, p. 575-598.

a new creature, named man and it is not called drop. Like this finally (man) comes to nothing, so that he is not man. Likewise we see the beginning of all creatures from nothing, and then it becomes something, and after that it comes to nothing and thus it is nothing.

This latter text is a passage from the *Sirru 'l-ḥalīqa*[62], 'das Buch über das Geheimnis der Schöpfung und die Darstellung der Natur', attributed to Apollonius of Tyana or Balinus, chapter VI 3. The title itself tells enough about the context of this text. It seems to be one of the *Problemata Inedita*, not existing in the BU-version or in the *Problemata* of pseudo-Alexander of Aphrodisias, but still belonging to this genre of texts. The question itself seems to be part of the same category as Id. I 1 and 2. In all texts, food is important for the formation of moistures. Moistures are important for the hair. Of course, the next question is what causes hair to turn grey. As we have seen in the *Problemata Inedita* 45, but also in other texts from the *Problemata*, it is the coldness that causes hair to turn grey. In these texts, too, the developing of grey hair depends on moistures in the head, but it is not mentioned that the origin of moistures depends on the food that man consumes. We may have to study the rest of the text to find the background of reasoning in this case.

The origin of the question surely is the *Problemata Inedita* or, per-haps better, the *Problemata Physica*, in the Arabic version XI 61, be-cause here the same question is formulated. The answer is that there is a great deal of moisture in man's body and there is only little heat, espe-cially in the head and the brain. White hair is the result of the corruption and putrefaction of the phlegm. Besides, the hair of other animals falls out every year and therefore the hair is always young and so it is darker and stronger. But when man is growing older, his hair becomes weak and turns white, and also because man lives a very long time, his hair grows weak and white. The life of most animals is short.

Whereas in the text of the *Sirru 'l-ḥalīqa* there is some emphasis on the beginning and the end of man's life, in the PPA the long duration of life is to be found. In the PG X 63, too, we only find the long term of man's life. The first part of the moisture and the slight heat in head and brain is missing, as is the putrefaction of the phlegm. In Arabic, we don't find the question in XI 4 as in Greek X 5, but that again may be

62. Apollonius Tyanensis, *Sirru 'l-ḥalīqa wa-ṣana'atu 'ṭ-ṭabī'ati. Kitābu 'l-'ilāli, Buch über das Geheimnis der Schöpfung und die Darstellung der Natur (Buch der Ursachen)*, Edited by U. WEISSER (Aleppo: Sources & Studies in the History of Arabic-Islamic Science, Natural Sciences Series I), Aleppo: Institute for the History of Arabic Science, University of Aleppo, 1979, p. 440-441. Cf. also WEISSER U., *Das 'Buch über das Geheimnis der Schöpfung' von Pseudo-Apollonius von Tyana*, Berlin-New York: De Gruyter, 1980, p. 137 and 220-221.

caused by the text having been re-edited. The text of the PPA is a combination of PG X 63, the long life of man, PIA 45 the coldness of the head and furthermore the moisture of the head and the putrefaction of the phlegm.

In the *Book of Treasures* we can go further back to the Syriac text in chapter XV, the origin of the *Sirru 'l-ḥalīqa*, as it seems, the *Book of Treasures* by Job of Edessa[63]. Here, too, the different kinds of food, even after satisfying his hunger, gives rise to many superfluities. Especially during puberty these moistures with their superfluities cause black hair to grow all over his body, but when he is getting old, his body becomes cold and so his hair turns white, first his head and his beard, because of all the residues there. But all other animals take kinds of food that are greatly different. Therefore they have less residues, and the residues they have are hard and dry. Because the nature of animals is thick and the residues which are collected near the skin are dry, their pores are narrow. Consequently, less evaporation takes place and therefore their heat is enclosed inside and so their hair remains black.

Conclusion

There is much more to be said about the motions and changes of different kinds of *Problemata* and still much more to investigate. In this respect, I refer to the studies of Gutas and Biesterfeldt[64] and that of Raven[65] about Ibn Dāwūd and the malady of love. We may conclude that the *Problemata* has proved to be a useful instrument to change the text and to adapt it on the basis of new knowledge and insights. The method of question and answer provides scope for additions, but also for changing the texts. Because of these changes, this genre will be found in all types of literature. Therefore, it will be interesting to investigate especially also the Arabic and Syriac literature, as they have used this genre extensively.

Aristoteles Semitico-Latinus
Universiteit Leiden

63. Job of Edessa, *Book of Treasures, Encyclopaedia of Philosophical and Natural Sciences as taught in Baghdad A.D. 817*, Syriac text edited and translated with a critical apparatus by A. MINGANA (Woodbrooke Scientific Publications 1), Cambridge: W. Heffer & Sons Limited, 1935.

64. GUTAS D. – BIESTERFELDT H.H., 'The malady of love', *Journal of the American Oriental Society* 104 (1984), (Reprint in: GUTAS D., *Greek Philosophers in the Arabic Tradition*, Aldershot-Burlington USA-Singapore-Sydney: Ashgate, 2000), p. 21-55.

65. RAVEN W., *Ibn Dāwūd al-Iṣbahānī and his Kitāb al-Zahra*, diss. Leiden, Amsterdam, 1989.

Graziella Federici VESCOVINI

L'*EXPOSITIO SUCCINTA PROBLEMATUM ARISTOTELIS* DE PIERRE D'ABANO

In this article, I would like to discuss the sources of Pietro d'Abano's Expositio succinta, *and whether he wrote a translation of the* Problemata *or not. Several indications indeed suggest that he might have written such a translation, e.g. expressions like 'transduxi', 'translinguavi', but the matter is complicated. I will also study the characteristics of Pietro's work, in order to give it its due place in the* Problemata *tradition.*

Introduction

L'*expositio succinta Problematum Aristotelis* pose beaucoup de problèmes qu'il ne me sera pas possible de résoudre. Je me bornerai à traiter du status quaestionis – ainsi que l'on aurait dit au moyen âge – par rapport à la question générale: *quicquid agitur?* de quoi s'agit-il? Je laisserai de côté, malgré leur importance, tous les problèmes philologiques et textuels concernant les manuscrits et les éditions, que personne n'a traités jusqu'aujourd'hui d'une façon exhaustive. Je me réfère à la connaissance complète de tous les exemplaires manuscrits des *Problemata* de Pierre, à la collation entre ces exemplaires manuscrits et les rédactions des premières éditions à la fin du 15e siècle et au commencement du 16e siècle (Kuksewicz a déjà fait une première exploration en comparant le texte de Pierre et l'*expositio* de Jean de Jandun)[1]; enfin, à la collation de tous les documents recensés et étudiés de la version dite de Barthélémy de Messine et de celle de Théodore Gaza. Autrement dit, même si nous avons déjà quelques renseignements précieux concernant les manuscrits des *Problemata* de Pierre qui nous ont été donnés par S. Ferrari, L. Thorndike, L. Nortpoth, par L. Minio-Paluello[2], par C. Marchesi, par L. Marenghi et L. Olivieri, nous sommes persuadée que le recensement de tous les manuscrits n'est pas encore achevé.

Au préalable, après avoir abordé les problèmes philologiques que j'ai cités, on doit aussi engager une recherche des sources pour retrouver la

---

1. KUKSEWICZ J., 'Les *problemata* de Pietro d'Abano et leur rédaction par Jean de Jandun', *Medioevo* 11 (1985), p. 113-138.
2. MINIO-PALUELLO L., *Aristoteles latinus, Codices, Pars posterior*, Cambridge: Typys Academiae, 1955.

stratification composite de la tradition textuelle des *Problemata* de Pierre d'Abano. De plus, à cet égard, il faut tenter d'identifier ses intérêts scientifiques et philosophiques à la lumière de son interprétation de la philosophie d'Aristote. Celle-ci aboutit à une transformation de l'ontologie même d'Aristote, à cause de l'exigence de Pierre de construire une philosophie de la médecine[3], qui est l'application de la science de la nature en mouvement à l'homme physique. Cette philosophie, comme j'ai essayé de le démontrer dans mes études précédentes[4], est fondée sur des doctrines issues de l'astrologie médicale des savants arabes qui les avaient développées en interprétant le *Quadripartitum* de Ptolémée et, surtout, le *Centiloquium* d'Alì. L'aristotélisme de Pierre d'Abano provenait aussi d'une nouvelle élaboration de la métaphysique d'Avicenne, et de l'interprétation des concepts d'*ars* et de science élaborés par Aristote dans l'*Éthique à Nicomaque,* livre VI, chap. 2 (1139a1-30) et 4 (1140a5-20), grâce à la médiation byzantine du commentaire d'Eustrace, dont on sait très peu de choses mais auquel Pierre se réfère souvent.

Troisièmement, on devrait essayer de lier le contenu des *Problemata* d'Aristote avec les *Parva naturalia*[5], le *De generatione et corruptione*, et le *De animalibus*[6]; on devrait aussi chercher à déceler les différences, si elles existent, dans le commentaire de Pierre. Mais ceci rejoint le problème de l'identification du contenu philosophique de l'œuvre de Pierre.

Dans cette contribution, je me bornerai à traiter deux sujets, sans aborder la question controversée de l'authenticité des *Problèmes* d'Aristote (connus au moyen âge) et de la tradition de la transmission du texte grec avec toutes ses contaminations. Par conséquent:

1) j'examinerai le problème de la valeur (et de l'interprétation) des expressions employées par Pierre d'Abano dans certains passages de

---

3. Voir en particulier mon étude 'La médecine, synthèse d'art et de science selon Pierre d'Abano', dans: R. RASHED – J. BIARD (éds), *Les doctrines de la science de l'antiquité à l'âge classique*, Leuven: Peeters, 1999, p. 237-255.

4. En particulier, cf. mon introduction à l'édition critique du *Lucidator dubitabilium astronomiae*: FEDERICI VESCOVINI G. (éd.), *I trattati di astronomia: Lucidator dubitabilium astronomiae, De motu octavae sphaerae e altre opere* (Il mito e la storia 3), Padova: Programma, 2e éd., 1992, p. 1-104.

5. Cf. aussi FEDERICI VESCOVINI G., 'Parva Naturalia', dans C. Crisciani – R. Lamberti – R. Martorelli (éds), *Saperi medievali, natura e vita. Atti dell' XI Convegno della Società Italiana per lo studio del Pensiero Medievale, Macerata, 7-9 dicembre 2001*, Pisa–Roma: Istituti Editoriali e Poligrafici Internazionali, 2004, p. 125-142.

6. Sur le *De animalibus* cf. aussi DE LEEMANS P., 'Internal senses, intellect and motivation. Some evidence from the medieval commentaries on Aristotle's *De motu animalium*', dans: G. FEDERICI VESCOVINI – C. VINTI (éds), *Corpo e anima, sensi interni e intelletto dal secolo XIV ai post-cartesiani e spinoziani* (Atti del Convegno, Firenze 18-20 sett. 2003), Louvain-La-Neuve: Brepols, 2005, p. 139-160.

ses œuvres, en me demandant dans quelle mesure il a, ou n'a pas, traduit le texte des *Problemata* attribués à Aristote, en essayant d'interpréter correctement certains termes qu'il emploie, tels que *traduxi, translinguavi, transduxi*, etc.

2) j'examinerai brièvement, d'un point de vue philosophique et scientifique, le caractère de cet *Exposé*, en soulignant la transformation accomplie par Pierre à l'égard de la physique d'Aristote selon les principes philosophiques, astronomiques et astrologiques de la science hellénistique tardive, à savoir de la science de Ptolémée, de Galien, d'Alexandre d'Aphrodisie, d'Eustrace. Cette science nous est connue grâce à l'interprétation très stimulante des philosophes et des médecins arabes et juifs, surtout d'Avenzoar (un des maîtres d'Averroès)[7]. La doctrine de ce dernier est très controversée, mais si son interprétation n'est pas acceptée par Pierre, c'est à cause de sa condamnation de l'astrologie comme science, de sa limitation du champ de la médecine au seul niveau opérationnel et mécanique. Aussi, bien que Pierre d'Abano en discute souvent les doctrines, est-il très proche de l'ontologie d'Avicenne et de sa conception de la médecine en tant que science spéculative. En outre, dans son interprétation des *Problemata*, on remarque aisément une influence aussi bien de la médecine juive (surtout de Maimonide et du livre *De diffinitionibus* de Isaac Israeli) que de l'astrologie de Abrame Ibn Ezra, dont il traduit presque tous les ouvrages.

Notre conclusion provisoire sera que Pierre n'a pas traduit les *Problemata* attribués à Aristote, mais qu'il a rédigé une compilation résumée (*expositio succinta*) et qu'il nous propose une interprétation que personne, à son avis, n'avait faite jusqu'alors, *nullo interpretante*. Dans son texte, il propose un bref commentaire des *Problemata*, dont il attribue la paternité à Aristote. À notre avis, son interprétation est soumise à l'influence de la physique ou de la théorie de la génération, de l'*inchoatio materiae*, d'Albert le Grand, dont Pierre d'Abano semble accepter la doctrine, comme l'avait démontré Bruno Nardi dans ses études[8]. C'est ainsi que sa conception de la nature biologique et psychologique représente un gauchissement de la métaphysique d'Aristote, dans le sens d'une philosophie de la médecine ou *physis*, d'après laquelle les princi-

7. À propos de Ibn Zuhr Avenzoar Gabd al-Malek ibn abi-l-Alazahr (1130-1163), voir COLIN G., *Avenzoar, sa vie et ses œuvres* (Publication de la Faculté des Lettres d'Alger, Bulletin de Correspondance Africaine, Tome 44), Paris, 1911; ULLMANN M., *Die Medizin im Islam*, Leiden-Köln: Brill, 1970, p. 162.

8. NARDI B., 'Le dottrine filosofiche di Pietro d'Abano', dans: *Saggi sull'aristotelismo padovano dal secolo XIV al XVI*, Firenze: La Nuova Italia, 1958, p. 19-74.

pes théoriques d'Aristote seraient assez contaminés par ceux de la médecine astrologique du *Quadripartitum* de Ptolémée, par la théorie de la complexion de Galien, et surtout par la théorie de l'intellect d'Alexandre d'Aphrodisie et, en particulier d'Avicenne, pour la notion ontologique de la matière et de la *dispositio materiae.* C'est ainsi qu'il transforme radicalement l'image traditionnelle de ce qu'on appelle l'aristotélisme de Padoue, en faisant appel surtout à l'influence d'Avicenne avec la médiation d'Albert le Grand. De plus, à cause de cette élaboration de Pierre d'Abano, il résulte que cet aristotélisme est profondément modifié aussi par des interprétations de commentateurs non seulement arabes, mais surtout grecs et byzantins (tels qu'Alexandre, Themistius, Simplicius, Cassius Iatrosophiste et Eustrace). Par conséquent, l'image traditionnelle de l'école aristotélicienne appelée 'de Padoue' a été renouvelée par la philosophie de Pierre, au point d'entraîner la modification de la doctrine canonique de l'ontologie physique d'Aristote: sa conception de la nature (*physis*), qui est l'objet primaire de la médecine et qui concerne l'être en mouvement (*fieri*) ou contingent, et non pas l'*esse* nécessaire, immuable, l'*esse est esse* du divin. Il en résulte, en particulier, que Pierre d'Abano, loin d'être un averroïste, était plutôt un adepte d'Alexandre d'Aphrodisie et qu'il soutient surtout les transformations de la notion de matière, développée dans un sens néoplatonicien par Avicenne.

1. *Pierre d'Abano, traducteur des* Problemata?

Si on examine les citations proposées par Pierre dans son *Conciliator*, Diff. 1ª dans le prologue, Diff. 5ª propter tertium[9], dans *Lucidator* diff. 1ª propter primum, on voit que Pierre emploie explicitement des termes tels que *mea translatio, transduxi*. Nous constatons, surtout dans le *Conciliator*, mais aussi dans une ligne de son *Lucidator dubitabilium astronomiae*, que Pierre d'Abano parle de *translatio* ('in quibusdam problematibus Aristotelis attributis per me translatis'); nous remarquons aussi quelques expressions aussi barbares que: *translinguavi* dans son *Lucidator*: 'secundum illud exordium Problematum Aristotelis ascriptorum que in latinum translinguavi'[10].

Pourtant, dans ces citations, nous devons signaler aussi le terme qui indique l'attribution de cette œuvre à Aristote, ce qui révèle que Pierre

9. *Conciliator*, Diff. 5 propter tertium, Venezia: Giunta, 1565, f. 9.

10. Cf. mon édition du *Lucidator dubitabilium astronomiae*: FEDERICI VESCOVINI (éd.), *I trattati...*, p. 123.

se réfère à une tradition qui n'est pas certaine de l'authenticité de ce *corpus* des *Problèmes*. Aussi Pierre d'Abano s'efforce-t-il de l'établir avec des mots qui ressemblent à ceux d'Albert le Grand. Il affirme donc, dans son *Conciliator*, diff. 5ª propter tertium, 'Aristoteles in quibusdam problematibus eidem ascriptis';… dans diff. 53ª, diff. 94ª, diff. 146ª on peut lire les mêmes affirmations: 'In problematibus, que transtuli Aristotelis ascriptis'. En outre, il déclare avoir traduit les *Problemata* d'Alexandre d'Aphrodisie[11].

Quant à la valeur des affirmations de Pierre d'Abano déclarant avoir traduit les *Problemata*, on peut rappeler brièvement la position de Nancy Siraisi, qui les accepte sans les discuter, celle de Franco Alessio, qui les cite sans les discuter lui aussi, celle de M. Thérèse d'Alverny, qui constate la faible crédibilité des propositions de Pierre, et enfin celle de Luigi Olivieri, qui les discute et propose une interprétation[12]. À ce propos, je me rapporte aux citations même de l'exorde des *Problemata*, où il faut souligner l'adverbe [*cum*][13] *post diu* par lequel Pierre d'Abano nous suggère qu'il a commencé une agrégation (ou *summa*) concernant l'exposition des problèmes. Il déclare que, pour mieux apprendre le grec, il était parti à Constantinople, où il avait trouvé un autre exemplaire des *Problèmes* d'Aristote, qu'il avait traduit en latin (cfr. *Annexe*, p. 66).

Les expressions que nous venons de présenter sont très difficiles à interpréter. Néanmoins, nous supposons que Pierre d'Abano avait commencé une *Expositio succinta* des *Problèmes* attribués à Aristote à partir de la traduction de Barthélémy de Messine. En effet, ces expressions le suggèrent, tout comme les gloses attribuables à Pierre d'Abano concernant la première version latine de *Problèmes* par Barthélémy de Mes-

11. Cf. l'étude de R.W. Sharples dans le présent recueil à propos de la tradition manuscrite grecque. Cette attribution, niée par Thorndike et Cranz, est acceptée par Marangon et Olivieri, s'appuyant aussi sur le ms. de Madrid, Escorial, Real Biblioteca, Monastero de San Lorenzo, ms. f. I, 11, (Antolin, II, 137) ff. 31-42, et sur un fragment qu'on trouve à la Bibliothèque Vaticane. On peut y lire la datation de 1302, 'Incipiunt Problemata Alexandri Affrodiseos translata per magistrum Petrum Aponensem Padue de greco in latinum'; f. 42: 'aut diversa inferiorum et superiorum molle figuratione. Explicit liber Problematum Alexandri Affrodiseos translatus per Petrum Padubanensem Padue de greco in latinum MCCC secundo XV die Decembris et sunt omnia problemata numero 197'.

12. Olivieri L., *Pietro d'Abano e il pensiero neolatino, filosofia, scienza e ricerca dell'Aristotele greco tra i secoli XIII e XIV*, Padova: Antenore, 1988, p. 180 ss.; Siraisi N., 'The *Expositio Problematum Aristotilis* of Pietro d'Abano', *Isis* 61 (1970), p. 323-24; Alessio F., 'Filosofia e scienza, Pietro d'Abano', dans: G. Arnaldi – M. Pastore Stocchi (éds), *Storia della cultura veneta*, II, *Il Trecento*, Vicenza: Neri Pozza Ed., 1976, p. 171-206; D'Alverny M.T., 'Pietro d'Abano traducteur de Galien', *Medioevo* 11 (1985), p. 19-64.

13. Cf. la note 27 de l'annexe. La phrase n'est pas claire.

sine, qui paraît conservée dans le ms. de Padoue, Antoniano 370, déjà décrit et étudié par Concetto Marchesi. Ensuite, (*post diu*) lors de son voyage à Constantinople pour mieux apprendre le grec, il aurait retrouvé un nouvel exemplaire des *Problemata*. On suppose qu'à cette occasion il aurait pu aussi comparer son exposé avec l'original grec trouvé à Constantinople. Voilà que se pose ici le problème de la datation du voyage de Pierre à Constantinople et de l'exemplaire précis qu'il y avait retrouvé. À cet effet, nous pouvons nous rapporter à l'*explicit* de quelques-uns des exemplaires les plus anciens, comme par exemple celui de Paris (Paris, BN lat. 6540). Nous pouvons y lire qu'il avait commencé son exposé pendant son séjour à Paris et qu'il l'avait achevé à Padoue en 1310. Nous savons que Pierre était à Paris jusqu'en 1298 (selon un document accepté par Hauréau et par Bruno Nardi)[14] et qu'il y avait achevé sa *Compilatio physiognomiae* en 1295. En 1302, il devait être de retour à Padoue, où il acheva sa version des *Problemata* d'Alexandre, comme le suggère l'*explicit* du codex de l'Escorial déjà cité. Il avait donc achevé la rédaction des *Problemata* en 1310, selon le codex de Paris BN 6540 et l'édition de Mantoue, 1475. Nous lisons dans ce codex, f. 1ra: 'Incipit scriptum super libro de problematibus a magistro Petro de Padua: «Sententiam Aristotelis secundo celi et mundi»'; f. 236va: 'Explicit expositio succinta compilationis Problematum quam Petrus edidit Padubanensis in ea nullo interpretante incepta quidem Parisius et laudabiliter Padue terminata anno legis chrispianorum M°CCC°X° cum laude dei altissimi, cuius nomen dei sit benedictum per secula'.

On peut toutefois se demander quand il a fait son voyage à Constantinople? Si en 1302 il termine à Padoue sa version des *Problemata* d'Alexandre, et qu'il dit dans l'*explicit* aussi bien de ce ms. de Paris, que de l'édition de Mantoue 1475, qu'il a commencé l'*expositio* (*incepta*) à Paris et terminé en 1310 à Padoue, on peut supposer qu'il l'avait rédigée à Paris avant 1298. C'est pendant les années des révisions finales de toutes ses œuvres (*Conciliator, De motu octavae sphaerae, Lucidator*), faites en 1303-1310 (comme il le déclare lui-même dans son *Conciliator*)[15], qu'il aurait corrigé et révisé son *Expositio problematum*. Aussi nous est-il permis de supposer qu'il est allé sans doute à Constantinople avant sa traduction des *Problemata* d'Alexandre (1302). Je reviendrai là-dessus, parce que mon hypothèse reste toujours *sub iudice*, puisqu'il

14. HAURÉAU B., *Notices et extraits de quelques manuscrits latins*, tome IV, Paris, 1982, p. 290-94; NARDI B., 'Le dottrine filosofiche…', p. 20.

15. *Conciliator*, Diff. 2ª propter tertium et Diff. 9ª.

aurait pu aussi aller en Grèce pendant son long séjour à Paris[16]. Pour l'instant, en comparant la copie manuscrite (Paris BN lat. 6540) avec la première édition de Mantoue de 1475, on peut soutenir sans trop de certitude cette conclusion.

L'*Expositio* présente aussi des affirmations expliquant de quoi il s'agit (*quicquid agitur*), selon la forme littéraire de cette œuvre de Pierre de Padoue (*expositio*), qui par cela même n'est pas une simple traduction. Il ne faut pas prétendre, à l'instar d'Angelo Poliziano, de trouver un texte philologiquement parfait des *Problemata* dans l'*Expositio* de Pierre d'Abano, parce que, comme tous les médiévistes le savent, les œuvres de Pierre sont l'expression de la tradition scolastique de son temps. C'est dire qu'il rédige une *Expositio succinta*, un abrégé d'un texte que nous supposons qu'il possédait déjà, et où il y avait des fautes. Aussi fait-il une *expositio succinta* qui n'est ni une traduction, ni une simple interprétation littérale, mais une nouvelle formulation en latin d'un texte qui, paraît-il, existait déjà. L'*accessus* du prologue est très important pour cette raison et nous éclaire sur plusieurs points.

Pierre écrit ici que son œuvre appartient au genre de la compilation (cf. *Annexe*, p. 66): 'In hoc libro inveniuntur fere totius philosophie *per modum cuiusdam allegationis* sermones compilati'. En d'autres termes, il a fait un recueil de sermons concernant la philosophie dans son ensemble, qu'il entend rapporter aux problèmes de la médecine. La forme de cette compilation sera une explication tirée de ce livre d'Aristote, où il introduira des doutes et des remarques pour résoudre les difficultés qui pourraient se présenter. C'est à lui que revient l'organisation des livres et la répartition des problèmes. Il ajoute aussi que, même si quelqu'un nie qu'Aristote soit l'auteur de cet ouvrage, on doit le lui attribuer, parce que Aristote parle de ces arguments à plusieurs endroits, comme dans le second livre de la *Métaphysique* et dans les *Parva naturalia*. Cette formulation nous rappelle les mots d'Albert le Grand dans son *De somno et vigilia*, I, 25[17], où Albert, comme Pierre d'Abano, souligne le rapport entre le *De somno et vigilia* et les *Problemata*: 'Dictum est in librum de

16. Pour la discussion de cette question et cette même conclusion, cf. MARANGON P., *Alle origini dell'aristotelismo padovano (sec. XII-XIII)*, Padova, 1977, p. 35-7; 'Per una revisione dell'interpretazione di Pietro d'Abano', dans: *Il pensiero ereticale nella Marca Trevigiana e a Venezia dal 1200 al 1350*, Abano Terme (Padova): Francisci Editore, 1984, p. 66-104.

17. *De somno et vigilia* I, 25, dans *Opera*, ed. BORGNET A., Paris, 1890-99, vol. IX, p. 145. (Cf. aussi KLIBANSKY R. – PANOFSKY E. – SAXL F., *Saturno e la malinconia*, Torino: Einaudi, trad. it. di Renzo Federici, 1983, p. 67-70, à propos des citations d'Albert le Grand et de Pierre d'Abano).

Problematibus ab Aristotile, qui liber ad me non pervenit, licet viderim quaedam excerpta de ipso'[18].

Revenons à la datation du voyage à Constantinople, d'où découle le problème de l'attribution de la traduction à Pierre. Dans les mss. connus, en particulier Cesena, Malat. Plut VI, Sin. 2, ff. 1r-202v, mais surtout, Malat. Plut. VI, Sin. 3, ff. 1r-191v, et Paris, BN lat. 6540[19], on lit que la compilation a été commencée à Paris, et qu'elle a été achevée à Padoue en 1310, comme je l'ai dit plus haut.

Nous sommes en face du problème de la première datation de l'*Expositio succinta* et de sa rédaction finale par rapport à la date du voyage de Pierre à Constantinople. Il se pourrait aussi qu'il ait commencé ce travail très tôt, pendant son long séjour à Paris; et ce serait plus tard que – selon l'interprétation de l'adverbe *post diu* – il l'aurait perfectionné grâce à sa meilleure connaissance du grec, acquise pendant son voyage à Constantinople. Il aurait donc fait des corrections après sa première rédaction, lorsqu'il a cru aussi devoir faire une nouvelle traduction du grec des œuvres de Galien[20], n'étant pas satisfait des traductions faites à partir de l'arabe (c'est du moins ma supposition). Mais pourquoi aurait-il voulu faire une nouvelle traduction des *Problemata*? Nous ne savons avec certitude ni la date de son voyage, ni si cette nouvelle traduction existe. Il faudra donc tout d'abord étudier les manuscrits et les éditions de la traduction de Barthélémy de Messine et du commentaire de Pierre pour résoudre la question des différentes rédactions de la version médiévale des *Problemata* d'Aristote et du commentaire. Il s'agit là d'une exigence philologique primaire et fondamentale, qui nous renvoie aussi à la solution du problème relatif à la date du voyage de Pierre en Grèce.

La conclusion provisoire de mon analyse de l'*accessus* de la Compilation de Pierre sera donc qu'il n'a pas fait dans cette édition un travail de traduction, mais qu'il a utilisé une traduction déjà existante, qu'il a commentée ou interprétée dans cette forme littéraire de l'enseignement scolastique médiéval qui est l'*Expositio succinta* et non *longa*. Ces formes existaient déjà dans la tradition scolaire de la Scolastique. Il est en effet

18. Sur les citations des *Problèmes* dans les œuvres d'Albert le Grand, voir VUILLE-MIN-DIEM G., 'Zum Aristoteles Latinus bei David von Dinant', *Archives d'Histoire Doctrinale et Littéraire du Moyen Âge* 70 (2003), p. 27-135.

19. L'autre copie de Paris, BN 6541 ne porte pas la date de 1310, quoiqu'elle ait le même explicit.

20. Cf. en particulier l'étude de D'ALVERNY M.-T., 'Pietro d'Abano,...', p. 40: 'en divers cas, il nous paraît probable qu'il a utilisé des manuscrits grecs pour faire des traductions à son usage ou pour revoir ses versions précédentes'.

généralement admis que la version précède la formulation du *Commentaire,* sous la forme d'une *expositio,* qui est aussi une interprétation. Pierre nous dit qu'il présente une édition brève concernant les mêmes problèmes que ceux développés dans un autre ouvrage, le *Conciliator,* sous forme prolixe, à savoir les questions relatives à la théorie de la médecine.

La polémique d'Angelo Poliziano[21] ou les critiques des autres humanistes à propos de celle qu'on appelle la 'rédaction de Pierre', n'ont pas de fondement, parce que Pierre ne veut faire ni une œuvre littéraire dans un latin pur, ni une traduction élégante. Il veut seulement expliquer et interpréter un texte qui probablement existait déjà, pour mieux connaître les doctrines physiques concernant les intérêts qu'il avait dans le domaine de la biologie, afin d'établir une théorie philosophique de la médecine qui soit différente aussi bien de la théorie opérationnelle d'Averroès, que de la théorie entièrement spéculative d'Avicenne. On n'a pas encore bien évalué le rôle plus ou moins important joué par la connaissance du grec de Pierre par rapport à ce texte. C'est ainsi que le sens du mot *traduxi* dans le contexte où Pierre s'en sert dans l'*Accessus,* est encore assez ambigu, et nous sommes du même avis que Marie T. d'Alverny qui propose d'accorder peu de crédibilité à cette affirmation. Aussi devrons-nous démontrer que Pierre d'Abano a employé la *translatio vetus,* où il a introduit des changements, et vérifier s'il a amélioré le texte des *Problemata* dans les différentes rédactions de son *Expositio*[22]. Ce sera le sujet – très important – de notre prochaine recherche. Pour l'instant, l'ouvrage de Pierre se présente comme une compilation fondée sur la traduction de Barthélémy et influencée par les erreurs de celle-ci.

En effet, le ms. d'Oxford, Canonici Misc. lat. 46, très important – il contient la *Compilatio physionomiae (Construxit presentem libellum)* –, propose la liste des ouvrages de Pierre de Padoue et de ses traductions,

---

21. Poliziano Angelo, *Miscellaneorum centuria secunda,* edité par V. BRANCA, M. PASTORE STOCCHI, Firenze, 1972, *Introduzione,* p. 51-3; à propos de Pierre d'Abano, *Centuria Prima,* cf. aussi ANTONIO LUIZ, *Liber de erroribus Petri Apponensis in Problematibus Aristotelis exponendis,* dans: ANTONII LODOVICI Medici Olyssipponensis, *De re medica opera,* Olyssipione 1540; cf. aussi LUDOVICO SETTALA, *Aristotelis Problemata commentaria,* vol. III, Lygduni 1632, qui soutient que Pierre avait peut-être à sa disposition l'exemplaire retrouvé à Constantinople.

22. Sur l'utilisation de la traduction de Barthélémy par Pierre, voir aussi GOYENS M. – DE LEEMANS P., 'Traduire du grec au latin et du latin au français: un défi à la fidélité', in: P. ANDERSEN (éd.), *Pratiques de traduction au Moyen Âge, Actes du colloque de l'Université de Copenhague, 25 et 26 octobre 2002,* Copenhagen: Museum Tusculanum Press, University of Copenhagen, 2004, p. 204-224.

où il n'est pas question d'une traduction des *Problemata* mais seulement
d'un *Commentum*. Et pourtant, on y trouve la liste de ses traductions du
grec. Je lis à la f. 30v: 'vir clarissimus Petrus de Appono Patavinus
huius libri compositor [la Physiognomie][23] infrascripta voluit: partim
composuit, partim ex greca lingua in latinum traduxit'. C'est dire qu'il
avait composé une partie, alors qu'il avait traduit une autre du grec.
C'est ainsi qu'il avait composé: 'Primum quidem librum in medicina
conciliatores litium [...] librum de motu octave sphere [...], librum de
discondantiis utriusque partis astrologie [le Lucidator]'[24]. Et pour finir,
un 'Commentum super libro problematum Aristotelis'.

Donc, d'après cette liste, l'*Expositio Problematum* ne serait pas une
version du grec de Pierre, alors que quelques lignes plus loin on affirme
qu'il a bien traduit du grec les *Problemata* d'Alexandre et les livres de
Galien: 'item...transtulit librum de colera nigra Galeni, transtulit librum
de utilitate particularium Galeni ex greco. Item eius libro de optima
complexione. [...] Item transtulit librum eiusdem de regimine sanitatis
de verbo ad verbum non sicut ille que abreviavit. [...] Item transtulit
librum de tabe Galenis. Item transtulit librum creticorum. [...] Item
transtulit problemata Alexandri medici'. Si les versions du grec aussi
bien des œuvres de Galien que des *Problemata Alexandri* sont ponctuellement énumérées, la traduction des *Problemata* d'Aristote n'est pas citée.

Mais alors quel sens faut-il donner au mot *traduxi* du prologue des
Problemata dont Pierre aurait trouvé un nouvel exemplaire à Constantinople?

Je suppose que Pierre d'Abano n'a pas fait une nouvelle version intégrale du texte, et qu'il a amélioré ses connaissances du grec, surtout
parce qu'il souhaitait mieux connaître les œuvres de Galien sans la médiation de la version arabe, et traduire les *Problemata* d'Alexandre.
Peut-être, voulait-il aussi améliorer son *Expositio*. Quoi qu'il en soit,
nous n'en connaissons pas encore le résultat: il faudra contrôler les différentes versions des rédactions de l'*Expositio* de Pierre d'Abano, dans
les manuscrits et dans les différentes éditions.

Et en ce qui concerne ce nouvel exemplaire, une autre question se
pose: quel exemplaire des *Problèmes* d'Aristote avait-il trouvé à Cons-

23. À propos de sa *Physiognomie*, voir FEDERICI VESCOVINI G., 'La simmetria del
corpo umano nella Physiognomica di Pietro d'Abano, un canone estetico', dans: G. PIAIA
(éd.), *Concordia discors, Studi offerti a Giovanni Santinello*, Padova: Antenore, 1993, p.
347-360.
24. Voir mon édition avec une préface de E. Garin, et la 2e éd., *I trattati di astronomia...*

tantinople? D'Aristote seulement ou aussi d'Alexandre d'Aphrodisie? Le problème n'est pas résolu, parce qu'on n'est pas encore certain que – par rapport à la *Vetus* – Pierre ait fait une nouvelle traduction des *Problèmes* d'Aristote. Et on n'a pas encore mis en relation les trois exemplaires, du pseudo-Aristote, d'Alexandre, de Pierre, faute d'éditions critiques et à cause de nos doutes sur leur authenticité.

2. *Le profil scientifique et philosophique du commentaire de Pierre d'Abano*

Si nous voulons, pour conclure, avancer une appréciation générale sur l'importance de l'*Expositio succinta* de Pierre d'Abano dans l'ensemble de l'*Aristoteles latinus*, nous pouvons affirmer que cet ouvrage représente un itinéraire de médiation dans le cadre de l'*Aristoteles latinus*. L'*Expositio* sort en effet du *Corpus* aristotélicien pur surtout parce qu'elle subit l'influence de certains ouvrages de la période hellénistique, de savants tels que Galien et Ptolemée, et plusieurs contaminations de la philosophie arabe et juive, à cause des développements par les Arabes de l'astrologie de Ptolemée, qui est la partie principale et fondamentale de la philosophie de la médecine de Pierre. Aussi sommes-nous en présence de beaucoup de doctrines qui ne sont pas d'Aristote.

Si on veut indiquer brièvement les problèmes de Pierre d'Abano étrangers à la physique d'Aristote, on en trouve en fait un grand nombre, surtout concernant l'astronomie, l'astrologie, la cosmologie, la génération des formes, les espèces, la matière, la classification des sciences, la musique, la perspective. Il s'agit de matières fortement influencées par l'encyclopédie latine médiévale des arts libéraux (*quadrivium* et *trivium*), de Boèce à Isidore de Séville, modifiée par l'organisation des sciences d'Avicenne et d'Alfarabi (*De scientiis*), qui avait introduit la perspective, la médecine et l'astrologie comme des sciences spéculatives, et qui avait traité aussi des sciences *ingegnorum (ingenium)*[25].

Mais il nous faut signaler quelque chose d'assez curieux: c'est que l'*Expositio succinta Problematum Aristotelis* de Pierre d'Abano représente un véritable paradoxe. En effet, il soumet à une critique acharnée qui mène à une nouvelle élaboration, les théories les plus importantes des grands médecins arabes – surtout Averroès et Avicenne – pour revenir à Galien, à Hippocrate. Mais c'est surtout chez Aristote qu'il cherche

---

25. À ce sujet, on peut voir aussi l'étude de RASHED R., *Les mathématiques de la terre*, dans: *Ratio et Superstitio*, *Études en hommage de G. Federici Vescovini* (Textes et études du Moyen âge latin 24), Louvain-La Neuve: Fidem, 2003, p. 285-318.

des appuis philosophiques, pouvant l'acheminer vers la construction
d'une philosophie de la nature et de la science de la médecine, autre que
celle de la *Métaphysique* d'Aristote même. Pierre veut bâtir une science
de l'individuel, et non de l'essence nécessaire, une science de la maladie
et de la santé de l'homme qui est un *esse in fieri*, c'est-à-dire un orga-
nisme continuellement en mouvement (la nature comme un être en mouvement). Aussi, n'est-il pas d'accord avec Aristote le métaphysicien sur
bien des sujets concernant les sciences, telles que l'astronomie des sphères dont il refuse le nombre donné par Aristote (*Problemata* XV, 3), les
arts libéraux, qui lui venaient de Boèce et d'Isidore de Séville, aussi à
propos de la musique, de la psychosomatique, de l'hygiène, de la phar-
macologie, de la perspective, de la magie, de la mélancolie. Pierre critique Avicenne et Aristote, à propos de la nature des étoiles; et c'est grâce
à sa critique de la théorie de la *latitatio* générale de la matière (ou pré-
disposition générale) d'Avicenne (*Problemata* I, 22) qu'on peut saisir
comment Pierre se situe en tant que philosophe aussi bien par rapport à
Avicenne qu'à Aristote. Mais c'est surtout lorsqu'il traite de l'intellect,
des vertus de l'âme, de l'art et de la science, que l'on peut avoir un
aperçu de ce qu'il y a de nouveau dans la théorie de la science de Pierre
d'Abano, en abrégé dans son *Expositio Problematum,* par rapport aux
Arabes et à Aristote lui-même (*Problemata* XXX 1, XXX, 2 et ss.).

Conclusion

Nous sommes ici en présence d'un exemple exceptionnel concernant
la médiation des théories des savants arabes sur le texte d'Aristote et de
ses commentateurs grecs, s'orientant dans une direction nouvelle indiquée par Pierre. Si jusqu'à présent on ne l'a pas très bien comprise, c'est
aussi à cause de la polémique acharnée menée par les humanistes, et surtout par Pico della Mirandola et Angelo Poliziano, contre l'œuvre de
Pierre et des savants arabes, d'où l'incompréhension dont il a été l'objet
et qui est loin d'être dépassée. Ceci est dû aussi à certains stéréotypes
historiographiques – tel que ce qu'on appelle l'aristotélisme averroïste
de Padoue – dont l'origine remonte assez loin (Renan). Il s'agit d'erreurs de compréhension historique que la présente recherche doit dé-
mentir en répondant aux questions historiques que nous avons énoncées.
La tâche est ardue, l'entreprise longue et difficile, mais elle vaut la peine
qu'on lui consacre beaucoup de temps.

Annexe
Expositio succinta problematum Aristotelis
Mantoue, 1475

(Prol. *Inc*): «Iuxta sententiam Aristotilis 2° celi et mundi promptitudinem inquisitionis difficultatis dignum quidem magis est verecundie, id est honestati, quam audatie seu presumptioni imputare, cum percunctator veritatis et amictus rite multorum non qua exteriori fortune cupiditate detentus, non etiam falsa ambitione gloriatus posterorum assertione hanc satagat indagare, sed potius quodam naturali instinctu quo quisque hominum secundum Aristotelem in principio metafisice anelat ad sciendum. Ideo, si ego Petrus de Ebano paduanus phylosophye minimus alumpnorum sim conatus librum compilationis artis problematum Aristotelis exponere, in quo ardua et difficilima pene circa unamquanque artem et scientiam plurimis occultantur, arrogantie autem presumptioni nullatenus asscribatur, cum huic operi diutius insudaverim non nisi desiderio sapiendi et scientiam queritantium hanc amore et precipue quia nihil hiis inveniebatur omnino a meis progenitoribus antea in lucis manifestationem redactum....

Forma autem in hoc opere observata erit seriatim nominibus lucidis propriisque succintis, que quidem clausa est ex sententia in hoc libro Aristotelis exposito, declarationes et notabilia nonnullas adiungendo; cum hoc etiam interdum litterales quasdam dubitationes motivis illarum plerumque[26] reticitis (*sic*) breviter removere. Et insinuabo itidem problemata per numerum algorismi et ut facilis ratio fiat et sine scriptura ipsorum inventio, nec si qua in hac videatur fore prolixitas, mihi nullatenus imputetur, sed potius quandam ubique interpretationem materie peregrine sibi ac dissone perquirentis, propter quod questiones in quibus per ampliora declarantur separatim in quadam alia edictione locavi, ne operis prolixitate in fastidium decidant sensibus delicati et intelligentium lecturis sufficiat hec cum illa scriptura etc. Et nunc illa octo preambula que in exordiis librorum solent tangere glosatores, breviter explicentur. Secundum nanque Ciceronem in Rethorica Veteris Prohemio 'promptiores nos reddunt ad inquirendas artis intrinsecas rationes'.

Materia sive subiectum huius libri vel scientie est scibile pene commune sub dubitatione prolatum, sive in alia edictione ubi hoc queritur ostendetur et ex hoc potest huius operis ubique intentio apparere.

---

26. plerumque *scr.*] plerunquam *ed. Mant.*

Forma autem huius est duplex: scilicet tractatus consistens in distinctione partium libri universalium et particularium ut videbitur subsequenter.

Et forma tractandi dicta modus agendi est triplex in doctrinis Aristotelis earum usitata: efficiens siquidem huius scientie fuit Aristotiles peripatheticus filius Nichomaci sapientissimus Grecorum: qui secundum Averroem magis dignius mereretur dici divinus quam humanus, neque est quod hic liber non fuerit Aristotelis, sicut asserunt quidam mendaciter abnegantes, cum de ipso in 2° Metaphisice ac in plerisque locis Parvorum naturalium ac Libris animalium, faciat multotiens mentionem, ac in hiis quidem derelicta hoc opere compleantur. Verumtamen extimo quod Aristotiles problemata omnia nndum ad nostram linguam pervenere cum et quedam in libris De sompno et vigilia atque animalium semitradita adhuc transmissa, librum in ipso fideliter inspiciens minime valeam reperire. Post[27] diu huius executionis problematum agregationem ut discerem cum in Constantinopoli me transtuli, volumen aliud problematum Aristotelis volui reperire quod quidem in linguam iam (?) latinam transduxi.

Est autem libri titulus, liber problematum Aristotelis secundum speciem compilationis incipit: problema quidem est grecum latine probationem importans. Est etenim questio difficilis, aliquid continens quod disputationem solvendum quod et voraginem videtur denotare, ut enim 'voret' et accipiat propositum est problema.

Dico autem compilationis speciem, id est modum, quia in hoc libro inveniuntur fere totius phylosophie per modum cuiusdam allegationis sermones compilati. Ex quo quidem deducitur quod liber hic non potest plene intelligi nisi ab illo qui phylosophiam secundum omnem eius partem inspexerit, propter quod fortasse in eius expositione pigritarunt glosatores et demum apparet quis huius scientie ydoneus existat auditor et non cuidam parti philosophie hic liber ut alii supponitur. Sed in eo pene sermo phylosophye totius simpliciter reperitur in ipso nanque tractantur dubitabilia problemata in unaquaque arte sicut Nicolaus Perypateticus in suis problematibus protestatur. Dixi autem 'pene' quoniam rationem non invenio explicitam in ipso de hiisque sunt gramatice et phylosophie supreme parumper.

Est autem forma tractatus quoniam Aristotiles premittit huic operi rubricas quasi per modum prohemii hic suam universaliter tangens intentionem que sunt in se ipsis patientes....

___

27. post] cum *praem. ms. Cesenas, Plut. VI, sin. 2.*

(*explicit*) Explicit expositio succinta Problematum Aristotilis quam Petrus edidit Paduanus ea nullo prius interpretante incepta quidem Parisius et laudabiliter Padue terminata anno legis Chrispianorum 1310, cum laude dei altissimi cuius nomen sit per secula benedictum. Amen. Et impressa Mantue sub divo (*sic*) Marchione Ludovico Mantue secundo per me Paulum Johannis de Puzpach Almanum Magontinensis dyocesis sub anno Jubilei M°CCCC°LXXV° cuius utilitas erit omni creature in universo orbe que apponet huic operi studium summa cum diligentia.

Université de Florence

Maaike VAN DER LUGT

ARISTOTLE'S *PROBLEMS* IN THE WEST:
A CONTRIBUTION TO THE STUDY
OF THE MEDIEVAL LATIN TRADITION[*]

Cet article est consacré à quatre commentaires sur les *Problemata* du XIVe siècle encore méconnus: a) une adaptation latine anonyme d'origine italienne (Vat. lat. 2481); b) un commentaire anglais, *Felix qui poterit*; c) deux commentaires qui circulaient en Europe orientale. Il y est étudié la tradition manuscrite de ces textes, leur contexte codicologique (public, possesseurs, notes marginales etc.). L'attribution de *Felix qui poterit* au philosophe et théologien Walter Burley est discutée en détail. Enfin, nous analysons la division en sections de ces différents commentaires. L'analyse de ces textes confirme que le commentaire de Pietro d'Abano était l'ouvrage de référence pour l'étude des *Problemata* au Moyen Âge. Elle éclaire aussi la place des *Problemata* dans le champ scientifique médiéval entre médecine, philosophie naturelle et littérature encyclopédique.

Introduction

Translated from Greek into Latin by Bartholomew of Messina between 1258 and 1266, the *Problems* were a late-comer in the flow of new Aristotelian texts that were to become available in the medieval West. Their attribution to Aristotle, which apparently met with little doubt[1], destined the *Problems* for university use. However, despite a rather large manuscript distribution – some sixty copies remain of it to-day[2] – they were never officially included in the Arts curriculum, which had already been fixed by the 1250's. Its integration in the school pro-

[*] Earlier versions of this article have been presented at the conference in Leuven and in several seminars. I wish to thank all participants for their comments. Many thanks also to Mariana Giovino and Matthew Hall, who kindly accepted to correct my English. Remaining Dutchisms are, of course, my own. A substantial part of the research for this article has been financed by a post-doctoral fellowship, which I received from the Niels Stensen Stichting (Amsterdam, the Netherlands) in 1999.

1. However, Peter of Abano felt obliged to defend its authenticity in the prologue of his *Expositio*, an indication that there was some doubt about the *Problems'* authenticity in Paris in the 1290's. See also WILLIAMS S., 'Defining the Corpus Aristotelicum: Scholastic Awareness of Aristotelian Spuria in the High Middle Ages', *Journal of the Warburg and Courtauld Institutes* 58 (1995), p. 29-51.

2. Cf. LACOMBE G., *Aristoteles Latinus. Codices*, Roma – Cambridge, 1939-1955, 2 vol., index s.v. *Problemata*.

gramme may also have been hampered by the structure and content of the text. The *Problems* lack a coherent plan, do not respect disciplinary boundaries and are made up of particulars, rather than universal truths, and thus – paradoxically – do not meet the Aristotelian standard for scientific knowledge[3].

However, if not officially, the *Problems* do seem to have figured at least *de facto*, albeit discretely, in university teaching. To be sure, in 1315 John of Jandun regretted, in the prologue to his *Physics* commentary, that 'the book of *Problems* is generally found in corrupted form and full of mistakes'. According to Jandun, this was why 'the book is hardly commented upon by anyone known or famous, and few study it'[4]. At the time of writing these lines, John of Jandun was apparently unaware of the commentary that Peter of Abano had started at Paris and completed at Padua in 1310[5], and which, ironically, he, Jandun, was later to disseminate in Paris[6]. There are other indications of early interest in the *Problems* in the medieval schools. One of their first readers seems to have been Roger Bacon, who cites them in his *Opus majus* (1267), attributing his failure to understand a crucial passage to the bad quality of the Greek original, or the botched job of the translator[7]. In 1304, the

---

3. On the epistemological status of the *Problems*, see BLAIR A., 'The *Problemata* as a Natural Philosophical Genre', in: A. GRAFTON – N. SIRAISI (eds.), *Natural Particulars. Nature and the Disciplines in Renaissance Europe*, Cambridge Mass., 1999, p. 180 and below p. 101-102. On Aristotle's philosophy of science, see HANKINSON R. J., 'Philosophy of Science', in: J. BARNES (ed.), *The Cambridge Companion to Aristotle*, Cambridge: Cambridge University Press, 1995, p. 109-139.

4. John of Jandun, *Quaestiones super VIII libros Aristotelis de physico auditu*, prologue: 'Et scias, quod liber ille de problematibus communiter invenitur corruptus et incorrectus, et non est multum expositus ab aliquo noto aut famoso, et ideo pauci student in eo, et pauciores intelligunt eum sufficienter: quia multa et pulcherrima theoremata mirabilis delectationis sunt in eo congregata, unde indubitanter ei qui illum librum bene corrigeret et exponeret competenter multas et magnas gratias deberent reddere studiosi' (Venezia 1551, repr. Frankfurt, 1969).

5. On Peter's *Expositio*, see SIRAISI N., 'The *Expositio Problematum Aristotelis* of Pietro d'Abano', *Isis* 61 (1970), p. 321-339; OLIVIERI L., *Pietro d'Abano e il pensiero neolatino, filosofia, scienza e ricerca dell'Aristotele greco tra i secoli XIII e XIV*, Padova: Antenore, 1988; BURNETT C., 'Hearing and Music in Book XI of Pietro d'Abano's *Expositio Problematum Aristotelis*', in: N. VAN DEURSEN (ed.), *Tradition and Ecstasy: The Agony of the Fourteenth Century*, Ottawa: The Institute of Mediaeval Music, 1997, p. 153-190, and Graziella Federici Vescovini's contribution to the present volume, as well as many of her other studies on Peter of Abano.

6. John of Jandun added a short prologue but did not alter the *Expositio* in any substantial way, cf. KUKSEWICZ Z., 'Les *Problemata* de Pietro d'Abano et leur 'rédaction' par Jean de Jandun', *Medioevo* 11 (1985), p. 113-37. The date of the copy John of Jandun made of the *Problems* cannot be determined more precisely than after 1315, more likely after 1317, see KUKSEWICZ, 'Les *Problemata*...', p. 121.

7. Roger Bacon, *Opus majus*, pars quinta, De scientia perspectiva, pars prima dist. viii, cap. ii: 'Tertium est oppositio visibilis respectu visus. Hoc enim exigitur in visu

Problems occur in a Parisian list of texts available as *peciae*, the university controlled system for the reproduction and correction of manuscripts[8]. They had been discussed in quodlibetal debates held at the Paris Arts faculty several years earlier[9]. Later in the century, Jean Berblengheem, a master of Arts, medical student and future professor in that discipline, lectured on the *Problems* in front of sixty Parisian Arts students[10], and the *Problems* figured in the medical *palaestrae* of John of Spello at the university of Perugia[11]. More generally, the *Problems* were often cited in scholastic works on philosophy, medicine[12], and even theology[13]. They

fracto secundum lineas rectas, sicut hic est intentio, quamvis per reflexionem et fractionem possit res videri sine oppositione. Sed mirabile est hoc, cum nos audiamus undique et olfaciamus, et in fronte sentiamus calorem ignis retro positi, si multus sit et fortis; et visus, qui est sensus nobilior, non facit sic. Et causa hujus rei est valde occulta et adhuc inaudita et invisa apud sapientes. Aristoteles enim in libro Problematum debuit nos certificare de hoc, nam ibi tangit istud inter alia sua problemata secreta. Sed vel mala translatio, vel falsitas exemplaris Graeci, vel aliqua alia causa nos impedit in hac parte' (Roger Bacon, *Opus majus*, ed. J.H. BRIDGES, Oxford, 1897, II, p 56). Bacon apparently refers to problem 11, 58.

8. Taxation list of the *stationarius* Andreas de Senonis dated February 25th 1304 (DENIFLE H.S. – CHÂTELAIN E. (eds.), *Chartularium Universitatis Parisiensis*, Paris: Delalain, 1891, II, p. 107), cf. DE LEEMANS P. – GOYENS M., 'La transmission des savoirs en passant par trois langues: les cas des *Problemata* d'Aristote traduits en latin et en moyen français', in: P. NOBEL (ed.), *La transmission des savoirs au Moyen Âge et à la Renaissance*. Vol. 1. *Du XIIe au XIVe siècle*. Besançon: Université de Franche-Comté – Université de Tours, 2005, p. 231-257, who have found explicit traces of the *pecia* system in at least one manuscript of the *Problems*, Venezia, Bibl. Nazionale Marciana, lat. VI, 43 (= 2488). On the *pecia* system, see BATAILLON L. J. – GUYOT B. G. – ROUSE R. H. (eds.), *La production du livre universitaire au Moyen Âge*. Exemplar *et* pecia, Paris: Éditions du CNRS, 1991.

9. The famous manuscript lat. 16089 from the Bibliothèque Nationale de France contains several series of quodlibetal questions debated by different *artistae*. Several of these questions discuss subjects taken from the *Problems*. See also COVA L., 'Il corpus zoologico di Aristotele nei dibattiti fra gli 'artisti' parigini alle soglie del XIV secolo', in: O. WEIJERS – L. HOLTZ (eds.), *L'enseignement des disciplines à la Faculté des arts (Paris et Oxford, XIIIᵉ-XVᵉ siècles)*, Turnhout: Brepols Publishers, 1997, p. 281-302, esp. p. 292, 294, 297, 299-300. One of the participants, Jean Vath, already used the *Problems* in his commentary on Aristotle's *Generation of Animals* (ca. 1285-1294), cf. COVA, 'Il corpus zoologico...', p. 285.

10. These lectures took place in 1334, cf. JACQUART D., *La médecine médiévale dans le cadre parisien,* Paris: Fayard, 1998, p. 176.

11. *Palaestrae* were a particular kind of disputations, held every evening during Lent in several Italian universities. The *palaestrae* by John of Spello took place in 1355, cf. BAKKER P., 'Les *palaestrae* de Jean de Spello: Exercices scolaires d'un maître en médecine à Pérouse au XIVᵉ siècle', *Early Science and Medicine* 3 (1998), p. 288-322, especially p. 300, and p. 314-315 and 321-322 for an edition of the two questions taken from the *Problems*.

12. For instance, Gentile da Foligno cites the *Problems* in a disputed question on the means to rebalance complexion (ms. Città del Vaticano, BAV, Vat. lat., 2481, fol. 1r).

13. The *Problems* figure among the favourite philosophical authorities in the Biblical commentaries attributed to the 14th century English Dominican Thomas Waleys, cf. SMALLEY B., 'Thomas Waleys OP', *Archivum Fratrum Praedicatorum* 24 (1954), p. 81.

clearly enjoyed authoritative status, although they never became central in scholastic learning.

When Jandun and Bacon complained about the quality of the text at their disposal, they were rehearsing a scholastic topos to disculpate the authorities. It is true however, that Bartholomew of Messina's word-to-word translation of the *Problems* adds to the difficulty of understanding this diverse and often obscure text. Peter of Abano's *Expositio*, the first effort to comment the *Problems* in their entirety, certainly filled a need and quickly became recognised as the standard gloss. Often transmitted together with the original *Problems* in manuscripts[14] and early prints, it remained the most influential commentary throughout the medieval period and beyond.

Nevertheless, Peter of Abano was not the only one to turn his mind to the *Problems*. Several other Latin commentaries exist, as well as a French translation and commentary by Evrart de Conty, professor of medicine at Paris and physician to Charles V[15]. There is no proof that Evrart wrote on the king's request, and he certainly finished the work after his patron's death in 1380[16], but by preferring the vernacular over Latin, Evrart clearly aimed for a wider readership than a strictly scholastic one, although the precise nature of his audience remains difficult to determine. Compared to both Peter's *Expositio* and Evrart de Conty's work, the other Latin commentaries are much shorter and less scholastic in form, and are more like compilations. Alongside these commentaries, Problem material also found its way into all sorts of late medieval reference works in Latin and in the vernacular and the title *Aristotle's Problems* was given to collections that have little to do with Aristotle, although they may contain some Problem material and adopt a similar structure of questions and answers. The so-called *Summa 'omnes homines'* is an important case in point[17]. The encyclopaedical scope of

It must be noted that the attribution to Waleys of one of the texts analysed by Smalley, the commentary on Genesis printed in some editions of Thomas Aquinas's works, has no basis. Sylvain PIRON, 'Note sur le commentaire sur la Genèse publiée dans les œuvres de saint Thomas', *Oliviana* 1 (2003) (www.oliviana.org) has recently argued that the commentary was written by a Franciscan influenced by Pierre de Jean Olivi.

14. For instance: Cesena, Bibl. Malatestiana, Plut, VI Sin. 2 and Sin. 3; and Plut XXIV Dext. 2.

15. For more information on Evrart de Conty and further bibliography, see the contributions of Annelies Bloem, Caroline Boucher, Joëlle Ducos and Françoise Guichard-Tesson in the present volume.

16. See the contribution of Caroline Boucher in the present volume, p. 186-187 and note 45. As noted by Caroline Boucher, section 27 was certainly written after 1377, since Evrart de Conty refers to Nicole Oresme as bishop of Lisieux.

17. For derivatives of the *Problems* as a genre or the use of the Aristotelian *Problems* in encyclopaedical literature of the later Middle Ages, see LAWN B., *The Salernitan Ques-*

the *Problems* (ranging from medicine, physiology, ethics, philology, mathematics, astronomy, meteorology, to music) and their often amusing character may explain the coexistence of both specialised and more 'popular' traditions.

Although the general pattern of the reception of the *Problems* is starting to become clearer, most individual commentaries are still awaiting edition. For the most part, their content, context of production and diffusion, and readerschip remain shadowy. In this article, I shall concentrate on several of these little or still unstudied Latin commentaries and adaptations. Four 14th century texts will receive attention: a Latin adaptation of the *Problems* from Italy, a commentary attributed to the English philosopher and theologian Walter Burley[18], and two commentaries that circulated in Central and Eastern Europe. We will see that the works under discussion confirm the special status of Peter of Abano's commentary as a guide and standard, and raise questions about the origin of an alternative division of the *Problems*. They also exemplify each in their own way, the strategies brought to bear on the text, to make it more accessible, understandable and useful. More generally, these commentaries help us to further specify the status and place of the *Problems* in medieval learning.

1. An anonymous Latin reconstruction of the Problems (BAV, Vat. lat. 2481)

Our first example is a Latin version of the *Problems* in a medical manuscript now kept at the Vatican library[19]. The manuscript in question is an in folio made of paper and copied by several contemporary hands. The *Problems* form its last item, while the rest of the manuscript contains a series of medical disputations by several eminent 14th century physicians active in the universities of Northern Italy[20]. Some of these

tions, *An Introduction to the History of Medieval and Renaissance Problem Literature*, Oxford: Clarendon Press, 1963, p. 99-103; BLAIR, 'The Problemata...'; VENTURA I., '*Quaestiones* and Encyclopaedias: Some Aspects of the Late Medieval Reception of the Pseudo-Aristotelian *Problemata* in Encyclopaedic and Scientific Culture', in: A.A. MACDONALD – M.W. TWOMEY (eds.), *Schooling and Society. The Ordering and Reordering of Knowledge in the Western Middle Ages*, Leuven-Paris-Dudley: Peeters, 2004, p. 23-42 and Iolanda Ventura's contribution to the present volume.

18. Of the texts discussed in this article, the commentary attributed to Burley has attracted the most attention by historians, see below note 30. Part of the research on the commentary attributed to Walter Burley will also be integrated into an article that I am presently co-writing with Caroline Boucher.

19. Bibliotheca Apostolica Vaticana, Vat. lat., 2481, fol. 89ra-96rb.

20. The disputations are by Gentile da Foligno (see *Dizionario degli italiani* 53

disputed questions were copied by one Willem Wael van Gelre, who also signed the *Problems*. The only scribe to identify himself, Willem Wael dates the *Problems* and the disputations to 1385, while indicating in the colophon of the latter that the manuscript is destined for one Nicholas of Ravenna, a 'doctor and master'. The manuscript contains no other signs of ownership or provenance, but everything (except the name of the scribe, who may well have been a Dutch student making some money by copying books) points to a university setting in northern Italy. The disputed questions in the manuscript are highly specialized scholastic medical texts and we may surmise that Nicholas of Ravenna was a medical man himself.

The Vatican manuscript does not contain the complete text of the *Problems*: it covers sections one to nine and the beginning of ten only, and breaks off in the middle of problem 10, 11. It bears no title and Aristotle's name is not mentioned, while the 15th century index refers to it as 'quidam tractatus problematum'[21]. Rather than doubt about the authenticity of the text, this lack of information probably reflects some ignorance on the part of the scribes. In fact, the *Problems* do not appear in Bartholomew of Messina's translation – for one thing, the incipit is different[22] – but in a form close to the paraphrase of the text that Peter of Abano offered (in good scholastic fashion) at the beginning of his commentary to each individual problem. Without always copying Peter *verbatim*, the correspondences between the adaptation of the *Problems* in the Vatican manuscript and Peter's *Expositio* on the one hand, and the differences with respect to Bartholomew of Messina's translation on the other are evident[23].

The anonymous adaptation also incorporates material not found in the *Problems* themselves, but in Peter of Abano's *Expositio* only, such as cross-references, indications of repetitions and citations. Problem 1, 37 on the influence of purslane and salt on toothache contains, for example,

(1999), p. 162-167), Marsiglio di Santa Sofia (d. 1405, see GLORIA A. (ed.), *Monumenti della Università di Padova 1318-1405*, Padua: Tipografia del seminario, 1888, I, p. 390-395, cited by SIRAISI N.G., *Avicenna in Renaissance Italy: the Canon and Medical Teaching in Italian Universities after 1500*, Princeton: Princeton University Press, 1987, p. 62, n. 73), Angelo da Siena and 'Garbensus' (Dino or Thomas Del Garbo?).

21. This index adds 'Ambroxo' in another, later hand. The manuscript also contains an Early Modern index reading 'Aristoteles particulae problematum'.

22. The incipit in the Vat. lat. 2481 is 'Que est causa quod maiores excessus' instead of 'Propter quid magne superhabundantiae'. More generally, Bartholomew of Messina renders διὰ τί by 'propter quid', while Peter of Abano uses 'que est causa', or, more frequently 'quare est' as an introductory formula to each question.

23. For an example, see Appendix 1, problem 10, 2.

a reference to the *Questiones Nicolai Peripatetici*, which is also found in Peter's *Expositio*[24]. In some cases, the adaptation summarises part or almost all of Peter of Abano's argument or renders its syllogistic structure[25]. Nevertheless, in the majority of cases, the adaptation is limited to the text of the *Problems* themselves. It should thus not be considered as an epitome of Peter of Abano's commentary, but rather as a conscious effort to reconstruct the Aristotelian work itself. The goal of its anonymous author seems to have been to provide a new and more accessible text of the *Problems*.

Admittedly, this adaptation, whether made for private use, or for a wider audience, did not have a lot of success. The copy in the Vatican manuscript, produced in 1385, apparently from an incomplete *Vorlage*[26], seems to be unique. However, it illustrates both the need for a clearer and more understandable text of the *Problems* and the extent to which Peter's *Expositio* had become part and parcel of the transmission of the *Problems*, to the point of becoming almost confounded with them[27].

2. Aristotle's Problems in England: Felix qui poterit

2.1. General presentation

Another deliberate effort to make the text more manageable and clear is found in an unedited commentary starting with a famous line from Virgil's *Georgics* 'Happy is he who can learn the causes of realities'

24. See Appendix 1, also for another example: problem 1, 28.
25. For example, problem 1, 37 (see Appendix 1); 'a' refers to the major, 'b' to the minor.
26. When and where the original adaptation was made is not easy to determine. Given the scholastic character of the copy, a university town of Northern Italy seems a likely environment for the *Vorlage* as well. The *terminus post quem* cannot be specified more precisely than 1310, i.e., when Peter of Abano had finished his *Expositio*.
27. Significantly, Evrart de Conty also used the paraphrase, rather than Bartholomew's translation, as a basis for much of his translation of the *Problems*, cf. GOYENS M. – DE LEEMANS P., *'Et samble qu'il woeille dire...'*: Evrart de Conty comme traducteur de Pierre d'Abano', in: O. BERTRAND (ed.), *Théorie et Pratique de la traduction au Moyen Age* (The Medieval Translator), Turnhout: Brepols Publishers (forthcoming). Another example of the use of Peter's paraphrase is found in a 15th century medical manuscript formerly owned by the cathedral of Metz and now kept at the municipal library there (Metz, BM, 280). The manuscript contains the first and part of the second section of the *Problems*. The scribe copied Bartholomew's translation, with Peter's paraphrase or, towards the end, only several words of this paraphrase as an interlinear gloss. The first problems are also followed by short commentaries. Bartholomew's translation lacks in the first problem, for which only Peter's paraphrase is given. This explains why the incipit is the same as in BAV, Vat. lat. 2481. I thank Joan Cadden for the reference to this manuscript.

('Felix qui poterit rerum cognoscere causas', or 'causas cognoscere rerum' in certain manuscripts)[28]. *Felix qui poterit*, or as the colophon of several manuscripts has it, the *Summa causarum problematum Aristotelis*[29], has been attributed to the English theologian and philosopher Walter Burley. I will return to the question of authorship later on.

Felix qui poterit circulated in two different versions: an original one, divided into thirty-eight sections, each of which is then subdivided into problems, and an adaptation in alphabetical order. In the latter, the subject matter, including the prologue, is cut up and rearranged by keyword, with references to section and problem numbers. The commentary has thus been transformed into a sort of encyclopaedical dictionary. Moreover, in two manuscripts of the original version, the latter is followed by an alphabetical index. The manuscripts and tables will be discussed in more detail below[30].

Although obviously influenced by Peter of Abano, the author of *Felix qui poterit* hints of this only in the prologue, when he defines the subject matter as 'things of common knowledge that are subject to doubt'[31].

28. Virgil, *Georgics*, 2. 490. Virgil has 'potuit', not 'poterit'. This line also occurs in the prologue of another English work on *Problems*, the *De causis naturalibus* by the carmelite Richard Lavenham (d. ca. 1381). In a short version of this work, which eliminates most of the prologue, *De causis naturalibus* has Virgil's line for an incipit. The work, which covers 16 meteorological questions (13 in the short version) has been edited by R. KEELE, 'Richard Lavenham's *De causis naturalibus*: a Critical Edition', *Traditio* 56 (2001), p. 113-147.

29. Oxford, Bodleian library, Digby 77, fol. 82rb; Digby 153, fol. 137r; Digby 161, fol. 35v; Digby 206, fol. 129rb. This title echoes a phrase in the prologue itself: 'causas problematum Aristotelis summaria brevitate perstringam'. A 15th century index in Digby 206 refers to the commentary as 'Problemata Aristotelis ffelix (!) qui poterit'.

30. *Felix qui poterit* seems to have been discovered by Lynn THORNDIKE, who wrote about it in a rather rushed manner: 'Peter of Abano and another Commentary on the *Problems* of Aristotle', *Bulletin of the History of Medecine* 29 (1955), p. 517-523. The comparative table in the article contains several errors; the number of problems given for several sections in *Felix qui poterit* is incorrect. LAWN, *The Salernitan...*, in his 1963 book on Problem literature (p. 95) identified more manuscripts and recognised the existence of two versions of the work. Much more recently, in an important article on problem 4, 26 about male homosexuality, Joan Cadden examined the section on sexuality, also taking into account questions about textual tradition, owner- and readership, cf. CADDEN J., "Nothing Natural Is Shameful': Vestiges of a Debate about Sex and Science in a Group of Late-Medieval Manuscripts', *Speculum* 76 (2001), p. 66-89. On problem 4, 26 see also CADDEN J., 'Sciences/Silences: the Natures and Languages of 'Sodomy' in Peter of Abano's Problemata Commentary', in: K. LOCHRIE – P. MCCRACKEN – J.A. SCHULTZ (eds.), *Constructing Medieval Sexuality* (Medieval cultures 11), Minneapolis: University of Minnesota, 1998, p. 40-57.

31. *Felix qui poterit* (*Summa causarum problematum Aristotelis*), prologue: 'causa materialis sive subiectum secundum Petrum Paduensem est scibile commune sub dubitatione prolatum' (ms. London, British Library, Royal, 12 E XVI, fol. 67r).

However, although based on the *Expositio*, there are also major differences between the two commentaries.

Felix qui poterit is much shorter than Peter's *Expositio*. Depending on the size of the script and the page, it runs between about thirty and a hundred leaves. The answers to the problems are only a couple of lines long (against several columns or even pages in Peter of Abano), each answer being organised as a numbered series of lapidary reasons or causes. The author leaves no room for doubt or qualification; the *Problems* are presented as small bits of unambiguous authoritative knowledge. This is a move away from the original *Problems*, where the answers are couched in the interrogative form (is it because...? or is it because...?), as suggestions or hypothesis. Even though the questions are largely rhetorical, this form invites discussion. Peter of Abano, by adopting a form close to the scholastic disputation, maintains something of this open-endedness, while the structure in *Felix qui poterit* is closer to the simple question and answer format of the Salernitan tradition[32]. This approach to what a problem is, is reflected in the author's definition of the formal cause, as the twofold procedure of posing a question and answering it[33], and in his explanation of the term *problema*. According to Peter of Abano, a problem is 'a difficult question containing something that is to be solved by disputation and appears to be a quagmire'[34]. In *Felix qui poterit*, any reference to the necessity of dialogue and debate has disappeared. A problem is just a knotty question[35].

---

32. For the Salernitan question, see LAWN, *The Salernitan...*

33. *Felix qui poterit* (*Summa causarum problematum Aristotelis*), prologue: 'Est duplex modus in eo procedendi, scilicet questivus et problematum responsivus' (ms. London, British Library, Royal, 12 E XVI, fol. 67r).

34. Peter of Abano, *Expositio problematum*, prologue: 'Est enim questio difficilis aliquod continens quod disputatione solvendum, quod et voraginem videtur' (ed. Venezia, 1482, without folio numbers). Unless specified otherwise, all citations are from this edition. The English translation of this phrase is Joan Cadden's ('Nothing Natural..., p. 69). Peter's definition is taken from the extremely popular *Liber derivationum* of Huguccio of Pisa (d. 1210), cf. OLIVIERI, *Pietro d'Abano...*, p. 107, n. 60, who cites mss. Padova, Bibl. Universitaria, 669, fol. 208va, Bibl. Antoniana, 11, fol. 147va, Bibl. Antoniana, 12 fol. 173ra: 'problematis, quod latine dicitur propositio, est questio difficilis habens aliquod quod disputatione solvendum sit [...] et videtur esse compositum a pro et lema, quod est vorago, quia proponitur ut voret et decipiat'.

35. *Felix qui poterit* (*Summa causarum problematum Aristotelis*), prologue: 'Problema est questio vel propositio difficilis ad solvendum secundum Huggucionem' (ms. London, British Library, Royal, 12 E XVI, fol. 67r). As can be seen in the preceding note, the author of *Felix qui poterit* truncates Huguccio's definition. For the progressive loss of the tentative and paradoxical quality of the *Problems*, see also BLAIR, 'The Problemata...', p. 177, 184.

In the prologue, the author of *Felix qui poterit* explicitly vindicates brevity as an intellectual virtue. Citing Cicero, he declares that brief statements are easier to understand than long ones and that longwindedness is revealing of a weak mind[36]. The *Problems* contain a lot of repetitions and these are very often tacitly omitted in *Felix qui poterit*, whereas Peter of Abano always signals these with cross references. To be true, the author of *Felix qui poterit* also introduced some new questions, most if not all of which have their origin in Peter's *Expositio*[37], and he added a prologue to the section on sexuality, which justifies study of that topic[38].

The section titles in *Felix qui poterit* diverge from Bartholomew's text, but echo Peter of Abano's paraphrases at the beginning of new sections[39]. The titles of the problems are more original. This reformulation often turns them into quite another direction[40]. The same is true of the answers. Here one example will suffice: problem 10, 2 on nose bleeds[41].

---

36. *Felix qui poterit* (*Summa causarum problematum Aristotelis*), prologue: 'Causas problematum Aristotelis summaria brevitate perstringam ut earum veritas facilius pateat intuenti: brevia enim facilius intelliguntur quam prolixa. Perpendens quod in multiloquio non deest peccatum; nec mirum cum verborum multitudo sit ingenii ebetudo, unde philosophorum mos laudabilis inolevit verba compendiosa succincte variis sentenciis sarcinare quapropter in omnibus quam ratio tollerat breviter est loquendum. Tullius in Rhetorica' (ms. Oxford, Bodleian library, Digby 153, fol. 102r). Neither the *De inventione*, nor the *Rhetorica ad Herennium* praise brevity in such a way, but the citation may echo *De inventione*, I, 61: 'Et breviter dicendum, ne in huiusmodi rebus diutius quam ratio praecipiendi postulat commoremur'.

37. This is for example the case for Peter's commentary to problem 30, 12, which is exceptionally long and gives rise to three new separate questions in *Felix qui poterit*: 'Quare gallici in puericia sunt sapientes et in senectute desipientes, sed ytalici econtrario'; 'Quare quidam in sompno deveniunt sapientes sicut prophete?'; 'Quare ardentes amantes non sompniant de amatis sicut zelotipi et concubinie' (ms. London, British Library, Royal, 12 E XVI, fol. 165v-166r). See also THORNDIKE, 'Peter of Abano...', p. 520-521.

38. On this prologue, see CADDEN, 'Nothing Natural...', p. 81-84.

39. For examples, see below, notes 138 and 139.

40. See also THORNDIKE, 'Peter Abano...', p. 519. The originality of *Felix qui poterit* led Brian Lawn (*The Salernitan...*, p. 95) to suggest that its author used a different Latin translation of the *Problems*. This is very unlikely, since there is no trace of such a translation. It is much more economical to suppose that the author paraphrased the text himself very freely, while also leaning on Peter's *Expositio*. The section titles in *Felix qui poterit* are clearly influenced by Peter of Abano, see note 139 below.

41. For the text, see Appendix 1. Caroline Boucher and I are preparing an article in which differences in content between *Felix qui poterit* with respect to the *Problems* in Bartholomew's translation and Peter of Abano's *Expositio* will be discussed in more detail. See also CADDEN, 'Nothing Natural...', p. 81-82, for the interesting case of problem 4, 26 on male homosexuality, which the author of *Felix qui poterit* replaced by a restatement of problem 4, 15, 'why is intercourse pleasurable'.

The original problem asks why, among animals, only man suffers from nose bleeds. The answer is that humans have a large and humid brain, the veins of which are full of blood mixed with superfluities; nose bleeds serve to eliminate this corrupted blood. In *Felix qui poterit* it is asked why all males suffer from haemorrhoids, the answer being that this is to clean themselves of putrid blood, which women expel by menstruation. Nose bleeds are thus replaced by haemorrhoids and menstruation, and a query about humans as opposed to other animals has become a question about sex difference.

The reformulation is not all the invention of the author of *Felix qui poterit*, who apparently took his cue from a remark in Peter of Abano's commentary on problem 10, 2. Peter first elaborated the answer given by Aristotle, then added some further reasons (for example: man has not only a big brain, but also a large liver, which produces a lot of blood). At the very end of his commentary, he noted, echoing Aristotle's *History of Animals*[42], that women, as opposed to men, rarely suffer from nose bleeds and from haemorrhoids, because they purify themselves by menstruation. However, whereas Peter mentions menstruation and haemorrhoids only in passing, almost as an afterthought, *Felix qui poterit* turns Peter's remark into his main subject.

The reformulation of the problem seems to be a part of a general fascination in medieval natural philosophy and medicine with menstruation. Menstruation, which is often likened, or even confounded with haemorrhoidic bleeding[43], is generally explained as a mechanism for women to expel impurities, which they cannot eliminate otherwise, due to their cold complexions. Menstruation is a good thing, but it remains a consequence of and a remedy for woman's imperfection. The view of menstruation and female physiology in *Felix qui poterit* is rather more positive: women purify themselves naturally every month, while men suffer from a horrible disease in order to do so[44].

42. Aristotle, *History of Animals*, III, 19, 521a29-31: women suffer less than men from varicose veins, haemorrhoids and nose bleeds. See also VI, 11, 587b: women who suffer from haemorrhoids lose less blood during menstruation than other females.

43. For the lack of distinction between different types of bleeding in medieval sources, see JACQUART D. – THOMASSET C., *Sexualité et savoir médical au Moyen Age*, Paris: PUF, 1985, p. 95-96 and MIRAMON C. de, 'La fin d'un tabou? L'interdiction de communier pour la femme menstruée au Moyen Age. Le cas du XIIe siècle', in: *Le sang au Moyen Age. Actes du quatrième colloque international de Montpellier Université Paul-Valéry (27-29 novembre 1997)*, Montpellier, 1999, p. 163-181, esp. p. 164-165.

44. For positive and negative judgements of menstruation, see CADDEN J., *Meanings of Sex Difference in the Middle Ages. Medicine, Science and Culture*, Cambridge: Cam-

Interestingly, there are other examples in *Felix qui poterit* of a positive opinion on female physiology, and even of a certain feminist attitude, admittedly with respect to older women only. The author thus attributes the fact that the old are wiser than the young, among other causes, to their phlegmatic temperament, adding that this is why old women (*vetulae*) are wise, whereas men get more and more stupid with age[45]. Likewise, in a question on prophetic dreams, he mentions prophets and old women in the same sentence[46]. Significantly, neither Aristotle nor Peter of Abano mention women. These examples, which can easily be multiplied, show that *Felix qui poterit* has a distinct voice of its own, and cannot simply be considered as an abridgment of Peter's *Expositio*.

The independence of *Felix qui poterit* with respect to Peter of Abano also shows in the conceptual organisation of the text. Of course, the *Problems* lack a clear plan – which is in itself an indication of their complicated textual history[47] – but medieval commentators nevertheless try to credit them with some sort of order. Peter of Abano divides the subject matter into three parts: a first on medicine and anthropology (*scientia medicinalis et naturalis prout ad hominis materiam*, sections 1-14); a second on liberal arts (sections 15-19); and a third, more heterogeneous group (sections 20-38), covering different subjects of natural science and moral philosophy (*naturalia tam composita universaliter et*

bridge University Press, 1993, p. 173-177. The author of *Felix qui poterit* is not alone in thinking that menstruation protects against certain diseases. Hildegard of Bingen claims that women suffer less from hernias and gout (the latter idea goes back, directly or indirectly, to the *Aphorisms* of Hippocrates), Héloïse cites Macrobius for the idea that women get drunk less easily, and Albert the Great attributes the greater longevity of women, among other causes, to menstruation, cf. CADDEN, *Meanings of Sex Difference...*, p. 175-176.

45. *Felix qui poterit*, 32, 4 (= 30, 5 in the original *Problems*): 'Quare senes sunt sapienciores iuvenibus. Respondeo [...]. 12° propter temperamentum fleugmatis (!), sicut vetule que in senectute deveniunt sapientes, ubi viri desipient in senectute' (London, British Library, Royal, 12 E XVI, fol. 163r-v). Conversely, the intellect of young men and voluptuous women is obstructed by their desires: *ibidem*, '6° propter carenciam voluptatum. Voluptates enim impediunt intellectum, sicut in iuvenibus et mulieribus delicatis'. Note that all young men, but not all young women are intellectually disqualified. On the ambivalent appraisal of old women in the Middle Ages, see AGRIMI J. – CRISCIANI C., 'Immagini e ruoli della 'vetula' tra sapere medico e antropologia religiosa (secoli XIII-XV)', in: A. PARAVICINI BAGLIANI – A. VAUCHEZ (eds.), *Poteri carismatici e informali. Chiesa e società medioevali* (Prisma), Palermo: Sellerio, 1992, p. 224-61.

46. *Felix qui poterit*, 32, 14 (this is an extra question, see note 37): '3° propter divinam influenciam, sicut vetule et prophete qui vere sompniant de futuris' (ms. London, British Library, Royal, 12 E XVI, fol. 165v).

47. See Pierre Louis' introduction to the Budé edition.

etiam in specie quam simplicia et similiter moralia). Peter announces and justifies this plan in his prologue; and the beginning of the sections he considers as the beginning of a new part[48]. By contrast, the author of *Felix qui poterit* divides the subject matter into four parts: medicine, natural philosophy, mathematics and moral philosophy, but without clearly indicating where these parts begin and end[49].

The division into sections and the section titles in *Felix qui poterit* also differ from Peter of Abano, as can be seen in Appendix 2. The author of *Felix qui poterit* divides the first section *Circa medicinalia* into two after problem 1, 29, and calls the two new sections *De egritudine* and *De medicinalibus* respectively. Section fifteen is also separated in two[50], and sections thirty-six, thirty-seven and thirty-eight (*Circa faciem, Circa totum corpus, Circa colorem*) are conflated into one, called *De facie*. The total number of sections is thus the same as in Bartholomew's translation, Peter's commentary and the original Greek text. The fact that the author of *Felix qui poterit* omits the last two section titles does not mean that he cuts the text. Apparently working from a defective Greek original, Bartholomew ended his translation at problem 37, 3[51], even though the table of contents accompanying his translation systematically mentions a section 38 *De colore*[52]. The last sections in the Latin translation contain so few problems that regrouping them in one section was quite a logical step. The origin of the alternative division in *Felix qui poterit* will be discussed later on.

We have already seen that the author of *Felix qui poterit* omits repetitious problems, while creating some new ones by cutting up Peter of Abano's answers. Of course, the divergent division into sections and numbering of problems could be confusing. Medieval scribes and readers were not unaware of this danger. The compiler of an alphabetical index on *Felix qui poterit*, one Johannes Bruyl, a Franciscan from Cam-

48. For the origin of this division into three parts, see below p. 96-100.

49. *Felix qui poterit*, prologue: 'Liber autem iste dupliciter est divisus, primo in partes 4 principales, scilicet medicinalem, naturalem, mathematicam et moralem, 2° subdividitur in 38 particulas speciales et quelibet particula in diversa problemata multipliciter est partita' (ms. Oxford, Bodleian, Digby, 153, fol. 102r).

50. Bartholomew's *Circa mathematica et circa celestia* becomes *De mathematicis* and *De supracelestibus* in *Felix qui poterit*.

51. Problems 37, 4-6 and 38, 1-11 thus lack in the Latin tradition. In Peter of Abano's *Expositio* problem 37, 3 is systematically renumbered 38, 1, masking the omission.

52. This is an indication that the textual tradition of the table of contents is separate from that of the text itself, see also *infra*. I thank P. De Leemans for drawing my attention to the text tradition of this table.

bridge, warns future users that his table cannot be used for Aristotle's text, but for this particular commentary only[53].

2.2. Manuscripts and codicological context

The way the problems are numbered in *Felix qui poterit* not only diverges substantially from the organisation in Bartholomew of Messina's translation, but it also differs from one manuscript of *Felix qui poterit* to the next, as scribes omit, divide or fuse problems[54]. These changes are often due to inattention, but some are more conscious and significant[55], such as the omission of the whole section on sexuality in one manuscript[56], and the existence of an abreviation which skips many problems and shortens others[57]. In like manner, the different manuscripts of the alphabetical version of *Felix qui poterit* do not contain the same number of keywords. It appears as if the latter remained continually under construction.

The instability of *Felix qui poterit* is typical of the problems as a genre, with its accumulative structure and lack of an encompassing theme[58], but it also reflects the type of manuscripts it was transmitted in.

53. Johannes Bruyl OFM: 'Volens hanc tabulam transcribere attendere debet quod presens tabula non deserviet pro textu Aristotelis sed pro exposicione ista. Quia exposicio multa addidit problemata que Philosophus non posuit, aliquando cum in uno problemate tractat de duabus materiis coincidentibus quas philosophus in textu tractat in duobus et ideo numeri illorum et istorum non concordant. Et ideo attendendum est ut servet noster numerus istius exposicionis super quam facta est hec tabula. Unde notandum est quod sicud in textu sunt 38 particule, sed particularum problemata ut dictum est variantur hic et ibi. Attendendum est ergo quod in prima particula sunt 29, in 2a 28, in 3a 42, in 4a 37, in 5a 31, in 6a 40, in 7a 8, in 8a 9, in 9a 21, in 10a 13, in 11a 69, in 12a 51, in 13a 10, in 14a 12, in 15a 15, in 16a 2, in 17a 9, in 18a 12, in 19a 3, in 20a 10, in 21a 50, in 22a 36, in 23a 24, in 24a 15, in 25a 38, in 26a 18, in 27a 21, in 28a 64, in 29a 10, in 30a 7, in 31a 14, in 32a 15, in 33a 32, in 34a 36, in 35a 12, in 36a 12, in 37a 9, in 38a 4or' (ms. Oxford, Bodleian Library, 153, fol. 138r). Unfortunately, his note, unlike the table itself, is of limited use because Johannes Bruyl does not indicate clearly where and how the division into sections diverges from the original *Problems*, and although he gives the number of problems in each section in *Felix qui poterit*, these do not always correspond to his own copy of that text.

54. For instance, ms. London, British Library, Royal, 12 E XVI, skips problems 2, 24 and 2, 25, while the scribe of Oxford, Bodleian Library, Digby, 206 has turned the end of the answer to problem 1, 21 ('Quare anni pluviosi magis sunt morbosi') into a new problem, numbered 1, 22 ('Quare mulieres quedam samaritane pariunt bufones').

55. In the second example in the preceding note, the scribe's intervention was probably prompted by the fact that the answer-turned-problem recalls a well known Salernitan question about women giving birth to toads (for this legend, see JACQUART – THOMASSET, *Sexualité et savoir...*, p. 223-224). Incidentally, the answer to problem 1, 21 is another example of originality with regards to Peter of Abano, who neither refers to toads, nor to the Salernitan legend.

56. Oxford, Bodleian Library, Digby, 206, cf. CADDEN, 'Nothing Natural...', p. 87.

57. London, British Library, Additional 62127. For this manuscript, see note 59 below.

58. On this point see also BLAIR, 'The Problemata...', p. 179.

Twelve manuscripts have been identified. Only ten of these hold the full text; the eleventh complete copy got divided between the remaining two manuscripts[59]. All date from the 14th and 15th century and are of English provenance[60]. The manuscripts are rather small and cheaply made, and in two cases we know for certain that they were copied by their owners[61]. They do not stand in the *pecia* tradition, and although most of them have links with the academic community of Oxford[62], and with members of the mendicant orders, especially Franciscans[63], these books were meant and used for extra-curricular discussion and consultation, rather than formal study or teaching[64].

There are seven copies of the original commentary; one manuscript contains an abbreviation of it, and three transmit the alphabetical version of the text[65]. Two 14th century copies of the original version also contain an alphabetical index. These tables are roughly organised in the same way as the alphabetical version of the commentary; however, they do not reproduce the whole work, and therefore cannot be used as a replacement.

59. See figure below. All manuscripts, except London, British Library, Additional 62127 (15th), had already been identified by Lynn Thorndike and Brian Lawn. The latter manuscript is of some interest because it contains an abbreviated version of the commentary. Apart from *Felix qui poterit*, the manuscript contains medical treatises, in Latin and English, written in England in several hands. Earlier owners include a certain John Irton, a 'magister' (late 15th), Robert Syddall (circa 1600), and John Byrom (d. 1763). The volume was bequeathed by Byrom to Chetham's Library Manchester (press mark MS.B.6.60) and purchased by the British Library from Alan G. Thomas Cat 143 no 8, 22 octobre 1981. Cf. *The British Library Catalogue of Additions to the manuscripts*. New series 1981-1985. Part 1 descriptions, The British Library, 1994, p. 57-58.

60. In her 2001 article 'Nothing Natural...', p. 86, Joan Cadden stated that Oxford, Bodleian Library, Digby, 206 once belonged to the prior of St Eloi. Although the copy contains a work by Pierre Bersuire, prior of that monastery, there is no indication that he owned the manuscript. The manuscript lacks any indication as to its owner or scribe.

61. Ms. Oxford, Digby 153, owned and copied by Johannes Bruyl OFM of Cambridge. Ms. Oxford, Magdalen college, 65, owned and copied by the humanist William Worcester (d. ca. 1482).

62. See CADDEN, 'Nothing Natural...', p. 86-87 for details.

63. In the late 14th or early 15th century, one Ralph Wyche of the Franciscan community of Chester copied the alphabetical version of *Felix qui poterit* (ms. London, Gray's Inn, 2). He also copied almost all the other texts in the manuscript. In the 15th century a friar Thomas Besforde owned a manuscript with the original text, which he later left to Reading abbey for study purposes (ms. Oxford, St John's college, 113). The manuscript owned and copied by Johannes Bruyl from the Franciscan convent of Cambridge has already been mentioned.

64. Cf. CADDEN, 'Nothing Natural...', p. 87.

65. See the figure below.

Manuscripts of *Felix qui poterit*

Date	Original version	Alphabetical version	Remarks
15th		Cambridge, Peterhouse, 220	
1466	Cambridge, University Library, 911		
15th	London, British Library, Royal, 12 E XVI		Attribution to Walter Burley
15th	London, British Library, Additional, 62127		Abbreviated form
late 14th/15th		London, Gray's Inn, 2	
14th	Oxford, Bodleian Library, Digby, 77		
14th	Oxford, Bodleian Library, Digby, 153		Contains alphabetical index
15th	Oxford, Bodleian Library, Digby, 161		Beginning of this copy in Oxford, Oriel College, 28
14th	Oxford, Bodleian Library, Digby, 206		Contains alphabetical index
late 14th		Oxford, Magdalen College, 65	Attribution to Walter Burley
15th	Oxford, Oriel College, 28		End of this copy in Oxford, Bodleian Library, Digby 161
14th	Oxford, St John's College, 113		

The first of these indexes, the one composed by Johannes Bruyl, has already been alluded to above. Bruyl, who copied *Felix qui poterit* himself as well, also compiled tables to other works in the manuscript, like the *Meteora* by Simon de Tunstede, a fellow Franciscan, and the *Aphorisms* of Urso, a 12th century Salernitan physician. The second manuscript, Digby 206, the owner and scribe of which we know nothing about, contains a combined table on the *Problems*, on Urso's *Aphorisms* and on Avicenna's *Canon*, and separate tables, in the same hand, on Urso's *Aphorisms* and on Bernard of Clairvaux's sermons.

The handy format of *Felix qui poterit*, as compared to Peter of Abano's lengthy work, and the simple question and answer format indicate that *Felix qui poterit* was intended as a reference work. The reorganisation in alphabetical order and the confection of alphabetical indexes can be understood as ways to make the text, which lacks a coherent plan, even more useful and accessible[66].

The combined table on the *Problems*, on Urso's *Aphorisms* and on the *Canon* in Digby 206 functions as a comprehensive medical dictionary, not unlike the *Concordances* on Galenic and Hippocratic works by Jean de Saint-Amand (1270-1274) and its continuation by Pierre de Saint-Flour around the middle of the 14th century[67]. The medical dimension of *Felix qui poterit* is confirmed by the texts it keeps company with in the manuscripts. These texts are varied in character, but medicine, next to natural philosophy, stands out. The strong link with Urso's *Aphorisms* is of particular interest on more than one account: *Problems* and *Aphorisms* are related genres[68] – both are short statements of very diverse character – and Urso of Salerno is not a prominent authority in scholastic medicine[69]. The type of medical works *Felix qui poterit* is associated with seem in fact to reflect a more general, less technical interest in medicine, than, for instance, the scholastic medical works found in the Vatican manuscript, which contains the anonymous reconstruction of the *Problems*. Several of the medical texts in *Felix qui poterit* are of a practical nature, and there is even a treatise on toothache in English[70].

66. The following two manuscripts of the alphabetical version of *Felix qui poterit* contain tables on other works as well: Ms. Oxford, Magdalen College, 65, which contains the alphabetical version copied by the one time owner of the manuscript, William Worcester, once also contained a table on another work, composed by the same William Worcester, as shown by the index: 'Tabula ultimi libri Petri de Crescenciis per W. Wyrcestre compilata'. Ms. London Gray's Inn, 2, also of the alphabetical version, contains many tables copied by the owner of the manuscript, a Franciscan called Ralph Wyche (see note 63 above). The presence of these indexes further enhances the encyclopaedical character of *Felix qui poterit*.

67. On these texts, see JACQUART, *La médecine médiévale...*, p. 170-173.

68. *Felix qui poterit* is associated with other texts of related genres, e.g. another English Problems text, Richard of Lavanham's *Tractatus de causis naturalibus* in ms. London, British Library, Royal, 12 E XVI (on this text, see KEELE, 'Richard Lavenham's...' and note 28 above); the *Quaestiones Nicolai Peripatetici* and the *Secreta Alberti* in ms. Oxford, Bodleian Library, Digby 153.

69. Urso of Salerno is cited by Evrart de Conty dans le *Livre des Problemes* (JACQUART, *La médecine médiévale...*, p. 254), but that is not a medical work in the strict sense of the term. Interestingly, Urso is also among the sources of Richard of Lavenham's *Tractatus de causis naturalibus*. In ms. Oxford, Bodleian Library, Digby, 161, *Felix qui poterit* is followed by another treatise by Urso of Salerno, the *De commixtionibus elementorum*.

70. Ms. London, British Library, Additional, 62127, contains, among other texts, the *Regimen salernitatum*, a tract in English on toothache, and a tract on urine. Ms. Oxford, Bodleian Library, Digby 161 contains recipes and a treatise on critical days.

2.3. The attribution to Walter Burley

Given the manuscript evidence, *Felix qui poterit* was almost undoubtedly written in England. The content of the text also suggests that the author was English or at least knew England well[71]. Attributions in two manuscripts make it possible to go further and propose the name of Walter Burley. In the first manuscript, which contains the alphabetical version and can be dated to the late 14th or early 15th century, the attribution is found in the incipit and in the colophon, which are written in the same hand as the text, and in the contemporary table[72]. In the second manuscript, a 15th century copy of the original commentary, the attribution has been added in a contemporary or slightly later hand.[73] In all the other manuscripts the text is anonymous[74], but, as Joan Cadden has argued, the fact that the attribution to Burley is found in copies of the two versions pleads in favour of its exactness, as does the presence, in three other copies, of authentic works by Burley[75]. Burley's biography also lends support to the attribution.

Born around 1275, probably in Yorkshire, Walter Burley belonged to the secular clergy and held several benefices. An Oxford Master of Arts by 1301, he taught Arts, probably at Oxford, until his departure for Paris around 1310, where he stayed until 1326, having obtained a Masters degree in theology by 1324. His star began to rise after 1327, when he was

71. In problem 1, 22, concerning the relationship between certain kinds of frogs and diseases, Peter of Abano asserts that such frogs often abound in Italy after rainfall. *Felix qui poterit* states that such is the case in England: '[...] cuiusmodi sunt rane anglicane in pratis et in fossis in mayo abundantes post pluviam' (ms. London, British Library, Royal, 12 E XVI, fol. 72v).

72. Ms. Oxford, Magdalen college, 65, fol. 1r: 'Hic incipiunt problemata Aristotelis secundum laborem magistri Wa<l>ter Burley'; fol. 58v: 'Explicit problemata Aristotelis secundum Burley' (in red). Next to this, in black, and underlined in red: 'Explicit abbreviacio libri problematum Aristotelis secundum ordinem alphabeti laborata per Walterum Burley, doctor in theologia universitatis Oxon. et pertinet iste liber Willelmo Worcestre nato de Bristollia Wigorniensis diocesis'. On flyleaf: 'Burley super problemata Aristotelis'.

73. Ms. London, British Library, Royal, 12 E XVI, fol. 67r: 'Magister Walterus Burlay super problemata Aristotelis'. The scribe of the text itself did not know who the author was, since he titles it 'Super problemata quedam expositio'.

74. Witness the note preceding his table (see note 53 above), Johannes Bruyl did not know who the author was.

75. Cf. CADDEN, 'Nothing Natural...', p. 79: 'Thus if, as seems likely, the ascription to Burley carried over from the first version to the second, the transfer would have occurred at most a couple of decades later than the production of the original text, in which case it is more likely to be accurate'. Mss Oxford, St John's college, 113 and London, Gray's Inn, 2 contain works by Burley although they are not labeled as such, whereas Oxford, Bodleian Library, Digby, 77 contains works explicitly attributed to Burley, although in a later hand than *Felix qui poterit*.

entrusted with a first diplomatic mission for Edward III, to Avignon. Other missions would follow, and benefices in their wake. Around 1333 Burley entered the service of the colourful and eccentric Richard de Bury (d. 1345), who had been appointed to the see of Durham that same year and whose patronage Burley enjoyed for about ten years. He was still alive on January 12, 1344 and it is generally assumed that he died shortly afterwards[76].

As an author of many works on Aristotelian logic, natural philosophy and ethics, Burley certainly had the interests to make him a candidate for having composed *Felix qui poterit*. He also had the opportunity[77]. We have seen that *Felix qui poterit* circulated mainly, or even exclusively in England. If Burley was indeed its author, he may have composed it at Paris and then brought it back with him to England. In Paris, he would have had easy access to both the *Problems* and to Peter of Abano's commentary, especially since he was acquainted with John of Jandun[78].

Burley may also have written or finished *Felix qui poterit* in England, while in the service of Richard de Bury[79]. The latter had surrounded himself with a group of eminent scholars, most of them Merton men like Burley, who probably hoped to gain royal patronage through their contact with the king's former tutor and principal advisor[80]. Besides Burley, the circle included Thomas Bradwardine, Robert Holcot, Thomas Fitzralph and Richard de Kilvington, to mention only the most well-known[81]. Even though these learned clerics probably were not all

76. For Walter Burley's life and works, see OTTMAN J. – WOOD R., 'Walter of Burley. His Life and Works', *Vivarium* 37 (1999), p. 1-23, who do not, however, mention *Felix qui poterit*. The attribution to Burley of an extremely popular *Liber de vita et moribus philosophorum* is now generally considered to be incorrect, cf. PRELOG J., '*De Pictagora phylosopho*. Die Biographie des Pythagoras in dem Walter Burley zugeschriebenen *Liber de vita et moribus philosophorum*', *Medioevo* 16 (1990), p. 192-95. However, according to OTTMAN – WOOD, 'Walter of Burley...', p. 22-23, the evidence for this conclusion is not entirely compelling.

77. See also CADDEN, 'Nothing Natural...', p. 79.

78. CADDEN, 'Nothing Natural...', p. 79, who cites an article by Katharine Park. The date of the copy John of Jandun made of the *Problems* cannot be determined more precisely than after 1315, more likely after 1317, see KUKSEWICZ, 'Les *Problemata*...', p. 121.

79. CADDEN, 'Nothing Natural...', p. 79 deems this unlikely, but without examining the possibility.

80. They were not unsuccessful in this. See COURTENAY W. J., *Schools and Scholars in Fourteenth Century England*, Princeton: Princeton University Press, 1987, p. 135-136. In 1337, Burley became the tutor of the Black Prince and the almoner of Queen Philippa.

81. Other known members of the household were Richard Bentworth, Walter Segrave, John Maudith and John Acton (for references see note 83). In at least one manuscript, London, Gray's Inn, 2, *Felix qui poterit* keeps company not only with another work by Burley (anonymous there), but also with a work by Holcot.

present at the same time – Bradwardine and Burley seem to have had the longest tenure – the episcopal court definitely provided a stimulating intellectual environment[82]. We know, both from Bury's own testimony, and from other contemporary sources, that at his household, table reading was followed by learned conversation, by discussion of controversial points and direct consultation of theological and profane authorities. Bury, a voracious book collector whose love of books bordered on the pathological, owned what was then probably the largest library in the British Isles[83]. In his bibliographical autobiography, the *Philobiblon*, Bury reports how he came by his books: receiving them as gifts or payment in exchange for his support and patronage, buying them on his many travels, especially to Paris, obtaining them from booksellers in England, France, Germany and Italy, and relying on the mendicant orders for supply[84]. He also employed scribes to copy books for him – indeed, he reports the presence, at his court, of all sorts of artisans of the book-trade[85]. Moreover, a certain number of Franciscans and Dominicans were engaged, as members of Bury's household, in the correction of his manuscripts, the composition of paraphrases and commentaries, the compilation and fabrication of all sorts of tables and indexes[86].

82. Bury travelled a lot on diplomatic missions. Before retiring semi-permanently to his diocese in 1340, his principal residence seems to have been Durham House in London.

83. On Bury, his circle and his library, see BRECHKA F.T., 'Richard de Bury. The Books he cherished', *Libri. International Library Review* 33 (1983), p. 302-315; GILBERT N.W., 'Richard de Bury and the 'Quires of Yesterday's Sophism'', in: E.P. MAHONEY (ed.), *Philosophy and Humanism. Renaissance Essays in Honour of Paul Oskar Kristeller*, Leiden: Brill, 1976, p. 229-257; CHENEY C.R., 'Richard de Bury, Borrower of Books', *Speculum* 48 (1973), p. 325-328, who offer some complements and corrections to two excellent older studies: DE GHELLINCK J., 'Un évêque bibliophile au XIVe siècle. Richard Aungerville de Bury (1345). Contribution à l'histoire de la littérature et des bibliothèques médiévales', *Revue d'Histoire Ecclésiastique* 18 (1922), p. 271-313; 482-508 and DENHOLM-YOUNG N., 'Richard de Bury (1287-1345)', *Transactions of the Royal Historical Society* 4, 20 (1937), p. 135-168 (reproduced in DENHOLM-YOUNG N., *Collected Papers on Mediaeval Subjects*, Oxford, 1946, p. 1-25).

84. Richard de Bury, *Philobiblon*, cap. 8 (*Philobiblon, o l'amore per i libri*, intr. M. FUMAGALLI BROCCHIERI, trans. and notes R. FEDRIGA, Milano: Biblioteca universale Rizzoli, 1998, p. 106-123). Bury enthusiastically praises Paris as a bibliophile's and intellectual's paradise.

85. Richard de Bury, *Philobiblon*, cap. 8, p. 122: 'Ceterum apud nos in nostris maneriis multitudo non modica semper erat antiquariorum, scriptorum, correctorum, colligatorum, illuminatorum et generaliter omnium, qui poterant librorum serviciis utiliter insudare'.

86. Richard de Bury, *Philobiblon*, cap. 8, p. 120: 'De istis ad statum pontificalem assumpti nonnullos habuimus de duobus ordinibus, Predicatorum videlicet et Minorum, nostris adsistentes lateribus nostreque familie commensales, viros utique tam moribus insignitos quam litteris, qui diversorum voluminum correctionibus, expositionibus, tabulationibus ac compilationibus indefessis studiis incumbebant' – the Italian translator renders the activities of the friars as 'correggere codici, compilare indici, catalogare e

It is generally assumed that members of Bury's circle used this tremendous library to compose their works. Such was the case, for example, of Thomas Bradwardine and his work on divine grace, the *De causa Dei contra Pelagianos*, a treatise that contains many references to obscure texts and which, like *Felix qui poterit*, does not adopt the scholastic format[87]. Bury certainly owned a copy of the *Problems*, since he cites the work very precisely in the *Philobiblon*[88]. Walter Burley thus would have had the work at his disposal at his patron's court.

Unfortunately, Bury's library was dispersed after he died a ruined man. Only a couple of manuscripts have been identified as his[89], and if a catalogue existed, as Bury claims in his *Philobiblon*[90], it has not survived. Under these circumstances, it is impossible to determine whether Bury's library contained a copy of *Felix qui poterit*. Whether or not Burley wrote it[91], we do know that his patron's court, with its large li-

trascrivere i miei molti volumi', which seems incorrect. In this respect, the situation at Bury's court was comparable to usage at the palace of pope John XXII. DE GHELLINCK, 'Un évêque…', p. 496, suggests that Bury may have been inspired by this model after an embassy to Avignon.

87. MOLLAND G., 'Addressing Ancient Authority: Thomas Bradwardine and *Prisca Sapientia*', *Annals of Science* 53 (1996), p. 213-233, especially p. 213-214. Of course, I do not mean to suggest that the *De causa Dei* and *Felix qui poterit* are similar in form and in content, but only that neither is a truly scholastic work.

88. Richard de Bury, *Philobiblon*, cap. 2, p. 46: 'Preterea Aristoteles De problematibus, particula 30a, problemate X, istam determinat questionem propter quid antiqui, qui pro gymnasticis et corporalibus agoniis premia statuerunt potioribus, nullum unquam premium sapientie decreverunt. Hanc questionem responsione tertia ita solvit: in gymnasticis exercitiis premium est eligibilius melius et illo, pro quo datur; sapientia autem nichil melius esse potest: quamobrem sapientie nullum potuit premium assignari. Ergo nec divicie nec delicie sapientiam antecellunt'. The content of Bury's citation is found in both the *Problems* (Latin 30, 10 = Greek 30, 11) and in Peter of Abano's *Expositio*. However, Bury does not cite his source *verbatim* and it is impossible to infer from his citation whether his copy of the *Problems* contained the *Expositio* as well. The fact that Bury so explicitly refers to the third answer may indicate that he used Peter of Abano, who indicates the division of the argument very clearly. Many thanks to Caroline Boucher for the reference to this passage of the *Philobiblon*.

89. BRECHKA, 'Richard de Bury…', p. 30.

90. Richard de Bury, *Philobiblon*, cap. 19, p. 198.

91. If Walter Burley did write *Felix qui poterit* while at Bury's service, it may seem odd that he did not dedicate the work to his patron, as he did with several other works from this period (his *Ethics* commentary, the last version of his *Physics* commentary, his *Super artem veterem* and his *Politics* commentary, see OTTMAN – WOOD, 'Walter of Burley…', p. 17 and the references there). Ottman and Wood, who do not mention the *Problems* commentary at all in their biographical article, point out (p. 20) that at least one passage in Walter Burley's authentical works is conspicuously sexist. In his *Ethics* commentary (ad VII, 6, 1048b, ed. Venezia, 1500, fol. 112rb), Burley says that women are for the most part led by their concupiscent desires and not by reason, which is why strong and wise women are hard to find. However, this statement is not necessarily contradictory with the positive view on women displayed in *Felix qui poterit*. First of all, as shown by Ottman and Wood, Burley relies heavily on Thomas of Aquinas' *Ethics* commentary.

brary, the presence of eminent scholars and a flock of mendicant specialists in the production of reference works, did constitute an ideal environment for the composition of such a work in either its original or its alphabetical guise.

3. Two commentaries on the Problems from Germany and Eastern Europe

As we have seen, *Felix qui poterit* circulated in England. Two other
14th century commentaries on the *Problems* were composed and copied
in Germany and Eastern Europe, the lands which, in the later Middle
Ages, also produced several encyclopaedias which incorporate material
from the *Problems*[92].

The first of our two anonymous (and still hardly studied[93]) commentaries is present in at least three manuscripts, the earliest of which was
copied at Erfurt in 1364[94]. It bears the title 'Aristotle's problems' in all
three manuscripts. For convenience I will call it the Erfurt commentary
here. The second commentary is found in, at least, two 14th century
manuscripts of Bavarian provenance. One manuscript presents it as a
work on natural problems[95]; in the other it lacks a title[96]. For our purposes, we will call it the Bavarian commentary.

Both works are comparable in length with *Felix qui poterit*, the Bavarian commentary being somewhat longer than the Erfurt one. As in

Thomas already claims that wise and strong women are rare. The significant difference
between the two commentaries is the shift from affections (in Thomas) to concupiscent
desires (in Burley) and the fact that Thomas repeatedly qualifies the lack of reason in
women as *ut in pluribus*. On the other hand, the author of *Felix qui poterit* has a positive
opinion on older women (*vetule*), while singling out voluptuousness of *iuvenes* and
mulieres as an obstacle to sagacity (see note 45 above). Precisely because it is desire
rather than affections as such that are at fault, *Felix qui poterit* judges the intelligence of
older women positively.

92. The *Summa omnes homines* was most likely compiled there; it certainly circulated
mainly in these regions, in both manuscript and printed form, and was translated into German long before any other vernacular version was made (see LAWN, *The Salernitan...*,
p. 101). Three further Latin encyclopedias influenced by Aristotle's *Problems* originated
in Northern Germany, Austria and Bohemia, cf. VENTURA, 'Quaestiones and...', p. 35.

93. The only reference to these commentaries seems to be the list of manuscripts
given by LAWN, *The Salernitan...*, p. 208, who presents them as a single text.

94. Göttingen, Niedersächsische Staats- und Universitätsbibliothek, 4° Theol. 124,
fol. 197r: 'Expliciunt probleumata Aristotelis Erfordie. Anno D. Myllesymo CCC S 4
(1364)'. Erfurt also appears in the colophon of several other texts in this miscellany,
which also contains some documents from Dresden.

95. Gent, Universiteitsbibliotheek, 178, fol. 90v: 'De probleumatibus circa naturalibus existentibus' (written in the hand of one of its owners, a canon of the Eichstätt chapter of Saint Willibald, see below p. 94).

96. München, Bayerische Staatsbibliothek, CLM, 12021.

Felix qui poterit, the problems take the form of simple questions and answers, rather than scholastic disputations[97]. The Erfurt and Bavarian commentary also have the same division into sections as *Felix qui poterit* (meaning that section one and fifteen are divided into two, and sections thirty-six, thirty-seven and thirty-eight combined into one), but the extra problems extracted from Peter's *Expositio* are absent here. The two German commentaries have, however, considerably less personality than *Felix qui poterit*: they lack a prologue, and as far as a rather rapid analysis can tell, they are much less original. This is especially true of the Bavarian commentary, which in many cases summarises Peter of Abano's answers, citing him explicitly, while the titles of the problems either copy Bartholomew's translation or are very similar to Peter of Abano's paraphrases. In the Erfurt commentary, the titles differ from both Bartholomew of Messina's translation and Peter of Abano's paraphrase, but compared to *Felix qui poterit*, they are much closer in meaning, if not in wording, to the original *Problems*[98]. Where the titles differ in content, this disagreement goes back to Peter of Abano. Such is the case, for instance, of problem 30, 9 (30, 10 in the Greek), on the dissolute character of 'artists of Dionysios' (Διονυσιακοὶ τεχνῖται), that is, actors[99]. Bartholomew translated this problem, literally, but obscurely, as 'Propter quid bachici artifices ut frequenter mali sunt'. Peter of Abano suggests that 'bachici' means here, not 'those who venerate Bacchus the wine God', as an interlinear gloss seems to have had it, but 'mechanici artifices', artisans 'who earn their living by working with their hands'[100]. Both the Erfurt and the Bavarian commentary adopt Peter's suggestion in their problem titles[101]. More generally, they can be qualified as derivatives of the *Expositio*.

97. In the German commentaries, however, the answers are not divided into numbered causes.

98. For some examples, see the comparative table of problem titles in Appendix 3. In the Erfurt commentary, the introductory formula to each problem is 'propter quid', as in Bartholomew of Messina, or, less frequently, 'quare', as in Peter of Abano's paraphrase and in *Felix qui poterit*, while the Bavarian commentary always uses 'propter quid'.

99. See *Aristote. Problèmes*, ed. P. LOUIS, 3 vols. (Collection des universités de France), Paris: Belles Lettres, 1991-1994, p. 40, note 75.

100. Peter of Abano, *Expositio Problematum*, 30, 9: 'Quare artifices dicti bachici ut frequenter sunt pravi, indiscreti et indisciplinati? Sciendum aliquod interlineasse bachici id est divinativi volentes id trahere ad id quod est dictum primo bachides, id est divini, vel bachici colentes festum bachi qui est deus vini. Melius quidem dicendum, quod sunt mechanici artifices victum manibus querentes'. Peter seems to refer to a gloss added by an early reader of Bartholomew's translation.

101. Erfurt commentary: 'Propter quid mechanici et artifices ut frequenter sunt mali et indiscreti et indisciplinati?' (ms. Göttingen, Niedersächsische Staats- und Universitätsbibliothek, 4° Theol. 124, fol. 193vb); Bavarian commentary: 'Propter quid agiti (!) et

Both abridgments circulated, and were most likely compiled in Germany and Eastern Europe. We have seen that the earliest copy of the Erfurt commentary was copied in that Thuringian town in 1364; many other texts in this miscellany, which contains scholastic works on theology, natural philosophy, logic, law, and astronomy (but also a lapidary), have Erfurt in their colophon as well. In 1364, Erfurt did not yet have a university, but there were important mendicant *studia generalia* and a host of other schools, which were equal or superior to the faculties of Arts[102]. Several texts in our manuscript (but not the *Problems*) are written by a certain Johannes de Corbae, a lector, suggesting that the manuscript originated and circulated in mendicant circles. The fact that in the 15th or 16th century, it belonged to the Franciscans of Göttingen points in the same direction[103].

The second copy of the Erfurt commentary was made in Prague in 1366 and later almost certainly belonged to Lucas de Magna Cosmin (or de Wielki Kozmin)[104]. Apart from the *Problems*, the manuscript contains notes by this Polish philosopher and theologian, and works by Jean Buridan, whom he was much influenced by[105]. Lucas probably acquired the *Problems* when he studied Arts in Prague in the last years of the 14th century – like many Polish scholars of that generation – and took them with him when he moved to Krakow, to pursue his studies in theology there[106]. Elected rector in 1411, Lucas died shortly afterwards, leaving

mechanici artifices ut frequenter sunt mali et indiscreti et indisciplinati? (ms. München, Bayerische Staatsbibliothek, CLM, 12021, fol. 175ra). The author of *Felix qui poterit* ignores Peter's remark and keeps the *bachici* as such, without mentioning artisans.

102. Cf. ASZTALOS M. 'The Faculty of Theology', in: H. DE RIDDER-SYMOENS (ed.), *Universities in the Middle Ages*, Cambridge: Cambridge University Press, p. 417 and SCHWINGES R.C., 'Admission', in: DE RIDDER-SYMOENS (ed.), *Universities...*, p. 175. The university was thus founded within an existing academic community. The Avignon pope first gave his approval in 1379, but the university did not open its doors before 1392.

103. Göttingen, Niedersächsische Staats- und Universitätsbibliothek, 4° Theol. 124, fol. 160r-197r (Erfurt, 1364), cf. *Verzeichnis der Handschriften im Preussischen Staate*, Berlin, 1893, p. 364-66. Ex-libris fol. 1: 'Liber fratrum minorum in Gottingen. J. II'.

104. Kraków, Biblioteka Jagiellońska, 654, fol. 1r-25v (Prague, 1366), cf. KOWALCZYK M. – KOZOWSKA A. – MARKOWSKI M. – WŁODEK Z. – ZATHEY J. – ZWIERCAN M., *Catalogus codicum manuscriptorum medii aevi latinorum qui in Bibliotheca Jagellonica Cracoviae asservantur*. Vol. 4. *Numeros continens inde a 564 usque ad 667*, Warszawa: Academiae scientiarium Polonae, 1988, I, p. 411-414.

105. There are no marginal notes in the part of the manuscript containing the *Problems*.

106. On Lucas de Magna Cosmin and his works, cf. TATARZYŃSKI R., 'Lucas de Magna Cosmin. *Duo sermones in festo Pentecostes*', *Przeglad Tomistyczny* 4 (1988), p. 59-60 and the bibliography cited. See also LOHR C.H., 'Medieval Latin Aristotle Commentaries', *Traditio* 27 (1971), p. 320-21; LOHR C.H., *Commentateurs d'Aristote au Moyen Age latin. Bibliographie de la littérature secondaire récente*, Fribourg: Éditions Universitaires, 1988, p. 161 and POTTHAST A., *Repertorium fontium historiae Medii aevi, primum ab Augusto Potthast digestum, nunc cura collegii historicum e pluribus nationibus emendatum et auctum*, Roma: Istituto storico italiano per il medio evo, 1962

his copy of the *Problems* commentary, like his other books, to the university[107]. No fewer than 43 manuscripts of his collection have survived[108].

The manuscripts from Erfurt and Prague were copied at a two year interval, they share common errors[109] and both circulated in urban environments with links to the university and mendicant circles. By contrast, the third copy, a 15th century miscellany, belonged to a Benedictine monastery somewhere in Germany. In terms of content it is not entirely dissimilar however; besides monastic texts, it contains a collection of *quodlibeta*, especially on philosophical subjects[110].

The Bavarian commentary can be found in, at least, two manuscripts. One belonged to the Benedictine monastery of Prüfening, in the diocese of Regensburg. The part of the manuscript that contains the *Problems* commentary is a self-contained unit dating from the 14th century, bound together with a miscellany of medical texts in various 15th century hands, which include a *Practica* and collections of recipes and *consilia* by several Italian physicians[111]. The second copy of the Bavarian commentary, also from the 14th century, bound with a historical work and a series of natural questions, belonged, in the 15th or 16th century, to the monastery of the Augustinian Canons at Rebdorf in the diocese of

sqq., VIII, p. 213. I wish to thank Anna Adamska for her help with the bibliography in Polish.

107. Two sermons were preached in his memory, bearing witness to his standing in the university community. Cf. KOWALCZYK e.a., *Catalogus codicum...*, p. 231 and 259.

108. 42 manuscripts are now in the Krakow university library, one in the chapter library, cf. TATARZYŃSKI, 'Lucas de Magna...', p. 60. For references to manuscripts owned or copied by Lucas de Magna Cosmin, see also the index of the excellent new manuscript catalogue of the Krakow university library by KOWALCZYK e.a., *Catalogus codicum...*

109. For example, the absence, in the table, of the part on the ears.

110. München, Bayerische Staatsbibliothek, CLM, 4710, fol. 262r-293r (15th century), cf. HALM C. – LAUBMANN G. – MEYER G., *Catalogus codicum latinorum Bibliotecae regiae Monacensis secundum Andreae Schmelleri indices, codices num. 2501-5250 complectentes*, München, 1871, p. 194-195. The first leaf contains a 15th century table and ex libris: 'Iste liber attinet venerabili monasterio Benedicten. pewrii'. The use of the letter *w* here and elsewhere in the manuscript points to a German provenance. I have not been able to determine the identity of this monastery any further; it seems not to be mentioned in KELLNER S. – SPETHMANN A., *Historische Kataloge der Bayerischen Staatsbibliothek München: Münchner Hofbibliothek und andere Provenienzen*, Wiesbaden: Harrassowitz, 1996. LAWN, *The Salernitan...*, p. 208, apparently following a suggestion in the Göttingen and Munich catalogues, cites a fourth manuscript: München, Bayerische Staatsbibliothek, CLM, 12021, fol. 118r-179r (cf. HALM C. – LAUBMANN G. – MEYER G., *Catalogus codicum latinorum Bibliotecae regiae Monacenses secundum Andreae Schmelleri indices, codices num. 11001-15028*, München, 1876, p. 52-53). However, this manuscript contains the Bavarian commentary.

111. München, Bayerische Staatsbibliothek, CLM, 12021, fol. 118r-179r (cf. HALM e.a., *Catalogus codicum latinorum...*, p. 52-53). It belonged to Prüfening at least as early as the 16th century.

Eichstätt[112]. Rebdorf, associated since 1458 with the Windesheim reform movement[113] and owner of a large library[114], received its copy by testament from a canon called Johann von Leonrot, a member of an aristocratic Bavarian familiy, which in the 15th and 16th century counted several canons in Eichstätt and other chapters in the region[115]. However, the first known owner of the manuscript was a canon of the Eichstätt chapter of St Willibald, also called Johann and whose last name may have

112. Gent, Universiteitsbibliotheek, n° 178, fol. 91r-155r. Fol. 1r contains several ex-libris in 15th or 16th century hands: 'Iste liber est Io. Vog[s or e] canonici ad S. Will<ibaldi> Eyst<etensis>.' A different, slightly later hand adds: 'sed modum canonicorum regularium Rebdorff ex testamento domini Ioh<anne>s Deleonrot canonici'. A third, even later hand adds: 'Iste codex est monasterii beatisimi Iohannis Baptiste in Rebdorff canonicorum regularium ordinis sancti augustini dyocesis eystetensis. Hic continentur Ystoria troyana et alia sequuntur'. The *Problems* are followed by a series of natural questions of the type found in ms. Paris, BNF, lat. 16089 (see above note 9) in another 14th century hand (fols 155r-157r) and by a table of contents listing the sections of the *Problems* in yet another contemporary hand. For this manuscript see also PATTIN A., *Repertorium commentariorum medii aevi in Aristotelem latinorum quae in bibliothecis belgicis asservantur*, Leuven: Leuven University Press, 1978, p. 118 (according to Adriaan Pattin the *Problems* are found on fol. 181r-313v; this seems to be a mistake, unless Pattin refers to folio-numbers that are undetectable on the microfilm I consulted).

113. For bibliography on Rebdorf, see *Lexikon des Mittelalters*, München: Artemis – Lexma, VII, 1994, col. 499.

114. RUF P., *Mittelalterliche Bibliothekskataloge Deutschlands und der Schweiz* 3. II, München: Bistum Eichstätt, 1933, p. 257-316 edits the 15th or 16th century catalogue of the Rebdorf library. The *Problems* commentary does not appear as such, but the *Historia troiana*, also found in the Ghent manuscript, does. According to the catalogue, the Rebdorf library did not contain a lot of manuscripts on natural philosophy or medicine. (pseudo)-Aristotle is represented by On the Soul, the *Economics*, *Politics*, *Rhetorics*, *Secret of Secrets*, the *Auctoritates Aristotelis*, and, a later addition, the *Physics*. Of (pseudo-) Albert the Great only the theological works and the *De mirabilibus mundi* figure. Avicenna and Peter of Abano are absent. The only (probably) medical work cited is an *Ysagogicus libellus Abdilazi*.

115. Cf. the ex-libris cited above note 112. On the von Leonrot family, first mentioned in 1235, cf. BRAUN H. A., *Das Domkapitel zu Eichstätt. Von der Reformationszeit bis zur Säkularisation (1535-1806). Verfassung und Personalgeschichte*, Stuttgart: F. Steiner, 1991, p. 342-345. FLACHENECKER H., *Eine Geistliche Stadt. Eichstätt vom 13. bis zum 16. Jahrhundert*, Regensburg: F. Pustet, 1988, p. 70, n. 182 and p. 244, n. 255 mentions a Johann von Leonrot, who was canon in Eichstätt in 1456 and Headmaster of the Hospital of the Holy Ghost in that town from 1455-1457. Braun (n° 150, p. 344-45) cites a Johann Georg von Leonrot (1512-1594), who held many benefices, among which canonries at Würzburg, Bamberg, Eichstätt (from 1532 to his death) and Ellwangen. Both are possible candidates; the first Johann is perhaps more likely given his name (Johann and not Johann Georg), and the date of the Rebdorf catalogue (15th/16th century) and the Rebdorf ex-libris (15th century) in the Ghent manuscript. The latter does not specify where our Johann von Leonrot was a canon, but this affiliation to Eichstätt seems likely, given the fact that an earlier owner of the manuscript (see below) was a canon there. There may have been other canons called Johann von Leonrot in 15th century Eichstätt. Braun's book does not cover the period before 1535.

been Vogt[116]. Several Vogts, a noble family like the Von Leonrots, held canonries in Eichstätt at least as early as the 16ᵗʰ century[117].

The readers and owners of the Bavarian commentary are monks and canons, rather than friars and university men. However, in the later Middle Ages, canons very often have a university education, and prosopographical studies on members of families like the Von Leonrots and the Vogts show that they all passed through university, typically starting in Germany, and pursuing their studies in Italy later in their career[118].

Two readers of the Bavarian commentary left traces in the manuscripts, which shed light on the way they read the *Problems*. The canon of St Willibald scribbled short notes in the margins of the *Problems* commentary, mostly indications of the subjects treated in the text. These notes are found throughout the commentary, but they are almost exclusively medical or anthropological: the signs of plague, for example, or the right *regimen* in case of fever, or the reason why melancholics stammer[119]. Likewise, in the late 15ᵗʰ century, a reader annotated the sections on medicine, on sweat and on sexual matters in the Prüfening manuscript[120]. He cites Averroes' *Colliget* and thus certainly had some medical knowledge[121]. The notes indicate that both readers conceived of the

116. Cf. the ex-libris cited above note 112. The last letter of this canon's name seems to be an *s* or an *e*. I have not found anyone named Vogs or Voge in either BRAUN, *Das Domkapitel...* or FLACHENECKER, *Eine Geistliche Stadt....* However, the name Vogt occurrs in both. In the 16ᵗʰ century, the Vogt von Altensummerau und Prassberg familiy, like the von Leonrots, counted several canons in the Eichstätt chapter (rather than the Willibaldschor), some of whom are called Johann (see BRAUN, *Das Domkapitel...*, p. 544-549). FLACHENECKER, *Eine Geistliche Stadt...,* p. 257, n. 341, cites a document from 1510 concerning a canon called Hans Vogt. Flachenecker does not indicate whether he was a canon at the cathedral chapter or at the chapter of St Willibald, an annex of the cathedral. Another identification seems possible as well. A register of 1453, which kept track of books lent to canons of St Willibald shows that a Johannes Vogler was at the time canon there, cf. RUF, *Mittelalterliche Bibliothekskataloge...,* p. 201: 'Nota libros spectantes ad chorum, confratribus accomodatos. Item Jo<hannes> Vogler habet concordanciam ewangeliorum. Compendium philosophiae et soliloquiorum et penitenciarum.' The Vogler family is not cited by either Flachenecker or Braun.

117. In 1477, the Eichstätt chapter decided to officialise the restriction of access to members of aristocratic families, cf. BRAUN, *Das Domkapitel...,* p. 11-12.

118. See the biographies in BRAUN, *Das Domkapitel...* Unfortunately, Braun does not indicate in what faculty they studied. Presumably, they studied arts in Germany.

119. The Ghent manuscript also contains a few annotations in another hand, but these merely indicate the authorities cited in the text. For instance, fol. 91r 'Ypocras'.

120. Sections 1-3 and 5 according to the alternative division followed here (1-2 and 4 according to the traditional division). The notes are written in a German hand. The section on sexuality also attracted special attention from the scribe: it is the only one where the title is capitalised in large black letters. Significantly, two manuscripts of *Felix qui poterit* also display interventions of scribes or readers in the section on sexuality, cf. CADDEN, 'Nothing Natural...', p. 85 and 87.

121. München, Bayerische Staatsbibliothek, CLM, 12021, fol. 130v.

Problems as a work on medicine or more generally on Man's physical dimension.

4. Some remarks on text division

Felix qui poterit, the Erfurt commentary and the Bavarian commentary share the same divergent text division[122]. The existence of three different commentaries with this alternative division, which circulated in different geographical areas naturally raises the question of its origin. First of all, it must be noted that the alternative division of the first and fifteenth section already appears in some of the best Greek manuscripts of the *Problems*, as well as in the Arabic and Hebrew translation[123]. Almost all Greek manuscripts, including the oldest one – Paris, BNF, gr. 2036 – contain an addition at the end of problem I, 29 indicating a transition to a discussion about remedies[124]. Moreover, several of these manuscripts insert this addition as a rubricated title, thus creating a new section[125]. Likewise, all the manuscripts in the sample I looked at insert a title at the beginning of problem 15, 5 indicating a transition to astronomy. However, these extra titles do not appear in the tables preceding the text. Peter of Abano, although adopting the standard division in his *Expositio*, seems to have been aware of the existence of a different organisation of the text. At the beginning of problem 1, 30 (the first problem of the second section according to the alternative division), Peter remarks that Aristotle's first section follows the Galenic distinction between theoretical and practical medicine: problems 1-29 pertain to theory, the rest to practice (a category Peter further divides into diet, medication and surgery)[126]. At the beginning of his commentary on sec-

---

122. See Appendix 2.

123. I wish to thank Lou Filius, editor of the translation in Arabic and in Hebrew of the *Problems* (*The* Problemata physica *attributed to Aristotle: the Arabic version of Ḥunain ibn Isḥāq and the Hebrew version of Moses ibn Tibbon*, Leiden: Brill, 1999) for his helpful remarks on this subject. The translation in Hebrew was made from the Arabic.

124. See the critical apparatus in Pierre Louis' edition.

125. For instance Paris, BNF, gr. 1865 and Paris, BNF, suppl. gr. 204, but not Paris, BNF, gr. 2036 and gr. 985.

126. Peter of Abano, *Expositio Problematum*, 1, 30: 'Expeditis causis egritudinis ad theoricam magis pertinentibus, nunc determinat problemata circa curas earum practice attinentia. Pars autem hec dividitur in tres, sicut triplex est medicorum instrumentum, scilicet dieta, potio, vel medicina et cyrurgia. Primo enim determinat problemata ad cyrurgiam spectantia, 2° ad dietam, 3° vero ad potum attinentia. 2a ibi in xxxvi problemate, 3a in xxxvii'. See also Peter of Abano, *Expositio Problematum*, 1, 37: 'Sequitur pars 3a principalis curative partis in qua determinat de problematibus curationis

tion fifteen, he announces that Aristotle first treats of mathematical problems *simpliciter*, before turning to mathematical problems with respect to the celestial bodies[127]. Moreover, Peter of Abano's division of the text in three parts (1-14; 15-19; 20-38) seems inspired by the titles of sections 15 and 20 in some Greek manuscripts, which announce the subject matter of sections that follow[128].

How did Peter of Abano acquire his knowledge on the alternative text division? We know that he started a first draft of his *Expositio* well before his departure for Constantinople to learn Greek, and finished it several years after his return, basing himself all the while on Bartholomew's translation[129]. As stated in an autobiographical note in the prologue to the *Expositio*, in Constantinople, Peter hoped to find some problems apparently lacking in the Latin text. He does not mean the problems omitted at the end of Bartholomew's version, but problems to which Aristotle refers in several of his other works[130]. One explanation for the presence of traces of the alternative division in the *Expositio* would be for Peter to have taken notes on the Greek text while at Constantinople, without transcribing the whole work. One of the first things a medieval reader of a new text or a new version of a text would do is to jot down the table, *incipit*, *explicit* and text division. However, if this were the case, it seems strange that Peter does not mention consulting the Greek text in the prologue to the *Expositio*, if only to remark that the missing problems he had been looking for are not in the Greek either. He merely says that he found and translated 'another volume of pro-

penes instrumentum medicine dictum potio vel medicina. Et quia practica est duplex, scilicet curativa et conservativa, primo determinat problemata de cura cuiusdem egritudinis vel accidentis dentium utputa stuporis, secundo de conservatione sanitatis tangit problemata et hoc in xxxix problemate, prima in duas secundum quod sermo duo de hoc ponit problemata 2a ibi in xxxix problemate'.

127. Peter of Abano, *Expositio Problematum*, 15, 1: '[...] Et primo determinat problemata circa mathematicas simpliciter, secundo circa quantitates relatas ad celorum corpora [...]'.

128. See the critical apparatus in Pierre Louis' edition at the beginning of sections 15 and 20. Peter of Abano announces and justifies the division in his prologue, and repeats it at the beginning of sections 15 and 20.

129. OLIVIERI (*Pietro d'Abano...*, chapter 3, especially p. 181-188) convincingly refutes the idea that Peter of Abano translated the *Problems* from the Greek, an idea based on erroneous interpretations of certain passages in the *Expositio* and the *Conciliator*. The autobiographical note in the prologue to the *Expositio* rather indicates that Peter had started a first version of his commentary (based on Bartholomew's translation) well before leaving for Constantinople. During his stay in Constantinople Peter made a translation of another collection of *Problems*.

130. See OLIVIERI, *Pietro d'Abano...*, p. 184-85.

blems'[131]. If Peter consulted the Greek text, and unless he consulted an incomplete copy, it also seems strange that he does not note that the Latin text is truncated at the end. It is thus much more likely to suppose that Peter used a manuscript of Bartholomew of Messina's translation carrying traces of the alternative division[132]. Indeed, some, if apparently not all[133], manuscripts of the Latin version do contain such indications[134]. However, as in the Greek manuscripts, the extra titles do not appear in the table of contents accompanying the *Problems*, the textual tradition of which seems to be quite separate. The presence of the extra titles does not necessarily influence the numbering of the sections in the text itself either[135]. Peter adopted the standard division, probably because it corresponded to the table of contents. The presence in this table

131. For this collection, see OLIVIERI, *Pietro d'Abano...*, p. 187-203 and note 129 above.

132. The manuscript of Bartholomew's translation used by Peter of Abano certainly contained rubrications indicative of something else than the traditional division into 38 parts. At the beginning of section 20, where Peter of Abano introduces the subject matter of what he considers as the third main part of the *Problems* (sections 20-38), he notes that rubrication indicates a link between sections 20 and 21: 'Etiam prima sequestratur in duas partes ut apparet per rubricam, primo enim determinat de problematibus circa ipsa vegetabilia, 2° circa illa que ex eis producuntur'. At the beginning of section 31 we find the following remark: 'Determinatis problematis circa moralia revertitur adhuc ad declarandum nunc de problematibus naturalibus existentibus circa organa sensuum (*ed. 1475*, sensum *ed. 1482*) hominis et maxime faciem et totum corpus, praemittens rubricam primo in quibus huiusmodi particule et sequentium apperitur intentio usque ad finem. Et dividitur in partes 8 sicut 8 tanguntur in ea ex quibus 8 consurgunt particule'. The manuscript used by Peter of Abano also seems to have contained interlinear glosses, see note 100 above.

133. I have not found any traces of an alternative division in Paris, BNF, lat. 3121A; 6327; 14725; 15081 and 16633.

134. Padova, Bibl. Antoniana, 370, an independent manuscript which according to Luigi Olivieri contains glosses in Peter of Abano's hand (OLIVIERI, *Pietro d'Abano...*, p. 109-111), carries remarks reflecting the additions in some Greek manuscripts. At the beginning of 1, 30 (fol. 3r): 'de problematibus que sunt circa medicinalia ad sanitatem'; at the beginning of 15, 5 (fol 30r): 'de hiis que sunt circa celestia'. Paris, BNF, lat. 6307, problem 1, 30 (fol. 189ra): 'de hiis que sunt medicativa ad sanitatem'; problem 15, 5 (fol. 226rb): 'de hiis que sunt circa celestia'. Venezia, Bibl. Marciana, lat. VI, 43 (= 2488), no division of the first section, but at problem 15, 5: 'de hiis que sunt circa celestia particula XVI'. I thank Pieter De Leemans for drawing my attention to the subdivisions and the numbering of the Sections (cf. n. 135) in these manuscripts. Further research on the manuscript is necessary to determine whether the Latin manuscripts also contain notes concerning the subdivision in three parts.

135. Gijs Coucke (K.U.Leuven), who prepares a Phd on section 4, has not found a single manuscript of Bartholomew's translation in which this section is referred to as section 5. Padova, Bibl. Antoniana, 370 does not number sections systematically, and the introduction of rubricated titles does not influence this numbering: sections 15 and 17 receive the corresponding numbers. In Paris, BNF, lat. 6307 the second part of section 15 receives the number 16, leading to a renumbering of the following sections, but these numbers seem to be a later addition. Venezia, Bibl. Marciana, lat. VI, 43 contains an original, non-systematic numbering in which the second part of 15 is numbered 16; the

of a section 38 'de colore', may also have led him to create such a section by renumbering the last problem in Bartholomew's truncated text as problem 38, 1[136].

The authors of *Felix qui poterit* and the two German commentaries go much further than Peter of Abano, because they systematically renumber the sections according to the alternative division, not only in the text, but also in the table of contents. Peter of Abano's *Expositio* is their most likely source of inspiration, even though he only provides indications for this division, without adopting it himself. A more serious enigma is the regrouping of the last three sections, 36, 37, 38, for which there hardly seem to be precedents in either Bartholomew's translation or Peter's *Expositio*. The most likely explanation seems the circulation of Peter's *Expositio* with the divergent division, possibly with alternative section titles and/or an alternative table as well. However, the manuscript tradition of the *Expositio* has not yet been studied in detail.

Another question is whether the authors of the three commentaries independently adopted the alternative division, or influenced each other. The latter possibility is not unlikely for the Erfurt and Bavarian commentaries, which circulated in more or less the same geographical area. Moreover, there are strong similarities between the section titles in the Erfurt and Bavarian commentaries (see Appendix 2), and in one manuscript, the Bavarian commentary is followed by the Erfurt table.[137] Taken together, the Erfurt and Bavarian commentaries show parallels with both Bartholomew's translation and *Felix qui poterit*, whereas the titles in the latter are farthest removed from Bartholomew's translation. Given their circulation in different areas, contact between *Felix qui poterit* on the one hand, and the German commentaries on the other seems much more improbable. The similarities between the titles in these three commentaries can, in fact, be traced back to the paraphrase at the beginning of new sections in Peter of Abano's *Expositio*[138], as can most of the section titles only found in *Felix qui poterit*, but not in the German commentaries[139]. These correspondences confirm yet again the

actual section 16 has no number, and section 17 has number 17; a younger hand numbers the second part of section 15 as 16, and continues this to the end of the manuscript.

136. In many, perhaps most manuscripts of Bartholomew's translation there is no distinction between sections 37 and 38.

137. Gent, Universiteitsbibliotheek, n° 178, fol. 157v. The table is written in another but contemporary hand.

138. Some examples of parallels between Peter of Abano and all three commentaries: Section 6 (7 in *Felix qui poterit* and the German commentaries), 'Ista est particula sexta in qua inquisitis causis accidentium ex labore et exercitio inquirit causas accidentium circa accubitum et figurationem membrorum labori seu exercitio oppositum'. Section 9

significance of Peter of Abano's paraphrase in shaping the form of the Latin *Problems*.

Conclusion

All four texts under discussion here bear witness to the hegemony of Peter of Abano's *Expositio* in the Latin tradition of the *Problems*. Peter's paraphrases at the beginning of each problem are used as a substitute for Bartholomew's translation in the reconstruction of the *Problems* in the Vatican manuscript. The section titles in *Felix qui poterit* and the two German commentaries also go back to the paraphrases found at the beginning of sections in the *Expositio*; and the alternative text division in these three commentaries is probably inspired by Peter's commentary. More generally, the Erfurt, and especially the Bavarian commentary can be qualified as derivatives and abridgments of the *Expositio*, and even though *Felix qui poterit* is a much more personal work, it is also deeply indepted to Peter of Abano.

The Vatican manuscript that holds the reconstruction of the *Problems* was copied for a member of the academic community, probably a physician, and the *Problems* are associated with disputed questions: scholasticism at its most technical and formal. By contrast, *Felix qui poterit* and the two German commentaries are not scholastic expositions in the strict sense of the word. Given the differences in titles and text division, they are of limited use for readers needing a linear commentary of the Aristotelian works. They adopt the simple question and answer format of the Salernitan tradition, rather than the form of the scholastic disputation, and present the *Problems* as a source of indisputable knowledge. Rather than an elucidation, these commentaries are new, independent reference works, closely based on the *Problems* and on Peter of Abano's *Expositio*; they can be used as replacements for these two works. The move away from the original *Problems* is taken even further in *Felix qui poterit*, which skips many problems, and changes their content; and the

(10), 'Ista est nona particula in qua causae assignantur accidentium contingentium circa albugines que apparent in oculis et cicatrices et vulnera'.

139. Some examples of parallels with *Felix qui poterit* only: Section 16 (18), 'Particula decimasexta in qua agit de problematibus circa quantitatem inanimatam que respiciunt ea que geometrie et utcumque perspective'. Section 20 (22), 'Determinat circa problemata circa ipsa vegetabilia'. Section 21 (23), 'Particula 21a in qua agitur de his que circa plantarum semina et primo circa farinam (*scr.*, farmam *ed. 1482*) ordei proprie et frumenti et pasta ipsorum et ceterorum per consequens similium'. However, the title of section 23 (25) in *Felix qui poterit* ('De aquis frigidis') has no parallel in Peter of Abano.

disconnection reaches an extreme in the alphabetical version of that work. The encyclopaedical character of these three commentaries does not imply that they were not read in scholastic circles. On the contrary, the profile of the owners of the manuscripts indicates that they circulated in academic communities. At the same time, these Problem commentaries seem to have been used in private consultation and conversation rather than formal study or teaching. The commentaries also reached a wider audience of monks, and canons.

Our four texts are transmitted with varied materials, but besides natural philosophy – the most obvious environment for an Aristotelian work – there is a substantial amount of medicine. The medical works in the Vatican manuscript are highly specialised, whereas *Felix qui poterit* and the Bavarian commentary keep company with less technical works, and which are often associated with medical practice. The existence of a combined table on *Felix qui poterit*, Avicenna's *Canon*[140] and Urso's *Aphorisms* in one manuscript, and the marginal notes by two readers of the Bavarian commentary, strongly suggest that the *Problems* were perceived as a medical work, even though their subject matter stretches far wider.

The perception and success of the *Problems* as a medical text cannot be explained solely by the fact that the text begins with a section on medicine. There would seem to be epistemological reasons as well. The *Problems* are a heterogeneous collection of natural particulars, without a clear plan or common theme, whereas the Aristotelian philosophy of science restricts scientific knowledge to what is universal and necessary. To be true, Aristotle's works on the sublunar world, and especially his biology, fall short of this ideal[141]. In his *Parts of Animals*, Aristotle justifies, not without difficulty, the importance of studying all animals, however diverse or vile, in detail, because all hold something divine and marvellous[142]. Interestingly, the author of *Felix qui poterit* cites precisely this passage in his prologue, assigning the *Problems* a place in the Aristotelian corpus after the books on animals and on plants[143]. But the

140. Avicenna's *Canon* is of course a major authority in scholastic medicine, but it was also quite widely read outside the medical community.

141. See HANKINSON, 'Philosophy...', p. 113-115.

142. Aristotle, *Parts of animals*, I, 5, especially 644ba21-645a24.

143. *Felix qui poterit*, prologue: 'Causa finalis est scire causas problematum collectorum et mirabilium diversorum in eis contentorum. Nec propter quorundam vilitatem est ab eis desistendum, quia non est spernendum vilia contemplari; in quolibet enim quantumcumque vili est aliquod divinum et mirabiles aliquos reperitur 13° De animalibus [*Parts of Animals*, I, 5, 645a15-19]. Liber autem iste dupliciter est divisus,

fact is, that no commentaries on botany were written after the 1250's and that commentaries on the *De animalibus* practically cease in the beginning of the 14ᵗʰ century. Their initial success and integration in the Arts curriculum seems mostly a side effect of the general enthusiasm for the new Aristotle.

The place of the *Problems* in natural philosophy is at best ambiguous, but medicine has more room for particulars. Medicine is based on general principles and rules, but every medical case is unique and asks for an individual approach, as when the physician describes a particular *regimen* for each patient, adapted to his constitution and complexion[144]. In structure, several medical genres such as aphorisms, collections of recipes, *experimenta* and *consilia*, are not unlike the *Problems*[145]. It is no coincidence that these kinds of medical texts are found in several manuscripts of the *Problems* under discussion here[146].

As far as they can be identified, none of the owners of *Felix qui poterit* and of the German commentaries were physicians. Apparently, the *Problems* and the medical material it was associated with appealed

---

primo in quartes partes principales, scilicet medicinalem, naturalem, mathematicam et moralem, 2° subdivitur in 38 particulas speciales et quelibet particula in diversa problemata multiplicata est, puta ordo talis, quod liber iste librum de animalibus et vegetabilibus subsequitur' (ms. London, British Library, Royal, 12 E XVI, fol. 67v-68r). Admittedly, in *Felix qui poterit*, the reference to the vileness of the subjects treated in the *Problems* also has a moral connotation.

144. In a well known passage in the *Metaphysics* (1, 1, 981a15-20), Aristotle states that 'the physician does not cure man, except in an incidental way, but Callias or Socrates or some other called by such individual name, who happens to be a man'. See also the *Auctoritates Aristotelis*: 'Actus et operationes sunt circa singularia, quia medicus non sanat hominem in communi, sed Socratem vel aliquem alium in particulari, similiter et in aliis' (HAMESSE J., *Les* Auctoritates Aristotelis. *Un florilège médiéval. Étude historique et édition critique*, Louvain: Publications universitaires – Paris: Béatrice-Nauwelaerts, 1974, p. 115). On the place of the particular in medicine, see also AGRIMI J. – CRISCIANI C, 'Per una ricerca su *experimentum-experimenta*: riflessione epistemologica e tradizione medica (secoli XIII-XV)', in: P. JANNI – I. MAZZINI (eds.), *Presenza del lessico greco e latino nelle lingue contemporanee*, Macerata: Università degli Studi di Macerata, 1990, p. 9-49, esp. p. 30-39 and MCVAUGH M. R., 'The Nature and Limits of Medical Certitude at Early Fourteenth-Century Montpellier', *Osiris*, 6 (1990), p. 62-84, especially p. 68-75. On the efforts to justify the scientific status of scholastic medicine, as opposed to the medicine of the empirics, see also AGRIMI J. – CRISCIANI C., *Edocere medicos. Medicina scolastica nei secoli XIII-XV*, Milano, 1988, p. 29, 34, 41-46.

145. On this literature, see AGRIMI – CRISCIANI, 'Per una ricerca...', p. 44-47; AGRIMI J. – CRISCIANI C., *Les consilia médicaux* (Typologie des sources du Moyen Age occidental 69), Turnhout: Brepols Publishers, 1994.

146. The *Problems* are also copied with philosophical texts with a similar structure, see note 68 and note 112 above.

to a more general readership[147]. In this respect, the reception of the *Problems* fits the pattern of the evolution of encyclopedical literature in the Later Middle Ages. These encyclopedias, which often include Problem material, tend to concentrate more and more on medicine, physiology and more generally anthropology: subjects that seem to correspond to an audience looking for knowledge, which is above all useful and practical[148].

Université Paris 7

Appendix 1

BM= Bartholomew of Messina's Latin translation of the *Problems* (in the edition of Peter of Abano's *Expositio*)
PA = Peter of Abano, *Expositio Problematum* (ed. Venezia, 1482)

1. Problem 1, 28

BM: Propter quid in hyeme minus sunt egritudines quam estate; mortifere magis in hyeme? Aut quia in estate quidem a parva occasione egritudines, in hyeme vero non; magis digestibiles enim et saniores sumus nobis ipsis, quare merito que a maiori occasione fiunt maiora et magis destructiva. Hoc idem autem in athletis et omnino in dispositis sane videmus. Aut (*scr.*, autem *ed. 1482*) enim non occupantur a morbo, aut ut cito occupenter magna causa indigent ad egrotandum et corrumpendum.

Vat. lat. 2481: Quare est quod pauciores egritudines fiunt in yeme quam in estate sed magis mortales? **Et est repetatio 25°**. Ratio et si in yeme procedunt a forciori causa, nam sumus saniores yeme, ideo si accidat egritudo est a fortiori causa. Sequitur.

PA: **Repetit XXV problema** ut magis exponatur et perfectius habeatur causa, maxime illius partis dubitabilis quare plus moriuntur hyeme homines. [...]

---

147. Johannes Bruyl's copy seems to lend some support to the hypothesis of a special interest in medicine among English Franciscans, see ZIEGLER J., '*Ut dicunt medici*. Medical Knowledge and Theological Debate in the Second Half of the Thirteenth Century', *Bulletin for the History of Medicine* 73 (1999), p. 208-37 and VAN DER LUGT M., *Le ver, le démon et la vierge. Les théories médiévales de la génération extraordinaire. Une étude sur les rapports entre théologie, philosophie naturelle et médecine*, Paris: Les Belles Lettres, 2004, p. 467. Of course, at the same time, mendicants were specialists in the use and production of reference works, aide-memoires, encyclopaedias and dictionaries.
148. See the contribution of Iolanda Ventura in the present volume.

2. Problem 1, 37

BM: **Propter quid congelationem dentium dissolvit portulaca et sal?** Aut quia hec humiditatem quandam habet? Manifeste autem hec confecta si apponatur quodam tempore; attrahitur enim humiditas. Viscosum autem ingressum extrahit acutum. Etenim quia cognota acuitas congelationem dentium significat; habet enim quandam acuitatem humor. Sal autem liquefaciens extrahit et acuitatem.

Vat. lat. 2481: **Quare est quod portulaca et sal habent dissolvere congellationem dencium et stuporem, cum unum sit frigidum et aliud calidum?** Ratio: illa removent stuporem dencium que acritudinem vel humiditatem aeris ab illis removent; portulaca et sal sunt huiusmodi ergo etc. **a. est nota** quia illa humiditas aeris est causa stuporis **b. nota Nycholaus Perypateticus** dicit: portulaca enim diu masticata viscositatem habet subintrantem dentes et attrahentem illud acetositatis quod adheret dentibus; nam et ipse succus portulace parum acetositatis habet, ideo similitudinis causa attrahit quod acetosum est; sal autem liquefaciens adducit acetositatem dentibus inherentem.

PA: **Quare est quod portulaca et etiam sal habet dissolvere congelationem et stuporem dentium, cum unum frigidum sit et alterum calidum?** Sermo autem **Nicolai peripathetici** (*ed. 1475*: peripotheci *ed. 1482*) talis est de hoc: stuporem dentium aufert sal, necnon et portulaca quamvis sit frigida et sal calidus; portulaca diu masticata viscositatem habet subintrantem dentes et attrahentem id acetositatis quod adheret dentibus, nam et ipse sucus portulace parum acetositatis habet, ideo similitudinis causa attrahit quod acetosum est; sal autem liquefaciens educit acetositatem dentibus inherentem. [...]

3. Problem 10, 2

BM: **Propter quid homini soli animalium sanguis fluit ex naribus?** Aut quia cerebrum habet plurimum et humiditatem a quo vene replete superfluitate per poros emittunt fluxum? Morbidum enim subtilius fit puro sanguine, hoc autem est quod commiscetur cerebri superfluitatibus et est sicut sanies.

Vat. lat. 2481: **Quare est quod homini inter cetera animalia sanguinis fluxus accidit ex naribus?** Ratio, quia homo ut dictum est habet cerebrum maius et humidius et venas valde plenas sanguinem (!), quare.

PA: **Quare est quod homini inter cetera animalium fluxus sanguinis ex naribus accidit?** Deinde. Aut quia. Solvit dicens causam esse quoniam homo ut dictum est prius habet plurimum de cerebro secundum rationem sui corporis et humidissimum; in quo etiam sunt vene magne valde replete humiditatibus sanguinis superfluis, quibus repletis emittunt eas extra per poros venarum terminantes exterius circa collatorium nasi in locum ubi fiunt emoroides nasi. Propter quod contingit fluxus sanguinis superflui, eo quod humidum sangui-neum est factum subtilius potentia sanguinis; tale autem est morbidum, quare natura movetur ad expellendum ipsum per fluxum factum ex naribus. [...] Fit autem tale humidum sanguineum morbidum et superfluitatibus cerebri commiscetur subalbidis; quibus quidem admixtis inficitur ex eis et incurrit quasi naturam saniei et secundum colorem fere et substantiam. [...] Et nota quod sunt alia plura propter que homo solus incurrit fluxum sanguinis narium. Unum quidem est quia est magni epatis secundum rationem sui corporis [...]. Item est recte stature, propter quod sanguis cum calido ascendit sursum ad cerebrum sub quo est quedam involutio veniens ex tunicis venarum et artariarum dicta rete mirabile [...]. Item cutis in homine est subtilior quam in reliquo animalium et maxime in facie [...] **Notandum quod mulier raro incurrit fluxum sanguinis narium et emoroidarum et maxime si vita utatur mensurata et convenienter purgetur menstruis.**

Felix qui poterit, 11, 2 (ms. London, British Library, Royal, 12 E XVI, fol. 112r): **Quare omnes homines patiuntur emoroydos?** Respondeo propter superfluitatem sanguinis putrefacti; mulieres raro patiuntur emoroydes propter menstruum.

Appendix 2: Comparative table of the division into sections

- Bartholomew of Messina, in Peter of Abano, *Expositio Problematum* (ed. Venezia, 1482).

- *Felix qui poterit*, according to London, British Library, Royal, 12 E XVI. The title of section 36 is given according to the table in this manuscript. It lacks in the text itself.

- Erfurt commentary according to the table in München, Bayerische Staatsbibliothek, CLM, 4710. This table is also found in Kraków, Biblioteka Jagiellońska, 654 and Göttingen, Niedersächsische Staats- und Universitätsbibliothek, 4 Theol. 124, with some minor variants. None of these manuscripts indicate section titles in the text itself.

- Bavarian commentary, according to the table in München, Bayerische Staatsbibliothek, CLM, 12021. In this manuscript, section titles are not given in the text itself. The section titles of the table are partially found in the text in Gent, Universiteitsbibliotheek, 178. However, the table in Gent, written in another hand than the text hand, corresponds to the table of the Erfurt tradition.

Bartholomew of Messina	Felix qui poterit
1. Circa medicinalia	{ 1. De egritudine 2. De medicinalibus
2. Circa sudores	3. De sudoribus
3. Circa ebrietatem	4. De ebrietate
4. Circa venerea	5. De coitu et venereis
5. A labore	6. De fatigacione et labore
6. Ex modo iacendi	7. De accubitu
7. Ex conpassione	8. De compassione
8. Ex rigore et horripilatione	9. De rigore et horripilacione
9. Circa vestigia oculorum et vulnerum et tumoris	10. De cicatricibus
10. Particula naturalium	11. De passionibus communibus et diversis
11. Circa vocem	12. De voce
12. Circa odorabilia	13. De odore
13. Circa fetida	14. De fetore
14. Circa complexiones	15. De complexione
15. Circa mathematica et circa celestia	{ 16. De mathematicis 17. De supracelestibus
16. Circa inanimata	18. De quantitatibus inanimatorum (*scr.* in animatis)
17. Circa animata	19. De quantitatibus animatorum
18. Circa philologiam	20. De philologia
19. Circa armoniam	21. De armonia
20. Circa plantas et olera	22. De vegetabilibus
21. Circa polentam et massam	23. De farmaciis
22. Circa fructum	24. De fructibus
23. Circa aquam salsam et mare	25. De aquis frigidis
24. Circa calidas aquas	26. De aqua calida
25. Circa aerem	27. De aere
26. Circa ventos	28. De ventis
27. Circa timorem et fortitudinem	29. De audacia et timore
28. Circa temperantiam et intemperantiam	30. De continentia et incontinentia, temperantia et intemperantia
29. Circa iustitiam et iniustitiam	31. De iustitia et iniustitia
30. Circa prudentiam et intellectum et sapientiam	32. De sapientia et intellectu
31. Circa oculos	33. De visu
32. Circa aures	34. De auditu
33. Circa nasum	35. De olfactu
34. Circa os	36. ⟨De ore et gustu⟩
35. Circa subtactum	37. De tactu
36. Circa faciem	} 38. De facie
37. Circa totum corpus	
38. Circa colorem	

Erfurt Commentary	**Bavarian Commentary**
1. De temboribus sanis et egris	1. De differentia temporum et ventorum
2. De medicinalibus	2. De variis medicinalibus
3. De sudoribus	3. De sudoribus
4. De ebrietate	4. De ebrietatibus
5. De veneriis	5. De venereis et coytu
6. De laborantibus	6. De laboribus
7. De accubitu	7. De accubitu
8. De passionibus humanis	8. De passionibus humanis
9. De frigore (!) et horore	9. De horripilacionibus et rigore
10. De cicatricibus	10. Que est circa cicatrices et albugines oculorum
11. De naturalibus	11. De hiis que contingunt circa naturam
12. De voce	12. De hiis que accidunt circa vocem
13. De odoribus	13. De odoribus
14. De fetidis	14. Circa fetida
15. De compleccionibus	15. De complexionibus
16. De matematicis	16. De mathematicabus
17. De corporibus celestibus	17. De celestibus
18. De inanimatis	18. De inanimatis
19. De animatis	19. De animatis
20. De phylosophia	20. De phylosophia
21. De armonia	21. De armonia
22. De oleribus et plantis	22. Circa plantas et olera
23. De pasta et farina	23. De (!) pastam (*scr.* pastum) et farinam
24. De fructibus	24. De hiis que queruntur circa fructus
25. De aquis salsis	25. De aquis salsis et marinis
26. De aquis calidis	26. De hiis que circa aquas calidas fiunt
27. De aere	27. Circa aerem
28. De ventis	28. De ventis
29. De timore et formidine	29. De timore et formidine
30. De continentia et incontinentia	30. Circa continentia
31. De iustitia et iniustitia	31. De iustitia et iniustitia
32. De sapientia et intellectu	32. De intelligentia et prudentia
33. De oculis	33. Circa oculos
34. De hiis que accidunt circa aures	34. De hiis que sunt circa aures
35. De naso et sternutatione	35. De naso et sternutatione
36. De ore	36. De ore
37. De tactu	37. De tactu
38. De facie	38. De hiis que apparunt in facie

Appendix 3
Comparative table of some problem titles

- Bartholomew of Messina's Latin translation of the *Problems* in the edition of Peter of Abano's *Expositio*, Venezia, 1482.
- Peter of Abano, *Expositio Problematum* (ed. Venezia, 1482).
- *Felix qui poterit* (ms. London, British Library, Royal, 12 E XVI).
- Erfurt commentary (ms. München, Bayerische Staatsbibliothek, CLM, 4710).
- Bavarian commentary (ms. München, Bayerische Staatsbibliothek, CLM, 12021).

Problem (original division)	Bartholomew of Messina	Peter of Abano
1, 7	Propter quid quandoque pestilentialis sola egritudinum maxime approximantes eis qui curantur replet?	Quare est quod egritudo pestilentialis ipsa sola quandoque interficit illos qui (*ed. 1475*, que *ed. 1482*) approximant seipsis qui curantur ab ipsa hoc est patientibus hanc egritudinem?
1, 37	Propter quid congelationem dentium dissolvit portulaca et sal?	Quare est quod portulaca et etiam sal habeat dissolvere congelationem et stuporem dentium, cum unum frigidum sit et alterum calidum?
10, 2	Propter quid homini soli animalium sanguis fluit ex naribus?	Quare est quod homini inter cetera animalium fluxus sanguinis ex naribus accidit?
10, 10	Propter quid aliis animalibus genita magis secundum naturas assimilantur quam hominibus?	Quare est quod in aliis animalibus secundum naturam genita cum gignentibus intensiorem habent similitudinem, ut bos generans cum bove genito et capra cum capra etc quam in hominibus, non enim in ipsis sic patri aut matri filius assimilatur?
30, 1	Propter quid omnes quicumque excellentiores fuerint viri aut secundum philosophiam aut politicam aut poesim aut artes videntur melancolici esse et hi quidem ita quod et occupantur egritudinibus que sunt a nigra colera, ut dicuntur ab heroicis ea que sunt circa herculem?	Quare omnes viri ad differentiam mulierum quibus talia per nature frigiditatem et imperfectionem non adveniunt, quicunque fuerint illustres et excedentes alios in philosophia politica etc videntur fuisse complexionis melancolice?
30, 9	Propter quid bachici artifices ut frequenter mali sunt?	Quare artifices dicti bachici ut frequenter sunt pravi indiscreti et indisciplinati? Sciendum aliquod interlineasse bachici id est divinativi volentes id trahere, ad id quod est dictum primo bachides id est divini vel bachici colentes festum bachi qui est deus vini. Melius quidem dicendum quod sunt mechanici artifices victum manibus querentes

Problem (original division)	*Felix qui poterit*	Erfurt commentary	Bavarian commentary
1, 7	Quare morbus pestilentialis inficit homines sicut basiliscus?	Propter quid generatis febribus pestilentialibus propinquantes sepius infirmantur quam ipsi a febribus convalescentes?	Propter quid quandoque pestilencia solum egritudinum maxime approximantes eis qui curantur replet?
1, 37	Quare sal et portulaca mittigant dolorem dencium in gingivis?	Propter quid cum sale solvit congelationem dentium portulaca?	Propter quid congelatio (!) dencium solvit portularia (!) et sal?
10, 2	Quare omnes homines patiuntur emoroydos?	Quare soli homini a naribus fluit sangwis?	Propter quid homini soli animalium sangwis fluit ex naribus?
10, 10	Quare proles humana minus assimilatur parentibus quam proles brutorum?	Quare aliorum animalium plus corpora filii sunt similes eis homini autem minus?	Propter quid aliis animalibus genita magis secundum naturam assimilantur quam homo?
30, 1	Quare omnes sapientes sunt malencolici?	Propter quid heroes viri illustres excedentes in phylosophia et politica speculativa et scientia dicuntur fuisse melancolici complexionis sicud recitatur de Platoni, Aristotele Socrate, similiter de Hercole et de aliis multis?	Propter quid heroes viri illustres excedentes in philosophia et polithica et speculativa et scientia et poetica videntur fuisse complexionis melancolice?
30, 9	Quare bachici deveniunt indiscreti?	Propter quid mechanici et artifices ut frequenter sunt mali et discreti (!) et indisciplinati?	Propter quid agiti (!) et mechanici artifices ut frequenter sunt mali et indiscreti et indisciplinati?

Iolanda VENTURA

ARISTOTELES FUIT CAUSA EFFICIENS HUIUS LIBRI: ON THE RECEPTION OF PSEUDO-ARISTOTLE'S *PROBLEMATA* IN LATE MEDIEVAL ENCYCLOPAEDIC CULTURE

Pendant le Moyen Âge et la Renaissance, un type particulier de texte encyclopé-dique se répand dans la littérature européenne: les recueils de questions natu-relles liés à la tradition des Problemata *pseudo-aristotéliciens et des* Quaes-tiones salernitanae. *Ce genre d'encyclopédie connaît un très grand succès, car il présente la matière scientifique d'une forme très claire et accessible. De plus, le système d'organisation de la matière sous forme de questions et de réponses, utilisé dans ces recueils, donne la possibilité aux auteurs de créer des textes encyclopédiques variés, qui peuvent s'adapter aux besoins et aux différents ni-veaux des lecteurs potentiels. Pourtant, le panorama présenté par ce genre en-cyclopédique est très varié, et comprend des collections d'orientation populaire, des recueils écrits pour les prêcheurs, ou même des textes qui montrent un ni-veau culturel plus élevé. Ces textes, en tout cas, ont des points en commun, qu'on peut identifier dans l'orientation 'humaine' de l'encyclopédie, et dans le rôle joué par la discipline médicale et par les sciences liées à l'homme, à son corps, à sa vie. Le but de cette étude est de donner un aperçu de ce genre de texte encyclopédique, en montrant les différentes typologies d'œuvres qu'on y trouve, d'après une sélection de textes écrits en latin entre le 14e et le 16e siècle.*

Introduction

The Late Middle Ages, and especially the thirteenth century, are char-acterized by the redaction of the most famous medieval encyclopaedias and, more generally, by a strong development of the encyclopaedic cul-ture: as J. Le Goff pointed out in 1992, the thirteenth century can be de-fined as 'the golden era of medieval encyclopaedic culture'[1]. Works like Thomas of Cantimpré's *De natura rerum*, Bartholomew the English-man's *De proprietatibus rerum*, or the huge *Speculum maius* written by Vincent of Beauvais are known among the scholars of Latin literature of the Middle Ages and of history of science[2]. These texts are, in fact, good

1. LE GOFF J., 'Pourquoi le XIIIe siècle a-t-il été plus particulièrement un siècle d'encyclopédisme?', in: M. PICONE (ed.), *L'enciclopedismo medievale. Atti del Convegno San Gimignano, 8-10 Ottobre 1992* (Memoria del tempo 1), Ravenna: Longo, 1994, p. 23-40.
2. On the literary genre of the encyclopaedias see BINKLEY P. (ed.), *Pre-Modern En-cyclopaedic Texts. Proceedings of the Second COMERS Congress, Groningen, 1-4 July 1996* (Brill's Studies in Intellectual History 79), Leiden-New York-Köln: Brill, 1997;

witnesses of the level of the late medieval scientific culture: they allow
us to identify the most famous and used sources, to analyze the role
played by a single branch of knowledge (medicine, theology, etc.), to
discover what both the compiler and his public considered as the necessary cultural background which had to be collected and handed over
through the encyclopaedia.

Less known, however, is the fact that in the Middle Ages, as well as
in other periods of the cultural history, various methods of organizing
and transmitting scientific knowledge, showing different possibilities of
'displaying culture', are developed. Beside the collections arranged according to the elements of nature (*ordo rerum*) or to the branches of
knowledge regrouped by the author in his *canon disciplinarum* (this system is known as *ordo artium*), we can distinguish among many other
forms of transmission of scientific culture: scientific *florilegia*, *compen-
dia*, handbooks, but also *regimina sanitatis*, books of secrets, and medical treatises. Within the literary genre of the texts handing over scientific
culture, a particular role is played by the encyclopaedias written in a
question-answer form or, on a higher literary level, by the fictive dialogues taking place, for example, between a master and a pupil[3]. This
second form of transmission of encyclopaedic culture with the help of a
question-answer structure is witnessed by the anonymous dialogue
called *Placides et Timeo* or by the anonymous *Livre de Sydrac*[4]. This

MEIER C. (ed.), *Die Enzyklopädie im Wandel vom Hochmittelalter bis zur frühen Neuzeit.
Akten des Kolloquiums des Projekts D im Sonderforschungsbereich 231 (29.11.-1.12.
1996)* (Münstersche Mittelalter-Schriften 78), München: Fink, 2002.

3. On the encyclopaedias written in a question-answer form cf. LAWN B., *The
Salernitan Questions*, Oxford: Clarendon Press, 1963; LAWN B., 'Medical *Quaestiones
Disputatae* c. 1250-1450', in: B. LAWN, *The Rise and the Decline of the Scholastic
'Quaestio Disputata' with Special Emphasis on its Use in the Teaching of Medicine and
Science* (Education and Society in the Middle Ages and Renaissance 2), Leiden-New
York-Köln: Brill, 1993, p. 66-84; BLAIR A., 'Authorship in the Popular "Problemata
Aristotelis"', *Early Science and Medicine* 4 (1999), p. 190-227; BLAIR A., 'The
Problemata as a Natural Philosophical Genre', in: A. GRAFTON – N. SIRAISI (eds.), *Natu-
ral Particulars. Nature and Disciplines in Renaissance Europe* (Dibner Institute Studies
in the History of Science and Technology 1), Cambridge-London: The MIT Press, 1999,
p. 171-204; VENTURA I., '*Quaestiones* and Encyclopaedias: Some Aspects of the Late
Medieval Reception of the Pseudo-Aristotelian *Problemata* in Encyclopaedic and Scientific Culture', in: A.A. MACDONALD – M.W. TWOMEY (eds.), *Schooling and Society. The
Ordering and Reordering of Knowledge in the Western Middle Ages* (Groningen Studies
in Cultural Change 6), Leuven-Paris-Dudley: Peeters, 2004, p. 23-42.

4. On the *Placides et Timéo* cf. *Placides et Timéo ou Li secrés as philosophes.* Édition
critique avec introduction et notes par C.A. THOMASSET (Textes littéraires français 289),
Genève: Droz, 1980; THOMASSET C.A., *Commentaire au Dialogue de Placides et Timéo*
(Publications romanes et françaises 161), Genève: Droz, 1982. On the *Livre the Sydrac*
see *Livre de Sydrac. Edition des enzyklopädischen Lehrdialogs aus dem XIII. Jahrhundert*, herausgegeben von E. RUHE (Wissensliteratur im Mittelalter 34), Wiesbaden: Dr.
Ludwig Reichert Verlag, 2000 (with further bibliography).

type of texts, which shows some particular features and is ruled by special strategies of redaction aiming at entertaining the readers, will be left
aside in this paper.

Aim of the present study is to describe the development of the genre
of the encyclopaedias written in a question-answer form, focusing particularly on the role played by the pseudo-Aristotelian *Problemata* both
as source and as a pattern for the redaction of different types of texts. In
order to give a complete panorama, and to emphasize some problematic
aspects shown by the literary genre of the collections of *naturales
quaestiones*, different aspects should be taken into account, viz. the description of some representative Latin texts written in a question-answer
form, the definitions of the types of encyclopaedia and of transmission
of encyclopaedic culture shown by the considered works, and the role
played by the *Problemata* as source for scientific culture as text combined with other scientific texts within late medieval miscellaneous manuscripts (the so-called *Mitüberlieferung*). Some miscellaneous manuscripts and printed texts, in fact, do not preserve the *Problemata* in a
complete form, but hand over only the parts of them whose content
could be connected with other works dealing with the same topic or
branch of knowledge. These manuscripts or printed texts can be considered as an attempt to offer a 'specialized encyclopaedic culture' or a
'portable library of similar texts' (for example, the medical sections of
the *Problemata* can be found in miscellaneous medical manuscripts).

Before starting the discussion of some medieval collections of
quaestiones naturales, I will briefly describe the different stages of the
development of the genre of the *quaestiones* literature within the Middle
Ages and the history of the reception of the texts which furnished the
pattern for the *quaestiones* and the *problemata* collections. Here, we do
not face a linear development or the reception and imitation of a standard work, but a stratified assimilation, where questions handed over by
different textual traditions integrate or overlap each other. The Late Antiquity hands over to the High Middle Ages a collection of *Problemata*,
which regroups 262 questions derived from the pseudo-Aristotelian text,
from Theophrastus, and from Alexander of Aphrodisia; a part of the
content can also be connected with the medical theories developed by
Hippocrates or Galen[5]. Some of these *quaestiones* can be found, in a

5. On the pseudo-Aristotelian *Problemata* see following editions: FLASHAR H.,
Aristoteles. Problemata Physica (Aristoteles Werke in deutscher Übersetzung 19), Ber-
lin: Akademie Verlag, 1962, p. 295-384 (esp. p. 372-382 on the Latin Tradition);
MARENGHI G., *Aristotele. Problemi di fonazione e di acustica*, Napoli: Libreria scientifica
editrice, 1962; MARENGHI G., *Aristotele. Problemi di medicina*, Milano: Istituto
Editoriale Italiano, 1966; MARENGHI G., *Aristotele. Problemi musicali*, Firenze: Sansoni,

Latin translation, in the manuscripts preserving the so-called *versio vetustissima*: this is the only form of the text read during the High Middle Ages[6]. A collection of *Problemata* is also transmitted by a Latin miscellaneous medical codex written in Germany during the eighth century, the so-called *Lorscher Arzneibuch*[7]. The version of the text preserved in this codex witnesses a combination of material derived from the pseudo-Aristotelian *Problemata* and from the *Problemata* attributed to Cassius Iatrosophista. The indirect tradition of the *Problemata* is especially represented by the use of the text shown by Macrobe in his *Saturnalia*[8].

Between the ninth and the twelfth centuries, the *Quaestiones salernitanae*, a popular scientific and medical text composed by various material derived from different sources, furnished a new approach to the natural world[9]. This text is characterized by an evident rationalism in the perception of nature, which emphasizes the possibility of giving a logical explanation to different kinds of natural phenomena, including some *mirabilia*. Another key feature of this text is the particular role played by medicine, anatomy, and physiology. The large presence of medical content in the *Quaestiones salernitanae* has lead some scholars to point to the existence of a connection between this text and the Medical School of Salerno; this 'supposed' connection also explains the current title given to the collection by modern scholarship. The relationship between the *Quaestiones salernitanae* and the texts written within the Medical

1958; MARENGHI G., *Aristotele. Profumi e miasmi*, Napoli: Arte tipografica editrice, 1991; LOUIS P., *Aristote, Problèmes*, Paris: Les Belles Lettres, 1991-1994, vol. I, p. VII-LIV.

6. A list of the manuscripts containing this version of the text can be found in: LACOMBE G. – BIRKENMAJER A. – DULONG M. – FRANCESCHINI A., *Aristoteles Latinus Codices*. Pars I, pars II, supplementa altera, Roma-Cambridge-Bruges-Paris: Libreria dello Stato/Desclée de Brouwer, 1939-1961, *passim*.

7. On the *Lorscher Arzneibuch* see following editions and studies: KEIL G. (ed.), *Das Lorscher Arzneibuch und die frühmittelalterliche Medizin. Verhandlungen des medizinhistorischen Symposiums im September 1989 in Lorsch*, Lorsch: Verlag Laurissa, 1991; KEIL G. (ed.), *Das Lorscher Arzneibuch. Faksimile der Handschrift Msc. Med. 1 der Staatsbibliothek Bamberg*, Stuttgart: Wiss. Verl. Gesellschaft, 1989, 2 vol.; STOLL U., *Das 'Lorscher Arzneibuch'. Ein medizinisches Kompendium des 8. Jahrhunderts (Codex Bambergensis Medicinalis 1). Text, Übersetzung und Fachglossar* (Sudhoffs Archiv, Beihefte 28), Stuttgart: Franz Steiner Verlag, 1992.

8. Cf. for instance WILLIS J. (ed.), *Macrobius, Saturnalia*, 7.13, 19-20, Lipsiae: In Aedibus B.G. Teubnerii, 1973. Here, Macrobe refers to *Problemata*, XXIII, 8.

9. LAWN, *The Salernitan Questions…*; *The Prose Salernitan Questions*. Edited from a Bodleian Manuscript (Auct. F.3.10) by B. LAWN (Auctores Britannici Medii Aevi 5), London: The British Academy – Oxford University Press, 1979. See also BALDWIN J.W., *The Language of Sex. Five Voices from Northern France around 1200* (The Chicago Series on Sexuality, History, and Society 1), Chicago-London: University of Chicago Press, 1994, *passim*.

School of Salerno is, however, more complex: the *Quaestiones salernitanae* show, in fact, an intricate manuscript tradition which implies the existence of an original small collection enlarged through the interpolation of new material derived from different sources, also from works related to the Salernitan Medical School. In the *Quaestiones salernitanae*, some aspects of the world of nature are gathered together and summarized in the form of questions followed by brief and clear answers, which perfectly summarize the dynamics of natural phenomena or describe the characteristics of some elements of nature.

The *Quaestiones salernitanae* were used, in an earlier and still unidentified form, by Adelard of Bath in his *Quaestiones naturales* and by William of Conches in his *Dragmaticon*; later, some questions originally belonging to these learned dialogues were incorporated into some versions of the *Quaestiones salernitanae*[10]. A collection of 'quaestiones naturales' is also included in the *Liber introductorius* written by Michael Scot[11]. The reception of the *Quaestiones salernitanae* continues, however, until the end of the Middle Ages, in different forms, e.g. as original text, as source for original collections, and finally as a reference text for the rich literature of scientific (especially medical) *quaestiones*. A certain interest for the literature of *naturales quaestiones* was also shown by the late medieval Italian literature: an Italian adaptation of Adelard of Bath's *Quaestiones naturales* is witnessed by two manuscripts written in Tuscany during the fourteenth century[12]. The success of the *Quaestiones salernitanae* was not limited to the lecture of the original text: also some encyclopaedic texts written in the thirteenth century such as Bartholomew the Englishman's *De proprietatibus rerum* or Thomas of Cantimpré's *De natura rerum* testify to the use of the collection.

10. On Adelard of Bath's *Quaestiones naturales* see BURNETT C. – RONCA I. – MANTAS ESPAÑA P. – VAN DEN ABEELE B., *Adelard of Bath, Conversations with his Nephew: On the Same and the Different. Questions on Natural Science and On Birds* (Cambridge Medieval Classics 9), Cambridge: Cambridge University Press, 1998. On William of Conches' *Dragmaticon* cf. RONCA I. – BADIA L. – PUJOL J. (eds.) *Guillelmus de Conchis, Dragmaticon* (Corpus Christianorum Continuatio Mediaevalis 152), Turnhout: Brepols Publishers, 1997. On both texts see SPEER A., 'Ratione duce. Die naturphilosophischen Dialoge des Adelard von Bath und des Wilhelm von Conches', in: K. JACOBI (ed.), *Gespräche lesen. Philosophische Dialoge im Mittelalter* (Scriptoralia 115), Tübingen: Günter Narr Verlag, 1999, p. 199-229.

11. Cf. THORNDIKE L., *Michael Scot*, London-Edinburgh: Nelson, 1965.

12. For this text see *«Questioni filosofiche» in volgare mediano dei primi del Trecento*. Edizione critica con commento linguistico a cura di F. GEYMONAT, Pisa: Scuola Normale Superiore, 2000, 2 vol.

The 'stratification process' ends with the translation of the genuine *Problemata*, completed by Bartholomew of Messina before 1265[13]. Bartholomew's translation, accomplished under the reign of King Manfred, the son of Frederick II, represents the only form of access the medieval culture had to the *Problemata*: a former translation by David of Dinant, a controversial philosopher whose *Quaternuli* were condemned by the Church and are preserved only in form of fragments, remained unknown[14]. The existence of the translation of the *Problemata*, whose text is now lost, is known only through Albert the Great's testimony in his *Politicorum libri VIII*[15].

Bartholomew's translation first became accessible when the most important encyclopaedic texts of the Late Middle Ages were already written; even the huge philosophic encyclopaedias written between the second half of the thirteenth and the end of the fourteenth century, like Henry Bate of Maline's *Speculum quorumdam rerum divinarum et naturalium*[16], Henry of Herford's *Catena aurea entium*[17], or Ramon Lull's *Arbor scientiae*[18], did not witness an extensive of the pseudo-Ar-

13. On Bartholomew of Messina see SELIGSOHN R., *Die Übersetzung der ps.-aristotelischen Problemata durch Bartholomaeus von Messina. Text und textkritische Untersuchungen zum ersten Buch*, Diss. Berlin, 1934; MARENGHI G., 'Un capitolo dell'Aristotele medievale: Bartolomeo da Messina traduttore dei "Problemata physica"', *Aevum* 36 (1962), p. 268-283; VENTURINI L., 'La traduzione latina di Bartolomeo da Messina del "De mirabilibus" dello Pseudo-Aristotele (dal codice Patav. Antoniano XVII 370)', *Atti dell'Accademia Patavina di Scienze, Lettere e Arti. Memorie della Classe di Scienze Morali, Lettere e Arti* 88/3 (1975-1976), p. 69-78; *Liber de pomo (Buch vom Apfel)*. Eingeleitet, übersetzt und kommentiert von E. ACAMPORA-MICHEL (Klostermann-Texte; Philosophie), Frankfurt a.M.: Klostermann, 2001.

14. On David of Dinant cf. SCHULTESS P. – IMBACH R., *Die Philosophie im lateinischen Mittelalter. Ein Handbuch mit einem bio-bibliographischen Repertorium*, Zürich-Düsseldorf: Artemis & Winckler, 1996, p. 140, 161 and 411-412; PICKAVÉ M., 'Zur Verwendung der Schriften des Aristoteles in den Fragmenten der *Quaternuli* des David von Dinant', *Recherches de Philosophie et Théologie Médiévales* 64 (1997), p. 199-221; CASADEI E., 'David di Dinant traduttore di Aristotele', *Freiburger Zeitschrift für Theologie* 45 (1998), p. 381-404.

15. BORGNET A. (ed.), *Albertus Magnus, Politicorum libri VIII*, Paris: Vivès, 1899, vol. VIII, here II, 7.

16. On Henry Bate of Malines see GULDENTOPS G., 'Henry Bate's Encyclopaedism', in: P. BINKLEY (ed.), *Pre-Modern Encyclopaedic Texts. Proceedings of the Second COMERS Congress, Groningen, 1-4 July 1996*, Leiden-New York-Köln: Brill, 1997, p. 227-237.

17. Cf. on this text SCHUMANN K.P., *Heinrich von Herford. Enzyklopädische Gelehrsamkeit und universalhistorische Konzeption im Dienste dominikanischer Studienbedürfnisse* (Veröffentlichungen der Historischen Kommission für Westfalen. Quellen und Forschungen zur Kirchen- und Religionsgeschichte 4), Münster: Aschendorff, 1996, p. 53-70.

18. See on this encyclopaedia DOMÍNGUEZ REBOIRAS F. – VILLALBA VARNEDA P. – WALTER P. (eds.), *Arbor scientiae. Der Baum des Wissens von Ramon Lull. Akten des*

istotelian work. The difficult access to the content, its complex structure and maybe the suspicion that the original work could not be authentic, probably did not encourage its use. The few exceptions are represented by some commentaries, among them the huge exposition written by Peter of Abano between the end of the thirteenth century and 1310 and also preserved in the version composed by John of Jandun[19], by the literary genre of the medical *quaestiones*, and by some late medieval or early modern encyclopaedic texts which will be discussed in the next pages.

Among the encyclopaedias written between 1300 and 1500 and influenced by the *Problemata* and, in general, by collections of *quaestiones naturales*, we can distinguish the following types of texts[20]:

a) Some 'popular' encyclopaedias concerning both science and medicine written between 1350 and 1400, whose aim was to offer to the readers a better knowledge not only of the natural world, but specifically of their own body, and to provide rules for the preservation of health and for the correct use of the elements of nature, for example in form of food, drink, or medical remedy[21]. Among these encyclopaedias, we find the *Problemata Aristotelis ac philosophorum medicorumque complurium* (known also as *Summa 'Omnes homines'*, a title derived from the *incipit*, that is the famous Aristotle's sentence concerning the human thirst for knowledge), the *Responsorium curiosorum*, the *Summa recreatorum*, the *Mensa philosophica*.

b) Two moralizing encyclopaedias written by members of the Dominican order, namely the *Lumen animae*, whose first version (we know of three) was composed between 1300 and 1320 by Beranger de Landorre, and Conrad of Halberstadt's *Liber similitudinum naturalium*, a work which can be dated between 1340 and 1350. Both works are collections of *similitudines naturales* written for the needs of preachers to

Internationalen Kongresses aus Anlaß des 40-jährigen Jubiläums des RAIMUNDUS-LULLUS-INSTITUTS der Universität Freiburg i. Br. (Instrumenta Patristica et Mediaevalia. Research on the Inheritance of Early and Medieval Christianity, XLII. Subsidia Lulliana 1), Turnhout: Brepols Publishers, 2002.

19. On Peter of Abano cf. G. FEDERICI VESCOVINI's contribution in this volume. On John of Jandun's version of the commentary to the *Problemata* see KUKSEWICZ Z., 'Les *Problemata* de Pietro d'Abano et leur "rédaction" par Jean de Jandun', *Medioevo* 11 (1985), p. 113-137.

20. On these works see VENTURA, '*Quaestiones* and Encyclopaedias...'.

21. The pseudo-Aristotelian *Problemata* are also to be found among the sources of an Italian *regimen sanitatis*, viz. Michele Savonarola's *Libreto de tutte le cosse che se magnano*. Cf. on this text the edition published by NYSTEDT J. (ed.), *Michele Savonarola, Libreto de tutte le cosse che se magnano; un'opera di dietetica del sec. XV* (Acta Universitatis Stockolmiensis. Romanica Stockolmiensia 13), Stockholm: Alqvist & Wiksell International, 1988.

provide them examples drawn from the natural world which could be related to human vices and virtues. In both works, the *Problemata* are used as a scientific source which supports the explanation of natural phenomena; the two texts, however, show some differences in the role played by the *Problemata* as source and, in general, in the interpretation and the treatment of the reference text.

c) An Early Renaissance encyclopaedia where the section devoted to medicine ends with a book composed of medical questions. The mammoth encyclopaedia (divided into 49 books) written by Giorgio Valla and published posthumously in 1501, the *De expetendis et fugiendis rebus*, closes its large section devoted to medicine (Books 24-30) with Book 30, a collection composed of 150 *quaestiones*. The insertion of scientific and medical questions into a humanistic encyclopaedia witnesses some intriguing phenomena, which deserve a closer discussion, viz. the interest shown by the humanist for medical culture and the discussion of the texts transmitting it, and the re-discovery of the Greek production of scientific works, which lead to a conflict with the Latin background inherited from the Middle Ages. Valla's encyclopaedia can be used in this context as a good witness not only to examine the role played by the *Problemata* literature during the fifteenth and the sixteenth century, but also to analyze the Renaissance medical culture and its sources.

1. The 'Popular Encyclopaedias' between the Late Middle Ages and the Renaissance

Let us commence with examining the first type, the texts we define as 'popular encyclopaedias' both because of the success achieved by some of them (e.g. by the *Problemata Aristotelis* and by the *Mensa philosophica*) and because of their content, which supposed a well-educated reader, but not necessarily a person specialized in medicine or science. The *Problemata Aristotelis ac medicorum complurium* (viz. the *Summa 'Omnes homines'*) is an anonymous collection of ca. 350 *quaestiones* concerning nature divided into 34 sections organized *a capite ad calcem* devoted to different aspects of human anatomy and physiology[22]. Each of them deals with a single aspect of human

22. Edition: *Problemata Aristotelis philosophorum ac medicorum complurium*, Paris: pro Alexandro Alyate, 1501. Cf. on this text SCHLEISSNER M., 'Sexuality and Reproduction in the Late Medieval "Problemata Aristotelis"', in: J. DOMES - W.D. GERABECK – B.D. HAAGE (eds.), *Licht der Natur. Medizin in Fachliteratur und Dichtung. Festschrift für Gundolf Keil zum 60. Geburtstag* (Göppinger Arbeiten zur Germanistik 585),

anatomy, moving from the head to the sexual organs, and the problems related to conception, the embryo and birth; some changes in the order, in the number, and in the content of questions included in each section characterize the different editions[23]. This first group of questions closes with the explanations of problems related to abortion and birth of monstrous beings, such as *hermafrodita* and *monstra*. A second part begins with questions concerning some *curiosa* of nature and has two functions: to continue with some aspects of human physiology which were neglected in the previous section, and to make a change of subject to draw the attention of the readers to some natural phenomena. Here, we find a small number of various *quaestiones*, separated from the rest of the collection by some introductory lines. Their structure and content may change in different manuscripts or printed versions: while the printed texts in this section include 28 questions, the version preserved in a Bolognese manuscript to which we will return, comprised 45 problems, followed by two paragraphs concerning animal eggs and the influence of the planets on human birth. The text had considerable success between 1350 and 1700, and we know of many manuscripts and about 20 printed editions (the first published probably in 1475). The *Summa 'Omnes Homines'* was translated into German, French and English, and was reprinted until the twentieth century. The sources of the *Summa 'Omnes Homines'* can be identified among medical texts, viz. in the *Quaestiones salernitanae*, in Hippocrates' *Aphorismi* and in the pseudo-Galenic work *De semine*, in Avicenna's *Liber canonis*, and in Constantine the African's translations. Zoological data are drawn from the Aristotelian *De animalibus*, and from Albert the Great's *De animalibus* and *Quaestiones super de animalibus*. The pseudo-Aristotelian *Problemata* are not frequently used: the role as reference texts is played by the *Quaestiones salernitanae*, a work which might have been considered as easily accessible and understandable, even by not specialized readers. We can recognize the presence of the pseudo-Aristotelian *Problemata* only in the last section of the work, a kind of *appendix* which does not deal with medicine and human physiology, but with questions generally related to the world of nature. A different status of the text is witnessed, to my knowledge, only by the version of the text preserved in a Bolognese manuscript and bearing the title *Problemata varia anatomica*:

Göppingen: Kümmerle Verlag, 1994, p. 383-396; BLAIR A., *The Theatre of Nature. Jean Bodin and Renaissance Science*, Princeton, New Jersey: Princeton University Press, 1997, *passim*; BLAIR, 'Authorship...'; BLAIR, 'The *Problemata*...'; VENTURA, '*Quaestiones* and Encyclopaedias...'.

23. Cf. BLAIR, 'Authorship...', p. 201-202.

the anonymous author of this version, who wrote in the fifteenth century, showed a more developed interest not only for the pseudo-Aristotelian *Problemata*, but also for a more specialized medical and scientific academic culture[24]. He also included in his collection a section discussing the influence of planets on human generation and birth, stressing a combination between medicine and astrology and a need of discussing both topics that the other collections do not reflect. The anonymous author shows his well-developed scientific culture and his knowledge of an academic milieu in different ways: the problems he puts together in the last section, for example, do not only concern problems related to everyday life, which might have been interesting for a larger public, but some more specialized questions to be discussed in an University *aula*. Moreover, his references to the sources are more precise, pointing not only to the author, but also to the title of the text, to the section, and to the chapter (e.g. 'ut dicit Avicenna primo Canonis fen prima de humoribus' or 'solutio vicesima problematum 54 problemate'): this way of reproducing references, which is not witnessed by the manuscripts and by the printed version of the vulgate version of the *Problemata Aristotelis*, where we find only some general indications like 'ut dicit Aristoteles', 'secundum Albertum' etc., is adopted in order to allow the readers to verify the references in the original sources. These texts, obviously, ought to be accessible in the library the readers used; on the other hand, the readers also had to be well acquainted with them.

The *Responsorium curiosorum*, the *Summa recreatorum* and the *Mensa philosophica* can be considered together, because they share the same purpose and the same aim of the author[25]. Here, the collection of scientific data is written in order to provide the readers with some useful material which could be used during a conversation; the presence of the scientific arguments gathered together in the encyclopaedia can transform the convivial situation into an occasion not only of entertainment,

24. Edition of this text in LIND L.R., *Problemata Varia Anatomica. The University of Bologna, MS 1165* (Humanistic Studies 38), Lawrence: The University of Kansas Publications, 1968.

25. Editions: *Responsorium curiosorum*, Lübeck: Lucas Brandis, 1476; *Mensa Philosophica. Faksimile und Kommentar.* Herausgegeben von E. RAUNER und B. WACHINGER, in Verbindung mit C. RUPRECHT-ALEXANDER und F. SCHANZE (Fortuna Vitrea 13), Tübingen: Max Niemeyer Verlag, 1995. The *Summa recreatorum* was never printed. For a list of the manuscripts containing this work, see RAUNER E., 'Summa recreatorum', in: *Die deutsche Literatur des Mittelalters. Verfasserlexikon* IX, Berlin-New York: De Gruyter, 1981, col. 503-506. A critical edition is currently prepared by D. Ruzickova (Brno).

but also of cultural and spiritual progress[26]. The meaning of the conversation for the transmission and the diffusion of culture, and the important role played by science within a social occasion is stressed by the anonymous authors in their Prologues[27]. The concrete purpose of the works and the close relationship between the material included in the collections and its practical use during a conversation is, however, made evident by the choice of the discussed topics: the problems the works deal with reflect natural phenomena the readers could experience and verify in everyday life, with the characteristics of their own bodies, or include information concerning important aspects of human life such as food, drink, sleep etc.

Let us firstly sketch the structure of these texts. The *Responsorium curiosorum*, preserved only in the printed version published in Lübeck in 1476, is a collection of 881 *problemata* divided into four books and opened by a General Prologue, where the anonymous author explains structure and aim of his work[28]. The interest of the compiler focuses on the human and the animal body: Books 2, 3, 4 are respectively dedicated to the anatomy of living beings, both human beings and animals *a capite ad calcem* (Book 2), to the human anatomy *a capite ad calcem* (together with some aspects of human life such as food, drink, and the properties of the eye and sight; Book 3), to the world of animals (Book 4). On the contrary, the whole world of nature (meteorology, precious stones, plants etc.) is comprised in the first book, and considered as a unitary complex opposed to the living beings. The number of questions included in the books varies from section to section: while the first, the second, and the fourth book respectively comprise 214, 142, and 182 questions,

26. WACHINGER B., '*Convivium Fabulosum*. Erzählen bei Tisch im 15. und 16. Jahrhundert, besonders in der *Mensa Philosophica* und bei Erasmus und Luther', in: W. HAUG – B. WACHINGER (eds.), *Kleinere Erzählformen des 15. und 16. Jahrhunderts* (Fortuna Vitrea 8), Tübingen: Max Niemeyer Verlag, 1993, p. 256-286; WACHINGER B., *Erzählen für die Gesundheit. Diätetik und Literatur im Mittelalter* (Schriften der Philosophisch-historischen Klasse der Heidelberger Akademie der Wissenschaften 23), Heidelberg: Carl Winter Verlag, 2001.

27. For the Prologue of the *Summa recreatorum*, see WACHINGER, *Erzählen...*, p. 43. The prologue of the *Mensa philosophica* has been reprinted in *Mensa philosophica...*, p. 9-10.

28. Reproduction of the Prologue in: VENTURA I., 'Der "Liber similitudinum naturalium" Konrads von Halberstadt und seine Quellen: ein Fallbeispiel aus der naturwissenschaftlichen Textüberlieferung im Spätmittelalter', *Frühmittelalterliche Studien* 35 (2001), p. 349-406, here p. 406. On the *Responsorium curiosorum*, see also SCHIPPERGES H., 'Handschriftliche Untersuchungen zur Rezeption des Petrus Hispanus in die "Opera Ysaac" (Lyon 1515)', in: G. KEIL – R. RUDOLF – W. SCHMITT – H.J. VERMEER (eds.), *Fachliteratur des Mittelalters. Festschrift für Gerhard Eis*, Stuttgart: Metzler, 1968, p. 311-318 and VENTURA, '*Quaestiones* and Encyclopaedias...'.

the third section, which is devoted to the human body, is divided into 343 problems! At first glance, this variation in the number of questions seems to destroy the internal equilibrium of the collection; however, it also clearly shows the main interests of the compiler and the bulk of the work, which is represented by medicine, human anatomy, and physiology.

The principal sources are mentioned in the General Prologue: the author declares he has drawn his material from pseudo-Aristotelian *Problemata*, from Albert the Great's works (e.g. the *De animalibus*, the *Quaestiones super de animalibus*, the *De proprietatibus elementorum*, and the *De mineralibus*), from Roger Bacon's *Perspectiva*, from Constantin the African's *Viaticum*, and from the commentary to this work written by Peter of Spain.

The *Summa recreatorum* is preserved in five manuscripts. Written before 1412, it is a collection of both scientific and literary material which can be used during a conversation at table[29]. The encyclopaedia consists of five books: the first (arranged in a question-answer form) and the second books establish a relationship between enjoyment at table (*recreatio mensalis*) and a correct knowledge of food and dietetics, while the other three books are devoted to the different kinds of conversation which can be developed at table. Therefore, Book 3 gathers together some scientific topics, dealing especially with medicine and nutrition, around which the *quaestiones mensales* can be developed. This section can be defined, because of its content, as a kind of small *regimen sanitatis*. The last two books leave aside science, to turn the interest to literature and spirituality: therefore, Book 4 gathers together some *iocundae historiae* and *laeta carmina*, while the whole of Book 5 is devoted to some *virtuosa exempla*. The *Mensa philosophica*, on the other hand, is divided into four books and was probably composed during the second half of the fifteenth century. The first book discusses eating habits, and concerns different kinds of food (bread, wine, meat, vegetables etc.), the right time to eat and the order of meals. The second gathers together different typologies of *exempla* organized according to the social class of one's table companions. The third section is devoted to some dietetic *quaestiones* organized into 13 chapters dealing with all kinds of food. The work ends with a collection of sentences, a *florilegium* composed

---

29. On this text cf. WACHINGER, *Erzählen...*; VENTURA, '*Quaestiones* and Encyclopaedias...'; BAUMANN W., *Die Literatur des Mittelalters in Böhmen: deutsch-lateinisch-tschechische Literatur vom 10. bis zum 15. Jahrhundert* (Veröffentlichungen des Collegium Carolinum 37), München-Wien: Oldenburg, 1978, p. 193-194.

for the purpose of entertaining table companions. The sources of both texts can be identified in the pseudo-Aristotelian *Problemata* and in the *Quaestiones salernitanae*, in Albert the Great's *Quaestiones super de animalibus* and in Peter of Spain's *De animalibus*, as well as in some medical or dietetic texts such as Isaac Israeli's *De diaetis*, Avicenna's *Cantica* with the commentary written by Averroes, Arnald of Villanova's *Regimen Sanitatis*, Constantin the African's *De gradibus*, and Rhazes' *Liber ad Almansorem*. The *Summa recreatorum* and the *Mensa philosophica* show very close similarities in the content: Book I of the *Mensa philosophica* reproduces, with few exceptions, the content of Books II and III of the *Summa recreatorum*, while the third book of the *Mensa* reflects, with small differences, the sequence of questions included in the first section of the *Summa recreatorum*. The close relationship between the two collections can be explained with the fact that both derived their material from a common source, probably a small encyclopaedia written in the German-speaking area during the second half of the fourteenth century. The work, which has not been identified yet, might have been one of the sources of the *Responsorium curiosorum*.

In the *Responsorium*, as well as in the *Summa recreatorum* and in the *Mensa philosophica*, the pseudo-Aristotelian *Problemata* are one of the principal sources; they are, however, considered and used together with a group of extremely specialized medical and scientific works which show the cultural level of the compiler and his aim to collect data related to 'technical' texts more than to the cultural background established, for example, by the encyclopaedias of the thirteenth century. If we consider, for instance, the presence of works like Peter of Spain's *Problemata*, Rhazes' *Liber ad Almansorem*, or Avicenna's *Cantica*, we notice that the cultural background of the compilers was close to the *curriculum studiorum* of the Faculties of Medicine of Paris and Montpellier, although no evidence can be found in the texts about the studies accomplished by these authors. The same level of cultural background was probably expected to be shared by the readers, too. To enjoy the reading of these works, they might have had at least some knowledge of medicine and natural science. Thus, although these encyclopaedias may be defined as 'popular works', the cultural *niveau* of their readers should have been relatively high[30]. A clue pointing to the cultural level of the

30. On the concept of 'popularization of science' cf. KRETSCHMANN C., 'Einleitung. Wissenspopularisierung – ein altes, neues Forschungsfeld', in: C. KRETSCHMANN (ed.), *Wissenspopularisierung. Konzepte der Wissensverbreitung im Wandel* (Wissenskultur und Gesellschaftlicher Wandel 4), Berlin: Akademie Verlag, 2003, p. 7-21.

public of these collections can also be found in the presence of the pseudo-Aristotelian *Problemata* among the sources: this work, in fact, cannot be as easily read as the *Quaestiones salernitanae*, and its interpretation requires certain skills and a solid scientific culture. Therefore, if we compare the structure and the content of the *Summa 'Omnes homines'* with the group of texts represented by the *Responsorium curiosorum*, the *Summa recreatorum*, and the *Mensa philosophica*, we may notice that they are not situated on the same cultural *niveau*.

On the other hand, these collections shared some common features, which allow us to affirm that they all shared a very pragmatic aim: their content is, in fact, oriented to the everyday life, and their attention focuses on the human body, on its characteristics, on the rules which should be followed for the preservation of health, while the world of nature represents only the frame of the encyclopaedia. These works can be considered as human-oriented encyclopaedias, where the centre of the text is represented by the sciences related to the human body, e.g. medicine, anatomy, dietetics, and physiognomy; the world of nature, viz. plants, precious stones, and aspects of meteorology are completely neglected, or else only described when related to their effects on the human body and their role within human life. The 'human orientation' is especially evident in the *Summa 'Omnes homines'*, which presents itself as a kind of 'handbook for private lecture', or as a sort of small encyclopaedia, whose data are compiled with the aim of providing a useful cultural background which can come in handy in everyday life: for example, for practical purposes like a more correct nurture or a better knowledge of one's own body and its characteristics. The same 'pragmatic' purpose of the scientific culture is also shown by the *Responsorium curiosorum* whose structure, however, reflects and reproduces the *ordo rerum*, the hierarchy of the parts of nature (non organic, organic, animal, human world) handed over by medieval encyclopaedias, more than a human-centred path. Finally, the human orientation takes another aspect in the *Summa recreatorum* and in the *Mensa philosophica*: here, the combination between scientific and cultural elements is more closely connected with the idea of spiritual improvement; we can argue that in this case, the encyclopaedia becomes a *vademecum*, a collection of data gathered together with the aim of furnishing not only scientific culture, but a spiritual background, of providing a bodily and spiritual *regimen*.

Finally, it can be suggested that in the case of the mentioned encyclopaedias, the representation of nature through a group of questions – or better, of *problemata* – has the function of displaying science in a clearer and more attractive way, and not of describing natural phenomena as an enigma to be solved with the help of logic. Here, the representation of nature is related to the aim of delighting the readers by presenting to them the world of nature and the features of their bodies in a dynamic way, emphasizing all phenomena taking place within and around them, even the most curious ones. This form of delight, however, is only a first step to the acquisition of knowledge, since it should be transformed into an occasion of cultural and spiritual improvement. The choice of the question-answer form helps, in this context, to reach this goal by awakening the curiosity of the readers, by providing delight, by allowing them to learn quickly, so that they can reach the cultural and spiritual progress aimed at.

2. The Preachers' Encyclopaedias and the Moralization of the Problemata

By turning our attention to the second type of encyclopaedias influenced by the pseudo-Aristotelian *Problemata*, we must firstly notice that in this case we face a very limited number of texts, which can be referred to a particular cultural and spiritual milieu. The two collections we will examine are, to my knowledge, the only encyclopaedias written for preachers witnessing the use of the pseudo-Aristotelian *Problemata* and, more generally, a developed interest for natural science. The background of sources the compilers used is large, comprises some highly specialized texts, and points to a very skilled scientific education. Moreover, both works were written by Dominican friars, viz. by two members of a Mendicant Order known to have shown a special interest for natural philosophy and science[31].

Beranger of Landorre (died 1330), a Dominican friar who later became the *vicarius generalis* of the Order and archbishop of Compostela, wrote his *Lumen animae* between 1300 and 1320. The text, a moralizing encyclopaedia organized alphabetically according to the *significata* (vices and virtues), is divided into three books, the first of which is a small collection of moralizations of elements of nature gathered in 73 lemmas regarding God, Christ, the Virgin Mary, and some vices and vir-

---

31. Cf. FRENCH R. – CUNNINGHAM A., *Before Science. The Invention of Friars' Natural Philosophy*, Aldershot: Scolar Press, 1996.

tues[32], while the second and the third books are, respectively, a treatise concerning vices and virtues where moral aspects of human life are represented in form of personifications, and a *florilegium* of literary *auctoritates* heavily depending upon Thomas of Ireland's *Manipulus florum*[33]. The work is preserved in three different versions; my own researches are, for the moment, based on the so-called *versio B*, viz. a later redaction of the text composed around 1332 by Gottfried of Vorau, and preserved in only three manuscripts and three incunabula. The world of nature is the object of the first section: here vices and virtues, as well as Christ or the Virgin Mary, are compared with rain, wind, precious stones, and other aspects of nature. Pseudo-Aristotelian *Problemata* are one of the principal sources of this book, together with some of pseudo-Albert the Great's works (among others, the *De mineralibus* and the *De impressionibus aeris*); surprising is also the mention of Theophrastus, a Greek philosopher and scientist whose works became famous only in the Renaissance[34]. These texts, however, are only a part of the huge corpus of sometimes extremely rare or specialized reference texts used by the compiler; a list of them is given by him in the Prologue of the work. Sometimes, however, the authors quoted by Beranger cannot be identified; therefore, some scholars argued that the compiler included some names of fictive authors, maybe in order to increase the importance of

32. On the literary genre of the moralized encyclopaedias see WELTER J. TH., *L'exemplum dans la littérature religieuse et didactique du Moyen Age*, Paris-Toulouse: Occitania, 1927 (repr. Genève: Slatkine, 1973); MEYER H., 'Zum Verhältnis von Enzyklopädik und Allegorese im Mittelalter', *Frühmittelalterliche Studien* 24 (1990), p. 290-313; MEYER H., *Die Enzyklopädie des Bartholomäus Anglicus. Untersuchungen zur Überlieferungs- und Rezeptionsgeschichte von 'De proprietatibus rerum'* (Münstersche Mittelalter-Schriften 77), München: Fink Verlag, 2000, p. 296-324; VAN DEN ABEELE B., 'Moralisierte Enzyklopädien in der Nachfolge von Bartholomäus Anglicus: das "Multifarium" in Wolfenbüttel und der "Liber de exemplis et similitudinibus rerum" des Johannes de Sancto Geminiano', in: C. MEIER (ed.), *Die Enzyklopädie im Wandel vom Hochmittelalter bis zur frühen Neuzeit. Akten des Kolloquiums des Projekts D im Sonderforschungsbereich 231 (29.11.-1.12. 1996)*, München: Fink, 2002, p. 278-304.

33. Edition: *Lumen Animae*, Straßburg: Drucker der "Legenda Aurea", 1482. On this text, see ROUSE R.H. – ROUSE M.A., 'The Text called *Lumen Animae*', *Archivum Fratrum Praedicatorum* 41 (1971), p. 5-113; VENTURA, '*Quaestiones* and Encyclopaedias...'; VENTURA I., 'Die moralisierten Enzyklopädien des späteren Mittelalters: ein Überblick unter Berücksichtigung der Fallbeispiele des «Lumen Anime», des «Liber de exemplis et similitudinibus rerum» und des «Liber Similitudinum Naturalium»', *Reti Medievali: Rivista* 4 (2003) (to read on www.retimedievali.it).

34. SHARPLES R.W., 'Some Medieval and Renaissance Citations of Theophrastus', *Journal of the Warburg and Courtauld Institutes* 47 (1984), p. 186-190; SHARPLES R.W., 'Snow Blindness and Underground Fish-Migration', *Journal of the Warburg and Courtauld Institutes* 51 (1988), p. 181-184.

the cultural background of his work[35]. This hypothesis, I daresay, is not convincing: the quotation of fictive authors is, in fact, a strategy the Dominican compilers do not adopt, since it would have diminished the value of the scientific data included in the collection. Moreover, Beranger of Landorre was *lector physicae*; he must have achieved a good knowledge of natural science, since he seems to have used all the works he mentioned at first hand and not through other collections or encyclopaedia, and to have been acquainted with authors like Theophrastus. Thus, an insertion of fictive authors seems rather improbable; perhaps some names were disfigured by later copyists.

As far as the treatment of the *Problemata* as source concerns, we can notice that Beranger seems to have been well acquainted with the text, and to consider it useful. He draws scientific data not only from the books dedicated to medicine or physiognomy, but from the whole text; he derives the largest part of his material from the meteorological sections. His way of inserting and using the *Problemata*, however, does not suggest a real understanding of the text and of its logical background: the quotations of the text are shortened, if compared to the original work, Aristotle's explanation is summarized, and the special approach to the world of nature and the logic explanation of natural phenomena made possible by Aristotelian logic has not been recognized. The superficial use of the pseudo-Aristotelian *Problemata* should not be connected with a low evaluation of the text, but, more generally, with the small role played by natural science in the *Lumen anime*. For its compiler, the bulk and the purpose of the collection are not represented by the description and the scientific interpretation of the natural phenomena, but by their possible moralization, and by the correct connection with a moral lesson to be used during the sermon.

Conrad of Halberstadt (died after 1355), a German Dominican friar who also was one of the first members of the *Studium generale* in Prague, designed with his *Liber similitudinum naturalium*, a collection of *similitudines naturales* divided into six books written around 1350, a completely different project[36]. His *Liber similitudinum naturalium* can be defined as a twofold work: the first five books consist of a collection based upon the *Liber de exemplis et similitudinibus rerum* composed by

35. Cf. ROUSE, 'The Text...'.

36. On this text, see VENTURA, 'Der *Liber similitudinum naturalium*...'; VENTURA, '*Quaestiones* and Encyclopaedias...'. I am currently preparing a critical edition of this work; cf. VENTURA I., *Il Liber similitudinum naturalium di Corrado di Halberstadt*, Phd. Diss. Firenze, 1998 (unpublished).

John of San Gimignano at the beginning of the fourteenth century[37], while the sixth one is devoted to a moralization of the whole content of the *Problemata*, as the author declares in his Prologue. All the books share the same structure, since they are organized alphabetically according to the human vices and virtues the compiler wanted to represent through some aspects of the natural world. The meaning the *Problemata* had for the compiler is also made evident by the content of the sixth book: 100 of its 107 lemmas are based on scientific material drawn from the pseudo-Aristotelian work. The others deal with medicine and optics, and show the use of Avicenna's *Cantica* and *De medicinis cordialibus*, of Roger Bacon's *Perspectiva*, and of John Peckham's *Perspectiva communis*. The combination of natural problems, medicine, and optics, and the correspondent use of some types of sources belonging to the University *curriculum studiorum* more than to the background of the preacher's encyclopaedias suggests that Conrad of Halberstadt might have had at disposal a rich scientific library, and that natural science plays an important role in his culture and, consequently, in his work. In the *Liber similitudinum naturalium*, the *Problemata* are the principal source of the sixth book, and one of the most important reference texts of the whole collection; the text was also used by the compiler, together with other sources such as Albert the Great's works, to insert some new data into the first five books, and to 'update' the scientific background provided by John of San Gimignano. Moreover, the content is copied so extensively that some chapters can be used for an eventual collation of the pseudo-Aristotelian text; a short comparison between the content of the *Liber similitudinum* and the transcription of Book I published by R. Seligsohn in 1934 suggests that the manuscript used by Conrad was related with the codex Erfurt, Universitätsbibliothek, Coll. Amploniana, MS Fol. 16[38]. In the *Liber similitudinum*, all sections of the *Problemata* are represented, even the books dedicated to acoustics and music, rhetoric and physics; the sections dedicated to medicine are, however, more extensively used than the other ones. Last but not least, he seems to have been acquainted not only with the pseudo-Aristotelian text translated by Bartholomew of Messina, but also with the indirect tradition represented by Macrobe's *Saturnalia*.

The most interesting aspect of the presence of the *Problemata* in the encyclopaedia written by Conrad of Halberstadt is, on the other hand,

---

37. On John of San Gimignano, cf. VAN DEN ABEELE, 'Moralisierte Enzyklopädien...', p. 288-296.

38. SELIGSOHN, *Die Übersetzung...*

the role played by the source within a collection composed for preachers: firstly, by devoting a whole book to the *Problemata* and organizing it like the other ones, he tries to combine two literary genres, the moralized encyclopaedia and the allegorization of a complete scientific work, creating a mixed product which presupposes from his public a high-level scientific culture and certain skills in connecting the complete dynamic of a natural phenomenon with an allegorical meaning. Second, by reading the *Liber similitudinum naturalium*, we can recognize that the compiler is more interested in reproducing the scientific content of the *Problemata* than in moralizing it: the lemmas usually offer a very short and banal allegorization, which is confined to some general features of the single items without reflecting the whole description of natural phenomena derived from the *Problemata*. Therefore, we can argue that Conrad aims at providing a scientific *compendium*, a 'scientific library' for preachers, more than an allegorical tool for the homiletics. In this sense, Beranger of Landorre and Conrad of Halberstadt may have shared the use of the same source, viz. the *Problemata*, but not the same goals.

Some final considerations can be made: is it a chance that two Dominican compilers use the *Problemata* in the same context, viz. within the homiletic culture? Moreover, could it be considered as a chance that both texts are diffused in the German-speaking area, where also the other encyclopaedias, namely the *Summa 'Omnes homines'*, the *Responsorium curiosorum*, and the *Mensa philosophica* were written? At the moment, it is not possible to answer these questions; however, it can be suggested that the success and the influence of the *Problemata* considered as scientific text in the German libraries and in the works written in the German-speaking area represent two interesting cultural phenomena, which might have been connected. Moreover, the fact that two Dominican compilers use the pseudo-Aristotelian *Problemata* for two preachers' encyclopaedias can also be related with the meaning that natural science had for the Dominican culture and also for their activity as preachers. As it has been pointed out by R. French and A. Cunningham, the Dominican order was characterized by a deep interest for natural science, which led their members to privilege scientific studies more than any other Mendicant order[39].

Nevertheless, the meaning of the *Problemata* and, more generally, of a highly specialized scientific culture within the Dominican order should not be overestimated. Actually, I have not found neither a clue of a con-

---

39. FRENCH – CUNNINGHAM, *Before Science...*, esp. p. 173-201 (Chapter 8: *Dominican Education*).

crete use of the pseudo-Aristotelian *Problemata* within the literary genre of the sermons, nor any other quotations of the work as a reference text in other tools written for preachers; I have not found any traces of a large diffusion of the text within the Dominican libraries either. Moreover, the presence of the *Problemata* in a preachers' encyclopaedia presupposes a high-level culture not only from the preacher, but also from the public of his sermon; in other terms, the public targeted for this type of collections of *similitudines naturales* must have been extremely competent. The relatively limited public who could have access to this scientific material may explain the small success of the *Problemata* and of the collections based on this work within the homiletic literature: while the *Lumen anime* enjoyed a very big success only with its latest version (the so-called *versio C*), which is characterized by a substantial exemplification of the content, Conrad's *Liber similitudinum naturalium* is preserved only in the manuscript Berlin, SBPK, Theol. Lat. Fol. 315. Thus, despite the efforts made by the two Dominican friars, we can argue that the pseudo-Aristotelian *Problemata* never became part of the cultural background of the preachers, and were not used for the redaction of sermons. On the contrary, they only became part of the well-stocked 'virtual library of scientific texts' owned by the Dominican order.

3. Giorgio Valla's Medical Encyclopaedia and the Role of the Problemata in the Humanistic Scientific Culture

To analyze the third type, we reach the world of the Renaissance encyclopaedia. Giorgio Valla's work, the *De expetendis et fugiendis rebus*, published posthumously in 1501, is a mammoth encyclopaedia divided into 49 books and arranged according to the seven liberal arts[40]. The sequence of the books, however, does not follow the usual structure provided by the *trivium* and the *quadrivium*, but the opposite order; the en-

---

40. Edition: Georgius Valla, *De expetendis et fugiendis rebus*, Venetiis: Aldus Romanus, 1501, 4 vol. On this encyclopaedia, see *Giorgio Valla tra scienza e sapienza*. Studi di G. GARDENAL, P. LANDUCCI RUFFO, C. VASOLI. Raccolti e presentati da V. BRANCA, Firenze: Olschki, 1981; ZEDELMAIER H., *Bibliotheca universalis et bibliotheca selecta. Das Problem der Ordnung des gelehrten Wissens in der frühen Neuzeit* (Beihefte zum Archiv von Kulturgeschichte 33), Köln-Weimar-Wien: Böhlau, 1992; VENTURA, '*Quaestiones* and Encyclopaedias...'; MAURO L., 'La "musica del polso" in alcuni trattati del Quattrocento', in: C. CASAGRANDE – S. VECCHIO (eds.), *Anima e corpo nella cultura medievale. Atti del V Convegno di Studi della Società Italiana per lo Studio del Pensiero Medievale (Venezia, 25-28 settembre 1995)* (Millennio Medievale 15; Atti di Convegni 3), Firenze: SISMEL-Edizioni del Galluzzo, 1999, p. 235-257, esp. p. 244-248.

cyclopaedia opens with natural science and ends with the branches of knowledge related to the *trivium*. Thus, the first three books are devoted to mathematics, the following five to music, the next six to geometry and optics; the section related to natural science ends with four books dedicated to astronomy and astrology. The medical part of the encyclopaedia consists of four books devoted to physiology, and of seven dealing with medicine. This section is completed by a book of *naturales quaestiones*. The small collection of *quaestiones* has, I argue, two functions: firstly, it integrates the section devoted to medicine; secondly, it separates the part of the encyclopaedia dealing with natural science from the following one dedicated to the *trivium*, to ethics, and to politics. This part is structured as follows: after four books dealing with grammar, three concerning dialectic, one devoted to poetic, and two to rhetoric, the author comes to treat the *moralis philosophia* (one book), the *oeconomica* (four books), the *politica* (one book). The encyclopaedia ends with four books *de corporis commodis et incommodis* dedicated to the soul and, again, to some medical topics, and with a section *de rebus externis*.

Medicine is one of Valla's main interests, and represents one of the largest sections of the encyclopaedia. That does not surprise us when we consider that Valla was a physician, translated Galen's medical works, and was the first editor of Aetius of Amida's œuvre. His skilled medical culture, as well as his deep knowledge of Greek medicine, is perfectly reflected by the encyclopaedia: among his sources we find Galen's works (which can be identified as the principal reference text), Hippocrates, Paul of Egina, and Aetius of Amida. What, however, surprises the modern reader of Valla's encyclopaedia, is the fact that the medical section closes with a collection of 150 *quaestiones*. The aim of this section, the author affirms in the small Prologue opening the book, is to integrate the discussion of medicine by taking up some *ambiguitates naturales* which had not been explained in the previous books[41]. The collection is divided in two parts, and it is not strictly medical: the first

41. Giorgio Valla, *De expetendis et fugiendis rebus*, XXX, Prologus: 'In proximis sex libris medicamina, quae bona, quaeque mala sint pro morborum varietate, ut a praestantissimis prodita sunt authoribus, Nos quoque prodidimus, ut admittenda, utque fugienda esse videantur. Reliquum nunc est, ut naturales quasdam ne omittamus ambiguitates, quas cognitu esse putamus necessarias, tum quod bene institutae menti conveniant, tum quod vel earum non ignari vitae opem ferre suae possint. Sunt enim eiusmodi, ut neminem scisse possit poenitere, quas ut rerum Conditor maximus Optimus clarissimorum virorum mentibus infundit Ita nos ab eis mutuati, Lingua nostra putavimus effundendas divino menti nostrae aspirante nutu, Cuius lenitate haec omnia quantacumque sunt, scriptis concredere potuimus'.

part, in fact, deals with organic and non-organic nature (e.g. the sea, the rain, some plants and animals), the second with the human being *a capite ad calcem*, focusing on medicine, physiology, and anatomy (where the human body is compared to that of animals). The sources of the *quaestiones* can be found in Plutarch's *Quaestiones mensales*, in both Cassius Iatrosophista's and in the pseudo-Aristotelian *Problemata*, especially in the collection known as *Problemata inedita*. While Valla's encyclopaedia remained an isolated literary product, and was never printed after 1501, Book 30 enjoyed a certain success; it was also published as an independent text, such as in the edition Strasbourg, 1529, where it bears the title *De physicis quaestionibus*, and is accompanied by Section XII of the pseudo-Aristotelian *Problemata*[42].

The presence of some medical and scientific *quaestiones* within a Renaissance encyclopaedia deserves some considerations. The humanist and Renaissance encyclopaedia, in fact, improved and perfected both the medieval technique of the *excerptatio* from the sources and the related concept of the encyclopaedia as reproduction of a universal knowledge, but with a different aim: for the Renaissance compilers, the goal of the encyclopaedia was not the gathering of the *notions*, of the *scientific data* forming the practical background of a branch of knowledge, but the presentation and the evaluation of the *texts* forming the necessary virtual library which the encyclopaedia incorporates into a single book. Therefore, the encyclopaedia is transformed into a sort of *compendium* of erudition related to a canon of books (this is the purpose, for example, of Conrad Gessner's *Pandectae* and, in general, of the so-called *commonplaces books*), into a virtual library destined not for the people who cannot have access to the sources, but for a well-educated public who already knows the texts. This attempt of a 'philological reconstruction' of a canon of books and authors through the encyclopaedia permeates the whole cultural project realized by Valla with his work.

Is it possible, however, to consider the insertion of some questions in the encyclopaedia as an attempt to relate their content to an established intellectual and cultural tradition? And which is the tradition Valla intends to refer to? It can be suggested that Valla's attempt to insert medi-

42. The combination between a section of Giorgio Valla's encyclopaedia and a book of the *Problemata* is also represented in the separate edition of the section *de corporis commodis et incommodis* printed in Strasbourg around 1530. Here, the text is accompanied by some *Problemata Aristotelis de re medica* (viz. by Book I of the pseudo-Aristotelian work). The combination Valla – pseudo-Aristotle is also shown by a printed version of the *De natura oculorum* (s.l., s.d.), where the work is contained in a volume together with the *Problemata que ad oculos pertinent* (viz. Book XXXI).

cal and scientific questions in his encyclopaedia should be seen in relation to the discovery and the revaluation of Cassius Iatrosophista's and Alexander of Aphrodisia's works which took place in the sixteenth century, and not as a the result of the influence of the literary genre of the medical *quaestio* developed, for example, in the faculties of medicine. Giorgio Valla is interested in texts and in textual traditions related to the Greek medical questions, not in the (medieval) technique connected with the use of the *quaestio disputata* within medicine. As far as the texts influencing Valla's use of the medical and scientific *problemata* concerns, it is interesting to notice that, while Cassius Iatrosophista's and Alexander of Aphrodisia's texts deeply permeated Valla's work, Aristotle's influence is surprisingly limited. Only the two last questions mention Aristotle as source, once in connection with Alexander of Aphrodisia; the *Problemata* are never mentioned[43]. Surprising is also the fact that Giorgio Valla does not seem to have become aware of the new translation of the *Problemata* completed by Theodore Gaza some decades before, or to have considered it as a potential source[44]. Probably, Valla's 'refuse' of the Latin translation of the *Problemata* can be explained, however, with the tendency shown by some erudite Humanists to evaluate Aristotle's Greek text more than the Latin version. This preference for the Greek original version against the (even most perfect) translation represents a trend characterizing the approach to Aristotle during the Early Modern Time; its origin, however, can be already found in the Italian Humanism[45]. A good example of this is the library owned by Nicolò Leoniceno, which contained a considerable amount of Greek manuscripts[46].

On the other side, it is interesting to analyze the way in which the public of the encyclopaedia considered the *quaestiones*. The fact that

43. Perhaps, the absence of any mention of the *Problemata* depends on the fact that Giorgio Valla does not quote the title of the works, but only refers shortly to the authors he draws material from.

44. On Gaza's translation of the pseudo-Aristotelian *Problemata*, see John Monfasani's contribution in this volume. Cf. also MONFASANI J., 'The Pseudo-Aristotelian *Problemata* and Aristotle's *De animalibus* in the Renaissance', in: A. GRAFTON – N. SIRAISI (eds.), *Natural Particulars: Nature and the Disciplines in Renaissance Europe*, Cambridge, Mass.: MIT Press, 1999, p. 205-247.

45. SCHMITT C.B., *Aristotle in the Renaissance*, Cambridge Mass.: Harvard University Press, 1983; SCHMITT C.B., 'Philosophy and Science in Sixteenth-Century Italian Universities', in: C.B. SCHMITT (ed.), *The Aristotelian Tradition and Renaissance Universities*, London: Variorum Reprints, 1984, nr. XV.

46. Cf. MUGNAI CARRARA D., *La biblioteca di Nicolò Leoniceno. Tra Aristotele e Galeno: cultura e libri di un medico umanista*, Firenze: Olschki, 1991; see also FORTUNA S., 'A proposito di manoscritti di Galeno nella biblioteca di Nicolò Leoniceno', *Italia medioevale e umanistica* 35 (1992), p. 431-438.

Book 30 was published as an independent work together with other
medical or pharmacological works, means that at least a part of Valla's
readers did not consider the questions neither as a part of the encyclopaedic project of the humanist nor as an attempt to refer to a 'cultural' or
'textual' tradition, but used the text as an example of medical *Fachliteratur*, perhaps as a part of the tradition of the *quaestiones medicales*.

The use of the Greek tradition of the *problemata* literature (e.g.
Cassius Iatrosophista, Plutarch, or Alexander of Aphrodisia) shown by
Giorgio Valla in his encyclopaedia can also be related to a particular
phenomenon characterizing the medical and, more generally, the scientific culture of the Renaissance. Between the fifteenth and the sixteenth
century, some scientific works were translated from Greek into Latin;
sometimes, the new versions overlap the pre-existent ones, often the result of an Arabic-Latin translation completed during the Middle Ages.
Moreover, the reception of the Greek works led some erudite Humanists
to compare the background handed over by the texts used since the Middle Ages with the content of the works made accessible through the recent Greek-Latin translations. Often, the contrast was solved in favour
of the new Greek-Latin texts against both the Arabic and the medieval
Latin works, since the former were supposed to hand over an original
and reliable scientific or medical culture that the Arabs and the Middle
Ages had misunderstood; a good example of this process is represented
by texts like Avicenna's *Liber canonis*, whose value as medical handbook declined during the Renaissance[47]. Since the sixteenth century,
their former function as reference texts was attributed, among others, to
the works belonging to the Galenic corpus, which was also newly translated into Latin from the Greek. The process of return to the Greek
medicine is well witnessed by Giorgio Valla and by the corpus of texts
he used as sources for his encyclopaedia; here, it seems that no Latin
translations of Arabic medical writings seem have been used. His work
can be used, therefore, as a good witness to analyze the changes in the
scientific culture in the first phase of the Renaissance, and the introduction into the early modern science of a new tradition of Greek
Problemata; these collections, and especially Plutarch's *Quaestiones
mensales*, played an important role in the early modern literary genre of
the *problemata* collections.

With our journey across the encyclopaedias, we have reached the
threshold of the early modern encyclopaedic culture; now, a little over-

---

47. Cf. D'ALVERNY M.-TH., *Avicenne en Occident. Recueils d'articles de Marie-
Thérèse d'Alverny réunis en hommage de l'auteur*, Paris: Vrin, 1993.

view of the development of the *problemata* collections in Early Modern Time can be offered. From the sixteenth century onwards, the literary genre of the *problemata* collections enjoyed a big success[48]. A huge *corpus* of texts bearing titles like *Problemata*, *Quaestiones*, *Fragen*, etc. can be found by consulting the catalogues of the most famous European libraries. Which kind of text will we read if we open these books? And for which kind of public were they written? A single paper would not suffice to answer these questions, since the literary genre is too wide to allow us to trace its history. One feature of these texts, however, can be stressed here: most parts of the *problemata* written in the sixteenth, seventeenth, and eighteenth century are, more or less, collections describing wonders of nature, exotics and strange things; we can define them as '*Wunderkammer* in form of books'. What are the reasons for this development? It can be argued that the early modern culture develops a deep interest for the *mirabile*, for the *curiositates naturae*, for all curious, strange, exotic things the world of nature displays, changing profoundly the idea of the *mirabile* handed over by medieval works[49]. The reasons for this change can be found in the progress of natural sciences which made people aware of both manifest and occult powers of nature, and in the discovery of new geographic areas showing exotic, unknown plants, animals, and human beings, which enlarges the catalogue handed over by classical and medieval scientific texts; moreover, in the enlargement and diversification of the public because of the invention of printing. This public needs not only practical information, but also entertainment;

48. For an overview of the literary genre of the *problemata* collections during the Early Modern Time see CHERCHI P., 'La selva rinascimentale: profilo di un genere', in: P. CHERCHI (ed.), *Ricerche sulle selve rinascimentali* (Seminario 'Susan and Donald Mazzoni' 2), Ravenna: Longo, 1999, p. 9-41, esp. p. 18-26; CHERCHI P., 'Il quotidiano, i "Problemata" e la meraviglia. Microstoria di un microgenere', *Intersezioni* 21/2 (2001), p. 243-275 (repr. in CHERCHI P., *Ministorie di microgeneri* [Il Portico, 132], a cura di C. FABBIAN, A. REBONATO, E. ZANOTTI CARNEY, Ravenna: Longo, 2003, p. 11-40); VENTURA I., 'The collections of natural questions: development and evolution forms of a type of "popular encyclopaedic literature" between thirteenth and sixteenth century', to be published in: P. MICHEL - F. DE CAPITANI (eds.), *All you need to know: Encyclopaedias and the idea of general knowledge (Conference, Prangins, Switzerland, 18-20 September 2003)*, in preparation.

49. On the idea of the *mirabile* see DASTON L. – PARK K., *Wonders and the Order of Nature, 1150-1750*, New York: Zone Books, 1998; ROTHMANN M., 'Zeichen und Wunder. Vom symbolischen Weltbild zur *scientia naturalis*', in: G. MELVILLE (ed.), *Institutionalität und Symbolisierung. Verstetigungen kultureller Ordnungsmuster in Vergangenheit und Gegenwart*, Köln-Weimar-Wien: Böhlau, 2001, p. 347-392; ROTHMANN M., '*Mirabilia vero dicimus, quae nostrae cognitioni non subiacent, etiam cum sint naturalia*. "Wundergeschichten" zwischen Wissen und Unterhaltung: der "Liber de mirabilibus mundi" ("Otia imperialia") des Gervasius von Tilbury', in: M. HEINZELMANN – K. HERBERS – D.R. BAUER (eds.), *Mirakel im Mittelalter. Konzeptionen, Erscheinungsformen, Deutungen* (Beiträge zur Hagiographie 3), Stuttgart: Franz Steiner Verlag, 2002, p. 399-432.

the readers buy books to be informed, but also to satisfy their curiosity. This development, however, causes some important changes, as in the use and in the interpretation of the *problema* form, which is not considered as a way to draw the attention of the readers to some features of the world around them, but as a technique to describe *mirabilia*, in the use of the sources (the compiler consults the books in search of unusual data; Aristotle, for example, assumes the identity of an *Aristoteles curiosus*), and in the way of describing the world of nature. All these changes lead to the transformation of the collections of natural *problemata* from a literary genre related to everyday life to a text form dealing with *mirabilia* and *exotica* and to a product of pure erudition.

The triumph of the collections of *mirabilia naturae* does not mean, however, that the literary genre of the encyclopaedias structured in question-answer form and dealing with medicine or natural science completely disappeared. On the contrary: the *Problemata* and the literature of natural questions experience a big success during the Early Modern Time, thanks to authors like Julius Caesar Scaliger or Girolamo Cardano[50], or to texts like the *Problemas* written by Francisco Lopez de Villalobos[51]. At the same time, however, during the Early Modern Time the pseudo-Aristotelian *Problemata* attracted more readers than during the Middle Ages, although they do not reach the success of other works like the *Ethics*, the *Politics*, or the works *De animalibus*. The reason for the success of the *Problemata* during the Early Modern Time can be firstly identified in the publication of a new Latin translation completed by Theodore Gaza in 1454 and published for the first time in 1474; although this translation did not satisfy the needs of the erudite people, who reproached Theodore to have both misunderstood and mistranslated the Aristotelian text, it made the work more accessible and easily understandable than Bartholomew of Messina's version[52]. From the sixteenth century onwards, the publication of the Greek text provided a more di-

50. On Girolamo Cardano, see INGEGNO A., *Saggio sulla filosofia di Cardano*, Firenze: La Nuova Italia, 1980; KESSLER E. (ed.), *Girolamo Cardano. Philosoph, Naturforscher, Arzt* (Wolfenbütteler Abhandlungen zur Renaissanceforschung 15), Wiesbaden: Harrassowitz Verlag, 1994.

51. F. Lopez de Villalobos, *Die Problemata des Villalobos*. Auszugsweise zum ersten Male ins Deutsche übersetzt, erläutert und mit einer Einleitung versehen, von Dr. med. et phil. F. LEJEUNE, Greifswald: Verlag Ratsbuchhandlung L. Bamberg, 1923.

52. On the Renaissance reception of the *Problemata*, cf. VENTURA I., 'Translating, Commenting, Re-translating: the Medical Sections of the Pseudo-Aristotelian *Problemata* and Their Readers', in: M. GOYENS – A. SMETS – P. DE LEEMANS (eds.), *Science Translated. Latin and Vernacular Translations of Scientific Treatises in Medieval Europe* (Mediaevalia Lovaniensia), Leuven: Leuven University Press, forthcoming.

rect access to the work; the erudite people, who were able to read the text in the original language, preferred this version. Finally, the composite nature and the particular structure of the text, where medicine, meteorology, dietetics, and physiognomic are gathered together, led the early modern scientists, philosophers, and some savants to consider even the pseudo-Aristotelian *Problemata* as a 'big encyclopaedia' summarizing a large part of the antique science. Therefore, the pseudo-Aristotelian *Problemata* became the 'genuine' collection of natural questions the erudite people read to get scientific information concerning some natural phenomena, while the collections produced during the Late Middle Ages and the Early Modern Time were considered more like a 'popular product' the readers used to be informed and delighted by the description of the 'curiosities of nature'.

4. Problemata *and* Quaestiones *Collections in the Manuscript Tradition*

After having described the texts, it is now possible to make some hypotheses concerning the role played by the *Problemata* as source and as pattern in the encyclopaedic literature discussed above. First of all, the introduction of pseudo-Aristotelian *Problemata* in the Latin West does not create a new literary genre; on the contrary, it continues a tradition established since the High Middle Ages, especially through the *Quaestiones salernitanae*; the aim of all these texts is to explain natural phenomena exclusively with the help of a rational interpretation, without connecting them to a supernatural or divine power or to an allegorical or moral meaning. This tradition leads, however, to the creation of different types of encyclopaedia witnessing the presence of pseudo-Aristotelian *Problemata* and of a net of related texts in very different milieus. It can be suggested, for example, that the pseudo-Aristotelian *Problemata* are used by compilers when they target for their encyclopaedias a public characterized by a high level of scientific culture, while the *Quaestiones salernitanae* are represented in the works we can locate on a lower cultural *niveau*.

As far as the use of the *Problemata* as source concerns, we can argue that the compilers did not refer to the pseudo-Aristotelian text because of its use of logic in describing the world of nature, but because of its intriguing content which shows 'the strange aspects of the reality'. The authors of the *quaestiones* collections do not seem to understand the perception of the natural phenomena shown by the *Problemata*; even Conrad of Halberstadt, who reproduces whole questions without summarizing the content, seems to have been more interested in excerpting a source he considered as important and in offering a complete text than in reproducing the logical process of the pseudo-Aristotelian work. In other terms, he seems to have aimed at creating a 'scientific *florilegium*' more than a philosophic encyclopaedia. For the other authors, the *Problemata* are only one of the possible scientific sources, among which they can choose to collect data, or a source which could offer new material and integrate the background provided by the scientific, philosophic, and encyclopaedic tradition with unusual rather than traditional topics. Giorgio Valla, on the other side, emphasizes another aspect of a possible interpretation of the *Problemata*: in his *De expetendis et fugiendis rebus*, the *Problemata* are considered neither as a source nor as a way of describing and explaining natural phenomena, but as a textual tradition to be reproduced in an encyclopaedia structured as a *Bibliotheca universalis*. On the other hand, although the logic legacy of the *Problemata* was not perceived by the compilers, this text gives an important contribution to improve a tendency already shown by the *Quaestiones salernitanae*, namely the attempt not only to display the features of natural phenomena, but to analyze the causes of their existence, the reasons for their occurrence. For the world of the encyclopaedias, which was used to describe the properties (*proprietates*) of things, it means a very different point of view.

As far as the scientific panorama offered by the encyclopaedias concerns, it is easy to recognize their 'human medical orientation': the most represented branches of knowledge are, of course, medicine, anatomy, physiognomic, dietetics, sometimes pharmacology. The human being, its body, its features and its illnesses represent the centre, the bulk of the encyclopaedia. The world of nature turns, we may say, around mankind: natural phenomena are displayed when they show a direct reference to the human world. At the same time, the *Problemata* are used within these encyclopaedias combined with other – sometimes extremely specialized – sources which belong to the cultural background of the scientists and especially of the physicians, but were not used in the literary genre of the encyclopaedias before. Let us only think of Avicenna's *Cantica*, a text used by Conrad of Halberstadt and by the anonymous author of the *Responsorium curiosorum*, whose presence can be traced only in the *curriculum studiorum* of the faculties of medicine, and whose reception in the collections of problems might have been the result of the use of a medical *florilegium* or of a *Pratica medicinae* like the one attributed to Arnald of Villanova.

The 'medical orientation' shown by the most part of the collections does not surprise us, if we consider not only the structure, the purpose, and the public of the encyclopaedias of *naturales quaestiones*, but also the nature and the reception of the *Problemata*. The text has been used, in fact, more as a scientific, especially as a medical reference text, than as a philosophical handbook. Beside the rich literature of *quaestiones medicales*, the *Problemata* become a reference text for physicians and are quoted in works written for a medical milieu. Moreover, compared with this strong reception within the medical literature, which especially involved Books I-IV, X-XIII, XX-XXII, and the sections concerning physiognomic, the influence of the sections dealing with mathematics, rhetoric, philology, music as well as human psychology can be defined as limited.

Furthermore, if we consider the manuscript tradition of the pseudo-Aristotelian collection, we face a twofold way to hand over the text: the *Problemata* are, in fact, preserved not only as complete work in manuscripts containing the Aristotelian *corpus*, but also in miscellaneous books dealing with science, particularly with medicine. This is the case, for example, of the manuscript Erfurt, Universitätsbibliothek, Coll. Amploniana, MS 4° 192, where the *Problemata* are preserved together with other medical texts, of the codex München, BSB, Clm 666, which contains only the fourth book in a medical miscellany formerly belonging to the library of Hartmann Schedel, of the manuscript München, BSB, Clm 8742, where the complete text of the pseudo-Aristotelian work is preserved together with other medical writings, or of the codex Augsburg, Universitätsbibliothek, III. 1. 2° 43, which shows the same combination between the *Problemata* and texts concerning medicine. Moreover, parts of the *Problemata* are printed together with other works dealing with similar topics, becoming parts of highly specialized *Wissenskomplexe*. For example, the sections concerning water (Books XXIII-XXIV) were included into a miscellany about thermal baths published in Venice in 1553[53]. As far as the role of the *Problemata* within these miscellanies concerns, I argue that here the pseudo-Aristotelian text is considered in a different way compared to the encyclopaedia written in a question-answer form: in the original collections they were used as a scientific source in a concrete context and related to the pragmatic aim to *explain the world of nature*, in the books of miscellanies (both in the manu-

---

53. García Ballester L., 'Sobre el origen de los tratados de baños (*de balneis*) como género literario en la medicina medieval', *Cronos* 1 (1998), p. 7-50, here p. 42.

scripts and in the printed texts) they provide the theoretical background that integrate the practical data handed over by medical or pharmaco-logical works.

An intriguing panorama is also offered by the *Mitüberlieferung* of the *Summa 'Omnes homines'*. The printed versions are usually handed down within two groups of texts: 1) together with works belonging to the early modern *problemata* tradition (e.g. with Marco Antonio Zimara's *Problemi*, with Plutarch's *Quaestiones*, with Alexander of Aphrodisia's work), 2) together with other scientific or pseudo-scientific texts, such as pseudo-Albert the Great's works (*Secreta mulierum, Experimenta seu Secreta, De mirabilibus mundi*), or with Julius Caesar Scaliger's *Problemata gelliana*. The manuscripts, on the contrary, show different ways of preserving the work and of combining it, creating various forms of *Wissenskomplexe*. As far as I know, we meet three alternative forms of preserving the *Summa 'Omnes homines'*, namely with other medical texts (as we have seen in the case of the pseudo-Aristotelian *Proble-mata*; this is the situation we face, for example, in the manuscript München, BSB, Cgm 4206), or with other encyclopaedias, as in the codex Frankfurt a.M., Stadt- und Universitätsbibliothek, MS Praed. 44, a miscellaneous codex also containing Beranger of Landorre's *Lumen anime* and some excerpts derived from Bartholomew the Englishman's *De proprietatibus rerum*, or of the manuscript München, BSB, Clm 27153, where the text is accompanied by some *exempla* and by a work *de hominibus monstruosis* probably related to Book III of Thomas of Cantimpré's *De natura rerum*. The third type of transmission is repre-sented by some miscellaneous manuscripts preserving works related to the homiletics: the manuscript Dresden, Sächsische Landesbibliothek, App. 2300 shows, for example, a combination between the *Summa 'Om-nes homines'*, Jacopo of Voragine's *Legenda aurea*, and some other tools written for the needs of the preachers. Although we do not have a complete list of the manuscripts preserving the *Summa 'Omnes homi-nes'*, the types of *Mitüberlieferung* I have presented show how different the reception, the use, the interpretation of this work can be. Maybe it will be reductive to affirm that the *Summa 'Omnes homines'* was only a 'popular', a low-profile text, as some scholars pointed out; it was not considered by its readers as such. On the contrary, it was a complete en-cyclopaedia, showing a great flexibility and adaptability to different kinds of public and to different needs, exemplifying perfectly the con-cept of usefulness (*utilitas*) that the most compilers stress while writing their works. Perhaps, the *Summa 'Omnes homines'* was a 'popular' text only because it gave an important contribution to the diffusion of medical and scientific knowledge between the Late Middle Ages and the Early Modern Time.

Conclusion

As we have seen during our journey through the *problemata* literature, both the reception within the late medieval and early modern encyclopaedic culture and the *Mitüberlieferung* of the *Problemata* show how the interpretation and the treatment of a text can change when it reaches different cultural contexts. A text written in order to explain the nature with the help of the Aristotelian logic became a source to describe natural phenomena, even the unusual ones, and to find an explanation for them. By being adapted both to the aims of the compilers and to the needs of the writers and readers of manuscripts, the *Problemata* experience transformations in the use of their content, in the interpretation of their form, and in their 'place within a canon of texts'.

If we try to identify the changes in the use of the content of the *Problemata*, we notice that the human orientation of the encyclopaedias deeply influences the use of the pseudo-Aristotelian text. The bulk of these collections is constituted by all sciences related to the human body; this choice transforms them into a kind of encyclopaedic *regimen sanitatis*. The use of the *Problemata* is adapted to this aim: the medical sections are more used than the others, the interest for the phenomena involving the human body becomes more evident. A second consequence of this 'human orientation' is the pragmatic content of the encyclopaedias: in the case of the tradition of the collections of natural questions, the encyclopaedia is not written in order to list and present the properties of nature in a general way, but to describe the elements of nature which can be useful for the reader to discover himself and to reorganize the world of nature around him.

As far as the changes in the interpretation of the form concerns, we notice that the most evident feature of the adaptation of the *Problemata* to the encyclopaedic literature is the *excerptatio* made from throughout the work by the compilers, viz. the extraction of the content and the extreme summarizing of it. The extraction of the material from its original context and its reorganization within the encyclopaedia particularly touch the logical structure which almost disappears. The only trace the *Problemata* left on these collections is the 'dynamic way' to describe natural phenomena, which was meant to help by describing the causes and the reasons for them.

Finally, we have noticed some changes in the classification and the interpretation of the work: Bartholomew of Messina translated a philosophical-scientific source, but Peter of Abano emphasized some years later the encyclopaedic character of the work. Within the literary genre of the encyclopaedias, the *Problemata* were incorporated into the established textual tradition built up by the *Quaestiones salernitanae* and became connected with a net of scientific texts, among these some reference texts of the medical and scientific literature. Therefore, they became part of canons of texts displayed by the encyclopaedias as well as by miscellaneous manuscripts, of a kind of virtual library used by different readers who were searching not only for collections providing concrete and useful data, but also for texts which could be read by everyone who could build up his own encyclopaedic culture. By establishing this connection between the attempt of acquisition of an encyclopaedic culture through private lecture and the production of encyclopaedic texts devoted to the needs of a larger public, the process of evolution from the medieval encyclopaedia to the modern encyclopaedism had begun.

University of Münster

Françoise GUICHARD-TESSON

ÉVRART DE CONTY, POÈTE, TRADUCTEUR ET COMMENTATEUR

With the impending publication of Évrart de Conty's translation of the Problemata, *this article will situate the author's venture within the scope of his work. Adopting G. Raimondi's hypothesis that Évrart is also the author of the poem* Eschés Amoureux, *we shall ponder the conception and the objectives of the commentary in the three works recognized as his, as well as consider the readership to which they were addressed. Finally, the article will explore the linkage between the works created by the use of common elements. Évrart's* Problemes *is seen to be the connective text: the exposition of scholarly truths within a very restricted structure subsequently led the physician and doctor to develop a technique which undoubtedly induced a less austere creation synthesizing both his moral and scholarly concerns and destined to a larger readership, the* Livre des Eschez Amoureux Moralisés.

Introduction

Dans son livre sur *La Médecine médiévale dans le cadre parisien*, Danielle Jacquart fait remarquer que 'le petit nombre de maîtres parisiens qui écrivirent sur le sujet de leur enseignement ne laisse pas d'étonner'[1]. Ainsi, parmi les dix-huit maîtres qui apparaissent sur la liste de 1379, Évrart de Conty fait-il figure d'exception, au point qu'elle le considère comme 'le seul véritable auteur'[2], puisque deux œuvres monumentales, la traduction / commentaire des *Problemes* et le *Livre des eschez amoureux moralisés*, lui sont d'ores et déjà attribuées. Une édition de cette dernière œuvre étant disponible, il est pertinent de rendre également accessible les *Problemes*[3], d'autant que nous disposons d'un outil précieux et riche d'enseignements: l'autographe[4].

---

1. JACQUART D., *La médecine médiévale dans le cadre parisien*, Paris: Fayard, 1998, p. 160.
2. JACQUART, *La médecine médiévale…*, p.153.
3. Évrart de Conty, *Le Livre des Eschez amoureux moralisés,* éd. critique par F. GUICHARD-TESSON et B. ROY, Montréal: CERES, 1993. L'édition des *Problemes* a été entreprise grâce à la collaboration de Michèle Goyens, Joëlle Ducos et moi-même.
4. Paris, B.N.F. fr. 24281-24282. Le premier volume (24281) contient les parties I à XV, le second (24282) les parties XVI à XXXVI. Toutes nos citations sont faites d'après ce manuscrit; nous indiquons successivement la partie, le problème, le folio du manuscrit correspondant.

Si l'objet de ce volume était la transmission des *Problemes* d'Aristote, notre intérêt pour la traduction d'Évrart de Conty a néanmoins suivi un itinéraire différent puisque, travaillant sur une œuvre anonyme, le *Livre des eschez amoureux moralisés*, nous avons pu identifier Évrart comme son auteur. Aussi notre étude se situera-t-elle dans un cadre plus large, de manière à souligner les liens qui unissent ces œuvres au-delà de leurs évidentes différences.

Ainsi, après avoir, dans une première partie, fait le bilan actuel de l'œuvre d'Évrart, nous évoquerons dans un deuxième temps la transmission textuelle et l'intérêt du manuscrit autographe des *Problemes*. Nous nous interrogerons ensuite sur les visées et le public de ces diverses œuvres, avant d'analyser pour finir certaines techniques d'écriture de notre glossateur.

Outre les *Problemes*, il sera ici question de deux œuvres, le poème des *Eschés amoureux* – que nous désignerons comme les *Eschés* dans la suite de l'article – et le *Livre des eschez amoureux moralisés*[5] – que nous désignerons comme les *EAM*. Du poème, il existe un manuscrit très incomplet, celui de Venise, partiellement édité en 1977[6], et le manuscrit de Dresde, d'environ 30000 vers, maintenant restauré; ce sont sur ces deux manuscrits que s'appuie G. Raimondi dans l'édition qu'il a entreprise[7]. Dans la continuité du *Roman de la Rose*, le poème raconte l'aventure du narrateur qui, découvrant à son tour le jardin de Déduit, livre, sur l'invitation du dieu d'amour, une partie d'échecs à une belle demoiselle. Chacune des pièces du jeu porte un emblème qui représente une qualité ou un comportement relatif à l'amour. Après sa défaite – très tôt dans le poème –, le narrateur reçoit les commandements du dieu d'Amour et doit ensuite écouter un très long discours de Pallas, qui semble inachevé. Quant au *Livre des eschez amoureux moralisés* d'Évrart de Conty, il

5. Ce sont les titres retenus par les éditeurs.

6. KRAFT C. (éd.), *Die Liebesgarten-Allegorie der Echecs amoureux, Kritische Ausgabe und Kommentar*, Frankfurt-a.-M. – Bern – Las Vegas: Peter Lang, 1977.

7. RAIMONDI G. (éd.), '*Les Eschés amoureux*. Studio preparatorio ed edizioni', *Pluteus* 8-9 (1990-1998), p. 67-241. Cette édition couvre les vers 1 à 3662. L'édition des vers 3663 à 5538 paraîtra dans le prochain numéro de *Pluteus*. Ces vers correspondent aux vers 1 à 1876 de l'édition Kraft qui en comprend 5664. Ce sont donc les 9326 premiers vers qui sont désormais accessibles en lecture continue. Des éditions partielles sont également disponibles, notamment: KÖRTING G., *Altfranzösische Übersetzung der* Remedia amoris *des Ovid. Ein Theil des allegorisch-didactischen Epos* Les Echecs amoureux *nach des Dresdener Handschrift hrsg.*, Genève: Slatkine Reprints, 1971 (réimpression de l'édition de Leipzig, 1871). Pour un relevé complet de ces éditions, voir RAIMONDI (éd.), '*Les Eschés...*', p. 240-41 et Évrart de Conty, *Le Livre des Eschez...*, éds GUICHARD-TESSON – ROY, *Introduction*, p. LXIX-LXX.

constitue, sur plus de 350 folios, une glose du poème (en fait seulement des 2000 premiers vers)[8].

1. *L'homme et l'œuvre*

1.1. L'homme

En ce qui concerne la vie d'Évrart de Conty, les renseignements dont nous disposons ne sont pas extrêmement nombreux[9]. Sa date de naissance nous est inconnue, mais on sait qu'il meurt en 1405 alors qu'il était chanoine d'Amiens, ville dont il est originaire et avec laquelle il a toujours entretenu des liens. Il était sous-diacre du diocèse en 1362.

C'est la similitude des rares indications autobiographiques qui nous a conduite à faire l'hypothèse d'une paternité commune des œuvres[10]. D'une part, l'auteur rappelle dans les deux cas l'histoire de l'étourneau qui, à Amiens, chantait une grande partie d'un virelai: cette indication, présentée à la première personne dans les *Problemes*, est à nouveau racontée de façon impersonnelle dans les *EAM*, mais il y ajoute des précisions qui ne figuraient pas dans les *Problemes*. D'autre part, les deux textes rappellent un parhélie observé quelques années auparavant: cette fois, ce sont les *EAM* qui présentent l'observation comme un souvenir personnel: 'et ce ai je veu a Paris en mon temps'[11].

Il y relate un autre souvenir de jeunesse: le cas de cette riche dame d'Amiens incapable de boire dans le hanap qu'on lui présentait parce qu'elle le pensait plein d'araignées[12]. Les *Problemes*, quant à eux, contiennent un certain nombre d'indications en relation avec la Picardie, telles les couronnes que l'on a coutume de faire pendant la nuit de la Saint-Jean (XX, 22) ou les boules avec une bosse qui en déséquilibre le poids 'en la maniere c'on les fait communement en Pycardie' (XVI, 3, 14r); faut-il l'accuser de chauvinisme lorsqu'il déclare, à propos de la mutation des eaux, que celle-ci serait pire que celle de l'air pour qui irait de Picardie en Flandres 'ou il ha malvaises yaues par nature' (I, 13, 20r)? Non, sans doute, puisque cette mauvaise réputation est déjà véhiculée

8. Sur le choix du titre, voir Évrart de Conty, *Le Livre des Eschez...,* éds GUICHARD-TESSON – ROY, *Introduction*, p. X-XI.

9. Sur l'origine de ces renseignements, voir Évrart de Conty, *Le Livre des Eschez...,* éds GUICHARD-TESSON – ROY, *Introduction*, p. LIV-LVI.

10. GUICHARD-TESSON F., 'Évrart de Conty, auteur de la *Glose des Échecs amoureux*', *Le Moyen Français* 8-9 (1981), p. 118-119.

11. Évrart de Conty, *Le Livre des Eschez...,* éds GUICHARD-TESSON – ROY, p. 440.

12. Évrart de Conty, *Le Livre des Eschez...,* éds GUICHARD-TESSON – ROY, p. 200.

par Pierre d'Abano, mais Évrart ne manque pas de reprendre l'exemple[13]!

Ces rapports étroits avec la ville et la Picardie incitent d'ailleurs à penser qu'il fait partie de cette famille amiennoise d'hommes de lois et de lettres étudiée par l'historien Philippe Contamine[14].

Évrart semble avoir eu une longue carrière comme maître régent à la Faculté de médecine de Paris, puisqu'il fête son jubilé en 1403. Il y aurait donc enseigné dès 1353. Dès 1357, il semble avoir atteint un statut enviable, puisque, lors d'une dissension sur le mode d'élection du doyen, il est l'un des deux maîtres chargés de rédiger le rapport. Toutefois, rien n'atteste qu'il ait été doyen et son nom n'est plus mentionné après 1379; il ne figure pas sur les listes tenues à partir de 1395[15].

Sachant qu'on était en général maître régent après cinq ou six années d'études, vers l'âge de vingt-cinq ans, on peut présumer qu'il est né vers 1330. Il serait donc venu à Paris vers 1345 et c'est sans doute comme étudiant ou comme jeune maître qu'il a observé, avant 1360, le parhélie dont Oresme a également parlé à Buridan[16].

Comme pour la plupart des maîtres de son temps[17], sa carrière de professeur se double d'une activité de praticien: dès 1363, il est le médecin du futur Charles V et le demeurera pendant tout le règne. Il est aussi au service de la reine Blanche, veuve de Philippe V. Comme les autres maîtres également, il s'attire de nombreuses prébendes.

1.2. L'œuvre

Comment situer, dans une vie aussi remplie, l'activité d'écriture de notre médecin? Nous avons, à vrai dire, peu de certitudes quant à la date de rédaction de ces deux œuvres de longue haleine que sont les *Problemes* et les *EAM*.

Il semble acquis que la traduction des *Problemes* aurait fait l'objet d'une commande de Charles V et notre Évrart paraît en effet tout désigné pour cette tâche. A.D. Menut et A.J. Denomy, les éditeurs du *Livre du ciel et du monde* d'Oresme, datent la commande royale des

---

13. 'sicut apparet cum quis in Pichardia se transferret in Flandria ubi pessime sunt aque...' (I, 13), Pierre d'Abano, *Expositio Problematum Aristotelis*, éd. Mantoue, 1475.
14. Évrart de Conty, *Le Livre des Eschez...*, éds GUICHARD-TESSON – ROY, *Introduction*, p. LIII et JACQUART, *La médecine médiévale...*, p. 283.
15. JACQUART, *La médecine médiévale...*, p. 153.
16. 'Reverendus magister Nicolaus Oresme dixit mihi se semel vidisse ex utroque latere Solis unum.' Voir à ce sujet GUICHARD-TESSON, 'Évrart de Conty, auteur...', p. 115.
17. JACQUART, *La médecine médiévale...*, p. 152.

Problemes de 1372, et A.D. Menut, dans son édition du *Livre de
ethiques*, en situe la réalisation vers 1375, mais dans aucun des cas, ils
ne précisent leurs sources[18]. Il est en tout cas certain qu'Évrart y travaille encore en 1377 puisque, dans la 27ᵉ partie, il fait référence à Nicole Oresme, 'evesque de Lisieux, excellent philosophe' (XXVII, 1,
153v) et l'on sait que ce dernier accéda à cette dignité en novembre
1377 et mourut en 1382. Au moment où il fait cette allusion, Évrart a
encore le sixième de l'œuvre à rédiger, ce qui accrédite l'hypothèse selon laquelle elle n'était pas achevée en 1380, date de la mort du roi.
L'ouvrage ne porte d'ailleurs pas de dédicace et ne figure pas, à cette
date, dans la bibliothèque royale. C'est seulement en 1410 que le duc de
Guyenne en fait placer une copie au Louvre[19]. On peut en revanche penser que la mort d'Oresme nous fournit un *terminus ad quem*, étant donné
la manière dont notre médecin parle de lui[20].

Dans notre étude d'attribution des *EAM* à Évrart, nous remarquions
que les relations entre les trois œuvres (*Eschés*, *EAM* et *Problemes*)

18. Nicole Oresme, *Le Livre du ciel et du monde*, éd. A.D. Menut et A.J. Denomy,
Madison: The University of Wisconsin Press, 1968, p. 5 et *Le Livre de ethiques d'Aristote*, éd. A.D. Menut, New York: G.E. Stechert & Co, 1940, p. 56. La date de 1395, fournie pour la rédaction dans Ducos J., *La météorologie en français au Moyen Âge (XIIIᵉ-
XIVᵉ siècles)*, Paris: Champion, 1997, p. 181, n. 11, et Jacquart, *La médecine
médiévale…*, p. 275, n. 124, nous semble donc une erreur. Sur ce problème de la datation,
voir aussi dans ce volume la contribution de C. Boucher, l'appendice II. Cherchant à re-
tracer l'origine de ces renseignements, la plus ancienne référence à la commande royale
que nous ayons trouvée nous est fournie au XVIIᵉ siècle par G. Naudé: 'Evrardus de
Conti, luculentum commentarium Problematum Aristotelis, in gratiam sui regis, lingua
vernacula edidit; qui etiamnum hodie in instructissima Sancti Victoris inter muros
bibliotheca inter magni nominis manuscriptos codices, diligenter asservatur.' *De anti-
quitate et dignitate scholae medicae Parisiensis*, p. 44. Ce passage est cité à deux reprises
par Franklin A., *Histoire de la bibliothèque de l'abbaye de Saint-Victor à Paris*, Paris:
Aubry, 1865, p. 90 et *Les anciennes bibliothèques de Paris*, Paris: Imprimerie impériale,
1867-70, I, p. 169. Franklin écrit également: 'Evrard de Conti était très-instruit; il fit pour
Charles V une traduction des *Problèmes* d'Aristote.' *Recherches sur la bibliothèque de la
faculté de médecine de Paris*, Paris: Aubry, 1864, p. 17, n. 1. Nous n'avons trouvé aucun
document antérieur qui en fournisse la confirmation et justifie les dates données par
A.D. Menut et A.J. Denomy. Notons l'ambiguïté de la formule 'in gratiam sui regis' qui
n'implique pas une commande comme telle. On peut, de toute manière, considérer que
l'œuvre a été entreprise dans cette période. Sur les traductions commandées par Charles
V, voir Lusignan S., *Parler vulgairement. Les intellectuels et la langue française aux
XIIIᵉ et XIVᵉ siècles*, Paris: Vrin, Montréal: Presses de l'Université de Montréal, 1986,
p. 129-171 et particulièrement 136-137; Boudet J.-P., 'Le bel automne de la culture médiévale (XIVᵉ – XVᵉ siècles)', dans: J.-P. Rioux – J.-F. Sirinelli (éds), *Histoire cultu-
relle de la France*, 1. *Le Moyen Âge*, Paris: Seuil, 1997, p. 276-83.

19. Voir *infra*, n. 35.

20. Il reste évidemment possible que l'œuvre d'Évrart ait été achevée après cette date,
sans qu'il ait éprouvé le besoin de revenir sur le texte antérieur. Dans tous les cas, on peut
penser que l'œuvre fut terminée dans les premières années de la décennie.

étaient complexes, puisque les *Problemes* connaissent manifestement fort bien le poème dont on situe la composition entre 1370 et 1380 à cause d'une allusion à Du Guesclin[21]. Ainsi s'établirait la séquence *Eschés* (1370-1380), *Problemes* autour de 1380, *EAM* autour de 1390.

1.3. Évrart, auteur du poème

Faisant un pas de plus, Gianmario Raimondi, qui est actuellement en train d'éditer le poème, propose d'en attribuer également la paternité à Évrart, et ses arguments emportent l'adhésion. À vrai dire, B. Roy et moi avions envisagé cette hypothèse, mais nous manquions alors des preuves convaincantes. Envisageant les relations entre le poème et le commentaire en prose, nous mentionnions le problème qui se pose du fait que le poème n'explicite pas la valeur allégorique des emblèmes portés par les pièces d'échecs et servant à les désigner au cours de la partie.

Cette signification, absente de la trame narrative mais indispensable à la compréhension du déroulement du jeu, est néanmoins donnée, dans le manuscrit de Venise, par un diagramme de l'échiquier qui fournit les noms allégoriques des pièces. Elle l'est également par les gloses latines qui figurent dans les marges de ce même manuscrit, alors que celui de Dresde en est dépourvu. 'L'ensemble de ces gloses formait, dans l'esprit de l'auteur, l'ébauche d'un commentaire destiné à accompagner le poème et à le rendre intelligible', écrivions-nous alors[22]. Ainsi imaginions-nous un précepteur-commentateur capable de fournir oralement les explications nécessaires, tout comme il pouvait le faire pour les récits mythologiques, eux aussi accompagnés du même type de gloses qui fourniront la base du commentaire en prose.

Nous résumerons donc la démonstration de G. Raimondi, telle qu'il nous l'a aimablement communiquée. La pièce maîtresse en est l'identification de la main même d'Évrart, dans les gloses latines ainsi que dans sept passages du texte en vers. Cette identification est indiscutable: il suffit de les comparer avec le manuscrit autographe pour voir qu'il s'agit bien de la même écriture cursive avec ses lettres caractéristiques (d oncial, boucle du g, y, etc.).

De plus, parmi les sept passages qui ont été grattés et réécrits par Évrart, l'un d'eux concerne la marche des pièces et propose une sé-

---

21. KRAFT (éd.), *Die Liebesgarten-Allegorie...*, p. 31: 'Bertrans li nobles connetables / Qui tant est preux et honnourables...' (Dresde, f. 100b). Or c'est en 1370 qu'il a accédé au rang de connétable, et il meurt en 1380.

22. Évrart de Conty, *Le Livre des Eschez...*, éds GUICHARD-TESSON – ROY, *Introduction*, p. LVII.

quence de mouvements absente du manuscrit de Dresde, mais reprise dans le commentaire en prose. Est-il pensable qu'un auteur revoie ainsi, modifie et commente l'ouvrage d'un autre, pour en arriver à une œuvre en prose d'une telle longueur? On peut en outre noter que, pas plus que dans le poème, on ne sait ce qu'il adviendra des relations entre l'acteur et la belle joueuse! Est-il vraisemblable, se demande G. Raimondi, qu'un commentateur ne s'interroge pas sur la morale finale de l'histoire? N'est-il pas plus raisonnable de penser, d'une part, que le texte en vers n'a jamais été terminé, d'autre part que seul l'auteur lui-même peut juger cet aspect comme sans importance[23]? Et, pourrions-nous ajouter, on comprend mieux la désinvolture avec laquelle il règle, en une trentaine de lignes à la fin du commentaire en prose, le discours d'Amour et surtout celui de Pallas qui représente, en termes de longueur, l'essentiel de l'œuvre (115 folios sur les 144 du manuscrit de Dresde!).

Faut-il alors s'étonner que le commentateur ne s'identifie pas comme l'auteur du poème, écrivant au début des *EAM*: 'Ce present livre fu fait et ordené principalment a l'instance d'un autre, fait en rime nagueres, et de nouvel venu a congnoissance, qui est intitulé *Des Eschez amoureux* ou *Des Eschez d'amours*'[24]? Non, répond G. Raimondi! Dans la mentalité médiévale, l'autocommentaire paraît peu praticable: gloser un texte, c'est reconnaître son importance, c'est juger la lettre digne d'une lecture allégorique, ce qui paraît inconvenant appliqué à soi-même. Tel est le cas de Dante qui, dans la *Vita nova* par exemple, désigne toujours à la troisième personne l'auteur de l'œuvre commentée[25].

Ainsi, conclut G. Raimondi, si aucun de ces éléments ne constitue une preuve irréfutable de la paternité d'Évrart, un faisceau de remarques concordantes vient la confirmer. Par exemple, le poème respecte rigoureusement les règles qui seront ensuite exposées dans le commentaire en prose: l'octosyllabe lui apparaît, parmi les rimes, 'la meilleure de toutes et de la plus raisonnable mesure'[26]; le compte des syllabes et l'élision du *e* muet à l'intérieur du vers sont strictement appliqués dans le poème.

---

23. Voir sur ce point: RAIMONDI (éd.), '*Les Eschés…*', p. 100, n. 55. Sur les éléments d'attribution du poème à Évrart, voir aussi p. 218-9, 1851-G et p. 89, n. 32.

24. Évrart de Conty, *Le Livre des Eschez…*, éds GUICHARD-TESSON – ROY, p. 2.

25. Il est intéressant de noter que A.J. Minnis, réfléchissant sur le statut des *EAM* en tant que commentaire et sur la volonté de l'auteur de donner à une œuvre en langue vernaculaire le poids d'une 'autorité', effectue précisément un rapprochement avec les autocommentaires de Dante, pressentant le lien intime qui unit le poème et sa glose. Voir MINNIS A. J., *Magister amoris, The* Roman de la Rose *and Vernacular Hermeneutics*, Oxford: Oxford University Press, 2001, p. 257-319, en particulier p. 272-77 et 289-92.

26. Évrart de Conty, *Le Livre des Eschez…*, éds GUICHARD-TESSON – ROY, p. 170.

Ainsi le vers: 'Et je trais ainsi de autre part'[27], qui doit être lu en élidant le e de de, illustre ce que dit Évrart lorsqu'il commente, dans l'œuvre en prose: 'S'amours n'estoit plus poissans que nature'. On devrait, dit-il, écrire se pour différencier le mot, même s'il ne fait qu'une syllabe avec la voyelle qui suit[28].

Quant à la coïncidence des sources, c'était déjà un argument employé dans notre article sur l'attribution du commentaire à Évrart de Conty, pour montrer qu'il connaissait et avait utilisé le poème lorsqu'il rédigeait les Problemes, et G. Raimondi étend aux Eschés les remarques que nous avions faites sur la parenté des styles entre les Problemes et les EAM.

Pour finir, G. Raimondi retrouve, dans les derniers vers du prologue du poème, l'anagramme utilisant le nom de l'auteur, que nous proposions d'y voir dans les huit vers qui terminent le commentaire[29].

Ainsi sommes-nous en présence d'un fascinant triangle textuel et pouvons-nous reconstituer la séquence suivante. Évrart entreprend, au plus tôt en 1370, le poème. Qu'il y ait eu ou non commande de Charles V, on peut penser que le commentaire des Problemes a effectivement été entrepris à son intention aux environs de 1375, en ces temps d'effervescence traductrice; on peut même envisager qu'il n'a pas terminé le poème quand il se lance dans cette nouvelle entreprise, sans doute achevée vers 1382. Il est encore plus difficile de dater précisément les EAM, certainement commencés après l'achèvement des Problemes, car on envisage mal qu'il ait pu mener de front deux œuvres d'une telle envergure. À la suite de P.-Y. Badel, nous avons fait l'hypothèse que l'œuvre était sans doute achevée en 1401, qui marque le paroxysme de la fameuse querelle autour du Roman de la Rose, à laquelle Évrart ne fait aucune allusion[30].

Or revenons à notre propos: les Problemes!

---

27. Il s'agit de l'un des huit vers réécrits de la main d'Évrart sur le manuscrit de Venise. KRAFT (éd.), Die Liebesgarten-Allegorie…, v. 1583, p. 131.

28. Évrart de Conty, Le Livre des Eschez…, éds GUICHARD-TESSON – ROY, p. 172. Sur l'art poétique d'Évrart, voir ROY B., 'Eustache Deschamps et Évrart de Conty théoriciens de l'art poétique' dans: Cy nous dient. Dialogue avec quelques auteurs médiévaux, Orléans: Paradigme, 1999.

29. 'OR VuEilliés DONCquEs la mATIeRe (evrart de con[t]i) / bien CONsiderer [s']a misTIere (conti) / caR je Vous CONTERAY sans DouTE (evrart de conti) / DE mon mAT l'aVEntuRe toute.' (evra[r]t de), RAIMONDI (éd.), 'Les Eschés…', v. 39-42, p. 108. Sur les vers qui terminent le commentaire, voir Évrart de Conty, Le Livre des Eschez…, éds GUICHARD-TESSON – ROY, Introduction, p. LIV et p. 766. Deux de ces vers: 'Je lairay donc ceste matere / Tant soit elle de grant mistere' (p. 766) sont également très proches du poème:'Mais je lairay cete matiere / pour ce qu'elle est d'autre mistiere' (v. 1213-14, p. 131).

30. BADEL P.-Y., Le Roman de la Rose au XIVe siècle. Étude de la réception de l'œuvre, Genève: DROZ, 1980, p. 290.

2. Les Problemes

2.1. La transmission textuelle

Le texte semble avoir fait l'objet d'un nombre assez important de copies, à la fin du XIVe et au début du XVe siècle, mais jamais d'une impression. Nous en connaissons actuellement sept versions complètes, dont trois en deux volumes séparés, auxquelles il faut ajouter les fragments provenant d'un manuscrit dont on semble avoir détaché les folios qui contiennent des miniatures[31].

Ce qui frappe, c'est la qualité des manuscrits conservés, qui sont des ouvrages de parchemin, ornés d'une miniature initiale. Il n'est toutefois pas aisé de faire le lien entre ces manuscrits et ceux dont on entend parler dans les inventaires médiévaux. Le seul qui soit sur papier et dont l'histoire soit presque parfaitement claire grâce aux travaux de G. Ouy sur la bibliothèque de St-Victor[32] est précisément le manuscrit autographe, conservé dans la bibliothèque de Simon de Plumetot, le collectionneur d'autographes. On ne sait toutefois pas comment il l'a acquis et on peut penser qu'il eut aussi entre les mains l'autographe des *EAM*.

Ces copies soignées attestent donc l'intérêt des princes pour de tels ouvrages. En 1399, Louis d'Orléans donne '70 écus à Jean Doche, maître es arts, pour la traduction des *Problemes*'. Ce manuscrit figure dans les inventaires de 1417 et 1466 de la bibliothèque de Blois[33]. Le duc de Berry en a également une copie qui lui a été offerte en 1405 par son conseiller Guillaume de Boisratier[34], mais on ne sait ce qu'elle devient lors de la dispersion de la bibliothèque qui suivit la mort du duc. Enfin, si le texte n'entre pas au Louvre du vivant de Charles V – il était vraisemblablement inachevé –, Louis de Guyenne y fait cependant placer une copie en 1410, mais elle ne contenait que la deuxième moitié du texte[35]. De ces trois volumes, nous perdons la trace et il est malaisé de les identifier avec ceux que nous avons conservés.

31. Paris, B.N.F. fr. 24281-24282 (autographe); Paris, B.N.F. fr. 210, 211, 563-564; Paris, B.N.F. n.a.fr. 3371 (12 folios); Cambrai, Bibl. Mun. 894 (797); Iéna, Gall. 81; s' Gravenhage, Koninklijke Bibliotheek, 133 A 3. Le manuscrit Chantilly, Musée Condé 990 (section musicale) copie la 19e partie consacrée à la musique.

32. OUY G., 'Simon de Plumetot (1371-1443) et sa bibliothèque', dans: P. COCKSHAW – M.-C. GARAND – P. JODOGNE (éds), *Miscellanea Codicologica F. Masai dicata*, Gand: Story-Scientia S.P.R.L., 1979, p. 351-381.

33. DELISLE L., *Le Cabinet des manuscrits de la Bibliothèque impériale*, Paris: Impr. impériale, 1868-81; réimpr. New York: Burt Franklin, 1973, I, p. 103 et 117.

34. DELISLE, *Le Cabinet...*, I, p. 60.

35. Il s'agit d'un des volumes provenant de la librairie de Jean de Montaigu, grand maître de l'hôtel du roi, qui avait été décapité. DELISLE, *Le Cabinet...*, I, p. 23 et 48.

On retrouve des copies au siècle suivant dans les bibliothèques des grands seigneurs. Un exemplaire de parchemin figure, en 1516 et 1523-24, dans les inventaires de la bibliothèque de Marguerite d'Autriche[36]. Deux manuscrits semblent avoir appartenu aux princes de Clèves, celui qui est conservé à Iéna et celui de La Haye qui passe ensuite dans la famille des princes de Nassau[37]. En outre, le comte d'Urfé (1501-58) en a une copie dans sa bibliothèque[38].

Le texte semble avoir toutefois circulé dans un autre milieu, celui des pairs d'Évrart: c'est à un maître ès arts que Louis d'Orléans a acheté sa copie et le manuscrit de Cambrai, quant à lui, fut acquis par Philippe Parent, membre du chapitre de Cambrai; il la tenait de Nicolas Lamant, maître de théologie, doyen du chapitre de Cambrai.

Ainsi voit-on l'œuvre circuler dans un double milieu, intéressant les clercs mais surtout les milieux princiers, comme le faisaient les *Eschés* et les *EAM*.

2.2. L'intérêt du manuscrit autographe

G. Ouy a été le premier à souligner l'intérêt de ce manuscrit qui permet de saisir sur le vif les caractéristiques de la langue de l'auteur et les différentes étapes de son travail[39]. Prenant appui sur la partie traitant des questions musicales, qui présente de nombreuses additions et ratures, nous avons étudié ces différents aspects et les conclusions auxquelles nous sommes parvenue peuvent évidemment être étendues à l'ensemble de l'œuvre[40]. Rappelons-les brièvement.

---

36. DEBAE M., *La Bibliothèque de Marguerite d'Autriche. Essai de reconstitution d'après l'Inventaire de 1523-24*, Louvain-Paris, 1995, p. 292. D'après M. Debae, ce manuscrit serait passé en 1530 à Marie de Hongrie; emporté par elle en Espagne, il aurait brûlé en 1671.

37. DEXEL W., *Untersuchungen über die französischen illuminierten Handschriften der Jenaer Universitätsbibliothek vom Ende des 14. bis zur Mitte des 15. Jahrhunderts*, Strassburg: Universitäts-Buchdruckerei Heitz & Mündel, 1917, p. 20-21. FINOT J., *Inventaire sommaire des archives départementales antérieures à 1790, Nord, Archives civiles série B. Chambre des comptes de Lille*, tome VIII, Lille, 1895, n° 3664.

38. DE BURE G., *Catalogue des livres de feu M. le duc de La Vallière, Ire partie*, Paris: éd. G. de Bure fils aîné, 1783, p. 374; DELISLE, *Le Cabinet...*, II, p. 420-21.

39. OUY, 'Simon de Plumetot...', p. 368 et 378 et OUY G.,'Les orthographes de divers auteurs français des XIVe et XVe siècles. Présentation et étude de quelques manuscrits autographes', dans: S. CIGADA – A. SLERCA (éds), *Le Moyen Français: recherches de lexicologie et de lexicographie. Actes du VIe Colloque international sur le Moyen Français. Milan, 4-6 mai 1998*, Vol. I, Milan: Vita e Pensiero, 1991, p. 98-102.

40. GUICHARD-TESSON F., 'Le souci de la langue et du style au XIVe siècle: l'autographe des *Problèmes* d'Évrart de Conty', *Le Moyen Français* 33 (1993), p. 57-84.

2.2.1. La langue

Ce qui frappe est le respect de l'orthographe grammaticale, se remarquant entre autres dans les corrections, la stabilité – relative – des graphies et, bien sûr, l'observation scrupuleuse de la déclinaison. Cette conscience aiguë de la langue se sent aussi dans l'attention à la formation des mots, séparés en raison de leur composition, alors que l'usage tend à les accoler. Ainsi écrit-il presque toujours en deux mots *aucune fois, desus dit, nient mains, toute fois*, etc. *Li prins tans* sera donc la forme naturelle du cas sujet. Si le système n'est pas parfaitement rigoureux, il révèle néanmoins des choix qui ne seront pas gardés dans les autres manuscrits.

Dans l'édition des *EAM*, nous remarquions que certaines leçons fautives de notre manuscrit de base, copié par Simon de Plumetot, pouvaient aisément être corrigées en rétablissant la flexion casuelle qu'offrait le manuscrit source (ex.: 'le pole sont porté'; il suffirait de remplacer *le* par *li*); notre copiste travaillait sans doute sur un manuscrit proche de l'autographe, si ce n'est sur l'autographe lui-même[41]. Il serait donc intéressant de savoir si Évrart avait déjà mis en place un tel système dans les *Eschés*. On serait tenté de le penser en examinant le manuscrit de Venise (V) sur lequel il a travaillé. G. Raimondi remarque que le non respect de la déclinaison est rare dans ce manuscrit, mais très fréquent dans celui de Dresde (D)[42]. Il arrive même que le compte des syllabes soit incorrect dans ce dernier, alors qu'il suffit de rétablir un cas sujet pour rendre son aplomb au vers, par exemple: 'Li arbre (les arbres D) aussy se reverdissent'(v. 95).

La comparaison des deux manuscrits montre également que V est beaucoup plus proche des choix habituels d'Évrart dans l'autographe des *Problemes*, par exemple l'emploi exclusif de *li* en fonction de régime indirect, les formes *lor, as, u*, etc. (*leur, aux, ou* D), des graphies telles que *coer, foeilles, voelt*, etc. (*cuer, fueilles, veult* D).

2.2.2. Les corrections du manuscrit autographe

Si l'on excepte les corrections proprement linguistiques, destinées à pallier les inadvertances – mot oublié ou répété, confusion entre deux mots –, à corriger la syntaxe, etc., on voit que les interventions sont de

---

41. Évrart de Conty, *Le Livre des Eschez...*, éds GUICHARD-TESSON – ROY, *Introduction*, p. XXXII.

42. RAIMONDI (éd.), '*Les Eschés...*', p. 103. Nous avons conscience de la limite de ces remarques dans la mesure où le manuscrit V n'offre que de rares passages écrits de la main même d'Évrart, mais on peut penser que la copie a été effectuée sous sa supervision.

deux types: certaines sont d'ordre stylistique et montrent un homme conscient de ses choix d'écriture; il s'agit d'alléger, de trouver un terme adéquat, etc. D'autres relèvent véritablement du commentaire et permettent de mesurer les hésitations, voire les changements d'avis de l'auteur, comme nous avons pu le montrer à propos de la musique. Ceci explique qu'on puisse trouver sur une même page plusieurs couches de corrections: certaines sont faites au fil de la plume ou lors d'une relecture immédiate; pour d'autres, la différence du module ou de l'encre montre qu'elles sont le fruit d'une relecture postérieure. Comme il est généralement possible de lire sur le manuscrit ce qui a été raturé, on peut s'interroger sur le sens de ces modifications.

Ainsi, si on regarde les premiers folios de l'œuvre, on voit que tout le développement du début sur les choses naturelles, non naturelles et contre nature (I, 1, 1v-8v) qu'il choisit d'ajouter ne fait l'objet que d'infimes corrections visant la précision et la qualité du style. Le seul changement majeur apparaît au moment où il a fini sa revue et passe à la conclusion. Il barre la phrase: 'les choses dont natureles desus dites sont proprement santés et cause de ycelle ...' pour en préciser la formulation:

> Ainsi appert il, par ce que dit est, que les choses natureles demourans
> en lor naturalité sont cause de santé pour le cors humain, et les choses
> non natureles deuement appliquies le gardent et conservent, et fina-
> blement les choses contre nature le destruient et corrumpent[43]. (I, 1, 9r)

Dans le 5e problème, il ajoute une référence à Galien (12r), d'ailleurs empruntée à Pierre d'Abano, et dans le 6e, il ajoute en bas de page (12v) un paragraphe qui constituera désormais le début de la partie *glose*, où il tente de reformuler clairement à l'intention de son lecteur la question posée, dit-il, 'par maniere de merveille'. De même, dans le 9e problème, un paragraphe ajouté en marge (17r), introduit par l'expression 'aucun exposent que', clarifie un passage du texte à propos des enfants nés pendant un printemps froid et sec en proposant une explication différente; il ne fait d'ailleurs que reprendre un passage du commentaire latin, même si l'*expositeur* n'est pas évoqué ici, et se termine par une phrase de transition.

Ainsi voit-on, par ces quelques exemples, les différentes strates de corrections: corrections de premier jet montrant l'effort de formulation, corrections de second jet, additions notamment, liées à la relecture. Ce travail résulte essentiellement d'un souci pédagogique: comment refor-

---

43. A noter que cette phrase fait elle-même l'objet de quatre corrections: *finablement* raturé après *il* et remplacé, en marge, par *par ce que dit est*; *santé et cause d'ycelle* raturé après *sont*; *au co* raturé après *appliquies*; *finablement* suscrit.

muler la question, quelle explication ajouter pour que l'ensemble soit clair et accessible au lecteur?

Un exemple (II, 2, 60r; voir la reproduction en annexe) illustrera l'attention minutieuse requise des copistes... et des éditeurs pour respecter l'ordre du texte. Évrart ajoute un passage en bas du folio, qu'une paire de signes placés dans le texte et avant la note permet de situer après *se fourme* (l. 9). Le retour au texte est aussi indiqué à la fin: *et c'est chose samblable*. Mais ce paragraphe est à son tour complété de deux nouvelles additions: l'une, en bas à droite, est clairement située par une nouvelle paire de signes. La place de l'autre – en bas, à gauche – est moins évidente: alors que les signes invitent à la situer à la toute fin de l'ajout, avant le retour au texte principal, deux copistes (B.N.F. fr. 563 et Cambrai), trompés par l'indication de retour au texte *et pour ce* qui clôt la première addition, la placent immédiatement après celle-ci.

3. *Le métier de traducteur et de commentateur*

Tout ce travail de révision montre le soin que le commentateur apporte à sa tâche et nous amène à revenir sur la manière dont il la conçoit et sur les buts recherchés. Nous nous contenterons de faire ici quelques rappels qui permettront d'établir des liens entre les *Problemes* et les deux autres œuvres d'Évrart qui les encadrent, du point de vue chronologique[44].

3.1. Translater

Pour Évrart de Conty, traduction et commentaire sont des opérations indissociables, comme le montre, dès les premières lignes, l'équivalence

---

44. Sur le travail d'Évrart comme traducteur et commentateur, voir GUICHARD-TESSON F., 'Le métier de traducteur et de commentateur au XIVᵉ siècle d'après Évrart de Conty', *Le Moyen Français* 24-25 (1990), p. 131-167 et 'Le souci de la langue...'; DUCOS , *La météorologie...*, en particulier p. 195-204 et 'Traduction et lexique scientifique: le cas des *Problèmes* d'Aristote traduits par Évrart de Conty', dans: C. BRUCKER (éd.), *Traduction et adaptation en France au Moyen Âge et à la fin de la Renaissance. Actes du colloque organisé par l'Université de Nancy II, 23-25 mars 1995*, p. 237-247; GOYENS M., 'Le développement du lexique scientifique français et la traduction des *Problèmes* d'Aristote par Évrart de Conty (c. 1380)', *Thélème, Revista Complutense de Estudios Franceses* (2003), p. 199-217; GOYENS M. – DE LEEMANS P., 'Traduire du grec au latin et du latin au français: un défi à la fidélité', dans: P. ANDERSEN (éd.), *Pratiques de traduction au Moyen Âge, Actes du colloque de l'Université de Copenhague, 25 et 26 octobre 2002*, Copenhagen: Museum Tusculanum Press, University of Copenhagen, 2004, p. 204-224; 'La transmission des savoirs en passant par trois langues: le cas des *Problemata* d'Aristote traduits en latin et en moyen français', dans: P. NOBEL (éd.), *La transmission des savoirs au Moyen Âge et à la Renaissance. Vol. 1. Du XIIᵉ au XIVᵉ siècle*. Besançon: Université de Franche-Comté – Université de Tours, 2005, p. 231-257.

sémantique posée par la conjonction *ou*: 'chils livres des problemes a present empris a *translater ou exposer* aucunement de latin en françois...' (1r). Elle est à nouveau formulée dans l'explicit, présent dans tous les manuscrits: 'Explicit le livre des *Problemes* de Aristote *translaté ou exposé* de latin en françois' (B.N.F. fr. 24282, 245r).

C'est d'ailleurs avec ces mêmes verbes qu'il se réfère au *Livre de ethiques* d'Oresme, l''excellent phylosophe qui *translata et exposa* le livre desus dit en la langue françoise, moult souffisamment' (XXVII, 1, 153v).

Entreprise difficile en effet que cette translation qui est en réalité une traduction 'seconde' – l'épithète est employée par Évrart lui-même –, puisque le texte grec a d'abord fait l'objet d'une mise en latin par Barthélémy de Messine[45]. L'inadéquation du latin pour rendre certains mots grecs, notre médecin l'expérimente à son tour lorsqu'il s'efforce de passer au français, comme il le fait remarquer dès le premier problème:

> Sans faille, la translation du grec en latin poet bien ausi faire aucunement a le obscurté de cest livre pour la diversité des langaiges qui ne s'acordent mie aucune fois tres bien, ains avient souvent que on ne troeuve pas en une langue mos proprement correspondans as mos et a la maniere de parler de l'autre, et ce veons nous meismes souvent avenir entre le latin et le françois. (I, 1, 1v)

Faisant preuve de véritables qualités de philologue, il est conscient que les difficultés de son entreprise se situent à deux niveaux: avant même d'affronter celles qui concernent la traduction du latin au français, il doit faire face à celles qui concernent la transmission du texte qui, dit-il à plusieurs reprises, peut être 'corrumpus par le vice des escrisans ou par aventure des translateurs' (XV, 5, 6v). A défaut de remettre en question l'authenticité de l'œuvre de celui qu'il appelle 'le prince des phylosophes' (1r), il est conscient, comme l'était déjà Pierre d'Abano, d'avoir à faire à une compilation de problèmes 'trouvé depuis en divers lieus', puis 'recueilli et assemblé'; ainsi Aristote n'est-il pas responsable de l'organisation interne, il n'a pas 'ordené' les questions, ce qui explique notamment les redites, comme il le fait remarquer par exemple dans le chapitre *Des Sueurs* (II, 39, 78v). De telles remarques abondent. À ses

---

45. Sur la notion de *translation* et le lien avec la *translatio studii*, voir Lusignan S., 'La topique de la *translatio studii* et les traductions françaises de textes savants au XIVe siècle', dans: G. Contamine (éd.), *Traduction et traducteurs au Moyen Âge, Actes du colloque international du CNRS organisé à Paris, Institut de recherche et d'histoire des textes, les 26-28 mai 1986*, Paris: Éditions du CNRS, 1989, p. 303-315, et Ducos, *La météorologie...*, p. 183.

yeux, comme le dit J. Ducos, 'il n'existe pas de texte complètement fiable en latin et (…) le sens d'Aristote, connu par des intermédiaires, risque d'avoir disparu ou de s'être obscurci'[46].

Nous ne multiplierons pas les exemples, mais nous nous contenterons de rappeler ici un passage situé à la fin de l'ouvrage, où Évrart fait la synthèse des difficultés auxquelles il se heurte et qu'il a maintes fois évoquées tout au long de l'ouvrage[47].

> Li textes de Aristote en cest probleme est moult lons et moult ausi *obscurs* en aucun pas et moult *confus,* et samble de premiere faice qu'il soit *mal ordenés* et par aventure est ce pour la translation du grec en latin, car comme il fu touchié au commencement de cest livre, li translateur anciennement voloient ensievir communement les paroles du texte, en metant *mot pour mot* au plus pres qu'il pooient. Et pour ce que la maniere de parler en une langue n'est mie tele qu'elle est en l'autre et *c'on ne troeuve mie proprement mos correspondans ensamble* d'une langue a l'autre bien souvent, pour ce n'est ce mie merveilles se la translations fait a le fois aucunement varier la sentence ou au mains la biauté.
>
> Et pour ce poet il estre que li textes de Aristote en cest probleme et en pluseurs lieus autres samble estre confus et obscurs, et que les parties aucune fois ne se continuent pas bien ne n'entresievent. Sans faille, a ce poet bien ausi aucune chose faire le corruption du texte par les *mal escrisans* ou aultrement, ou par le espoir *malvaisement entendre.* Et pour ce n'est ce mie ausi merveilles se la translation seconde du latin en françois qui doit le texte ausi aucunement ensivre, si comme il fu promis, aucunement s'en sent. (XXX, 1, 179v)

Les quelques passages cités montrent qu'Évrart a su envisager, sinon dans le bon ordre, du moins de manière assez exhaustive, les accidents possibles dans la chaîne de transmission: compilation et non œuvre originale, mauvaise compréhension du traducteur, fidélité excessive à la lettre du texte au détriment du sens, fautes des copistes. Ainsi s'impose la tâche de 'desclairier' autant que possible le propos d'Aristote, d'en fournir la 'sentence' à celui qui veut l''entendre'.

Il est intéressant de constater qu'Évrart emploie un lexique identique lorsqu'il parle de son poème qui, d'emblée, semble solliciter un commentaire. Ainsi met-il en garde le lecteur qui serait tenté de blâmer l'auteur,

> car mesprent moult villainement
> chilz qui reprent aucune chose
> s'il n'entend bien et texte et glose[48].

---

46. Ducos, *La météorologie…*, p. 198.
47. A noter que Pierre d'Abano ne se plaint pas ici de l'obscurité du texte.
48. Raimondi (éd.), 'Les Eschés…', v. 24-26, p. 107.

S'agit-il simplement ici des gloses marginales latines écrites de sa main dans le manuscrit de Venise, ou envisage-t-il déjà le lourd appareil didactique que constituera la glose en prose? Toujours est-il que le poème demande à être commenté et que le passage à la prose est ressenti comme une opération d'élucidation. Tel est bien l'avis du copiste du manuscrit Paris, B.N.F. fr. 19114 des *EAM*, qui fait précéder le texte de la mention suivante: 'Le jeu des Eschez amoureux translaté de rithme en prose et exposé.' Quant à l'auteur lui-même, il exprime dès les premières lignes sa volonté de 'declairier aucunes choses que la rime contient, qui semblent estre obscures et estranges de prime face', justifiant ainsi le choix de la prose, 'plus clere a entendre que n'est rime'[49].

Si différent que soit le propos des œuvres, toutes deux reposent donc sur une démarche identique. Les 'fortes questions' posées par Aristote s'adressaient en priorité 'aus anciens et aus sages' déjà exercés en l'art de philosophie; c'est pourquoi les propos concis et complexes du Philosophe demandent à être éclaircis, car 'parole briefve et de grant sentence est communement obscure' (*Problemes* I, 1, 1v). De même, la 'fainte maniere de parler des poetes' contient 'aucune grant sentence secrete moult souvent'[50], ce qui rend les éclaircissements fournis par les *EAM* nécessaires à l'intention des non-initiés.

On voit donc qu'un réseau sémantique commun s'impose à l'auteur pour analyser sa démarche: 'texte / glose; translater, exposer, declairier, ordener, sentence, entendre'[51].

3.2. Exposer (plaisir et profit)

Il y a loin, évidemment, de la matière des *EAM* à celle des *Problemes*, mais le même souci de plaire et d'émerveiller reste présent.

En affirmant qu'il veut procurer à ses lecteurs plaisir et profit, l'auteur des *Problemes* ne fait que reprendre un topos des traducteurs et, plus généralement, des écrivains de son époque. Aristote a choisi, sur les divers sujets, les questions 'esmerveillables et delitables', et le plaisir éprouvé résidera essentiellement dans la satisfaction de l'intelligence qui acquiert la 'cognoissance des causes'. Ainsi la formule 'par maniere de merveille' revient-elle comme un leitmotiv! Le profit plus immédiat

---

49. Évrart de Conty, *Le Livre des Eschez...*, éds GUICHARD-TESSON – ROY, p. 2.
50. Évrart de Conty, *Le Livre des Eschez...*, éds GUICHARD-TESSON – ROY, p. 2.
51. Parlant de Paris, Pallas dit aussi dans le poème: 'Tant y treuve on textez et gloses / Et d'escolet et d'escoliers...' Cité dans GALPIN S.L., '*Les Eschez amoureux*: A Complete Synopsis with Unpublished Extracts', *Romanic Review* 11 (1920), p. 283-307, ici p. 293.

n'est pas oublié non plus: l'ouvrage parle d'abord de médecine, science qui nous est 'plus necessaire et plus pourfitable'[52].

Nous avons déjà eu l'occasion de souligner que, dans le commentaire du poème, Évrart s'exprime dans les mêmes termes et reprend mot pour mot une phrase de la *Rhétorique* d'Aristote, 'les choses esmerveillables sont par nature delitables', identifiée en marge dans les *Problemes*, non identifiée dans les *EAM*. Ce sont cette fois les poètes qui auront à tâche d''esmerveiller l'entendement' en s'exprimant sous le manteau de la fiction: elle enveloppe 'une sentence plaisant et delitable et moult souvent une moralité qui est de grant profit'[53]. S'il est ici question de poésie en général, Évrart a été encore plus précis sur les intentions du poète des *Eschés* dans les toutes premières lignes, et qui de mieux autorisé que l'auteur lui-même pour en parler?

> Et affin que ce livre rimé fut plus agreablement et plus generalment receu de tous, jones et anciens, l'aucteur avec l'amoureuse matiere entremella et adjousta pluseurs choses estranges qui profitent grandement a traictier des meurs et au gouvernement de nostre vie humaine, affin que ceulx qui y regardent, avec la recreacion et le delit qu'ilz y pourront prendre, aucun profit aussi en puissent raporter[54].

Le corps n'est pas oublié non plus, et le sage médecin rappelle ensuite que le plaisir éprouvé à la lecture des poètes 'recree moult et resjoïst nature, dont grandement vault mielx la corporele disposition; et le profit aussi que on en raporte parfait l'ame et amende'[55].

L'auteur était moins explicite au début du poème. Mais le lecteur y est invité à lire 'par bonne diligence' et à 'bien considerer s'a mistiere'[56] sous la matière de ce qui s'annonce comme le récit d'une partie d'échecs et l'aventure d'un jeune homme – le narrateur du poème, l'acteur du commentaire en prose – maté en l'angle par une jeune fille. Récit lui aussi destiné à émerveiller l'entendement: bien subtil en effet celui qui comprendra, par le seul recours au texte, la signification allégorique de la partie d'échecs.

---

52. Déjà dans le poème, Pallas affirmait: 'Premierement nous trouverons / Qu'il n'est chose a la verité / Plus desiree de santé' (manuscrit de Dresde 70a); cité par HÖFLER H., *Les Échecs amoureux. Untersuchungen über die Quellen des II. Teiles* (Inaug.-Diss. München, 1905), Neustadt, 1907, p. 23.

53. Évrart de Conty, *Le Livre des Eschez...*, éds GUICHARD-TESSON – ROY, p. 25.

54. Évrart de Conty, *Le Livre des Eschez...*, éds GUICHARD-TESSON – ROY, p. 2.

55. Évrart de Conty, *Le Livre des Eschez...*, éds GUICHARD-TESSON – ROY, p. 3.

56. RAIMONDI (éd.), '*Les Eschés...*', v. 32 et 40, p. 107-108.

3.3. Le lectorat

Ceci nous amène, on le voit, à poser la question des destinataires. Est-ce aux mêmes lecteurs que s'adressent ces trois œuvres? On a peine à le croire tant les sujets sont différents. Le poème et le commentaire des *Problemes* semblent a priori aux antipodes, puisqu'il s'agit, dans le premier cas, d'une œuvre de fiction dans laquelle l'auteur est libre de puiser sa matière où il l'entend (*Roman de la Rose* ou *Régime des princes*). Les *Problemes*, eux, sont une œuvre philosophique, et le déroulement en est imposé par l'organisation du texte à traduire.

Le poème s'adresse

> A tous les amoureux gentilz,
> especialement aux soubtilz
> qui aiment le beau jeu nottable
> le jeu plaisant et delitable[57],

celui des échecs, bien sûr. On peut penser que ces jeunes amoureux experts au jeu ont peu en commun avec ceux qui liront les *Problemes*. Mais on a vu précédemment qu'Évrart prétendait s'adresser aux jeunes et aux anciens, et si l'on regarde attentivement le déroulement du poème, on remarque que la narration est très vite envahie de discours qui abordent des sujets fort sérieux. Déjà Nature et Diane ont mis l'*acteur* en garde contre l'amour. À partir du moment où Pallas prend la parole, il est presque relégué au rôle d'auditeur muet. Ses interventions se font de plus en plus rares et si on en croit les rubriques du manuscrit de Dresde, il n'ouvre plus la bouche dans le dernier quart de l'œuvre. Après la traditionnelle mise en garde contre l'amour, c'est un traité de bonne vie qu'elle lui propose; le destinataire visé est clair: huit folios parlent de chevalerie, la fin de l'œuvre est consacrée au mariage, aux femmes, aux enfants, à la maison, etc. 'Formule renouvelée du «régime des princes»', disions-nous dans l'introduction des *EAM*[58]. En somme, on appâte le lecteur par l'aventure amoureuse pour lui servir ensuite un discours édifiant.

Ceux qui liront les *Problemes* savent, eux, à quoi s'attendre dès le Prologue. Il s'agit de rendre un savoir accessible sur des sujets clairement annoncés et les destinataires iront y puiser matière à satisfaire leur désir de comprendre. Ainsi le texte est-il toujours accompagné de sa glose. Ce qui constitue l'originalité de l'œuvre, c'est évidemment la présence constante des indications marginales en latin, qui identifient les

---

57. RAIMONDI (éd.), '*Les Eschés...*', v. 1-4, p. 107.
58. Évrart de Conty, *Le Livre des Eschez...*, éds GUICHARD-TESSON – ROY, *Introduction*, p. LXVIII.

sources utilisées dans le texte ou ajoutent de nouvelles références. Ainsi, tout fonctionne comme si le texte des *Problemes* pouvait offrir deux lectures. L'une, qui se passerait des indications marginales, offrirait les éclaircissements essentiels sur ces fortes questions, le commentaire étant clairement distingué de la traduction par l'indication *glose*[59]. L'autre, plus érudite, identifie, pour chaque champ de savoir, les principales autorités et permettra à un lettré de retrouver, dans les textes anciens, la matière qui n'est pas 'propre a exposer en françois' ou celle qui est 'trop soubtile'.

Les gloses marginales du poème identifiaient certes quelques sources, mais essentiellement destinées à préparer l'interprétation allégorique de certains épisodes. Qu'en était-il du manuscrit autographe des *EAM*? On peut raisonnablement penser que de telles indications marginales n'y figuraient pas si l'on considère l'état de la tradition manuscrite: notre manuscrit de base, proche de l'autographe, n'en comporte que quelques-unes. On ignore à quel moment le projet du commentaire en prose a été élaboré, mais ne peut-on penser qu'Évrart a voulu se livrer, à partir d'une matière moins austère, sur des sujets qui se recouvrent partiellement, à une même entreprise de vulgarisation du savoir? Ici, plus d'indications marginales; les indications seront intégrées au fil du texte – certains copistes en identifieront en marge. La volonté d'instruire complète la volonté d'édifier.

On sent toutefois l'ambivalence d'Évrart, désireux de mettre à la portée de ceux qu'il désigne dans les *Problemes* comme 'la gent laye' le savoir des philosophes, mais conscient des difficultés de l'entreprise. Il semble penser que la langue française a ses limites et n'est pas aussi propre que le latin à exprimer certaines notions. Ainsi, dans le 10e problème de la 3e partie traitant de l'ivresse, et plus particulièrement du fait que ceux qui sont 'fort yvre' voient double, il juge nécessaire de parler de perspective et de la composition de l'œil, mais après avoir précisé qu'il est composé de trois humeurs et de sept tuniques, il décide de se 'taire atant de ceste composition, pour ce que c'est chose trop forte a entendre et a mettre en françois' (III, 10, 87v)[60]. Une phrase identique est em-

---

59. Après survol des trois premières parties (136 problèmes), on constate que le cas de loin le plus fréquent est la présence d'une seule indication *glose*. Elle manque dans cinq cas, (I, 19, 47, 56; II, 37; III, 21). Mais le problème II, 37 ne comporte qu'un paragraphe. Dans les trois cas de la 1re partie, elles semblent être le résultat d'un oubli, alors que nous retrouvons les formules initiales usuelles: 'C'est la sentence de Aristote en cest probleme...' (45r et 53v).

60. Il faut toutefois noter qu'il y reviendra dans la 9e partie sur les cicatrices: 'Et combien que ce soit fort de bien entendre ceste composition et de la metre entendement en françois, nient mains, pour l'ocasion de la matiere, je y woeil un petit arrester...' (IX, 10, 156r).

ployée dans les *EAM* à propos des *beles soutiletés* et des *grans misteres* qui ont trait à l'arc-en-ciel, ce qui est 'chose trop estrange et trop forte a entendre et a metre en françois'[61]. Ainsi semble-t-il lier les difficultés de compréhension et les limites de la langue. De même, la variation de la taille des ombres portées par les objets lui paraît-elle, dans les *Problemes*, 'chose moult estrange a comprendre a la gent laye et mal aussi seant en françois' (XV, 5, 6v). Aussi décide-t-il de mettre 'la sentence de ce qu'il woelt dire par example', c'est-à-dire qu'il l'accompagnera d'une figure. Là encore un rapprochement s'impose avec les *EAM*: c'est à propos des miroirs qu'il décide de laisser 'les grans soutilletés et les demonstracions fortes qui ne sont pas bien seans en françois'[62]. Là encore, il accompagnera de schémas ses explications sur les différents types de miroirs. Il est intéressant de constater que tous ces sujets sont liés à la vue et à la science naissante de perspective[63].

4. *La construction du commentaire*

Problemes et *EAM* offrent des analogies de structure. La trame est dans les deux cas offerte par un texte-source, mais l'auteur s'accorde une grande souplesse. Le commentaire est linéaire, mais pas de manière aussi stricte que chez Pierre d'Abano qui renvoie précisément au passage commenté. Évrart opère par enchâssements et digressions, et les *EAM* vont pousser plus loin une méthode déjà en place dans les *Problemes*. Le texte est aussi le prétexte à fournir un ensemble de connaissances minimales qui semblent nécessaires au lecteur sur certains sujets.

Ainsi le commentaire de Pierre d'Abano est-il très inégalement utilisé d'un problème à l'autre, presque toujours abrégé et simplifié, allégé de nombreuses citations. Mais Évrart y insère à l'occasion de longs excursus. Le premier problème de la première partie, par exemple, qui occupe moins d'une page dans l'*Expositio Problematum Aristotelis* de Pierre d'Abano – Mantoue 1475 –, va donner lieu à un développement de plus de huit folios, parce qu'Évrart juge nécessaire d'exposer, à l'intention d'un lecteur qui n'est pas nécessairement versé dans l'art de la médecine, les principes qui en constituent la base, en s'appuyant sur l'*Isagoge*

---

61. Évrart de Conty, *Le Livre des Eschez...*, éds GUICHARD-TESSON – ROY, p. 642. Les causes en sont 'rendues et sceues des soubtilz philosophes'.
    62. Évrart de Conty, *Le Livre des Eschez...*, éds GUICHARD-TESSON – ROY, p. 702.
    63. Ces remarques sont aussi faites à propos des proportions musicales (XIX, 2).

de Johannitius. Dans le 11ᵉ problème, qui traite de la mutation des eaux et de l'air, après avoir repris l'essentiel du commentaire latin en l'abrégeant et en le réorganisant à sa manière, il juge bon d'ajouter 'pour le occasion de ceste matiere' un développement sur les trois conditions du bon air et les cinq conditions d'une eau bonne et saine, en s'appuyant sur Avicenne et Palladius. Il ira encore plus loin dans les *EAM* où l'évocation du jugement de Pâris sera l'occasion d'insérer tout un traité de mythographie, la figure d'Apollon permettant elle-même d'insérer une série de traités sur les arts libéraux. Cette construction assez lâche lui permet de réutiliser la matière des *Problemes* jugée pertinente, de même qu'il avait déjà repris dans ces derniers certains passages du discours de Pallas.

Pour montrer la manière dont notre médecin travaille et dont il réutilise plus tard la matière des *Problemes*, nous utiliserons deux exemples.

4.1. De Pierre d'Abano aux *Problemes*, des *Problemes* aux *EAM*

Dans la première partie consacrée aux problèmes médicinaux, le troisième problème pose la question: 'Pour quoy est ce que la mutation des tans et des vens engendrent et font maladies, et ausy les curent et garissent?' (I, 3, 10r) Après avoir traduit assez fidèlement la réponse, Évrart propose un commentaire dont l'ensemble des éléments sont déjà présents dans le texte de Pierre d'Abano, mais il les réorganise; il les réutilisera quelques années plus tard lorsqu'il rédigera les *EAM*.

Déjà Pierre d'Abano lui-même s'intéressait essentiellement aux dernières lignes du problème, notamment au passage: 'Et ortus stellarum sicut Orion et Arcturus et Pleias et Canis' qui occupe près de la moitié de son commentaire. Cette partie s'organise de la façon suivante (voir aussi infra *Figure 1*):

- il passe en revue les quatre étoiles fixes citées dans le texte original;
- il présente ensuite les trois manières de distinguer les saisons:
  sensibilis valde medicinalis;
  secundum astrologos;
  sicut tradunt quidam astronomi et poetizantes magis;
- il revient ensuite au commentaire général pour dire que le lever et le coucher des étoiles sont plutôt des signes, tandis que le soleil est la cause;
- il commente enfin les derniers mots: *serenitatum et tempestatum.*

Le commentaire qu'en offre Évrart de Conty montre la liberté avec laquelle il procède et les choix qu'il effectue. Il abrège et réorganise la

matière fournie par l'*expositeur*, de sorte que les considérations astronomiques occupent une place accrue, alors que tout le début de la réponse est commenté en quelques lignes, les seules références à Galien et Avicenne étant renvoyées dans les marges. La matière empruntée sur ce sujet à Pierre d'Abano, introduite par: 'Nous devons aussi entendre…' est ainsi réorganisée:
- les trois manières de considérer les saisons viennent en premier: considération médicinale;
  considération des *astronomiens*;
  considération des poètes;
- cette dernière amène un développement supplémentaire, 'pour ceste matere encor miex desclairier' (10v), car il y a trois manières de considérer le lever et le coucher des étoiles, 'mondaine, cronique, heliatique'. Elles n'étaient qu'énumérées chez Pierre d'Abano et donnent ici lieu à un développement d'une vingtaine de lignes;
- il reprend la remarque de Pierre d'Abano sur les étoiles qui sont plutôt des signes tandis que le soleil est cause;
- c'est ensuite seulement qu'il reviendra à la présentation des quatre étoiles citées par Aristote – 'pour ce devons nous encore savoir…' –, supprimant certaines précisions astronomiques et certaines références, rappelant en revanche le nom sous lequel on désigne les Pléiades en langue vulgaire: 'l'Estoile pouchiniere'. Le Chien fournit par contre une des très rares citations latines intégrées au texte des *Problemes*: 'sub cane et ante canem moleste sunt purgationes';
- la fin est assez proche de Pierre d'Abano. Évrart y reprend de façon très générale – 'on poet dire que…' – ce qui était assumé à la première personne par Pierre d'Abano: 'intelligo'.

Si l'on s'interroge sur les intentions d'Évrart lorsqu'il procède à cette réorganisation, il semble qu'il s'efforce de partir d'une constatation proche de l'expérience quotidienne: le passage des saisons. A partir de là, il va éveiller la curiosité, 'esmerveiller', en proposant des regards différents sur ce sujet simple qui sera l'occasion d'instruire en donnant lieu à des considérations plus savantes sur les étoiles.

Quand on replace ce passage dans le contexte de l'ensemble de l'œuvre d'Évrart, il est intéressant de constater que la 'reverdie' par laquelle l'*acteur* du poème évoque le printemps et qui occupe une soixantaine de vers – inspirés, dit le commentaire en prose, du *Gouvernement des princes* d'Aristote – rappelle le passage des *Problemes* où Évrart évoque le printemps sous le patronage d'Avicenne:

[Li] arbre aussy se reverdissent
et font fueilles et se flourissent...(v. 95-96)
La naige *se degaste et font*,
Li airs s'adoulcist et attempre
Si qu'il n'y a, ne tart ne tempre,
ne trop chaleur ne trop froidure...[64] (v. 104-07)

Et selon ce dit Avicennes que li prins tans est quand li arbre commencent a foeillir et que les naiges des montaingnes *se fondent et
degastent* et que nous n'avons mie trop grant mestier de nous vestir et
couvrir pour le froit ne de trop grant eventation pour la chaleur. (10v)

Au-delà de la formulation poétique, la reprise du doublet *degaster /
fondre*, qui traduit le verbe *cadunt* employé par Pierre d'Abano, ne nous
paraît pas un hasard: quand il compose le poème, Évrart a sans doute en
tête le texte de Pierre d'Abano[65]!

Le commentaire en prose ne manquera pas de reprendre la citation
d'Avicenne, en des termes presque identiques à ceux des *Problemes*[66];
elle s'inscrit dans un long développement sur les quatre saisons, qu'il
estime nécessaire 'pour l'occasion de ceste matiere', c'est-à-dire le fait
que l'aventure amoureuse se déroule au mois de mai. Après avoir rap-
pelé en médecin les qualités propres à chacune, il reprend, en l'introdui-
sant par une formule quasi identique – 'nous devons oultre aussi secon-
dement entendre...' – une grande partie du développement analysé
précédemment, organisé cette fois dans l'ordre suivant:

- les trois considérations sur les saisons – selon les médecins, les
astronomiens, les poètes – sont formulées dans les mêmes termes.
On y retrouve, inséré au fil du texte, le nom de Galien qui figurait

---

64. RAIMONDI (éd.), '*Les Eschés...*', p. 109. G. Raimondi note que dans les gloses latines du manuscrit de Venise comme dans les *EAM*, le livre *Du gouvernement des princes*
est attribué à Aristote (p. 191-92), autre indice renforçant l'identité de l'auteur. En réalité,
Évrart ne renvoie pas ici à l'œuvre de Gilles de Rome, comme le pense G. Raimondi,
mais au *Secretum secretorum*, utilisé à plusieurs reprises dans les *EAM*. Voir STEELE R.
(éd.), *Opera hactenus inedita Rogeri Baconi, Fasc. V, Secretum secretorum*, Oxford:
Oxford University Press, 1920, p. 76-77. Rappelons que la traduction de Jofroi de
Waterford et de Servais Copale était intitulée *Livre du gouvernement des rois et des princes*.
65. 'Dicit enim quod ver est principium frondendi arborum et quod nives de montibus
cadunt neque multis tunc indigemus cooperimentis propter frigus neque paucis propter
eventationem.' (I, 3)
66. 'Pour ce dit Avicennes que li printemps commence quant les arbres commencent a
foeillir et que les naiges des montaignes se fundent et degastent, et que nous n'avons pas
aussi trop grant nécessité de nous vestir ne couvrir pour le froit, ne de eventacion aussi
trop grant pour la chaleur.' Évrart de Conty, *Le Livre des Eschez...*, éds GUICHARD-TES-
SON – ROY, p. 20. Sur le rapprochement entre ces trois textes, voir aussi dans ce volume la
contribution de C. BOUCHER.

en marge dans les *Problemes*, tandis que la référence au *De aere et aqua* disparaît; seul le nom d'Ypocras est retenu;
- le développement sur les trois sortes de lever des étoiles est escamoté, mais Évrart reprend, associée aux considérations des poètes, la présentation des Pléiades et d'Arcturus. Orion et le Chien, qui ne sont pas nécessaires au développement sur le déroulement des saisons, sont ici omis;
- enfin, notre médecin indique sa préférence pour la considération des poètes en rappelant, dans la continuité de Pierre d'Abano et des *Problemes*, que les étoiles sont 'plus signe que cause', tandis que le soleil est 'cause principal'.

Une conclusion abrupte nous ramène ensuite au poème: ce qu'il dit du printemps s'applique au mois de mai!

On voit donc Évrart reprendre la matière des *Problemes* de façon très proche, supprimant toutefois ce qui n'est pas nécessaire à son propos, insérant dans le texte les références qu'il juge nécessaires à cet effort accru de vulgarisation, se rapprochant de son lecteur en rappelant les noms courants de 'l'Etoile pouchiniere' ou du 'char a IIII roes'.

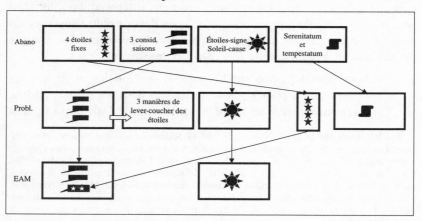

Figure 1: *Réutilisation de la matière savante*

4.2. Des *Problemes* aux *EAM*

Notre deuxième exemple est emprunté à la 27e partie qui traite 'des problemes morauls qui appartienent a l'ame' et plus particulièrement 'des problemes appartenans a force ou a hardiesce et aussi a peur, son contraire, pour ce qu'il y ha ausi en ceste matere aucunes grans merveilles' (XXVII, 152r).

Le premier problème est ainsi formulé:

> Pour quoy est ce que a ciaus qui ont peur, les membres lor tramblent?
> A ce respont Aristotes et dit ainsi que c'est pour le infrigidation des
> membres de dehors de la persone qui ha peur, car la chaleur naturele
> s'en retrait et eslonge. Et pour ce ausi en avient il que li ventres lor
> lache et le orine meismes aucune fois involuntairement. (XXVII, 1,
> 152r)

C'est à cet endroit que se trouve placée la mention *Glose*; celle-ci oc-
cupera deux folios et demi, et c'est seulement alors que l'on reviendra à
la question posée et à l'aspect physique de la peur, ce retour au sujet
étant introduit par la formule très lâche: 'Pour quoy nous devons savoir
quant au propos present...' Entre les deux, le développement est d'ordre
moral et s'inscrit dans ce type de petits traités qui permettent à l'auteur
de faire le point, de manière simple et claire, sur un sujet qu'il juge important[67]. Nous en analyserons rapidement la composition pour montrer
ensuite que l'ensemble s'en retrouve, de manière éclatée, dans les *EAM*
(voir aussi infra *Figure 2*).

Le passage offre peu d'indications marginales; elles renvoient toutes
à Aristote: deux au 2ᵉ livre de l'*Éthique*, une au 8ᵉ de la *Politique*, une
au 2ᵉ de la *Rhétorique* et enfin une au 3ᵉ livre de l'*Éthique*. Deux sont ici
d'un intérêt particulier pour nous, car elles montrent la construction du
passage.

- Un premier développement – celui qui renvoie au 2ᵉ livre de l'*Éthique* – va être consacré aux vertus, comme le montre la formule d'introduction: 'Pour le occasion de ceste matiere qui a regart a la vertu
  moral...' (152r). Après avoir défini la vertu en général, il donnera
  une liste des douze vertus, parmi lesquelles figure *force*. Les pages
  suivantes développent une à une ces douze vertus et ce passage se
  clôt par l'allusion à Oresme dont nous avons déjà parlé.
- Un deuxième développement, en marge duquel nous trouvons la référence à la *Rhétorique*, est relié au précédent par un lien extrêmement lâche:

> Nous devons oultre ausi savoir que tout ausi qu'il y a .xii. vertus qui
> nous enclinent, comme dit est, a bonnes oeuvres, tout ausi y a il .12.
> manieres de passions ou de affections de ame qui nous esmoeuvent les
> coraiges en diverses manieres, des queles Aristotes parle en sa *Retho-
> rique*... (153v)

---

67. Le commentaire de Pierre d'Abano est ici beaucoup plus court et Évrart s'en
écarte considérablement. Nous ne le prendrons donc pas en compte dans le développement qui suit.

Elles sont ensuite énumérées et rapidement commentées; parmi elles figurent *peur* et *hardiesce*.

- Évrart y ajoute, toujours de l'autorité d'Aristote, mais sans plus de précision, six autres passions qu'il énumère et commente brièvement (153v-154r). C'est alors seulement que le lien est établi: les vertus 'repriment et amoderent' les passions.
- La digression semble terminée et, après un retour à la ligne, Évrart déclare: 'Quant est dont a nostre pourpos qui regarde la vertu de force...' (154r). C'est l'occasion d'une nouvelle distinction entre force de corps et force d'âme. C'est cette dernière qui permet de n'être 'ne trop hardis ne trop couars', ce qui entraîne un développement sur *hardiesce* et *peur* (154r-v).
- Ces passions altèrent aussi le corps. Nous voici réellement revenus au 'pourpos present'; la réponse est alors éclairée par des considérations médicales sur la chaleur.

Le lecteur des *EAM* remarquera bien sûr que ces énumérations s'y retrouvent en des termes quasiment identiques.

- Elles sont amenées cette fois par la découverte des figures peintes sur le mur du verger de Deduit, dont la première est *Haine* qui est 'une passion d'ame ou une affection qui nous esmeut a vouloir mal a aucune personne, ainsi que amours est une passion qui nous esmeut a bien vouloir a aucune personne'[68]. On se contente ici de nous fournir une simple liste, complétée, comme dans les *Problemes*, par six autres énumérées dans le même ordre: 'grace, jalousie, desdaing, misericorde, et envie, et vergoigne'.
- Sans autre justification que la liaison 'Aristote aussi en son livre d'*Ethiques* fait mencion de .XII. notables vertus', nous nous trouvons devant une reprise quasi littérale des *Problemes*. À défaut de pouvoir nous livrer à une comparaison détaillée des deux textes, nous donnons en exemple la définition de la vertu comme juste milieu:

Problemes	*EAM*
...en toutes les œuvres humaines ou il y a defaute et superhabondance qui font a blasmer, c'est a dire ou on poet errer et falir par trop faire ou trop peu, li moyens est loables, u quel gist la vertus. (152v)	...en toutes les oeuvres humaines ou ly hons peut errer par trop et trop peu faire, il y a deux extremités vituperables, dont l'une excede en trop et l'autre en trop peu faire, entre lesquelles le moien est loable ouquel la vertu gist. (p. 442) (repris en des termes identiques p. 448)

---

68. Évrart de Conty, *Le Livre des Eschez...*, éds GUICHARD-TESSON – ROY, p. 441.

- Après cette revue des vertus[69], on revient aux passions précédemment mentionnées: la définition générale et la présentation en sont
là encore très proches. (153v, p. 445)
- Les six autres passions ne seront pas définies ici, mais le commentateur y reviendra à propos de la troisième flèche à pointe de plomb
du dieu d'amour: *Honte*. Ce sera l'occasion de reprendre presque
littéralement les définitions de ces six passions[70].

Les rapports entre les deux textes s'arrêtent-ils là? Non, puisque nous
identifierons plus tard deux autres passages de ce problème.

- L'un des deux cavaliers de l'acteur est *Hardement*, c'est-à-dire
Hardiesse, qui a le lion pour emblème[71]. Avatar de la vertu de
force, il est donc redéfini en des termes qui rappellent fortement
notre problème; on y retrouve notamment la distinction opérée entre force de corps et force d'âme.

Problemes	*EAM*
Tout ausi que force corporele gist en poissance de soubstenir et de porter grans fais et pesans, ausi gist ceste force de ame en bien envaÿr et en bien soubstenir les choses perilleuses et terribles… (154r)	Tout aussi que force corporele est neces-saire pour soustenir et pour porter grant faiz, tout aussi est force d'ame requise a cest besoing pour acomplir les œuvres de vertu qui sont grandes et fortes, car vertu a regard a choses fortes… (p. 721)

- Quant à la fin du problème qui constitue l'explication médicale, elle
sera réinvestie dans le commentaire des cavaliers de la jeune fille,
Honte et *Peur*. *Peur*, dit-il dans les *EAM*, est 'une maniere de
infrigidacion' (p. 656); c'est le terme employé au début du problème. C'est ce qui explique la pâleur du visage, explication qui a
bien évidemment été fournie dans notre problème.

Problemes	*EAM*
… pour ce avient il ausy, en acordant a l'ame qui bien woelt eslongier le peril et eviter, que la chaleur naturele proportion-nelment se eslonge des membres de dehors et de desus as quels la resistence devroit apartenir, et s'en fuit non mie au coer mais es parties basses du cors, aussi comme pour	… et c'est pour la naturele chaleur qui se depart des parties foraines et se retrait dedens le corps en bas au plus loings que elle peut, aussi come pour eslongier le peril apparant, et pour ce encline aussi pa-reillement paour, quant elle est grande, la personne a fuir en enssivant l'affection de

---

69. A noter que quatre de ces vertus, *amative de honneur, debonnaireté, amiableté,
jocundité,* seront à nouveau évoquées en des termes très proches lors du commentaire des
couleurs de l'arc-en-ciel (Évrart de Conty, *Le Livre des Eschez…*, éds GUICHARD-TESSON –
ROY, p. 640).
70. Évrart de Conty, *Le Livre des Eschez…*, éds GUICHARD-TESSON – ROY, p. 567.
71. Évrart de Conty, *Le Livre des Eschez…*, éds GUICHARD-TESSON – ROY, p. 720.

plus eslongier le peril ou pour les membres conforter as quels la fuite est plus apartenans, et pour ce en avient il que li peureus est toudis pales... en peur la chaleur naturele se depart des membres de dehors et se retrait dedens... pour ce s'ensieut le infrigidation des membres desus dis de dehors. (154v)	l'ame; pour ceste cause donc demeurent la face et les parties haultes de chalour desnuees. Et pour ce dit Aristote aussi que paour est une maniere de infrigidacion. (p. 656)

Le passage sur les vertus et passions que nous venons de commenter et qui figure dans les deux œuvres donne aussi l'occasion d'attirer l'attention sur un autre aspect, soit l'héritage de Gilles de Rome, dont l'apport dans le poème a déjà été mis en évidence[72]. C'est lui qui, dans le *De regimine principum,* ajoute six nouvelles passions aux douze de la tradition aristotélicienne; le classement des vertus lui est aussi redevable, ainsi que certains des noms en français, par exemple *amative de honneur* ou *jocundité*[73].

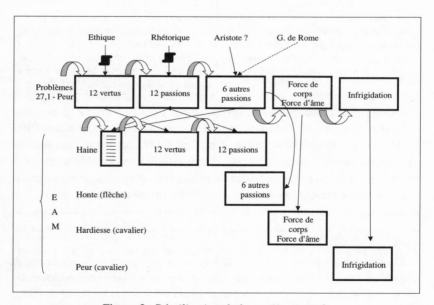

Figure 2: *Réutilisation de la matière morale*

72. HÖFLER, *Les Échecs amoureux. Untersuchungen...*, et HÖFLER H., '*Les Échecs amoureux*', *Romanische Forschungen* 27 (1910), p. 625-689.

73. On se rappellera que *Jocus* est l'autre nom de Déduit, fils de Vénus, que le poème présente comme le dieu 'des soulas du monde et des jieux'. RAIMONDI (éd.), '*Les Eschés...*', v. 2070, p. 149. Par ailleurs, le mot *jocundité* n'est pas employé par Oresme.

On voit donc comment, malgré la trame bien différente imposée par les deux ouvrages, Évrart reprend largement la matière des *Problemes*, par le jeu de formules de transition extrêmement lâches. Nous avions déjà fait des constatations identiques en comparant les développements sur l'ivresse, à propos de la figure de Bacchus, et sur la musique à laquelle est consacrée une section des *Problemes*, mais aussi une partie du traité des arts libéraux contenu dans les *EAM*[74].

Ces techniques de construction, de réduction et d'assemblage dans les ouvrages d'Évrart, nous pouvons aussi noter qu'elles sont au service de quelques intentions-clés: susciter la curiosité, élargir le sujet, proposer plusieurs angles de vue, simplifier ce qui est trop compliqué, procurer des exemples à la portée de son public. Bref, garder l'intérêt de son lecteur quelle que soit l'aridité de la matière, en authentique pédagogue.

Conclusion

Voici donc un enseignant–écrivain, qui s'intéresse à de multiples sujets, qui habite une bibliothèque, et pour lequel il faudrait pouvoir reconstituer l'ensemble de ses sources, comme G. Raimondi a commencé de le faire pour les *Eschés*.

Voici un témoin de la fin du XIVe siècle, familier des princes et des lettrés, qui participe à la vulgarisation du savoir de son époque et s'est fait une idée de ce que doit être un comportement sage et de ce que doit connaître un homme cultivé.

Il y a déjà plus de dix ans, nous commencions la présentation des *EAM* en remarquant qu'Évrart de Conty était 'un de ces auteurs médiévaux pour qui l'histoire littéraire s'est montrée ingrate'[75]. Incontestablement, les choses ont changé et justice lui est rendue puisqu'il est désormais reconnu comme l'auteur de trois œuvres majeures de genre fort différent, qui pourtant présentent entre elles bien des ressemblances et des liens qu'on n'a pas fini d'élucider. On peut espérer disposer de l'œuvre intégrale dans un avenir proche.

Et, justement, les *Problemes* apparaissent comme la pièce charnière dans l'œuvre d'Évrart: l'occasion qui lui est donnée d'exposer des vérités savantes, mais selon un cadre très contraint, lui permet de développer une technique et lui donnera sans doute le goût de faire une œuvre moins austère, plus large, qui fera la synthèse de ses préoccupations morales et savantes et destinée à un plus large public.

Université de Montréal

---

74. GUICHARD-TESSON, 'Évrart de Conty, auteur…', p. 125-136.
75. Évrart de Conty, *Le Livre des Eschez…*, éds GUICHARD-TESSON – ROY, *Introduction*, p. VII.

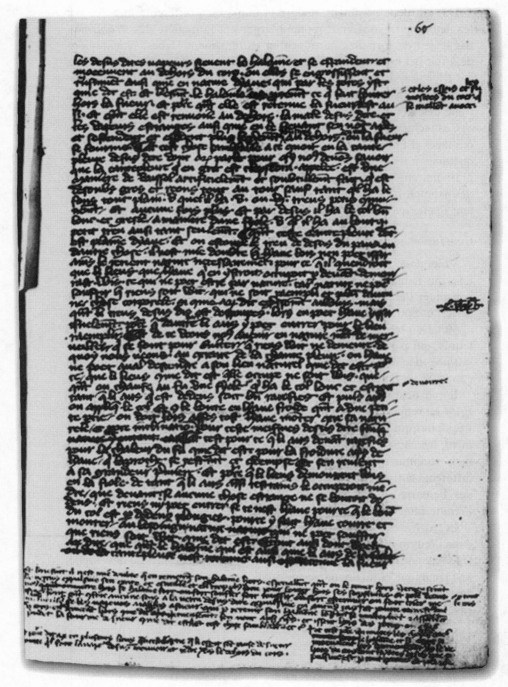

Paris, Bibliothèque nationale de
France, ms. 24.281, f. 60r

Caroline BOUCHER

DES PROBLÈMES POUR EXERCER L'ENTENDEMENT DES LECTEURS: ÉVRART DE CONTY, NICOLE ORESME ET LA RECHERCHE DE LA NOUVEAUTÉ

Évrart de Conty draws the reader's attention to the originality of the solution he proposes to some Aristotelian problemata *and to the novelty of the developments he adds in his* Livre des eschez amoureux moralisés. *I intend to study this 'claim to originality' by comparing Évrart de Conty's remarks to those of Nicole Oresme in his* Livre du ciel et du monde, *a translation and commentary of Aristotle's* De celo *almost contemporary with Évrart de Conty's works. I suggest that both translators are set apart from the previous vernacular translators by their quest for novelty and that they invite their reader to go further with the commentary, to argue and debate in a competitive spirit. Such statements of Évrart de Conty and Nicole Oresme contribute to define their work as recreative; they are stressed here as key passages for the very status of vernacularization.*

1. Introduction: la prétention à l'originalité

La place étonnante qu'occupe Évrart de Conty dans son *Livre des problemes*, presque démesurée par rapport au texte aristotélicien, offre plusieurs pistes de lecture pour aborder la traduction et le commentaire des *Problemata* en français[1] et pour mieux comprendre, sinon l'intention de l'auteur, du moins le genre auquel appartient ce texte. La manière dont Évrart de Conty revendique la nouveauté des solutions qu'il propose à certains problèmes d'Aristote est, à cet égard, particulièrement significative. Bruno Roy avait déjà souligné cet aspect de l'œuvre d'Évrart de Conty, en mentionnant comment Évrart, tout en affectant l'objectivité, marque aussi la nouveauté de son entreprise et attire très

---

1. Cf. GUICHARD-TESSON F., 'Le métier de traducteur et de commentateur au XIVᵉ siècle d'après Évrart de Conty ', *Le Moyen Français* 24-25 (1990), p. 131-167. Rappelons en effet que les traductions vernaculaires des grandes *auctoritates* médiévales se définissent à l'aune du commentaire universitaire et que les traducteurs se proposent à la fois de traduire et d'*exposer* le texte latin qu'ils mettent en français: voir en particulier COPELAND R., *Rhetoric, Hermeneutics, and Translation in the Middle Ages: Academic Traditions and Vernacular Texts*, Cambridge: Cambridge University Press, 1991.

explicitement l'attention de son lecteur sur l'originalité des opinions qu'il défend[2]. Évrart conclut ainsi l'art poétique qu'il introduit dans la partie sur la musique de son *Livre des eschez amoureux moralisés* en affirmant que cette 'ymaginacion' 'semble assez nouvelle; au moins n'ay je pas dusques a cy veu personne qui s'en soit avisee ne qui y ait pris garde, dont j'aye eu toutesfoiz congnoissance'[3]. Il y réclame semblablement l'originalité d'une explication sur l'existence présupposée du vide, affirmant que 'ceste ymaginacion est quant a moy nouvelle'[4].

Évrart de Conty vante également l'originalité de son commentaire dans le *Livre des problemes*, où il expose deux autres 'imaginations' qu'il n'a pas 'oy dire ne veu ne en escript', soit en XX, 24 à la question de savoir pourquoi les petites myrtilles n'ont pas de pépins, et en XV, 6 dans un problème d'optique[5]. La solution de ce dernier problème est particulièrement intéressante de par le raisonnement géométrique qu'elle implique et de par l'écho qu'on en retrouve dans l'œuvre littéraire d'Évrart de Conty. L'originalité effective de l'explication d'Évrart de Conty nous intéresse moins ici que sa manière de la présenter au lecteur. Ce problème retiendra ainsi notre attention et nous amènera à sortir du

2. LEGARÉ A.M. – ROY B., ' Le 'je' d'Évrart de Conty: Du texte à l'image ', dans: B. BAILLAUD – J. DE GRAMONT – D. HÜE (éds), *Auteurs, lecteurs, savoirs anonymes. 'Je' & encyclopédies*, Rennes: Presses Universitaires de Rennes, 1996, p. 39-55, ici p. 42-3.

3. GUICHARD-TESSON F. – ROY B. (éds), *Le livre des eschez amoureux moralisés*, Montréal: Ceres, 1993 (désigné par la suite par *EAM*), p. 173. La nouveauté de ce développement à propos 'des rimes et des mectres et mesmes des proses' semble d'ailleurs conforter l'affirmation d'Évrart de Conty et pourrait ici justifier ce morceau de bravoure; cf. ROY B., 'Eustache Deschamps et Évrart de Conty théoriciens de l'art poétique', dans: *Cy nous dient. Dialogue avec quelques auteurs médiévaux*, Orléans: Paradigme, 1999, p. 25-40.

4. 'On pourroit bien aussi ymaginer que ceste replecion du lieu dont nous parlons ne se fait pas tant seulement de l'entencion de nature affin qu'il ne soit riens de vuit, ainz se peut bien, ce semble, faire de neccessité de nature aussi come par une maniere de compression; car ce bas monde cy dessoubz que le ciel avironne de toutes pars est tout plain et doit par nature estre et par raison aussi. Et pour ce, quant aucune chose d'une part se condense ou restraint, l'autre le sieut et se boute en son lieu, aussi come contrainte des autres qui sont entour ly, qui se veulent pareillement estendre. Et c'est aussi ce que on voit en une grant multitude de gent ou il y a grant presse que, quant les uns boutent fort d'une part et de leur lieu se muent, les autres les sievent aussi, non mie pour le lieu remplir principalment, maiz pour ce qu'ilz en sont contraint des autres qui les boutent. Et ceste ymaginacion est quant a moy nouvelle, et c'est assez, ce semble, raisonable, qui l'entendroit bien.' (*EAM*, p. 223). Cette image de la foule ne se retrouve pas parmi les 'expériences de pensée' sur le vide étudiées par GRANT E., *Much Ado About Nothing. Theories of Space and Vacuum from the Middle Ages to the Scientific Revolution*, Cambridge: Cambridge University Press, 1981, ch. 4: 'Nature's abhorence of a vacuum', p. 67-100.

5. Ms. BnF fr. 210, fol. 261va et 206vb respectivement. Ces passages avaient déjà été signalés par GUICHARD-TESSON, 'Le métier de traducteur…', p. 162 n. 67.

cadre des *Problemata* pour mieux comparer le *Livre des problemes* au *Livre des eschez amoureux moralisés* d'Évrart de Conty, commentaire prolixe de ses *Eschés amoureux*[6], qui recoupe largement la matière des *Problemes* et donne à voir une autre lecture des *Problemata*, une manière de lire et d'exposer qui entremêle aisément les genres et les conventions. Il sera question également du *Livre du ciel et du monde* de Nicole Oresme, traduction et commentaire du *De celo* d'Aristote quasi contemporaine des *Problemes*, où les positions d'Évrart de Conty trouvent un éloquent précédent[7]. Les traductions de Nicole Oresme et d'Évrart de Conty invitent à la comparaison, tant elles se rejoignent sur de nombreux points: leur argumentation en faveur de la traduction en langue vernaculaire, l'ampleur des textes et des savoirs qu'ils mettent en français, leur intérêt pour les questions scientifiques et les développements mathématiques, leur souci d'utiliser une terminologie précise en français, leur prédilection pour des thèmes (la musique, par exemple) et des exemples communs – sans compter les rapprochements multiples entre les personnes des deux traducteurs et les milieux où ils se sont, très vraisemblablement, entrecroisés. Ces 'personnages' nous semblent d'autant plus accessibles que leurs traductions laissent entendre leur voix, le 'je' du traducteur dont la présence s'impose, à la lecture, à l'égal de l'auteur qu'il traduit. Leur prétention à l'originalité fournira ici le point de départ d'une discussion sur le rôle du traducteur et la 'vulgarisation' des savoirs scientifiques en français.

2. Une 'ymaginacion' nouvelle

Commençons donc par cette nouvelle 'imagination' qu'Évrart de Conty introduit dans son commentaire des problèmes de la XVe *parti-*

---

6. F. Guichard-Tesson a montré comment cette œuvre, longtemps tenue pour anonyme, devait être attribuée à Évrart de Conty ('Évrart de Conty, auteur de la *Glose des Echecs amoureux*', *Le Moyen Français* 8-9 (1982), p. 111-148; cf. aussi le résumé de ses principaux arguments dans l'introduction à l'édition des *EAM*, p. LIII-LIV). Cette œuvre encyclopédique se veut un commentaire du poème des *Eschés amoureux* (voir l'introduction à la 1re partie de son édition par RAIMONDI G. (éd.), '*Les eschés amoureux*. Studio preparatorio ed edizione (I. v. 1-3662)', *Pluteus* 8-9 (1990-98), p. 67-241), réécriture du *Roman de la Rose* dont Évrart de Conty serait lui-même l'auteur (cf. appendice II). Les *EAM* s'inscrivent ainsi dans la tradition du *Roman de la Rose* et dans la mouvance des premiers commentaires d'œuvres vernaculaires; cf. MINNIS A.J., *Magister Amoris: The 'Roman de la Rose' and Vernacular Hermeneutics*, Oxford: Oxford University Press, 2001.

7. MENUT A.D. – DENOMY A.J. (éds), *Nicole Oresme, Le Livre du ciel et du monde*, Madison: The University of Wisconsin Press, 1968. La traduction de Nicole Oresme du *De celo* est explicitement datée de 1377 et précède vraisemblablement le travail d'Évrart de Conty.

cula, répondant à la question de savoir pourquoi le soleil, lorsqu'il passe à travers un quadrilatère, ne produit pas une figure rectangulaire mais circulaire[8]. L'explication fournie par le texte des *Problemata* s'appuie sur la représentation géométrique de la lumière sous la forme d'un cône, soit, dans les termes géométriques qu'emploie Évrart de Conty, d'une pyramide ronde. La *glose* du traducteur ajoute d'abord deux exemples permettant d'illustrer comment les rayons du soleil se projettent ainsi sur la terre sous la forme d'un cône lumineux, soit l'éclipse de la lune et le cas fictif de la 'terre percée'[9]. Le commentaire en français introduit alors l'idée que l'intensité de la lumière permettrait d'expliquer l'ombre circulaire que fait une source sphérique de lumière en traversant un quadrilatère – par analogie à la luminosité d'un miroir concave qui reflète la lumière en la condensant, voire en brûlant ce qui se trouve au point opposé[10]. Évrart de Conty insiste bien sur l'originalité de cette solution,

---

8. 'Propter quid sol per quadrilatera transiens non rectilineas facit figuras sed circulos?' (suivant la traduction de Barthélémy de Messine qui se trouve dans PIETRO D'ABANO, *Expositio problematum Aristotelis*, Mantoue: Petrus de Butzbach, 1475, non folioté), soit: 'Pour quoy est ce que li rais du soleil quant ils passent par aucuns treus quarrés ne font, en passant oultre, pas figures quarrees, mais reondes et circulieres, si comme il appert par experience quant on met a l'encontre du soleil aucune chose quarree?' (XV, 6, ms. BnF fr. 210, fol. 206vb). On trouvera l'ensemble du commentaire d'Évrart (soit, faute d'espace, la *glose* du traducteur sans le *texte* proprement dit de la version de Barthélémy de Messine) dans l'appendice I; ce texte n'a nullement valeur d'édition mais se veut un accès au commentaire d'Évrart de Conty, que je résume ici très sommairement.

9. En l'absence de schéma dans le *Livre des problemes*, on peut se rapporter ici à la figure qu'insère Nicole Oresme dans son traité de la sphère pour illustrer les éclipses de lune (ms. BnF fr. 1350, fol. 35vb), où la lune (*l*) se retrouve dans le cône d'ombre formé par la terre (*t*), elle-même éclairée par le soleil (*s*):

Imaginant ensuite que la terre serait percée de part en part, Évrart de Conty suppose que la lumière du soleil éclairant la terre en ressortirait du côté opposé sous la forme d'un cône inversé. On notera à ce propos que l'image de la 'terre percée' a été abondamment utilisée dans la littérature scolastique, mais davantage, semble-t-il, pour expliquer des questions de mécanique, non d'optique; cf. l'étude de RIBÉMONT B., 'Un exemple d'image didactique dans l'encyclopédisme et le milieu savant: la terre percée', *De Natura Rerum. Études sur les encyclopédies médiévales*, Orléans: Paradigme, 1995, p. 217-67. Elle est employée en français notamment dans le *Livre du ciel et du monde*, où Nicole Oresme 'pose que la terre fust perciee et que l'on veist par un grant treu tout d'oultre en oultre siques de l'autre part la ou seroient les antipodes se la terre estoit partout habitee' (MENUT – DENOMY (éds), *Le livre du ciel et du monde*, II, 31, p. 572).

10. Il n'est pas dans le propos de cet article de discuter de l'originalité proprement dite de la solution d'Évrart de Conty, qui ne vient pas ici de Pietro d'Abano. On notera cependant que ce problème, de même que la question des 'miroirs ardents', a suscité,

'ceste ymaginacion' qu'il n'a 'pas ailleurs veue escripte ne oye', qui vient alors compléter le texte d'Aristote et en renouveler l'exposition.

Il est intéressant de noter que le *Livre des eschez amoureux moralisés* fait largement écho aux questions d'optique des *Problemes*. Évrart de Conty y évoque explicitement la question XV, 6 parmi les différentes 'merveilles' dont les causes peuvent être rendues par la science de 'perspective'[11], où il n'expose ni ne résout cependant la question. L'analogie avec le miroir, dont les propriétés 'merveilleuses' devaient être bien connues des lecteurs, introduit par ailleurs un motif qui, manifestement, intéressait Évrart de Conty par ailleurs. Le *Roman de la Rose*, l'illustre modèle des *Eschés amoureux*, y avait déjà consacré une digression notable, incluant les miroirs ardents[12]. Un long développement de la 6e partie des *Eschez amoureux moralisés* est semblablement consacré aux différents types de miroirs, puisque l'un des pions du jeu d'échecs (Souvenir) a un miroir concave pour emblème[13]. On retrouve dans ce passage le miroir 'pyramidal' concave qui a la propriété 'merveilleuse' de concentrer les rayons lumineux en un point et d'enflammer ainsi ce qui s'y trouve[14]: en l'occurrence, dans la trame des *Eschez amou-*

dans l'Antiquité comme au Moyen Âge, plusieurs commentaires. Roger Bacon est le premier à en proposer une solution essentiellement géométrique dans son *De speculis comburentibus*, développement qui influencera par la suite John Pecham dans sa *Perspectiva communis*; voir à ce propos les travaux de LINDBERG D.C., 'A Reconsideration of Roger Bacon's Theory of Pinholes Images', *Archive for History of Exact Sciences* 6 (1970), p. 214-23, et 'Roger Bacon and the Origins of *Perspectiva* in the West', dans: E. GRANT – J.E. MURDOCH (éds), *Mathematics and its Applications to Science and Natural Philosophy in the Middle Ages. Essays in honor of Marshall Clagett*, Cambridge: Cambridge University Press, 1987, p. 249-268, surtout p. 260-261.

11. Ce développement sur la 'science de perspective' (la *perspectiva* du moyen âge désignant la géométrie optique) se trouve dans la partie sur la géométrie, qui elle-même trouve place dans la longue introduction aux arts libéraux et aux sciences qu'Évrart de Conty introduit dans la 2e partie sur les dieux et les déesses. La question y est formulée en termes quelque peu différents: 'pourquoy la lumiere du soleil passant parmy un treu quarré ou de troiz angles se moustre en la paroy opposite neantmoins, ou sur la terre, de figure ronde' (*EAM*, p. 108).

12. Cf. STRUBEL A. (éd.), *Guillaume de Lorris et Jean de Meun, Le Roman de la Rose*, Paris: Le livre de poche, 1992, v. 18017-18064 et 18157-18302; voir en particulier v. 18171-6 sur les miroirs ardents: 'Autre miroer sont, qui ardent / Les choses quant il les regardent, / Qui les set a droit compasser / Pour les rais ensemble amasser / Quant li soleuls resflambaianz / Est seur les miroers raianz.'

13. 'Souvenir fu après le paonnet sisiesme, sy come assez secretement le miroer concave segnefie, dont il portoit en son escu l'enseigne'; 'Pour declairier aussi aucune chose du miroer concave dont cel paonnet ot en son escu l'ensaigne et la samblance, sy come l'acteur faint, nous devons cy noter, selon les anciens sages de perspective, que on treuve .vij. manieres de miroers qui sont de diverses natures [...].' (*EAM*, p. 696 et 700, introdui-sant ainsi le développement sur les miroirs, p. 700-710).

14. 'cest miroer concave a encore une autre proprieté sur toutes merveilleuse, car il art et enflamme les choses qui sont devant ly en certaine distance.' (*EAM* p. 709).

reux moralisés, le cœur de l'amant[15]. Cette propriété du miroir concave était d'ailleurs déjà évoquée par l'une des gloses latines qui accompagnent le texte des *Eschés amoureux*[16] que le *Livre des eschez amoureux moralisés* entend commenter, complétant – et compliquant d'autant plus – le va-et-vient qui s'opère entre les *Problemes*, les *Eschez amoureux moralisés* et le poème qu'il commente, entre tradition scolastique et littéraire.

3. L'explication par 'manière de géométrie'

À la lecture, les *Problemes* et les *Eschez amoureux moralisés* n'épuisent pourtant pas la question et la traduction semble ici rencontrer un écueil, négligeant apparemment l'explication des causes pour en retenir surtout l'effet merveilleux produit par le miroir concave. L'exposé des *Eschez amoureux moralisés* décrit ainsi précisément les formes géométriques des différents types de miroirs, ces 'figures, en laquelle chose gist, selon la verité, consideracion tres soutille et tres belle', comme l'explique Évrart de Conty à son lecteur, pour mieux laisser de côté cependant 'les grans soutilletés et les demonstracions fortes qui ne sont pas bien seans en françois'[17]. La *glose* des *Problemes*, semblablement, ne propose pas de solution purement mathématique, mais semble construire son explication sur des analogies. Il est vrai que le raisonnement 'par maniere de geometrie', selon ce que nous dit Évrart par ailleurs, est une manière de procéder difficile à comprendre pour les laïcs et inhabituelle

15. Cf. GUICHARD-TESSON F., 'Le pion Souvenir et les miroirs déformants dans l'allégorie d'amour', dans: B. ROY – P. ZUMTHOR (éds), *Jeux de mémoire. Aspects de la mnémotechnie médiévale*, Montréal-Paris: Presses de l'Université de Montréal-Vrin, 1985, p. 99-108, en particulier p. 105-6. Comme l'a souligné F. Guichard-Tesson, le pion Souvenir est d'ailleurs déterminant pour la suite du récit, causant la défaite de l'amant qui sera 'maté' par l'aimée.

16. Cf. *Les eschés amoureux*, vv. 4880-4882 ('li sisimes, de l'aultre part, / avoit aussy un mireoir / concave, mout bel a veoir'), glose: 'Sextus est *Souvenir*, qui per speculum concavum figuratur, quia comburit et quia conversas ymagines representat, que optime ad propositum applicantur.' RAIMONDI G. (éd.), '*Les eschés amoureux*. Studio preparatorio ed edizione (II. vv. 3663-5538)', à paraître dans *Pluteus*; je remercie G. Raimondi de m'avoir fait parvenir, avant publication, la 2e partie de son édition).

17. 'Or venons donc a leurs proprietés et regardons come celz miroers diversement esmeuvent la veue et la deçoivent, selon aussi leurs diverses figures, en laquelle chose gist, selon la verité, consideracion tres soutille et tres belle, qui bien vouldroit toute ceste matiere reveler et entendre. Maiz nous lairons les grans soutilletés et les demonstracions fortes qui ne sont pas bien seans en françois, et du surplus dirons aucunes choses briefves, tant qu'il doie souffire a cest present propos ou il nous fault parler du miroer concave' (*EAM*, p. 702), introduisant ainsi quelque six folios d'explication.

en langue vernaculaire[18] – rappelant ainsi le clivage traditionnel entre langues latine et vernaculaire, réservant à l'une les *démonstrations* géométriques et les *subtilités* mathématiques des clercs, procédant dans l'autre par exemples et cherchant à y convaincre le lecteur de la vérité du texte, suivant un jeu d'oppositions constituées en véritables *topoi*. Le *Roman de la Rose* illustrait déjà cette dichotomie: Jean de Meun, sous prétexte de brièveté, omettait de son exposé sur l'optique les démonstrations géométriques, explications difficiles à comprendre, surtout pour les laïcs qui ne sauraient croire aux effets merveilleux des miroirs à moins que des clercs, instruits en la science de perspective, ne veuillent l'exposer[19]. C'est d'ailleurs encore cet idéal de brièveté qu'invoque Évrart de Conty lorsqu'il ne développe pas le problème XV, 6 dans les *Eschez*

18. 'Et ce veult il apres declarier par la maniere de geometrie, laquelle chose est moult obscurement mise, et communement le texte quant a ce est corrompu par le vice des escrivains, ou par aventure des translateurs. Et ausi est ce chose moult estrange a comprendre a la gent laye, et mal ausi seant en françois. Et pour ce je mettray la sentence de ce qu'il veult dire par example, au plus briefment que je pourray' (XV, 5, ms. BnF fr. 210, fol. 205vb), où Évrart traduit du latin le *texte* du problème posé en termes géométriques sans développer cependant l'analyse géométrique dans sa *glose* où il s'en tient à la signification générale du problème d'Aristote. Cf. également XXVI, 52 sur les illusions d'optique causées par le vent, où Évrart de Conty explique que 'la propre cause et la vraye raison de ceste chose ne peut estre sceue sans le dangier de la science de perspective, car c'est celle qui tracte des diverses manieres de veoir, et qui la droite verite enseingne des merveilles c'on y troeuve. Sans faille ce seroit moult longue chose de desclairier au long la merveille qui est touchie en cest probleume, et si seroit ausi estrange chose et forte a le faire entendent a ceulx qui ne sont pas entroduiz es principes de ceste science, si que je m'en passeray briefment quant a present' (ms. BnF fr. 210, fol. 331rb), où Évrart introduit cependant ainsi une explication géométrique, 'par figure', à l'intention explicite des lecteurs 'qui ont l'entendement soubtil' (fol. 332va); sur ce passage, voir Ducos J., *La météorologie en français au Moyen Âge (XIIIᵉ-XIVᵉ siècles)*, Paris: Champion, 1998, p. 202, ainsi que sa contribution dans cet ouvrage.

19. 'Mais ne vueill or pas metre cures / En desclaroier les figures / Des miroers, ne ne dirai / Comment sont reflechi li rai / Ne leur angles ne vueill descrivre: Tout est aileurs escrit en livre [...] Ce ne desploieré je mie / N'il ne le couvient ores pas; / Ainçois les tais et les trespas /Avoec les choses devant dites, / Qui ja n'ierent par moi descriptes; / Car trop y a longue matire, / Et si seroit grief chose a dire, / Et mout seroit fort a entendre, / S'il ert qui le seüst aprandre / As genz lais especialment, / Qui nes diroit generalment. / Si ne porroient il pas croire / Que la chose fus ainsi voire / Des miroers meesmment / Qui tant oevrent diversement, / Se par estrumenz nes veoient, / Se clers moustrer le lor voloient / Qui seüssent par demoustrance / Ceste merveilleuse sciance. [...]' (*Le Roman de la Rose...*, v. 18251-90). On rapprochera ce passage des vers suivants, sur les effets d'optique provoqués par les miroirs: '[...] qui raconter / Le vorroit et l'avroit veü, / Ce ne porroit estre creü / D'omme qui veü ne l'avroit / Ou qui les causes ne savroit. / Si ne seroit ce pas creance / Puis qu'il en avroit la sciance' [...] 'Pour ce les vueill ci trespasser / Ne si ne vueill or pas lasser / Moi de parler ne vous d'oïr: / Bon fait prolexité foïr' (*Le Roman de la Rose...*, v. 18058-18064 et 18299-18302). Sur ces 'subtilités' qu'omet Jean de Meun en français, voir les remarques de Bruni F., *Testi e chierici del medioevo*, Genova: Marietti, 1991, p. 124-8.

amoureux moralisés[20], et ne prétend expliquer dans son exposé sur les miroirs qu''aucunes choses briefves, tant qu'il doit souffire a cest present propos'[21]; semblablement, le traducteur n'explique les problèmes posés en termes géométriques qu''au plus briefment' qu'il pourra[22].

Or, ces *topoi* ne trouvent en réalité qu'une place fort limitée au sein de l'œuvre d'Évrart de Conty[23]. L'idéal de brièveté peut ainsi servir, tout au contraire, à introduire des passages difficiles, et plusieurs des remarques sur ce qu'il ne convient pas d'exposer en français renvoient en fait à un développement ultérieur[24]. À défaut d'exposer ses hypothèses par une analyse géométrique, Évrart de Conty ne néglige nullement les questions d'optique, qui l'intéressent au contraire tout particulièrement, ni n'exclut les *subtilités* mathématiques. La *glose* du problème XV, 6 implique ainsi *de facto* un raisonnement géométrique et renvoie explicitement aux 'figures' qu'il conviendrait d'ajouter pour en démontrer l'explication: le commentaire suppose d'emblée une représentation géométrique de la lumière ('si comme il appert clerement qui ymagine bien la chose et ausi par figure'), qu'il décrit soigneusement[25], et l'exemple de la 'terre percée' est laissée à l'imagination du lecteur (qui doit 'ymaginer

---

20. 'ce seroit trop longue chose a faire et c'est aussi trop loings de ma matiere' (*EAM* p. 107).

21. *EAM*, p. 702.

22. Cf. supra n. 18.

23. J'ai tâché de montrer par une étude du terme *subtilité* comment certains traducteurs comme Nicole Oresme et Évrart de Conty pouvaient ainsi renverser les *topoi* de la traduction: 'De la *subtilité* en français: vulgarisation et savoir dans les traductions d'*auctoritates* des XIIIe-XIVe siècles', dans: R. VOADEN – R. TIXIER – T. SANCHEZ ROURA – J.R. RYTTING (éds), *The theory and practice of translation in the Middle Ages* (The Medieval Translator VIII), Turnhout: Brepols, 2003, p. 89-99.

24. C'est le cas, par exemple, dans les problèmes relatifs à la composition de l'œil: en III, 10, Évrart laisse la question de côté, puisque c'est 'chose trop forte a entendre et a metre en françois' (ms. BnF fr. 210, fol. 70ra), pour l'exposer en IX, 2, 'combien que ce soit fort de bien entendre ceste exposicion et de la metre en françois' (fol. 125ra) et y revenir plus longuement en XXXI, 2, où 'il est bien cy seant que la composicion de l'oeil soit si a plain declairie et monstree' (fol. 374ra), explication qu'il évoque encore en XXXI, 25 (cf. fol. 387ra).

25. On notera qu'Évrart de Conty s'attarde plus longuement à la description géométrique du cône dans ses *EAM*, où il ajoute cette fois un schéma: 'Les autres miroers sont appellés pyramidal pour ce qu'ilz sont semblables a une pyramide de ronde maniere, ou qu'ilz contiennent une partie d'elle; et est ceste figure dessoubz large et ronde, et agu dessus come un alambic est, ou un clochier rond. Et se nous voulons bien aussi ceste figure entendre, ymaginons un triangle rectangle, c'est a dire un triangle qui ait un de ses angles droit, sy come seroit le triangle .a.b.c., et qu'il se meust et tournast tout entour de la ligne .a.b. et tant qu'il revenist en son droit lieu premier: cel triangle lors descriroit une pyramide ronde.' (p. 701, où le schéma est reproduit). On trouve la même comparaison à propos des éclipses dans le traité de la sphère, où Nicole Oresme décrit ce cône de lumière 'en la maniere d'un clochier d'eglise' (ms. BnF fr. 1350, fol. 35ra; cf. supra n. 9).

ausi que…'); la solution d'Évrart de Conty, en particulier, 'pourroit bien estre ausi declairie par figure' et c'est cette figure qu'on retrouve en marge du problème, schéma géométrique que n'utilise pourtant pas le commentaire mais qui est destiné, vraisemblablement, à l'intention du lecteur 'subtil', initié à la science de perspective, qui saura apprécier l'originalité de cette 'imagination'[26]. L'enjeu de la traduction apparaît ici comme la capacité, non seulement de traduire la matière des *Problemata*, mais aussi d'utiliser le langage mathématique – dont l'emploi reste malaisé, sinon inhabituel en langue vernaculaire – pour mieux exposer le texte d'Aristote. S'il est difficile de suivre ici l'explication de la *glose* sans recourir à la géométrie, l'explication en termes géométriques n'en pose pas moins certaines difficultés et le traducteur semble *a priori* renoncer à l'analyse mathématique, passant sous silence la démonstration géométrique de sa solution qu'il inclut cependant sous la forme d'une 'figure'.

Ces remarques d'Évrart de Conty sur l'originalité de sa *glose* trouvent un contrepoint intéressant dans le *Livre du ciel et du monde*, où Nicole Oresme vante semblablement l'originalité de la figure qu'il ajoute pour illustrer sa glose sur les proportions mathématiques, qu'il décrit comme 'un merveilleus signe, lequel je n'ay pas apris par doctrine d'autre'[27]. Le commentaire s'appuie sur cette figure, exposée en termes géométriques, mais renvoie le lecteur à la démonstration mathématique développée précédemment par Nicole Oresme dans son *Algorisme de proporcions*. Tout en impliquant le recours à l'explication par 'figure', ce passage soulève comme dans le *Livre des problemes* les difficultés du raisonnement mathématique en langue vernaculaire, puisque la traduction, certes 'savante', n'en relègue pas moins la démonstration au latin, une 'demonstraison pure mathematique a laquelle nul ne pourroit par raison contredire'[28]. En l'absence de preuves conclusives, 'évidentes', en lan-

26. Voir la reproduction de ce schéma géométrique dans l'appendice II, et n. 56 pour une explication du schéma.
27. Soit la *glose* sur II, 18, MENUT – DENOMY (éds), *Le livre du ciel et du monde*, p. 484, à propos de la musique des sphères. À défaut de comparer plus avant les deux traductions sur cette question, on notera à tout le moins la proximité de la position de Nicole Oresme et d'Évrart de Conty sur la musique des sphères comme abstraction mathématique; cf. MENUT – DENOMY (éds), *Le livre du ciel et du monde*, II, 17, p. 472, 476, et *EAM*, p. 161.
28. 'Et tout ce ay je autrefois declairé evidanment en un livret que je nommay *Algorisme de proporcions* et par demonstraison pure mathematique a laquelle nul ne pourroit par raison contredire.' (MENUT – DENOMY (éds), *Le livre du ciel et du monde*, p. 484; le schéma est reproduit p. 485). Nicole Oresme renvoie ainsi à son *Algorismus proportionum*, écrit dans les années 1350 et dédié à Philippe de Vitry; cf. GRANT E., 'Part I of Nicole Oresme's *Algorismus Proportionum*', *Isis* 56 (1965), p. 327-341.

gue vernaculaire, les remarques des traducteurs insistant sur l'originalité de leur solution servent peut-être ici d'artifice rhétorique pour persuader le lecteur de la véracité de la solution trouvée[29]. On peut penser cependant qu'elles s'adressent aussi, de manière plus polémique, à des lecteurs à même d'en apprécier la teneur, invités ainsi, comme on le verra, à rechercher, s'il est possible, de nouvelles solutions, au-delà des explications des commentateurs.

4. La recherche de la nouveauté

La prétention d'Évrart de Conty et de Nicole Oresme à renouveler l'exposition des problèmes posés par les textes qu'ils mettent en français modifie, en effet, la lecture qu'on peut en faire. Cette recherche de la nouveauté est d'abord liée à l'idée d'un plaisir de la lecture et de la recherche des causes. C'est là un thème qui appartient vraisemblablement à la tradition des *Problemata*, mais qu'Évrart de Conty aura développé et repris avec insistance. Le prologue de sa traduction affirme ainsi que les problèmes sont 'esmerveillables au proposer et delitables a exposer', car, comme le dit Aristote, ce qui suscite l'étonnement est cause de plaisir, 'les choses esmerveillables sont par nature delitables'[30]. Cette cita-

---

29. Suivant ici l'opposition médiévale entre persuasion et démonstration, et les différentes manières de procéder qu'elle suppose, comme l'explique ainsi Nicole Oresme: 'Persuasion est raison vraysemblable non pas evidente, et induit a soy assentir a la conclusion; mais elle n'y contraint pas. [...] Et n'a point de lieu en mathematiques, mais tant seulement demonstracion qui est tres certainne, neccessaire et evidente.' (MENUT A.D. (éd.), *Livre de Ethiques*, New York: G.E. Stechert & Co., 1940, I, 2, glose 5, p. 107). L'opposition dans la manière de procéder – démontrer ou convaincre – s'appuie par ailleurs sur la distinction aristotélicienne (telle qu'exposée dans la *Rhétorique*) entre arguments (*entimematibus aut sillogismis*) et exemples (*exemplis et similitudinibus*); voir à ce propos la traduction d'Évrart de Conty à la question de savoir 'Pourquoy est ce que es sermons et es paroles ou persuasions notables on se esjoist plus de examples que de argumens quelconques?', où il explique 'que les choses particulieres qui se monstrent a l'oeil et au sens prestement sont mieuls sceues de nous que les choses universeles, qui ne se monstrent fors a l'entendement, ne sont, especialment de la commune gent qui vivent de la vie active, li quels n'ont cure que de choses grosses et sensibles, et de ceuls parle ausi Aristote en cest probleume principalment pour ce donc que la commune gent s'esjoissent de ce qu'il aprennent legierement' (XVIII, 3, ms. BnF fr. 210 fol. 221ra-b et *Expositio problematum*...).

30. Cf. Aristote, *Rhetorica* III, 2 (1404b12): 'admiratores enim advenarum sunt, delectabile autem quod mirabile est'; SCHNEIDER B. (éd.), *Rhetorica, Translatio Guillelmi de Moerbeka* (Aristoteles Latinus 31, 1-2), Leiden: Brill, 1978, p. 283. Évrart de Conty cite cependant le texte tel qu'on le retrouve dans les *Auctoritates Aristotelis*: 'Quod mirabile est delectabile est.' (HAMESSE J., *Les Auctoritates Aristotelis. Un florilège médiéval. Étude historique et édition critique*, Louvain: Publications universitaires – Paris: Béatrice-Nauwelaerts, 1974, p. 267 n° 56).

tion d'Aristote revient comme un leitmotiv dans l'œuvre d'Évrart, à différents passages clefs: outre le prologue du *Livre des problemes*[31], on la retrouve dans la glose du problème XXX, 6, où l'on apprend qu'il y a plus de plaisir dans l'explication des causes que dans les effets des phénomènes[32], et enfin dans le prologue du *Livre des eschez amoureux moralisés*, où Évrart justifie l'obscurité des *Eschés amoureux* (qu'il va commenter) par le plaisir que procure l'explication des matières subtiles[33].

Ce thème suggère ici que l'exposition des *Problemes* en français cherche volontiers à susciter l'étonnement et la curiosité du lecteur. Le *Livre du ciel et du monde*, où l'idée d'un plaisir dans la recherche des causes n'est cependant pas explicite[34], semble partager ce rapport au lecteur. La recherche de la nouveauté pour le plus grand plaisir des lecteurs trouve de fait sa contrepartie dans les passages où les traducteurs interpellent directement leurs lecteurs et les incitent à trouver, s'ils le peuvent, une meilleure solution au problème posé par le texte. On peut parler ici d'un

---

31. 'Et au voir dire, elles sont esmerveillables au proposer et delitables a exposer. Et pource met Ar<istotes> premierement la question par maniere de merveille en demandant pour quoy c'est, pour enquerre la cause. Et apres ce, tantost il meismes respont et met la solution, qui fait l'entendement devant esmerveillie deliter tres grandement. Car les choses esmerveillables sont par nature delitables, selonc ce qu'il meismes dit ailleurs (*3° rethorice: quod admirabile est delectabile est*)' (ms. BnF fr. 24281, fol. 1r).

32. 'Car nous nous esmerveillons plus des causes que nous ne cognoissons mie de premiere face que nous ne faisons des effetz que nous veons de fait. Et se nous nous en esmerveillons aucunefoiz se n'est ce fors pour le ignorance de la cause et par consequens nous nous delitons plus es causes que es effetz car ce qui est esmerveillable est delitable, si comme Aristote dit ailleurs (*tercio rethorice*) de tant aussi que les causes des choses de nature nous sont plus occultes, de tant les desirons nous plus a savoir.' (ms. BnF fr. 210, fol. 367ra). Ce problème est à rapprocher des *EAM* de par la comparaison qu'y introduit Évrart de Conty entre le jeu d'échecs et la résolution des angles d'un triangle dont parle Aristote (cf. appendice II).

33. 'les choses qui sont subtilement faites ou dites font plus esmerveillier l'entendement, et par consequant deliter, car les choses esmerveillables sont par nature delitables, sy come dit Aristote ailleurs' (*EAM*, p. 24-25). On trouve encore cette idée exprimée en des termes légèrement différents en d'autres passages, notamment dans une digression sur la connaissance par les sens: 'Et pour ce nous delitons nous en moult de choses que les sens nous presentent, qui de riens ne profitent au salut de la vie, pour ce que elles nous font esmerveillier et nous donnent matiere de aprendre et de enquerre les causes de pluseurs merveilles que nous veons, en laquelle chose gist grant delectacion, come Aristote dit.' (*EAM*, p. 747).

34. On lit toutefois dans le *De configurationibus qualitatum et motuum* de Nicole Oresme, à propos des causes qui rendent un son agréable à l'écoute, que la nouveauté suscite le plaisir: 'ex [...] novitate generatur admiratio et admiratio illa causat delectationem'; CLAGETT M. (éd.), *Nicole Oresme and the Medieval Geometry of Qualities and Motions. A Treatise on the Uniformity and Difformity of Intensities, known as Tractatus de configurationibus et motuum*, Madison: The University of Wisconsin Press, 1968, p. 326, II, 22.

véritable esprit d'émulation qui anime tant le *Livre du ciel et du monde* que le *Livre des problemes*, où Nicole Oresme et Évrart de Conty invitent leur lecteur, par jeu ou par défi, à égaler ou à surpasser leur travail. Ainsi, à différents problèmes, Évrart de Conty semble insatisfait de son commentaire et s'en remet au lecteur. Au 12e problème de la XXIXe *particula*, par exemple, il conclut en insistant sur le fait que ce problème est 'obscur' et 'long', lançant à son lecteur: 'qui mieuls saura, mieuls die'[35]. En de nombreux passages également, il invite son lecteur, 'qui volroit', à compléter la matière dont il n'a pas traité, pour cause de brièveté[36]. Particulièrement révélateur à cet égard est le commentaire à la XXVIe *particula* où Évrart de Conty explique que la cause de ce problème n'est sans doute pas encore connue et qu'Aristote a peut-être posé ce problème afin qu'on y recherche une solution, 'pour excerciter l'entendement des survenans et esmouvoir a ce que aucunes cause souffisant, s'il est possible, en fust trouvee'[37], justifiant ainsi les hypothèses qu'il va proposer à la suite. Cette remarque est significative du genre même des *Problemata*, où les conclusions importent moins que les arguments permettant de résoudre un problème[38], mais suggère plus généralement l'idée d'un débat, où l'exposition du texte prendrait l'aspect d'un jeu et où les lecteurs seraient invités, 'esmeus', à trouver de nouvelles solutions. En des termes semblables, Nicole Oresme vante la nouveauté et l'originalité de son *Livre du ciel et du monde* 'pour animer, exciter et esmouvoir les cuers des jeunes honmes qui ont subtilz et nobles engins et desir de science, afin que il estudient a dire encontre et a moy reprendre pour amour et affection de verité'[39], appelant ainsi ses lecteurs à dé-

35. XXIX, 12, ms. BnF fr. 210, fol. 355rb.

36. Comme on l'a vu ainsi dans l'exposé sur les miroirs des *EAM*, où Évrart de Conty souligne l'intérêt des 'figures' géométriques, pour 'qui bien vouldroit toute ceste matiere reveler et entendre' (p. 702). Pour un autre exemple dans les *Problemes*, voir notamment XIX, 13: 'Finablement on pourroit, qui volroit, par samblable maniere trouver les proporcions de toutes les consonances et de tous les sons qui pevent estre en nostre game, et en tous instrumens quelconcques, et les comparisons qu'il ont ensamble et par nombres certains, dont je me passe a present pour cause de briefté.' (ms. BnF fr. 210, fol. 232va).

37. XXVI, 17, ms. BnF fr. 210, fol. 316vab, à la question de la présence du vent précédant une éclipse de lune.

38. L'exposition des *Problemes* apparaît bien ici comme la recherche de nouvelles explications à des phénomènes dont on ne questionne cependant pas l'existence; voir à ce propos BLAIR A., 'The *Problemata* as a Natural Philosophical Genre', dans: A. GRAFTON – N. SIRAISI (éds), *Natural Particulars. Nature and the Disciplines in Renaissance Europe*, Cambridge (Mass.): The MIT Press, 1999, p. 187-8.

39. Il s'agit de la conclusion du *Livre du ciel et du monde*, où Nicole Oresme 'ose dire et me faiz fort que il n'est honme mortel qui onques veist plus bel ne meilleur livre de philosophie naturele que est cestui, ne en ebreu, ne en grec ou arabic ne en latin, ne en françois.' (MENUT – DENOMY (éds), p. 730).

battre des arguments qu'il a exposés. Les œuvres de Nicole Oresme et d'Évrart de Conty incitent à la discussion, au débat, à la confrontation d'idées: il y a ainsi tout lieu de les lire comme un ensemble d''exercices intellectuels' plutôt que d'œuvres doctrinaires[40]. Au-delà du texte *in extenso* d'Aristote que les traductions rendent en français, c'est le commentaire des traducteurs qui s'impose à la lecture, allant bien au-delà du texte pour introduire de nouvelles hypothèses, en faisant largement appel aux fictions géométriques et aux raisonnements 'par imagination', cherchant à renouveler l'exposition du texte et encourageant son lecteur, s'il est possible, à faire mieux[41].

5. *La présomption des traducteurs*

Un autre aspect des *Problemes* et du *Ciel et du monde*, lié à ce caractère polémique des traductions, mérite encore d'être souligné: ces appels invitant le lecteur à 'reprendre' l'auteur et à débattre des solutions trouvées supposent un certain statut des traducteurs qui portent ici l'entière responsabilité de leur commentaire, en vantant leur originalité, en se mettant littéralement en scène, et surtout en ne s'effaçant pas derrière la personnalité d'un dédicataire. Peu de traducteurs, en effet, ont revendiqué ne serait-ce que l'initiative de leur traduction, qu'ils attribuent plus généralement au dédicataire présenté comme le commanditaire de l'œuvre. Par cette invention de la requête[42], les traducteurs affirment presque tous écrire de par la volonté, sinon par ordre d'un personnage

40. Il est intéressant de voir par ailleurs Nicole Oresme distinguer les deux 'genres' dans le prologue de son *De configurationibus qualitatum et motuum*, écrit non seulement comme 'exercice', mais comme 'discipline': 'non solum exercitationi prodesset sed etiam discipline' (CLAGETT (éd.), *Nicole Oresme and the Medieval Geometry...*, p. 158). Sur la lecture des *Problemata* comme des exercices intellectuels, voir tout particulièrement la contribution de Joan Cadden dans cet ouvrage.

41. Il me semble ainsi qu'on ne peut pas lire simplement la conclusion de Nicole Oresme comme un appel à défier l'autorité, comme le suggère Edward Grant, ni comme une œuvre s'adressant spécifiquement aux 'jeunes hommes' de la cour royale (cf. GRANT E., 'Nicole Oresme, Aristotle's *On the Heavens*, and the Court of Charles V', dans: E. SYLLA – M. McVAUGH (éds), *Texts and Contexts in Ancient and Medieval Science. Studies on the Occasion of John E. Murdoch's Seventieth Birthday*, Leiden: Brill, 1997, p. 191), mais qu'il convient de replacer ces passages dans la tradition médiévale du débat, où il est attendu d'arguer *pro* et *contra*.

42. Sur les requêtes et dédicaces, qui constituent déjà un lieu commun dans l'Antiquité classique, cf. JANSON T., *Latin Prose Prefaces. Studies in Literary Conventions*, Stockholm: Almqvist & Wiksell, 1964, p. 120-4, et CURTIUS E.R., *La littérature européenne et le Moyen Âge latin*, traduit de l'allemand par J. Bréjoux, Paris: Presses Universitaires de France, 1991 (1956, éd. originale allemande 1948), p. 154-158, en particulier p. 157.

politique, protecteur ou ami. Les prologues des traducteurs consistent ainsi le plus souvent en une dédicace au roi, à un prince ou à un personnage important, et les traducteurs, l'un après l'autre, se récusent bien d'avoir eu la *présomption* d'entreprendre une telle traduction, mais affirment au contraire écrire sous le *commandement* d'un haut personnage à qui ils ne pouvaient désobéir. Martin de Saint-Gille affirme ainsi traduire les *Aphorismes* d'Hippocrate non 'par orgueil ne par presumption, mais pour l'un de mes meilleurs amis, auquel je ne doy ne ne veul reffuser chose qu'il me prie ou commande'[43], et Raoul de Presles explique longuement au début de sa traduction de la *Cité de Dieu* qu'il n'a pas été 'si hardi ou si oultrecuidié' d'avoir entrepris cette traduction de son propre chef, mais qu'il obéit ainsi au commandement du roi qui lui a longtemps réclamé ce travail et à qui il n'ose désobéir[44]. On pourrait ici multiplier les exemples, les traducteurs rappelant soit l'arrogance, l'orgueil, la témérité ou la présomption qu'il y aurait à traduire en français de sa propre initiative, déléguant ainsi au dédicataire toute responsabilité quant au contenu de l'œuvre traduite.

Les prologues introduisant au *Livre du ciel et du monde* et au *Livre des problemes* se démarquent notablement au sein de cette tradition. Il est connu que Nicole Oresme et Évrart de Conty étaient des maîtres de l'université, mais également des personnages importants de l'entourage d'un roi dont le mécénat allait devenir légendaire, et l'on a, conséquemment, beaucoup associé ces traductions à la figure royale et au prestige de la cour. Rappelons cependant que le *Livre des problemes* ne contient pas de dédicace: le prologue d'Évrart de Conty s'articule autour des thèmes propres à la tradition des *Problemata* – l'émerveillement et l'étonnement, le plaisir lié à l'explication des causes – et l'exposition du premier problème, qui tient lieu d'un second prologue du traducteur,

43. JACQUART D., 'Hippocrate en français', dans: D. JACQUART (éd.), *Les voies de la science grecque. Études sur la transmission des textes de l'Antiquité au dix-neuvième siècle*, Genève: Droz, 1997, p. 305.
44. 'Et pour ce que l'en ne cuide pas que par arrogance ou par moy ingerer je l'aie voulu entreprendre, je appelle Dieu a tesmoing et vous le savez assez comment et par quel temps je l'ay refusé et differé a entreprendre, et les excusacions que je y ai pretendues tant pour ce que je savoie et sai la foiblesse de mon engin, la grandeur de l'euvre, et l'aage dont je sui qui me deüsse, si comme il me semble dorenavant reposer. Si ne tiengne vous ne autre moy avoir esté si hardi ou si oultrecuidié de l'avoir entreprist de moy, car se je ne cuidasse avoir commis plus grant offence et que l'en me tenist plus oultrecuidié de le vous avoir refusé que de vous avoir obeÿ a vostre commandement, je l'eüsse a plain refusé. [....]' (BEER J., 'Patronage and the Translator: Raoul de Presles's *La Cité de Dieu* and Calvin's *Institutio religionis Christianae*', dans: J. BEER – K. LLOYD-JONES (éds), *Translation and the Transmission of Culture between 1300 and 1600*, Kalamazoo (Michigan): Medieval Michigan University, 1995, p. 125).

n'évoque aucunement un lecteur privilégié à qui Évrart de Conty aurait destiné son texte. S'il est généralement tenu pour acquis que la traduction d'Évrart de Conty aurait été entreprise du vivant de Charles V qui l'aurait commanditée, le *Livre des problemes* a tout lieu d'être plus tardif: l'explicit du manuscrit autographe situe ainsi la fin de la rédaction après la mort de Charles V[45].

Quant au *Livre du ciel et du monde*, que Nicole Oresme a pour sa part explicitement dédié au roi, on n'y trouve, en lieu de dédicace, que quelques lignes introductives où se trouvent indiqués brièvement l'auteur, le titre de l'œuvre et son dédicataire. Nicole Oresme dit ainsi traduire 'du commandement tres souverain et tres excellent prince Charles, quint de cest nom, par la grace de Dieu roy de France, desirant et amant toutes nobles sciences', avant de se présenter lui-même: 'je, Nychole Oresme, doien de l'eglise de Rouen, propose translater et exposer en françoys'[46]. Si l'épilogue du traducteur rappelle de manière élogieuse le patronage de Charles V, c'est, semble-t-il, pour mieux insister sur sa nomination comme évêque de Lisieux, obtenue en récompense de cette traduction[47]. La place de la dédicace reste, malgré tout, peu développée, et il est frappant de voir Nicole Oresme revendiquer ici clairement l'initiative de la traduction: 'je, Nychole Oresme, propose translater et exposer en françoys', déclaration qui contraste avec la formule, classique, où le traducteur se retire derrière la figure du dédicataire qui lui a, certes, *com-*

45. 'Explicit le livre des problemes de Ar. translaté ou exposé de latin en françois par maistre Évrart de Conty jadis phisicien du Roy Charles le quint.' (ms. BnF fr. 24282, fol. 245r). Cette indication se retrouve encore au début du second manuscrit autographe (ms. BnF fr. 24282) où une note latine identifie le texte comme l''expositio in gallico edita a magistro Evrardo de Conti quondam phisico Karoli quinti francorum regis super secundam partem principalem Probleumatum Aristotilis [...]'. On notera d'ailleurs que la rédaction de la XXVIIe *particula* doit être à tout le moins postérieure à 1377 puisqu'Évrart de Conty se réfère alors explicitement à Nicole Oresme comme évêque de Lisieux, position que celui-ci obtient au moment d'achever sa traduction du *De celo* (cf. infra note 48).

46. 'Ou nom de Dieu, ci commence le livre d'Aristote appelé *Du Ciel et du monde*, lequel du commandement tres souverain et tres excellent prince Charles, quint de cest nom, par la grace de Dieu roy de France, desirant et amant toutes nobles sciences, je, Nychole Oresme, doien de l'eglise de Rouen, propose translater et exposer en françoys. Et est cest livre ainsi intitulé quar il traite du ciel et des elemens du monde [...]' (MENUT – DENOMY (éds), *Livre du ciel et du monde*, p. 38).

47. 'Et ainsi a l'aide de Dieu, je <ay> acompli le livre *Du Ciel et du monde* au commandement de tres excellent prince Charles, quint de ce nom, par la grace de Dieu roy de France, lequel en ce faisant m'a fait evesque de Lisieux'. Le *Livre du ciel et du monde* se termine enfin sur des vers latins à la louange de Charles V: 'Ecce librum celi. Karolo pro rege peregi. / Regi celesti gloria, laus et honor. / Nam naturalis liber unquam philosophie / Pulcrior aut potior nullus in orbe fuit.' (MENUT – DENOMY (éds), *Le livre du ciel et du monde*, p. 730).

mandé de traduire Aristote en français, mais sur qui ne revient pas ici exclusivement le prestige de l'entreprise.

Les traductions de Nicole Oresme et d'Évrart de Conty sont révélatrices ainsi de l'autorité nouvellement acquise du traducteur en langue vernaculaire et du statut que peut conférer l'exposition en français des *auctoritates* médiévales. Il est significatif à ce propos qu'Évrart de Conty se réfère explicitement, dans un passage des *Problemes*, à 'la translacion de Nicole Oresme, evesque de Lisieux, excellent philosophe'[48]. Si l'on imagine bien que les traducteurs devaient être également les premiers lecteurs des traductions vernaculaires, les références explicites d'un traducteur à l'autre sont cependant rarissimes. Dans l'allusion, par exemple, que fait Simon de Hesdin dans son *Valère-Maxime* à la traduction de la *Cité de Dieu* de Raoul de Presles, le traducteur n'est évoqué que par l'intermédiaire de son dédicataire, le roi Charles V[49]. Jean de Meun est peut-être l'une des seules figures de traducteurs en langue vernaculaire auxquelles on se réfère directement, comme le fait par exemple Raoul de Presles en citant le *Roman de la Rose*[50], et auquel Évrart de Conty rend hommage par ses *Eschés amoureux* et son commentaire[51]. Mais le traducteur est le plus souvent passé sous silence au

48. 'Qui en volroit estre bien a plain enfourmé, il convenroit voir le livre de *Ethiques* ou Aristote en traitta excellentement bien. Et qui pourroit avoir la translacion de Nicole Oresme, evesque de Lisieux, excellent philosophe, qui translata et exposa le livre dessus dit en langue françoise moult souffisaument, il y trouveroit de ceste matiere delitables merveilles.' (XXVII, 1, ms. BnF fr. 210, fol. 337a). Sur ce passage, voir GUICHARD-TESSON F., *La 'Glose des Échecs amoureux' d'Évart de Conty. Les idées et le genre de l'œuvre d'après le commentaire du Verger de Déduit*, Thèse de doctorat, Université de Montréal, 1980, p. 294, ainsi que sa contribution dans cet ouvrage.

49. 'De moult de merveilles parles aussi Saint Augustin ou .xxie. livre *de la Cité de Dieu*, si le puet la veoir qui veult, car je le laisse a raconter pour ce especialment que le roy a cellui livre mieulx translater que je ne le sauroie faire, mais toutesvoies pour l'excellence d'aucunes merveilles qu'il raconte ou .xviiie. livre, je ne m'en vueil taire.' (ms. BnF fr. 282, fol. 69va).

50. '[...] qui en vouldra veoir plus a plain voie Alain in *Anticlaudiano* en son .vii^e. livre, du quel maistre Jehan de Mehun ou livre *de la Rose* ou chapitre de fortune prinst son texte et la sentence [...]' (IV, 18, ms. BnF fr. 22912, fol. 204ra); cf. aussi plus loin: 'de ce l'en a example en Virgile qui dit *frigida o pueri fugite hinc <latet> anguis in herba*, le quel ver expose nottablement et declare maistre Jehan de Meun en son livre qu'il fist *de la Rose* ou chapitre du labour [...]' (IV, 10, fol. 195rb). Sur l'autorité de Jean de Meun comme traducteur de Boèce, et plus généralement sur la manière dont les traductions (et leurs traducteurs) s'approprient, en partie du moins, l'autorité de leurs sources latines, voir COPELAND, *Rhetoric...* p. 127-150.

51. L'autorité de Jean de Meun et de son *Roman de la Rose* dépasse bien évidemment ici le cadre de la 'traduction', Jean de Meun apparaissant tout à la fois comme traducteur, commentateur, compilateur, mais aussi *auctor* au plein sens du terme; c'est d'ailleurs à

profit de 'son' auteur, qu'il traduit, expose et défend au mieux de ses compétences – les sources latines constituant toujours le texte de référence auquel les traductions médiévales ne vont jamais se substituer. En ce sens, l'allusion d'Évrart de Conty à Nicole Oresme ne souligne pas tant l'autorité d'un traducteur à l'égard de l'auteur qu'il met en français[52], que la notoriété d'un commentateur devenant lui-même une autorité et à l'œuvre de laquelle on peut désormais se référer, fût-elle écrite en langue vulgaire.

6. Conclusion

La figure du traducteur que mettent en scène les *Problemes* et le *Livre du ciel et du monde* est de fait imposante: l'omniprésence des traducteurs-commentateurs au sein du texte, leurs remarques soulignant la nouveauté de leurs explications, le dialogue qui s'ouvre avec le lecteur, l'effacement du dédicataire, tous ces aspects contribuent à mettre de l'avant la voix du traducteur, véritable personnage qui s'interpose entre l'auteur et le lecteur. Il est vrai que cette présence du traducteur dans le texte marque l'ensemble du corpus des traductions des grandes *auctoritates* du savoir médiéval en langue vernaculaire des XIIIe-XIVe siècles, si elle n'en est pas la caractéristique la plus manifeste permettant de distinguer ces traductions, notamment, des traductions humanistes qui suivront, où le traducteur cherchera à s'effacer pour mieux laisser le lecteur dialoguer seul avec l'auteur.

Le *Livre du ciel et du monde*, sinon plus encore le *Livre des problemes*, poussent cependant cette logique à sa plus grande extrémité. Les deux traducteurs sont ici devenus, si l'on peut renverser le *topos* habituel, des traducteurs présomptueux, qui prennent l'initiative de traduire

---

l'autorité du *Roman de la Rose* que puisent *Les eschés amoureux* et son commentaire. Sur toutes ces questions, voir MINNIS, *Magister Amoris*...., surtout chap. 5-6.

52. On a souvent relevé l'aspect critique d'Évrart de Conty et de Nicole Oresme à l'égard d'Aristote. Le statut équivoque et la réelle difficulté que posait le texte latin des *Problemata* expliquent en partie cependant la position d'Évrart de Conty, qui en souligne les contradictions et répétitions (cf. GUICHARD-TESSON, 'Le métier de traducteur...', p. 146-57; pour la position de Nicole Oresme, voir notamment les remarques de GRANT, 'Nicole Oresme, Aristotle's *On the Heavens*...', p. 192). Quoi qu'il en soit, il convient de rappeler que les traducteurs ne remettent pas directement en cause l'autorité prestigieuse d'Aristote et cherchent au contraire à sauver, par l'interprétation, le texte du Philosophe; les solutions présentées prennent ainsi la forme d'hypothèses, où le fait d'exposer une opinion contraire n'est qu'une façon d'exposer plus complètement le texte d'Aristote.

Aristote en français, revendiquent l'originalité de leur commentaire et invitent le lecteur à trouver mieux et à débattre des solutions présentées, assumant la pleine responsabilité de leur travail. Les remarques de Nicole Oresme et d'Évrart de Conty vantant la nouveauté de leur solution renforcent de fait l'autorité des traducteurs-commentateurs; elle leur permet notamment d'introduire des développements mathématiques que la langue vernaculaire, dans le jeu des conventions qui l'opposent traditionnellement au latin, devait pour l'essentiel omettre.

Il a été suggéré d'expliquer cet aspect tout à la fois savant et ludique, sinon polémique, de leurs traductions, par le genre même auquel elles appartiennent, et de voir ainsi dans le *Livre des Problemes* et le *Livre du ciel et du monde* un ensemble d''exercices intellectuels', dans un genre qui emprunte manifestement aux disputes scolastiques et aux formes d'enseignement, mais également aux traditions littéraires et aux conventions des milieux de cour[53] – un entrecroisement que suggère également la lecture des *Problemata* qu'offrent les *Eschez amoureux moralisés*. Cette parenté formelle entre le *Livre du ciel et du monde* et le *Livre des problemes* permet alors d'expliquer la prétention à l'originalité des deux traducteurs et leur recherche manifeste de la nouveauté; elle éclaire également le contexte, ambigu, de ces traductions scientifiques et – à défaut d'indices plus précis sur les lecteurs des traductions d'Évrart de Conty et de Nicole Oresme – la manière dont on a pu lire ces textes. Si l'effacement, voire l'absence de dédicataire, devrait nous mettre sur la piste d'un lectorat qui ne se confine pas au milieu de la cour et à l'entourage du roi, suivant des modes de diffusion peut-être plus personnalisés, à même de se passer de l'entremise d'un prestigieux commanditaire, la forme même des traductions de Nicole Oresme et d'Évrart de Conty, avec ses adresses au lecteur, renvoie l'image d'un public lettré, capable d'apprécier les développements mathématiques des commentateurs. Nicole Oresme et Évrart de Conty ne cherchaient pas tant, ou pas seulement du moins, à initier des lecteurs à un savoir et à transmettre une 'discipline', de maître à élève, qu'à exercer l'entendement des lecteurs, c'est-à-dire à disputer des arguments d'Aristote et à défendre, sous prétexte d'hypothèses, des 'imaginations' nouvelles que le lecteur n'aura 'ailleurs veue escripte ne oye'.

53. Cf. CADDEN J., 'Charles V, Nicole Oresme, and Christine de Pizan: Unities and Uses of Knowledge in Fourteenth-Century France', dans: E. SYLLA – M. MCVAUGH (éds), *Texts and Contexts in Ancient and Medieval Science*, Leiden: Brill, 1997, p. 208-44, ici p. 243, et p. 234-44 sur la notion de débat en langue vernaculaire.

Appendice I: Problème XV, 6, *Glose* (ms. BnF fr. 210, fol. 207ra-207va)

'[207ra] Pour la declaracion de la response de Aristote, nous devons ymaginer que combien que toute chose lumineuse envoie ses rais et sa lumiere de toutes pars a la maniere d'une espere, si comme il a esté autrefois dit, toutefois toute chose lumineuse au regart d'aucune autre chose meindre de li, pour ce qu'elle le regarde de toute sa grandeur, envoie ses rais et estent sur la chose en les restraingnant et en les aguisant a la maniere d'une pyramide, qui est devers la chose lumineuse lee, et devers la chose enluminee estroite et agüe, si comme il appert clerement qui ymagine bien la chose et ausi par figure.

Et ainsi veons nous que le soleil, qui est plus grant que n'est toute la terre cent soixante et six fois, si comme Ptholomee demonstre (*in quinto Almagesti*)[54], envoie ses rais sur la terre et l'embrace de sa lumiere selonc ceste figure. Et pour [207rb] ce veons nous que le umbre que la terre fait a l'opposite du soleil s'estent et procede tousdis en aguysant comme une pyramide dont le coing et la pointe ataint tout oultre l'espere de la lune jusques a l'espere de mercure, de quoy il avient oultre que quant la lune passe parmy ceste umbre, comme elle fait aucunefois a l'eure de l'opposicion, elle pert sa lumiere qu'elle recevoit par devant du soleil et lors est il eclipse. Et devons ymaginer ausi que se la terre estoit partie tout oultre, si que se fust ausi que un treu, ce qui passeroit oultre de la lumiere du soleil se multiplieroit et procederoit selonc la fourme et la figure pyramidele de le umbre desus dicte.

Tout ausi donc samblablement convient il dire, quant le soleil envoie sa lumiere et ses rais par aucun treu qu'il encontre en sa voie, que sil rais et sa lumiere descendent sur le treu et passent oultre de necessité pyramidelement. Et suppose que aucuns des rais qui sont a l'opposite du treu dyametrelement se puissent oultre estendre quarreement et droit, se convient il dire que li rais qui vienent de la perifere du soleil et des parties de entour, les quelles ne pevent passer oultre le treu desus dit tout droit pour sa petitesce, passent nient mains tout oultre obliquement et selonc la figure pyramidele desus dicte.

54. Cf. *EAM*, où on lit que 'par cest art [de la géométrie] savons nous que le soleil est plus grant que la terre cent .lxvj. foiz, sy comme le demoustre Ptholomeus, et tant de grans merveilles que enviz le croiroit qui ne seroit bon geometrien' (p. 106). La référence à Ptolémée, indiquée en marge dans les manuscrits d'Évrart de Conty, vient ici du commentaire de Pietro d'Abano sur les *Problemata*.

Et pour ce convient il ausi, ce samble, de necessité dire que cils rais obliques qui ainsi se joingnent et asamblent au moilon de la pyramide, entour le dyametre, avec la lumiere qui des autres rais du milieu du soleil ausi y sera envoiee, facent la lumiere desus dicte plus intense et plus forte, et par consequens qu'elle se monstre a la veue mieuls et plus efficaument en l'air et en tous lieus qu'elle pourra ataindre, pource qu'elle sera ausi comme doublee pluseurs fois pour l'addicion des rais obliques desus dis. Et ceste ymaginacion n'ay je pas ailleurs veue escripte ne oye. Et ce pourroit bien estre ausi declairie par figure[55].

Pour ce voit on, quant li rais du soleil descendent sur la face du mireoir concave, laquelle ils raemplissent toute de lumiere et l'air tout environ, que nient mains cils qui sont repercutés se refroissent et se assamblent ausi comme en un point en faisant une pyramide et par ainsi, [207va] pource que la lumiere y est ausi comme doublee et repliquie par infinites fois, il la font si intense et si forte qu'elle a vertu de fu et art tout ce qui en peut estre ataint. Et pource ausi est il que la pyramide petite desus dicte, qui ainsi art et esprent comme fu, notablement se monstre a la veue et se differe des autres parties environ pour sa tres grande luminosité.

Aristote donc veult dire, en confourmant aus choses desus dictes, que quant la lumiere du soleil encontre en sa voie aucun treu, soit quarré ou autre, elle se multiplie et espant tout oultre en aguysant tous dis comme une pyramide. Et pource que ceste figure aproche plus et resamble a figure reonde et circuliere que autre, pource dit il que es lieus ou elle arreste, elle se monstre de reonde figure, et non pas de quarree quant a la premiere raison.

Et quant a la raison seconde ausi qui est confirmatoire de la premiere, pource que la lumiere, qui est enclose en la pyramide desus dicte qui est reonde, se monstre mieuls a la veue et plus notablement que la lumiere qui passe oultre es angles, pource qu'elle est ainsi doublee et enforcie, comme dit est, par quoy elle vaint l'autre et le rent ausi comme nule et umbraige, pource briefment samble il que la lumiere du soleil desus dicte passant par aucun treu quarré, quant a le impression qu'elle fait oultre en aucun lieu ou elle est arrestee, soit de figure circuliere et reonde et non pas de quarree. Et pource convient il que ceste impression se face loings du treu et de la veue, comme Aristote pretent, car con plus la lumiere des angles desus dis se estent loings, plus afeblie, et ausi fait la vertu de veoir.'

55. Cf. figure reproduite infra.

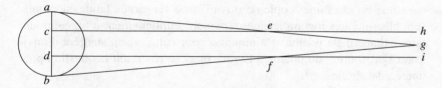

Figure, fol. 207rb, marge inférieure[56]

Appendice II: Les *Eschés amoureux* d'Évrart de Conty

La discussion dans cet article sur les relations entre les *Problemes*, les *Eschez amoureux moralisés* et les *Eschés amoureux* présupposant que ce poème soit également d'Évrart de Conty, il convient d'exposer ici les principaux arguments qui sous-tendent cette attribution. Seule l'attribution du poème à Évrart de Conty permet en effet de résoudre de manière satisfaisante une difficulté majeure que pose la relation du texte à sa glose, difficulté qu'ont soulevée tous les commentateurs modernes: le poème ne se suffit pas à lui-même et appelle le commentaire, puisqu'il ne dévoile pas l'identité allégorique des pièces de l'échiquier, nécessaire à la compréhension de l'œuvre[57]. La clé de cette interprétation est fournie cependant par les gloses latines et le schéma des pièces du jeu d'échec contenus dans l'un des deux manuscrits (celui de Venise) des *Eschés amoureux*, qui forment ainsi 'l'ébauche d'un commentaire'[58]; ces gloses se retrouvent à nouveau en marge de l'adaptation anglaise qu'en fait, vers 1410, John Lydgate[59]. L'étude minutieuse de Gianmario Raimondi sur les manuscrits des *Eschés amoureux* conforte ici l'idée que ce commentaire à l'état d'ébauche n'est autre que celui d'Évrart dans le *Livre des eschez amoureux moralisés*: le manuscrit de Venise, avec ses nombreuses corrections, ratures et révisions d'une même main,

---

56. Il me semble qu'on doit lire ce schéma de la manière suivante: si *ef* représente l'ouverture de forme carrée, le cône (ou 'pyramide ronde') *abg*, formé par les rayons obliques du soleil se rejoignant en *g* au 'moilon' ou vertex de la pyramide, apparaîtra plus lumineux que les zones éclairées seulement par les rayons 'du milieu du soleil' *ch* et *di* qui seuls conservent la forme carrée de l'ouverture; c'est pourquoi, à partir d'une certaine distance, la lumière apparaît sous la forme d'un cercle.

57. Cf. GUICHARD-TESSON – ROY (éds), *EAM*, p. LIX-LXIII; RAIMONDI (éd.), 'Les eschés amoureux (I)...', p. 87-89, et MINNIS, *Magister Amoris...*, p. 289-90.

58. GUICHARD-TESSON – ROY (éds), *EAM*, p. LXII.

59. Cf. SIEPER E., *Lydgate's Reason and Sensuallyte*, London: Early English Text Society, 1901-03.

constitue en effet une 'copie de travail'[60] où les gloses latines apparaissent elles-mêmes incomplètes et renvoient implicitement à un commentaire exhaustif du poème: Raimondi a pour cette raison suggéré d'envisager l'attribution du poème à Évrart, mais en réservant la question pour
une étude ultérieure[61].

Cette hypothèse apparaît d'autant plus probante à la relecture des
Problemes. On notera ainsi que le poème des *Eschés amoureux* introduit
dans la trame du *Roman de la Rose* deux motifs chers à Évrart: les
échecs, pour lesquels l'intérêt d'Évrart est manifeste dans les *Problemes*
XXX, 1 et XXX, 6, voire XV, 1, et les dieux et déesses, dont l'explication des attributs représente la deuxième partie, fort imposante, du *Livre
des eschez amoureux moralisés*[62]. Le motif du miroir concave, on l'a vu,
se retrouve également dans les trois textes. Un autre point de comparaison mérite d'être signalé ici: le prologue du *Livre des eschez amoureux
moralisés* met l'accent sur l'obscurité de l'œuvre qu'il commente, justifiant ainsi son propre travail, de la même manière que le prologue du
Livre des problemes insiste sur l'obscurité du texte d'Aristote, liant dans
les deux textes l'obscurité du texte au plaisir de le lire et de l'exposer
(utilisant d'ailleurs à l'appui la même citation de la *Rhétorique* d'Aristote)[63], alors que le prologue des *Eschés amoureux* évoque le 'mistiere'
de la matière de l'œuvre[64]. Enfin, c'est un rapprochement du poème au
Livre des problemes qui fournit l'argument le plus conclusif, l'attribution à Évrart offrant la solution la plus économique pour expliquer les
correspondances textuelles entre les trois œuvres – correspondances
qu'avait fort justement notées Françoise Guichard-Tesson[65], en soulignant 'le fait que les *Problemes* semblent, dans certains cas, aussi proches des *Echecs* que de la *Glose*', mais pour en conclure 'qu'Évrart connaissait déjà les *Echecs* lorsqu'il rédigea la *Glose*'. Ma conviction que le
poème est l'œuvre d'Évrart de Conty s'appuie ainsi plus précisément sur
un parallèle entre les trois textes – la description du printemps qu'on
trouve au début de chacune des œuvres, soit dans les *Problemes* I, 3[66],

---

60. Suivant l'expression de RAIMONDI (éd.), '*Les eschés amoureux* (I)…', p. 94-97.
61. Voir RAIMONDI (éd.), '*Les eschés amoureux* (I)…' p. 218-9, note sur la glose
1851-G, et '*Les eschés amoureux* (II)…', notes sur les v. 4695-4920 et sur les gloses latines explicitant la signification des pièces du jeu d'échecs – en attendant la parution du
travail de Raimondi portant spécifiquement sur ces questions d'attribution.
62. GUICHARD-TESSON – ROY (éds), *Eschez amour. moral.*, p. 63-347.
63. Cf. supra note 30.
64. RAIMONDI (éd.), '*Les eschés amoureux* (I)…', p. 108 v. 40.
65. GUICHARD-TESSON, 'Évrart de Conty, auteur de la *Glose*…', p. 111-148, en particulier p. 133-136.
66. 'Et selont ce dit Avic<ennes> (*1° Can. f. 2ª*) que li prins tans est quant li arbre
commence a foeillir et que les naiges des montaingnes se fondent et degastent. Et que

les *Eschés amoureux*, v. 95-109[67], et *Le livre des eschez amoureux moralisés*, lignes 8r38-8r42[68] – qui trouve sa source dans le commentaire latin de Pietro d'Abano à ce problème[69]. Ces passages suggèrent de revoir la datation respective de ces œuvres (le *Livre des Problemes* devant vraisemblablement précéder les *Eschés amoureux*); ils illustrent bien, enfin, comment le 'projet' littéraire d'Évrart de Conty s'entremêle dès l'origine avec sa traduction et son commentaire des *Problemata*[70].

École Pratique des Hautes Études
Institutionen für historisk Studier, Umeå universitet

nous ausi n'avons mie trop grant mestier de nous vestir et couvrir pour le froit ne de trop grant eventation pour la chaleur.' (ms. BnF fr. 24281, fol. 10v).

67. '[Li arbre] aussy se reverdissent / et font fueilles et se flourissent, / pour fruit porter en la saison / tel qu'il doivent selon raison. / Li fleuve aussy et les fontaines / se renouvellent en leurs vaines, / et commencent habondanment / a croistre et courre radement / et grant proufit au monde font. / La naige se degaste et font, / li airs s'adoulcist et attempre, / si qu'il n'y a, ne tart ne tempre, / ne trop chaleur ne trop froidure, / pour le souleil qui par mesure / ses rais a la terre presente' (RAIMONDI éd., '*Les eschés amoureux...*', p. 109).

68. 'Pour ce dit Avicennes que le printemps commence quant les arbres commencent à foeillir et que les naiges des montaignes se fundent et degastent, que nous n'avons pas aussi trop grant necessité de nous vestir ne couvrir pour le froit, ne de eventacion aussi trop grant pour la chaleur; et ce dit il pour la bonne attemprance de sa nature.' (*EAM*, p. 20).

69. 'Una quidem est sensibilis valde medicinalis penes effectum data que quidem describitur ab Avicen. primo can. fen. 2ª. Dicit enim quod ver est principium frondendi arborum et quod nives de montibus cadunt neque multis tunc indigemus cooperimentis propter frigus neque paucis propter eventationem' (*Expositio problematum...*).

70. Les journées d'études sur les *Problemata* ont très heureusement permis de confronter les recherches en cours sur ces questions; je renvoie ici bien évidemment à la contribution de F. Guichard-Tesson dans cet ouvrage.

Joëlle DUCOS

LECTURES ET VULGARISATION
DU SAVOIR ARISTOTÉLICIEN:
LES GLOSES D'ÉVRART DE CONTY (SECTIONS XXV-XXVI)

The translation of Aristotle's Problems *by Evrart de Conty is in many respects original: appearing as a landmark in Aristotelian translations in French, it is part of a long tradition of paraphrastic translations accompanied by a commentary. The commentary that comes with the translation is nevertheless a true creation of the translator, which, while inspired by sources borrowed from scholasticism, reveals Evrart's personal culture and his true reflection on the writing process of popularization. Books XXV and XXVI are both concerned with air. The way glosses are organised, sources are laid out in the margin and the text, and personal developments are introduced, displays the personal choices of Evrart de Conty in the reading of the Aristotelian text and its commentaries, while they reflect his general practice, but also evince his appropriation of the text, which leads to a rewriting of it and a genuine creation. That is why both books seem to exemplify the popularization of knowledge, which involves the choice of sources, some active reading, but also the invention of textual forms and themes.*

Introduction

Si les questions médicales constituent la majorité des *Problèmes* d'Aristote, plusieurs sections de cette œuvre sont consacrées à des interrogations sur la physique et spécialement sur l'eau et l'air, c'est-à-dire sur les deux éléments qui sont essentiels à la fois dans la météorologie aristotélicienne et dans la médecine hippocratique, où ils apparaissent comme des causes des maladies ou du bon état de santé. Il n'est pas étonnant dans ces conditions que les sections XXV à XXVI donnent lieu à un commentaire original d'Évrart de Conty qui, médecin de formation et écrivain hors du commun[1], ne peut avoir le même regard que le com-

---

1. Voir les travaux de GUICHARD-TESSON F., 'Évrart de Conty, auteur de la *Glose des Echecs amoureux*', *Le Moyen Français* 8-9 (1983), p. 111-148; 'Le métier de traducteur et de commentateur au XIVᵉ siècle d'après Évrart de Conty', *Le Moyen Français* 24-25 (1990), p. 131-167; 'Le souci de la langue et du style au XIVᵉ siècle: l'autographe des *Problèmes* d'Évrart de Conty', *Le Moyen Français* 33 (1993) p. 57-84 ; voir aussi sa contribution à ce volume. LÉGARÉ A. M. - ROY B., 'Le 'je' d'Évrart de Conty: Du texte à l'image', dans: B. BAILLAUD – J. DE GRAMONT – D. HÜE (éds), *Auteurs, lecteurs, savoirs*

mentateur Pierre d'Abano dont les choix et la lecture reflètent la pensée scientifique. Nous nous intéresserons donc à son commentaire pour tenter de mettre à jour la culture du traducteur et pour nous interroger sur son projet: choix et lecture personnels de l'œuvre d'Aristote ou commentaire orienté pour une vulgarisation spécifique, dans une théorie générale de la vulgarisation des savoirs?

1. Un commentaire séparé de la traduction.

La mise à distance du texte d'Aristote par rapport à la voix du commentateur se mesure d'abord matériellement dans les folios des manuscrits puisque la glose est signalée en marge par l'abréviation gl^2. Cette mise en page, qui est l'un des moyens des manuscrits français de signaler le commentaire, n'est cependant pas le seul indice d'un texte polyphonique. Les interventions du traducteur-commentateur sont nombreuses et marquent un regard critique particulièrement étonnant dans un texte français qui traduit une autorité. Mahieu le Vilain, au 13e siècle, ou Nicole Oresme, qui traduit plusieurs traités d'Aristote, ne font guère de commentaire défavorable sur la nature du texte ou sur l'organisation ou la cohérence du texte, en dehors de quelques passages où ils peuvent relever des contradictions. Ils mettent en avant l'extrême rigueur de l'argumentation dans chaque préliminaire de chapitre et en soulignent les articulations[3]. Au contraire Évrart de Conty n'hésite pas à relever les obscurités et les répétitions du texte. Il refuse ainsi de traduire:

> Cy aprés repete Aristotes le 23e probleme de la premiere partie et demande comme devant pourquoy c'est que li homme sont plus pesant et plus dangereus quant li vens austrins vente qu'en aultre tans et respont Aristotes comme devant et pour ce que cils probleme fu de-

anonymes. «JE» et encyclopédies (Cahiers Diderot 8), Rennes: Presses universitaires de Rennes – Association Diderot, 1996, p. 39-55; voir aussi les analyses de JACQUART D. sur la mise en scène du savoir médical par Évrart de Conty dans La médecine médiévale dans le cadre parisien, Paris: Fayard, 1998. Voir également sur les procédés de traduction et les relations au texte latin, GOYENS M., 'Le développement du lexique scientifique français et la traduction des Problèmes d'Aristote par Évrart de Conty (c. 1380)', Theleme. Revista Complutense de Estudios Franceses, Número Extraordinario (2003), p. 189-207; GOYENS M. - DE LEEMANS P., 'Traduire du grec au latin et du latin au français', dans: P. ANDERSEN (éd.), Pratiques de traduction au Moyen Âge, Actes du colloque de l'Université de Copenhague, 25 et 26 octobre 2002, Copenhagen: Museum Tusculanum Press, University of Copenhagen, 2004, p. 204-224.

2. Voir en particulier le manuscrit autographe BNF fr. 24281 et 24282.

3. Cf. EDGREN R. (éd.), Mahieu le Vilain, Livre des Meteores, Uppsala, 1945; MENUT A.D. - DENOMY A.J. (éds), Nicole Oresme, Le livre du ciel et du monde, Madison: University of Wisconsin Press, 1968.

vant desclairiés souffisamment et qu'il ne ajouste riens ycy endroit qui la n'ait esté dit, pour ce n'y faut il ja plus arrester et par aventure n'est il cy repetés fors pour le ramener a la memoire por ce qu'il est bien seans a ceste matere des vens[4].

Aristotes dont respont comme devant et pour ce qu'il n'y aidjouste riens combien que ce soit une aultre translation et qu'il fut exposés ausi devant assés souffisamment, pour ce n'y fault il ja plus arrester et de ceste matere fu il ausi parlé ou 19e probleme[5].

Mais toutefois pour ce qu'il fut devant exposés assés souffisamment et qu'il ne ajoute riens qui ne soit devant dit, pour ce ne fault il ja plus ycy arrester[6].

La répétition des questions l'autorise à supprimer certains passages, sans apport nouveau. La traduction permet de simplifier un texte répétitif et d'en donner une version expurgée de ses redondances. Le traducteur souligne aussi dans son commentaire plusieurs défauts:

- les redites:

Ceste response est assés clere, selont la doctrine de Aristote, ja devant souvent ditte[7].

La response de Aristote est de soy assés clere parmi ce qui fu dit ausi devant u 23e probleme[8].

Ceste matere en partie fut touchie devant u 19e probleme et se sera encores cy aprés repetee ou 44e[9].

- les insuffisances de certains passages:

Cil problemes est moult obscurement translatés et exposés aussi assés legierement[10].

Pour ce que la premiere raison est rude et aussi comme nulle, car elle ne aprent riens ne ne desclaire tant soit pou du probleme, ains demeure la chose aussi obscure ou plus comme devant, pour ce met il la seconde raison qui est plus claire et satefie miex[11].

Aristotes ne respont mie a son probleme completement, mais par ce qu'il en dit qui soubtilment sa response ymagine, il poet legierement le remanant comprendre[12].

4. BNF fr. 24282, XXVI, 41, fol. 142r. Toutes les références au texte d'Évrart de Conty sont tirées de ce manuscrit autographe, et plus en particulier des parties 'glose'.
5. BNF fr. 24282, XXVI, 44, fol. 142v.
6. XXVI, 30, fol. 136v; voir aussi XXVI, 43, fol. 142v.
7. XXVI, 32, fol. 138r.
8. XXVI, 35, fol. 139r.
9. XXVI, 38, fol. 141r.
10. XXVI, 43, fol. 142v.
11. XXVI, 19, fol. 130r.
12. XXVI, 20, fol. 130v.

- les additions:

> Ceste matere fut touchie par devant ou probleme second quant a une
> partie, mais Aristotes y ajouste en cest probleme une autre question
> pour le miex desclairier[13].

- les différences:

> Cils problemes se differe du quart probleme devant dit en ce que
> Aristotes y compere les parties de miedi et de mienuit[14].

Ce regard critique peut aussi amener une récapitulation et une reconstruction du raisonnement:

> Aristotes en cest probleme demande 4 choses ou 5, premierement
> pourquoy Zephyrus est li plus douls vens et li plus souefs de tous et de
> ce fu il parlé u 31e probleme et s'en parlera encores cy aprés u 54e
> pour le miex desclairier, secondement pourquoy il est frois et de ce fu
> il parlé aucunement ou 21e probleme en la desclairation, tiercement
> pourquoy il vente en certain tamps determiné de l'an comme en
> printans et en autonpne et de ce fu il ausi parlé ou probleme 31e
> desusdit, quartement pourquoy il vente volentiers bas et pres de la
> terre, de quoy il fut aussi parlé ou 21e probleme et quintement pour
> quoy il vente volentiers au soir vers soleil esconsant et se cesse par
> nuit et de ce fu il aussi parlé devant u 33e et 36e problemes[15].

Cette mise à distance du texte d'Aristote, où est démontrée la structure particulière des *Problèmes*, parfois répétitive ou au contraire contra-
dictoire, et en tout cas très différente de la structure argumentative de ses
traités, n'est cependant pas une innovation d'Évrart dans la lecture médiévale d'Aristote. Elle apparaît aussi dans le commentaire de Pierre
d'Abano[16] et relève clairement de l'exercice scolastique de la *lectio* où
sont marqués les articulations logiques, les échos ou les écarts. Évrart de
Conty ne se distingue pas sur ce point de ses prédécesseurs dans la pratique de la traduction aristotélicienne en français: Mahieu le Vilain le fait
systématiquement et Nicole Oresme procède de la même manière, mais
sans le regard critique si présent dans la traduction d'Évrart de Conty[17].
Le médecin montre ainsi sa formation universitaire, en adaptant la tech-

---

13. XXVI, 50, fol. 145v.
14. XXV, 7, fol. 115r.
15. XXVI, 51, fol. 146r.
16. Pierre d'Abano, *Expositio problematum Aristotelis quam Petrus edidit paduanus*,
Mantoue, 1475.
17. DUCOS J., *La météorologie en français (XIIIe-XIVe siècles)*, Paris: Champion,
1998, p. 185-195; 'Traduction et autorité: le cas des *Météorologiques* d'Aristote', *Bien
dire et bien aprandre* 14 (1996), p. 307-318.

nique de lecture couramment pratiquée à l'université : lire un texte, que ce soit pour le commenter ou le traduire, suppose une mise en évidence de sa structuration logique et des relations internes à l'œuvre. Ainsi le traducteur signale systématiquement les échos entre les problèmes, comme le fait aussi Pierre d'Abano, et ce souci se manifeste continuellement chaque fois qu'une thématique a déjà été traitée[18]. Cette insistance sur la cohérence d'une œuvre, pourtant disparate, amène le traducteur à indiquer non seulement les relations entre les problèmes d'un même livre, mais aussi en dehors du livre. Il montre à la fois sa maîtrise du texte, malgré son extrême dispersion et souligne la structure des livres où une même interrogation peut amener une série d'explications, en particulier au livre XXVI. Le lecteur est orienté et invité à comparer des passages parfois éloignés. L'œuvre n'est pas prise comme une succession de questions sans relation, mais comme un tout où des niveaux successifs d'explication sont proposés par Aristote. Évrart de Conty paraît ainsi comme un commentateur imprégné des principes de la lecture scolastique dans sa pratique d'écriture.

D'autres remarques sont plus originales par rapport aux autres traducteurs. C'est d'abord la présence du commentateur qui est indiquée à plusieurs reprises, parfois pour souligner son apport, mais aussi pour le critiquer :

> Le expositeur ausi de Aristote expose ceste premiere response aultrement en disant ainsi que aucun dient que Subsolanus atrait a soy les nues[19].

> Et briefment l'autre exposition s'acorde miex au texte de Aristote et est plus raisonnable a mon avis[20].

> Cils probleme briefment est moult obscurs et moult obscurement est ausi exposés et pour ce ne poet on mie bien comprendre ce qu'il woelt dire[21].

> Cils problemes est moult obscurement proposés de Aristote et la response ausi est moult obscure, ne li expositeres ausi ne desclaire point bien l'entente de Aristote[22].

Or, si la traduction d'autorité française suppose la présence d'un commentaire, les références à des auteurs qui ne relèvent pas de l'autorité sont habituellement absentes. À titre d'exemple, Mahieu le Vilain cite

18. Voir le tableau en annexe. Des écarts de référence en particulier dans les chiffres peuvent apparaître, mais ils sont sans signification en l'absence d'édition scientifique du commentaire de Pierre d'Abano.

19. XXVI, 29, fol. 136r.

20. XXVI, 29, fol. 136r.

21. XXVI, 8, fol. 125r.

22. XXV, 12, fol. 117v.

de temps en temps Alexandre d'Aphrodisias, en le nommant[23]. En revanche sa source principale, qui est le commentaire de Thomas d'Aquin sur les *Météorologiques,* n'est jamais indiquée alors que le traducteur mêle la traduction du texte de Guillaume de Moerbeke à la paraphrase de Thomas d'Aquin[24]. De même, dans le *Livre du ciel et du monde* traduit par Nicole Oresme, si des références à certains auteurs apparaissent[25], il n'y a guère d'allusion aux commentaires du traité aristotélicien traduit. Dans les *Problemes,* le nom de ce commentateur n'est pas donné: c'est *l'expositeur,* appellation pour le moins ambiguë. Mais il est clair qu'il s'agit de Pierre d'Abano, commentateur par excellence des *Problèmes*: il n'est pas nommé, peut-être en raison de ses idées contestées, mais surtout parce que son œuvre est inséparable de la traduction de Barthélémy de Messine. Le traducteur marque donc trois niveaux. Le premier est constitué du texte de traduction où, après la question traduite directement, Évrart signale ostensiblement la voix d'Aristote par la proposition attributive suivante ou par ses variantes: *A ce respont Aristote.* Le deuxième niveau s'inspire du commentaire latin parfois signalé, réorganisé, réécrit ou même négligé dans la glose. Enfin on peut parler d'un commentaire autonome d'Évrart de Conty, signalé séparément du texte d'Aristote et reprenant des éléments du commentaire, d'autres œuvres aristotéliciennes et d'autres références ou compléments. Il ne s'agit donc pas dans ce dernier niveau d'une simple compilation, mais bien d'une écriture personnelle du commentateur qui manifeste sa culture et ses intérêts.

Une autre originalité du texte est aussi la conscience claire que le texte-source est lui-même une traduction dont la qualité est parfois défaillante, en fonction de la capacité aux traducteurs à tenir compte des adaptations indispensables du grec au latin.

> Cil probleme est moult obscurement translatés et exposés aussi assés legierement... On porroit dire aussi que li textes est corrompus en ceste partie[26].

23. Ducos J. (éd.), *Mahieu le Vilain, Livre des meteores,* III, Champion: à paraître: 'Et por ce dist Alixandres qui exposa cest livre que en aucun lieu avint que .I. estorbellon hurta si en la mer que il esleva et emporta grant plenté d'eve, et en .I. autre lieu emporta il une nef et grans pierres et bestes de la terre.'

24. Ducos J., 'L'œuvre de Mahieu le Vilain: traduction et commentaire des *Météorologiques*', dans: J. Hamesse (éd.), *Les traducteurs au travail, leurs manuscrits et leurs méthodes* (Textes et études du Moyen Age 18), Turnhout: Brepols, 2001, p. 285-309.

25. Voir par exemple les références citées dans Menut – Denomy (éds), *Le Livre du ciel et du monde,* II, 16, p. 452-468, où Nicole Oresme traite de l'image et de la nature de la lune: Albert le Grand, *Libri Meteororum,* Averroès, Macrobe, Avicenne, Pline.

26. XXVI, 43, fol. 142v. Cette mention est absente du commentaire de Pierre d'Abano et est originale.

Ce commentaire, philologique en quelque sorte, pourrait paraître comme une amorce de la réflexion humaniste sur la transmission des textes antiques. De fait, si ce type de remarques est rare en français, elles sont beaucoup plus fréquentes dans les commentaires scolastiques où sont comparées des versions successives d'un même texte. Que ce soit Jean Buridan ou Thémon le juif, ils n'hésitent pas à comparer les versions latines, indiquant les différences, voire les insuffisances de telle ou telle version. Elles montrent ainsi un souci du texte original, ce qui est révélateur de la réflexion sur la traduction dans le cercle de Charles V dont Nicole Oresme est le représentant le plus notable, lui qui a présenté une théorie originale[27]. Toutefois cette appréciation de la qualité du texte à traduire, qui est nettement mise en doute par Évrart de Conty, est rarement exprimée aussi explicitement chez les autres traducteurs en dehors d'un prologue. Évrart de Conty reproduit des habitudes scolastiques et témoigne par là même d'un souci de vulgarisation, en faisant du français et de son œuvre les réceptacles d'une attitude universitaire face au texte d'autorité traduit en latin. Mais surtout, il ne présente pas sa traduction comme la seule étape entre le grec et le français, mais comme la deuxième. La difficulté du texte paraît ainsi liée moins à l'écart entre le français et le latin qu'à un texte dont le sens a déjà été transformé par un premier traducteur. Ce sont donc des problèmes généraux de traduction, lexicaux ou de sens auxquels est confronté Évrart, qui doit non seulement trouver un équivalent en français, mais aussi comprendre une langue qui n'est peut-être qu'une adaptation maladroite du texte grec d'Aristote. Cette conscience clairement exprimée se retrouve dans la section XXVI où le traducteur signale à plusieurs reprises que tel ou tel problème est une nouvelle version de la même thématique: il utilise le terme *translation*, indiquant ainsi qu'il peut s'agir d'une variante du traducteur plutôt que de la pensée d'Aristote.

> La response de Aristote en cest probleme est samblable a la response du 20e probleme, combien que la translation soit par aultres paroles et plus longues[28].

Le texte traduit ainsi présenté paraît un résultat parfois aléatoire qui peut perdre de sa lisibilité et de sa clarté d'origine. La mise à distance

---

27. Voir LUSIGNAN S., *Parler vulgairement: les intellectuels et la langue française aux XIIIᵉ et XIVᵉ siècles,* Paris-Montréal: Vrin-Presses de l'Université de Montréal, 1986, p. 154-166.

28. XXVI, 53, fol. 148v: ce même commentaire se trouve aussi dans le commentaire de Pierre d'Abano qui insiste sur la longueur; en revanche, mention originale dans XXVI, 29, fol. 135v: 'Cy repete Aristotes le premier probleme de ceste partie et briefment c'est une autre translation qui fut trouvee et cy par aventure mist pour miex avoir l'entente de Aristote.'

nécessaire invite alors à la glose, espace de liberté de la parole, où le traducteur peut développer à partir d'Aristote, mais aussi en dehors de lui et de son commentateur latin.

2. Des gloses révélatrices d'une culture aristotélicienne et médicale

Le commentaire d'Évrart de Conty se développe largement à la suite de la traduction. Toutefois, cette glose séparée n'empêche pas différents types d'interventions du traducteur qui se mêlent et s'ajoutent pour mettre en évidence un savoir: la marge, les commentaires internes à la traduction et les commentaires externes constituent les trois espaces où la voix du traducteur apparaît.

2.1. Les références bibliographiques

L'usage de la marge est réservé aux références en latin. Mais des noms d'autorités ou de livres sont nommés dans le texte ou, ce qui est le plus fréquent, des allusions imprécises sont faites dans le texte[29]. La comparaison entre les deux types de référence est instructive sur l'usage du texte[30]. Les références marginales renvoient majoritairement aux textes d'Aristote, parfois à Avicenne ou encore au *Pantegni* de Constantin et à Abu Mashar, c'est-à-dire aux ouvrages qui sont d'usage universitaire, alors que celles qui sont citées dans le texte relèvent davantage d'une culture commune, soit par la notoriété du nom, soit parce que les théories citées sont vulgarisées ailleurs, ce qui laisse supposer deux types de lecteurs ou de lecture. La culture aristotélicienne que l'on trouve en marge renvoie tout spécialement aux ouvrages importants pour la météorologie, ce qui n'est pas étonnant: la thématique des sections XXV et XXVI est centrée sur les questions météorologiques puisqu'elles traitent de l'air et des vents. Or l'ouvrage de référence pour l'explication physique des phénomènes météorologiques est, au Moyen Age, le traité d'Aristote traduit en latin depuis le 12e siècle[31].

---

29. Elles sont annoncées par les formules: *comme il est dit ailleurs, comme Aristotes le dit ailleurs.*

30. Voir tableau en annexe: les références données se séparent de celles de Pierre d'Abano: s'il y a parfois conformité, certaines peuvent être supprimées ou ajoutées.

31. Deux traductions latines ont été faites, l'une dite *vetus,* par Gérard de Crémone, l'autre par Guillaume de Moerbeke *(nova).* À cela s'ajoute une traduction en hébreu. SCHOONHEIM P.L., *Aristotle's Meteorology in the arabico-latin tradition*, Leiden, 2000. Pour la *nova*, une édition est en préparation par VUILLEMIN-DIEM G., à paraître dans la série *Aristoteles Latinus*. Le texte peut être consulté dans l'édition léonine de THOMAS D'AQUIN, *Opera omnia iussu impensaque Leonis XIII*, T. III, Rome, 1886. Pour l'édition en hébreu, voir FONTAINE R. (éd.), *Otot ha-Shamayim. Samuel Ibn Tibbon's Hebrew version of Aristotle's Meteorology,* Leiden, 1995.

Mais les théories exposées dans les *Problèmes* présentent des écarts par rapport à la théorie aristotélicienne, en particulier pour les vents, au point que l'on a pu hésiter à les attribuer au philosophe et qu'on les a rapprochées du livre sur les vents de Théophraste[32]. La culture météorologique affichée dans les marges permet, pour un lecteur qui a à la disposition ces textes ou qui les connaît, d'établir des liens entre les textes et de les comparer.

Le problème XXVI, 29 sur le vent d'est est l'une des questions qui marquent des divergences entre le traité aristotélicien et l'explication des *Problèmes*. La glose d'Évrart de Conty témoigne à la fois d'une réflexion sur les deux textes et sur le commentaire. La question posée porte sur le vent d'est qui attire les nuages de toutes parts alors que les autres vents ne les attirent que sur leur passage[33]. La réponse d'Aristote dans les *Problèmes* est double. La première vient de la présence d'un vent contraire qui renvoie les nuages vers lui. La deuxième hypothèse repose sur la différence entre le concave et le convexe. Le vent d'est a une ligne concave au contraire des autres vents et par conséquent il attire les nuages. Le traducteur, après avoir paraphrasé Aristote, commence par utiliser, ce qui est extrêmement rare dans cette section[34], une observation pour justifier la première théorie :

> Ainsi veons nous souvent que les nues se moeuvent d'une part et sont cachies, ce qui ne se poet faire sans aucun vent et nientmains les banieres et les coches des tours et des esglises et des haus edefices se moeuvent au contraire des nues. Meismes voit on que les basses qui sont pres de la terre se moeuvent d'une part et sont cachies moult violentement et les hautes sont quoyes sans mouvoir ou elles se remouevent au contraire des autres, lesquels choses ne se poeent faire sans vens contraires[35].

Cette observation faite, le traducteur résume l'opinion de Pierre d'Abano, qui repose sur un vent qui souffle de tous les côtés :

> Le expositeur ausi de Aristote expose ceste premiere response aultrement en disant ainsi que aucuns dient que Subsolanus atrait a

32. Voir, sur cette question, la synthèse de P. LOUIS dans son introduction à son édition des *Problèmes,* Paris, 1991, p. XXIII-XXXV.

33. XXVI, 29, fol. 135v.

34. L'absence d'observation dans les textes météorologiques est presque de règle, car il s'agit d'explications théoriques. Généralement, les exemples donnés relèvent de topiques et sont répétés de commentaires en commentaires. Les observations ou les témoignages apparaissent ainsi ponctuellement, sauf chez certains auteurs comme Jean Buridan qui en fait un élément constitutif de son argumentation. Sur cette place, voir DUCOS J., 'Théorie et pratique de la météorologie médiévale: Albert le Grand et Jean Buridan', dans: C. THOMASSET – J. DUCOS (éds), *Le temps qu'il fait au Moyen Age,* Paris: Presses de l'Université de Paris-Sorbonne, 1998, p. 45-58.

35. XXVI, 29, fol. 135v.

soy les nues pour ce que il meïsmes vente a parties contraires tout
ensamble et par ainsi, en retournant a soy aussi comme circulerement,
il ramaine les nues et les ratrait a soy ou au lieu dont il vint
premierement ausi que s'il wolsist dire que, quant Subsolanus est ve-
nus ou occident, il s'en retorne aprés par un autre cemin en orient,
aussi comme s'il se meüst circulerement. Mais ceste response ne
samble pas estre bien raisonnable[36].

Le jugement final détruit l'explication et marque un scepticisme du
traducteur. Évrart de Conty va même jusqu'à refuser complètement cette
hypothèse au nom de la raison:

Il n'y ha point d'autre maniere qui me apere de ymaginer comment cis
vens porroit venter as parties contraires (…) Et briefment l'autre exposition s'acorde miex au texte de Aristote et est plus raisonnable a
mon avis. Aristotes toutefois ce samble reproeuve ceste response, quar
pour ce met il aprés sa response plus vraye en reprendant une raison
qui fut devant touchie u probleme premier[37].

Ce passage montre ainsi la relation entre raisonnement et vérité: deux
voies sont suggérées et ne relèvent pas du même domaine. L'une est
l'accord avec l'autorité, mais peut amener une discordance avec la raison, ce qui en détruit la force. L'autre est l'imagination qui permet
d'élaborer des hypothèses, mais qui doit aussi correspondre à la vérité
pour avoir valeur assertive. La raison est donc l'élément fondamental
dans la détermination du vrai et est même supérieure à l'argument
d'autorité[38]. Toutefois la réponse *plus vraye* d'Aristote ne le satisfait pas
non plus et il termine à l'aide d'un autre problème, en mettant l'accent
sur l'illusion et la chaleur:

Finablement la plus raisonnable response a cest probleme fut toucie
en l'autre probleme ou il samble que Aristotes woelt dire que cils
Subsolanus n'est mie vens impetueus ne fors, ains est petis et febles et
souefs et pour ce n'esmoet il mie moult les nues qu'il encontre, ains
samble miex qu'elles ne se moeuvent et pour ce qu'elles demeurent
par derriere le vent, il samble lors qu'il les atraye a soy ou il se moet
espoir desoubs les nues et ne les atrait point. A ce poet faire ausi
aucune chose la grant chaleur acquise du lieu dont il se part ou il est
longuement soubs les rais du soleil et ce touce Aristotes quant il dit
qu'il n'est mie moiste ausi que s'il wolsist dire qu'il est chaus et secs
et pour ce dit il finablement qu'il samble qu'il faice ce qu'il ne fait
mie[39].

36. XXVI, 29, fol. 136r.
37. XXVI, 29, fol. 136r.
38. Cette relation est très différente de celle que l'on trouve un siècle plus tôt dans le
texte de Mahieu le Vilain qui affirme la supériorité aristotélicienne, sauf pour les questions qui touchent à la théologie.
39. XXVI, 29, fol. 136v.

Ce commentaire marque clairement la réflexion d'Évrart de Conty. Il
se démarque à la fois de l'Aristote des *Problèmes* et du commentateur
pour conclure sur une proposition qui est bien plus proche de la physique aristotélicienne: tout repose sur une question de températures, si
importante dans la météorologie aristotélicienne, puisque c'est en fonction du chaud et du froid que peuvent s'élever et s'épaissir les exhalaisons. L'observation qui est indiquée au départ fait partie également de
l'ensemble des exemples de la scolastique et permet de justifier la question de l'apparence, parfois lointaine par rapport à la cause. L'ensemble
prouve à l'évidence qu'Évrart de Conty fait un développement éloigné
de celui de Pierre d'Abano et manifeste une culture qui n'est pas la simple reproduction de citations.

D'autres passages sont très évidemment des résumés de la théorie
aristotélicienne des *Météorologiques*: ainsi a-t-on un condensé de la
théorie de la double exhalaison[40], de l'explication des précipitations[41], de
celle des étoiles filantes[42] ou encore de la définition de l'air et des zones
de l'air[43], exposé classique de tout début de commentaire sur les *Météorologiques*[44]. Il est clair qu'Évrart de Conty connaît la physique aristoté-

40. XXVI, 1, fol. 121v: 'Pour le occasion de ceste matere, nous devons savoir que li
vens n'est aultre chose que une exalation ou une fumee soubtille qui est eslevee de la
terre et des choses terrestres qui sont cy desoubs, laquele se moet en l'air et li airs avoec
elle entour la terre et pour ce convient il que ceste matere soit froide et seche combien
qu'elle soit ainsi par chaleur eslevee et n'est mie doubte selont la doctrine de Aristote que
la vertu du ciel et des estoiles et principalment du soleil est la principal cause qui ainsi en
eslieve la matere et li donne fourme et mouement et toute sa nature.' Voir aussi XXVI,
22, fol. 132r.

41. XXVI, 55, fol. 150r: 'Les ploeuves s'engendrent en l'air por ce que les vapeurs et
les nues se condempsent et espoississent si par la froidure de la moyenne region de l'air
qu'elles revienent a la nature d'yaue.' Voir aussi XXVI, 22, fol. 132r.

42. XXVI, 22, fol. 132r: 'L'autre fumee est eslevee de la terre et des choses terrestres
laquele est froide et seche de sa propre nature comme la terre dont elle est eslevee combien qu'elle soit chaude accidentelement por la raison de la chaleur qui se esmoet et
eslieve et ceste est proprement appelee exalation et de ceste se font aussi moult de impressions seches comme le vent, le tonoirre, le espart, les estoiles volans et les cometes,
rougeurs et fus et inflammations de diverses manieres et briefment moult de choses
esmerveillanles qui de ceste matere se font en l'air.'

43. XXV, 19, fol. 120r: 'Pourquoy nous devons oultre considerer que li airs en son
espere contient 3 parties: la premiere et la souveraine qui joint a le espere du fu laquele
est chaude et seche u regart des autres parties et de ceste parle Aristotes quant il dit que li
airs est plains de fu et qu'il ne se poet pourrir. L'autre partie de l'air est celle qui est cy
desoubs qui nous avironne sans moyen, laquele retient plus proprement la nature de l'air
que les autres ne font et pour ce est plus proprement ausi chaude et moiste comme li airs
doit estre par nature que les autres parties ne sont combien qu'elles soient toutes de ceste
nature u regart des autres elemens. Et la tierce partie est la moyenne qui est entre ces 2,
laquele est froide et moiste de le ordenance de nature universele pour les impressions
necessaires au monde qui s'i font et qui sanz ceste froidure ne se porroient convenable-
ment faire.'

44. Voir Ducos, *La météorologie en français...*, p. 66-88.

licienne et le traité des *Météorologiques*, comme tout universitaire, et considère comme indispensable de les exposer dans une œuvre qui s'en inspire tout en étant différente.

Les renvois qu'effectue Évrart de Conty sont donc conformes à une culture universitaire et marquent une réflexion réelle sur les deux œuvres, réflexion qui peut l'amener à citer d'autres traités comme la *Physique* ou le *De anima*, cette dernière référence étant indispensable à propos de tout ce qui touche à la vue. Il en va de même pour un autre auteur, Albert le Grand, qui est cité avec abondance dans les commentaires du 14e siècle à propos de météorologie[45]. Évrart de Conty l'utilise en particulier quand il s'agit de nuancer le système aristotélicien, en marquant le relativisme et l'importance des conditions locales dans la naissance d'un vent.

> Pourquoy Zephyrus vente quant li solaus esconse ou environ, plus volentiers que a nule autre heure[46].
> Et ce desclaire aussi expressement Aulbers, uns moult grans philosophes qui dit que li solaus ne enlumine onques de ses rays plainement nostre orizon, fors quant il est vers le milieu du ciel ou en la ligne de nostre myedy et pour ce qu'il est adont fors et de plus grant vertu que a nule autre heure et qu'il regarde a plain septentrion et myedy, pour ce y eslieve il lors et atrait moult de vapeurs mais pour ce d'autre part qu'il ne arreste pas longuement en cest point, ains decline et se part tantost de celle ligne meridional, pour ce ne degaste il pas lors ne ne consume les vapeurs desusdites qu'il eslieve, ains les espart et cache par sa chaleur es 2 extremités de myedi et de septentrion[47].

Or c'est justement l'un des apports d'Albert le Grand dans le domaine de la météorologie: à partir de la notion d'accident et de l'importance qu'il accorde à la causalité du lieu et du temps, il permet de compléter et de nuancer le système aristotélicien, en rendant compte de toutes les situations possibles[48]. Évrart de Conty utilise ainsi à juste titre ce passage dans un problème qui se détache de la théorie aristotélicienne, puisqu'il suppose une ressemblance entre le mouvement de l'eau et celui de l'air,

---

45. C'est le cas en particulier dans les questions sur les *Météorologiques* de Jean Buridan, de Nicole Oresme ou de Thémon le Juif, mais aussi dans le commentaire de Pierre d'Abano. Nicole Oresme cite également Albert le Grand dans sa traduction du *De caelo,* voir *supra*. Albert le Grand est une référence indispensable pour la météorologie du 14e siècle.

46. XXVI, 35, fol. 138v.

47. XXVI, 35, fol. 139v. Cette référence se trouve aussi dans le commentaire de Pierre d'Abano et est accompagnée d'un renvoi à Abu Mashar et à Ptolémée.

48. Cf. Ducos, *La météorologie en français...,* p. 162-165; 'Théorie et pratique de la météorologie', p. 53-54.

alors que le Stagirite considère que le vent est un ensemble d'exhalaisons[49]. La citation d'Albert le Grand permet au traducteur de confirmer la première théorie, mais aussi d'indiquer que celle des *Problèmes* permet d'expliquer l'étape suivante de la formation des vents:

> Li vent vienent tuit d'une racine et d'un commencement comme li floeuve font, c'est a dire que tout ausi que uns floeuves poet venir de une fontaine comme de son premier commencement, combien que pluseurs aultres fontaines et ruyssiaus puissent cheïr dedens qui le font croistre, tout ausi vient et s'engendre uns seuls vens d'une asamblee de vapeurs faite en 1 certain lieu, lesqueles sont ainsi deboutees des nues et meues sur costé comme nous veons tout autour de la terre[50].

Cette citation explicite confirme l'influence du savant médiéval, en particulier pour la variation du vent en qualités quand il a quitté son lieu d'origine. Évrart de Conty mentionne aussi l'importance du relief ou des marais[51], ce qui est l'une des idées majeures d'Albert le Grand qui insiste sur la variabilité des phénomènes selon les lieux[52].

Il n'est pas non plus surprenant de voir apparaître le nom de Sénèque ou celui d'Abu Mashar: l'un est couramment cité aussi à propos de météorologie, en particulier pour les comètes, pour les tonnerres et les éclairs ou encore pour les sources d'eau. Quant à Abu Mashar et son *Introductoire*, c'est l'une des sources les plus fréquemment citées dans les commentaires à propos de l'astrométéorologie, mais aussi pour la hauteur des différentes régions de l'air[53]. C'est justement ce point qu'évoque Évrart de Conty, témoignant par là même d'une culture scolastique évidente[54].

---

49. Cet écart entre la théorie exprimée dans les *Problèmes* et celle des *Météorologiques* est l'un des arguments pour réfuter l'authenticité de cette section des *Problèmes* qui est, pour cette définition, plus proche des traités de Théophraste. Toutefois, cette divergence entre les écrits aristotéliciens se trouve pour d'autres théories, en particulier pour la vue dont la théorie est différente entre le *De anima* et le troisième livre des *Météorologiques*.
50. XXVI, 35, fol. 139v-140r.
51. XXVI, 5, fol. 123v, et 38, fol. 141v.
52. Voir HOSSFELD P. (éd.), *Albert le Grand, De natura loci; De causis proprietatum elementorum; De generatione et corruptione*, Münster: Aschendorff, 1980.
53. Cette référence à Abu-Mashar apparaît dès les premiers commentaires sur les *Météorologiques*, par exemple dans celui d'Alfred de Sareshel, cf. OTTE J.K. (éd.), *Alfred of Sareshel. Commentary of the Metheora of Aristotle*, Leiden: Brill, 1988, p. 38. Les valeurs numériques ne sont cependant pas constantes, voir l'introduction de l'éditeur p. 25.
54. XXVI, 35, fol. 140r: 'Et de ce dit aussi Albumasar que les vapeurs ne s'eslievent mie sus la terre en l'air plus de 16 stades qui valent environ 2 milles ou une lieue françoise et aussi s'i acorde Seneques en son livre des natureles questions.'

La personnalité d'Évrart de Conty comme représentant de la médecine universitaire, et tel que D. Jacquart l'a fait apparaître[55], se manifeste ainsi dans un domaine qui est à la frontière de la médecine, mais qui relève davantage de la physique. Il est vrai que la question de l'air est fondamentale comme cause de maladies et que l'intérêt pour les conditions météorologiques et climatiques fait partie des connaissances préliminaires du médecin[56]. Évrart de Conty est ainsi représentant d'une formation universitaire. Elle apparaît aussi par la présence d'autorités médicales qui ne sont pas dominantes dans ces questions, mais toujours appropriées. Ainsi trouve-t-on le *Pantegni* de Constantin, qui lui-même cite Galien:

> Ceste froidure ausi excite le appetit pour ce qu'elle refroide aucunement le orifice de l'estomac, car ceste infrigidation fait bien a ce comme Galiens tesmoigne quant il dit que li frois ventres c'est a dire li frois estomas par nature doit bien appeter; ceste froidure toutefois ne doit pas si grande estre qu'elle tresperce ce trop avant le cors feble, car lors elle afeblieroit la chaleur naturele desusdite et nuiroit trop a la digestion et pour ce dit il ausi que li cors maygre et feble ne se doivent pas baignier en esté en l'yaue froide[57].

La citation est appropriée dans une question qui porte sur la digestion facilitée par le vent du nord, contrairement à ce qui se passe par le vent du sud. Le *Canon* d'Avicenne est aussi cité à propos de l'haleine froide[58]. En dehors de ces références, certains développements ne surprennent pas, comme, à propos du nombre trois, un exposé sur le tiers jour critique en médecine[59], un autre sur la position des astres favorable aux purgations[60] ou encore sur la définition de la fièvre[61]. Ces défini-

---

55. JACQUART, *La médecine médiévale...*, p. 250-255, 281-286 par exemple.

56. Voir par exemple sur les vents et la putréfaction de l'air, JACQUART, *La médecine médiévale....*, p. 247-248.

57. XXVI, 42, fol. 142r-142v.

58. XXVI, 47, fol. 143v.

59. XXVI, 13, fol. 127r: 'La premiere raison est fundee sur la nature du tiers jour qui est de grant vertu en tant qu'il est nonmés des medecins entre les jours critiques es quels les maladies se finent volentiers et determinent par nature.'

60. XXVI, 11, fol. 126r: 'Et est ceste estoile ou constellation celle dont le jour caniculer sont denommé et est ausi celle dont Ypocras parle en ses Amphorismes quant il dit que desoubs le chien ne au contraire du chien ne sont mie convenables les purgations a faire.'

61. XXVI, 49, fol. 145r: 'Fievre n'est aultre chose que une maniere de chaleur supehabondant u cors humain et pour ce dit Avicennes que fievre est une chaleur estrange imprimee u coer qui de la s'espant et espart par tout le cors entierement. Et li autre dient que c'est une chaleur innaturele qui premierement assaut le coer et de la se espant et se multeplie par tout le cors. Li autre ausi redient que ce n'est autre chose que la chaleur naturele transmuee en chaleur excessive et samblable a chaleur de fu qui procede du coer et finalement se espant par tout le cors et toutes ces manieres de parler sont en sentence ausi comme tout un.'

tions font toutes l'objet de débats universitaires et le développement du traducteur est souvent une compilation des opinions différentes[62]. En revanche on a pu noter l'originalité de ses développements sur la mélancolie[63]. Sa culture médicale et scolastique imprègne le commentaire au point de se révéler dans le lexique qui décrit les phénomènes: les qualités des vents sont ainsi nommées par le lexème *complexion*. Le phénomène d'*antiperistasis* est désigné par le syntagme *purgation et decoction*. Ces pratiques lexicales portent la trace d'une culture médicale, à la différence de la tradition physique généralement plus présente à propos de météorologie[64]. Le lexique n'est en effet pas purement référentiel, mais il témoigne d'un savoir spécifique à une époque où les usages lexicaux diffèrent entre les disciplines. La traduction d'Évrart de Conty est ainsi marquée par la culture médicale et ses usages lexicaux.

2.2. Apports didactiques et controverses

Toutefois il ne faudrait pas considérer que le commentaire n'est que le reflet d'une pratique médicale. Il présente en effet une grande diversité de remarques, tout comme des types de glose. S'il est parfois une simple paraphrase du texte[65], il sert avant tout à communiquer un savoir aristotélicien ou scientifique. Ainsi s'expliquent les exposés de météorologie aristotélicienne ou les définitions physiques. C'est le cas de la chaleur et de l'humidité, qualités actives selon les principes médicaux: l'exposé témoigne d'un élargissement de perspective par rapport à la question posée qui portait sur le froid occasionnel de l'air[66]. Ce sont aussi des exposés didactiques sur des notions astronomiques ou astrologiques comme la notion de lever cosmique et héliaque[67], Orion[68], l'étoile du chien[69], la relation entre vents et planètes[70]. On peut s'interroger sur la présence de ces développements dans une œuvre où ils ne sont guère indispensables. L'influence du commentaire de Pierre d'Abano peut appa-

---

62. Voir par exemple sur la fièvre les débats évoqués par JACQUART, *La médecine médiévale* ..., p. 379-391: ces débats naissent de la définition d'Avicenne face au flou du corpus galénique. La phrase d'Évrart de Conty évite le débat en ne mentionnant pas la notion de chaleur étrangère et en refusant la distinction entre chaleur naturelle et chaleur non naturelle qu'il considère comme purement rhétorique.

63. JACQUART, *La médecine médiévale* ..., p. 275-283.

64. DUCOS, *La météorologie en français* ..., p. 231-232.

65. XXV, 4; XXVI, 57 par exemple.

66. XXV, 10, fol. 117r: 'Pourquoy est ce que li airs est aucune fois fais frais sans atoucier a l'yaue et si n'en est point moistes ja soit ce qu'il le atouche?'

67. XXVI, 11, fol. 126r.

68. XXVI, 12, fol. 126v.

69. XXVI, 11, fol. 126r; 35, fol. 137v.

70. XXVI, 47, fol. 144r.

raître comme décisive. Les développements astronomiques y sont certes importants, mais ne sont pas du même ordre, l'astronomie d'Évrart de Conty étant beaucoup plus simple. C'est donc un choix du traducteur d'en proposer une version élémentaire. Toutefois la question de l'influence des planètes reste un point pour lequel la position d'Évrart de Conty est très ambiguë. À plusieurs reprises, il évoque cette possibilité à propos des vents et des variations de température, en l'attribuant parfois à Aristote. Mais il reste peu clair et il insiste bien davantage sur l'influence du soleil attestée par Aristote, contrairement à celle des autres planètes, comme le montre la glose suivante :

> Ceste response est assés clere selonc la doctrine de Aristote ja devant souvent dite car li solaus est la principal cause des vens et de lors mutations combien que les 15 estoiles desusdites et aucunes autres constellations y faicent bien aucune chose selonc les astronomiens[71].

Cette position, qui semble admettre deux théories contradictoires, est évidemment surprenante. Elle est à mettre en relation avec deux faits, d'une part l'intérêt du milieu royal pour l'astronomie et l'astrologie, mais aussi l'opposition à cette dernière discipline aussi bien par Nicole Oresme que par l'Église. L'embarras du traducteur s'explique, car il hésite entre l'affirmation du rôle des planètes et la dénonciation d'une influence. Le commentaire de Pierre d'Abano à l'inverse affirme le rôle des planètes dont celui du soleil au lever et au coucher. Évrart de Conty préfère s'abriter derrière l'autorité des *astronomiens* pour justifier une influence astrale dans son commentaire[72], ce en quoi il témoigne des controverses universitaires, des pôles d'intérêt aussi bien de l'université que de l'entourage de Charles V.

L'œuvre d'Évrart de Conty est d'ailleurs souvent en écho avec celle de Nicole Oresme. Si l'on ne peut parler d'imitation ni de réponse à certaines questions traitées par Nicole Oresme, une correspondance évidente apparaît avec des thèmes communs. Par exemple, à propos du bruit qui peut émaner de la terre, Évrart de Conty termine son commentaire par une allusion aux croyances du peuple à propos des feux follets :

> Et c'est ausi que les communes gens dient et croient des chandailes ardans c'on voit aucune fois de nuyt que ce soient ames humaines qui ainsi vont par l'air pour faire la peneance de lors peciés et toutefois se font tels choses par nature pour aucune matere crassete et unctueuse, de legier inflammable qui ainsi s'enflamme de nuit pour la froidure

71. XXVI, 33, fol. 138r.
72. Voir également XXVI, 47 où il termine aussi sur la théorie planétaire des vents, en précisant qu'elle est exposée par les spécialistes d'astronomie.

circonstant de l'air qui les asamble ainsi et fortefie lor chaleur tant qu'elles se alument et enflamment. Et pour ce qu'elles sont de matere soubtille, pour ce y soufist petis vens et petite cause a les ainsi mouvoir de lieu en autre et par aventure pour ce que tels petites flammes se alument et s'engendrent volentiers es cymentieres et entour les gibés, pour ce sont il meü et ramené a ceste oppinion. Et ceste oppinion vient en partie et vint originalment de la doctrine de Platon et de ciauls qui ensievent sa phylosophie car cils Platons metoit une maniere de esperis et d'ames qui, si comme il disoit, habitent et conversent cy en l'air pres de nous, liquel moult de merveilles et moult de mouvemens poent faire en cest monde. A ce fait moult aussi la doctrine des loys si comme Averroys dit[73].

Cette évocation s'articule sur la dénonciation des croyances erronées des ignorants, que les commentaires scolastiques identifient souvent avec les vieilles femmes, représentantes de tout savoir superstitieux et non universitaire. C'est l'un des rares passages où le traducteur commente des croyances populaires qu'il ignore le plus souvent. Or ce développement n'est pas sans rappeler l'*Inter impressiones* de Nicole Oresme qui évoque plusieurs fois les feux follets et la croyance qui leur est associée et donne semblable explication dans les mêmes termes[74]. La fin de ce problème en revanche est un apport du commentateur français qui fait le rapprochement avec la théorie des démons platoniciens, théorie rappelée d'ordinaire dans les commentaires scolastiques à l'occasion des tornades qui enlèvent les hommes et les bêtes[75]. Cette glose paraît ainsi comme un résumé des croyances dénoncées par la scolastique médiévale et tout spécialement par Nicole Oresme.

L'écho entre Nicole Oresme et Évrart de Conty, manifeste dans cet extrait, n'est cependant pas unique. Une autre question sur le *Zephire, le*

---

73. XXV, 2, fol. 113r-113v.

74. MATHIEU R. (éd.), 'Nicole Oresme, Inter omnes impressiones', *AHDLMA* 34 (1959), p. 283-284: 'Et juxta apparet nobis sepe, quod a locis terre, suppositis patibulis, in quibus homines suspenduntur, apparet de nocte inflammacio, prima hora noctis vel secunda et a cemiteriis. Et hoc pro tanto, quia in die, agendo in corporibus mortuorum; facit fumare materiam unctuosam, elevando illam a corporibus mortuis. Materia unctuosa faciliter in die inflammatur et illam inflammationem impressam supervenientem retinet per certas horas. Et tunc ista materia movetur in modo serpentis, quia flexuose, quia ingrossatur a frigiditate noctis. Et sepe vetule indicaverunt mortuos corizare, id est trepidare, in patibulis et animas eorum cruciari. Et sepe visum est quod hujusmodi inflammacio applicatur vestibus hominum equitancium de nocte, quia illa materia viscosa et adhaeret statim vestibus. Et quia ista materia est multum habilis ad motum, propter suam levitatem, videtur sepe fugere dum homines volunt capere illam, et hoc de prima difficultate.'

75. Voir sur cette question du démon aérien, DUCOS, *La météorologie en français...*, p. 389-394.

plus souef et le plus delitable de tous les vens[76], amène Aristote à définir dans sa réponse la droite et la gauche du ciel, la droite étant la plus douce[77]. A cette occasion, Évrart de Conty rapproche ce passage du *De caelo* d'Aristote[78] et évoque la figure d'un géant en ces termes:

> Pour ce devons nous savoir qu'il n'y ha u ciel proprement a parler ne destre ne senestre mais tant seulement improprement et par similitude as hommes et as bestes parfaites ou ces 2 choses sont proprement trouvees et selonc ce dit Aristotes ailleurs que la destre partie du ciel est en orient et la senestre en occident pour laquel chose miex donner a entendre il ymagine que uns grans gaians soit estendus dedens le ciel telement qu'il ayt ses piés u pole de septentrion c'on appele le pole artique et sa teste au contraire u pole de myedi c'on appele antartique et puis se ait son bras destre estendu devers orient et le senestre ausi en occident, comme s'il feïst par sa vertu mouvoir le ciel de orient en occident. Selonc donc ceste ymagination dit Aristotes que la partie du ciel qui est devers le pole meridionnal ou li gayans desusdis ha sa teste est le deseure et l'autre partie opposite est le desoubs et la partie ou il ha sa faice tournee et qu'il regarde c'est le devant et l'autre partie contraire c'est le derriere et oriens est la destre partie et occidens est la senestre[79].

Cette question signifie une orientation au nord de la rose des vents. Or cette interprétation n'est pas partagée et la fin du problème souligne d'ailleurs la contradiction:

> Selonc donc ceste ymagination dit Aristotes que la partie du ciel qui est devers le pole meridionnal ou le gayans desusdit ha sa teste est le deseure et l'autre partie opposite est le desoubs et la partie ou il ha sa face tournee et qu'il regarde, c'est le devant et l'autre partie contraire c'est le derriere et oriens est la destre partie et occidens est la senestre mais Aristotes ne prent mie ainsi le destre partie du ciel ne le senestre en cest probleme, ains entent, selonc ce que son expositeur li met sus par la partie destre la partie meridionnal qui est oultre le equinoctial, et par la senestre la partie septentrional qui est dessa, mais il n'est ja neccessités pour le exposition de cest probleme qu'il y ayt destre ne senestre u ciel fors ou regart du droit point de occident comme dit est[80].

Cette question et cette comparaison avec le géant sont longuement débattues dans Nicole Oresme, qui, en plaçant son géant dans toutes les

76. XXVI, 31, fol. 136v-137r: 'Pour quoy est ce que Zephyrus est li plus souefs vens et li plus delitables de tous les autres selonc ce meismes que Homers tesmongne qui dit que tous dis vente li vens zephirus tres delitables en 1 certain tans et en 1 certain lieu que cils Homers nommoit?'

77. XXVI, 31, fol. 136v: 'Il dit que c'est pour ce que tout li vent qui ventent ou il sont en la partie destre ou en la partie senestre du ciel desqueles la partie destre si comme il est esprouvé est la plus douce et la plus debonnaire.'

78. Aristote, *De caelo*, II, 2, 284b6-285b33.

79. XXVI, 31, fol. 137r.

80. XXVI, 31, fol. 137r.

positions possibles dans le ciel, montre le relativisme de la notion de droite et de gauche dans les considérations astronomiques[81]. Évrart de Conty prouve ainsi une connaissance de ce débat, voire de ce texte en français, et par ce développement qui n'est pas indispensable à la compréhension du texte d'Aristote, montre comment un vulgarisateur, à partir d'un exemple et d'une question issus de la scolastique, réécrit et développe différemment son projet de commentaire: Nicole Oresme l'utilise comme point d'appui pour un raisonnement théorique alors qu'Évrart en fait un exemple didactique.

On peut constater une semblable nécessité de rendre compte de questions importantes dans la scolastique à propos de l'optique. Dans la question XXVI, 52[82], Évrart de Conty renvoie d'abord au *De anima* en rappelant l'importance fondamentale du milieu dans la vue, théorie sur laquelle il avait également insisté dans une glose didactique au problème XXV, 9[83] où il avait parlé du cristal et du verre. Or dans ce commentaire, après ce court passage sur le moyen, il affirme que ce genre de question relève de l'optique et semble refuser d'en parler[84]. Pourtant ce qui suit est un exposé de perspective, accompagné d'une description d'un schéma introduit par la phrase suivante: *nous poons toutefois aucunement desclairier par figure ce que dit est*[85]. Cette contradiction apparente entre une affirmation et son contraire est déconcertante dans un commentaire, plus cohérent d'ordinaire. Elle ne peut s'expliquer que par la présence de plusieurs théories sur la vue couramment exposées dans les textes scolastiques. Évrart de Conty choisit l'approche physique d'Aristote et insiste sur la notion de milieu. Mais la *science de perspective* est difficile à éviter à une époque où, entre autres, la théorie de Witelo bouleverse les connaissances, comme en témoigne Nicole Oresme[86]. Les illusions d'optique, les effets de grandeur ou de petitesse font partie des questions privilégiées par la scolastique médiévale et Évrart de Conty marque ainsi l'évolution de la science médiévale où la

81. MENUT – DENOMY (éds), *Nicole Oresme, Le Livre du ciel et du monde ...*, p. 328-344.

82. XXVI, 52, fol. 147r.

83. XXV, 9, fol. 117r: 'C'est ce que Aristotes woelt dire en cest probleme. Ceste matere aussi en le 11e partie fu desclairie assés souffissamment.'

84. XXVI, 52, fol. 147v: 'Mais il ne afiert pas cy de tout desclairier comment c'est ne pour quoy.'

85. XXVI, 52, fol. 147v. Une figure géométrique figure d'ailleurs en marge au folio 148r.

86. MAC CLUSKEY S. (éd.), *Nicole Oresme, On Light, Color and the Rainbow, an Edition and Translation with Introduction and Critical Notes of Part of Book Three of his Questiones super quatuor libros Metheororum,* Unpublished dissertation, U. of Wisconsin, Madison, 1974.

théorie aristotélicienne devient seconde par rapport à celle de l'optique.

Cette présence de la science scolastique qui infléchit le commentaire se mesure très clairement dans les questions purement météorologiques. Si l'on examine attentivement les gloses et la relation avec les affirmations des *Problèmes* d'Aristote, plusieurs tendances se dégagent. Les actions de la chaleur, dont celle du soleil et du froid, sont nettement mises en avant, de même que l'importance de l'origine du phénomène et des lieux traversés. Enfin la distinction entre air élémentaire et air élémenté est fondamental. Ces trois aspects sont à mettre en relation avec les références marginales et montrent un écart par rapport à l'Aristote des *Problèmes*. De fait, il est clair qu'Évrart privilégie une lecture médiévale de la théorie météorologique du philosophe, vraisemblablement celle d'Albert le Grand cité plusieurs fois dans son commentaire. Ainsi à une explication générale, le commentateur substitue un système plus local où la géographie a largement sa place: la causalité du lieu est semblable à celle du père pour le fils, selon Albert le Grand[87]. Toutefois, il ne va pas, comme Jean Buridan, jusqu'à mettre en cause la description aristotélicienne du régime des vents avec un vent du nord dominant, et, comme la majorité des commentaires, il garde le même système, malgré des contradictions évidentes entre la théorie exposée et la réalité géographique et météorologique qu'il connaît.

La relation avec le milieu et les débats scolastiques est donc évidente. Il serait trop long d'en multiplier les exemples[88]. La place d'Albert le Grand y est importante de même que dans les commentaires scolastiques contemporains. L'œuvre d'Évrart de Conty apparaît ainsi comme un témoignage fiable des questions météorologiques de l'université et comme un représentant des lectures médiévales de l'œuvre aristotélicienne.

3. Vulgariser et écrire

3.1. Une écriture différente

Toutefois il ne faudrait pas réduire l'écriture de la glose à une simple mise en relation entre un savoir scolastique et le texte d'Aristote. À plusieurs reprises, Évrart de Conty marque une réelle originalité dans son

---

87. HOSSFELD (éd.), *Albert le Grand, De natura loci...*, c. XX. Sur cette influence du lieu, voir dans le livre XXVI, la glose des questions 1, 5, 14, 35, 38, 51 et surtout 55, 56, 57.

88. Par exemple la question de la continuité de l'air, XXV, 21; la définition du vent, XXVI, 1.

commentaire. La rose des vents qui figure dans la partie XXVI, question 1[89] en est l'image emblématique. Alors que Pierre d'Abano, comme presque tous les commentateurs, énumère longuement les noms et les places des vents sur une rose composite et décrite par un texte, Évrart de Conty refuse une énumération sans rapport avec les connaissances du lectorat et présente une rose constituée de trois nomenclatures, celle des marins, celle des philosophes et celle du peuple commun. Cette rose met en évidence l'inadéquation et l'impossibilité à juxtaposer des noms entre les usages linguistiques différents. Elle prouve aussi l'importance de la rose maritime, mais surtout elle marque son originalité par son orientation au sud et non à l'est ou au nord, ce qui prouve un ordre alphabétique et non d'orientation géographique ou astronomique[90].

Cette figure, dit le traducteur, est donnée pour *desclairier*, de même que la description optique qui doit permettre de rendre claire l'explication complexe de la vue[91]. Ce rôle d'explication pédagogique attribué à la figure n'est cependant pas la seule technique d'exposé dans le commentaire. C. Boucher, dans un très récent article où elle étudie la notion de subtilité chez les traducteurs[92], a mis en évidence le rôle de l'imagination dans le raisonnement et l'examen des possibles, en montrant comment elle permettait de renouveler l'explication. De fait, le verbe *ymaginer* et son dérivé *ymagination* sont fréquents dans les deux sections XXV et XXVI. Leur apparition n'est jamais fortuite, mais correspond à des moments précis dans l'argumentation et l'explication quand elles quittent le schéma explicatif, la définition didactique ou le résumé de théories. Ainsi Évrart de Conty fait appel à l'imagination pour l'image du géant, pour l'hypothèse d'une intersection astronomique dans l'éclipse de la lune, pour celle d'une succession entre *evaporation* et exhalaison sèche plutôt qu'une concomitance ou encore pour la justification de la présence simultanée de deux vents contraires[93]. L'imagination

89. Fol. 122r.

90. Sur le détail de l'analyse, voir DUCOS J., 'Traduction et lexique scientifique: le cas des *Problèmes* d'Aristote traduits par Évrart de Conty', dans: C. BRUCKER (éd.), *Traduction et adaptation en France, Actes du colloque organisé par l'université de Nancy II, 23-25 mars 1995,* Paris: Champion, 1997, p. 243-245.

91. XXVI, 52, fol. 147v: 'Nous poons toutefois desclairier par figure'; XXVI, 1, 121v: 'On porroit cy endroit aussi noter et describe la figure des vens pour desclairier comment il sont communement.'

92. BOUCHER C., 'De la subtilité en français: vulgarisation et savoir dans les traductions d'*auctoritates* des XIII-XIVe siècles', dans: R. VOADEN – R. TIXIER – T. SANCHEZ ROURA – J.R. RYTTING (éds), *The Theory and Practice of Translation in the Middle Ages* (The Medieval Translator 8), Turnhout: Brepols, 2003, p. 89-99.

93. Eclipse de lune, XXVI, 17, fol. 129v: 'Et pour ce porroit on ymaginer que ce seroit pour la propreté des desus dites intersections dont la lune se aproceroit plus que

paraît ainsi avoir deux fonctions, soit celle d'une comparaison qui permet de mieux comprendre, le raisonnement par analogie se substituant aux argumentations habituelles, soit celle d'une hypothèse souvent liée à une difficulté de conception et qui, comme l'a indiqué justement C. Boucher, marque une subtilité du raisonnement. Cette *ymagination* se distingue clairement de l'argumentation dialectique et est généralement opposée au raisonnable. De même le verbe *considerer* intervient dans le raisonnement et marque un type d'argument différent de l'explication didactique ou de l'hypothèse: le plus souvent, il s'agit d'un appel à l'examen d'un nouveau fait ou d'une observation. Cet emploi signale que le commentateur quitte le domaine théorique pour envisager soit une conséquence concrète, soit un fait couramment connu et qui peut être éclairé ou intervenir dans la démonstration[94]. Ce verbe dont l'équivalent latin est fréquent dans les commentaires scolastiques, n'a pourtant pas la même signification, mais marque une étape dans le déroulement d'une question et signale un élargissement à de nouveaux faits dans une pratique à la fois inspirée et détachée du latin[95].

autrefois'; à propos de Zephirus et de Subsolanus, XXVI, 20, fol. 131v: 'Se nous volons bien soubtilement ymaginer selont l'ymagination d'Aristote'; sur la succession des exhalaisons: XXVI, 24, fol. 133r: 'Nous devons ausi oultre ymaginer que, quant la matere des vens se commence a eslever en aucune partie tousdis, la plus vaporeuse partie et la plus yaueuse s'eslieve premierement et per consequens la plus grosse et puis après la plus seche partie et la plus soubtille finablement se eslieve'; vents contraires: XXVI, 29, fol. 136r: 'Il n'y ha point d'autre maniere qui me apere de ymaginer comment cils vens porroit venter as parties contraires, se ce n'estoit toutefois que aucun deist selont l'ymagnation touchie u 20ᵉ probleme'; pour le géant, XXVI, 31, fol. 137r: 'Pour laquel chose miex donner a entendre il ymagine que uns grans gaians soit estendus dedens le ciel (…); selonc donc ceste ymagination dit Aristotes que la partie du ciel (…) est le deseure'. Voir également XXVI, 40.

94. Examen d'une situation précise d'observation: XXVI, 5, fol. 123v: 'Mais se nous volons bien considerer la nature des vens, li aucuns font plouvoir communement en une region.' Nouvel argument emprunté à l'observation commune XXVI, 6, fol. 124v: 'Et c'est ce que la parole assés commune dit quant on dit: «De rouge vespree, belle matinee» et li autre dient: «Rouge vespree et blanc matin, c'est le jornee au pelerin», pour quoy nous devons considerer que la rougeur du soleil (…) se fait pour aucunes vapeurs ou aucunes fumees.' Examen d'une hypothèse dont on tire une considération pratique: XXVI, 20, fol. 130v-131r: 'Se nous considerons dont soubtilment, nous trouvons que quant li solaus esconse a nous, il lieve as antipodes.'

95. Sur la pratique scolastique et le lexique des disputes, voir BAZÀN B.C., 'Les questions disputées, principalement dans les facultés de théologie', dans: *Les questions disputées et les questions quodlibétiques dans les facultés de théologie, de droit et de médecine* (Typologie des sources du Moyen Age occidental) Turnhout: Brepols, 1985, p. 15-144; WEIJERS O., *La terminologie de la philosophie au XIIIᵉ siècle*, Rome: Edizioni dell'Ateneo medievale, 1987; *Le maniement du savoir. Pratiques intellectuelles à l'époque des premières universités (XIIIᵉ-XIVᵉ siècles)* (Studia artistarum: subsidia), Turnhout: Brepols, 1996.

L'écriture du commentaire n'est donc pas uniquement celle d'un raisonnement rhétorique à la manière des pratiques universitaires. Il échappe ainsi à la pure argumentation scolastique, en mettant en évidence d'autres choix. Le traducteur opère d'abord une sélection dans ce qu'il veut commenter et expliciter: Évrart de Conty le marque clairement au problème XXVI, 32, où il affirme après une succession de gloses didactiques scandées par *nous devons dont savoir* :

> Ce sont les 3 persuasions que Aristotes touce en sa response; tout le sourplus n'est pas de grand pourfit[96].

Cette affirmation démontre le rôle déterminant du commentateur qui dirige ainsi la lecture du texte d'Aristote en mettant en valeur ce qui lui semble important et en glosant ce qui lui semble utile. Ce choix amène alors une variété des gloses et des types d'écriture: gloses didactiques (*nous devons savoir*) où sont donnés de brefs exposés de science médiévale pour *desclairier* et *rendre entendible*, gloses universitaires où le commentateur se fait l'écho de débats et de controverses, en utilisant toutes les possibilités rhétoriques de l'argumentation et intégrant aussi l'imagination et les figures, et gloses personnelles où le traducteur marque véritablement ses options et ses goûts.

3.2. Choix du traducteur

Plusieurs développements en effet ne se justifient pas sans cette marque personnelle qu'imprime le traducteur à son œuvre: c'est par exemple l'image d'Atlas qui revient à plusieurs reprises[97], c'est aussi l'évocation du mont Athos et des marques anciennes d'un sacrifice qui demeurent en raison de l'absence de vent et de neige, étant donnée la haute altitude[98], c'est l'importance du nombre trois chez les Pythagoriciens et dans la religion chrétienne[99], ce sont les Antipodes[100], ou encore les proverbes[101]. Tous ces développements, souvent très éloignés du propos initial, permettent à Évrart de Conty d'évoquer des épisodes mythologiques, ou des évocations religieuses dans des récits ou des anecdotes toujours brefs. Ce goût qu'il développe dans le *Livre des eschez amoureux moralisés*[102] paraît en filigrane dans cette œuvre plus scientifique

96. XXVI, 32, fol. 138r.
97. XXVI, 51, fol. 140v-141r; XXVI, 31, fol. 137r.
98. XXVI, 35, fol. 140.
99. XXVI, 9, fol. 125.
100. XXVI, 20, fol. 130v.
101. XXVI, 6, fol. 124v; XXVI, 19, fol. 130v.
102. GUICHARD-TESSON F. – ROY B. (éds), *Évrart de Conty, Le livre des eschez amoureux moralisés,* Montréal: Ceres, 1993.

qu'il teinte d'échos littéraires, voire poétiques. Ainsi ne peut-il s'empêcher de rappeler périodiquement que Zephyr est le vent des fleurs selon
les poètes[103]. Cette pratique pourrait paraître une continuité du rôle
scientifique de la poésie latine au Moyen Age[104]. Or s'il est vrai
qu'Ovide, Lucain sont encore cités par Albert le Grand, les poètes n'in-
terviennent guère dans l'argumentation scolastique en cette fin du 14e
siècle. C'est donc un choix d'écriture, esquissé dans cette œuvre et largement développé ailleurs.

Cette déviation par rapport au texte scolastique, plus codé et plus ra-
tionnel, marque clairement que l'écriture n'est pas latine et savante,
mais celle d'une vulgarisation où l'anecdote annexe peut exister. De fait
on ne peut qu'être frappé par la liberté d'Évrart de Conty par rapport aux
conventions du genre. S'il s'y réfère, c'est pourtant pour s'en détacher
dans une écriture où il juxtapose, développe en dépassant le strict cadre
didactique qu'il semble parfois s'imposer (*nous devons savoir*). L'adverbe *briefment* y paraît comme l'emblème de son écriture[105], procédant
par condensés successifs et s'éloignant de la matière aristotélicienne,
frôlant l'écriture de fiction, narrative voire poétique, et marquant ainsi
une originalité d'écrivain et non plus seulement de simple traducteur. Si
on peut rapprocher ce type d'écriture d'une esthétique de l'*abbreviatio*
que l'on trouve dans d'autres genres didactiques où elle fonctionne
comme élément indispensable de l'écriture paraphrastique[106], il semble
bien qu'il s'agit ici d'un choix volontaire d'écriture, plutôt que la reproduction du genre du *compendium*. Évrart de Conty ne se contente en effet pas de résumer un contenu théorique ou des connaissances indispensables. Ses développements personnels sont aussi sous le signe de
l'abrégé, l'écriture de vulgarisation devenant comme une succession de
touches allusives, d'esquisses qui seront développées dans d'autres formes, littéraires, didactiques ou universitaires.

103. XXVI, 21, fol. 132r; XXVI, 31, fol. 137r.
104. Sur cette question, voir l'illustration qu'en propose VIARRE S., *La survie d'Ovide
dans la littérature scientifique des XIIe et XIIIe siècles*, Poitiers: Centre d'Etudes Supé-
rieures Médiévales, 1966.
105. Voir à ce sujet les remarques de GUICHARD-TESSON, 'Évrart de Conty, auteur… ',
p. 137.
106. Sur cette question, voir les analyses de POUZET J.P. à propos d'une paraphrase de
la Bible: 'Entre *abbrevatio* et *auctoritas,* les modes de l'écriture vernaculaire dans un
compendium moyen-anglais de la Bible', dans: R. VOADEN – R. TIXIER – T. SANCHEZ
ROURA – J.R. RYTTING (éds.), *The Theory and Practice of Translation in the Middle Ages*
(The Medieval Translator 8), Turnhout: Brepols, 2003, p.101-111.

Conclusion

Traduire le texte d'Aristote, mais surtout le commenter paraît ainsi comme un choix. C'est d'abord celui du commentateur qui n'éclaire que ce qui lui semble nécessaire à la lumière des débats scolastiques, et cherche avant tout à supprimer l'obscurité, en développant aussi ce qui l'amuse ou l'intéresse. Le commentaire est ainsi guide de lecture qui reproduit les habitudes universitaires, d'où les références à un savoir universitaire introduites dans le texte et autour du texte, d'où les rappels, les renvois, les annonces. Mais la variété d'écriture ou des procédés où le commentateur peut aussi bien évoquer une question compliquée que se lancer dans une anecdote laisse incertain sur l'enjeu véritable du texte. Le commentaire des *Problèmes* paraît comme un ensemble de tentatives pour différents lecteurs ou différents modes d'écriture. Ainsi la rose des vents est compréhensible à la fois pour l'ignorant et le lettré, et la structure des *Problèmes* facilite la diversité des commentaires et des approches. L'ensemble donne l'impression de fragments qui sont autant de tentatives d'explicitation mais aussi de modes d'écritures: la culture manifeste du médecin se déploie, s'étale et veut atteindre plusieurs publics, comme le montre la différence entre la marge latine et le texte où les références sont plus vagues et en français. Vulgariser, c'est donc jouer des lecteurs potentiels, de leur culture ou de leur désir de savoir, mais surtout c'est un chantier d'écriture où tous les genres de raisonnement rhétorique et tous les types d'écriture peuvent être introduits dans une variété de motifs et de styles qui restent pourtant dans le cadre restreint et bref de la glose. C'est cette diversité qui, au-delà de l'intérêt culturel et intellectuel du commentaire d'Évrart de Conty, prouve la qualité d'écriture d'un médecin médiéval, vulgarisateur et écrivain.

Université Michel de Montaigne-Bordeaux III

Appendice: Références – sections XXV-XXVI

Chapitres	Renvois à d'autres problèmes	Références en marge	Références dans le texte
XXV, 2	XXIII, 4, XXIV, 19	Averroes, 2. Metaphysica Prob. 4, 19ᵉ particula	Platon Averroes
XXV, 5	VIII, 16		
XXV, 7	XXVI, 15; XXV,4		Albumasar
XXV, 9	XI, 49; XI, 57	49 et 57 problema	
XXV, 10	XXIII, 4	2° De generatione	Aristote
XXV, 12		4° Celi 4° Methe 1° Celi	Aristote
XXV, 14	XXV, 5		
XXV, 16	XXII, 4		
XXV, 19		4° Metheo.	
XXV, 20	XXV, 17	Primo Metheororum	Aristote
XXV, 21	XXIII, 5	4. Physica 5° prob.	Aristote
XXVI, 1	XXVI, 19	2. Metheora	Aristote, livre de metheores
XXVI, 2		Ibidem	
XXVI, 5	XXVI, 55		
XXVI, 9		Primo celi (deux fois)	Aristote
XXVI, 10		2. Meteora	Aristote
XXVI, 11		Avicenne. Pr. Can. F. 3	Amphorismes, Ypocras
XXVI, 12	XXVI, 9		Ypocras
XXVI, 13	XXVI, 9		
XXVI, 15		Meteora. 2	Aristote
XXVI, 16		Meteora. 2	Aristote
XXVI, 26		4° Celi lib. Ethimologiarum 1° metheororum	Aristote Ysidorus Aristote
XXVI, 28	I, 53		
XXVI, 29	XXVI, 1; 20		
XXVI, 30	XXIII, 16		
XXVI, 31		Celi. 2	Aristote
XXVI, 32	XXVI, 11; I, 3		
XXVI, 34		Lib. Meteororum	Aristote

Chapitres	Renvois à d'autres problèmes	Références en marge	Références dans le texte
XXVI, 35	XXVI, 33	2. Meteora Albert, lib. Meteo Albumasar, 2 Mag. Introd. Libro de ascensione imbrium 1. Metheororum	Aristote Aulbers Albumasar Aristote Seneque, livre de Questions Naturelles
XXVI, 36	XXIII, 9	2. Meth	
XXVI, 38	XXVI, 19; 44; 47		
XXVI, 39	XXVI, 7; XXVI, 8		
XXVI, 40	XXVI, 19; 38; 44		
XXVI, 41	XXVI, 24		
XXVI, 42		3. Physica 3. Tegni	Aristote Galien
XXVI, 43	XXVI, 21; 26	Libro primo	Lucain
XXVI, 44	XXVI, 38; 19		
XXVI, 47	XXV, 18; XXVI, 27	1. Meth 1. Can. Fen 2	Aristote Avicenne
XXVI, 48	XXVI, 15	2° Meth;	Aristote
XXVI, 49			Avicenne
XXVI, 50	XXVI, 2		
XXVI, 51	XXVI, 21, 31; 54; 33; 35; XXV, 18		
XXVI, 52	XI, 57; II, 20	2° De anima 57 prob.	Aristote 11ᵉ partie
XXVI, 53	XXVI, 20		
XXVI, 54	XXVI, 31; 51		
XXVI, 55	XXVI, 5		
XXVI, 57	XXIII, 4		
XXVI, 58	XXVI, 20; 9; 23		
XXVI, 59	XXVI, 50		
XXVI, 60	XXV, 20		

Geneviève DUMAS

ÉVRART DE CONTY ET PIERRE D'ABANO: COMMENTATEURS D'ARISTOTE

The first chapter of Évrart de Conty's French translation of Aristotle's Problemata *shows some 225 references to medical and scientific sources which mirror the author's academic knowledge. The work is based on a Latin translation by Bartholomaeus de Messina and a Latin commentary by Peter of Abano, a known Paduan doctor who studied in Paris. Therefore, both scholars who tackled the* Problemata *were coming from the same educational milieu but at very different times. In their respective use of the citation and references one can see links with their academic learning, the cultural context in which they produced their work and their theoretical and doctrinal orientations. Also, despite the fact that they display the same background and basically the same knowledge, both works do not seem to be destined for the same public.*

Introduction

Un des problèmes les plus épineux lors de l'édition d'un texte universitaire médiéval consiste dans l'identification et la mise en contexte des différentes sources citées et utilisées par les auteurs. On les retrouve en grand nombre soit dans le texte et référencées en marge, soit entièrement en notes marginales, difficiles donc à repérer et à lire. L'état de conservation des documents ajoute encore à la difficulté de l'identification. Pourtant, l'examen des sources relève d'une préoccupation qui dépasse les simples impératifs éditoriaux. Cet examen nous apprend beaucoup sur les connaissances de l'auteur et sur les destinataires possibles de l'entreprise d'écriture. Dans le cas des *Problèmes* d'Aristote traduits et commentés par Évrart de Conty, cet examen s'avère des plus instructifs pour plusieurs raisons.

D'abord, bien que les recherches récentes aient permis de mieux connaître l'écrivain d'envergure que fut Évrart de Conty[1], il nous reste à le

---

1. Voir GUICHARD-TESSON F., 'Évrart de Conty, auteur de la *Glose des Echecs amoureux*', *Le Moyen Français* 8-9 (1982), p. 111-148, 'Le métier de traducteur et de commentateur au XIVe siècle d'après Évrart de Conty', *Le Moyen Français* 24-25 (1990), p. 131-167 et l'introduction de l'édition critique, GUICHARD-TESSON F. – ROY B. (éds), *Livre des Eschez amoureux moralisés*, Montréal: CERES, 1993. Voir aussi GATHERCOLE P.M., 'Medieval Science: Évrart de Conty', *Romance Notes* 6 (1965), p. 175-81 et surtout

situer dans le contexte de l'histoire parisienne de la médecine[2]. Ensuite, l'exercice de la traduction des autorités dans ce même contexte demande encore à être documenté et analysé. En effet, les aspects politiques et littéraires des traductions ont été bien étudiés[3], notamment dans le contexte de l'entourage de Charles V, mais l'étude des contenus médicaux est encore à faire puisqu'elle se situe en marge des préoccupations royales.

Une telle démarche ne pourra se faire sans effectuer une dialectique constante entre la version latine des *Problèmes* de Pierre d'Abano et la traduction française d'Évrart, mais aussi en tentant de comparer l'utilisation des sources dans d'autres formes de traductions ou de commentaires. Évrart de Conty était un médecin parisien, influencé par son temps, son cadre professionnel, les modalités de son cursus académique. C'est la même chose pour Pierre d'Abano, médecin padouan mais dont l'activité scientifique s'est déroulée en grande partie à Paris.

L'axe de réflexion que je me suis proposé à l'intention de cette contribution consiste à mettre en relief, par le biais de l'étude des sources, certains aspects du contexte académique, socioprofessionnel et culturel de la traduction par Évrart de Conty des *Problèmes* d'Aristote, dans une perspective d'histoire de la médecine. Il s'agit, ici, de remarques préliminaires puisque cette analyse est uniquement basée sur la première section des *Problèmes* et se situe dans une entreprise qui vise à analyser les sources des quatre premières *particulae* de ce texte immense. Les questions qui orientent cette analyse sont les suivantes: que nous apprennent les sources citées sur le médecin qu'était Évrart de Conty, sur son cheminement académique et sur les connaissances requises pour comprendre, assimiler et commenter la médecine médiévale? S'il est permis d'émettre une hypothèse, on pourrait dire que cette étude préliminaire des sources montre que la traduction d'Évrart et le commentaire de

MINNIS A.J., *Magister Amoris, The Roman de la Rose and Vernacular Hermeneutics*, Oxford: Oxford University Press, 2001, chap. 6, 'Pruning the Rose: Évrart de Conty and European Vernacular Commentary', p. 257-319.

2. Entreprise déjà amorcée par Danielle Jacquart qui, à l'aide de passages des *Problèmes* d'Aristote, a documenté les réponses parisiennes au fléau de l'épidémie de peste de 1347. JACQUART D., *La médecine médiévale dans le cadre parisien*, Paris: Fayard, 1998; voir les nombreux passages sur Évrart, notamment ceux qui traitent de la peste au chapitre III, p. 229-324.

3. Voir entre autres LUSIGNAN S., 'La topique de la *translatio studii* et les traductions françaises de textes savants au XIVe siècle', dans: *Traduction et traducteur au Moyen Age, Colloque International du CNRS, IRHT, 26-28 mai 1986*, Paris: Éditions du CNRS, 1989, p. 303-315. Ou encore *Parler vulgairement. Les intellectuels et la langue française aux XIIIe et XIVe siècles*, Montréal: Presses de l'Université de Montréal, 1986, du même auteur.

Pierre n'ont pas les mêmes destinataires. Pierre d'Abano, qui cite plus largement qu'Évrart, le fait dans le contexte plus rigide de la scolastique et de l'exégèse des textes d'autorités. Il annonce d'emblée dans son prologue que la matière des *Problemata* est complexe et qu'elle ne peut être comprise que par ceux qui ont maîtrisé les rudiments de la philosophie et ses nombreuses branches. Bien qu'il ne spécifie pas à quel auditoire il s'adresse, il semble évident que l'œuvre est destinée à des philosophes ou du moins à des érudits chevronnés[4]. Évrart, dans ce premier chapitre, semble vouloir donner les rudiments de la médecine tels que conçus par Johannitius et Avicenne, à l'image d'un cours d'introduction à la médecine à de futurs étudiants. On y décèle une tentative didactique qui va au-delà du commentaire académique par son souci de vulgarisation scientifique.

Le cadre académique des deux médecins

C'est une généralisation fort répandue que de considérer la médecine médiévale comme une médecine archaïque et primaire. Elle ne se réfère pas au même paradigme que la nôtre, mais quiconque s'est déjà penché sur des textes médicaux conçoit bien qu'elle est complexe. Si l'on se fie aux universitaires médiévaux, sa complexité est due au caractère parfois obscur des propos des Anciens sur lesquels elle se base. Ces propos doivent être explicités, éclairés, commentés. D'où l'exercice universitaire de la *lectio* à l'oral et du commentaire à l'écrit, qui servent justement à mettre en relief les diverses parties d'un texte de façon à l'éclairer, à faire la lumière sur l'obscurité du texte[5].

La médecine médiévale est complexe aussi parce que la théorie qui la sous-tend, celle des humeurs appelée hippocratique, est le fruit d'une accumulation de connaissances, lesquelles ne sont pas toujours en concordance. Les Anciens, dont le savoir jalonne le chemin de cette connaissance, ne sont pas toujours d'accord sur un même point. Un exemple souvent cité est celui de la double semence de Galien, laquelle s'oppose

---

4. Sur la difficulté du texte et les possibles destinataires de la traduction latine des *Problemata*, voir SIRAISI N., 'The *Expositio Problematum Aristotelis* of Peter of Abano', *Isis* 61 (1970), p. 324-25.

5. Sur l'exercice universitaire de la *lectio*, on peut consulter WEIJERS O., *Terminologie des universités au XIIIe siècle*, Rome: Lessico Intellettuale Europeo, Edizioni dell'Ateneo, 1987 et WEIJERS O. – HOLTZ L. (éds), *L'enseignement des disciplines à la Faculté des Arts (Paris et Oxford, XIIIe-XIVe siècles)* (Studia Artistarum 4), Turnhout: Brepols, 1997. Sur le commentaire voir entre autres MINNIS A.J. – BRIAN SCOTT A. (éds), *Medieval Literary Theory and Criticism c. 1100-c. 1375, The Commentary Tradition*, Oxford: Clarendon Press, 1988 (édition révisée).

en maints points à la théorie aristotélicienne de la reproduction[6]. Cette divergence donne lieu à de multiples tentatives de réconciliation. Pierre d'Abano, à qui ce volume fait une large place, a écrit son *Conciliator* dans le but de réconcilier les nombreuses divergences entre des autorités qui ont toutes le sceau de l'excellence[7]. La médecine médiévale est complexe encore parce qu'elle fait appel à des connaissances et des savoirs qui relèvent à la fois d'une approche théorique et donc pouvant se baser sur des principes universels mais aussi sur des savoirs techniques qui eux ne s'apprennent pas à l'université, se maîtrisent avec la pratique et concernent le particularisme individuel.

Devant la complexité de la médecine médiévale, les médecins ont recours à diverses méthodes pour assimiler et intégrer le nombre croissant de connaissances qui les submergent. En effet, à partir du 12e siècle, on assiste à un mouvement massif de traductions de l'arabe au latin des textes médicaux anciens qui augmentent considérablement le bassin des connaissances[8].

Jean de St-Amand, médecin parisien, établit par exemple une table de concordance pour compiler les extraits de Galien qui sont indispensables à la pratique. Certains, plus nombreux, commentent les textes fondamentaux des Anciens selon l'exercice du commentaire scolastique. D'autres produisent des traités théoriques dans lesquels ils exposent des principes qu'ils appuient sur les savoirs antiques. D'autres, enfin, écrivent des traités de pratique qui tentent d'adapter ces savoirs théoriques universels à l'univers aléatoire de la pratique. Que dire des traductions de ces œuvres latines? Lorsqu'elles sont entreprises par des universitaires, ce qui est généralement le cas, elles gardent le caractère hautement académique qui a servi à former leurs auteurs, dans le sens du propos mais aussi et surtout dans le sens de la forme.

6. Pour un développement sur cette question, on consultera JACQUART D. – THOMASSET C., *Sexualité et savoir médical au Moyen Âge*, Paris: Presses universitaires de France, 1985, p. 84-98.

7. VESCOVINI G.F., *Il 'Lucidator dubitabilium astronomiae' di Pietro d'Abano ed altre opere, Presentazione di Eugenio Garin, Introduzione, edizione, indici e note*, Padoue: Ed. Programma, 1988, 1992, aussi de la même auteure, 'Peter of Abano and Astrology', dans: P. CURRY (éd.), *Astrology, Science and Society. Historical Essays,* New York: The Boydell Press, 1987, p. 19-39, ainsi que SIRAISI N., *Arts and Sciences at Padua, The Studium of Padua before 1350*, Toronto: Pontifical Institute of Mediaeval Studies, 1973.

8. Sur ces entreprises multiples d'acquisition des savoirs antiques voir, entre autres, JACQUART D. – MICHEAU F., *La médecine arabe et l'Occident médiéval*, Paris: Maisonneuve-Larose, 1990, ainsi que les nombreux articles de *Traduction et traducteurs au Moyen Age, Colloque International du CNRS, IRHT, 26-28 mai 1986*, Paris: Éditions du CNRS, 1989.

Martin de Saint-Gille, auteur d'une traduction des *Aphorismes* d'Hippocrate et ancien maître de l'Université de Paris, dit qu'il a traduit ce livre, entre autres, parce que:

> L'œuvre me plaist à faire, car quant je ne la puis lire en escolles et en estude general, il me semble et est advis que le lise publiquement en la translatant, car plus fort est de la translater que de la lire en escolles[9].

Martin de Saint-Gille fait ici référence à l'exercice de la lecture publique ou *lectio*, équivalant au cours universitaire, et compare son entreprise de traduction à une démarche didactique mais aussi et surtout académique. À preuve, il destine son œuvre à 'tous ceux qui estudieront'[10].

Qu'en est-il alors de l'œuvre de traduction d'Évrart sur les *Problèmes*? À l'inverse des *Aphorismes* d'Hippocrate qui sont un *sine qua non* de l'enseignement médical, les *Problèmes* ne font pas partie du curriculum médical universitaire, du moins pas du programme formel.

Les autorités médicales avaient différentes fonctions dans le système hippocratico-galénique médiéval, c'est la raison pour laquelle les nombreuses contradictions pouvaient continuer à coexister sans grands heurts. Aristote était considéré d'emblée comme l'autorité sur les questions philosophiques et biologiques. Indépendamment des opinions divergentes sur la nature de la médecine, il était généralement convenu qu'elle devait se baser sur la philosophie naturelle et s'articuler selon la logique aristotélicienne[11].

C'est que l'art médical aspire à être considéré comme une science et ainsi à intégrer aisément le cadre universitaire[12]. Tous les étudiants en médecine se devaient d'avoir fait d'abord la faculté des arts et c'est là qu'ils apprenaient les rudiments de la logique aristotélicienne. À Paris, après la longue période d'introduction des traités d'Aristote, le pro-

---

9. JACQUART D.,'Hippocrate en français. *Le livre des Amphorismes* de Martin de Saint-Gille (1362-1363)', dans: D. JACQUART (éd.), *Les voies de la science grecque, Études sur la transmission des textes de l'Antiquité au dix-neuvième siècle,* Genève: Droz, 1997, p. 245.

10. JACQUART,'Hippocrate en français...', p. 245.

11. OTTOSON P.-G., *Scholastic Medicine and Philosophy, A study of Commentaries on Galen's* Tegni, Naples: Bibliopolis, 1984, p. 283.

12. Voir, à ce sujet, GARCIA-BALLESTER L., 'Medical Ethics in Transition in the Latin Medicine of the Thirteenth and Fourteenth Centuries: New Perspectives on the Physician-Patient Relationship and the Doctor's Fee', dans: A. WEAR – J. GEYER-KORDESCH – R.K. FRENCH (éds), *Doctors and Ethics: The Earlier Historical Setting of Professional Ethics* (Clio Medica / The Wellcome Institute Series in the History of Medicine 24), Amsterdam-Atlanta: Rodopi, 1993, p. 38-71; MCVAUGH M., *Medicine before the Plague. Practitioners and their Patients in the Crown of Aragon 1285-1345,* Cambridge: Cambridge University Press, 1993.

gramme de la faculté des arts était bien connu et il incorporait l'ensemble du corpus aristotélicien; les matières étant divisées, comme on le sait, en trivium et quadrivium[13]. En ce qui regarde la philosophie naturelle, l'étudiant en arts devait suivre les lectures sur la *Physique*, le *De generatione et corruptione*, le *De anima*, le *De caelo et mundo*, les *Météorologiques* et le traité *De animalibus*[14]. Par contre, lorsque qu'il arrivait en médecine, il ne pouvait plus ni lire ni suivre de lectures sur Aristote, sauf sur le *Traité des animaux* et les *Météorologiques*[15]. On remarque que, même si la médecine doit se baser sur la philosophie naturelle, celle-ci est absente des cursus médicaux dans les universités françaises.

Pourtant, il importe de situer l'œuvre pseudo-aristotélicienne dans le développement de la scolastique médicale. Bien qu'une version complète des *Problèmes* n'ait été disponible qu'au 13ᵉ siècle grâce à la traduction de Barthélémy de Messine, des fragments circulaient déjà entre les 11ᵉ et 13ᵉ siècles. L'école de Salerne avait utilisé le genre pour développer une méthode d'apprentissage basée sur le modèle des questions-réponses dont une compilation nous est connue sous le nom des *Quaestiones Salernitanae*[16]. Ce genre introduisait d'abord des notions de philosophie naturelle dans la médecine mais aussi un style de débat qui allait déterminer la forme des disputes médicales dans les futures universités occidentales.

En effet, les questions disputées médicales ont ceci de particulier qu'elles se présentent sous une forme hybride de questions naturelles, c'est-à-dire questions-réponses, et des *dubia,* c'est-à-dire des disputes scolastiques[17]. À la base de cette forme particulière d'exercice scolastique se trouvent dans un premier temps les questions salernitaines versifiées et les questions salernitaines en prose qui sont en partie inspirées

13. KIBRE P.,'The Quadrivium in the Thirteenth Century Universities (with special reference to Paris)', dans: *Studies in Medieval science: Alchemy, Astrology, Mathematics and Medicine*, London: Hambledon Press, 1984, I.

14. KIBRE P., 'Arts and Medicine in the Universities in the Later Middle Ages', dans: *Studies in Medieval Science: Alchemy, Astrology, Mathematics and Medicine*, Londres: Hambledon Press, 1984, XII, p. 222-223.

15. KIBRE, 'Arts and Medicine...', XII, p. 222-223.

16. Voir LAWN B., *The Salernitan Questions. An Introduction to the History of Medieval and Renaissance Problem Literature*, Oxford: Clarendon Press, 1963 et du même auteur, *The Prose Salernitan Questions*, Londres: Oxford University Press, 1979.

17. JACQUART D., 'La question disputée dans les facultés de médecine', dans: B.C. BAZÀN (éd.), *Les questions disputées et les questions quodlibétiques dans les facultés de théologie, de droit et de médecine* (Typologie des sources du moyen âge occidental 44-45), Turnhout: Brepols, 1985, p. 279-315, ici p. 292-293.

des *Problèmes* d'Aristote. C'est donc que les *Problèmes* d'Aristote revê-
taient pour le médecin une importance que Pierre d'Abano et Évrart de
Conty ont voulu mettre en relief[18].

L'utilisation des sources par les deux médecins

Une première constatation s'impose quant à l'utilisation des sources
chez Évrart par rapport à Pierre d'Abano. Il utilise beaucoup moins que
ce dernier les renvois aux sources, du moins dans son premier chapitre,
avec 225 citations contre 293 chez Pierre[19]. Cette première observation
quantitative n'a valeur que d'indication; il importe surtout de voir quand
et comment chacun des médecins utilise les sources. En effet, si Évrart
cite moins dans certains problèmes, d'autres lui donnent l'occasion de se
reprendre. On peut y voir des liens avec la formation académique, le
contexte socioculturel de la production littéraire et les inclinaisons théoriques que Pierre d'Abano et Évrart de Conty adoptent face à leur matière. Un regard même sommaire sur les textes et les sources montre que
l'entreprise d'Évrart se pose comme un prétexte au commentaire, tant
l'adaptation peut y être libre[20]. Le premier problème semble constituer
pour Évrart une occasion de démontrer ce fait. Alors que Pierre y cite
six références, Évrart y va de plus d'une vingtaine.

Avicenne est la première source citée en importance chez Évrart, avec
66 références. Le même auteur fait l'objet de 79 citations dans la version
latine de Pierre d'Abano, chez qui pourtant Galien arrive en tête de la
liste des citations avec quelque 120 références contre 40 chez Évrart.
Comment expliquer cet écart? Pierre était-il un plus fervent admirateur
de Galien? Notons que le moment de la rédaction du commentaire latin
des *Problèmes* par Pierre d'Abano correspond à une période d'assimilation de ce qu'il convient d'appeler le Nouveau Galien[21]. Ce contexte
particulier de production explique peut-être la préférence de Pierre
d'Abano pour les traités galéniques.

Le *curriculum* universitaire des médecins est connu principalement
par les statuts des universités. Dans le cas des programmes médicaux, on

18. JACQUART, 'La question disputée...', p. 292-293.
19. Ces chiffres excluent les références aux autres traités d'Aristote que je n'ai pas
encore examinés. Ils sont le résultat de calculs préliminaires qu'une vérification ultérieure
pourrait modifier.
20. Comme l'avait constaté GUICHARD-TESSON, 'Le métier de traducteur...', p. 134,
163 et *passim*.
21. GARCIA-BALLESTER L., 'Arnau de Villanova (c.1240-1311) y la reforma de los
estudios médicos en Montpellier (1309): El Hippocrates latino y la introducción del
nuevo Galeno', *Dynamis* 2 (1982), p. 97-158.

se réfère souvent aux trois plus importantes écoles de médecine du bas Moyen Âge, soit Paris, Montpellier et Bologne. Pour Paris, nous n'avons que les textes au programme de la licence en 1270-74. Mais, ils 'marquent davantage la fin d'une période qu'ils n'en inaugurent une nouvelle'[22], en ce sens qu'ils se basent essentiellement sur les textes primitifs de l'*Ars medicine*, un ensemble de textes provenant de différentes sources et antérieur à l'avènement des universités[23]. L'*Ars* primitif comptait les textes suivants: l'*Isagoge* de Johannitius[24], auquel on avait ajouté les *Aphorismes* et les *Pronostics* d'Hippocrate, le *Traité du pouls* de Philarète et le *Traité des urines* de Théophile. Au milieu de 13e siècle, de nouveaux textes apparaissent, issus principalement des mouvements de traduction espagnols et italiens. On y ajouta le *Tegni* ou *Ars parva* de Galien, auquel on incorpora le *Traité des maladies aiguës* d'Hippocrate ainsi que les très nombreux commentaires de Galien aux œuvres de cet auteur. C'est donc un apport certain de Galien à l'*Ars medicine* qui s'ajoute au noyau primitif et que l'on désigne désormais plutôt comme l'*Ars commentata* ou l'*Articelle* de la Renaissance[25]. Compte tenu de cet apport, Galien devient au tournant du 13e siècle la source par excellence du savoir médical, comme en témoignent par exemple les nouveaux programmes scolaires de Montpellier en 1309.

Pourtant, au tournant du 13e siècle, l'immense *Canon* d'Avicenne fait aussi son apparition dans la traduction latine de Gérard de Crémone[26]. Dans les programmes successifs des universités, Avicenne en viendra à dominer l'enseignement médical de premier degré et à supplanter Galien, qui demeurait pourtant l'autorité principale après Hippocrate lui-

22. JACQUART – MICHEAU, *La médecine arabe...*, p. 175.

23. Voir KRISTELLER P.O., *Studi sulla scuola medica salernitana*, Naples: Instituto Italiano per gli Studi Filosofi, 1986.

24. Malgré les changements aux divers programmes dont je parlerai plus loin, l'*Isagoge* continua d'être le texte d'introduction par excellence à l'étude de la médecine, surtout à cause de sa forme abrégée et de ses propos clairs et concis. Évrart de Conty, dans sa traduction commentée des *Problèmes,* ne le mentionne qu'une fois, à l'instar de la version latine de Pierre d'Abano, mais il en fait largement usage dans ces premiers propos sans le citer nommément.

25. Voir O'BOYLE C., *The Art of Medicine, Medical Teaching at the University of Paris,* Leiden: E.J. Brill, 1998. On verra aussi ARRIZABALAGA J., 'The Death of a Medical Text: The *Articella* and the Early Press', dans: R. FRENCH – J. ARRIZABALAGA – A. CUNNINGHAM – L. GARCIA-BALLESTER (éds), *Medicine from the Black Death to the French Disease*, Aldershot: Ashgate, 1998, p. 184-220.

26. Sur Avicenne en latin, on verra les codices de l'*Avicenna Latinus*, Leiden: E.J. Brill, 1994. Aussi JACQUART D., 'La réception du *Canon* d'Avicenne: comparaison entre Montpellier et Paris aux XIIIe et XIVe siècles', *Actes du 110e congrès des sociétés savantes,* Montpellier, 1985, II, p. 69-77.

même. Dès 1340 à Montpellier, le premier livre du *Canon* d'Avicenne sert désormais de lecture obligatoire, même si les œuvres galéniques forment l'essentiel du curriculum[27]. Cette tendance ira en s'accentuant. Dans les dernières décennies du 15e siècle, la rotation des cours à l'école de médecine de Montpellier montre non seulement que le livre 1 est le livre le plus lu et le plus commenté en cours, mais que parmi les lectures, il est le seul à être présenté en permanence[28]. Comment expliquer cet engouement face au *Canon* d'Avicenne? Cela tient principalement à la forme que prend cet ouvrage: une présentation systématique, en chapitres faciles à repérer, en sentences faciles à mémoriser, qui rendait la médecine hippocratico-galénique compréhensible et accessible. Mais encore, Avicenne avait déjà fait l'exercice de tenter de concilier les sources antiques; 'Par sa double qualité de philosophe et de médecin, Avicenne pouvait jouer le rôle de médiateur entre Aristote et Galien'[29]. Entre le début du 14e siècle et sa fin, Avicenne a envahi les curriculums et est devenu beaucoup plus accessible. Évrart mentionne Avicenne plus de 60 fois dans son premier chapitre et une grande majorité de ces références proviennent précisément du premier livre d'Avicenne[30].

Une autre autorité largement utilisée dans les *Problèmes* est Hippocrate: 57 références chez Évrart et 40 chez Pierre. Si on y retrouve quelques références aux *Pronostics* et au traité *De la Nature humaine*, les références proviennent principalement des *Aphorismes* et du traité *Air, eaux et lieux*. En ce qui concerne les *Aphorismes* d'Hippocrate, il n'y a pas à s'en étonner. Les *Aphorismes* sont une compilation de sentences courtes qui résument les enseignements hippocratiques. Leur traduction du grec au latin date du 5e siècle[31] et on y trouve des sentences sur tout. Ils figurent en bonne place dans les programmes des écoles. Dans la rotation des leçons du 15e siècle à Montpellier par exemple, ils arrivent au deuxième rang après le *Canon* d'Avicenne, ce qui montre que leur popularité ne diminue pas avec les années.

Pour le traité *Airs, eaux et lieux,* c'est une autre histoire. Non qu'il ne soit pas populaire[32], mais on se demande pourquoi utiliser presque ex-

27. GERMAIN A. (éd.), *Cartulaire de l'Université de Montpellier I*, Montpellier: Ricard et frères, 1890, p. 347-348.

28. Bibliothèque de la Faculté de médecine de Montpellier, E2, *Livre des leçons*, sans foliotation.

29. JACQUART – MICHEAU, *La médecine arabe...*, p. 178.

30. Ces chiffres sont à confirmer lors des dernières vérifications des sources citées avec le manuscrit autographe, dont je n'ai actuellement que le microfilm.

31. KIBRE P., 'Arts and Medicine ...', p. XII, 214.

32. Ce traité était très connu au Moyen Âge, il aurait été traduit en latin dès le 5e siècle. KIBRE P., 'Hippocratic Writings in the Middle Ages', *Bulletin of the History of Medicine* 18 (1945), p. 393.

clusivement celui-ci? Les passages des *Problèmes* sur les maladies pestilentielles en justifient certainement l'usage. Peu de textes des Anciens
préparaient adéquatement les médecins médiévaux à faire face au fléau
qui sévit d'abord en 1347 et qui affecta de nouveau Paris entre 1361 et
1381. Ces dates correspondent assez avec l'évaluation que l'on fait de la
traduction en français des *Problèmes* par Évrart et qui justifie qu'il ait
recours bien davantage que Pierre d'Abano à ce traité. Danielle Jacquart
y a consacré plusieurs pages de son livre sur la médecine parisienne et
elle y utilise abondamment les passages du premier chapitre des *Problèmes* par Évrart de Conty. Il est certain que cette expérience traumatisante
a marqué le médecin et qu'elle l'a conduit à faire des choix. Le problème de la peste monopolise d'ailleurs une grande partie des efforts
d'écriture des médecins dans le dernier quart du 14e siècle. Environ
vingt-cinq traités médiévaux sur la peste sont parvenus jusqu'à nous en
partie ou en totalité[33]. Le *Problème* 7 qui traite du mal pestilentiel est
éclairant sur ce point. Même s'il ne contient pas plus de sources dans la
traduction française que dans la version latine, on remarque qu'Évrart y
utilise le *Compendium des maîtres de l'Université de Paris* sur la peste
de 1348. Même s'il ne le cite qu'une seule fois, il est clair qu'une partie
du contenu y a été transférée[34]. Le *Compendium* de la Faculté de médecine constitue une référence nouvelle, qui n'existait pas du temps de
Pierre. D'ailleurs, le traitement du *Problème* 7 par Évrart de Conty montre que la réflexion sur les maladies pestilentielles et principalement sur
le concept de contagion avait considérablement évolué suite aux épisodes successifs de peste[35]. Pourtant l'utilisation du traité *Airs, eaux et
lieux* se justifie aussi par des raisons intrinsèques au texte. En effet, il
appert que le livre 10 de ce même traité a servi à la compilation des problèmes. Les *Problèmes* I, 8-12 et I, 19-20 en portent la trace à peu près
certaine[36]. Nul doute qu'il était aisé de commenter les *Problèmes* avec
ce traité hippocratique puisque les matières s'y confondent.

33. La plupart ont été publiés par Karl Sudhoff dans *Sudhoffs'Archiv* au début du
20e siècle; on en trouvera une liste dans SUDHOFF K., ' Pestschriften aus den ersten 150
Jahren nach der Epidemie des schwarzen Todes 1348, XX ', *Sudhoffs' Archiv* 17 (1925),
p. 264-291.

34. Voir l'édition du texte du *Compendium* dans REBOUIS É., *Étude historique et critique de la peste*, Paris: Picard, 1888, ainsi que les passages qui y sont consacrés dans
JACQUART, *La médecine médiévale...*, p. 252-253.

35. JACQUART, *La médecine médiévale* ..., p. 254-55. Voir, entre autres, la note 69 sur
le *Problème* 7 et ses possibles origines salernitaines. Voir aussi CHASE M., 'Fevers, Poi-
sons and Apostemes: Authority and Experience in Montpellier Plague Treatises', dans:
P. LONG (éd.), *Science and Technology in Medieval Society*, New York: Annals of the
New York Academy of Sciences, 1985, p. 153-69.

36. DILLER H., 'Die Überlieferung der Hippokratischen Schrift', *Philologus*,
Supplementband XXXIII, 3 (1932).

Pour sa part, le *Problème* 13 sur la corruption de l'air et des eaux donne lieu chez Évrart à un développement beaucoup plus long. Un premier regard montre qu'il fait une large place au *Canon* d'Avicenne, où notamment la qualité de l'eau fait l'objet de longs passages[37]. Mais Évrart a recours à une source pour le moins inattendue: Le *Traité d'agriculture* de Palladius, qu'il avait déjà cité dans les *Eschez amoureux moralisés* et auquel il aurait eu accès par le biais du *De regimine principum* de Gilles de Rome[38]. Le *Traité d'agriculture* de Palladius est un compendium agronomique axé sur la pratique agricole, comme en témoigne l'organisation originale de la matière de façon chronologique: le premier livre contient des informations générales et les douze livres suivants traitent des différents mois de l'année. On y trouve une grande variété d'informations relatives à la santé et la salubrité. Le texte était connu au Moyen Âge et avait même fait l'objet de nombreuses traductions en langue vernaculaire[39]. De fait, l'utilisation de Palladius par Évrart au *Problème* 13 est non seulement extensive et nominale (6 citations), mais il s'en sert en conjonction avec Avicenne sur les questions de la corruption de l'air et des eaux et lui accorde visiblement beaucoup de crédit. D'abord, les références proviennent du livre 1 de Palladius qui présente les conditions générales de l'agriculture et dont les chapitres premiers traitent des conditions de l'air et des eaux[40]. Ensuite, le livre 9, qui couvre les particularités du mois d'août, est mis à contribution pour au moins trois citations en raison de son chapitre sur les puits. Il serait intéressant d'examiner davantage l'association de ce texte à la médecine.

Il ne faut pourtant pas confondre ce Rutilius Taurus Aemilianus Palladius avec un autre, plus tardif et auteur d'un commentaire sur le 6ᵉ li-

---

37. AVICENNE, *Liber Canonis*, IV, 1-4-1, Venise, 1507, fol. 416r.

38. GUICHARD-TESSON F., *La Glose des Échecs amoureux d'Évrart de Conty, les idées et le genre de l'œuvre d'après le commentaire du Verger de Déduit*, Thèse, Institut d'Études Médiévales, Université de Montréal, 1980, voir le passage sur les vertus, p. 321 et *passim*. Pierre d'Abano, pour sa part, cite le *De agricultura* aux sections 20-22 qui traitent des plantes. SIRAISI, *Arts and Sciences at Padua ...*, p. 129.

39. On en trouve des traductions en espagnol, en moyen anglais et en catalan. Voir à ce sujet CIFUENTES L., 'La volgarizzazione della scienza in Catalano', dans: *Filosofia in volgare nel Medioevo*, Louvain-La-Neuve: Fidem, 2003, p. 247-263, où il est question de la traduction en langue catalane de ce traité: édition de GINER SANCHEZ A.J., *El 'Tractat d'agrucultura' de Palladi: una copia feta de la traducció de Ferrer Sayol*, Testi di laurea della Università di València, 1986.

40. Sur Rutilius Taurus Aemilianus Palladius, voir RODGERS R.H., *An Introduction to Palladius* (Institute of Classical Studies, Bulletin n° 35), London: Institute of Classical Studies, 1975, l'édition du texte par le même auteur, *Palladii Rutilii Tauri Aemiliani viri inlustris; Opus agriculturae, De veterinaria, De insitione* (Bibliotheca scriptorum Graecorum et Romanorum Teubneriana), Leipzig: Teubner, 1975, ainsi que la traduction française et le commentaire de MARTIN R., *Palladius, Traité d'agriculture, livre 1-2*, Paris: Les Belles-Lettres, 1976.

vre des *Épidémies* d'Hippocrate[41]. Cet opuscule aurait tout aussi bien pu se trouver en référence du problème 13 puisqu'il traite justement de l'air et des eaux. De fait, le texte complet des *Épidémies* ne fut disponible en Occident qu'au 16e siècle[42], sauf le 6e livre qui semble être de facture différente et postérieure à l'ensemble et qui est tenu pour être d'origine cnidienne. Il donne des informations générales d'hygiène assorties de témoignages sur la pratique, mais surtout il recense un grand nombre de maladies et de fièvres méridionales[43]. Il était donc d'une grande utilité, on le trouvait associé dès l'Antiquité tardive avec un commentaire de Galien[44]. Le commentaire de Palladius sur le Livre 6 des *Épidémies* constituait un accès privilégié au texte d'Hippocrate et un manuscrit datant du 12e siècle atteste de sa popularité précoce[45]. Or, le texte des *Épidémies* semble lui aussi avoir été connu des compilateurs des *Problèmes*[46]. Bien que les deux incidences que l'on puisse associer au chapitre I concernent les *Problèmes* 50, 53 et 54, il reste que le texte a pu éveiller un souvenir chez nos commentateurs[47]. Une des particularités du texte de Palladius est qu'il commente le contenu hippocratique en y intégrant les concepts galéniques sur la contagion, comme en témoigne sa compréhension du terme 'miasmes' tirée complètement du *Traité des fièvres* de Galien[48]. Mais comme nous l'avons vu, aucune des références

---

41. ROSELLI A. – MANETTI D., *Ippocrate Epidemie: libro sesto: Introduzione, testo critico, commento e traduzione*, Firenze: La nuova Italia, 1982. Sur Palladios le iatrosophiste, on peut consulter le passage qui lui est dédié par TOUWAIDE A., 'Palladios 5', dans: *Der Neue Pauly* IX (2000), p. 194.

42. KIBRE P., *Hippocrates Latinus, Repertorium of Hippocratic Writings in the Latin Middle Ages*, New York: Fordham University Press, 1985, p. 139-142. Ou encore du même auteur, 'Hippocratic Writings …'.

43. KIBRE, *Hippocrates Latinus…*, p. 139.

44. On en trouve un exemplaire dès le 12e siècle en Angleterre et au 13e siècle dans la bibliothèque de Richard de Fournival. KIBRE, *Hippocrates Latinus…*, p. 139 et 'Hippocratic Writings … ', p. 396. Voir aussi BIRKENMAYER A.,'La bibliothèque de Richard de Fournival, poète et érudit français du XIIIe siècle et son sort ultérieur', dans: *Studia Copernica* I, *Études d'histoire des sciences et de la philosophie au Moyen Age*, Breslau-Varsovie-Cracovie: Wydawnictwo Polskiej Akademii Nauk, 1970, p. 117-154.

45. WOLSKA-CONUS W., 'Stéphanos d'Athènes (d'Alexandrie) et Théophile le Protospathaire, commentateurs des Aphorismes d'Hippocrate sont-ils indépendants l'un de l'autre?', *Revue d'études byzantines* 52 (1994), p. 9, note 7.

46. BERTIER J., 'À propos de quelques résurgences des *Épidémies*, dans les *Problemata* du Corpus aristotélicien', dans: G. BAADER – R. WINAN (éds), *Die Hippokratischen Epidemien, Theorie-Praxis-Tradition*, Actes du Ve Colloque International hippocratique, Stuttgart: Franz Steiner, 1989, p. 261-269.

47. Pierre d'Abano ne cite apparemment ce traité qu'une seule fois, à la section I, 50.

48. 'Ainsi, bien que Palladius commente directement Hippocrate, sa lecture de l'hippocratisme sur la question de l'air, des miasmes et de la pestilence semble tributaire de Galien '. JOUANNA J., 'Air, miasmes et contagion à l'époque d'Hippocrate et survivance des miasmes dans la médecine post-hippocratique', dans: S. BAZIN-TACCHELLA –

d'Évrart à Palladius ne concerne ce traité ni même ce Palladius puisque il ne s'agit pas du même personnage. Ce dernier était un médecin grec du début du 6e siècle sur lequel nous avons, par ailleurs, peu d'informations et qui a laissé un certain nombre de commentaires d'œuvres hippocratiques, dont les *Aphorismes*[49]; le premier était un agronome du 5e siècle, mais Évrart et les médecins médiévaux le savaient-ils?

Au chapitre des références attendues chez Évrart se trouvent celles de Galien (plus de 40 contre 120 chez Pierre), mais en moins grand nombre qu'Avicenne ou Hippocrate. Outre le *Tegni* et le *Methodus medendi*, il n'y a pas beaucoup d'ouvrages généraux dans l'œuvre de Galien, mais plutôt une quantité de textes plus spécialisés[50]. Alors que la majorité des références à Avicenne proviennent du livre 1 du *Canon* et que la majorité de celles à Hippocrate proviennent des *Aphorismes*, pour Galien la diversité des sources est plus grande[51].

Viennent ensuite les sources qui, sans être nommément prescrites par les statuts universitaires, faisaient partie du corpus des textes indispensables[52]. Averroès, pour sa part, est cité 11 fois chez Pierre contre 5 chez Évrart. Le seul ouvrage cité est le *Colliget* ou *Collectorium*. Ce traité avait été traduit en latin autour de 1285 et était donc particulièrement nouveau au temps de Pierre d'Abano, ce qui explique peut-être son plus grand nombre de références[53]. Les commentaires d'Averroès au *Traité de l'âme* et à la *Metaphysique* d'Aristote, pourtant prisés des commentateurs médicaux[54], auraient eu leur utilité pour commenter les *Problèmes*, mais nos auteurs ne les utilisent pas, du moins dans le premier chapitre.

D. QUÉRUEL – E. SAMAMA (éds), *Air, miasmes et contagion: Les épidémies dans l'Antiquité et au Moyen Âge* (Hommes et textes de Champagne), Langres: Dominique Guéniot, 2001, p. 28.

49. Pour une mise au point récente, voir MAGDELAINE C., avec la collaboration de S. DIEBLER, 'Le commentaire de Palladius aux *Aphorismes* d'Hippocrate et les citations d'Al-Ya'qubi ', dans: A. GARZYA – J. JOUANNA (éds), *Trasmissione e ecdotica dei testi medici greci, Atti del IV Colloquio internazionale*, Paris: Sorbonne, 2003, p. 324-334.

50. Sur le Galien médiéval et les traités qui étaient disponibles aux médecins du 14e siècle, voir DURLING R.J., 'Corrigenda et addenda to Diel's Galenica', *Traditio* 23 (1967), p. 461-76 et 37 (1981), p. 373-381.

51. Rappelons qu'une meilleure évaluation pourra être faite après vérification auprès de l'autographe.

52. KIBRE, 'Arts and Medicine …', p. 224.

53. Voir à ce sujet MCVAUGH M., *Arnaldi de Villanova Opera Medica Omnia. II. Aphorismi de gradibus,* Granada-Barcelona: Seminarium historiae medicae Granatensis, 1975, p. 61. Danielle Jacquart suggère la possibilité d'une date plus précoce, JACQUART – MICHEAU, *La médecine arabe…*, p. 182-85.

54. Comme en témoigne leur utilisation chez Taddeo Alderotti, Jacopo da Forli et Petrus Turisanus dans leur commentaire respectif à Galien; OTTOSON, *Scholastic Medicine and Philosophy…*, p. 291, ainsi que Jacques Despars dans son commentaire au *Canon* d'Avicenne, JACQUART, *La médecine médiévale…*, p. 542.

Abulcassis (Abu al-Qasim al-Zharawi) est cité le même nombre de fois chez Pierre et chez Évrart. Les 28e et 30e livres du *Tasrif* avaient été traduits par Gérard de Crémone en Espagne dans la deuxième moitié du 12e siècle[55]. La traduction de sa *Chirurgie* eut un retentissement immense et fut à la base des grands traités européens de chirurgie à partir du 13e siècle[56]. L'utilisation de citations d'Abulcassis par Pierre et par Évrart s'explique par la présence du long développement au *Problème* 31 qui traite de chirurgie dans la première section des *Problèmes*.

Étrangement, le traité de chirurgie d'Abulcassis n'est jamais mentionné dans les statuts universitaires. Ceci s'explique par le fait que la chirurgie représentait une opération manuelle et était le propre des chirurgiens, exclus des universités. Or, il appert qu'une majorité de médecins ont lu ce traité. S'il n'est pas toujours cité dans les commentaires aux textes des autorités, c'est bien sûr parce qu'il concerne principalement la chirurgie. Les traités chirurgicaux y font une large place avec notamment près de 200 citations chez Guy de Chauliac[57]. Il en est de même du 28e livre du *Tasrif* d'Abulcassis, cité sous le titre *Liber servitoris*, qui explique les différentes étapes de préparation des simples pour leur utilisation médicale[58]. Bien que cet ouvrage se retrouve rarement dans les programmes des universités, il était lu par beaucoup de médecins qui s'en servaient dans leur pratique[59].

Alors qu'on se serait attendu à une plus grande utilisation de Ptolémée chez Pierre qui, on le sait, était un fervent astrologue, on en retrouve nettement plus chez Évrart avec cinq citations contre une. Pour les savants, Ptolémée représentait le témoin le plus respectable du sérieux de la

55. Sur cet auteur, LECLERC L., 'Abulcassis, son œuvre pour la première fois reconstituée ', dans: F. SEZGIN (éd.), *Abul-Qasim Al-Zahrawi (d. after 400/1009), Texts and Studies. Collected and Reprinted* (Islamic Medicine 37), Frankfurt a.M.: Institute for the history of Arabic-Islamic science at the Johann Wolfgang Goethe University, 1996, p. 30-45.

56. JACQUART – MICHEAU, *La médecine arabe...*, p. 150.

57. LECLERC, 'Abulcassis, son œuvre ...', p. 32.

58. La mise au point la plus récente se trouve dans ENGESER M., *Der 'Liber servitoris' des Abulkasis (936-1013), Übersetzung, Kommentar und Nachdruck der Textfassung von 1471*, Stuttgart: Deutscher Apotheker, 1986.

59. Une étude que j'effectue depuis quelques années sur un texte de la pratique impliquant des médecins parisiens, suggère que les médecins utilisaient beaucoup cet ouvrage et en connaissaient probablement de grands pans par cœur. Guillaume Boucher, le médecin-vedette de ce *consortium in practica*, tardait d'ailleurs à en remettre l'exemplaire qu'il avait emprunté à la bibliothèque de la Faculté de médecine de Paris. WICKERSHEIMER E., 'Les secrets et conseils de maître Guillaume Boucher et ses confrères', *Bulletin de la société française d'histoire de la médecine* 8 (1909), p. 199-205 et *Commentaires de la Faculté de médecine de l'Université de Paris (1395-1516)*, Paris: Imprimerie Nationale, 1915, p. 2.

science astrologique[60]. Le *Centiloquium* n'est pas une œuvre de Ptolémée, mais les astronomes médiévaux le considéraient comme tel. Cité par un grand nombre d'auteurs médiévaux, dont Jacques da Forli et Jacques Despars, le *Centiloquium* était consulté avec le commentaire d'Ali ibn Ridwan et on le trouvait souvent avec une œuvre authentique de Claude Ptolémée, le *Tetrabiblos* ou le *Quadripartitum* latin aussi commenté par Ali ibn Ridwan[61]. C'est ainsi qu'on le trouve cité chez Évrart, parfois sous le nom de Ptolémée, parfois sous celui d''Alibeuridian'. L'autre source relevant aussi de l'astrologie se trouve uniquement chez Pierre, c'est Alcabitus. Il s'agit du *Liber introductorius ad magisterium iudiciorum astrarum* d'Al-Qabisi et traduit au 12ᵉ siècle par Johannes de Luna Hispalensis. Bien que cet ouvrage d'astrologie ait fait partie, comme le précédent, du programme des arts à l'Université de Bologne en 1405[62], les statuts parisiens ne le mentionnent pas.

On notera aussi chez Évrart l'utilisation d'Al-Ghazali, absent chez Pierre. Ce philosophe arabe (1058-1128) était connu des milieux de traduction tolédans et dès le début du 12ᵉ siècle, une partie de son œuvre avait déjà fait l'objet d'une traduction[63]. Le *Maqashid* est un ouvrage didactique dont le dessein ultime était la réfutation des erreurs des philosophes, plus particulièrement d'Aristote et de ses disciples. L'œuvre était divisée en deux parties: logique et métaphysique. La première exposait les idées des philosophes de façon objective et factuelle, la deuxième réfutait leurs arguments un par un. Commentée par Raymond Lulle au 13ᵉ siècle, la *Logique* fut traduite et comprise en domaine latin. La deuxième partie, la *Métaphysique*, a surtout servi à la division des sciences. La préface qui indiquait les intentions de l'auteur a pour sa part été négligée par les traducteurs, il n'en subsiste qu'une copie et il semble que peu l'aient connu au Moyen Âge[64]. On a donc pris Al-Ghazali pour un commentateur d'Aristote. Par ailleurs, sa *Métaphysique* est citée par

60. NORTH J.D., 'Medieval Concepts of Celestial Influence: A Survey', dans: P. CURRY (éd.), *Astrology, Sciences and Society, Historical Essays*, New York: The Boydell Press, 1987, p. 6-7.

61. Sur cet auteur arabe du 10ᵉ siècle, voir SEYMORE J.A., *The life of Ibn Ridwan and his commentary of Ptolemy's Tetrabiblos*, University of Michigan, UMI, 2001.

62. MALAGOLA C. (éd.), *Statuti delle Università e dei Collegi dello Studio Bolognese*, Bologna, 1888, p. 276.

63. Probablement par l'archidiacre Dominique Gundisalvi, le même qui avait traduit la *Shifa* d'Avicenne; D'ALVERNY M.-T., 'Algazel dans l'Occident latin', dans: Ch. BURNETT (éd.), *La transmission des textes philosophiques et scientifiques au Moyen Âge*, Aldershot: Variorum Reprints, 1994, VII, p. 5.

64. Salomon MUNK en donne une traduction partielle dans ses *Mélanges de philosophie juive et arabe*, Paris: J. Vrin, 1988, p. 270-371. D'ALVERNY, 'Algazel...', VII, p. 8.

un grand nombre d'auteurs[65]. On la retrouve, entre autres, dans l'une des quatre *Divisiones scientiarum* provenant de l'Université de Paris au 13e siècle, ce qui atteste de son utilisation en milieu universitaire. Mais surtout, elle fait l'objet d'un chapitre dans les *Erreurs des philosophes* de Gilles de Rome et c'est peut-être par là qu'Évrart y trouve accès, puisqu'il cite lui aussi la *Métaphysique*[66].

En dernier lieu, il convient d'examiner brièvement l'utilisation chez nos auteurs des classiques antiques, poètes ou rhéteurs. Vu les expériences d'écriture d'Évrart, notamment la récente attribution du poème des *Échecs amoureux*[67], il est normal de trouver des références aux classiques dans ses *Problèmes* : Évrart mentionne Fulgence et Ovide, lesquels, on le sait, étaient lus et étudiés à Paris à la Faculté des arts[68]. Les références à Ovide sont attendues; l'intérêt qu'Évrart portait à la tradition ovidienne telle que transposée dans le *Roman de la Rose* a été bien documenté[69]. Pierre d'Abano, pourtant un ardent défenseur de la rhétorique, n'utilise de Boèce que la *Consolation de la philosophie*[70].

Conclusion

Bien entendu, il reste beaucoup à faire pour que cette étude des sources citées dans les *Problèmes* par Évrart de Conty soit complète. Il s'agit, ici, d'une ébauche qui tente d'établir une approche. Cette approche s'établit sur la dialectique entre les sources citées, les savoirs transmis et les lieux de provenance de ces savoirs: curriculums universitaires, traductions, diffusion. Pour avoir une idée plus complète de la question, il faudrait d'abord examiner les traités de l'*Ars medicine* et les ouvrages des lectures obligatoires universitaires avec plus de soin, déterminer les modalités de leur utilisation chez les deux médecins, et établir des liens

65. LAFLEUR C., *Quatre introductions à la philosophie au XIIIe siècle, Textes critiques et étude historique*, Montréal-Paris: Institut d'études médiévales-Vrin, 1988, p. 297-303

66. On sait que pour certaines sources citées dans *Les échecs amoureux moralisés*, Évrart avait souvent recours à Gilles de Rome. GUICHARD-TESSON, *La Glose des Échecs amoureux...*, p. 321.

67. Cette attribution n'a pas encore fait l'objet d'une étude publiée. Pour une mise au point sur la question, on consultera l'article de Françoise Guichard-Tesson ainsi que l'annexe fournie par Caroline Boucher dans le présent recueil.

68. Voir les propos de DE CLAMANGES N. et D'AILLY P. dans: DENIFLE – CHÂTELAIN (éds), *Chartularium Universitatis Parisiensis*, Paris: Delalain, 1889-97, t. III, p. XI et 589-90. Cité dans KIBRE, 'Arts and Medicine ...', XII, p. 220.

69. Voir, entre autres, MINNIS, *Magister Amoris...*

70. KIBRE, 'Arts and Medicine ...', XII, p. 219-20.

plus précis entre les différents passages cités et les propos des *Problemata*. En dernier lieu, il faudrait tenter d'évaluer les méthodes d'appropriation des savoirs et voir comment ceux-ci sont ensuite retransmis par le biais du commentaire ou de la traduction.

Ce bref survol montre néanmoins que les médecins suivaient les lectures obligatoires du cours de médecine, mais que pour être médecin, érudit, commentateur et traducteur, il fallait aller beaucoup plus loin. Si les sources citées se retrouvent pour la plupart dans les statuts universitaires ou dans des curriculums connus, d'autres lectures supplémentaires et autodidactes étaient jugées indispensables pour parfaire la formation d'un médecin. Les sources citées chez Pierre et chez Évrart montrent l'étendue du savoir nécessaire à la compréhension de la science médicale.

Université de Sherbrooke

Annexe 1

Sources citées dans le premier chapitre des *Problèmes*, classées selon leur fréquence

Évrart de Conty		Pierre d'Abano	
Avicenne	66	Galien	120
Hippocrate	57	Avicenne	79
Galien	41	Hippocrate	40
Haly abbas (Ali ibn al-Abbas al-Magusi)	11	Averroès	11
Palladius	7	Haly Al-Magusi	7
Ptolémée (Pseudo-Ptolémée)	5	Haly abbas (Ali ibn al-Abbas al-Magusi)	5
Mésué (Pseudo-Mésué)	4	Haly ibn Ridouan (Ali ibn Ridwan)	4
Averroès	3	Johannitius (Hunain ibn Ishaq)	4
Johannitius (Hunain ibn Ishaq)	3	Mésué (Pseudo Mésué)	4
Abulcassis (Abu al-Qasim al- Zharawi)	3	Abulcassis (Abu al-Qasim al-Zharawi)	3
Algazel (Al-Ghazali)	2	Sérapion (Yuhanna ibn Sarabiyun)	3
Albert (Albert le Grand)	2	Boèce	2
Constantin (Haly al-Magusi)	2	Razès (Al-Razi)	2
Sérapion (Yuhanna ibn Sarabiyun)	2	Alcabitus (Al-Qabisi)	1
Damascène (Ibn Massawayh)	1	Dioscoride	1
Dioscoride	1	Damascène (Ibn Massawayh)	1
Faculté de médecine de Paris	1	Ptolémée (Pseudo-Ptolémée)	1
Fulgence	1	Théophile	1
Haly Abeuridiam/Phtolomee (Ali ibn Ridwan)	1		
Isidore de Séville	1		
Ovide	1		
Platearius	1		
Urso de Salerne	1		
Razès	1		
Isaac	1		

Annexe 2

Sources citées dans le premier chapitre des *Problèmes*, tableau comparatif

Source citée	Évrart de Conty	Pierre d'Abano
Abulcassis (Abu al-Qasim al-Zharawi)	3	3
Albert (Albert le Grand)	2	
Alcabitus (Al-Qabisi)		1
Algazel (Al-Ghazali)	2	
Averroès	3	11
Avicenne	66	79
Boèce		2
Constantin (Haly al-Magusi)	2	
Damascène (Ibn Massawayh)	1	1
Dioscoride	1	1
Faculté de médecine de Paris	1	
Fulgence	1	
Galien	41	120
Haly abbas (Ali ibn al-Abbas al-Magusi)	11	5
Haly Abeuridiam/Phtolomee (Ali ibn Ridwan)	1	
Haly Al-Magusi		7
Haly ibn Ridouan (Ali ibn Ridwan)		4
Hippocrate	57	40
Isaac	1	
Isidore de Séville	1	
Johannitius (Hunain ibn Ishaq)	3	4
Mésué (Pseudo-Mésué)	4	4
Ovide	1	
Palladius	7	
Platearius	1	
Ptolémée (Pseudo-Ptolémée)	5	1
Razès	1	2
Sérapion (Yuhanna ibn Sarabiyun)	2	3
Théophile		1
Urso de Salerne	1	

Annelies BLOEM

À LA RECHERCHE DE LA SUBJECTIVITÉ DANS LES *PROBLEMES* D'ÉVRART DE CONTY: UN COMMENTATEUR JUCHÉ SUR LES ÉPAULES D'ARISTOTE?

The aim of this study is to describe the degree of 'subjectivity' of Évrart de Conty in his Middle French translation of the Latin pseudo-Aristotelian Problemata. *More precisely, we discuss how Évrart de Conty adopts the ideas of Aristotle in his translation. In this, we re-examine a question treated by Françoise Guichard-Tesson: how Évrart balances the conflict between the loyalty towards Aristotle and his desire to present his own perception and even criticism with respect to the various topics under discussion. In this article, we focus on the first book which deals with medical problems. This permits us to consider Évrart's treatment of problems that were particularly familiar to him, given his job as teacher at the faculty of medical science.*

Introduction*

Comment étudier la 'subjectivité' d'un traducteur du 14ᵉ siècle par le biais de sa traduction? Avant de répondre à cette question, il est nécessaire de situer la traduction dans l'histoire et d'élucider brièvement ce que nous entendons par 'subjectivité'.

Évrart de Conty, connu grâce à son *Livre des échecs amoureux moralisés*, a entrepris dans les années 1380, peut-être à la demande du roi Charles V le Sage[1], la traduction des *Problemata*, un traité pseudo-aristotélicien. Il s'agit d'un ouvrage scientifique, qui comporte 38 sections. Chaque section se compose d'un certain nombre de problèmes axés sur une problématique particulière. En gros, on entrevoit trois grandes parties, à savoir une partie consacrée à la médecine, une partie traitant des arts libéraux et une troisième partie parlant de la philosophie naturelle et morale.

La traduction des *Problemata*, réalisée par Évrart de Conty, remonte d'une part à la traduction latine de la main de Barthélémy de Messine

* Cette contribution cadre dans le projet de recherche 'De la langue source à la langue cible: l'expression du mouvement et du changement dans les traductions médiévales des *Problèmes* d'Aristote' (Fonds de la Recherche Scientifique – Flandre, G.0110.03; directeur: Michèle Goyens; co-directeurs: Willy Van Hoecke et Pieter De Leemans).

1. Voir, pour une discussion, les contributions de Françoise Guichard-Tesson et Caroline Boucher dans ce volume.

(1260 environ), et d'autre part au commentaire de Pierre d'Abano (début du 14e siècle)[2]. Différentes études ont déjà relevé les stratégies de traduction d'Évrart de Conty[3].

Par la piste de la 'subjectivité', nous déterminerons le rôle qu'Évrart de Conty adopte dans sa traduction. Nous étudierons la relation multiple qu'il établit par le biais de sa traduction entre le lecteur, les *Problemata* aristotéliciens originaux, la traduction latine et lui-même. À l'intérieur de cette problématique, nous nous concentrerons essentiellement sur la position qu'adopte Évrart de Conty face aux idées d'Aristote. De cette façon, nous examinerons la relation complexe présentée déjà par Françoise Guichard-Tesson concernant le rapport entre Évrart de Conty et Aristote, balançant entre d'un côté le 'respect pour l'autorité' et, de l'autre, le 'recul critique'[4].

Dans notre contribution, nous nous focaliserons sur la première partie des *Problemes*, consacrée à la médecine, car cette partie permet de mesurer l'attitude critique ou non d'Évrart de Conty à l'intérieur de son domaine professionnel. En d'autres mots, nous regarderons comment Évrart se profile à l'intérieur de sa traduction et s'il exploite ses connaissances médicales ou pas.

Nous analyserons avant tout le prologue et la première section, plus en particulier les interventions d'Évrart dans la partie 'texte' et la 'partie glose'[5] puisque, comme Charles Brucker l'a affirmé dans sa présentation d'une typologie des traductions[6], la présence, l'absence et le contenu du prologue et des gloses sont des critères externes donnant 'une informa-

---

2. Pierre D'ABANO, *Expositio problematum Aristotelis quam Petrus edidit paduanus* (Mantoue: Paulus de Butzbach, 1475). Cette édition contient la traduction de Barthélémy suivie, pour chaque problème, du commentaire de Pierre d'Abano.

3. Voir entre autres GUICHARD-TESSON F., 'Le métier de traducteur et de commentateur au XIVe siècle d'après Évrart de Conty', *Le Moyen Français* 24-25 (1990), p. 131-167; GOYENS M. – DE LEEMANS P., 'Traduire du grec au latin et du latin au français: un défi à la fidélité', dans: P. ANDERSEN (éd.), *Pratiques de traduction au Moyen Age, Actes du colloque de l'Université de Copenhague,* Copenhagen: Museum Tusculanum Press, University of Copenhagen, 2004, p. 204-224; DE LEEMANS P. – GOYENS M., 'La transmission des savoirs en passant par trois langues: le cas des *Problemata* d'Aristote traduits en latin et en moyen français', dans: P. NOBEL (éd.), *La transmission des savoirs au Moyen Âge et à la Renaissance.* Vol. 1. *Du XIIe au XVe siècle,* Besançon: Presses Universitaires de Franche-Comté, 2005, 231-257.

4. GUICHARD-TESSON F., 'Le souci de la langue et du style au XIVe siècle: l'autographe des *Problèmes* d'Évrart de Conty', *Le Moyen Français* 33 (1993), p. 75-79.

5. Sur la distinction entre 'texte' et 'glose', voir GUICHARD-TESSON, 'Le métier de traducteur ….', p. 134.

6. BRUCKER C., 'Pour une typologie des traductions en France au XIVe siècle', dans: C. BRUCKER (éd.), *Traduction et adaptation en France. Actes de Colloque organisé par l'Université de Nancy II 23-25 mars 1995,* Paris: Honoré Champion, 1997, p. 63-79, ici p. 64.

tion sur l'attitude du traducteur à l'égard de son propre travail et à l'égard de son modèle faisant l'objet de la traduction'.

1. Le prologue et le premier problème

Dès la première phrase du manuscrit, Évrart commence par se mettre en scène de façon très humble en disant que selon la possibilité de son 'petit engien, la grace divine a empris a translater ou exposer aucunement en françois'[7]. En même temps, il renvoie à Aristote en le nommant 'li princes des phylosophes'[8]. En effet, conformément à l'esprit médiéval, cette traduction fait preuve d'un grand respect pour Aristote.

Dans la suite du prologue, Évrart se contente essentiellement de communiquer l'organisation du livre des *Problemes*, tout en mentionnant très brièvement son approbation vis-à-vis de cette structure. Ainsi, il se réjouit du fait qu'Aristote a mis la partie sur la médecine au début du livre, probablement puisqu''elle nous est plus necessaire et plus pourfitable et pour ce doit elle estre mise en presence devant les autres sciences humaines selonc ce que dit Constantins'[9]. Ces idées se retrouvent aussi dans le commentaire de Pierre d'Abano.

L'illustration contenue dans une des copies du texte d'Évrart, à savoir le manuscrit Iena, Gallica 81, offre d'ailleurs un beau témoignage de l'importance de la structure du livre des *Problemes*. Plus précisément, la miniature montre d'abord Aristote, siégé sur un trône, devant lequel se présentent trois groupes de personnes. Ces trois groupes correspondent à la structure tripartite des *Problemes*. La première partie contient les problèmes relatifs à la médecine. Par conséquent, il faut identifier dans le premier groupe de personnes, à l'exemple de Dexel[10], Hippocrate et Galien. Le deuxième groupe présente un joueur de harpe et des chevaliers qui représentent la seconde partie axée sur les arts libéraux. Le troisième

---

7. Voir à cet effet aussi JACQUART D., *La médecine médiévale dans le cadre parisie*n : *XIVe-XVe siècle* (Penser la médecine), Paris: Fayard, 1998, p. 278. Nous citons toujours le texte d'après l'autographe d'Évrart de Conty, à savoir le manuscrit Paris BNF fr. 24281-24282, ici fol. 1r du premier volume.

8. Ms. Paris BNF fr. 24281, fol. 1r.

9. Ms. Paris BNF fr. 24281, fol. 1r.

10. DEXEL W., *Untersuchungen über die französischen illuminierten Handschriften der Jenaer Universitätsbibliothek vom Ende des 14. bis zur Mitte des 15. Jahrhunderts*, Strasbourg: Heitz & Mündel, 1917, p. 21: '[...] die ersten beiden links sind als Vertreter der medizinischen Disziplin anzusehen und ihre namentliche Fixierung erscheint nicht unmöglich. Die nächsten drei Figuren, ein Harfenspieler und zwei Rittergestalten, sollen wohl die sieben freien Künste repräsentieren, während die letzten vier Gestalten der Natur- und Moralphilosophie angehören. In dem Philosophen mit der Kugel dürfte Hermes trismegistos zu erkennen sein, während die übrigen nicht weiter gekennzeichnet sind.'

groupe renvoie à la philosophie naturelle et morale. Walter Dexel pense reconnaître Hermes Trismegistos.

Un peu plus loin dans le prologue, Évrart de Conty montre en renvoyant à l'adage aristotélicien 'quod admirabile est delectabile est'[11], que la structure sous forme de question[12] qu'adopte Aristote se prête à merveille à stimuler l'entendement, qui est d'ailleurs un désir humain naturel. En outre, 'savoir et cognoistre les causes de merveilles de nature fait deliter souverainement'[13] et la connaissance rend heureuse. Ces mots préliminaires indiquent selon nous les deux soucis principaux d'Évrart de Conty, à savoir stimuler 'l'entendement' et 'deliter souverainement', c'est-à-dire favoriser la compréhension et plaire. Tout compte fait, le prologue joue sur le motif de 'plaire et instruire'[14]. Notons que ce prologue témoigne ainsi du succès de la *translatio studii,* qui connaît son essor depuis le 13e siècle[15]. Au 14e siècle, le savoir est passé à l'Université de Paris. La *translatio studii* est perçue comme la relation 'de fille à mère', surtout sous Charles V qui désignait dans ses ordonnances l'Université de Paris comme sa 'fille aimée'[16].

Plus loin, lorsqu'il glose le premier problème, Évrart de Conty nous communique également, à l'instar de Nicole Oresme, ses réflexions concernant la question de la langue. Comme d'autres chercheurs l'ont déjà repéré, Évrart de Conty est très conscient du fait que traduire littéralement corrompt souvent le texte. Voilà pourquoi Évrart traduira 'ad sensum' [17], tout en veillant à rester près de ses textes sources à l'instar de la méthode de traduction de Nicole Oresme et Simon de Hesdin[18], deux

11. Ms. Paris BNF fr. 24281, fol. 1r.
12. Il apprécie aussi la façon selon laquelle Aristote opère, car tout problème est introduit par la question 'pour quoy est ce que', après laquelle suit une réponse, ce qui 'fait l'entendement, devant esmerveillié, deliter tres grandement' et, après tout, la 'verité, ceste cognissance des causes fait moult a la perfection et a la felicité humaine' (ms. Paris BNF fr. 24281, fol. 1r).
13. Ms. Paris BNF fr. 24281, fol. 1r.
14. Voir aussi Jacquart, *La médecine médiévale* …, p. 278 et Guichard-Tesson, 'Le métier de traducteur ….', p. 143.
15. Lusignan S., 'La topique de la *translatio studii* et les traductions françaises de textes savants au XIVe siècle', dans: G. Contamine (éd.), *Traduction et traducteurs au Moyen Âge. Actes du colloque international du CNRS organisé à Paris, Institut de recherche et d'histoire des textes les 26-28 mai 1986*, Paris: Centre National de la Recherche Scientifique, 1989, p. 313.
16. Lusignan, 'La topique de la *translatio studii*…, p. 314.
17. Voir entre autres Guichard-Tesson, 'Le métier de traducteur et …'; Goyens – De Leemans, 'Traduire du grec au latin …', p. 204-224; De Leemans – Goyens, 'La transmission des savoirs …'.
18. Voir entre autres Brucker, 'Pour une typologie des traductions …', p. 69. Observons que cette façon de traduire pourrait être due au fait qu'ils éprouvaient assez souvent beaucoup de difficultés à comprendre le texte, chose dont Évrart de Conty se plaint assez souvent. De même, comme le signale Jacques Monfrin, ces remarques à propos de la dif-

traducteurs de la même période. Dès lors, on retrouve maintes fois dans les gloses 'et c'est la sentence de cest probleme[19]'.

Plusieurs éléments sont donc à retenir du prologue. Évrart de Conty y déclare son respect pour Aristote surtout à travers l'appréciation de la structure du livre. Il se pose comme but principal la *translation* et l'*exposition*[20] du texte afin de rendre ses lecteurs heureux en leur offrant *les causes de ce qui émerveille*. Dès lors, il n'est point étonnant que le souci de l'entendement joue un rôle important dans ce qui suit.

Afin de déterminer l'attitude d'Évrart de Conty face à sa tâche de traduction, plusieurs analyses doivent être effectuées. Il faut notamment regarder son apport personnel à travers la manipulation de la traduction latine. Plus précisément, nous dresserons le bilan des différentes espèces de gloses. À cet effet, nous nous livrons dans un premier instant à la catégorisation des interventions. Concrètement, nous distinguons deux catégories, à l'intérieur desquelles il convient d'apporter encore différentes subdivisions.

Premièrement, nous discernons des interventions à tendance purement pédagogique, explicative, et assez souvent lexicographique, quasiment neutre vis-à-vis des idées d'Aristote. Ces interventions peuvent se retrouver tant dans la partie 'texte', que dans la partie 'glose'. À l'intérieur de cette classe se démarquent les observations qui sont calquées sur celles de Pierre d'Abano et les remarques 'personnelles' d'Évrart de Conty. Deuxièmement, nous entrevoyons dans la partie 'glose' des commentaires à tendance critique, parmi lesquelles on peut différencier des remarques puisées dans le texte de Pierre d'Abano, des observations pour lesquelles Évrart emprunte les idées de Pierre d'Abano tout en les adaptant quelque peu, et des interventions personnelles d'Évrart de Conty, absentes du commentaire de Pierre d'Abano. Il convient de remarquer que ces catégories ne peuvent être délimitées de façon rigide. Il faut les considérer comme des points de repère sur une ligne continue des tendances qu'on peut entrevoir dans la méthode de travail d'Évrart de Conty. Schématiquement, on pourrait les représenter comme suit:

---

ficulté du texte servaient peut-être non seulement à 'mieux faire estimer leur mérite, mais il semble bien y avoir quelque vérité et pas seulement le développement d'un thème littéraire '. Voir: MONFRIN J., 'Les traducteurs et leur public en France au Moyen Age', dans: A. FOURRIER (éd.), *L'humanisme médiéval dans les littératures romanes du XIIe au XIVe siècle* (Actes et colloques 3), Paris: Klincksieck, 1964, p. 260.

19. Voir entre autres ms. Paris BNF fr. 24281, fol. 16v, 24v, 27r, 28r, 31v, 35v.

20. Voir aussi ms. Paris BNF fr. 24282, fol. 245r, où Évrart de Conty écrit en guise d'explicit: 'Explicit le livre des problemes de Aristote translaté ou exposé de latin en françois par maistre Evrart de Conty, jadis physicien du roi Charles le quint. Deo gratias.' Notons également qu'il est intéressant de voir qu'Évrart de Conty mentionne explicitement son nom vers la fin de l'œuvre. Voir 3.3.

1. Interventions générales, pédagogiques, *neutres* :

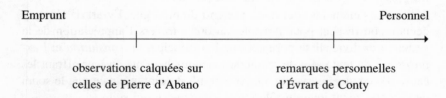

2. Commentaires à tendance *critique* dans la partie 'glose' :

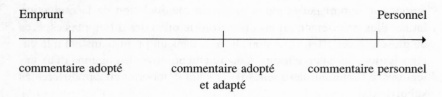

2. *Interventions à tendance purement pédagogique, 'explicative', quasiment neutre vis-à-vis des idées d'Aristote*

Avant de classifier les interventions, éclairons d'abord de façon générale la méthode de travail d'Évrart de Conty. Plusieurs études ont montré qu'Évrart ne traduit pas mot à mot[21]. Qui plus est, il semble même paraphraser les données qu'il trouve dans les textes latins. Dès lors, il est très difficile de définir sa façon de travailler.

Conformément aux attentes créées dans le prologue, la plupart des interventions peuvent être classées dans la première catégorie, celle des gloses pédagogiques[22], qui se caractérise par l'attitude quasiment neutre vis-à-vis des idées d'Aristote, puisqu'Évrart y explique soigneusement les paroles d'Aristote.

D'ailleurs, à maintes reprises, Évrart signale que le texte d'Aristote est difficile à comprendre. Ainsi, il commence la glose du problème 52 par la remarque que 'li textes de Aristote en cest probleme est moult obscurs. Toutefois, il samble qu'il woeille principalment enquerre pour

---

21. À propos de la problématique concernant la manière de traduire d'Évrart de Conty, voir GUICHARD-TESSON, 'Le métier de traducteur ...', p. 131-167. Sur la méthode de traduction de Barthélémy de Messine, voir GOYENS – DE LEEMANS, 'Traduire du grec au latin ...'; DE LEEMANS – GOYENS, 'La transmission des savoirs en passant par trois langues ...'.
22. Nous empruntons ce terme à BRUCKER, 'Pour une typologie des traductions ...', p. 76.

quoy c'est que li medecin regardent les signes qui se moustrent en le orine'[23].

Comme Guichard-Tesson et Goyens l'ont déjà montré, Évrart de Conty recourt à toute une série de procédés pédagogiques afin de rendre le texte compréhensible[24]. Dans la manipulation des données encyclopédiques qu'Évrart retrouve essentiellement chez Pierre d'Abano, plusieurs techniques sont à distinguer. Dans ce qui suit, nous rappelons quelques-unes de ces méthodes, tout en mesurant l'apport personnel ou non d'Évrart de Conty.

Dans beaucoup de cas, Évrart soigne les transitions entre les différents problèmes en explicitant le lien qui existe entre eux. Ainsi, afin d'assurer la cohérence de son texte, Évrart introduit le 22e problème par la phrase suivante: 'Aprés ce met Aristotes encor .1. probleme de pestilence seignefiie par aucuns autres signes, et demande ainsy'[25]. On retrouve fréquemment des phrases telles que: 'Aprés ce met Aristote .1. probleme qui resamble au .32e. devant dit et samble qu'il le woeille repeter pour plus plainement respondre y et par especial a la seconde partie. Il demande donc ainsy'[26].

Remarquons en outre que, ici, la partie 'glose' commence par quelques paragraphes d'explications supplémentaires que nous ne retrouvons pas dans les textes latins. De même, Évrart introduit le problème 36 par une phrase explicitant la cohérence du texte:

> Aprés ce que Aristotes ha mis aucuns problemes appartenans a cyrurgie, il en woelt mettre aucuns apartenans a diete, et demande ainsy a savoir (...) se la ptisane de orge est plus legiere et meillour pour curer les maladies, que la ptisane de fourment[27].

Évrart ajoute aussi indépendamment des textes latins une phrase introductive au problème 37, à savoir 'Cy aprés woelt Aristotes proposer aucuns autres problemes appartenans a potion, et parle premierement de la maladie des dens, et demande ainsy'[28]. Il signale au début du pro-

---

23. Ms. Paris BNF fr. 24281, fol. 49v.
24. Ces procédés ont été décrits de façon méticuleuse dans GUICHARD-TESSON, 'Le métier de traducteur...', p. 131-167; GUICHARD-TESSON, 'Le souci de la langue ...', p. 75-79. De même, à propos de la reformulation chez Évrart de Conty, voir GOYENS M., 'Comprendre Aristote au Moyen Âge: le procédé de reformulation dans la traduction des *Problèmes* par Évrart de Conty', dans: P. NOBEL (éd.), *Textes et cultures: réception, modèles, interférences. Volume I: Réception de l'Antiquité*, Franche-Comté: Presses Universitaires, 2004, p. 145-163.
25. Ms. Paris BNF fr. 24281, fol. 28v.
26. Ms. Paris BNF fr. 24281, fol. 35v.
27. Ms. Paris BNF fr. 24281, fol. 36v-37r.
28. Ms. Paris BNF fr. 24281, fol. 38r.

blème 30, que 'Aprés ce que Aristotes ha proposé pluseurs problemes apartenans a la partie speculative de medecine, il commence a proposer autres problemes qui appartienent plus a la practique'[29]. Évrart veille donc à apporter plus de structure à l'intérieur de cette section et explicite ainsi les différentes parties qu'il faut discerner.

Une autre preuve du souci de l'organisation se trouve dans la glose du 35e problème, traitant des cautérisations. Évrart rend assez fidèlement le commentaire de Pierre d'Abano dans sa glose et ils renvoient tous les deux à un autre livre d'Aristote, à savoir le 4e livre de la *Météorologie*. Cependant, il semble qu'Évrart de Conty explicite un peu plus les transitions dans le raisonnement. Afin de les signaler, il emploie fréquemment des phrases telles que:

> On porroit bien ausy, qui volroit, autrement exposer cest probleme, et dire que par les adustions dont Aristotes parle en ceste partie, il entent les chalours et les inflammations des fievres, en disant que les inflammations des membres nutritis, c'est a dire des humours qui norrissent le cors, qui font fievres pourries, se garissent tost, et les inflammations des membres se garissent tart, comme fievre ethique, mais ce n'est mie bien au porpos[30].

D'une façon analogue, Évrart rend fidèlement la problématique du problème 17, telle qu'on la retrouve chez Barthélémy de Messine, tout en la structurant un peu plus. Évrart ajoute notamment des phrases telles que:

> [Aprés les problemes desus dis retourne Aristotes as impressions qui se font par le mutation du tans et demande ainsy.] […] A ce respont Aristotes et premierement a la premiere partie […] Aprés ce respont Aristotes a la seconde partie[31].

Notons que certaines phrases sont prises du texte de Pierre d'Abano, comme par exemple, relativement au problème cité ci-dessus: 'Adhuc Aristoteles revertitur ad impressiones que fiunt in mutationibus temporum ut sit sermo eius sufficiens in illis'[32].

Évrart aide le lecteur à classer les problèmes rigoureusement, afin de garantir une bonne compréhension. Dès lors, Évrart intervient non seulement en tant que 'traducteur', mais également en tant que véritable 'translateur' de sciences et 'commentateur', veillant sur l'organisation logique de son texte.

---

29. Ms. Paris BNF fr. 24281, fol. 33r.
30. Ms. Paris BNF fr. 24281, fol. 36v.
31. Ms. Paris BNF fr. 24281, fol. 25v.
32. Pierre d'ABANO, *Expositio problematum…*, fol. 15ra.

D'ailleurs, Évrart compile et ordonne assez librement les données qu'il retrouve chez Pierre d'Abano. Il ajoute des passages entiers afin de faciliter la compréhension du texte, comme l'ont déjà fait remarquer De Leemans et Goyens:

> Dans certains cas, Évrart n'hésite pas à ajouter des développements par rapport à la traduction de Barthélémy de Messine ou au commentaire de Pierre d'Abano, afin d'améliorer son texte. Pour ce faire, il semble s'être inspiré de certaines sources, auxquelles il renvoie régulièrement dans la marge de son manuscrit autographe[33].

Les ajouts personnels qu'Évrart de Conty insère déjà dès le début du livre à propos de la division de la science des médecines, confirment l'idée qu'il veille à transmettre le message d'une façon aussi transparente que possible:

> Pour ce donc que Aristotes parle en ces premiers problemes de materes medicinauls qui meismes sont touchies es livres notables de medecine, et par especial es *Amphorismes* de Ypocras et en son livre *De aere et aqua* ou il les prist par aventure principalment, lesquels materes se doivent par raison exposer medicinalment, car les paroles se doivent tousdis exposer selonc ce que la matere desire, si comme il meismes dit aillours, pour ce convient il aucunes choses desclairier apartenans a la science de medecine, au mains generalment et tant qu'il doie soufire aucunement a la declaration des materes medicinauls qui sont touchies en cest livre.
> Nous devons dont savoir que la science de medecine traicte du cors humain et, selonc ce que dit Avicennes, elle fait congnoistre sa disposition en tant qu'il est recevables de santé et de maladie, a la fin que la santé, s'il l'a, li soit gardee, et la maladie, s'elle li sourvient, li soit ostee.
> Et c'est a entendre, selonc Averroy, en tant qu'il est possible en cascun cors humain, car selonc ce qu'il dit, la science de medecine n'est pas ordenee pour garir de toutes maladies ne en tous tans, mais en tant qu'il est possible par nature, car nulle science ne nulle vertus purement humaine ne poet faire plus que ce qui est faisable par nature.
> Et pour ce dit Ypocras que se li medecins pooit garir de toutes maladies, il ne seroit pas seulement prophetes, mais plus devins que nuls aultres prophetes[34].

Suivent alors 753 lignes ayant pour but d'introduire ses lecteurs dans la science des médecines. Évrart note d'ailleurs au début du manuscrit que:

---

33. DE LEEMANS – GOYENS, 'La transmission des savoirs ...', p. 249. Nous reviendrons à ce propos sous la partie 'digressions scientifiques'.
34. Ms. Paris BNF fr. 24281, fol. 2r. Certains fragments cités ici, à savoir les extraits des folios 1r-30r, sont issus de la transcription provisoire de Françoise Guichard-Tesson, réalisée dans le cadre de l'édition en cours.

> Et pour ce ausi que Aristotes suppose pluseurs choses en cest pro-
> bleme et en pluseurs autres dont cil ne se donnent de garde qui n'ont
> pas la congnissance ne les termes de la science de medecine *pour ce*
> *convient il aucunes choses prenoter et devant dire pour mieux avoir*
> *la declaration et l'entendement de ses paroles, meesmement pour* ce
> que cil livres doit estre translatés en françois, si ne porra qu'il ne
> viengne aucune fois entre les mains d'aucuns qui autrement ne le
> porroient pas si bien comprendre[35].

Quoiqu'il soit clair qu'Évrart reprend certaines idées de l'introduction
de Pierre d'Abano, ce long exposé ne figure pas comme tel dans celle-ci.

Dans le même souci pédagogique, Évrart explique des mots ou il
reformule[36] des mots inconnus: 'lors il descript par son mouvement
jornal entour la terre .1. cercle, que li astronomien appelent le tropique
estival, c'est a dire le conversion de esté, car *tropos* en grec, c'est *con-*
version en françois'[37]. Évrart tient aussi à expliciter que 'pourcelaine'
constitue 'une herbe assés commune qui est froide u tiers degré, et
moiste u secont, et est moult medicinal herbe, et moult pourfitable en
pluseurs cas, et entre les autres choses, elle ha proprieté de oster la
congelation des dens'[38]. Cette précision ne figure pas dans les textes latins, contrairement à certains passages où la description des caractéristiques médicales du pourpier et du sel est presque identique à celle de
Barthélémy de Messine.

À l'intérieur du problème 10, Évrart insère également une remarque
lexicographique[39] dans le texte pour expliquer le mot *phtisie*:

> Et nous devons savoir que la maladie dont Aristotes fait ycy mention,
> qui est appelee ptysis, c'est une maladie a laquele s'ensieut la
> consumption et le degastement de tout le cors pour le ulceration du
> poumon, car ceste dispositions ne poet estre sans fievre qui
> continuelment l'acompaigne. Et pour ce, tous pthisiques est ethiques,
> mais tous ethiques n'est pas ptisiques. Et pour ce est ceste maladie
> ainsi appelee, car *ptisis* en grec, c'est *consumption* en françois[40].

---

35. Ms. Paris BNF fr. 24281, fol. 1v-2r.
36. Voir GOYENS, 'Comprendre Aristote...', p. 145-163.
37. Ms. Paris BNF fr. 24281, fol. 31r.
38. Ms. Paris BNF fr. 24281, fol. 38r.
39. Pour un aperçu plus complet des procédés lexicologiques chez Évrart de Conty,
voir notamment DUCOS J., 'Traduction et lexique scientifique: le cas des problèmes
d'Aristote traduits par Évrart de Conty', dans: C. BRUCKER (éd.), *Traduction et adapta-*
tion en France. Actes du colloque organisé par l'université de Nancy II, 23-25 mars 1995
(Colloques, congrès et conférences sur la Renaissance 10), Paris: Honoré Champion,
1997, p. 237-247; GOYENS M., 'Le lexique des plantes et la traduction des *Problèmes*
d'Aristote par Evrart de Conty (c. 1380)', *Le Moyen Français* 55-56 (2004-2005), p. 145-
165.
40. Ms. Paris BNF fr. 24281, fol. 18v.

Cette remarque correspond à ce qu'on trouve dans le commentaire de Pierre d'Abano: 'Notandum quod in omni ptisi est consumptio'[41]. Ces observations peuvent donc être calquées sur le modèle latin que constitue le texte de Pierre d'Abano.

On trouve un cas pareil dans le problème 53, où la remarque d'Évrart (EDC) est une traduction de ce qui se trouve dans le texte de Pierre d'Abano (PDA):

> PDA: Notandum est quod raritas quam hic Phylosophus iniungit ad sanitatem non est raritas superflua ex qua corpus ledatur ab exterius occurentibus magis[42].
>
> EDC: Nous devons ausi considerer que la rarité dont Aristote parle en cest present probleme qui pourfite a la santé du cors humain n'est mie rarités superflue dont li cors puist estre adamagiés des choses de dehors[43].

De même, Évrart rend une précision de Pierre d'Abano dans le 54e problème:

> PDA: Et scias quod per pustulas intelligo tumores[44].
>
> EDC: Par les pustules dont Aristotes parle, on doit entendre les petites tumeurs […][45]

Parfois, Évrart tient non seulement à préciser ce qu'Aristote entend par certains mots ou par certaines idées, mais il vise également à clarifier comment il ne faut pas interpréter ses mots:

> Et n'entent mie Aristotes c'on boive fort vin, ne tant c'on en soit yvres, mais c'on boive bon vin, cler et net, et soubtil et flairant souef, avoec certaine quantité de yaue, bonne, saine et loable, tant qu'il appartient selonc la force du vin, et la complexion de la personne, et ausy la chalour du tans, et c'on en boive raisonnablement et par bonne mesure[46].

Évrart insère souvent des moments de récapitulation, comme il le fait à l'intérieur du problème 56:

> C'est la sentence de Aristote en cest probleme. *Pour laquele un petit miex comprendre, nous poons dire que la sentence de Aristote et la response en cest probleme gist en .3. poins generalment.*
> Li premiers regarde le gouvernement qui appartient es fievres continues u commencement et par especial quant au boire, et quant a ce woelt dire Aristotes en respondant au probleme que on doit donner en

---

41. Pierre d'ABANO, *Expositio problematum*..., fol. 12ra.
42. Pierre d'ABANO, *Expositio problematum*..., fol. 32rb.
43. Ms. Paris BNF fr. 24281, fol. 52r.
44. Pierre d'ABANO, *Expositio problematum*..., fol. 32va.
45. Ms. Paris BNF fr. 24281, fol. 52r.
46. Ms. Paris BNF fr. 24281, fol. 39r.

cest cas au patient a boire en petite quantité quant a une foys et souvent, pource que li boires donnés en grant quantité passe oultre[47].

Ailleurs dans le texte, on retrouve des phrases telles que: 'on trouve
donc u cors humain [...]', faisant preuve de son esprit synthétisant.

Une autre tendance pédagogique consiste en l'insertion d'anecdotes et
d'exemples frappants. Plus précisément, çà et là, Évrart de Conty essaie
d'illustrer son discours en y ajoutant des exemples très concrets. De
même, il raconte assez souvent des situations anecdotiques, qui servent à
garder l'attention du lecteur ainsi qu'à le stimuler à continuer à lire.
Ainsi, lorsqu'il déclare dans sa digression à propos de la science médicale que 'nulle science, ne nulle vertus purement humaine ne poet faire
plus que ce qui est faisable par nature'[48], il y ajoute une note assez hu-
moristique de la part d'Hippocrate disant que 'se li medecins porroit
garir de toutes maladies, il ne seroit pas seulement prophetes mais plus
divins que nuls autres prophetes'[49].

Afin d'illustrer que 'il est chose bien faisable que une meismes chose
soit cause de .ii. contraires en diverses manieres'[50], il introduit de nouveau un exemple concret: 'le fus fait le charbon noir et puis se fait la
cendre blance'[51]. Notons qu'Évrart répète cet exemple dans la glose du
problème 55:

> [...si comme il fu dit u probleme de devant] et pource dit Aristotes
> aillours que une meismes chose poet bien estre cause de .2. choses
> contraires, *si comme chaleurs poet bien estre cause et de blanc et de*
> *noir, comme nous veons es charbons et es cendres. Ce n'est mie dont*
> *merveilles se chaleurs et froidure poeent engendrer aucunes maladies*
> *et les ausi garir par diverses manieres*[52].

De même, au septième problème, Évrart veut rendre son discours plus
clair pour illustrer que le ciel peut changer. Voilà pourquoi il renvoie, à
l'instar des poètes, à l'histoire de la chute de Phaeton avec la charrette
de Soleil, pour expliquer que l'air peut se corrompre et altérer de façon
naturelle[53]. D'une façon analogue, il insère une anecdote à propos de
Galien pour exemplifier que certains fruits peuvent être 'de malvaise digestion' et 'principal cause de putrefaction, si comme dit Galiens qui se
complaint de ce qu'il en avoit trop mengié en sa jonesce pource qu'il en

---

47. Ms. Paris BNF fr. 24281, fol. 53v.
48. Ms. Paris BNF fr. 24281, fol. 21r.
49. Ms. Paris BNF fr. 24281, fol. 21r.
50. Ms. Paris BNF fr. 24281, fol. 9v.
51. Ms. Paris BNF fr. 24281, fol. 9v.
52. Ms. Paris BNF fr. 24281, fol. 52v.
53. Ms. Paris BNF fr. 24281, fol. 13v.

encouru moult de malvaises maladies'[54]. Afin de rendre son discours plus expressif dans le 17e problème, Évrart observe entre autres que les anciens poètes appelaient Zephyrus le dieu des fleurs: 'Et pour ce ausy fu il appelés des anciens poetes li dieus des fleurs, pour ce que par sa douçour et par sa suavité il multeplie et fait croistre les fleurs'[55].

D'ailleurs, comme l'a démontré F. Guichard-Tesson, Évrart n'hésite pas à évoquer ses propres aventures pour illustrer certaines positions qui rendent son commentaire personnel[56]. Il adopte ainsi une tendance se manifestant déjà dans le texte de Pierre d'Abano, qui lui aussi intervenait de temps en temps pour communiquer ses propres expériences. Évrart les traduit d'ailleurs, comme en témoigne le passage suivant:

> Et de ce dit l'expositeur de Aristote en cest livre que cils problemes estoit en li trés grandement verifiés, car il avoit le cors si froit u tans de esté, si comme il aferme que les puces meismes gietees desus li, s'enfuioient pour la froidure[57].

En outre, Évrart n'hésite pas non plus à ajouter des données plus actuelles, une attitude relevée déjà par Danielle Jacquart. Ainsi, pour illustrer le problème 7 du premier livre par exemple, il fait allusion aux épidémies du 14e siècle[58].

Les modifications de la part d'Évrart évoquées ici se situent sur le plan pédagogique. Les tendances qu'on y retrouve peuvent dès lors être groupées dans ce que P. Dembowski appelle 'service aspects of the translation': 'explicate a given doctrine, make more transparent the organisation, facilitate the understanding of a given passage, or a given term in particular'[59]. En effet, comme l'ont montré F. Guichard-Tesson[60] et M. Goyens, les ajouts personnels d'Évrart visent avant tout à assurer une bonne compréhension du texte:

> Évrart de Conty, ayant reçu pour tâche de rendre accessible le texte d'Aristote (...), s'efforce non seulement de rendre en langue vulgaire un traité difficile, pour lequel il ne dispose que d'une (mauvaise?) tra-

---

54. Ms. Paris BNF fr. 24281, fol. 31r.

55. Ms. Paris BNF fr. 24281, fol. 26r.

56. GUICHARD-TESSON, 'Le métier de traducteur...', p. 165.

57. Ms. Paris BNF fr. 24282, fol. 240v.

58. JACQUART, *La médecine médiévale...*, p. 250.

59. Cf. DEMBOWSKI P.F., 'Scientific Translation and Translator's Glossing in Four Medieval French Translations', dans: J. BEER, (éd.), *Translation theory and practice in the Middle Ages* (Studies in medieval culture 38), Kalamazoo – Michigan: Western Michigan University, Medieval Institute Publications, 1997, p. 113-134, ici p. 113.

60. GUICHARD-TESSON, 'Le métier de traducteur...', p. 131-167, et 'Le souci de la langue ...', p. 75-79.

duction en latin et un commentaire, mais aussi d'en assurer la compréhension[61].

3. *Le commentaire à tendance critique dans la partie 'glose'*

Examinons maintenant le commentaire à tendance critique vis-à-vis
d'Aristote, que nous retrouvons essentiellement dans la partie 'glose'.

Rappelons pour commencer l'idée de P. Gathercole qui postulait déjà
que 'the book must have popularized some scientific ideas, awakened a
desire to question scientific dogma, rather than served as a practical
handbook for medecine and other related fields'[62].

Selon F. Guichard-Tesson, l'attitude d'Évrart face à Aristote est
d'ailleurs bien illustrée par la remarque suivante: 'On pourroit dire que
Aristote ne doit pas estre pour ce reprins car la science de medecine ne
la vertu des choses medecinauls n'estoient pas encore parfaitement
sceuez ne trouveez'[63]. Plus précisément, elle dit à ce propos: 'On voit
qu'Évrart fait preuve d'un certain sens historique. Il souligne que la
science a progressé; aussi est-il normal qu'Aristote ignore ce qui a été
découvert plus tard'[64]. De même, P. De Leemans et M. Goyens ont déjà
remarqué que la critique face à Aristote constitue un élément non négli-
geable à l'intérieur des *Problemes*[65].

Dans ces débats scientifiques, Évrart s'inspire essentiellement sur les
commentaires de Pierre d'Abano, qui, comme le dit N. Siraisi, avait des
idées très précises à l'égard des connaissances scientifiques:

> As a commentator, Peter of Abano repeatedly demonstrated interest in
> secondary rather than primary causes, readiness to question esta-
> blished authorities, and scepticism toward the marvellous. Moreover,
> Peter had very definite ideas about what constituted scientific know-
> ledge, holding only sciences depending upon inductive and deductive
> reasoning to be worthy of the name[66].

Ainsi, tant Évrart de Conty que Pierre d'Abano invoquent à maintes
reprises des opinions d'autres autorités telles que Hippocrate, Galien,
Avicenne, etc.[67]

61. GOYENS, 'Comprendre Aristote au Moyen Âge...', p. 160.
62. GATHERCOLE P.M., 'Medieval science: Évrart de Conty', *Romance Notes* 6
(1964), p. 181.
63. GUICHARD-TESSON, 'Le métier de traducteur ...', p. 152.
64. GUICHARD-TESSON, 'Le métier de traducteur ...', p. 152.
65. 'Dans certains cas, il [Évrart de Conty] (...) n'hésite pas à accuser Aristote
d'avoir tort': DE LEEMANS – GOYENS, 'La transmission des savoirs en passant ...', p. 253.
66. SIRAISI N.G., 'The *Expositio Problematum Aristotelis* of Peter of Abano', *Isis* 61
(1970), p. 321-339.
67. Voir la contribution de G. Dumas dans ce volume.

Dès lors s'impose la question de savoir dans quelle mesure et comment Évrart se positionne face à l'autorité du philosophe. Nous analyserons donc les parties 'glose' afin de voir le degré de correspondance des commentaires d'Évrart face à ceux de Pierre d'Abano. Nous aimerions ainsi classifier les commentaires de cette catégorie dans trois groupes. Dans un premier instant, nous regarderons les remarques purement 'translatees' du texte de Pierre d'Abano, dans un deuxième instant, les interventions dans lesquelles il adapte les idées de Pierre d'Abano, et troisièmement, les gloses plus personnelles, absentes des textes latins[68].

3.1. Remarques simplement 'translatees' du manuscrit de Pierre d'Abano

La première catégorie, à savoir celle des remarques reprises du commentaire de Pierre d'Abano, est la plus importante à l'intérieur des commentaires à tendance critique. À l'instar de N. Siraisi, on peut reconnaître certaines tendances dans la façon dont Pierre d'Abano se comporte face aux idées d'Aristote[69]. Ainsi, Pierre d'Abano essaie généralement d'opposer les différentes voix de plusieurs autorités afin de les réconcilier. Nous classifierons ces commentaires dans la catégorie des 'digressions scientifiques'. Un deuxième mouvement consiste à réfuter la thèse d'Aristote lorsque d'autres autorités et l'expérience prouvaient le contraire. Enfin, de temps en temps, Pierre d'Abano résout les contradictions dans le texte d'Aristote. Schématiquement, on pourrait représenter ces types de la façon suivante:

Commentaires empruntés à tendance critique dans la partie 'glose':

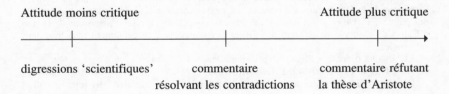

Attitude moins critique | Attitude plus critique

digressions 'scientifiques'   commentaire   commentaire réfutant
                              résolvant les contradictions   la thèse d'Aristote

3.1.1. Digressions 'scientifiques'

Pierre d'Abano et, partant, Évrart de Conty essaient fréquemment d'opposer les différentes voix de plusieurs autorités afin de les réconcilier[70].

---

68. Voir ci-dessus le schéma dans le paragraphe 1.

69. Siraisi, 'The *Expositio Problematum*...', p. 336.

70. Cependant, Évrart de Conty insère parfois des renvois qu'on ne retrouve pas dans le texte de Pierre. Un exemple est discuté dans De Leemans – Goyens, 'La transmission

Beaucoup de gloses se révèlent donc être 'scientifiques'. Ces digressions servent notamment à juxtaposer et à confronter différentes théories.

Dans le problème 43 par exemple, Pierre d'Abano et Évrart de Conty n'hésitent pas à mettre le doigt sur certaines contradictions repérables dans les théories des différents auteurs. Ainsi, ils mentionnent que la théorie d'Avicenne à propos du poivre semble être le contraire de ce qu'Aristote dit:

> PDA: Sed admirabitur aliquis cum inveniat sermonem Avicennae secundo canonis capitulo de pipere omnino huic contrarium; et est quod piper provocat urinam et eicit fetum et post choytum corrumpit semen cum fortitudine et paucum eius provocat urinam et multum eius solvit ventrem sed contrarium scamonea. *Quia tamen in Aristotelis insistitur expositione dicendum eius sermonem verum esse*[71].
>
> EDC: Toute fois sambl'il que Avicennes, u chapitre du poivre, woeille dire le contraire de ce que Aristotes dit en cest probleme, car il dit que poivre, en petite quantité, multeplie le orine; et en grant, il lasche le ventre, au contraire de scamonee, *mais le dit de Aristote est plus raisonnable et plus apparant estre vray*[72].

Notons que tant Pierre qu'Évrart mentionnent que le texte d'Aristote est plus logique.

Par la suite, les deux commentateurs signalent un problème d'interprétation. Ils résolvent le problème en disant qu'il s'agit ici tout simplement d'une question de terminologie: là où Avicenne parle d'une petite quantité, il faudrait interpréter ceci comme étant une grande quantité chez Aristote et lorsqu'il parle d'une grande quantité, il faut entendre une 'tres grande et excessive dose'[73]. Cependant, la glose dans la traduction française est légèrement différente. Évrart suppose notamment que

des savoirs …', dans lequel ils discutent les 'sources personnelles' d'Évrart de Conty à l'intérieur de la 20ᵉ section. Ce procédé est également discuté dans GOYENS, 'Le lexique des plantes…'. De ce point de vue, on pourrait considérer ce type d'insertions de la part d'Évrart de Conty comme étant des gloses personnelles. Voir également plus loin dans cet article.

71. PIERRE D'ABANO, *Expositio problematum…*, fol. 27ra.

72. Ms. Paris BNF fr. 24281, fol. 44r.

73. PDA: 'Dictum autem Avicennae incontrarium non intelligo nisi intelligat illud quod Aristoteles appellat multam quantitatem Avicenna parvam dicat et multam dicat Avicenna postea quantitatem maximam'. Voir: Pierre D'ABANO, *Expositio problematum…*, fol. 27va.

EDC: 'Il ne samble mie dont c'on doie arrester au dit de Avicenne en cest pas, se on ne le voloit ainsi exposer, et dire qu'il entent par le grant quantité, dont Aristotes parle, la petite, et aprés par la grant quantité, dont Avicennes parle, qu'il entent la tres grande et excessive dose, de laquel dose excessive il dit aprés que, quant on prent de scamonee la moitié de une dragme, elle restraint premierement le ventre et fait grant perturbation et grant angoisse et froide sueur. Mais finablement, aucune fois elle lasche et maine le pacient dusques a la mort. Ainsi les porroit on acorder aucunement et non pas bien plainement.' Ms. Paris BNF fr. 24281, fol. 44v.

cette erreur est due à une traduction fautive, tandis que Pierre mentionne que les savants ne s'entendent pas :

> PDA : Est autem causa istius sermonis Aristotelis curiosa et calumpniosa valde et maxime quia *sapientes non conveniunt* in causato ut iam patuit[74].
> EDC : Et pource porroit on dire que *ces mos de Avicenne furent mal translaté*, ou par inadvertence ou aultrement. Et ce sambl'il par ce qu'il dit u chapitre de scamonee ou il dit que la scamonee viese, selonc ce que aucun dient, prise en petite quantité multeplie le orine et ne lasce mie[75].

Dans le 19e problème, Évrart, à l'instar de Pierre d'Abano, signale que les propos d'Aristote dans ce problème vont à l'encontre de ce que dit Hippocrate dans son livre *De aere et aqua* :

> PDA : Notandum quod ista constitutio anni est contraria constitutioni anni saluberrimi[76].
> EDC : La constitution de tans de l'an que Aristotes met en cest probleme est droitement contraire a la bonne disposition du tans et de l'an dont Ypocras fait mencion en son livre *De aere et aqua*, ou il dit que li ans tres bons et tres sains entre les autres est cils u quel les elevations et les esconsemens des estoiles se font deuement, c'est a dire quant li tans de l'an se commencent naturelment et se continuent ausy aprés ainsy qu'il doivent, en tel maniere que li antompnes n'ayt que poy de yaues et de ploeuves, et li hyvers en ayt plenté et qu'il ne soit ne plus frois ne plus seris qu'il appartient, et que li prins tans et li estés ausy soient atempreement pluvieus. Comme dont la disposition de l'an dont Aristotes fait mention en cest probleme soit precisement contraire a celle tres bonne et tres saine constitution desus dite dont Ypocras parle, ce n'est pas merveilles s'elle est pestilentiele et mal saine[77].

3.1.2. Commentaires résolvant les contradictions apparentes dans le texte d'Aristote

Dans la partie 'glose' du problème 37, Évrart rend d'une manière assez fidèle le texte de Pierre d'Abano. Ainsi, il reprend même les paragraphes dans lesquels ce dernier émet des doutes à propos de ce qu'Aristote dit :

> Aristotes toutefoys parle du sel commun et artificiel en cest probleme. Aucuns qui regarderoit le texte de Aristote en cest probleme porroit doubter de ce qu'il dit que le humour qui est entre les dens, qui fait la congelation desus dite et l'entommissement, ha en li une acuité, car

---

74. Pierre d'Abano, *Expositio problematum*..., fol. 27va.
75. Ms. Paris BNF fr. 24281, fol. 44v.
76. Pierre d'Abano, *Expositio problematum*..., fol. 16ra.
77. Ms. Paris BNF fr. 24281, fol. 27r.

chose agüe est par nature chaude et seche u quart degré, et tel chose
ne poet faire tel congelation[78].

Évrart renforce, à l'instar de Pierre, cette idée en citant les paroles de
Haly Abbas à ce propos: 'et pource dit Haly Abbas que la congelation
des dens se fait quant aucuns masche aucune chose aygre ou sure ou
quant il ha en l'estomac aucune tele humour, et tel chose par nature
froide[79]'. Il résout le problème en démontrant qu'Aristote interprète
'acuité' d'une autre façon:

> A ce poet on respondre que Aristotes ne prent mie cy acuité en sa pro-
> pre signification, comme il fu dit u .32e. probleme, mais le prent pour
> acetosité ou aigreté, si comme nous disons que vins aygre ha aucune
> acuité quant il est fort, et communement on appele les choses sures et
> aigres, agües. Et au dire voir, il y ha volentiers aucune autre amellee
> avoec la sure ou le acetosité desus dite.
> Car ausy comme Galiens dit, on ne troeuve riens de pur, simplement
> ains est toute chose composee de tout, c'est a dire que en une chose
> est trouvee aucunement la nature de l'autre[80].

Dans le problème 48, il s'agit de la question de savoir si les plantes
bien odorantes sont digestibles et diurétiques. À l'exemple de Pierre
d'Abano, Évrart met le doigt sur un paradoxe dans le texte d'Aristote.
Plus tôt, dans le problème 40, Aristote avait expliqué que les choses diurétiques ne peuvent pas être digérées. À cet effet, Pierre d'Abano et
Évrart de Conty remarquent qu'il faut distinguer deux manières de
digestibilité. De cette façon, il n'y a donc pas de contradiction dans les
paroles d'Aristote, ce qu'Évrart tient à souligner dans une phrase con-
clusive:

> Et se aucuns faisoit doubte de ce que Aristotes dit que les choses bien
> odourables sont bien digestibles, et pource diuretiques, car il fu dit u
> .40e. probleme que les choses diuretiques qui multeplient le orine sont
> par nature yaueuses et plainnes de humidité; et tels choses sont
> medecinauls et per consequens indigestibles, *et ainsi sambleroit il que
> Aristotes se contredie.*
> On poet a ce respondre que une chose poet estre dite digestible en .ii.
> manieres, ou pource qu'elle est de sa nature convenable a estre
> digeree et a nourrir, ou pource qu'elle fait ayde a digerer les autres
> choses, ja soit ce qu'elle, de sa nature, ne soit mie convenable a estre
> digeree. Selonc donc la premiere maniere, les choses diuretiques ne
> sont mie digestibles, mais elles le sont selonc la seconde maniere, car
> tels choses ont une chaleur qui fait les autres choses digestibles
> digerer et pource dit Avicennes que raphanus digere, mais il ne poet

---

78. Ms. Paris BNF fr. 24281, fol. 38r-38v.
79. Ms. Paris BNF fr. 24281, fol. 38v.
80. Ms. Paris BNF fr. 24281, fol. 38v.

estre digerés *et ainsi poet on exposer les paroles de Aristotes et ramener a bon sens sans contradiction*[81].

Dans le 51ᵉ problème, Évrart parle à l'exemple de Pierre d'Abano des
doutes que soulève le texte d'Aristote à propos de la nourriture des ma-
lades. Plus précisément, ils mentionnent que les idées d'Aristote sem-
blaient s'opposer aux idées d'Hippocrate. Les deux commentateurs signalent d'ailleurs qu'Aristote traite ce problème d'une manière assez
insolite.

PDA: Aristoteles habuit modum insolitum proponendi problema[82].
EDC: Aristotes propose cest probleme par maniere inacoustumee[83].

Selon Évrart, cette manière d'exposer le problème est vraisemblablement influencée par les habitudes des médecins de son temps:

Aristotes dont propose ceste demande par maniere de doubte, pource
que aucun medecin a son tans commandoient que li malade au commencement de lor maladie ne mengaissent dusques au tiers jour, les
quels Galiens reprent moult aigrement[84].

Toutefois, les deux commentateurs résolvent la discordance entre les
idées d'Aristote et de Galien d'une part et la théorie d'Hippocrate
d'autre part. En signalant qu'il faut envisager différents cas de maladies,
Pierre et Évrart démontrent que la théorie de Galien s'accorde avec celle
d'Hippocrate: 'Et ainsi acorde Galiens les .ii. paroles de Ypocras desus
dites qui sambleroient au mal entendant de premiere faice contraires'[85].

À cet effet, Évrart souligne à maintes reprises l'importance du bon
entendement d'Hippocrate:

Pour desclairier dont ceste doubte des paroles de Ypocras, nous devons savoir que Ypocras dit bien et voir et sans contradiction qui bien
l'entent [...]. Selonc la verité ainsi entent Aristotes c'on doit regarder
la vertu du malade et les circonstances particuleres au commencement
de sa maladie[86].

3.1.3. Commentaire réfutant la thèse d'Aristote

À titre d'exemple, nous citons quelques cas dans lesquels Évrart formule à l'instar de Pierre d'Abano des remarques critiques vis-à-vis
d'Aristote. Bien qu'on les rencontre moins fréquemment que les digressions 'scientifiques', ce groupe représente quand même un nombre important.

81. Ms. Paris BNF fr. 24281, fol. 47r.
82. Pierre D'ABANO, *Expositio problematum*..., fol. 30r.
83. Ms. Paris BNF fr. 24281, fol. 48v.
84. Ms. Paris BNF fr. 24281, fol. 48v.
85. Ms. Paris BNF fr. 24281, fol. 49r.
86. Ms. Paris BNF fr. 24281, fol. 49r.

Déjà au cours du troisième problème, Pierre d'Abano et Évrart contredisent l'idée d'Aristote que les astres provoqueraient un changement de l'air. Il cite alors Ptolémée qui dit que c'est au contraire le soleil et les signes qui en sont la cause[87].

N. Siraisi a déjà montré que Pierre d'Abano ne réfute la thèse d'Aristote que lorsque d'autres autorités et l'expérience prouvaient le contraire de ce qu'il disait[88]. Évrart de Conty et Pierre d'Abano dénoncent aussi le fait qu'Aristote n'aurait pas proprement vérifié ce qu'ils déclarent au problème 42 : 'et aussy la parole de Aristote en cest probleme comme elle soit medecinal n'est verifiie ne ne doit estre estendue fors en l'omme et non pas es autres bestes'[89]. Plus précisément, Pierre d'Abano n'est pas d'accord avec Aristote quant au fait que le cuivre, l'argent et les matières de ce genre ne peuvent pas être digérés par la chaleur animale. Pierre d'Abano, ainsi qu'Évrart de Conty, argumentent que ceci est en désaccord avec ce que dit Averroès et qu'Aristote a uniquement vérifié sa thèse sur l'homme, sans la tester sur les animaux.

3.2. Interventions dans lesquelles Évrart de Conty adapte le commentaire de Pierre d'Abano

Le nombre d'interventions dans lesquelles Évrart de Conty modifie les idées de Pierre d'Abano, est beaucoup plus restreint, mais elles sont en général intéressantes. Citons à titre d'exemple le problème 9 de la première section. Évrart de Conty y commence la partie 'glose' en paraphrasant le discours de Pierre d'Abano. Cependant, il la structure différemment. Au lieu de commencer par invoquer ce que Hippocrate dit à ce propos, comme le fait Pierre d'Abano, Évrart préfère entamer sa glose en rendant d'abord le deuxième paragraphe du texte de Pierre, ce qui lui permet de continuer son texte en commentant la question posée par Aristote, et établit ainsi un lien avec le problème précédent :

> PDA : Unde in hoc videtur hoc problema conversum differre a priori[90]
> EDC : Cils problemes est ausi comme li revers de l'autre probleme precedent[91]

Évrart ne suivra pas le raisonnement de Pierre d'Abano tel quel dans ce commentaire. Ainsi, lorsqu'on parle de 'la superhabondance des hu-

---

87. Ms. Paris BNF fr. 24281, fol. 11r.
88. SIRAISI, 'The *Expositio Problematum...*', p. 336.
89. Ms. Paris BNF fr. 24281, fol. 42v.
90. Pierre D'ABANO, *Expositio problematum...*, fol. 11ra.
91. Ms. Paris BNF fr. 24281, fol. 16v.

midités assamblees en hiver⁹²', il abrège le texte de Pierre d'Abano d'une façon considérable, tout en signalant que certains commentent ce problème autrement: 'Aucuns exposent autrement ceste partie en le continuant a l'autre de devant'⁹³. Ensuite, il suit de nouveau le texte de Pierre d'Abano, tout en omettant certains passages. Vers la fin, Évrart reprend alors les idées-clés de ce problème après s'être plaint de la difficulté du texte:

> C'est la sentence de cest probleme dont li textes est moult obscurs et resamble moult a l'amphorisme que Ypocras met de ceste matere. Les maladies dont qui s'ensievent a l'yver austrin et au prin tans boreal sont .5. selonc Aristote. Premierement, les fames qui ont lor terme de enfanter en prin tans abortissent de legier pour la grant froidure contraire as enfans, et s'il vivent, si sont il feble et imparfait. Secondement, li colerique qui a ce sont disposé en ont mal es yeuls et obtalmies seches. Tiercement, li flegmatique en sont encombré de tous et rumes diverses⁹⁴.

Notons qu'Évrart introduit dans la suite lui-même tout un passage expliquant qu'il existe 5 manières de flegme.

Dans le 18ᵉ problème de la première section, Évrart traduit le texte très librement. Sa traduction se caractérise ici par quelques adaptations qui rendent le texte d'Aristote plus compréhensible. Ainsi, il commence la glose en précisant ce qu'Aristote comprend par *ulceres*: 'Aristotes en cest probleme entent par ulceres toutes manieres de plaies et toute solution de continuité qui se poet faire en la teste ou aillours u cors humain'⁹⁵. Dans le texte latin de Pierre d'Abano, on retrouve cette idée un peu plus loin dans l'exposé:

> Notandum est quod per ulcera contingit intelligere omnem solutionem continuitatis sive sit plaga que est solutio ex recenti tempore vel vulnus sive ulcus quod est ex longinqua iam habens saniem sive attritio sive excoriatio vel scarificatio aut fissura⁹⁶.

Évrart de Conty tend à expliciter le plus possible. Lorsque nous retrouvons dans le texte latin '[…] partes superiores ut partes capitis sunt bene expurgabiles emittentes superflua sua per multas vias vel digestibiles'⁹⁷, Évrart rend cette phrase par 'La teste ausy ha pluseurs voyes par lesqueles elle se delivre de ses superfluités diverses, si comme les

92. Ms. Paris BNF fr. 24281, fol. 17r.
93. Ms. Paris BNF fr. 24281, fol. 17r.
94. Ms. Paris BNF fr. 24281, fol. 17r.
95. Ms. Paris BNF fr. 24281, fol. 26v.
96. Pierre D'ABANO, *Expositio problematum...*, fol. 15vb.
97. Pierre D'ABANO, *Expositio problematum...*, fol. 15vb.

oreilles, les yeuls, les narines et le palais, et meesmement les os de la teste ou il ha pluseurs pieches et diverses coustures'[98], où il ajoute donc des exemples concrets tels que 'les oreilles, les yeuls', etc. pour expliquer ce qu'il faut entendre par 'voies'. Pierre d'Abano continue cette partie en donnant les renvois précis au problème 14 qui parle du même sujet. Évrart se contente ici de dire 'comme il fu dit devant'.

Il n'est pas très clair d'où Évrart de Conty prend certaines idées dans ce problème 18. Il semble parfois ajouter des observations personnelles. De même, il ajoute une conclusion qui ne se trouve pas dans le texte latin: 'Et la raison de toutes les choses desus dites si est pour ce que les ulceres ne les plaies ne se garissent point, comme dit Avicennes, s'elles ne sont ançois modefiies et desechies, laquel chose se fait mieuls ou il ha mains de superfluités'[99].

Dans beaucoup de cas d'ailleurs, Évrart ne suit pas servilement la structure du texte de Pierre. Assez souvent, il organise son texte d'une autre manière en employant les données du texte de Pierre. Parfois, il les abrège. De temps en temps, il explicite plus que Pierre[100].

3.3. Interventions personnelles d'Évrart de Conty, absentes du commentaire de Pierre d'Abano

La troisième subdivision renferme les interventions plus personnelles d'Évrart de Conty, absentes du commentaire de Pierre d'Abano, qui sont plutôt rares. Ainsi, nous avons déjà évoqué ci-dessus quelques cas dans lesquels Évrart ne suit pas le modèle latin de Pierre d'Abano (cf. 3.2.). L'observation suivante montre en outre qu'Évrart se rend compte du fait que son objectif principal de 'traduire' fidèlement le texte et le commentaire constitue en quelque sorte un désavantage. Ainsi, dans la section 33, Évrart admet que son texte pourrait être tout aussi difficile à comprendre suite au fait qu'il s'efforce de suivre les paroles d'Aristote:

> La translation du texte de Aristotes en cest probleme est un petit obscure et estrange de premiere faice et pource, comme il ha esté dit autrefois et promis des le commencement de cest livre que je voloie aucunement ensivre le texte et les paroles de Aristotes en ceste oeuvre, selonc ce qu'il me seroit possible, ce n'est mie merveilles se ceste premiere translation ou exposition en françois est aucunement obscure aussi[101].

98. Ms. Paris BNF fr. 24281, fol. 26v.
99. Ms. Paris BNF fr. 24281, fol. 26v.
100. Cf. supra: voir 2.1. sur les gloses à tendance purement pédagogique.
101. Ms. Paris BNF fr. 24282, fol. 226v.

À part les remarques à propos de l'obscurité du texte source et de sa traduction[102], Évrart de Conty donne également des précisions à propos de sa méthode. Ainsi, dans le problème 7 de la première section, il donne la cause qui l'a incité à développer un peu plus ce problème: 'Et pour ce dit Galiens que malvais airs nuit plus que malvaise viande et se apartient ausi miex a cest present pourpos, *et pour ce y arresterai ge un petit plus*'. De même, dans son introduction à la science de la médecine, Évrart de Conty parle maintes fois à la première personne. Ainsi, nous rencontrons des passages tels que:

> Ausy est il des .4. elemens comme *je* di[103], [...] et est pour la raison des .4. humours dont *je* parlerai cy après, qui sont de telle nature[104].
> Et de ce *me* samble il que les cysternes faites a la maniere de celles que on fait a Venice communement sont les meillours pour bien garder ceste yaue du ciel de putrefaction. La maniere que *je* di si est tele [...][105].

Par la formule 'il samble que'[106], ou en utilisant 'c'est ce que woelt dire selonc ma consideration'[107], Évrart offre une voie d'interprétation personnelle en imposant de façon subtile ses propres idées, tout en se disculpant d'une erreur d'interprétation, car assez souvent, le texte est 'moult obscurs'[108]. Ces justifications à propos de sa manière de travailler et la présence de son nom dans *l'explicit*[109] dénotent une fois de plus une certaine subjectivité[110].

En outre, Évrart se distancie parfois de certaines idées d'Aristote, sans toutefois suivre Pierre d'Abano[111]. Ainsi, dans son exposé sur l'organisation de la médecine, Évrart de Conty rejette catégoriquement l'idée que le corps ne serait composé que de sang, comme Aristote l'avait affirmé dans son *De animalibus*. Il précise alors que, sans aucun doute, les

---

102. Voir aussi la section 2 de cet article.

103. Ms. Paris BNF fr. 24281, fol. 3r.

104. Ms. Paris BNF fr. 24281, fol. 3v.

105. Ms. Paris BNF fr. 24281, fol. 22v.

106. Voir GUICHARD-TESSON, 'Le métier de traducteur ...', p. 160: 'Évrart est à la fois conscient des qualités qu'exige sa tâche et prudent dans ses interprétations, fréquemment introduites par 'il semble que''.

107. Voir par exemple: 'Et pource dit il ausi finablement que ceste humidités de dedens (...) se osteroit a grant painne (...), c'est ce que woelt dire selonc ma consideration'. Ms. Paris BNF fr. 24281, fol. 51v.

108. Voir par exemple ms. Paris BNF fr. 24281, fol. 24v.

109. Voir note 20.

110. Les anecdotes concernant sa propre expérience rendent le commentaire également 'personnel': voir notamment GUICHARD-TESSON, 'Le métier de traducteur ...', p. 165. Voir aussi plus haut dans cet article.

111. Comp. ci-dessus, sous 3.1.3. les cas où il se distancie des idées d'Aristote à l'exemple de Pierre d'Abano.

quatre humeurs sont d'une telle utilité au corps que, sans eux, le corps serait continuellement malade:

> Et supposé que li cors humains en sa premiere formation soit a la rei verité composés tant seulement de sanc et ausi depuys nourris et continués, tant que la vie dure, en tel maniere que les autres humours ne faicent riens a ceste chose quant a la substance materiele d'yceli, comme il samble que Aristotes woeille dire en son livre *de Animalibus* et Averroys ausy en son *Colliget, toute foys n'est il pas doute que elles sont toutes au sanc si necessairement acompaingnies* et ont u cors humain si grans utilités en pluseurs cas que sans elles toutes quatre, il ne porroit demourer un seul moment sanz corruption[112].

Dans la glose du 20ᵉ problème de la première section, Évrart de Conty recourt une fois de plus au livre *De aere et aqua* d'Hippocrate, à l'instar de Pierre d'Abano. Évrart de Conty ajoute ici l'idée qu'il existe une espèce de contradiction entre les affirmations d'Hippocrate et le texte d'Aristote, qu'il résout en même temps:

> Et s'il samble qu'il y ayt contradiction pour ce que Ypocras dit que li flegmatique en encourent fievres causoniques et Aristotes dit que cil qui sont rare les encourent, laquel disposition samble miex estre deue as coleriques et as sanguins, et ainsi il samble que ce que Ypocras dit des flegmatiques, que Aristotes die des coleriques, on poet respondre que li flegmatique ont la char plus rare, quant a nostre pourpos[113], que li colerique ne li sanguin qui sont bien composé et bien musculeus n'ont, car il ont la char mole et recevable de superfluités, combien que li colerique et li sanguin l'ayent plus poreuse, pour la raison de la chaleur de lor complexion qui purge miex la superfluité des pores[114].

Cette remarque semble venir de lui-même, puisqu'elle ne figure pas dans le commentaire de Pierre d'Abano. Qui plus est, dans la marge droite, Évrart ajoute auprès de ces phrases 'quant a nostre pourpos'.

Dans le problème 46, Évrart modifie quelque peu la partie 'glose' par rapport au texte de Pierre d'Abano. Ainsi, il invoque des paroles de Fulgentius. Évrart omet aussi la remarque de Pierre traitant de l'opposition apparente entre les idées d'Aristote et celles d'Hippocrate en ce qui concerne la conservation de la santé. Évrart insère dans sa glose une remarque à propos du fait qu'il faut louer le seigneur.

> Et pource se doivent resjoir cil qui criennent et doubtent les medecines laxatives et la sainnie, car s'il se woelent deuement exerciter, il n'auront mestier des choses desus dites. Car ceste

---

112. Ms. Paris BNF fr. 24281, fol. 4r.
113. En marge droite.
114. Ms. Paris BNF fr. 24281, fol. 28r.

excercitations les excusera de medecine de sainnie et de baingn et se
n'y ha en excercitation ne paour, ne amertume, ne despens, ains est
chose joieuse et recreations tres grande de cors et d'ame. Especialment quant ce se fait en biau lieu, net et plaisant, et en bon air et sain,
car nature humaine s'esjoist en veir diverses choses loingns et prés, si
comme le ciel et la terre, et la mer, et la verdure; et les autres choses
qui embellissent le monde, des quels choses on doit loer et magnefiier
le Createur qui ainsy ha tout ordené si esmerveillablement, et de tant
fait le excercitation desus dite aussi a recommender, qui finablement
ainsy ramainne le createur pardurable a la memoire de l'excercitation[115].

Il termine cette glose en s'adressant directement à son public en utilisant la première personne du singulier, le 'je', afin de dire qu'il n'expo-
sera pas comment il faut conserver une bonne santé:

De la maniere comment on se doit excerciter; et des diversités, des
excercitations, et de pluseurs choses qui toucent ceste matere ne
parleray *je* plus quant a present pour cause de brieté[116].

Ces fragments montrent qu'Évrart de Conty n'hésite pas à faire entendre sa propre voix, voire à mettre en relief ses propres idées, non seulement quant à l'organisation du texte, mais également au niveau de l'interprétation même.

Conclusion

Des données qui précèdent il ressort qu'Évrart suit pour la plupart du
temps fidèlement l'exemple de Pierre d'Abano en ce qui concerne la critique à l'égard d'Aristote.

Dès lors, les adaptations personnelles quant au contenu des gloses de
la part d'Évrart sont assez rares. L'apport personnel se situe souvent à
l'intérieur du domaine de l'organisation du savoir et de sa vulgarisation,
puisqu'il faut y percevoir les mêmes techniques pédagogiques que celles
présentées dans la première catégorie, à savoir celle des interventions
générales, pédagogiques, neutres.

En prenant le lecteur par la main d'une telle façon, Évrart de Conty
incarne le clerc-philosophe qui guide son public à travers la *matere obscure* d'Aristote, tout en la clarifiant par ses explications supplémentaires, par ses renvois, par des exemples éloquents et des anecdotes. De
même, il abrège le commentaire de Pierre d'Abano, il le rend plus lisible

115. Ms. Paris BNF fr. 24281, fol. 46r.
116. Ms. Paris BNF fr. 24281, fol. 46r.

en éliminant les critiques superflues et en signalant les passages difficiles.

La subjectivité d'Évrart de Conty se reflète donc à travers son souci
didactique, puisque les cas où il offre des remarques critiques originelles
qu'on ne retrouve pas chez Pierre d'Abano, sont moins fréquents.

Toutefois, derrière un effacement personnel se cache quand même un
translateur très conscient de sa tâche qui ne peut s'empêcher de venir à
l'avant-plan pour émettre de temps en temps ses idées personnelles.
Ainsi, Évrart de Conty se sent un nain par rapport au géant qu'est Aristote. Plus précisément, il se trouve sur les épaules d'un commentateur
qui lui, siégeait sur les épaules d'Aristote, ce qui le mettait dans une situation favorable. Les interventions et les ajouts 'scientifiques' doivent
alors être imputés à l'évolution du temps, ce qui jette une lumière différente sur les idées antiques. Dès lors, ces ajouts ne doivent nullement
être interprétés comme une dépréciation des idées d'Aristote. Bref,
Évrart de Conty se dessine comme un pédagogue, capable d'associer
science et *sentence* dans ses gloses, tout en essayant d'intégrer ses lecteurs au maximum dans le monologue encyclopédique qu'il leur adresse.
En effet, dans certains passages, Évrart s'adresse directement à son public en justifiant sa méthode de travail à travers l'emploi de la première
personne. L'insertion des exemples concrets et les digressions explicati-
ves peuvent également être considérées comme une manière d'attirer
l'attention de ses lecteurs.

Qui plus est, Évrart donne la possibilité au lecteur de s'approfondir en
la matière en renvoyant à maintes sources, souvent à l'instar de Pierre
d'Abano. Bref, la *translatio studii* n'ôte rien à la valeur scientifique de
cette 'vulgarisation'. Il vise en même temps à ouvrir le débat et à stimuler les réflexions médicales de façon théorique afin d'ouvrir de cette façon le débat en langue vernaculaire. Plus précisément, à côté du but
premier de 'translater', de respecter et d'expliquer les *Problemes* d'Aristote, Évrart réserve également une place à la discussion et à la réflexion
scientifique. Ainsi, il ne se lasse jamais de citer de façon très précise les
sources auxquelles il fait allusion.

Les observations dénotant le fait que le texte d'Aristote est parfois
'daté', ainsi que les adaptations parfois explicites par rapport aux idées
'aristotéliciennes', souvent à l'instar de Pierre d'Abano, indiquent que
les traducteurs-commentateurs n'hésitent pas à adhérer plutôt aux convictions médicales plus récentes qu'au texte d'Aristote. De même, l'utilisation de la première personne dans le commentaire d'Évrart et certaines remarques par rapport à la cohérence du texte d'Aristote, par rapport
au texte source et par rapport à sa traduction même, montrent qu'il ose

exposer sa position. De ce point de vue, Évrart de Conty donne une touche personnelle, avant tout à la traduction du commentaire mais parfois aussi à la paraphrase du problème, même s'il veut rester près du texte d'Aristote et quoiqu'il résolve souvent discrètement des paradoxes dans le texte d'Aristote.

D'une façon générale, Évrart de Conty doit être considéré comme un glossateur didactique des commentaires de Pierre d'Abano, offrant à son public une traduction des *Problemata* en moyen français et un commentaire scientifique, actualisé et assez personnalisé d'une édition des *Problemes* d'Aristote, tout en y ajoutant des notes de bas de page justifiant et corrigeant les idées du grand philosophe.

Katholieke Universiteit Leuven

John MONFASANI

GEORGE OF TREBIZOND'S CRITIQUE
OF THEODORE GAZA'S TRANSLATION
OF THE ARISTOTELIAN *PROBLEMATA*

L'invective Protectio Problematum Aristotelis *de Georges de Trébizonde contre Théodore Gaza reflète la collision d'idées opposées concernant la manière de traduire Aristote. En condamnant les traducteurs médiévaux comme des barbares ignorants, Gaza non seulement désira donner à Aristote une apparence 'oratoire', mais aussi crut-il nécessaire de corriger souvent radicalement le texte et même la structure des œuvres d'Aristote. Georges accusa Gaza de pervertir le texte d'Aristote plus qu'il ne le traduisit,* pervertere magis quam vertere. *Il analysa 20 passages de la traduction de Gaza pour démontrer que celui-ci ne comprenait pas Aristote. Il défendit avec verve les traducteurs médiévaux comme étant des* interpretes fidi *et indispensables pour l'essor de la philosophie et la théologie latines – Georges fut un grand admirateur de la scholastique latine. Enfin, Georges présenta une théorie flexible de la traduction dans le sens où il se permet des libertés en traduisant les œuvres littéraires, mais dans le cas des œuvres de science il serre le texte de près.*

George of Trebizond wrote the *Protectio Problematum Aristotelis*, his critique of Theodore Gaza's translation of the Aristotelian *Problemata*, in Rome in 1456[1]. George had completed his own translation of the *Problemata* four years earlier, in 1452 (though he only released it for publication in 1454)[2]; Gaza had followed with a new translation in 1453–54[3]. George's *Protectio* was unquestionably a polemical work, meant to discredit Gaza, who was his rival at the papal court, and to con-

---

1. For the date see my *George of Trebizond: A Biography and a Study of His Rhetoric and Logic*, Leiden: E. J. Brill, 1976, p. 163-165; and *Collectanea Trapezuntiana: Texts, Documents, and Bibliographies of George of Trebizond* (Medieval & Renaissance Texts & Studies 25; Renaissance Texts Series 8), Binghamton, New York: Medieval & Renaissance Texts & Studies, 1984, p. 411-421. The text is available in MOHLER L., *Kardinal Bessarion als Theologe, Humanist und Staatsmann*, 3 vols. (Quellen und Forschungen aus dem Gebiete der Geschichte 20: *Darstellung*; 22: *Bessarionis in Calumniatorem Platonis Libri IV*; 24: *Aus Bessarions Gelehrtenskreis*), Paderborn: Ferdinand Schöningh, 1923, 1927, 1942; reprint Aalen: Scientia Verlag – Paderborn: Ferdinand Schöningh, 1967; in vol. 3, p. 274-342. I am preparing a new edition of this work.

2. See MONFASANI, *George of Trebizond...*, p. 74-75, 150-151; and *Collectanea...*, p. 707-709.

3. See MONFASANI, *George of Trebizond...*, p. 150 n. 79.

demn his oppressors, most especially Cardinal Bessarion. As such, the *Protectio* can be fairly analyzed as a rhetorical *invectiva*, the main goal of which was victory rather than truth. Nonetheless, the *Protectio* is also an extraordinarily interesting work of scholarship and theorizing on the art of translation.

Theodore Gaza had laid out his approach to translation in his preface to Pope Nicholas V, a text that has never been printed and only survives in a handful of manuscripts[4]. The preface that accompanies Gaza's widely available revised translation of the *Problemata*, published twenty years after the original translation, is not by Gaza, but by Gaza's disciple Nicolaus Gupalatinus[5]. In the original preface of 1454 to Nicholas V, Gaza proclaimed that he would transform the traditional scientific vocabulary into proper Latin, substituting *laxum intestinum* for *colon*, *transversum septum* for *diaphragma*, *sideratio* for *dolor*, *rationis victus* for *dieta*, and so forth, while introducing new words and phrases such as *levitas intestinorum*, *nervorum distentio*, *aqua intercutis*, etc. so that the *sententiae* of Aristotle would be truly revealed and in good Latin (*vere Latineque*)[6]. No less importantly, he insisted that Aristotelians should

4. At the moment I know of nine manuscripts of the first redaction of Gaza's translation and five of the second. For the editions see my 'The Pseudo-Aristotelian *Problemata* and Aristotle's *De Animalibus* in the Renaissance', in: A. GRAFTON – N. SIRAISI (eds.), *Natural Particulars: Nature and the Disciplines in Renaissance Europe*, Cambridge, Mass.: MIT Press, 1999, p. 205-247, at p. 205, 213, 232 n. 1, and 243-244 n. 64.

5. See the previous note. Gaza's revised translation (but not Gupalatinus' preface) is most easily available in ARISTOTLE, *Opera*. Ex recensione IMMANUELIS BEKKERI. Edidit Academia Regia Borussica, 5 vols., Berlin: G. Reimer, 1831-1870, vol. 3, p. 415-474; this volume is reprinted in KESSLER E. (ed.), *Aristoteles Latine interpretibus variis edidit Academia Regia Borussica Berlin 1831*, Munich: W. Fink Verlag, 1995.

6. For GAZA's preface and translation I shall cite the dedication copy, MS Biblioteca Apostolica Vaticana, Vat. Lat. 2111; in this case, f. 2v-4v: 'Quod si aequius agere mecum velint cum concoctionem audiunt, non digestionem, cum essentiam aut naturam aut constantiam, non substantiam, cum sunt, non existunt, cum interdum genus et modum potius quam qualitatem et quantitatem, cum aliquis, non quidam, quisque, non quilibet, iubam, non crinem, barbam, non mentum, cum syderationem, non dolorem, horrorem, non horripilationem, transversum septum, non diaphragma, pituitam, non phlegma, abscessum, non apostema, laxum intestinum, non colon, rationem victus, non dietam, cum levitatem intestinorum, nervorum distentionem aut rigorem, articulorum dolorem, aquam intercutem, anginam, gravedinem, destillationem, convulsa collisa, luxata, contusa, cum cetera prope omnia aliter a me audiunt quam ipsi nominare consueverunt, nolint me arbitrari vel qua de re ageretur ignorasse vel quo illi nomine uterentur minime animadvertisse, sed probent industriam qua suis quaeque vocabulis pro viribus interpretari conamur... Tum errores et sordes istorum interpretum adhuc legitis atque defenditis, qui tanti mali causam dederunt? Non in ignem proiicitis? Non nulla potius quam eiusmodi habere vultis? Sinite ista. Sinite pessum ire. Non deerunt vobis interpretationes quae sententias Aristotelis vere Latineque aperiant. Excultius disputare incipite. Nolite vereri ne oratores videamini. Res aliae sunt quae faciunt oratorem. Sermo Latinus ac integer communis omnium est. Sectatores, credo, philosophiae Aristotelicae esse vos vultis. Ergo

not fear to seem to be orators or to dispute in a more polished manner (*excultius*) inasmuch as Aristotle was, in the words of Cicero, a *flumen aureum eloquentiae*[7]. The medieval translator was as ignorant of Latin as he was of Greek. Up to this point, Gaza was simply recapitulating what Leonardo Bruni had said forty years earlier when he offered the first justification of the humanist rhetoricizing method of translating Aristotle[8]. But Gaza diverged from Bruni in two respects. First, as a Greek himself, he acknowledged what Bruni absolutely refused to acknowledge, namely, that Greek had a richer lexicon than Latin[9], though Gaza's solution was the same as Bruni's, namely, replacing the transliterated Greek and even vernacular *termini technici* of the medieval tradition with Latin periphrases of pure classical vocabulary. Second, whereas Bruni had as his foil the Greekless Alonso of Cartegena[10], whose knowledge of Latin literature was no match for Bruni's, Gaza provoked a response from George of Trebizond, a fellow Greek, much experienced as a translator and celebrated as a teacher of Latin eloquence.

In his preface, Gaza gave as an example of the incompetence of the medieval translator his rendering of *Probl.* 10.25, which asks why man lacks a mane, and responds as an answer: 'Is it because he has a beard[11]?' In the medieval version, the problem asks why man lacks a plume of hair (*crinis*) and responds because he has a chin (*mentum*)[12].

---

magistrum imitemini ipsum, qui, cum philosophus gravissimus atque acutissimus esset, studia eloquentiae adeo prae se tulit ut flumen aureum eloquentiae a M. Cicerone appellaretur [*Acad.* II / *Luc.* 119], qui (quod Strabon, Graecus insignis philosophus, scripsit [*Geogr.* 13: 2.4]), cum suos omnes discipulos eloquentia ornavit, tum Theophrastum suum eloquentissimum reddidit. Omnia credite. Aliquando credite, edocentius atque explanatius disputabitis siquem sermonis cultum servaveritis et ornatum.'

7. See the last part of the quotation in the previous note.

8. See BARON H. (ed.), *Leonardo Bruni Aretino Humanistisch-philosophische Schriften mit einer Chronologie seiner Werke und Briefe*, Leipzig: B. G. Teubner, 1928, p. 75-96; and GRIFFITHS G. – HANKINS J. - THOMPSON D., *The Humanism of Leonardo Bruni: Selected Texts, Translation, and Introductions* (Medieval & Renaissance Texts & Studies 46; Renaissance Text Series 10), Binghamton, NY: Medieval & Renaissance Texts & Studies, 1987, p. 213-51.

9. See his preface to Pope Nicholas V, MS Vat. Lat. 2111, f. 3r: 'Nescius non sum, viri docti, et Latinam linguam verborum esse interdum inopem et quae formari aliquando debent vocabula non a quolibet condi oportere, sed ab eo qui et doctrina valet et auctoritate.'

10. See BIRKENMAJER A., 'Der Streit des Alonso von Cartagena mit Leonardo Bruni Aretino', *Beiträge zur Geschichte der Philosophie des Mittelalters* 20 (1922), p. 129-246.

11. *Probl.* 893b17-19: Διὰ τί ὁ ἄνθρωπος χαίτην οὐκ ἔχει; ἢ διότι πώγωνα ἔχει, ὥστε ἡ ἐκεῖ ἀπελθοῦσα τροφὴ τῆς τοιαύτης περιττώσεως εἰς τὰς σιαγόνας ἔρχεται;

12. GAZA's preface to Pope Nicholas V, MS Vat. Lat 2111, f. 3v-4r: 'Quaerit dilucide ac explanate Aristoteles quam ob causam iuba homini nulla sit data a natura. [*Probl.*

Humanist translators had no difficulty pointing out the failings of medieval translators, but they almost never acknowledged their virtues. We shall see that George of Trebizond was different in this respect. Gaza totally ignored the fact that George had preceded him in translating this problem correctly, indeed, more correctly, rendering the problem as 'Quare homo iubam non habet? Vel quia barbam habet[13]?' as opposed to Gaza's 'Cur homini nulla iuba data a natura est? An quoniam barba data est?', which elaborates a simple *habet* (ἔχει in Greek) to *data est* with a dative noun and adds the prepositional phrase *a natura*, which has no basis in the Greek. Gaza was so successful in the pretense that George's translation did not exist that forty years later Angelo Poliziano knew nothing of George's translation when he criticized Gaza's translation of the *Problemata* in chapter 90 of the *Miscellaneorum Centuria*[14]. Even though Poliziano concluded that Gaza's translation of the *De Animalibus* was dependent on George's translation (no doubt because he had in his hands the dedication copy to Pope Nicholas V, the present day manuscript Plut. 84, 9 of the Biblioteca Mediceo-Laurenziana in Florence[15]), the only translation of the *Problemata* to which he could com-

---

10.25] Vester interpres sic vertit: 'Propter quid homo crinem non habet?' Reddit idem auctor rationem hoc modo: 'An propterea quia barba data est?' Interpres sic: 'Aut quia mentum habet?' O hominem rudem omnium ignarum! Crines, quos homines omnes habent, nisi quid praeter accidat, quaerit cur homo non habeat. Et causamne suo quidem errori congruam affert: 'Quia mentum habet'? The medieval translator is, of course, Bartolomeo da Messina. I have consulted MS Vat. Lat. 2112 of the Biblioteca Apostolica Vaticana and the *editio princeps*: Mantua: Paulus de Butzbach, 1475, where it accompanies PIETRO D'ABANO's *Expositio Aristotelis Problematum* (= *Gesamtkatalog der Wiegendrucke* 2453). Bartolomeo's translation of Bk. 1 is available in SELIGSOHN R., *Die Übersetzung der ps.-aristotelischen Problemata durch Bartholomaeus von Messina. Text und textkritische Untersuchungen zum ersten Buch*, Berlin: E. Eberling, 1934. His translation of Bk. 11 is available in MARENGHI G. (ed.), *Aristotele. Problemi di fonazione e di acustica*, Naples: Scientifica Editrice, 1962, p. 103-117; and of Bks. 34-37 in MARENGHI G. (ed.), *Aristotele. Problemi di medicina*, Milan: Istituto editoriale italiano, 1965, p. 337-349.

13. Pieter De Leemans has pointed out to me that Pietro d'Abano had also interpreted Bartolomeo's *crinis* to mean *iuba*. (PIETRO D'ABANO, *Expositio*, f. [120rI]: 'non habet crinem, id est, iubam'). George's translation was not printed in the Renaissance (see MONFASANI, *Collectanea...*, p. 707-709). I have consulted two dedication copies in the Bibliotheca Apostolica Vaticana: Urb. Lat. 1322 and Vat. Lat. 5790; in this instance, *Probl.* 10.25 is to be found on f. 44v and f. 55r respectively. G. MARENGHI has edited many parts of George's translation: Bks. 1, 6, 9, 14, 27-28, 31-33 in *Problemi di Medicina*; p. 275-336; Bk. 11 in *Problemi di fonazione e di acustica*, p. 121-135; and Bks. 12-13 in *Aristotele. Profumi e miasmi* (Università degli studi di Salerno. Quaderni del dipartimento di scienze dell'antichità 10), Naples: Arte Tipografica, 1991, p. 165-177.

14. Poliziano A., *Opera Omnia*, 3 vols., ed. I. MAÏER, Turin: Bottega d'Erasmo, 1970-1971 (vols. 1 and 2 = reprint of the Basel, 1553 edition), vol. 1, p. 301-303.

15. See MONFASANI, *Collectanea...*, p. 16-17, 705-707.

pare Gaza's was the medieval translation, which he ascribed to Pietro d'Abano.

George's *Protectio* consists of 35 chapters[16]. Seven of the first eight chapters deal with general and even personal issues; the middle chapters dissect 20 passages from Gaza's translation drawn from nine different books of the *Problemata*; the last chapters sum up George's indictment of Gaza and also digress to discuss extraneous matters, such as the correct interpretation of *Jn.* 21. 22[17], the difference between *loca* and *loci* in Latin[18], and the heathenism of George Gemistus Pletho[19].

The first and most devastating charge that George leveled against Gaza was that Gaza quite misunderstood what was an Aristotelian problem. A problem is not, as Gaza asserted to Nicholas V, a *quaestio*[20], because a *quaestio*, as everyone knows, is a *propositio dubitabilis*, a proposition about something that is in doubt. Rather a problem is the *inquisitio rationis rei sensu patentis*, the investigation of the reason for a thing that is plain to the senses. Not one in a thousand of the problems in the *Problemata*, George explained, corresponds to the definition of a *quaestio*, which concerns things that are in doubt[21]. In fact, although George did not say this, Gaza had confused an Aristotelian problem with a scholastic *quaestio*, where a proposition is stated and arguments given for and against it.

George developed this argument with a discussion of the Greek particle ἤ (or as George called it: *particula E longa*), which begins almost

16. This division of the work into chapters as found in the manuscripts does not correspond to the division MOHLER imposed on his edition, cited in n. 1 above. In references and quotations below, I shall cite the appropriate page and line numbers in MOHLER, but his marginal chapter divisions will be different as will, to a degree, his text since I shall be quoting my new edition, which is still in typescript.

17. Chap. 32 (MOHLER, *Kardinal...*, p. 330.12-337.23).

18. Chap. 33 (MOHLER, *Kardinal...*, p. 337.24-340.2).

19. Chap. 34 (MOHLER, *Kardinal...*, p. 340.3-341.17).

20. Gaza's preface to Pope Nicholas V, MS Vat. Lat. 2111, f. 1v: 'Nunc Aristotelis philosophi quaestiones, quae Problemata inscribuntur Encyclia...'

21. I quote from my unpublished edition and cite MOHLER's (in this case, p. 281.21-31) merely as a point of reference since his edition differs at various points from mine: 'Problema questionem esse ait, cum questio, ut omnes aiunt, propositio sit dubitabilis. Problema vero ne unum quidem inter innumerabilia pene Aristotelis Problemata inveniatur quod ambigue propositum sit, ut vel cuilibet ceco insanoque homini pateat sensu certius ipso quiddam ab Aristotele semper sic proponi ut nullo pacto de re sitne an minime ambigatur, sed vel per sensum certioris rei ratio queratur. Problema enim est, ut hic capitur, rationis rei sensu patentis inquisitio. Legite, legite ipsius philosophi libros Problematum (si qua rerum istiusmodi cura est), queso, si unum de mille vel alterum problema reperitis quibus aut questionis diffinitio conveniat aut hec problematis non congruat.'

every response to the opening question in a problem. George asserted
that in this context the particle was explanatory, *diasaphetice* (διασα-
φητικῶς) as one learns from the *vetusti codices* of Aristotle's *Physics*[22].
I have not found such scholia in the Aristotelian commentators, but one
can easily produce references to the explanatory ἤ from classical gram-
matical works and scholia on Homer[23]. Therefore, the translation of
Bartolomeo of Messina (whom George knew only as the *vetus interpretator*) was inaccurate in its use of the disjunctive *aut* to render the Greek
ἤ. Aristotle did not normally propose either/or solutions, which is what
aut suggests. More to George's point, Theodore Gaza's use of the interrogative particle *an* as a translation of ἤ was terribly misleading since
Aristotle was not proposing a doubtful solution, i. e., he was not proposing a genuine question prefaced by an interrogative. Aristotle's responses were assertions, framed as rhetorical questions. This is why
George translated as *vel quia* the formula ἤ ὅτι with which the *Problemata* normally begins the answer to the question that begins each
problem. *Vel* can carry an assertory sense and signals that the question is
rhetorical, demanding an affirmative response[24].

In point of fact, Helmut Flashar, who has written the most extensive
modern commentary on the *Problemata* (accompanied by a German
translation) fully agrees with George, though, like virtually everyone
else since the mid-Quattrocento, he knows nothing of the *Protectio*. In
the introduction to his commentary, Flashar specifically explains that the
'Antwortformel ἤ ὅτι was 'vorwiegend nur rhetorischen'[25]. Flashar fol-

---

22. (MOHLER, *Kardinal...*, p. 282.32-38): 'Nam et Greci plerisque in locis Physicorum Metaphysicorumque, ubicumque similiter eadem particula ponitur, solutionem per
eam significari <dicunt> solutivamque aut 'diasapheticam', idest, expositivam, nominant.
Nec est ullus mediocriter doctus qui hoc ignoret. In omnibus enim et maxime vetustis
codicibus Physicorum Aristotelis super huiusmodi particula expositio eadem invenitur.'

23. I could not find *diasaphetikos* in the *index verborum* of any of the commentaries
on the *Physics* and *Metaphysics* of the *Commentaria in Aristotelem Graeca. Edita
consilio et auctoritate Academiae Litterarum Regiae Borussicae*, 23 vols., Berlin: G.
Reimer, 1882-1909, nor in any of the anonymous comments reported in BRANDIS C.A.
(ed.), *Scholia in Aristotelem*, which is vol. 4 of ACADEMIA REGIA BORUSSICA, *Aristotelis
Opera*. Ex recensione IMMANUELIS BEKKERI, 5 vols., Berlin: G. Reimer, 1831-1870, nor
in the *Scholiorum in Aristotelem supplementum*, in vol. 5 of the same collection. The CD-
ROM (version E, November 1999) of UNIVERSITY OF CALIFORNIA, IRVINE, *Thesaurus
Linguae Graecae*, confirms these negative results, but also reports attestations in Porphy-
ry's *Quaestiones Homericae*, the *Scholia in Homerum*, Appollonius Dyscolus' *De
Coniunctionibus*, Aelius Herodianus' *De Prosodia Catholica*, and other works, including
two attestations in fragments of the Stoic Chrysippus.

24. This is the argument of George's chapter 6 (MOHLER, *Kardinal...*, p. 294.35-
297.35).

25. FLASHAR H. (tr.), *Aristoteles. Problemata Physica* (Aristoteles Werke in deutscher
Übersetzung 19), Berlin: Akademie Verlag, 1962, p. 341: 'Als ein Handbuch für den

lows through on this opinion in his German translation by putting the explanation of each problem in the form of a declarative sentence, thereby completely eliminating the question format. Hence, in his German translation each response to the opening question of a problem begins 'Doch wohl, weil...' Gherardo Marenghi, who more than anyone else in modern times has studied the manuscript tradition of the *Problemata*, in his earliest translation rendered ἢ ὅτι either as a declarative sentence ('Poiché...', 'Perché...') or as a rhetorical question demanding the answer 'yes' ('Non è perché...' or 'Non sarà perché...')[26]. In his next set of translations he preferred the rhetorical question[27]; and in his last translation (of Bks. 12-13), he did away with the interrogative mode completely and translated ἢ ὅτι as a declarative sentence: 'É perché...'[28]. Pierre Louis in his translation in the Guillaume Budé series uses the neutral interrogative formula 'Est-ce parce que...' rather than 'N'est-ce pas parce que...'[29]. But, as we shall see, Louis was overly influenced by a faith in the correctness of Gaza's translation.

George had one more related general point to make before getting to particular instances of Gaza's translation. Gaza frequently put into the subjunctive the main verb of the opening question of each problem. Not only does such a practice not reflect the Greek text, which is in the indicative, but, George strenuously argued, it perverts Aristotle's intent. The subjunctive in a main verb expresses potentiality; it implies ambiguity as to whether the statement is true or not. But the opening question to each problem asks not whether a phenomenon is a real fact or not, but rather the reason why the perceived phenomenon occurs. The reality of the phenomenon itself is not in question[30]. Of all the translators of the *Problemata*, medieval as well as modern, Gaza is unique in putting the opening question of a problem into modal form.

To dissect Gaza's translation, George used as points of comparison his own translation and that of Bartolomeo of Messina, the *vetus*

Gebrauch der Schule geben sich die Probl. vor allem durch ihre Form zu erkennen: durch die stets mit διὰ τί eingeleitete Frage und die dazugehörige Antwortformel ἢ ὅτι, wobei die Antwort ihrerseits in der Form einer – wenn auch vorwiegend nur rhetorischen – Frage gehalten ist.'

26. MARENGHI G. (ed.), *Aristotele. Problemi musicali* (Edizioni Fussi), Florence: Sansoni, 1957.

27. See his translations in *Problemi di medicina*; and *Problemi di fonazione...*

28. See MARENGHI, *Profumi e miasmi*.

29. LOUIS P. (ed.), *Aristote. Problèmes*, 3 vols. (Collection des universités de France), Paris: Belles Lettres, 1991-1994.

30. This is chapter 4 in the work (MOHLER, *Kardinal...*, p. 289.8-292.1). On the opening question of a problem not involving anything the reality of which is doubt, see FLASHAR, *Problemata ...*, p. 342: 'Da die Frage selbst immer schon eine Behauptung enthält, wird sie oft näher begründet.'

interpretator. Though the medieval translators rendered Aristotle into bad Latin ('alienioribus verbis, idest, minus Latinis'[31]), they were consistently faithful to the text ('veteres integre fideliterque traduxerunt'[32]). Consequently, George at times quoted the medieval translation as a substitute for the Greek text which his Latin audience could not have been expected to understand.

But George used the medieval translation as a witness to the Greek text more than simply for polemical purposes. He also used it as a witness to the Greek text in making his own translation. His translation stopped with Bk. 33 instead of continuing on to the end of Bk. 38 because, as George tells us in the colophon to his translation, that is all his Greek exemplar contained. We also know from a letter of his son Andreas that this Greek exemplar came from Cardinal Bessarion[33]. The Biblioteca Marciana in Venice preserves this Greek exemplar. It is Zan. Gr. 216 (coll. 404), copied by Ioannes Scutariotes for Cardinal Bessarion in 1445, which has the siglum O^a in the literature and which itself derives directly from one of the two oldest and most important manuscripts of the *Problemata*, the thirteenth-century Marcianus Graecus IV, 58 (coll. 1206). Gherardo Marenghi suggested forty years ago that Gr. IV, 58 (which carries the siglum K^a in the literature) was George's exemplar[34]. However, more recently Marenghi corrected his mistake[35]. On the basis of Marenghi's researches and my own edition of Bks. 1, 4, and 30 of George's translation I can confirm that the separative variants overwhelmingly prove that George's exemplar reflected what is called the β family of *Problemata* manuscripts, namely, O^a, K^a, and the Vatican's Palat. Gr. 164, which also derives from K^a and was also copied by Ioannes Scutariotes, in this case for Giannozzo Manetti[36]. But of these

31. MOHLER, *Kardinal...*, p. 299.15.
32. MOHLER, *Kardinal ...*, p. 325.40; see also p. 300.1-2: 'qui iam quantum ad rem integre fideliterque traducti fuerunt'; and 299.11-12: 'ut verbis barbara, ita sensu integerrima est.'
33. MONFASANI, *Collectanea...*, p. 787, §7.
34. MARENGHI, *Problemi di fonazione...*, p. 119 and 130 n. 15.
35. MARENGHI, *Profumi e miasmi*, p. 156-157, 167 ad lin. 6–7, 175 ad lin. 14, 176 ad lin. 2. For a detailed description of the manuscript, where Scutariotes is correctly identified as the scribe, see MIONI E., *Bibliothecae Divi Marci Venetiarum Codices Graeci manuscripti*, 7 vols. (Codices Graeci Manuscripti Bibliothecae Divi Marci Venetiarum), Rome: Istituto poligrafico dello Stato, Libreria dello Stato, 1960-1985, vol. 1, p. 330-31.
36. On the Greek manuscripts and their stemma, especially concerning the β family, MARENGHI has done the most work; in addition to *Problemi di fonazione...*; *Problemi di medicina*; and *Profumi e miasmi*; see his 'La tradizione manoscritta dei *Problemata physici* aristotelici', *Bollettino del Comitato per la preparazione dell'edizione nazionale dei classici greci e latini* n. s. 9 (1961), p. 47-57. The latest description of the manuscripts is by LOUIS, *Problèmes*, vol. 1, p. xxv-l. On Palat. Gr. 164 see STEVENSON E., *Codices*

three manuscripts, only O[a] would have plausibly been in George's hands in 1452. We have no evidence that Bessarion ever possessed K[a], but even if he did, it is not plausible to suppose that he would have sent to Rome from Bologna, where he was papal legate in 1452, such a precious *codex antiquus* rather than the copy O[a]. We do not know the date of Palat. Gr. 164, but it is even less likely that Giannozzo Manetti, who did not reside in Rome until 1453, could have been George's source[37]. More decisively, at Bk.12, probl. 1, 906a28, O[a] alone has the reading καθαρώ-τατον, which explains George's otherwise unique rendering *purissimus*, and at Bk. 13, probl. 6, 908a31, τῷ καυλῷ which explains George's otherwise unique rendering *in caule*[38].

But if George has an overwhelming number of variants peculiar to the β family, he also frequently differed from the β family. Some of these differences are corrections of obvious errors of the β family; some seem to be excellent conjectures; but there are a whole class of variants that he must have taken from Bartolomeo of Messina as his only source for the Greek text other than O[a]. For instance, at Bk. 1, probl. 33 (863a17) George's words 'quousque humidum influet, non consolidabitur' are clearly copied from Bartolomeo's 'quousque utique enim humidum fluit, non consolidabuntur' since the Greek text of the β family completely lacks this passage (ἕως δ' ἂν ὑγρορροῇ, οὐ συμφύσεται)[39]. To take another example, all the Greek manuscripts lack the opening question in problem 4 of Bk. 15, but Bartolomeo has it in his Latin version. So George relied on Bartolomeo's translation for the missing text, just as do all the modern editors of the *Problemata*[40]. In short, George relied on the medieval translation not simply as an aid in translating but also as an alternate source for the Greek text[41].

manuscripti palatini graeci Bibliothecae Vaticanae, Rome: Typographeus Vaticanus, 1885, p. 88, where Scutariotes is rightly identified as the scribe.

37. There is no good modern biography of Manetti, but see the notice by R. PAL-MAROCCHI in the *Enciclopedia Italiana*, vol. 22, Rome: Istituto della Enciclopedia italiana, 1934, p. 108-109.

38. See the apparatus in MARENGHI, *Profumi e miasmi*, p. 78 and 114.

39. See MARENGHI, *Problemi di medicina*, p. 287 and the apparatus to this line on p. 50 for George's translation, but Marenghi seems not to realize that George borrowed the missing words from Bartolomeo. For Bartolomeo's translation of this problem see SELIGSOHN, *Übersetzung...*, p. 37.

40. Bartolomeo's translation runs: 'Propter quid apparitiones figurarum videntur ipsis [ipsis *om. editio Petri Aponi*] nobis eedem? Quia terra centrum?' (Vat. Lat. 2112, f. 17vII; PIETRO D'ABANO, *Expositio*, f. [172rII]). George's runs: 'Quare apparitiones figure similes semper videntur? Vel quia terra centrum?' (Urb. Lat. 1322, f. 67r; Vat. Lat. 5790, f. 80v).

41. For another instance see MARENGHI G., 'Un capitolo dell'Aristotele medievale: Bartolomeo da Messina traduttore dei *Problemata physica*', Aevum 13 (1962), p. 268-83, at 279 for οἱ κιβδηλιῶντες in *Probl.* 1.4 (859b1).

In the *Protectio* George accused Gaza of mixing his own words with those of Aristotle[42]. In more modern times, some editors, such as Pierre Louis, have accepted as authentic Gaza's additions in the naive belief that he must have had access to a manuscript or manuscripts now lost[43]. Working on the principle that all the manuscripts were corrupt, as Nicolaus Gupalatinus tells us[44], Gaza felt authorized to manipulate the Greek text in a sovereign manner. Not only did he fabricate words and phrases that he thought the text needed, add glosses, and paraphrase at will, but he also reorganized the text in ways unrecognizable in the Greek manuscripts. Indeed, in an earlier publication I had to publish thirteen pages of concordances between the Greek text of the *Problemata* and Gaza's translation so that one could compare the two[45]. George complained about the difficulty of locating problems in Gaza's translation, but since, as he explained, he had only *nonnulli quinterniones* of Gaza's translation[46], he never really understood the extent of

42. George hurls this accusation many times; to give some examples: 'Nunc quid facis? Derogas Aristoteli. Multa de suis, quasi maledicta, tollis. Multa addis. Multa commutas. Et que non intelligis, quasi mendosa sint, emendas. Que non pauca sunt.' (MOHLER, *Kardinal...*, p. 299.3-6); and: 'Si multa addere, multa subtrahere, multa mutare in his libris impudenter audent, qui iam quantum ad rem integre fideliterque traducti fuerunt, unde levitas, perfidia, ignorantia sua prostitui potest, quid putatis eos aut fecisse aut facturos in libris qui nondum apud Latinos habentur?' (MOHLER, *Kardinal...*, 299.38-300.4); and: 'Subtrahit, addit, mutat, pervertit, confunditque omnia' (MOHLER, *Kardinal...*, 317.37). Almost all of George's chap. 15, on *Probl.* 15.3, concerns Gaza's additions and changes (*ibid.*, p. 304.11-306.32).

43. See his assertion in LOUIS, *Problèmes*, vol. 1, p. XLVI-XLVII: 'La traduction latine de Théodore Gaza ne concorde pas toujours avec le texte des manuscrits dont nous disposons. Force est donc de supposer que cet éminent helléniste du XVe siècle a utilisé un manuscrit qui n'existe plus aujourd'hui. L'un des intérêts de sa traduction est justement de permettre de retrouver les traces d'un témoin disparu.' KLEK, in his preface to RUELLE C.E. - KNÖLLINGER H. - KLEK J. (eds.), *Aristotelis Quae Feruntur Problemata Physica* (Bibliotheca scriptorum Graecorum et Romanorum Teubneriana 1096), Leipzig: Teubner, 1922, p. X, recognized that Gaza 'emendandi officio functum esse'; nonetheless, he still posited a wonderous lost codex: 'Neque tamen infitiamur Gazam codicem quoque nobile deperditum manibus tenuisse e quo nonnulla in suum usum converterat.' MARENGHI, *Profumi e miasmi*, p. 159, effectively shows that Gaza relied mainly on two manuscripts A^m (= A 174 sup. of the Biblioteca Ambrosiana, Milan; the shelfmark '67' cited by Marenghi is the serial number in MARTINI E. - BASSI L., *Catalogus Codicum Graecorum Bibliothecae Ambrosianae*, 2 vols., Milan: U. Hoepli, 1893-1906, vol. 1, p. 80) and D (= 233 of New College, Oxford) of the δ family. Marenghi had identified A^m as Gaza's source in earlier publications; see his 'Un capitolo dell'Aristotele medievale...', p. 278 and 281 n. 59; *Problemi di fonazione...*, p. 29 and 91 *ad probl. 62*; and *Problemi di medicina*, p. 270.

44. See MONFASANI, 'Pseudo-Aristotelian...', p. 238 n. 35 ('Depravati erant certe Greci codices omnes').

45. MONFASANI, 'Pseudo-Aristotelian...', p. 219-31.

46. MOHLER, *Kardinal ...*, p. 300.11-12: 'Non nullos quinterniones extorsimus, qui diutius apud nos morari nequeunt.'

Gaza's enormous transformation of the structure of the *Problemata*. Indeed, almost no one since the Renaissance has understood this because in 1501 an enterprising editor in Venice reordered Gaza's translation to conform to the commentary of Pietro d'Abano and, therefore, inadvertently, to the Greek text. It is in this reordered form that Gaza's translation was read for the rest of the Renaissance and up to today[47].

George, as I have said, complained about Gaza's unwarranted intrusions into the Greek text. George argued that if Gaza had comments and substantial corrections to make to the text, he should have done so in marginal glosses, just as he, George, had done for his own translation[48]. Given what we now know of his intrusions in the text, what Gaza should have done was write a full-fledged commentary on the *Problemata*, supplanting the standard commentary of Pietro d'Abano. But since Gaza's interest was primarily textual rather than philosophical, what he really needed to do was to anticipate Angelo Poliziano's style of textual criticism, elucidating with textual and literary evidence what the correct reading ought to be. Ironically, this is exactly what Poliziano did in correcting Gaza's translation some forty years after George's *Protectio*.

Poliziano's criticism in the *Miscellaneorum Centuria* concerned how Gaza misunderstood the opening section of the celebrated problem 1 in Bk. 30 (953a17-18) on the melancholy of Hercules[49]. Poliziano quoted

47. See MONFASANI, 'Pseudo-Aristotelian...', p. 212, 217-218, 241 nn. 54-55.

48. MOHLER, *Kardinal* ..., p. 298.38-299.3: 'Si vero non nulla obscura liquido tibi patere putas aut ambigua tibi certiora esse ducis, in marginibus, sicuti nos facere consuevimus, que sentis ascribe, nec tua cum alienis commisce. Ita enim et Aristoteles integer erit et sententia tua non erit ignota.'

49. Poliziano, *Opera Omnia*, vol. 1, p. 301-302 (I have modernized the punctuation): 'Sed in quo Problemate quaeritur, cur homines, qui ingenio claruerunt... melancholicos omnes fuisse videamus, et alios ita ut etiam vitiis atrae bilis infestarentur, in eo manifestius utique (ni fallor) insigniusque extitit interpretis erratum quam ut excusari iam dissimularive possit. Nam cum illic exempla subiiciat Aristoteles, heroum qui laborasse dicantur atra bile, primumque de Hercule agat, fuisse illum nimirum tali habitudine, signis argumentisque colligit istiusmodi, quod et comitialis morbus sacer ab eo sit dictus, et filios occiderit vecors, ut in Senecae tragoedia tractatur, et antequam obiret, scatentium ulcerum eruptione laboraverit, unde illa, puto, Nexea tunica venerit in fabulam, nam hoc quoque vitium atrae bilis est. Ex quo etiam Lysandro Lacedaemonio proxime ante obitum, genus id, inquit, ulcerum emersit. Theodorus itaque, quod ad filios et ad ulcera Herculis attinet, ita denique interpretatur: 'Puerorum quoque', inquit, 'motio mentis idem hoc explicat et eruptio ulcerum quae mortem interdum antecedit', cum sit ita Graece: καὶ ἡ περὶ τοὺς παῖδας ἔκστασις καὶ ἡ πρὸ τῆς ἀφανίσεως αὐτοῦ ἐντῇ ἑλκῶν ἔκφυσις γενομένη. Neque autem dubitem ex usu esse, antequam ipsi locum vertimus, perpendere diligentius quid sibi illud velit ἐντῇ, quod ille dissimulat, quaeve de praepositione articuloque illo abiuncto sententia elici possit. Et quidem ego sic arbitror legendum corrigendumque: ἐν Οἴτῃ, ut sit ad verbum sensus: 'Et in liberos suos pavor', seu mavis dicere, 'mentis excessus, et ante obitum ipsius in Oeta ulcerum eruptio.'... Quorsum enim

Gaza's rendering of a passage dealing with Hercules' children and his ulcers: 'the motion of the mind of boys shows the same thing as does the eruption of ulcers which sometimes precedes death', which quite distorts the Greek and completely ignores the fact that the text is supposed to be about Hercules and not about some vague group of the children or ulcers in general. To explain his emendation, Poliziano cited Seneca's description of Hercules killing his own children in a senseless rage and his suffering from an outbust of ulcers just before he died. He then proposed to correct the nonsensical ἐν τῇ of the Greek, which Gaza had left untranslated, to ἐν Οἴτῃ, i. e., 'on Mount Oeta,' where Hercules was said to have died. With this emendation Poliziano could then proceed to translate the Greek as: 'And Hercules' terror', or if you prefer to say, 'his derangement towards his children, and the outbreak of ulcers before his death on Mount Oeta [shows etc.]'). Poliziano's emendation, I should note, was silently accepted into the Aldine edition of the Greek text of Aristotle in 1498, and from the Aldine edition into every edition of the Greek text of the *Problemata* to this day, but with no editor ever recognizing that the emendation came from Poliziano. This emendation became the occasion for Poliziano's well known attack upon Gaza as a translator and his defense of George against Gaza. Poliziano, however, showed no sign of ever having read George's *Protectio* or his translation of the *Problemata*. So his defense of the beleaguered Cretan stemmed exclusively from his reading of George's translation of the Aristotelian *De Animalibus*, which he cites.

Of the twenty passages of Gaza's translation George analyzes in the *Protectio* seventeen clearly catch Gaza in mistakes or distortions of varying seriousness; one case depends upon whether or not you accept Gaza's emendation[50]; one case is unclear because of an ambiguity or perhaps a corruption in the Greek text[51]; and in one case Gaza is probably right, and certainly not wrong[52].

hic de pueris mente motis in mediis agatur heroibus, aut quae magis aetas a bile hac atra, quem furorem dicimus, quam puerilis abest? Quid autem generalem hanc ulcerum ante obitum eruptionem accipit, quod neque verba significant Aristotelis, et plane illius proposito voluntatique contrarium? Nempe qui probare nitatur ex argumentis quibuspiam atque exemplis, non pueros, non quoslibet atra bile, sed heroas maximosque viros inquietari. Quin illud etiam diligentius cogitandum, sacerne tantum morbus, ut Aristoteles ait, an etiam Herculeus, quod de suo Theodorus adicit, appelletur?'

50. See the discussion of *Probl.* 1.4 below.

51. See the discussion of *Probl.* 4.29 below.

52. See the discussion of *Probl.* 19.12 below. George discusses various problems in the following order (M = Mohler 's edition):

1.1 (chap. 7; M 298.1-24)	16.6 (chap. 18; M 308.12-24)
1.4 (chap. 9; M 299.12-300.14)	17.1 (chap. 19; M 308.25-309.18)

The one instance in which Gaza is certainly not wrong is Bk.19, probl. 12, where it is asked: Διὰ τί τῶν χορδῶν ἡ βαρυτέρα ἀεὶ τὸ μέλος λαμβάνει; (918a37), which W. S. Hett translate: 'Why is it that the lower of the two strings always has the tune[53]?' Both George and Bartolomeo of Messina translated τὸ μέλος λαμβάνει as 'accipit sonum'[54]. Gaza, however, rendered the Greek as 'huic actus modulandi committitur'[55]. His phrasing is not literal as is George's and Bartolomeo's, but *actus modulandi* does capture better than the ambiguous *sonus* of Bartolomeo and George the Greek *melos* in the sense of 'tune' or 'melody'. I note that modern scholars differ on how to read and emend the rest of this problem[56].

Of the seventeen instances of error or distortion, rightly listed by George, some involve Gaza's pretentious or inexact Latin, for instance, in Bk. 17, probl. 2 (916a12), instead of translating the Greek φυτά simply as *plantae* ('plants'), Gaza wrote 'ea quorum stirpes terra continentur' (those things whose stems are contained by the earth')[57]. More serious was Gaza's decision in 4.20 (878b36) to translate ἰξίαι as *varices* instead of keeping the transliterated Greek technical term *ixiae*[58], as did Bartolomeo and George. *Varices* means vericose veins, but the Greek text here is clearly referring to varicoceles, as George explained, which are tumors in vericose veins and not the veins themselves[59]. Also more

1.14 (chap. 10; M 300.15-22)	17.2 (chap. 20; M 309.19-310.3)
1.16 (chap. 11; M 300.23-301.2)	19.12 (chap. 21; M 310.4-310.21)
2.1 (chap. 12; M 301.3-302.9)	20.2 (chap. 22; M 310.21-311.14)
2.20 (chap. 13; M 302.9-303.4)	20.3 (chap. 23; M 311.15-311.30)
2.26 (chap. 14; M 303.5-304.11)	20.4 (chap. 24; M 311.31-313.8)
15.3 (chap. 15; M 304.11-306.32)	4.20 (chap. 25; M 313.9-315.7)
15.5 (chap. 16; M 306.33-307.29)	5.31 (chap. 26; M 315.8-317.38)
16.7 (chap. 17; M 307.30-308.11)	4.29 (chap. 30; M 324.30-328.3)

53. HETT W.S. (ed.), *Aristotle. Problems*, 2 vols. (Loeb Classical Library; vol. 2 includes the *Rhetorica ad Alexandrum*, tr. H. RACKHAM), Cambridge, Mass.: Harvard University Press – London: W. Heineman, 1936-1937.

54. For George (for whom this is 20.12): Urb. Lat. 1322, f. 77r, and Vat. Lat. 5790, f. 91v; for Bartolomeo: Vat. Lat. 2112, f. 20r, and *Petri Aponi Expositio*, f. [190v].

55. For Gaza (for whom this is 13.39): Vat. Lat. 2111, f. 161v.

56. See the long discussion in FLASHAR, *Problemata...*, p. 605-606. HETT, *Aristotle....*, p. 384 n. b, remarks 'The meaning of this problem is obscure and indeed with the MS. text nothing can be made of it.' See also FORSTER E.S. (tr.), *Aristotle. Problemata* (The Works of Aristotle 7), Oxford: Clarendon Press, 1927, *ad loc.*

57. Gaza (for whom this is 13.27): Vat. Lat. 2111, f. 100r.

58. Gaza (for whom this is 4.21): Vat. Lat. 2111, f. 39r.

59. George translates the passage as (Urb. Lat. 1322, f. 25r; Vat. Lat. 5790, f. 32r): 'Quamobrem ixie faciunt ne generent qui eas patiuntur?' Bartolomeo's translation runs (Vat. Lat. 2112, f. 7vII; *Expositio Petri Aponi*, f. [70rII]): 'Propter quid yschias habentes prohibent generare?' [eas (?) id est ysoliatice passiones *post* ischias *add. Vat. Lat. 2112*; cf. PIETRO D'ABANO, *Expositio*, f. [70rII]): 'Notandum quod ischia idem est quod siatica

serious were the changes Gaza imposed on the Greek text. For instance, in 1.16 (861a10-11), Gaza changed 'those who have lice' to 'those who have no lice'[60]; in 16.7 (914b1-2) he changed the assertion that the sum of the parts seems to be less than the whole to its opposite meaning, namely, that the sum of the parts seems to be more than the whole[61]; in 15.3 (910b23-24), he changed 'counting by tens' to 'counting up to ten', which means something very different[62]; in 1.14 (860b34-35), where the Greek text asks why a change of water is more likely to cause disease than a change of food, Gaza reversed the meaning of the proposition and asked why a change of food was more likely to produce disease than a change of water[63]. To take one last example, in 2.1 (866b11-13), Gaza gratuitously inserted into the text a new clause followed by a whole new sentence on the classical clepsydra totally fabricated by himself[64].

Some of Gaza's changes are defensible. For instance, in 1.4 (859a25-28), he changed a positive sentence into a negative by adding the word *minime* and then inserted a new sentence fabricated by himself[65]. In the revised version of his translation, he dropped the negative, probably be-

passio que est colectio…' I thank Pieter De Leemans for pointing out the possible influence of Pietro here]. Ἰξίαι, in a medical sense are varicoceles; see LIDDELL H.G. – SCOTT R., *A Greek-English Lexicon*, 9th ed., Oxford: Clarendon Press, 1940, *ad voc.*, citing Aristotle and Plutarch. HETT, *Problems*, agrees with George on varicocele: 'Why does varicocele prevent generation both in men who have it and in other animals? Is it because varicocele occurs when breath changes position'. See also FLASHAR, *Problemata…*, p. 465 n. *ad probl. 20*: 'Gemeint ist die Varikozele…'

60. Gaza, Vat. Lat. 2111, f. 8r: 'Cur mutationes aquarum faciant ut qui nullos pediculos habent, multos iam habere incipiant?'

61. Gaza (for whom this is 13.19), Vat. Lat. 2111, f. 97r: 'Cur omnis magnitudo divisa maior suo toto videatur?' Gaza reversed himself in his revised version (ACADEMIA REGIA BORUSSICA, *Aristotelis Opera*, vol. 3, p. 445a): 'Cur omnis magnitudo divisa minor esse suo toto videatur?' Pieter De Leemans tells me that Evrart de Conty also deviated from Bartolomeo's translation, translating: 'Pour quoy est ce que les choses devisees en pluseurs parties samblent estre plus grandes que devant?' In his *glose*, however, Evrart acknowledged that he changed the text: 'Nous devons savoir que selonc le commun texte de Aristote en cest probleme, il demande pour quoy c'est que les choses devisees samblent estre mendres que devant'.

62. Gaza (for whom this is 13.3), Vat. Lat. 2111, f. 91v: 'Cur omnes homines, tam barbari quam Greci, ad decem usque enumerare consueverunt?'

63. Gaza, Vat. Lat. 2111, f. 7v-8r: 'Cur ciborum mutatio magis quam aque gravis occurat?'

64. Gaza, Vat. Lat. 2111, f. 19r: 'Ut in aqua fit vasis quod in mare demissum dulcem intra se colligit humorem, clepsydraque ob id nominatum est. Nequit enim effluere cum quis pleno iam vase partem alteram obturavit.' See MONFASANI, 'Pseudo-Aristotelian…', p. 208.

65. Gaza, Vat. Lat. 2111, f. 5v-5 bis r: 'Cur vomitus cum tempora immutantur citari minime debeant? Ne conturbatio redundet cum varia excrementa materie inutilis ex mutandi ratione proveniant? Unde fit ut cibum etiam alii parum concoquant, alii parum cupiant.'

cause of George's criticism, but he kept the fabricated sentence[66]. The irony is that modern scholars, not knowing the first version of Gaza's translation, have independently inserted a negative at this point while discarding the fabricated sentence which he had inserted.

An even more interesting example is a difficult sentence in 4.29 (880a26-27). George began his analysis by quoting the literal but non-sensical medieval rendering, 'propter quod et quibusdam ventosorum piscium plintro[67] fetet mulier' (literally 'because also in certain things does a woman stink of the washbowl of windy fishes?)[68], which mimics the Greek διὸ καὶ ἐνίοις τῶν πνευματικῶν ἰχθύων πλύντρου ὄζει ἡ γονή, except that Bartolomeo read γυνή instead of the γονή found in the Greek editions. Gaza's translation of the passage in the first edition of his translation is even worse: 'Unde etiam piscium spirabilium quorundam virus genitale plautrum redolet.' ('Hence even the genital secretion of certain 'fishes has the fragrance of plautrum')[69]. George had great fun pointing out that 'respiratory fishes' makes no sense; that 'genital secretion' can in no way be a translation of *mulier* (George also read γυνή instead of γονή[70]); that *plautrum*/πλαύτρον is not a Latin nor a Greek word[71]; and that *redolet* is pretentious when the Greek here plainly has the sense of 'stinks'. George's solution to the difficult passage was: 'Ideo in non nullis spiritum natis reddere piscine, ubi lavatur, olet mulier' ('Therefore in some things born to emit fumes, the female gives off the smell of the fishpond, where she is washed')[72]. George's rendering makes better sense, but is not fully satisfactory. Gaza came up with a new solution in the second edition of his translation, emending τῶν πνευματικῶν ἰχθύων to τῶν περιττωματικῶν ἰχθύων, with the result that he translated the passage to mean that 'the *genitura* of some

66. He changed *minime* to *maxime* (ACADEMIA REGIA BORUSSICA, *Aristotelis Opera*, vol. 3, 415a). See MONFASANI, 'Pseudo-Aristotelian...', p. 208-209.

67. George reports *plyntri* and not *plintro*, but I follow Vat. Lat. 2112 (see the next note).

68. Bartolomeo: Vat. Lat. 2112, f. 8rI; *Expositio Petri Aponi*, f. 75vII [plintro *om.*]. Pieter De Leemans tells me that *plintro*, though rather exceptional in the manuscripts, is confirmed by one of the most important, viz., Padua, Bibl. Antoniana, Scaff. XVII, 370.

69. Gaza (for whom this is 4.30), Vat. Lat. 2111, f. 30v.

70. George's Greek exemplar, Zan. Gr. 216 (= 404), f. 188r, of the Biblioteca Marciana, Venice, has γυνή, just as does its exemplar, Gr. IV, 58 (= 1206), f. 60v, also of the Marciana.

71. LIDDELL – SCOTT, *ad voc.*, reports πλύτρον (as a variant of πλύτρις, 'fuller's *earth*'). The root word, πλυνεύς, is defined as '*trough, tank,* or *pit, in which dirty clothes were washed* by treading'. According to the *TLG*, 4: 29.880a27 is the only place the word appears in the Aristotelian corpus.

72. George: Urb. Lat. 1322, f. 27r; Vat. Lat. 5790, f. 34r.

who are abundant with waste matter has the fragance of fish wash'[73]. Some modern scholars accept Gaza's emendation, some do not[74]; but all differ from Gaza, George, and Bartolomeo by translating ἡ γονή as semen, which give much better sense. In short, this particular passage about which George contested Gaza is still contested today. If we were methodically to compare George's and Gaza's translations, we would undoubtedly find numerous instances of passages which are still today objects of debate.

But the overall pattern of George's criticism was on the mark. Gaza emended the Greek text, fabricated additions, and substituted elegant paraphrases for translation to a degree that would shock modern scholars as much as such things shocked George[75]. Indeed, George never realized the full extent of Gaza's restructing of the *Problemata*. Nor did he really understand Gaza's motivation. Because, as we have seen, Gaza considered all the manuscripts to be corrupt, he felt free to recreate in the guise of a Latin translation a new Greek text in some ways radically different from the extant manuscripts. All George knew was Gaza's statement in the preface to Pope Nicholas V for the first edition that he, Gaza, would expand a bit on Aristotle's *rationes compressae* and make them more pleasant to Latin ears[76]. George interpreted these words as reflecting a position in the traditional debate on how to translate. So he explained

73. ACADEMIA REGIA BORUSSICA, *Aristotelis Opera.*, vol. 3, p. 426b: 'unde etiam nonnullorum excrementis abundantium genitura lavamentum piscium redolet.' Gaza was clearly influenced by George's criticism because in the revised version he followed George in associating ἰχθύων with πλύντρον instead of with πνευματικῶν, as he had done in his first translation.

74. F. SYLBURG accepted it in his edition of the *Problemata* (Frankfort: A. Wecheli haeredes et al., 1585), as do the translators FLASHAR, FORSTER, and HETT. RUELLE – KNÖLLINGER – KLEK and LOUIS do not, however, in their respective editions.

75. Although he knew nothing of Gaza's restructuring of the *Problemata* or of his creative insertions in other books, of relevance here are the remarks of MARENGHI concerning Bks. 12-13 in *Profumi et miasmi*, p. 158-162, where he compares five passages in George's and Gaza's translations (12: 1.906a24, 12: 8.907a22, 13: 1.907a23, 13: 5.908a22, 13: 6.908a32-34) and notes some other passages. The comparison is a condemnation of Gaza, e. g.: 'Trapezunzio rende in modo lineare e corretto... Il Gaza non solo fraintende ἀκρατεστέρα [as had George] rendendo *validior* (che un efflucio odoroso, stemperandosi all'aria, diventi *piú forte* è, a dir poco, illogico!), ma per ἀπόρροια, termine empedocleo, scova una *vox inaudita*, '*delibatio*', qui è in XII 6, mentre in XIII 5 per lo stesso termine usa '*delatio*'' (p. 158); or 'chiaro che il Trapezunzio ha come fine primario di penetrare il testo e rendere in un latino piano e intelligibile, e insieme preciso e fedele, un discorso tecnico alieno da sbavature, mentre Teodoro Gaza ama calamistrarlo a scapito di una retta interpretazione' (p. 160).

76. Vat. Lat. 2111, f. 4v: 'Verum quoniam rationes illas Aristotelis compressas, argutas, parum moderari excolique patientes, nos conspectius, ni fallor, ad Latinas aures explicavimus...'

that for literary works, one translated *ornatiuscule*, i. e., in a literary manner, without regard to word order of the original Greek but with an intent to capture in Latin the literary quality of the Greek. In translating history, one should wish to replicate the *res* of the original, not the *verba*. But in translating scientific texts, especially Aristotle, one must follow the Greek as closely as possible within the limits of literate Latin, neither adding or subtracting anything lest the translator substitute his understanding of the material in place of Aristotle's or of readers more insightful than the translator[77]. In short, George applied to Aristotle the justification Jerome had given for translating Scripture as much as possible *verbum ad verbum*, and he differed from the medieval translators only in his adherence to a higher standard of Latinity[78]. Furthermore, he endorsed the medieval use of transliterated Greek as the basis for the creation of technical terms when appropriate Latin terms were wanting. Finally, while condemning Gaza's attempt to recast Aristotle in a new 'classical', non-medieval vocabulary, he strongly insisted that use of traditional vocabulary (*verba trita*) was the only way to maintain clarity, consistency, and continuity with the medieval tradition[79].

77. MOHLER, *Kardinal...*, p. 326.20-41: 'Accedit quod in iis rebus necesse est non nihil nunc addere, nunc omittere quas ornate studemus edere. Opus est enim ut, si ornatiuscule volumus dicere, Grecorum verborum ordinem omnino negligamus. Nam si a materna lingua in Latinam, que proxime sunt, aut contra vertenti ordo verborum servandus non est, quod facile intelliget qui periculum fecerit, quanto minus in longius multo remotis linguis ordo verborum servandus erit? Idcirco Hieronymus ille, vir doctrina, prudentia, sanctitate precipuus, divinas quidem scripturas, ornatu verborum neglecto, verbum de verbo transtulit. In sermonibus vero doctorum aut historie, rem, non verba secutus, et adiecit et subtraxit aliqua que tamen rebus non derogant... In Aristotelicis quidem traducendis, quantum fieri a nobis potuit, nihil pretermisimus, nihil addidimus, ordinemque ipsum Grecorum verborum ubique conati sumus inviolatum reddere. Minima enim tum propter magnitudinem rerum, tum quia de rebus naturalibus documenta sunt, textus immutatio aut verbi additio substractiove longe in alienum sepe sensum universam rem rapuit. In aliis vero maiore dicendi usi libertate, nunc evagatiores, nunc contractiores fuimus.'

78. See Jerome's famous ep. 57, *De optimo genere interpretandi*, where he rejected literal translation save in the case of Scripture (5.2): 'Ego enim non solum fateor, sed libera voce profiteor me interpretatione Graecorum absque scripturis sanctis, ubi et verborum ordo mysterium est, non verbum e verbo, sed sensum exprimere de sensu.' See Jerome, *Epistulae*, ed. I. HILBERG, 2ⁿᵈ ed., 3 vols. in 4 (Corpus Scriptorum Ecclesiasticorum Latinorum 54-56), Vienna: Österreichische Akademie der Wissenschaften 1996, vol. 1, pp. 503-506; and BARTELINK G.J.M., *Hieronymus Liber de optimo genere interpretandi (Epistula 57). Ein Kommentar* (Mnemosyne. Supplementum 61), Leiden: E.J. Brill, 1980, p. 46, *ad 5, 2 mysterium*.

79. George laid out his position especially in chap. 3 in criticism of Gaza's preface to Pope Nicholas V (MOHLER, *Kardinal...*, p. 283.33-289.7); e. g.: 'Que quadrigentorum, ut ipse scribis, annorum frequenti usu consuetudo trivit, ea tu revocasse ac in melius vertisse iactas' (288.19-21). See also elsewhere: 'propriis rerum tritisque consuetudine auctorum

George ended the *Protectio* with an appeal to King Alfonso of Naples to defend medieval philosophy against the attacks of Gaza and his allies[80]. George argued that for all their obvious flaws the medieval translators were essential for the rise of medieval philosophy and science. No medieval translators, then no Thomas, no Albert, no Giles of Rome, no John Scotus[81]. Rather than to be excoriated, the medieval translators should be honored for their achievement even when one wished to supplant them with more accurate translations in better Latin. Indeed, George expressed his gratitude towards them[82]. He saw Gaza's attempt to recreate a Latin Aristotle in a completely new Latin vocabulary, structure, and to a degree even new content as a conscious plan to destroy the medieval philosophical/scientific tradition[83]. Even though his friend

verbis facile ad earum intelligentiam legentes adduci, novis inusitatisque nihil recte intelligere posse. Trita vero usitataque scimus aliter plerumque ab aliis capi. Multa enim aliter philosophi, aliter rhetores; et Aristotelici aliter multa, aliter Platonici. Quare qui Aristotelem interpretatur, ipsum sequi debet, non alios. Nam si alios sequitur, non vertit, sed pervertit evertitque omnia.' (281.14-20). And: '... presertim cum nusquam a communi usu dicendi, quoad eius fieri potuit, diverterim, illudque Ciceronis semper ante oculos habuerim, quod re ipsa Cages aspernatur atque contemnit: 'Vitium', inquit [*De Orat.* 1.12], 'maximum est in dicendo a vulgari genere orationis atque consuetudine communis sensus abhorrere' (321.30-35). And: 'Verba semper nova querit; contemnit trita. Subtrahit, addit, mutat, pervertit, confunditque omnia, quod unico solum declarare verbo sat erit.' (317.36-38).

80. 'Reliquum est ut tua maiestas non aliter eorum omnium causam suscipiat quam regem philosophum decet. Id abste Aristoteles depravatus a Caguleis petit. Id abste prisci interpretes a Theodoro quasi magni mali causam prebuerint falso accusati postulant. Id abste Alberti, Egidii, Burlei, ceteri omnes veterum interpretamentorum commentatores, et maxime Thomas' (MOHLER, *Kardinal...*, p. 341.22-27).

81. 'Si nihil illi traduxissent, essent Alberti? Essent Scoti? Essent Egidii? Esset Thomas? Essent alii quam plures aut in philosophia aut in theologia aut in medicina preclarissimi viri, quorum scriptis nature secreta, theologie profunditas, medicine varia, multiplex, subtilisque ratio, que ante illas traductiones omnia iacebant in tenebris, hominibus patuerunt?' (MOHLER, *Kardinal...*, p. 319.23-28).

82. 'Debemus autem eis non parum. Nam nisi ipsi traduxissent, iuniores apud Latinos philosophi non extitissent. Qui si non fuissent, nec nos, quantulumcumque sit, quod in philosophia sumus assecuti, teneremus. Fatemur enim id totum a Latinis nos sic habere ut aliunde id habere impossibile fuerit. Nam philosophie quidem fundamenta nemo prorsus citra ducentos annos apud Grecos nisi Latinis doctus litteris tenuit. Nec modo, sed semper (ex quo aliquid percepi) sic me affectum erga ipsos esse argumento illud est, quod etsi multa philosophie nobis iam traducta volumina sunt, nunquam tamen verbum unum adversus ipsos scripsimus' (MOHLER, *Kardinal...*, p. 324.17-27).

83. 'Nec enim tantum potuit in Latinos furorem retinere. Exclamat melius esse nulla philosophie habere quam eiusmodi exempla [*see the next note*], cuiusmodi ad hos dies a priscis edita sunt. Egre fert quia non citius in ignem interpretamenta priscorum proiiciuntur [*see the next note*]. At his tunc sublatis, scientia omnis tollitur. Alia enim non erant. Et hoc est quod optat. Melius erat, inquit, nihil habere quam huiusmodi habere. Scientia vero sublata, cetera quoque propter ignorantiam facile vacillabunt' (MOHLER, *Kardinal...*, p. 320.16-23).

Lorenzo Valla published a work, the *Repastinatio Dialectice et Philosophie* which he, Valla, thought could replace traditional scholastic philosophy[84], Gaza actually never enunciated such a plan. He only promised that his translations would enable contemporary philosophers to dispute more elegantly in the manner of orators[85]. But by the same token Gaza's Aristotle was alien to the medieval tradition, and his translations were an inspiration to a later generation of humanists who wished to create a completely non-scholastic Aristotle. Ermolao Barbaro, who set out in the 1480s to render all of Aristotle into humanistic Latin and normally referred to scholastics as 'barbarians'[86], explicitly took Gaza as his model[87].

George of Trebizond was a Greek emigrant who greatly admired medieval scholasticism. It is not adequately appreciated that up to the mid-Quattrocento his attitude was the common one among Greek intellectuals who had become familiar with Latin culture. From the Demetrius Cydones to Cardinal Bessarion and John Agyropoulos, Greek émigrés happily assimilated Latin scholastic culture[88]. Gaza's stance toward scholasticism reflected not so much a Greek outlook as the attitude of the more militant currents of Italian humanism. Furthermore, Gaza's aggressive manipulation of the Aristotelian texts he translated corresponded to no Greek tradition, but was of a piece with the free reworking of Greek texts that Italian humanists sometimes practiced, starting with Leonard Bruni. The novelty of Gaza was to conceive his task as not simply to translate the Greek original in a way that would please Latins

---

84. See the critical edition in 2 vols. by ZIPPEL G., Padua: Antenore, 1982; and my review in *Rivista di letteratura italiana* 2 (1984), pp. 177-194, reprinted in my *Language and Learning in Renaissance Italy*, Aldershot: Variorum, 1994, as Essay VI. Valla had no compunction in declaring that he would rather be illiterate than be like scholastic logicians; see his *Epistole*, BESOMI O. – REGOLIOSI M. (eds.), *Epistole,* Padua: Antenore, 1984, p. 201.149-152: '... aut illos dialecticos, Albertum utrunque, Strodem, Occam, Paulus Venetum. Quos omnes tantum abest ut existimem doctos fuisse, ut (deum testor) mallem me illiteratum quam parem alicuius illorum esse.'

85. See the latter part of the quotation in n. 6 above.

86. The most recent discussion with relevant reference is BAUSI F., *E. Barbaro. G. Pico della Mirandola. Filosofia o eloquenza*, Naples: Liquori, 1998, p. 13, 23. 144 §46.

87. See the preface to his translation of Themistius in BRANCA V. (ed.), *Epistolae, orationes et carmina*, 2 vols., Florence: Bibliopolis, 1943, p. 9: 'Hic [Gaza] unus mihi certare cum vetustate ipsa visus est, hunc mihi quem colerem, quem imitarer proposui, ab huius scriptis adiutum me et fateor et predico.'

88. See my 'Greek Renaissance Migrations', *Italian History & Culture* 8 (2002), p. 1-14, at p. 7-10 (reprinted in my *Greeks and Latins in Renaissance Italy: Studies on Humanism and Philosophy in the 15th century* (Variorum Collected Studies Series 801), Aldershot: Ashgate, 2004).

but even more so to recreate the Greek original as he believed it must have been before it was distorted by classical editors and later scribes, a bold and brilliant plan in its general conception, worthy of the most audacious nineteenth- and twentieth-century classical scholars[89]. Unfortunately, not only did Gaza lack the tools and methods for such a task, but he also omitted to inform his readers of what he was doing.

The decisive event in the rivalry between George of Trebizond and Gaza was something rather banal. Both translations enjoyed a modest manuscript diffusion. But because of his reputation among humanists such as the young Angelo Poliziano, Gaza's translation was printed in the 1470s and George's was not. Once Gaza's translation became the standard version. George's *Protectio* as well as his translation of the *Problemata* faded into obscurity. Gaza's reputation, on the other hand, as an accurate translator with a supposed access to lost Greek exemplars maintained itself, except for an occasional critic, for the rest of the Renaissance and has continued in some degree to the present day[90].

The University at Albany, State University of New York

---

89. See MONFASANI, 'Pseudo-Aristotelian...', p. 209-210.
90. SEE MONFASANI, 'Pseudo-Aristotelian...', p. 205-206, 211.

ARISTOTLE'S PROBLEMATA
IN DIFFERENT TIMES AND TONGUES

A SELECTED BIBLIOGRAPHY

This bibliography does not offer a survey of all sources and studies mentioned in the present volume. We have instead asked specialists to compose a selected bibliography on the areas of their expertise in order to create an instrument for further research on the *Problemata* in different times and tongues:

1. The Greek *Problemata Physica* (R.W. Sharples)
2. Other Greek *Problemata* collections (R.W. Sharples)
3. The Arabic, Hebrew, and Syriac Tradition (L.S. Filius)
4. Medieval *Problemata* literature (I. Ventura)
5. Bartholomew of Messina (G. Coucke)
6. Peter of Abano (M. Klemm)
7. Évrart de Conty (C. Boucher – M. Goyens)
8. Renaissance (C. Martin)

These topics are thus not limited to the *Problemata Physica*, but also include other *Problemata* and *Quaestiones* collections both in antiquity and in the Middle Ages. Moreover, a more elaborate bibliography is provided for the three authors who have played a central role in the reception of the *Problemata Physica* in the Middle Ages: Bartholomew of Messina, Peter of Abano, and Evrart de Conty. In the Sections devoted to these authors, editions and studies that deal with other works than the *Problemata Physica* are also listed.

1. THE GREEK *PROBLEMATA PHYSICA*   R.W. Sharples

Fundamental is the introduction to: FLASHAR H., *Aristoteles: Problemata Physika* (Aristoteles Werke in Deutscher Übersetzung 19), Berlin: Akademie-Verlag, 1962 (1991⁴), p. 316-358 and 370-382. His bibliography (p. 382-384) should be consulted, especially for material on *Problems* on specific themes such as music. See also:

BERTIER J. – FILIUS L.S., 'Problemata Physica', in: R. GOULET – J.-M. FLAMAND – M. AOUAD (eds.), *Dictionnaire des philosophes antiques. Supplément*, Paris: CNRS éditions, 2003, p. 575-593.
FILIUS L.S., *The Problemata Physica attributed to Aristotle: the Arabic version of Hunain ibn Ishaq and the Hebrew version of Moses ibn Tibbon* (Aristoteles Semitico-Latinus 11), Leiden: Brill, 1999.

FORSTER E.S., *The Works of Aristotle: Problemata*, Oxford: Clarendon Press, 1927.

FORSTER E.S., 'The pseudo-Aristotelian *Problems*: their nature and composition', *Classical Quarterly* 22 (1928), p. 163-165.

LOUIS P., 'Les manuscrits parisiens des *Problèmes* d'Aristote', *Revue de Philologie* 60 (1986), p. 197-204.

LOUIS P. (ed.), *Aristote: Problèmes* (Collection des universités de France), Paris: Les Belles Lettres. *Tome 1: Sections I à X*, 1991; *Tome 2: Sections XI à XXVII*, 1993; *Tome 3: Sections XXVIII-XXXVIII, Index*, 1994.

MARENGHI G., 'La tradizione manoscritta dei Problemata physica aristotelici', *Bollettino del Comitato per la Preparazione della Edizione Nazionale dei Classici Greci e Latini* 9 (1961), p. 47-57.

MARENGHI G., 'Per una identificazione e collocazione storica del fondo aristotelico dei *Problemata*', *Maia* 1 (1961), p. 34-50.

MARENGHI G., *Problemi musicali*, Firenze: Fussi, 1958 (Section XIX).

MARENGHI G., *Problemi di fonazione e di acustica*, Naples: Libreria scientifica editrice, 1962 (Section XI).

MARENGHI G., *Problemi di medicina*, Milan: Istituto editoriale Italiano, 1966; 2nd ed. Bolsena: Massari, 1999 (= Sections I, VI-IX, XIV, XXVII-XXVIII, XXXI-XXXVIII).

MARENGHI G., *[Aristotele]: Profumi e miasmi*, Naples: Arte Tipografica, 1991 (Sections XII-XIII).

PRANTL C., 'Über die Probleme des Aristotles', *Abh. Königl. bayerischen Akad. der Wiss.* 6 (1851), p. 339-377.

PRANTL C., review of U.C. Bussemaker, ed., *Aristoteles, Opera Omnia*, vol. IV.1, Paris: Didot, 1857, *Gelehrte Anzeigen der Königlichen bayerischen Akad. der Wiss.* 25 (1858), p. 201-207.

RICHTER E., *De Aristotelis Problematibus*, diss. Bonn, 1885.

SUSEMIHL F., review of Richter 1885, *Wochenschrift für klassische Philologie* 1885, 1481ff.

2. OTHER GREEK *PROBLEMATA* COLLECTIONS R.W. Sharples

Again, the introduction to FLASHAR H., *Aristoteles: Problemata Physika* (Aristoteles Werke in Deutscher Übersetzung 19), Berlin: Akademie-Verlag, 1962 (1991[4]) is fundamental (p. 297-316 and 359-370). See also:

BUSSEMAKER U.C. (ed.), *Aristoteles, Opera Omnia*, vol. IV.1, Paris: Didot, 1857, p. 291-332 (the *Problemata inedita* = *Supplementary Problems*).

FILIUS L.S., forthcoming editions of the Arabic version of the Bussemaker *Problems* and the Syriac version of the Ideler *Problems*.

GARZYA A., 'La tradition manuscrite des *Problemata* de Cassius le iatrosophiste', in: A. GARZYA – J. JOUANNA (eds.), *Storia e ecdotica dei testi medici greci, Atti del II Convegno Internazionale, Parigi 24-26 maggio 1994*, Naples: M. d'Auria, 1994, p. 181-189.

GARZYA A., 'Ancora sulla tradizione manoscritta dei *Problemi* di Cassius iatrosofista', in: K.-D. FISCHER – D. NICKEL – P. POTTER (eds.), *Text and Tradition: Studies in Ancient Medicine and its Transmission presented to Jutta Kollesch*, Leiden: Brill, 1998, p. 85-89.

GARZYA A. – MASULLO R., *I Problemi di Cassio Iatrosofista* (Quaderni dell'Accademia Pontaniana 38), Naples: Accademia Pontaniana, 2004.

GUARDASOLE A., 'Prose rhythmique et ecdotique médicale: le cas des Problèmes "hippocratiques"', in: A. GARZYA – J. JOUANNA (eds.), *Transmission et ecdotique des textes médicaux grecs, Actes du IVème Colloque International (Paris-Sorbonne, 17-19 mai 2001)*, Naples: M. D'Auria, 2003, p. 187-197. (= *Hippocratic Problems*).

IDELER J.L. (ed.), *Physici et medici graeci minores*, Berlin: Reimer, 1841-2 (reprint: Amsterdam: Adolf M. Hakkert-Publisher, 1963), vol. 1, p. 3-80 (= pseudo-Alexander); p. 144-167 (= Cassius).

JOUANNA J., 'Pourquoi les plaies circulaires guérissent-elles difficilement', in: D. GOUREVITCH (ed.), *Maladie et maladies, histoire et conceptualisation: mélanges en honneur de Mirko Grmek*, Geneva: Droz, 1992, p. 95-108. (= *Hippocratic Problems*)

JOUANNA J., 'Présentation d'un nouveau corpus de *problemata médicaux et physiques*: les *Problèmes Hippocratiques*', in: U. CRISCUOLO – R. MAISANO (eds.), *Synodia, studia humanitatis Antonio Garzya... dicata*, Naples: M. D'Auria, 1997, p. 511-539. (= *Hippocratic Problems*).

KAPETANAKI S. – SHARPLES R.W. (eds.), *Pseudo-Aristotle (Pseudo-Alexander), Supplementary Problems*, Berlin: De Gruyter, *forthcoming*.

LINDQVIST C.-G., new edition of the Ideler pseudo-Alexander *Problems*, in preparation.

ROSE V., *Aristoteles Pseudepigraphus*, Leipzig: Teubner, 1863, p. 666-676 (= *Problemata Bambergensia* or *vetustissima*).

ROSELLI A., 'Ps.-Aristotele *Problemata Inedita* 2.153 in POxy 2744', *ZPE* 33 (1979), p. 9-12.

STOLL U., *Das "Lorscher Arzneibuch": ein medizinisches Kompendium des 8. Jahrhunderts (Codex Bambergensis medicinalis 1)* (Sudhoffs Archiv, Beihefte 28), Stuttgart: F. Steiner, 1992, p. 68-75 (= *Problemata Bambergensia* or *vetustissima*).

USENER H. (ed.), *Alexandri Aphrodisiensis quae feruntur Problematorum libri 3 et 4*, Berlin: Typis Academiae Regiae, 1859 (= the *Supplementary Problems*).

WEGEHAUPT H., 'Zur Überlieferung der Problemata des sogenannten Alexanders von Aphrodisias', *Berliner Philologische Wochenschrift* 35 (1915), p. 95-96 (= the *Supplementary Problems*).

WEGEHAUPT H., 'Zur Überlieferung der pseudo-Aristotelischen *problemata anekdota*', *Philologus* 75 (1918), p. 469-473 (= the *Supplementary Problems*).

3. THE ARABIC, HEBREW, AND SYRIAC TRADITION
L.S. Filius

For a systematic survey see BERTIER J. – FILIUS L.S., 'Problemata Physica', in: R. GOULET – J.-M. FLAMAND – M. AOUAD (eds.), *Dictionnaire des philosophes antiques. Supplément*, Paris: CNRS éditions, 2003, p. 575-593, esp. 593-598. See also the following primary sources (3.1.) and studies (3.2.).

3.1. Primary sources

(Pseudo-)Apollonius Tyanensis, *Sirr al-khalīqa wa-ṣana'atu 'ṭ-ṭabī'ati. Kitāb al-'ilāli, Buch über das Geheimnis der Schöpfung und die Darstellung der Natur (Buch der Ursachen)*, ed. U. WEISSER, (Sources & Studies in the History of Arabic-Islamic Science, Natural Sciences I), Aleppo: Institute for the History of Arabic Science, University of Aleppo, 1979.

Ar-Razi Abu Bakr Muhammad Ibn Zakariya, *Kitābu 'l-Ḥāwī fī 'ṭ-ṭibb*, I-XXIII, published by Dā'iratu 'l-Ma'ārifi 'l-Osmania, Haidarabad 1374-1389 / 1955-1970 (Reprint 1394/1974).

FILIUS L.S., *The Problemata Physica attributed to Aristotle: the Arabic version of Hunain ibn Ishaq and the Hebrew version of Moses ibn Tibbon* (Aristoteles Semitico-Latinus 11), Leiden: Brill, 1999.

Hunain ibn Ishaq, *al-Masā'il at-tibbiya*, ed. Muḥammad 'Alī Abū Rayyān, Mursī Muḥammad 'Azab and Djalāl Muḥammad Mūsā, Cairo, 1978 (Engl. transl. by P. GHALIOUNGI, Cairo, 1980).

Ibn an-Nadim, *Kitāb al-Fihrist*, ed. RIDA TAĞADDUD, Tehran, 1391/1971.

Ibn Abi Usaibi'a, *Kitāb 'Uyūn al-anbā'i fī tabaqāti 'l-atibbā'I*, ed. A. MÜLLER, Königsberg-Cairo: al-Matba'a al-Wahbiya, 1299-1301/1882-1884 (reprint: Westmead, 1972 and Frankfurt a/M., 1992).

Job of Edessa, *Book of Treasures, Encyclopaedia of Philosophical and Natural Sciences as taught in Baghdad A.D. 817*, Syriac text and translation with a critical apparatus by A. MINGANA (Woodbrooke Scientific Publications 1), Cambridge: W. Heffer & Sons Limited, 1935.

3.2. Studies

BAUMSTARK A., *Aristoteles bei den Syrern vom 5. bis 8. Jahrhundert*, Leipzig: Teubner, 1900 (reprint Aalen: Scientia Verlag, 1975).

CLERMONT J.T., *A checklist of Syriac manuscripts in the United States and Canada* (Orientalia Christiana Periodica 32), Roma: Pontificale Institutum orientalium studiorum, 1966.

DAIBER H., note to F.E. PETERS, *Aristoteles Arabus*, Gnomon 42 (1970), p. 538-547.

DAIBER H., *The Encyclopaedia of Islam*. New edition, Leiden-Boston-Köln: Brill, 1979 ff., vol. VI, 636a- 639b, s.v. Masā'il wa-adjwiba.

DAIBER H., 'New Manuscript Findings from Indian Libraries', *Manuscripts of the Middle East* 1 (1986), p. 26-48.

FILIUS L.S., 'The theory of vision in the *Problemata Physica*. A comparison between the Greek and the Arabic versions', in: G. ENDRESS – E. KRUK (eds.), *The ancient tradition in Christian and Islamic Hellenism. Studies on the transmission of Greek philosophy and Sciences, dedicated to H.J. Drossaart Lulofs on his ninetieth birthday*, Leiden: Research School CNWS-School of Asian, African and Amerindian Studies, 1997, p. 77-83.

FLASHAR H., *Aristoteles: Problemata Physika* (Aristoteles Werke in Deutscher Übersetzung 19), Berlin: Akademie-Verlag, 1962 (1991⁴), esp. p. 370-372.

GUTAS D. – BIESTERFELDT H.H., 'The Malady of Love', *Journal of the American Oriental Society* 104 (1984), p. 21-55 (reprint in: GUTAS D., *Greek Philosophers in the Arabic Tradition*, Aldershot-Burlington USA-Singapore-Sydney: Ashgate, 2000).

KRUK R., 'Pseudo-Aristotle: An Arabic version of *Problemata Physica* X', *Isis* 67 (1976), p. 251-256.

MEREDITH-OWENS G., 'A tenth-century Arabic miscellany', *The British Museum Quarterly* 20 (1955-1956), p. 33-34.

OESTERLEY W.O.E. – BOS G.H., *A short survey of the literature of rabbinical and mediaeval Judaism*, New York: Macmillan, 1920 (reprint New York: Lenox Hill, 1973).

PETERS F.E., *Aristoteles Arabus. The oriental translations and commentaries on the Aristotelian Corpus* (New York University, Department on Classics, Monographs on Mediterranean Antiquity II), Leiden: Brill, 1968.

PETERS F.E., *Aristotle and the Arabs. The Aristotelian Tradition in Islam* (New York University studies in Near Eastern civilization 1), New York: New York University Press, 1968.

RAVEN W., *Ibn Dawud al-Isbahani and his Kitab al-Zahra*, diss. Leiden, Amsterdam, 1989.

RENAN M.E., *Les Rabbins Français du commencement du quatorzième siècle*, Paris: Imprimerie Nationale, 1877 (reprint Westmead: Gregg International Publishers Limited,1969).

SCHACHT J. – MEYERHOF M. (eds.), *The medico-philosophical controversy between Ibn Buṭlān and Ibn Riḍwān of Cairo* (Faculty of Arts Publication 13), Cairo: The Egyptian University, 1937.

SEZGIN F., *Geschichte des arabischen Schrifttums*, Leiden: Brill, 1979-1984.

STEINSCHNEIDER M., *Die hebraeischen Handschriften der königlichen Hof- und Staatsbibliothek in Muenchen,* München, 1875.

STEINSCHNEIDER M., 'Bibliografia Orientale. Manoscritti arabici in caratteri ebraici', *Bollettino italiano degli studi orientali*, N.S. 4, Firenze 1878, p. 65-69.

STEINSCHNEIDER M., 'Schriften der Araber in hebräischen Handschrifte, ein Beitrag zur arabischen Bibliographie', *Zeitschrift der Deutschen Morgenländischen Gesellschaft* 47 (1893), p. 335-384.

STEINSCHNEIDER M., *Die arabischen Übersetzungen aus dem Griechischen*, Graz: Akademische Druck- und Verlagsanstalt, 1960.

ULLMANN M., *Die Medizin im Islam*, Leiden-Köln: Brill, 1970.

VOORHOEVE P., *Handlist of Arabic Manuscripts*, Leiden-The Hague-Boston-London: Leiden U.P., 1980.

WEISSER U., *Das 'Buch über das Geheimnis der Schöpfung' von Pseudo-Apollonius von Tyana*, Berlin-New York: De Gruyter, 1980.

WITKAM J.J., *Catalogue of Arabic manuscripts*, fasc. 1-5, Leiden: Brill, 1983-1989.

4. MEDIEVAL *PROBLEMATA* LITERATURE   I. Ventura

Fundamental is the general study by LAWN B., *The Salernitan Questions*, Oxford: Clarendon Press, 1963. Moreover, the following primary sources (4.1) and studies (4.2.) should be mentioned.

4.1. Primary sources (Selection, In Chronological Order)

KEIL G. (ed.), *Das Lorscher Arzneibuch. Faksimile der Handschrift Msc. Med. 1 der Staatsbibliothek Bamberg*, Stuttgart: Wiss. Verl. Gesellschaft, 1989, 2 vol.

STOLL U., *Das 'Lorscher Arzneibuch'. Ein medizinisches Kompendium des 8. Jahrhunderts (Codex Bambergensis Medicinalis 1). Text, Übersetzung und Fachglossar*, Stuttgart: Franz Steiner Verlag, 1992.

LAWN B. (ed.), *The Prose Salernitan Questions. Edited from a Bodleian Manuscript (Auct. F.3.10)*, London: The British Academy – Oxford University Press, 1979.

Adelard of Bath, *Conversation with his nephew: On the Same and the Different, Questions on Natural Science, and On Birds*, edited and translated by C. BURNETT, with the collaboration of I. RONCA – P. MANTAS ESPAÑA – B. VAN DEN ABEELE, Cambridge: Cambridge University Press, 1998.

Guillelmus de Conchis, *Dragmaticon* (CCCM 152), ed. I. RONCA, L. BADIA, J. PUJOL, Turnhout: Brepols Publishers, 1997.

Baudri de Bourgueil, *Adelae comitissae*, in: P. ABRAHAMS (ed.), *Les Oeuvres poétiques de Baudri de Bourgueil*, Paris: Champion, 1926, p. 196-253.

Livre de Sydrac. Edition des enzyklopädischen Lehrdialogs aus dem XIII. Jahrhundert, herausgegeben von E. RUHE, Wiesbaden: Dr. Ludwig Reichert Verlag, 2000.

Placides et Timéo ou Li secrés as philosophes. Edition critique avec introduction et notes par C.A. THOMASSET, Genève: Droz, 1980.

«Questioni filosofiche» in volgare mediano dei primi del Trecento. Edizione critica con commento linguistico a cura di F. GEYMONAT, Pisa: Scuola Normale Superiore, 2000, 2 vol.

Lumen Animae, Straßburg: Drucker der "Legenda Aurea", 1482.

Cecco d'Ascoli, *L'Acerba*, ed. M. ALBERTAZZI, Trento: La Finestra, 2003.

Mensa Philosophica. Faksimile und Kommentar. Herausgegeben von E. RAUNER und B. WACHINGER, in Verbindung mit C. RUPRECHT-ALEXANDER und F. SCHANZE, Tübingen: Max Niemeyer Verlag, 1995.

Responsorium curiosorum, Lübeck: Lucas Brandis, 1476.

Summa Recreatorum (MS Praha, Narodni Knihovna, Rodnice VI. Fc. 34).

Problemata Aristotelis philosophorum ac medicorum complurium, Paris: pro Alexandro Alyate, 1501.

Problemata Varia Anatomica. The University of Bologna, MS 1165, edited by L.R. LIND, Lawrence: The University of Kansas Publications, 1968.

Girolamo Manfredi, *Liber de homine. Il Perché*, ed. A. L. TROMBETTI BUDRIESI and F. FORESTI, Bologna: Edizioni Luigi Parma, 1988.

Girolamo Manfredi, *Quesits o perquens*, ed. A. CARRÉ, Barcelona: Editorial Barcino, 2004.

Georgius Valla, *De expetendis et fugiendis rebus*, Venetiis: Aldus Romanus, 1501, 4 vol.

Ortensio Landi, *Quattro libri de' dubbi, con le solutioni a ciascun dubbio accommodate. La Materia del Primo è Amorosa, del Secondo è Naturale, del Terzo è Mista, ben che per lo piu sia Morale, del Quarto è Religiosa*, In Vinegia: appresso Gabriel Giolito de' Ferrari, 1556.

Girolamo Garimberto, *Problemi naturali et morali*, Vicenza: Bolzetta, 1617.

F. Lopez de Villalobos, *Die Problemata des Villalobos*. Auszugsweise zum ersten Male ins Deutsche übersetzt, erläutert und mit einer Einleitung versehen, von Dr. med. et phil. F. LEJEUNE, Greifswald: Verlag Ratsbuchhandlung L. Bamberg, 1923.

Alessandro Tassoni, *Dieci libri de' Pensieri Diversi. Corretti, ampliati, e arricchiti in questa ultima impressione per tutto dall'Autore di nuove curiosità: Ne' quali per via di Quisiti con nuovi fondamenti, e ragioni si trattano le più curiose materie Naturali, Morali, Civili, Poetiche, Istoriche, e d'altre facoltà, che vogliono venire in discorso fra Cavalieri, e Professori di Lettere. Con due copiosissime Tavole: Una de' Libri, Quisiti e Capitoli, e l'altra delle cose più notabili e memorabili*, In Venetia: Per il Barezzi, all'Insegna dell'Abbondanza, 1646.

4.2. Studies

BALDWIN J.W., *The Language of Sex. Five Voices from Northern France around 1200*, Chicago-London: University of Chicago Press, 1994.

BERNT G., 'Dialog. Lateinisches Mittelalter', in: *Lexikon des Mittelalters*, III, München: Artemis Verlag, 1986, col. 951-955.

BILLER P., 'A "scientific" view of Jews from Paris around 1300', in: *Micrologus IX: Gli Ebrei e le scienze / The Jews and the Sciences*, Firenze: SISMEL, 2001, p. 137-168.

BILLER P., 'Black Women in Medieval Scientific Thought', in: *Micrologus XIII: La pelle umana / The Human Skin*, Firenze: SISMEL, 2005, p. 477-492.

BLAIR A., 'Authorship in the Popular "Problemata Aristotelis"', *Early Science and Medicine* 4 (1999), p. 190-227.

BLAIR A., 'The *Problemata* as a Natural Philosophical Genre', in: A. GRAFTON – N. SIRAISI (eds.), *Natural Particulars. Nature and Disciplines in Renaissance Europe*, Cambridge-London: The MIT Press, 1999, p. 171-204.

BLAIR A., *The Theatre of Nature. Jean Bodin and Renaissance Science*, Princeton, New Jersey: Princeton University Press, 1997.

BRANCA V., *Giorgio Valla tra sapienza e scienza. Saggi di Gianna Gardenal, Patrizia Landucci Ruffo, Cesare Vasoli*, Firenze: Olschki, 1981).

CADDEN J., '"Nothing Natural Is Shameful": Vestiges of a Debate about Sex and Science in a Group of Late-Medieval Manuscripts', *Speculum* 76/1 (2001), p. 66-89.

CADDEN J., 'Western Medicine and Natural Philosophy', in: V.L. BULLOUGH – J.A. BRUNDAGE (eds.), *Handbook of Medieval Sexuality*, New York – London: Garland, 1996, p. 51-80.

CARDELLE DE HARTMANN C., 'Diálogo literario y polémica religiosa en la edad media (900-1400)', in: A. ALBERTE GONZÁLEZ – C. MACÍAS VILLALOBOS, *Actas del Congreso Internacional «Cristianismo y tradición latina» (Málaga, 25 a 28 de abril de 2000)*, Madrid: Editorial del Laberinto, 2001, p. 103-123.

CARRÉ A. – CIFUENTES L., 'Quesits (Barcelona, Pere Posa, 1499): una traducció catalana desconeguda del Liber de nomine (Il perché) de Girolamo Manfredi amb filtre napolità', *Arxiu de Textos catalans Antics* 20 (2001), p. 543-560.

CHERCHI P., 'I *Dubbi* di Ortensio Lando in inglese erroneamente attribuiti ad Alain Chartier', in: P. CERCHI, *Ministorie di microgeneri*, a cura di C. FABBIAN, A. REBONATO, E. ZANOTTI CARNEY, Ravenna: Longo, 2003, p. 41-48.

CHERCHI P., 'Il quotidiano, i "Problemata" e la meraviglia. Microstoria di un microgenere', *Intersezioni* 21/2 (2001), p. 243-275, in: P. CHERCHI, *Ministorie di microgeneri*, a cura di C. FABBIAN, A. REBONATO, E. ZANOTTI CARNEY, Ravenna: Longo, 2003, p. 11-40.

CHERCHI P., 'La «selva» dei Marmi di A.F. Doni', in CHERCHI P., *Ministorie di microgeneri*, a cura di C. FABBIAN, A. REBONATO, E. ZANOTTI CARNEY, Ravenna: Longo, 2003, p. 129-156.

DOMÍNGUEZ REBOIRAS F. – VILLALBA VARNEDA P. – WALTER P. (eds.), *Arbor scientiae. Der Baum des Wissens von Ramon Lull. Akten des Internationalen Kongresses aus Anlaß des 40-jährigen Jubiläums des RAIMUNDUS-LULLUS-INSTITUTS der Universität Freiburg i. Br.*, Turnhout: Brepols Publishers, 2002.

EHLERT T., 'Komplexionlehre und Diätetik im 'Buch Sidrach'', in: J. DAEMS a. o. (eds.), *Licht der Natur. Medizin in Fachliteratur und Dichtung. Festschrift für Gundolf Keil zum 60. Geburtstag* (Göppinger Arbeiten zur Germanistik 585), Göppingen: Göppingen: Kümmerle Verlag, 1994, p. 81-100.

FRENKEN G., 'Die älteste Schwanksammlung des Mittelalters (Die Mensa Philosophica eines Kölner Dominikaners)', *Jahrbuch des kölnischen Geschichtsvereins* 8-9 (1927), p. 105-121.

HEMPFER K.W. (ed.), *Möglichkeiten des Dialogs. Struktur und Funktion einer literarischen Gattung zwischen Mittelalter und Renaissance in Italien* (Text und Kontext. Romanische Literaturen und Allgemeine Literaturwissenschaft 15), Stuttgart: Steiner Verlag, 2002.

KEIL G., 'Die frag ist, ob der arczet schuldig sey oder nit. Eine ortolf-haltige Bearbeitung der >Quaestiones de medicorum statu< aus dem spätmittelalterlichen Schlesien', in: K. KUNZE a. o. (eds.), *Überlieferungsgeschichtliche Editionen und Studien zur deutschen Literatur des Mittelalters: Kurt Ruh zum 75. Geburtstag* (Texte und Textgeschichte 31), Tübingen: Niemeyer, 1989, p. 189-209.

KEIL G. – SCHNITZER P. (eds.), *Das Lorscher Arzneibuch und die frühmittelalterliche Medizin. Verhandlungen des medizinhistorischen Symposiums im September 1989 in Lorsch*, Lorsch: Verlag Laurissa, 1991.

KRAYE J., 'The Printing History of Aristotle in the fifteenth Century: a bibliographical approach to Renaissance philosophy', *Renaissance Studies* 9 (1995), p. 189-211 (reprint in KRAYE J., *Classical Traditions in Renaissance Philosophy* (Variorum Collected Studies Series 743), Ashgate: Aldershot, 2002).

LAWN B., 'Medical *Quaestiones Disputatae* c. 1250-1450', in: B. LAWN (ed.), *The Rise and the Decline of the Scholastic 'Quaestio Disputata' with Special Emphasis on its Use in the Teaching of Medicine and Science*, Leiden-New York-Köln: Brill, 1993, p. 66-84.

PERI (PFLAUM) H., 'Die scholastische Disputation', in: M. LAZAR (ed.), *Romanica et Occidentalia. Etudes dédiées à la mémoire de Hiram Peri (Pflaum)*, Jerusalem: Magnes Press, 1963, p. 349-368.

RAUNER E., 'Summa recreatorum', in: *Die deutsche Literatur des Mittelalters. Verfasserlexikon* IX, Berlin-New York: De Gruyter, 1981, col. 503-506.

RAYMUND W., 'Mündliche Unterhaltungserzählungen im Due-Trecento. Zur historischen Pragmatik mündlichen Erzählens zwischen Alltag und Literatur', *Romanistisches Jahrbuch* 46 (1995), p. 47-73.

ROUSE R.H. – ROUSE M.A., 'The Text called *Lumen Animae*', *Archivum Fratrum Praedicatorum* 41 (1971), p. 5-113.

RUHE E., 'Wissensvermittlung in Frage und Antwort. Der enzyklopädische Lehrdialog 'Le Livre de Sidrac'', in: H. BRUNNER – N. R. WOLF (eds.), *Wissensliteratur im Mittelalter und in der Frühen Neuzeit* (Wissensliteratur im Mittelalter 13), Wiesbaden: Dr. Ludwig Reichert Verlag, 1993, p. 26-35.

SCHIPPERGES H., 'Handschriftliche Untersuchungen zur Rezeption des Petrus Hispanus in die 'Opera Ysaac' (Lyon 1515)', in: G. KEIL, R. RUDOLF, W. SCHMITT & H.J. VERMEER (eds.), *Fachliteratur des Mittelalters. Festschrift für Gerhard Eis*, Stuttgart: Metzler, 1968, p. 311-318.

SCHLEISSNER M., 'Sexuality and Reproduction in the Late Medieval "Problemata Aristotelis"', in: J. DOMES – W.D. GERABECK - B.D. HAAGE (eds.), *Licht der Natur. Medizin in Fachliteratur und Dichtung. Festschrift für Gundolf Keil zum 60. Geburtstag* (Göppinger Arbeiten zur Germanistik 585), Göppingen: Kümmerle Verlag, 1994, p. 383-396.

SCHUMANN K.P., *Heinrich von Herford. Enzyklopädische Gelehrsamkeit und universalhistorische Konzeption im Dienste dominikanischer Studienbedürfnisse*, Münster: Aschendorff, 1996, p. 53-70.

SPEER A., '*Ratione duce*. Die naturphilosophischen Dialoge des Adelard von Bath und des Wilhelm von Conches', in: K. JACOBI (ed.), *Gespräche lesen. Philosophische Dialoge im Mittelalter* (Scriptoralia 115), Tübingen: Gunter Narr Verlag, 1999, p. 199-229.

THOMASSET C., *Commentaire au Dialogue de Placides et Timéo*, Genève: Droz, 1982.

VAN DER LUGT M., 'La peau noire dans la science médiévale', in: *Micrologus XIII: La pelle umana / The Human Skin*, Firenze: SISMEL, 2005, p. 439-475.

VAN DER LUGT M., *Le ver, le démon et la vierge. Les théories médiévales de la génération extraordinaire. Une étude sur les rapports entre théologie, philosophie naturelle et médecine* (L'Ane d'or 16), Paris: Les Belles Lettres, 2004.

VENTURA I., 'Cecco d'Ascoli', in T.F. GLICK – S.J. LIVESEY – F. WALLIS (eds.), *Medieval Science, Technology and Medicine: An Encyclopedia*, London: Routledge, 2005.

VENTURA I., 'Der 'Liber similitudinum naturalium' Konrads von Halberstadt und seine Quellen: ein Fallbeispiel aus der naturwissenschaftlichen Textüberlieferung im Spätmittelalter', *Frühmittelalterliche Studien* 35 (2001), p. 349-406.

VENTURA I., 'Die moralisierten Enzyklopädien des späteren Mittelalters: ein Überblick unter Berücksichtigung der Fallbeispiele des "Lumen Anime", des "Liber de exemplis et similitudinibus rerum" und des "Liber Similitudinum Naturalium"', *Reti Medievali: Rivista* 4 (2003) (to read on www.retimedievali.it).

VENTURA I., *Il Liber similitudinum naturalium di Corrado di Halberstadt*, Phd. Diss. Firenze, 1998 (unpublished).

VENTURA I., '*Quaestiones* and Encyclopaedias: Some Aspects of the Late Medieval Reception of the Pseudo-Aristotelian *Problemata* in Encyclopaedic and Scientific Culture', in: A.A. MACDONALD – M.W. TWOMEY (eds.), *Schooling and Society. The Ordering and Reordering of Knowledge in the Western Middle Ages*, Leuven-Paris-Dudley: Peeters, 2004, p. 23-42.

VENTURA I., 'The collections of natural questions: development and evolution forms of a type of 'popular encyclopaedic literature' between thirteenth and sixteenth century', to be published in: P. MICHEL – F. DE CAPITANI (eds.), *All you need to know: Encyclopaedias and the idea of general knowledge (Conference, Prangins, Switzerland, 18-20 September 2003)*, in preparation.

VENTURA I., 'The Scholastic Quaestio as Encyclopaedic Structure: the Catena aurea entium of Henry of Herford', in: G. DE CALLATAŸ – B. VAN DEN ABEELE (eds.), *Une lumière venue d'ailleurs. Actes du Colloque International Louvain-la-Neuve, 20-21 Mai 2005*, in preparation.

VIDMANOVÁ A., 'Summa recreatorum', in: D. FLIEGER – V. BOK (eds.), *Deutsche Literatur des Mittelalters in Böhmen und über Böhmen. Vorträge der internationalen Tagung, veranstaltet vom Institut für Germanistik der Pädagogischen Fakultät der Südböhmischen Universität Česke Budějovice (Česke Budějovice, 8. bis 11. September 1999)*, Wien: Edition Praesens, 2001, p. 169-179.

WACHINGER B., '*Convivium Fabulosum*. Erzählen bei Tisch im 15. und 16. Jahrhundert, besonders in der ‚Mensa Philosophica' und bei Erasmus und Luther', in: W. HAUG – B. WACHINGER (eds.), *Kleinere Erzählformen des 15. und 16. Jahrhunderts*, Tübingen: Max Niemeyer Verlag, 1993, p. 256-286.

WACHINGER B., *Erzählen für die Gesundheit. Diätetik und Literatur im Mittelalter*, Heidelberg: Carl Winter Verlag, 2001.

WACHINGER B., 'Wissen und Wissenschaft als Faszinosum für Laien im Mittelalter', in: C. DIETL – D. HELSCHINGER (eds.), *Ars und Scientia im Mittelalter und in der Frühen Neuzeit. Ergebnisse interdisziplinärer Forschung. Georg Wieland zum 65. Geburtstag*, Tübingen-Basel: Francke, 2001, p. 13-29.

WEISEL B., 'Die Überlieferung des 'Livre de Sidrac' in Handschriften und Drucken', in: H. BRUNNER – N. R. WOLF (eds.), *Wissensliteratur im Mittelalter und in der Frühen Neuzeit* (Wissensliteratur im Mittelalter 13), Wiesbaden: Dr. Ludwig Reichert Verlag, 1993, p. 53-66.

WINS B., ''Le Livre de Sidrac' – Stand der Forschung und neue Ergebnisse', in: H. BRUNNER – N.R. WOLF (eds.), *Wissensliteratur im Mittelalter und in der Frühen Neuzeit* (Wissensliteratur im Mittelalter 13), Wiesbaden: Dr. Ludwig Reichert Verlag, 1993, p. 36-52.

YASSIF E., 'Pseudo Ben Sira and the 'Wisdom Questions' Tradition in the Middle Ages', *Fabula* 23 (1982), p. 48-63.

YASSIF E., *The tales of Ben Sira in the Middle Ages: a critical text and literary studies*, Jerusalem: Magnes Press, 1984.

5. BARTHOLOMEW OF MESSINA
G. Coucke

5.1. Editions

BRAMS J. – STEEL C. – TOMBEUR P. – DE LEEMANS P. – GOUDER E. (eds.), *Aristoteles Latinus Database ALD Release 2/2006*, Turnhout: Brepols Publishers, 2006.

> This CD-ROM contains critical editions of Bartholomew's translations of *De mundo* (ed. by Lorimer, see below), *De mirabilibus auscultationibus* (ed. by Livius-Arnold, see below) and the *Magna Moralia* (ed. by C. Pannier, unpublished). Moreover, it contains a faithful transcription of Bartholomew's translation of the *Problemata Physica*, as it is found in the Venice *ap. Ioh. Herbort de Seligenstadt* 1482 edition.

FÖRSTER K. (ed.), *Scriptores Physiognomonici Graeci et Latini*, Vol. I: *Physiognomonica Pseudoaristotelis, graece et latine, Adamantii cum epitomis Graece, Polemonis e recensione G. Hoffmanni arabice et latine continens* (Bibliotheca scriptorum Graecorum et Romanorum Teubneriana), Leipzig: Teubner, 1893, p. 1-91.

FRANCESCHINI E., 'Sulle versioni latine medievali del Περὶ χρωμάτων', in: *Autour d'Aristote. Recueil d'études de Philosophie ancienne et médiévale offert à Monseigneur A. Mansion* (Bibliothèque Philosophique de Louvain 16), Leuven: Publications Universitaires de Louvain, 1955, p. 451- 469. (partial edition + study)

GÜNSTER M., *Studien zu der vom Magister Bartholomäeus de Messina durchgeführten lateinischen Übertragung der griechischen Hippiatrica-Kapittel des Hierocles*, Hannover: Tierärztliche Hochschule, 1974 (Inaugural Dissertation; edition + study)

KLEY W., *Theophrasts Metaphysisches Bruchstück und die Schrift Περὶ Σημείων in der lateinischen Übersetzung des Bartholomaeus von Messina*, Würzburg: Dissertationsdruckerei und Verlag Konrad Triltsch, 1936 (edition + study).

LIVIUS-ARNOLD G., *Aristotelis quae feruntur De Mirabilibus Auscultationibus. Translatio Bartholomaei de Messana. Accedit Translatio Anonyma Basileensis*, Amsterdam, 1978 (unpublished doctoral dissertation; edition + study).

LORIMER W.L. – MINIO-PALUELLO L. (eds.), *De Mundo. Translationes Bartholomaei et Nicholai (Aristoteles Latinus XI, 1- 2)*, Bruges – Paris: Desclée De Brouwer, 1965.

MARENGHI G. (ed.), *Problemi di fonazione e di acustica*, Naples: Libreria scientifica editrice, 1962 (= Bartholomew's translation of Section XI on p. 105-117).

MARENGHI G. (ed.), *Problemi di medicina*, Milan: Istituto editoriale Italiano 1966; 2nd ed. Bolsena: Massari, 1999 (= Bartholomew's translation of Sections XXXIV-XXXVII on p. 337-349).

ROSE V., *Aristoteles Pseudepigraphus*, Leipzig: Teubner, 1863, p. 631-643 (Reprint: Hildesheim-New York: G. Olms, 1971) (translation of *De inundatione nili*).

SELIGSOHN R., *Die Übersetzung der ps.-aristotelischen Problemata durch Bartholomaeus von Messina. Text und textkritische Untersuchungen zum ersten Buch*, Inaugural Dissertation, Berlin: Ebering, 1934 (edition + study).

5.2. Studies

BRAMS J., *La Riscoperta di Aristotele in Occidente* (Eredità Medievale 3/22), Milano: Jaca Books, 2003 (esp. p. 89-103: 'Capitolo settimo: Bartolomeo di Messina').

DE LEEMANS P. – GOYENS M., 'La transmission des savoirs en passant par trois langues: les cas des *Problemata* d'Aristote traduits en latin et en moyen français', in: P. NOBEL (ed.), *La transmission des savoirs au Moyen Âge et à la Renaissance*. Vol. 1. *Du XIIe au XVe siècle* (Littéraire), Besançon: Presses Universitaires Franche-Comté, 2005, p. 231-257.

DEVIÈRE E., 'Traduction et spécialisation du vocabulaire au Moyen Âge: Les équivalents des mots de la famille de πνεῦμα dans la traduction latine des *Problemata* par Barthélémy de Messine', *Filologia Mediolatina* 15 (2007, forthcoming).

DOD B.G., 'Aristoteles Latinus', in: N. KRETZMANN – A. KENNY – J. PINBORG (eds.), *The Cambridge History of Later Medieval Philosophy. From the Rediscovery of Aristotle to the desintegration of scholasticism, 1100-1600*, Cambridge, 1982, p. 45-79 (esp. p. 62).

FISCHER K.-D., '"A horse! a horse! my kingdom for a horse!" Versions of Greek Horse Medicine in Medieval Italy', *Medizin Historisches Journal* 34 (1999), p. 123-138 (about the translation of Hierocles' *Hippiatrica*).

FLASHAR H., *Aristoteles: Problemata Physika* (Aristoteles Werke in Deutscher Übersetzung 19), Berlin: Akademie-Verlag, 1962 (1991⁴), p. 373 sqq.

GOYENS M. – DE LEEMANS P., 'Traduire du grec au latin et du latin en français: un défi à la fidelité', in: P. Anderson (ed.), *Medieval Translation Practices. Papers from the Symposium at the University of Copenhagen 25th and 26th October 2002*, Copenhagen: Museum Tusculanum Press, 2004, p. 204-223.

IMPELLIZZERI S., 'Bartolomaeo da Messina', in: *Dizionario Biografico degli Italiani* VI (1964), p. 729-730.

JOUANNA J. (ed.), *Hippocrate. La Nature de l'homme* (Corpus Medicorum Graecorum I 1,3), Berlin: Akademie-Verlag, 1975, esp. p. 127-130.

MARENGHI G., 'Un capitolo dell' Aristotele medievale: Bartolomeo da Messina, traduttore dei *Problemata physica*', *Aevum* 36 (1962), p. 268-283.

MINIO-PALUELLO L., 'Guglielmo di Moerbeke traduttore della Poetica di Aristotele 1278', *Rivista di Filosofia Neo-Scolastica* 39 (1947), 1-17 (p. 7) [= MINIO- PALUELLO L., *Opuscula. The Latin Aristotle*, Amsterdam: Adolf M. Hakkert, 1972, p. 40-56].

MINIO-PALUELLO L., 'Note sull'Aristotele Latino Medievale. III. I due traduttori medievali del *De Mundo*: Nicola Siculo (Greco) collaboratore di Roberto Grossatesta, e Bartolomeo da Messina', *Rivista di Filosofia Neo-Scolastica* 42 (1950), p. 232-237 [= *Opuscula...*, p. 108-113].

PANNIER C., 'La traduction médiévale des *Magna Moralia*. Une étude critique de la tradition manuscrite', in: L.J. BATAILLON – B.G. GUYOT – R.H. ROUSSE (eds.), *La production du livre universitaire au moyen âge. Exemplar et pecia*, Paris: CNRS, 1988, p. 165-204.

VUILLEMIN-DIEM G., 'La liste des Oeuvres d'Hippocrate dans le *Vindobonensis Phil. Gr. 100*: un autographe de Guillaume de Moerbeke', in: J. BRAMS – W. VANHAMEL (eds.), *Guillaume de Moerbeke. Recueil d'études à l'occasion du 700ᵉ anniversaire de sa mort (1286)* (Ancient and Medieval Philosophy De Wulf-Mansion Centre Series 1 VII), Leuven: Leuven University Press, 1989, p. 135-184, esp. p. 159-162.

VUILLEMIN-DIEM G., ' Zum Aristoteles Latinus in den *Quaternuli* des David von Dinant', *Archives d'Histoire Doctrinale et Littéraire du Moyen Âge* 70 (2003), 27-136, esp. p. 67-98 (= comparison between David of Dinant's and Bartholomew's translation of the *Problemata*).

6. PETER OF ABANO   M. Klemm

6.1. Primary sources

References to texts which lack modern editions or printings can be found in PASCHETTO E., *Pietro d'Abano medico e filosofo*, Firenze: Vallecchi, 1984.

FEDERICI VESCOVINI G. (ed.), *Il "Lucidator dubitabilium astronomiae" di Pietro d'Abano ed altre opera*. Presentazione di E. GARIN (Il mito e la storia 3), Padova: Editoriale Programma, 1988.

FEDERICI VESCOVINI G. (ed.), *Pietro d'Abano. Trattati di Astronomia. Lucidator dubitabilium astronomiae, De motu octavae sphaerae e altre opere* (Il mito e la storia 3), Padova: Editoriale Programma, 1992 (= second edition of the 1988 ed., with a revised introduction).

RIONDATO E. – OLIVIERI L. (eds.), *Pietro d'Abano, Conciliator. Ristampa fotomeccanica dell'edizione Venetiis apud Iuntas 1565* (I Filosofi Veneti. Sezione II – Ristampe 1), Padova: Editrice Antenore, 1985. Also includes Pietro's *De Venenis*.

6.2. Studies

A complete list of the publications by G. Federici Vescovini, several of which are devoted to Pietro d'Abano, is found in: G. MARCHETTI – O. RIGNANI – V. SORGE (eds.), *Ratio et Superstitio. Essays in Honor of Graziella Federici Vescovini* (FIDEM. Textes et études du Moyen Âge 24), Louvain-la-Neuve, 2003, p. 621-643.

ALESSIO F., 'Filosofia e Scienza. Pietro da Abano', in: G. ARNALDI – M. PASTORE STOCCHI (eds.), *Storia della cultura veneta, II: Il trecento*, Vicenza: Pozza, 1976, p.171-206.

BURNETT C., 'Hearing and Music in Book XI of Pietro d'Abano's *Expositio Problematum Aristotelis*', in: N. VAN DEUSEN (ed.), *Tradition and Ecstasy: The Agony of the Fourteenth Century*, Ottawa: Institute of Mediaeval Music, 1997, p. 153-190.

CADDEN J., ' "Nothing Natural is shameful": Vestiges of a debate about sex and science in a group of late-medieval MSS', *Speculum* 76 (2001), p. 66-89.

CADDEN J., 'Sciences/silences: The Natures and Languages of 'Sodomy' in Peter of Abano's *Problemata* Commentary', in: K. LOCHRIE – P. MCCRACKEN – J. SCHULTZ (eds.), *Constructing Medieval Sexuality* (Medieval Cultures 11), Minneapolis: University of Minnesota, 1997, p. 40-57.

CRISCIANI C., 'Filosofia e medicina in Pietro d'Abano: Note da un convegno', *Rivista di storia della filosofia* 41 (1986), p. 795-804.

D'ALVERNY M.-T., 'Pietro d'Abano et les 'naturalistes' a l'époque de Dante', in: V. BRANCA – G. PADOAN (eds.), *Dante e la cultura veneta: atti del Convegno di studi organizzato dalle Fondazione "Giorgio Cini", Venezia, Padova, Verona, 30 marzo – 5 aprile 1966*, Florence: Olschki, 1966, p. 207-219.

D'ALVERNY M.-T., 'Pietro d'Abano traducteur de Galien', *Medioevo* 11 (1985), p. 19-64.

FAVARO A., 'Pietro d'Abano ed il suo *Lucidator astrologiae*', *Atti del Reale Istituto Veneto* 75 (1916), p. 515-527.

FEDERICI VESCOVINI G., 'La médecine, synthèse d'art et de science selon Pierre d'Abano', in: R. RASHED – J. BIARD (eds.), *Les doctrines de la science de l'Antiquité à l'âge classique* (Ancient and Classical Sciences and Philosophy), Leuven: Peeters, 1999, p. 238-55.

FEDERICI VESCOVINI G., 'Pietro d'Abano e le fonti astronomiche greco-arabo-latine (a proposito del *Lucidator astronomiae* o *astrologiae)*', *Medioevo* 11 (1985), p. 65-96.

FEDERICI VESCOVINI G., 'Peter of Abano and astrology', in: P. CURRY (ed.), *Astrology, Science and Society: Historical Essays*, Woodbridge: Boydell and Brewer, 1987, p. 19-40.

FEDERICI VESCOVINI G., 'Pietro d'Abano e la medicina astrologica dello *Speculum physiognomiae* di Michele Savonarola', in: R. KECKS (ed.), *Musagetes. Festschrift für Wolfram Prinz* (Frankfurter Forschungen zur Kunst 17), Berlin: Gebr. Mann Verlag, 1991, p. 167-77.

FEDERICI VESCOVINI G., 'Pietro d'Abano tra Biografia e Fortuna', in: Ead. (ed.) *Pietro d'Abano. Trattati di Astronomia. Lucidator dubitabilium astronomiae, De motu octavae sphaerae e altre opere* (Il mito e la storia 3), Padova: Editoriale Programma, 1992.

FEDERICI VESCOVINI G., 'Profilo di Pietro d'Abano, Il Conciliatore', in: G. BENTIVEGNA – S. BURGIO e.a. (eds.), *Filosofia, Scienza, Cultura. Studi in onore di Corrado Dollo,* Soveria Mannelli: Rubbettino, 2002, p. 845-862.

FEDERICI VESCOVINI G., 'Il sole e la luna nelle citazioni di Pietro d'Abano dei segretti di Albumasar, di Sadan', *Micrologus* (2004), p. 185-194.

FERRARI S., *I tempi, la vita, le dottrine di Pietro d'Abano*, Genova, 1900.

HASSE D.N., 'Pietro d'Abano's "Conciliator" and the Theory of the Soul in Paris', in: J.A. AERTSEN – K. EMERY, Jr. – ANDREAS SPEER (eds.), *Nach der Verurteilung von 1277. Philosophie und Theologie an der Universität von Paris im letzten Viertel des 13. Jahrhunderts. Studien und Texte* (Miscellanea Mediaevalia 28), Berlin – New York: Walter de Gruyter, 2001, p. 635-653.

JACQUART D., 'Du Moyen Age à la Renaissance: Pietro d'Abano et Berengario da Carpi lecteurs de la Préface de Celse', in: G. SABBAH – P. MUDRY (eds.), *La Médecine de Celse: aspects historiques, scientifiques et littéraires* (Université de Saint-Etienne. Centre Jean Palerne. Mémoires 13), Saint-Étienne: Publications de l'Université de Saint-Etienne, 1994, p. 345-352.

JACQUART D., *Le milieu médical en France du XIIe au XVe siècle: en annexe au 2e supplément au «Dictionnaire» d'Ernest Wickersheimer* (Centre de Recherches d'histoire et de philologie de la IVᵉ Section de l'École Pratique des Hautes Études, V, Hautes études médiévales et modernes 46), Genève: Librairie Droz, 1981, esp. p. 202.

JACQUART D., 'L'influence des astres sur le corps humain chez Pietro d'Abano', in: B. RIBÉMONT, *Le corps et ses énigmes au Moyen Âge: Actes du colloque, Orléans, 15-16 mai 1992*, Caen: Paradigme, 1993, p. 73-86.

KLEMM M. – DE LEEMANS P., 'Pietro d'Abano', in: T.F. GLICK – S.J. LIVESEY – F. WALLIS (eds.), *Medieval Science, Technology and Medicine: An Encyclopedia*, New York-London: Routledge, 2005, p. 404-405.

KLEMM M., 'Medicine and Moral Virtue in the *Expositio Problematum Aristotelis* of Peter of Abano', *Early Science and Medicine* 11.3 (2006), p. 302-335.

MARANGON P., *Il pensiero ereticale nella Marca trevigiana e a Venezia dal 1200 al 1350*, Abano Terme: Francisci Editore, 1984 (esp. p. 67-104: 'Per una revisione dell'interpretatione di Pietro d'Abano').

Medioevo: Rivista di storia della filosofía medievale 11 (1985) (= special issue entirely devoted to Pietro d'Abano).

NARDI B., *Saggi sull'aristotelismo padovano dal secolo XIV al XVI*, Firenze: G.C. Sansoni, 1958 (esp. p. 19-74: 'Intorno alle dottrine filosofiche di Pietro d'Abano' and p. 1-17 'La teoria dell'anima e la generazione delle forme secondo Pietro d'Abano').

NARDI B., *Saggi di filosofia dantesca*, Firenze: La Nuova Italia, 1967² (esp. p. 43-65: 'Dante e Pietro d'Abano').

NORPOTH L., 'Zur Bio-, Bibliographie und Wissenschaftslehre des Pietro d'Abano, Mediziners, Philosophen und Astronomen in Padua', *Kyklos* 3 (1930), p. 292-353.

OLIVIERI L., *Pietro d'Abano e il pensiero neolatino: filosofia, scienza e ricerca dell'Aristotele greco tra i secoli xiii e xiv* (Saggi e Testi 23), Padova: Editrice Antenore, 1988.

OTTAVIANI D., 'La méthode scientifique dans le *Conciliator* de Pietro d'Abano', in: C. GRELLARD (ed.), *Méthodes et statut des sciences à la fin du Moyen-Âge*, Villeneuve d'Ascq: Presses Universitaires du Septentrion, 2004, p. 13-26.

PASCHETTO E., *Pietro d'Abano medico e filosofo*, Firenze: Vallecchi, 1984.

PASCHETTO E., 'La Fisiognomica nell'enciclopedia delle scienze di Pietro d'Abano', *Medioevo: Rivista di storia della filosofía medievale* 11 (1985), p. 97-112.

RANDALL J.H., Jr., 'The Development of Scientific Method in the School of Padua', *Journal of the History of Ideas* 1 (1940), p. 177-206 (repr. in *The School of Padua and the Emergence of Modern Science,* Padova: Editrice Antenore, 1961).

SIRAISI N., 'The *Expositio Problematum Aristotelis* of Peter of Abano', *Isis* 61 (1970), p. 321-339.

SIRAISI N., *Arts and Sciences at Padua: The* studium *of Padua before 1350* (Pontifical institute of mediaeval studies. Studies and texts 25), Toronto: Pontifical institute of mediaeval studies, 1973.

SIRAISI N., 'Pietro d'Abano and Taddeo Alderotti: Two Models of Medical Culture', *Medioevo: Rivista di storia della filosofía medievale* 11 (1985), p. 139-162.

STRUEVER N., 'Petrarch's *Invective contra medicum*: An early confrontation of rhetoric and medicine', *MLN* 108 (1993), p. 659-679.

THORNDIKE L., 'Relations of the Inquisition of Peter of Abano and Cecco d'Ascoli', *Speculum* 1 (1926), p. 338-43.

THORNDIKE L., *A History of Magic and Experimental Science*, 8 Vols., New York: Macmillan (vols. 1-2) and Columbia University Press, 1923-58 (esp. vol. II, p. 874-947).

THORNDIKE L., 'Manuscripts of the Writings of Peter of Abano', *Bulletin of the History of Medicine* 15 (1944), p. 201-19.

THORNDIKE L., 'Peter of Abano and Another Commentary on the Problems of Aristotle', *Bulletin of the History of Medicine* 29 (1955), p. 517-523.

TROILIO E., 'L'oroscopo delle religioni: Pietro d'Abano e Pietro Pompanazzi', *Sophia* 3 (1935), p. 49-63 and p.161-180.

WALLACE W., 'Circularity and the Paduan *Regressus*: From Pietro d'Abano to Galileo Galilei', *Vivarium* 33 (1995), p. 76-97.

7. EVRART DE CONTY[1]   C. Boucher – M. Goyens

7.1. General studies

BOSSUAT R., *Manuel bibliographique de la littérature française du Moyen Âge*, Melun: Librairie d'Argences (Bibliothèque elzévirienne. Nouvelle série. Études et documents 1), 1951, p. 531, n° 5509; p. 581, n° 5963; *Supplément (1949-1953)*, with Jacques MONFRIN, Paris: Librairie d'Argences, 1955, p. 118, n° 7108.

JACQUART, D., *La médecine médiévale dans le cadre parisien*, Paris, Fayard, 1998, p. 275-286.

LEFÈVRE S., 'Évrard de Conty', in: G. HASENOHR – M. ZINK (eds.), *Dictionnaire des lettres françaises: le Moyen Âge*, Paris: Fayard, 1992, p. 434-435.

ROY B., 'La cantillation des romans médiévaux: une voie vers la théâtralisation', *Le moyen français* 19 (1988), p. 148-162. – Reprint.: 'Évrart de Conty et la cantillation des romans', in: B. ROY, *Cy nous dient: dialogue avec quelques auteurs médiévaux*, Orléans: Paradigme, 1999, p. 13-24.

WICKERSHEIMER E., *Dictionnaire biographique des médecins en France au Moyen Âge* (Publications du Centre de recherches d'histoire et de philologie de la IVᵉ section de l'École pratique des hautes études, série 5: Hautes études médiévales et modernes, 34), Genève: Droz, 1936 [Reprint: G. BEAUJOUAN (ed.), Genève: Droz; Paris: Champion, 1979], vol. 1, p. 146; vol. 3: *Supplément*, par D. JACQUART, Genève: Droz; Paris: Champion (Hautes études médiévales et modernes, 35), p. 72.

---

1. This bibliography was prepared for a large part by Caroline Boucher and is to be found on the website of ARLIMA, *Archives de Littérature du Moyen Âge*, edited by Laurent Brun, (www.arlima.net). It has been completed and adapted for the purposes of this volume by Michèle Goyens.

7.2. Poem of the *Eschés amoureux*

7.2.1. Editions

GALPIN S. L., '*Les Eschez amoureux*: a Complete Synopsis with Unpublished Extracts', *Romanic Review* 11 (1920), p. 283-307. (partial edition)

KÖRTING G., *Altfranzösische Übersetzung der "Remedia amoris" des Ovids. Ein Theil des allegorisch-didaktischen Epos "Les échecs amoureux", nach der Dresdener Handschrift herausgegeben*, Leipzig, 1871 [Reprint: Genève: Slatkine, 1971]. (edition of verses 11120-13478).

KRAFT C., *Die Liebesgarten-Allegorie der Échecs amoureux. Kritische Ausgabe und Kommentar*, New York, Bern et Frankfurt: Lang, 1976. (edition of verses 3663-9326).

METTLICH J., *Ein Kapitel über Erziehung aus einer altfranzösischen Dichtung des XIV. Jahrhunderts*, Münster: Aschendorff, 1902. [edition of fol. 127-30 and 136-138 of the Dresden ms.]

RAIMONDI G., '*Les eschés amoureux*: studio preparatorio ed edizione (I. vv. 1-3662)', *Pluteus* 8-9 (1990-1998), p. 67-241.

RAIMONDI G., '*Les eschés amoureux*: studio preparatorio ed edizione (II. vv. 3663-5538)', *Pluteus*, in preparation.

RIVOIRE A., "*Li eschés amoureux"* : *frammenti trascritti dal codice marciano con introduzione e apendice*, Torre Pellice, 1915 [Reprint: 1920].

7.2.2. Studies

ABERT H., 'Die Musikästhetik der *Échecs amoureux*', *Romanische Forschungen* 15 (1904), p. 884-925.

ABERT H., 'Die Musikästhetik der *Échecs amoureux*', *Sammelbände der Internationalen Musikgesellschaft* 6 (1905), p. 346-355.

BADEL P.-Y., *Le "Roman de la Rose" au XIVe siècle: étude de la réception de l'oeuvre*, Genève: Droz, 1980. See p. 263-290.

GALLY M., 'Le miroir mis en abyme. Les *Échecs amoureux* et la réécriture du *Roman de la Rose*', in: F. POMEL (ed.), *Miroirs et jeux de miroirs dans la littérature médiévale*, Rennes: Presses universitaires de Rennes, 2003, p. 253-263.

GALLY M., *L'intelligence de l'amour d'Ovide à Dante*, Paris: CNRS Éditions, 2005. See p. 125-194: « L'(es) échec(s) de l'amour ».

HÖFLER H., "*Les Échecs amoureux"* : *Untersuchungen über die Quellen des II. Teiles*, Diss., München: Neustadt, 1905.

HÖFLER H., '*Les Échecs amoureux*', *Romanische Forschungen* 27 (1910), p. 625-689.

JUNG M.-R., *Études sur le poème allégorique en France au Moyen Âge*, Bern: Francke, 1971.

JUNKER H.P., 'Über das altfranzösische Epos *Les échecs amoureux*', *Berichte des freien Deutschen Hochstiftes* 3 (1886-1887).

LEFÈVRE S., 'Échecs amoureux', in: G. HASENOHR – M. ZINK (eds.), *Dictionnaire des lettres françaises: le Moyen Âge*, Paris: Fayard, 1992, p. 397-398.

MUSSAFIA A., 'Zu den altfranzösischen Handschriften der Marcus bibliothek in Venedig', *Sitzungsberichte der philosophisch-historischen Klasse der Akademie der Wissenschaften in Wien* 42 (1863), p. 313-328.

RAIMONDI G., *"Les eschés amoureux" : studio preparatorio all'edizione dei vv. 1-16300*, dottorato di ricerca, Università di Roma La Sapienza, 1997.
SIEPER E., *Les échecs amoureux: eine altfranzösische Nachahmung des Rosenromans und ihre englische Übertragung*, Weimar, 1898.
SIEPER E., 'Zu den *Échecs amoureux*', *Englische Studien* 2 (1900), p. 310-315.

7.3. Problemes

7.3.1. Edition

The translation by Evrart de Conty will be edited by a group of scholars, a.o. Françoise Guichard-Tesson, Michèle Goyens, and Joëlle Ducos. It will be published by Champion in the series *Classiques Français du Moyen Âge* in ten volumes. The first volume, which will contain the edition of Section I, is in preparation by F. Guichard-Tesson and M. Goyens, with a contribution by G. Dumas; publication is foreseen in the course of 2007:

GUICHARD-TESSON FR. – GOYENS M. – DUMAS G., *Les* Problemes *par Évrart de Conty. Partie I.* (avec la collaboration d'A. Bloem) (Classiques Français du Moyen Âge), Paris: Honoré Champion, in preparation.

7.3.2. Studies

BLAIR A., 'The *Problemata* as a Natural Philosophical Genre', in: A. GRAFTON – N. SIRAISI (eds.), *Natural Particulars. Nature and the Disciplines in Renaissance Europe*, Cambridge (MA): MIT Press, 1999, p. 171-204. See p. 180-181.
BLOEM A. – GOYENS M., 'À propos des mouvements et des affections de l'âme. Analyse du champ sémantique des émotions dans la traduction en moyen français des *Problemes* d'Aristote', in: O. BERTRAND – H. GERNER – B. STUMPF (eds.), *Constitution des lexiques scientifiques et techniques entre 1300 et 1600*, Paris: Les Editions de l'Ecole Polytechnique, in press.
BOUCHER C, *La mise en scène de la vulgarisation. Les traductions d'autorités en langue vulgaire aux XIIIᵉ et XIVᵉ siècles*, PhD École pratique des hautes études, Paris, 2005.
CADDEN J., '"Nothing Natural Is Shameful": Vestiges of a Debate about Sex and Science in a Group of Late-Medieval Manuscripts', *Speculum* 76 (2001), p. 66-89.
DE LEEMANS P. – GOYENS M., 'La transmission des savoirs en passant par trois langues: le cas des *Problemata* d'Aristote traduits en latin et en moyen français', in: P. NOBEL (ed.), *La transmission des savoirs au Moyen Âge et à la Renaissance*. Vol. 1. *Du XIIᵉ au XVᵉ siècle*, Besançon, Presses Universitaires de Franche-Comté, 2005, p. 231-257.
DE LEEMANS P. –GOYENS M., '"Et samble qu'il woeille dire...". Evrart de Conty comme traducteur de Pierre d'Abano', in: O. BERTRAND – J. JENKINS (eds.), *The Medieval Translator IX*, Turnhout: Brepols Publishers, in press.
DUCOS J., *La météorologie en français: réception des météorologiques d'Aristote (XIIIᵉ–XIVᵉ siècles)*, PhD Université de Paris IV-Sorbonne, 1993.
DUCOS J., 'Traduction et lexique scientifique: le cas des *Problèmes* d'Aristote traduits par Evrart de Conty', in: *Traduction et adaptation en France à la fin du Moyen Age et à la Renaissance. Actes du Colloque organisé par*

l'Université de Nancy II, 23-25 mars 1995, réunis et présentés par Charles Brucker (Colloques, congrès et conférences sur la Renaissance 10), Paris, Champion, 1997, p. 237-248.

DUCOS J., *La météorologie en français au Moyen Âge (XIIIe–XIVe siècles)* (Sciences, techniques et civilisations du Moyen Âge à l'aube des Lumières 2), Paris: Champion, 1998 [p. 195-204: 'Évrart de Conty et Jean Corbechon: l'évolution de la traduction scientifique'].

GATHERCOLE P. M., 'Medieval Science: Evrart de Conti', *Romance Notes* 6:2 (1965), p. 175-181.

GOYENS M., 'Le développement du lexique scientifique français et la traduction des *Problèmes* d'Aristote par Evrart de Conty (c. 1380)', *Thélème: revista complutense de estudios franceses*, número extraordinario (2003), p. 189-207.

GOYENS M., 'Comprendre Aristote au Moyen Age: le procédé de reformulation dans la traduction des *Problèmes* par Evrart de Conty', in: P. NOBEL (ed.), *Textes et cultures: réception, modèles, interférences*. Volume 1. *Réception de l'Antiquité* (Collection "Littéraire"), s.l.: Presses universitaires de Franche-Comté, 2004, p. 145-163.

GOYENS M., 'Évrart de Conty: traducteur, adaptateur et commentateur des *Problèmes* d'Aristote', in: M. COLOMBO TIMELLI – C. GALDERISI (eds.), *"Pour acquerir honneur et pris"*. *Mélanges de Moyen Français offerts à Giuseppe Di Stefano*, s.l.: Editions CERES, 2004, p. 123-135.

GOYENS M., 'Le lexique des plantes et la traduction des *Problèmes* d'Aristote par Evrart de Conty (c. 1380)', *Le Moyen Français* 55-56 (2004-2005), p. 145-165.

GOYENS M. – DE LEEMANS P., 'Traduire du grec au latin et du latin au français: un défi à la fidélité', in: P. ANDERSEN (ed.), *Medieval Translation Practices. Papers from the Symposium at the University of Copenhagen, 25th and 26th October 2002*, Copenhagen: Museum Tusculanum Press, 2004, p. 204-224.

GUICHARD-TESSON F., 'Le métier de traducteur et de commentateur au XIVe siècle d'après Évrart de Conty', *Le moyen français* 24-25 (1990), p. 131-167.

GUICHARD-TESSON F., 'Le souci de la langue et du style au XIVe siècle: l'autographe des *Problèmes* d'Évrart de Conty', *Le moyen français* 33 (1993), p. 57-84.

GUICHARD-TESSON F. – GOYENS M., 'Les *Problèmes* d'Aristote par Evrart de Conty, ou comment éditer l'autographe d'une traduction de traduction', in preparation.

JACQUART D., 'Médecine et morale: les cinq sens chez Évrard de Conty († 1405)', *Micrologus X* (2002), p. 365-379.

MAURO L., 'La musica nei commenti di *Problemi*. Pietro d'Abano e Évrart de Conty', in: L. MAURO (ed.), *La musica nel pensiero medievale*, Ravenna: Longo, 2001, p. 31-69.

OUY G., 'Simon de Plumetot (1371-1443) et sa bibliothèque', in: P. COCKSHAW – M.-C. GARAND – P. JODOGNE (eds.), *Miscellanea codicologica F. Masai dicata*, Gand: Story-Scientia, 1979, vol. 2, p. 353-381 and pl. 53-54.

OUY G., 'Les orthographes de divers auteurs français des XIVe et XVe siècles. Présentation et étude de quelques manuscrits autographes', in: *Le moyen français: recherches de lexicologie et de lexicographie*, Milano: Vita e pensiero, 1991, vol. 1, p. 93-139.

ROY B., 'Pilosité et horripilation dans les *Problèmes* d'Aristote d'Évrart de Conty', *Senefiance* 50 (2004), p. 357-363.

VEDRENNE I., 'L'homme sous la mer: la figure du plongeur dans le monde gréco-romain et l'occident médiéval', in: D. JAMES RAOUL – C. THOMASSET (eds.), *Dans l'eau, sous l'eau: Le monde aquatique au Moyen Âge* (Cultures et civilisations médiévales 25), Paris: Presses de l'Université de Paris-Sorbonne, 2002, p. 273-320. See p. 293, 295-313.

7.4. *Eschez amoureux moralisés*

7.4.1. Editions

LEGARÉ A.-M. (ed.), in coll. with F. GUICHARD-TESSON and B. ROY, *Le livre des échecs amoureux: Bibliothèque nationale [ms. fr. 9197]*, Paris: Éditions du Chêne, 1991. (fac-simile edition)

GUICHARD-TESSON F. – ROY B. (eds.), *Evrart de Conty. Le Livre des Eschez amoureux moralisés* (Bibliothèque du Moyen Français 2), Montréal: Ceres, 1993.

HYATTE R. L. – PONCHART-HYATTE M., *L'harmonie des sphères: encyclopédie d'astronomie et de musique extraite du commentaire sur les Échecs amoureux*, New York, Bern, Frankfurt: Lang, 1985. (partial edition)

7.4.2. Studies

BADEL P.-Y., *Le "Roman de la Rose" au XIVe siècle: étude de la réception de l'oeuvre*, Genève: Droz, 1980. See p. 290-315.

GALLY M., *L'intelligence de l'amour d'Ovide à Dante*, Paris: CNRS Éditions, 2005. See p. 125-194: 'L'(es) échec(s) de l'amour'.

GUICHARD-TESSON F., *La "Glose des Échecs amoureux" d'Évrart de Conty. Les idées et le genre de l'oeuvre d'après le commentaire du Verger de Déduit*, PhD Université de Montréal, 1980.

GUICHARD-TESSON F., 'L'*amour par amours*: l'héritage du *De Amore* dans la *Glose* des *Échecs amoureux*', *Fifteenth-Century Studies* 4 (1981), p. 93-103.

GUICHARD-TESSON F., 'Évrart de Conty, auteur de la *Glose des Echecs amoureux*', *Le moyen français* 8-9 (1982), p. 111-148.

GUICHARD-TESSON F., 'La *Glose des Échecs amoureux*. Un savoir à tendance laïque: comment l'interpréter?', *Fifteenth-Century Studies* 10 (1984), p. 229-260.

GUICHARD-TESSON F., 'Le pion Souvenir et les miroirs déformants dans l'allégorie d'amour', in: B. ROY – P. ZUMTHOR (eds.), *Jeux de mémoire: aspects de la mnémotechnie médiévale*, Montréal: Presses de l'Université de Montréal; Paris: Vrin, 1985, p. 99-108.

HUOT S., 'Sentences and Subtle Fictions: Reading Literature in the Later Middle Ages', in: F. CORNILLIAT – U. LANGER – D. KELLY (eds.), *What Is Literature? 1100-1600*, Lexington: French Forum, 1993, p. 196-209, esp. p. 205-208.

HYATTE R. L., 'The Manuscripts of the Prose Commentary (Fifteenth Century) on *Les Echecs Amoureux*', *Manuscripta* 26 (1982), p. 24-30.

JEAY M., 'La mythologie comme clé de mémorisation: la *Glose des Echecs amoureux*', in: B. ROY – P. ZUMTHOR (eds.), *Jeux de mémoire: aspects de la mnémotechnie médiévale*, Montréal: Presses de l'Université de Montréal; Paris: Vrin, 1985, p. 157-166.

LEGARÉ A.-M. – ROY B., 'Le 'je' d'Évrart de Conty: du texte à l'image', in: B. BAILLAUD – J. DE GRAMONT – D. HÜE (eds.), *Auteurs, lecteurs, savoirs anonymes, "je" et encyclopédies*, Rennes: Presses universitaires de Rennes, 1996, p. 39-56.

METTLICH J., *Die Schachpartie in der Prosabearbeitung der allegorisch-didaktischen Dichtung "Les Eschez amoureux"*, Münster: Aschendorff, 1907.

METTLICH J., *Die Abhandlung über "rymes et mettres" in der Prosabearbeitung der "Échecs amoureux"*, Münster, 1911.

MINNIS A. J., 'Authors in Love: the Exegesis of Late-Medieval Love Poets', in: C. COOK MORSE – P. REED DOOB – M. CURRY WOODS (eds.), *The Uses of Manuscripts in Literary Studies. Essays in Memory of Judson Boyce Allen* (Studies in Medieval Culture 31), Kalamazoo: Western Michigan University, 1992, p. 161-191. See p. 177-180.

MINNIS A. J., 'The Author's Two Bodies? Authority and Fallibility in Late-Medieval Textual Theory', in: P. ROBINSON – R. ZIM (eds), *Of the Making of Books. Medieval Manuscripts, their Scribes and Readers. Essays presented to M. B. Parkes*, Aldershot: Scolar Press, 1997, p. 259-279. See p. 278.

MINNIS A., *Magister Amoris: The "Roman de la Rose" and Vernacular Hermeneutics*, Oxford: Oxford University Press, 2001. See p. 256-319.

MINNIS A., 'Absent Glosses. A Crisis of Vernacular Commentary in Late-Medieval England', *Essays in Medieval Studies* 20 (2003), p. 1-17. See p. 3, 4 and 11.

ROY B., 'Eustache Deschamps et Évrart de Conty théoriciens de l'art poétique', in: B. ROY, *Cy nous dient: dialogue avec quelques auteurs médiévaux*, Orléans: Paradigme, 1999, p. 25-40.

8. RENAISSANCE   C. Martin

8.1. Primary sources (in alphabetical order)

Ellebodius Nicasius, *Aristotelis Problemata partes undecim cum notis Mss.*: Milano, Biblioteca Ambrosiana, D. 291. inf. 1r-72r [1609]; Milano, Biblioteca Ambrosiana, O. 246. sup., fol. 27r-39v [16th c.].

Gaza Theodore, *Problemata*, in: *Aristoteles Opera* edidit Academia Regia Borussica. *Volumen tertium. Aristoteles Latine Interpretibus variis*, p. 415-474 (= Gaza's revised translation; reprinted in: KESSLER E. (ed.), *Aristoteles Latine. Interpretibus variis edidit Academia Regia Borussica Berlin 1831* (Humanistische Bibliothek, Texte und Abhandlungen, Band 30), München: W. Fink Verlag, 1995.

Guastavini Giulio, *In priores decem Aristotelis Problematum sectionis*, Lyon: Horace Cardon, 1608.

Luiz Antonio, *Liber de erroribus Petri Apponensis in Problematibus Aristotelis exponendis,* in: Antonio LUIZ, *De re medica opera,* Lisbon: Rodrigues Luiz, 1540, fol. 109r-115r.

Manelfi Giovanni, *Urbanae Disputationes in primam Problematum Aristotelis sectionem,* Roma: Guglielmo Facciotti, 1630.

Manzoli Benedetto, *Adnotationes in Aristotelis Problemata.*
   Ms.: Milano, Biblioteca Ambrosiana, S. 98 sup., fol. 388r-401v [1562].

Montesauri Domenico, *Commentaria in Aristotelis Problemata.*
   Ms.: Milano, Biblioteca Ambrosiana, A. 113. inf., fol. 1r-374v [1546].

Settala Lodovico, *Commentariorum in Aristotelis Problemata Tomus 1* [= Bks. 1-7], Frankfurt: Andreas Wechel, Claude Marne, & Johann Aubrey, 1602.

Settala Lodovico, *Commentariorum in Aristotelis problemata Tomus 2* [= Bks. 8-14], Frankfurt: Claude Marne & Johann Aubrey, 1607.

Settala Lodovico, *In Aristotelis Problemata commentaria* [= Bks. 1-38], Lyon: Claude Landry, 1632.

Tizzi Roberto, *In Problemata Aristotelis notae* [= Bks 1-15.4].
   Ms.: Oxford, Bodleian Library, D'Orville 54 (S.C. 16932), fol 1r-206v, [circa 1600].

Trebizond George, *Aristotelis Problemata*
   - G. MARENGHI (ed.), *Problemi di fonazione e di acustica,* Naples: Libreria scientifica editrice, 1962, p. 121-135 (= Section XI).
   - G. MARENGHI (ed.), *[Aristotele]: Profumi e miasmi,* Naples: Arte Tipografica, 1991, p. 165-177 (Section XII-XIII)
   - MARENGHI G. (ed.), *Problemi di medicina,* Milan: Istituto editoriale Italiano 1966; 2nd ed. Bolsena: Massari, 1999, p. 275-336 (= Sections I, VI-IX, XIV, XXVII-XXVIII, XXXI-XXXIII).

Trebizond George, 'Adversus Theodorum Gazam in perversionem Problematum Aristotelis', in: L. MOHLER (ed.), *Kardinal Bessarion als Theologe, Humanist und Staatsmann.* Vol. III. *Aus Bessarions Gelehrtenkreis,* Aalen: Scientia Verlag; Paderborn: F. Schöningh, 1967 (reprint of Paderborn, 1942), p. 274-342.

Trebizond George, 'Postfatio in traductione Aristotelis Problematum', in: J. MONFASANI, *Collectanea Trapezuntiana*: Texts, Documents, and Bibliographies of George of Trebizond (Medieval and Renaissance Texts & Studies Series 8), Binghamton: Medieval & Renaissance Texts & Studies, 1984, p. 90.

Trebizond George, 'Protectio Aristotelis Problematum', in: J. MONFASANI, *Collectanea Trapezuntiana...,* p. 411-422.

Trebizond George, 'Scholia ad Problemata Aristotelis', in J. MONFASANI, *Collectanea Trapezuntiana...,* p. 640-666.

8.2. Studies

BLAIR A., 'Authorship in the popular *Problemata Aristotelis'*, *Early Science and Medicine* 4 (1999), p. 189-227.

BLAIR A., 'The *problemata* as a natural philosophical genre', in: A. GRAFTON – N.G. SIRAISI (eds.), *Natural Particulars: Nature and the Disciplines in Renaissance Europe,* Cambridge, Mass.: MIT Press, 1999, p. 171-204.

LAWN B., *The Salernitan Questions: An Introduction to the History of Medieval and Renaissance Problem Literature*, Oxford: Oxford University Press, 1963.

MARENGHI G., 'Giorgio di Trebisonda e la sua traduzione dei problemata', in: G. MARENGHI, *[Aristotele]: Profumi e miasmi*, Naples: Arte Tipografica, 1991, p. 149-164.

MONFASANI J., 'The pseudo-Aristotelian *Problemata* and Aristotle's *De animalibus* in the Renaissance', in: A. GRAFTON – N.G. SIRAISI (eds.), *Natural Particulars: Nature and the Disciplines in Renaissance Europe*, Cambridge, Mass.: MIT Press, 1999, p. 205-47.

INDEX CODICUM MANU SCRIPTORUM

Augsburg
Universitätsbibliothek
   III. 1. 2° 43: 141

Berlin
Staatsbibliothek zu Berlin
Preussischer Kulturbesitz
   Theol. Lat. Fol. 315: 132

Brugge
Openbare Bibliotheek
   476: 3, 4, 6

Cambrai
Bibliothèque Municipale
   894 (797): 153, 154, 157

Cambridge
Peterhouse Library
   200: 86
University Library
   911: 86

Cesena
Biblioteca Malatestiana
   D.XXII.2: 13
   D.XXIV.2: 5, 13, 74
   S.VI.2: 5, 62, 74
   S.VI.3: 62, 74

Chantilly
Musée Condé
   990: 153

Den Haag
Koninklijke Bibliotheek
   133 A 3: 3, 6, 8, 14-17, 19, 153

Dresden
Sächsische Landesbibliothek
   App. 2300: 142

Erfurt
Universitätsbibliothek Erfurt/Gotha
   Ampl. Fol. 15: 9, 10, 12
   Ampl. Fol. 16: 12, 130
   Ampl. Fol. 26: 12
   Ampl. Fol. 236: 12, 13
   Ampl. Fol. 263: 7, 10, 12
   Ampl. Qu. 16: 12
   Ampl. Qu. 192: 141
   Ampl. Qu. 237: 12

Escorial
Biblioteca del Monasterio de San
Lorenzo
   f. I. 11: 59, 60

Firenze
Biblioteca Mediceo-Laurenziana
   Plut. 84,9: 278
   Plut. 87,4: 37

Frankfurt a.M.
Stadt- und Universitätsbibliothek
   Ms. Praed. 44: 142

Gent
Universiteitsbibliotheek
   72: 14, 17, 18
   178: 92, 96, 97, 103, 178

Göttingen
Niedersächsische Staats- und
Universitätsbibliothek
   4° Theol. 124: 92-94, 107

Istanbul
Nuruosmaniye
   3610 (3095): 36, 52

Jena
Thüringer Universitäts- und Landes
bibliothek
   El.f.81: 5, 17, 19, 153, 154, 249

Kraków
Biblioteka Jagiellońska
    654: 94, 107
    2095: 8

Leiden
Universiteitsbibliotheek
    Or. 958 (11): 45, 50
    Voss. misc. 16: 27

London
British Library
    Add. 21978: 13
    Add. 62127: 84-87
    Royal, 12 E XVI: 78, 79, 82, 84,
        86-88, 104, 107
Gray's Inn
    2: 86, 88, 89

Metz
Bibliothèque Municipale
    280: 77

Milano
Biblioteca Ambrosiana
    A 174 sup.: 284

München
Bayerische Staatsbibliothek
    Cod. Hebr. 275: 46
    Cgm 4206: 142
    Clm 666: 141
    Clm 4710: 95, 107
    Clm 8742: 141
    Clm 12021: 12, 92, 94, 95, 97, 107
    Clm 27153: 142

Nürnberg
Stadtbibliothek
    Cent. III.38: 5, 12

Oxford
Bodleian Library
    Barocc. gr. 131: 28
    Canon. misc. lat. 46: 63
    Digby 77: 78, 86, 88
    Digby 153: 6, 7, 12, 78, 80, 83-87
    Digby 161: 78, 86, 87
    Digby 206: 9, 10, 12, 78, 84-87

Magdalen College
    65: 85-88
New College
    233: 27, 284
Oriel College
    28: 86
St. John's College
    113: 6, 7, 9, 14, 85, 86, 88

Padova
Biblioteca Antoniana
    370 Scaff. XVII: 59, 100
Biblioteca Universitaria
    669: 79

Paris
Bibliothèque Nationale de France
    fr. 210: 153, 176, 178, 181, 182,
        184, 186, 190, 193-195
    fr. 211: 15, 18, 153
    fr. 282: 190
    fr. 563-564: 153, 157
    fr. 1350: 178, 182
    fr. 19114: 160
    fr. 22912: 190
    fr. 24281-24282: 145, 153, 154-
        157, 200-205
    ancien gr. 2047A: 23
    gr. 985: 98
    gr. 1865: 98
    gr. 2036: 37, 98
    lat. 3121A: 100
    lat. 6307: 100
    lat. 6327: 100
    lat. 6540: 3, 5-8, 11, 14, 59, 61, 62
    lat. 6541: 5, 14
    lat. 6541A: 5
    lat. 6543: 14
    lat. 7064: 13
    lat. 14725: 6, 12, 100
    lat. 14728: 6, 9
    lat. 15454: 12
    lat. 15081: 12, 100
    lat. 16089: 73, 96
    lat. 16633: 100
    n.a.fr. 3371: 153
    suppl. gr. 204: 98
    suppl. gr. 690: 28

Prague
Národní Knihovna
   I.C.25: 11

's Gravenhage: see Den Haag

Vaticano
Bibliotheca Apostolica Vaticana
   Borgh. 37: 6
   Chis. E.VIII.254: 12
   Pal. gr. 164: 282, 283
   Urb. lat. 1322: 278-283, 287, 289
   Vat. lat. 901: 7
   Vat. lat. 2111: 276-279, 287-289
   Vat. lat. 2112: 9, 13, 15, 278, 283,
     287, 289, 290
   Vat. lat. 2174: 5
   Vat. lat. 2175: 5

Vat. lat. 2481: 12, 75-77, 105, 106
Vat. lat. 5790: 278, 283, 287, 289
Vat. lat. 10452: 13
Vat. lat. 14725: 6
Vat. lat. 14728: 6

Venezia
Biblioteca Nazionale Marciana
   Gr. IV, 58 (= 1206): 282-283, 289
   Lat. VI, 43 (= 2488): 100
   Lat. VI, 126 (=2465): 5
   Zan. Gr. 216 (= 404): 282, 283,
     289

Wien
Österreichische Nationalbibliothek
   med. gr. 49: 23

INDEX AUCTORUM

Abraham Ibn Ezra: 57
Abulcassis: 240
Adelardus Bathensis [of Bath]: 117
Aegidius Romanus: 167, 172, 237, 242
Aelius Herodianus: 280
Aetius Amidenus [of Amida]: 133
Albertus Magnus (incl. pseudo-): 57-59, 61, 62, 82, 96, 118, 121, 124, 125, 128, 130, 142, 210, 211, 218, 222
Albumazar: 210, 211
Alcabitus: 241
Alexander Aphrodisiensis (incl. pseudo-): 21-31, 33, 34, 36, 43, 49, 50-52, 57-60, 63, 65, 115, 135, 136, 142; see also *Problemata Inedita*
Algazel: 241
Ali ibn Ridwan: 56, 241
Alpharabius: 65
Angelo da Siena: 76
Angelo Poliziano: 66, 278, 285, 286
Apollonius Tyanensis: 53
Appollonius Dyscolus: 280
Aristoteles (incl. pseudo-): *passim*
  De caelo: 11, 232
  De anima: 11, 210, 232, 239
  De animalibus: 3, 6, 8, 56, 104, 121, 138, 232, 269, 270
  De generatione animalium: 30, 73
  De generatione et corruptione: 56, 232
  De historia animalium: 11, 25, 81
  De motu animalium: 3, 6
  De partibus animalium: 103
  De vegetabilibus: 6
  Ethica: 56, 138, 169, 170
  Metaphysica: 61, 66, 239
  Meteorologica: 8, 25, 209, 232, 254
  Parva Naturalia: 8, 11, 56, 61
  Physica: 6, 210, 232, 280

  Politica: 138, 169
  Problemata Physica: *passim*
  Rhetorica: 161, 169, 184, 196
  See also *Problemata Inedita, Problemata Bambergensia (= vetustissima), Problemata: anonymous Latin commentaries on -*
Arnaldus de Villanova: 125, 140
ar-Rāzī: *see* Rhazes
Athenaeus: 25
Avenzoar: 57
Averroes: 57, 65, 97, 125, 239, 266
Avicenna: 56, 58, 65, 66, 86, 96, 103, 121, 125, 130, 136, 140, 160, 165, 166, 212, 213, 229, 233-235, 237, 239, 262

Balinus: see Apollonius Tyanensis
Barbaro, Ermolao: see Hermolaus
Bartholomaeus de Messana: 2-4, 8-10, 12, 13, 55, 59, 62, 63, 71, 74, 76, 80, 83, 84, 93, 99-102, 105, 107, 118, 130, 138, 144, 158, 178, 232, 278, 280, 283, 285, 287, 289, 290
Bartholomaeus Anglicus: 113, 117, 142
Beranger de Landora: 119, 127-129, 131, 142; see also *Lumen animae*
Bernard Chaussade: 13
Bernardus de Claraevallensis [of Clervaux]: 86
Boethius: 65, 66, 242
Bruni: see Leonardo Bruni
Buridanus: see Ioannes Buridanus

Cardano, Girolamo: 138
Cassius Iatrosophista: 26, 34, 44-46, 49, 58, 116, 134-136
Chrysippus: 280
Cicero: 80
Conradus de Halberstadt: 119, 129-132, 139, 140

Constantinus Africanus: 121, 124, 125, 212

David de Dinant: 62, 118
Despars: see Jacobus de Partibus
Didymus Chalcenterus: 25

Erasistratus: 24, 56-58
Evrart de Conty: 145-274 (*passim*)
    Eschés amoureux: 146, 149-152, 154, 155, 159-162, 166, 167, 172, 177, 179, 180, 185, 190, 195-197, 199-223
    Livre des Problemes: 1-4, 6, 8, 9, 11, 12, 14-16, 19, 74, 77, 87, 145-274 (*passim*), 288
    Livre des eschez amoureux moralisés: 145-155, 160, 163-165, 167-173, 176-180, 182, 183, 185, 186, 192, 193, 195-197, 227, 237, 247

Felix qui poterit: see *Problemata*, anonymous commentaries on –
Francisco López de Villalobos: 138
Fulgentius: 242, 270

Gaufridus Voraviensis: 128
Galenus (incl. pseudo-): 24, 27, 30, 40, 43, 48-51, 57-59, 62, 64, 65, 115, 121, 133, 136, 156, 166, 167, 212, 229-235, 238, 239, 249, 258, 260, 264, 265
Gaza: see Theodorus
Gentile da Foligno: 73, 75
Georgius Trapezuntius: 13, 275-294 (*passim*)
Georgius Valla: 23, 120, 132-136, 140
Gerardus Cremonensis: 234, 240
Gessner, Conrad: 134
Gottfried of Vorau: see Gaufridus Voraviensis
Gualterus Burlaeus: 1, 2, 6, 7, 9, 14, 75, 78, 86, 88-91; see also *Problemata*, anonymous commentaries on -: 'Felix qui poterit'
Guillelmus de Conchis: 117
Guy de Chauliac: 240

Haly Abbas: 264
Hartmann Schedel: 141
Heloise: 82
Henricus Bate: 118
Henricus de Hervordia [of Herford]: 118
Hermolaus Barbarus: 293
Herophilus: 30
Hieronymus: 291
Hildegard von Bingen: 82
Hippocrates: 23, 24, 65, 115, 121, 133, 168, 231, 234, 235, 238, 239, 248, 255, 258, 260, 263, 265, 270
Ḥunain ibn Isḥāq: 34, 35

Ibn Abī Uṣaibiʿa: 35
Ibn an-Nadīm: 35, 38
Ibn aṭ-Ṭayyib: 36
Ibn Dāwūd: 54
Isaac Israeli: 57, 125
Isidorus Hispalensis: 65, 66

Jacobus de Forli: 241
Jacobus de Partibus [Jacques Despars]: 241
Jacopo da Varagine: 142
Jean de Meun: 181, 190
Joannes Alexandrinus: 44
Joannes Berblengheem: 73
Joannes Bruyl: 83-86, 88
Joannes Buridanus: 94, 148, 210
Joannes de Janduno: 6, 10, 72, 74, 89, 119
Joannes de Sancto Amando [Saint-Amand]: 87, 230
Joannes de Sancto Geminiano: 130
Joannes de Spello: 73
Joannes Grammaticus: *see* Yaḥyā an-Naḥwī
Joannes Vath: 73
Job of Edessa: 54
Johannitius: 165, 229, 234
John Lydgate: 195
John Peckham: 130, 179
Julius Caesar Scaliger: 138, 142

Leo: 24
Leonardo Bruni: 277

Livre de Sydrac: 114
Lorenzo Valla: 23, 293
Lorscher Arzneibuch: 116
Lucas de Magna Cosmin: 94, 95
Lumen animae: 119, 127, 132; see also Beranger de Landora

Macrobius: 25, 30, 82, 116, 130
Mahieu le Vilain: 200, 202-204, 208
Maimonides: 57
Marcus Antonius Zimara: 142
Marsilius de Sancta Sophia: 76
Martin de Saint-Gille: 188, 231
Meletius: 24
Mensa philosophica: 119, 120, 122-126, 131
Michael Scotus: 117; see also *Quaestiones Nicolai Peripatetici*
Michele Savonarola: 119
Moses ibn Tibbon: 35

Nicolaus Leonicenus: 135
Nicole Oresme: 148, 149, 158, 169, 172, 175-198 (*passim*), 200, 203-205, 210, 214-217, 250

Olympiodorus: 23
Omnes Homines: see *Summa Omnes Homines*
Oribasius: 30
Orion: 24
Ovidius: 242

Palladius [Rutilius Taurus Aemilianus] 165, 237, 239
Palladius [Iatrosophista]: 27, 237-239
Paulus Aegineta: 133
Petrus de Abano: 1-8, 10-15, 17, 55-111 (*passim*), 119, 144, 148, 156, 158, 159, 164-169, 178, 184, 193, 197, 227-273 (*passim*), 278, 279, 287-288
Petrus Hispanus: 124, 125
Philaretus 234
Pico della Mirandola: 66
Petrus Johannis Olivi: 74
Petrus de Sancto Floro [Saint-Flour]: 87

Placides et Timeo: 114
Plato: 24
Plutarchus: 25, 134, 136, 142
Poliziano: see Angelo Poliziano
Porphyrius: 280
Problemata, anonymous commentaries on –:
- 'Bavarian commentary': 92-93, 95, 98, 101, 102, 107
- 'Erfurt commentary': 92-94, 98, 101, 102
- 'Felix qui poterit': 77-89, 90-94, 97, 98, 101-104, 107
- *Vat. lat. 2481*: 75-77
Problemata Aristotelis (ac philosophorum medicorumque complurium): see *Summa 'Omnes homines'*
Problemata Bambergensia [= *vetustissima*]: 26, 34, 44-46, 49, 116
Problemata Inedita [= Supplementary Problems]: 21-31, 34, 44-53, 134
Problemata varia anatomica: 121-122
Psellus: 27-29
Ptolemaeus: 56-58, 65, 210, 240, 241

Quaestiones Nicolai Peripatetici: 77, 87
Quaestiones Salernitanae: 26, 44, 49, 116, 117, 121, 125, 126, 139, 140, 144

Raoul de Presles: 186, 188, 189
Raymundus Lullus: 118, 241
Regimen Salernitatum: 87
Responsorium curiosorum: 119, 122-126, 131, 140
Rhazes: 45, 125
Richard de Bury: 89-91
Richard Lavenham: 78, 87
Roger Bacon: 124, 130, 17

Scaliger: see Julius Caesar Scaliger
Schedel: see Hartmann
Scholia in Aristotelem: 280
Scholia in Homerum: 280
Seneca: 211
Simon de Hesdin: 190, 250
Simon de Tunstede: 86

Simplicius: 58
Stephanus: 24
Summa causarum problematum Aristotelis: see *Problemata*, anonymous commentaries on -: 'Felix qui poterit'
Summa 'Omnes homines': 74, 92, 119-122, 126, 131, 142, 143
Summa recreatorum: 119, 122-126

Themistius: 58
Themo Iudaei: 210
Theodorus Gaza: 13, 55, 135, 138, 276-294 (*passim*)
Theophilus: 234
Theophrastus: 23, 24, 34, 115, 128, 130, 211
Thomas Aquinas: 74, 91
Thomas Bradwardine: 90, 91
Thomas Cantimpratensis: 113, 117, 142

Thomas de Hibernia [of Ireland]: 128
Thomas Waleys: 73
Trapezuntius: see Georgius

Urso Salernitanus: 86, 87, 103

Valla: see Georgius
Vergilius: 77, 78
Villalobos: see Francisco López de Villalobos
Vincentius Bellovacensis [de Beauvais]: 113

Walter Burley: see Gualterus Burlaeus
William of Conches: see Guillelmus de Conchis

Yaḥyā an-Naḥwī: 35, 38

Zimara: see Marcus Antonius Zimara

PRINTED ON PERMANENT PAPER • IMPRIME SUR PAPIER PERMANENT • GEDRUKT OP DUURZAAM PAPIER - ISO 9706

N.V. PEETERS S.A., WAROTSTRAAT 50, B-3020 HERENT